The Caribbean

Edited by STEPHAN PALMIÉ

and FRANCISCO A. SCARANO

THE
Caribbean

A History of the Region and Its Peoples

The University of Chicago Press | Chicago and London

STEPHAN PALMIÉ is professor of anthropology and social sciences at the University of Chicago.
FRANCISCO A. SCARANO is professor of history at the University of Wisconsin–Madison.

The University of Chicago Press, Chicago 60637
The University of Chicago Press, Ltd., London
© 2011 by The University of Chicago
All rights reserved. Published 2011.
Printed in the United States of America

20 19 18 17 16   4 5

ISBN-13: 978-0-226-64506-3 (cloth)
ISBN-10: 0-226-64506-1 (cloth)
ISBN-13: 978-0-226-64508-7 (paper)
ISBN-10: 0-226-64508-8 (paper)

Library of Congress Cataloging-in-Publication Data

The Caribbean : a history of the region and its peoples / edited by Stephan Palmié and
    Francisco A. Scarano
        p. cm.
    Includes bibliographical references and index.
    ISBN-13: 978-0-226-64506-3 (cloth : alk. paper)
    ISBN-10: 0-226-64506-1 (cloth : alk. paper)
    ISBN-13: 978-0-226-64508-7 (pbk. : alk. paper)
    ISBN-10: 0-226-64508-8 (pbk. : alk. paper) 1. Caribbean Area—History. I. Palmié, Stephan.
    II. Scarano, Francisco A. (Francisco Antonio)
    F2175.C325 2011
    972.9—dc22

                                                                            2011012778

♾ The paper used in this publication meets the minimum requirements of the American
National Standard for Information Sciences—Permanence of Paper for Printed Library
Materials, ANSI Z39.48-1992.

CONTENTS

GENERAL MAPS

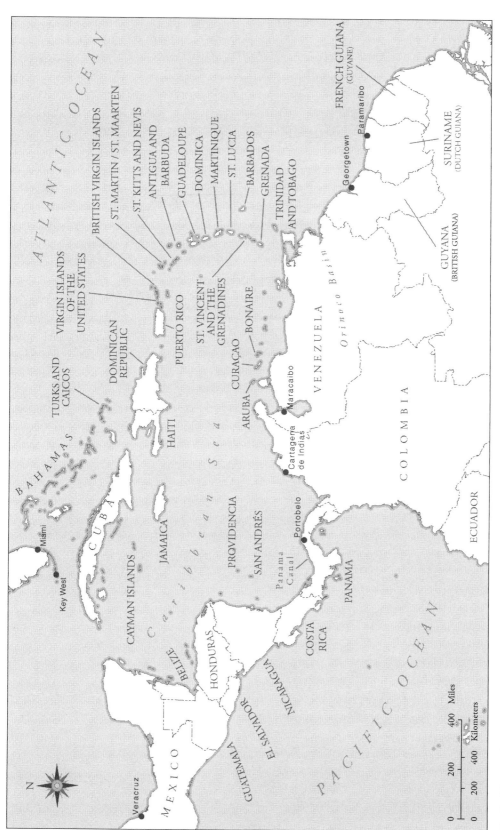

The Caribbean region

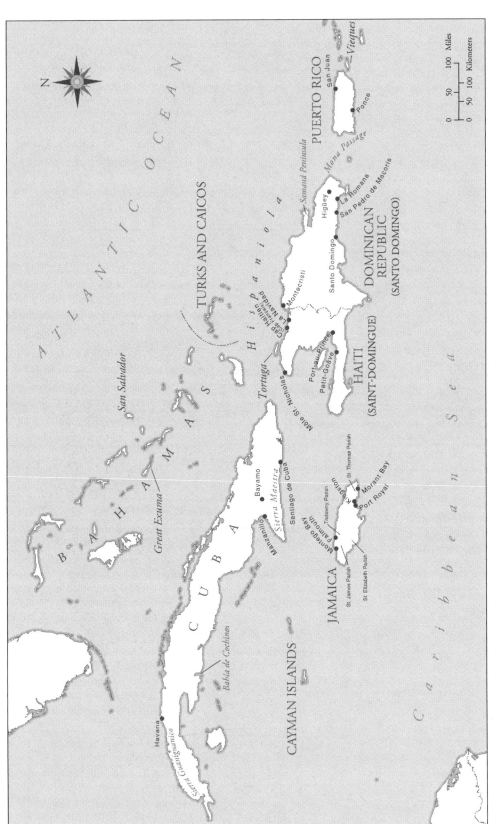

The Greater Antilles and the Northern Caribbean

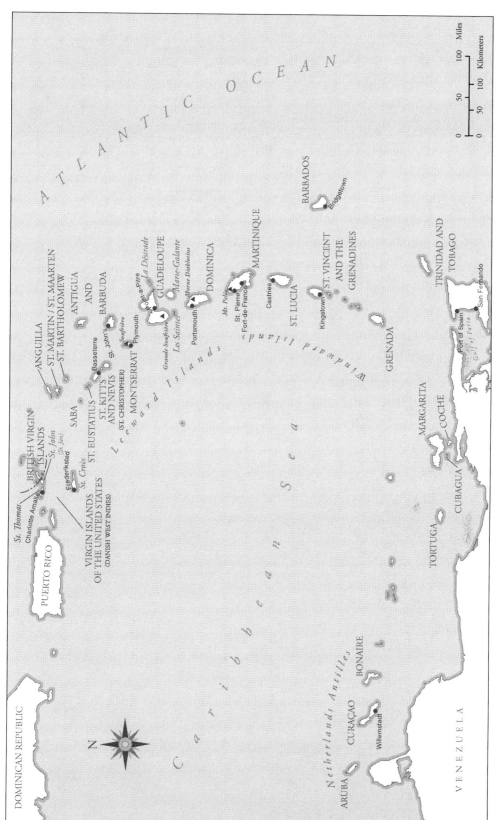

The Lesser Antilles and the southern Caribbean

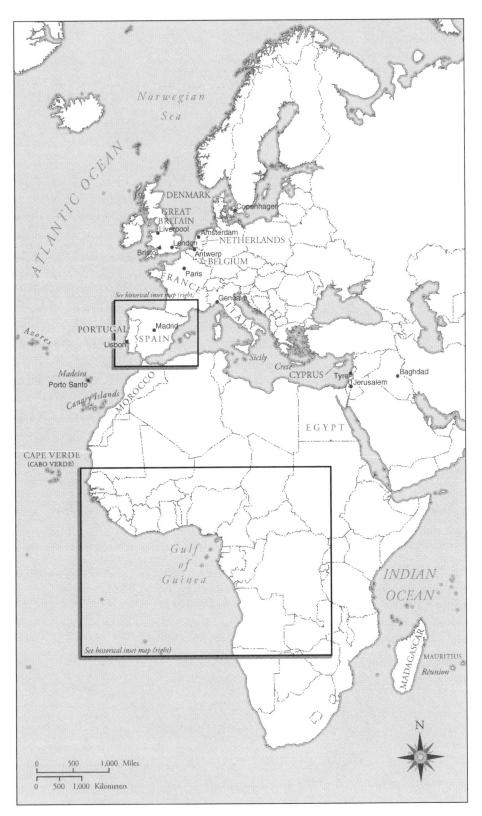

Europe, Africa, and the Middle East (key locations discussed in the text)

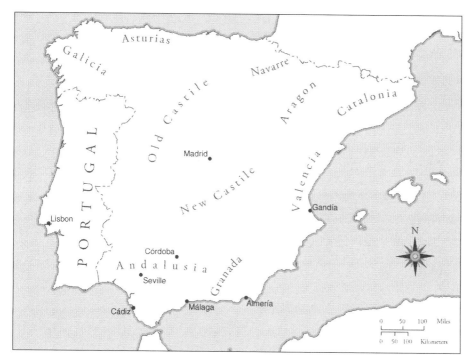

Selected locations in the Iberian Peninsula, ca. 1492

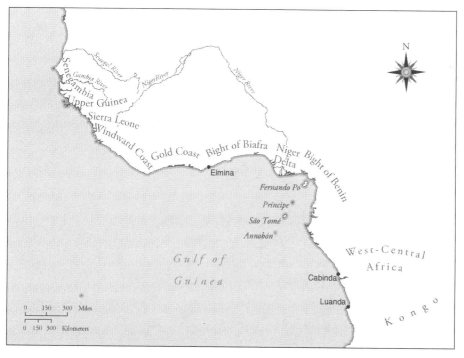

Selected locations in West Africa, 1500–1900

INTRODUCTION

Caribbean Counterpoints

STEPHAN PALMIÉ

FRANCISCO A. SCARANO

In historical writings about the Caribbean, it has been no easy task to maneuver the central streams and currents of the region's past while navigating the myriad backwaters, eddies, and obstacles along the way. Traditionally divided into a handful of imperial zones, each with a different European or creole language and imperial or national historiography, the string of islands and assorted continental regions spanning from the Florida Keys to the Orinoco delta around the Caribbean Sea has only in the past half-century lent itself to comprehensive histories, narratives that encompass the entire region and cover, at the very least, the five centuries of European occupation. This book, which brings together the expertise of 40 contributors, is a one-volume survey of the region's past and present, including its diverse geography, challenging ecology, Amerindian foundations, and intractable contemporary problems of poverty, economic stagnation, and migration, in addition to more conventional topics. Students and other readers not yet acquainted with Caribbean history will find in its pages an accessible and thorough introduction to this complex part of the world.

Long before it came to be considered a distinct "socio-cultural area" (Mintz 1966), or even a cohesive geographic entity except in the military or strategic sense, the Caribbean originally emerged as a collection of disparate colonies from which European powers, or metropoles, obtained profit and strategic value while exploiting hundreds of thousands of people who had been racialized as "inferior" and, in most cases until the 19th century, legally enslaved. European histories of the region at that time reflected the attempts to claim these colonial possessions. Unsurprisingly, those early narratives were partial either to a group of colonies (for example, the British West Indies or the Spanish Caribbean) or to a dominant social group (the white planters of the British colonies or the Spanish conquistadores), and often to both. The class and racial biases of their authors were readily apparent, as was their affiliation with the stories in support of the dominant classes. To paraphrase Karl Marx's somewhat misguided dictum, what they chronicled was "the work of Britain (or Spain, or France) in the Indies," not the histories made by people native to the Caribbean, often in contravention of the designs of imperial powers.

A new crop of historians emerged in the Caribbean after World War II when nationalism began to arise, however gradually, from the ashes of a grinding colonialism. The new nations created in the postwar years paraded their novelty, while a handful of former colonies inaugurated "postcolonial" arrangements with their former metropoles. During a promising era of economic modernization and robust nation-building, many of the new historians were themselves children of the Caribbean, and not a few were leading players in the anticolonial struggles just completed or underway. Some wrote paradigm-shifting monographs that garnered attention inside and outside the region. These included, among others, the Trinidadian historians and politicians C. L. R. James and Eric Williams; the outstanding historians Elsa Goveia, of Guyana, and Douglas Hall, of Jamaica; Cuban intellectuals such as Ramiro Guerra y Sánchez, Fernando Ortiz, and Manuel Moreno Fraginals; and Arturo Morales Carrión, the Puerto Rican historian, educator, and statesman. Their works collectively embraced the racial and ethnic diversity of the region while stressing commonalities and shared experiences across the archipelago and the continental colonies conventionally regarded as integral to it (such as Belize and the Guianas). When appropriate, they emphasized the African substratum of regional cultures that made their stories so compelling and universal.

General syntheses of Caribbean history grew organically from these novel treatments of the past. Some historians—many of whom became academic professionals—wrote ambitious narratives that tried to break the isolation of individual colonies or imperial zones while paying due attention to their working classes—for example, J. H. Parry and P. M. Sherlock's *A Short History of the West Indies*, first published in 1956. The most widely disseminated of these works treated single Caribbean territories and individual actors as important in their own right, while underscoring joint themes and outcomes. Histories such as *From Columbus to Castro: The History of the Caribbean, 1492–1969* (1970), by Eric Williams and *De Cristóbal Colón a Fidel Castro: El Caribe, frontera imperial* (1970), by Dominican writer and politician Juan Bosch, counterbalanced European conquest and Amerindian decline, plantation agriculture and its coercive labor systems, the formation of peasantries and the making of creole societies, the struggles over slavery and emancipation, imperial declension and transition, decolonization, and, in the late 20th and early 21st centuries, the multiple signs of an inconclusive or fractional nationalism (Knight 1978). Such works helped raise Caribbean history into a significant subfield of Western Hemisphere studies. In a crowning achievement, a major international effort sponsored by UNESCO resulted in a six-volume anthology of Caribbean history (published 1997–2010) written by a collective of leading scholars, most of them native to the region.

This volume provides an overview of the best of this contemporary scholarship on the region for readers who are new to the field. Its contributors include historians, anthropologists, geographers, political scientists, and sociologists, many of them authors of pathbreaking works; their essays are concise summaries of the state of knowledge about their respective topics, presented in accessible prose, with short bibliographic references and a minimum of scholarly clutter. Inevitably, there are areas of overlap among chapters, many of them designed to underscore issues of scholarly disagreement or polemical engagement rather than general consensus. But such points of contention show Caribbean historiography for what it is: a remarkably lively field of debate in which scholars at times disagree vigorously, but important discoveries continue to occur.

The book is arranged thematically and chronologically into seven parts. Part 1, "The Caribbean Stage," covers essential background topics, from the opportunities and constraints posed by the region's geography to the displacement of sugar production techniques westward across the Mediterranean and the eastern Atlantic islands, a key development in the transfer of colonial methods and institutions into the 16th-century Spanish Caribbean. Part 2, "The Making of a Colonial Sphere," explores the formation of Spanish colonial societies and traces the eventual replacement of Spanish hegemony by British, French, and Dutch dominance, with all that this transfer implied for the region. Part 3, "Colonial Designs in Flux," describes the economic, demographic, and social transformation of the Caribbean in the 17th century as the colonies of the northwest Europeans began to mature into full-fledged plantation societies and as the transatlantic slave trade, catalyzed by the demand for agro-industrial workers, escalated fatefully toward its historic 18th-century peaks. Part 4, "Capitalism, Slavery, and Revolution," takes an in-depth look at slave cultures, forms of resistance to enslavement, the interimperial rivalries that made war commonplace in the 1700s, and the revolutionary explosion of Saint-Domingue's slaves in the wake of the French Revolution that gave birth to Haiti and forever changed Atlantic and Caribbean history.

Part 5, "A Reordered World," focuses on how the paradoxes of the 19th century were lived in the region—how it was an age of progressive abolition of the slave trade's "imperial branches" and widespread slave emancipation in the old "sugar colonies," even while imperialist incursions into Africa and Asia and inequality based on racist, pseudoscientific theories arose collaterally. The same epoch that witnessed the reconstitution of a slave-based plantation economy and the emergence of deep racial fissures in Cuba and Puerto Rico saw a strengthening of national sensibilities there—a volatile combination of racism and nationalism that, in the larger of the two Antilles, erupted in a bloody 30-year anticolonial insurgency. In part 6, "The New Empire," six chapters explore various angles of US colonial or neocolonial influence in the most populous of regional societies, and the ways in which a succession of crises, from the 1930s Great Depression to the Cold War, helped shape local reactions and responses across the region. Finally, in part 7, "The Caribbean in the Age of Globalization," the chapters provide coverage of key themes in Caribbean history during the second half of the 20th century and the early years of the 21st: the struggles to define freedom in the face of dictatorship, the clash between democratic aspirations and persistent poverty, the long-standing Cuban experiment with socialism, and the dispersal of Caribbean peoples across the developed nations of the North Atlantic, with all its intrinsic promises and challenges.

Following the final chapter is an extensive list of suggested readings—some general, others keyed to each of the book's seven parts—that will allow readers to deepen their understanding of Caribbean history and learn about current debates among specialists. An appended glossary provides concise definitions of historical and specialized terms, many of which have evolved, like the Caribbean itself, from the creative friction between Old and New World people, events, and idioms.

All history is necessarily provisional; it ends in a present that only too soon becomes a moment of history in itself. That dynamic applies to the story told in this book. Just a few weeks after Haiti experienced a devastating earthquake in January 2010, a history graduate student at Duke University, Julia Gaffield, uncovered in Great Britain the only copy yet found of that nation's declaration of independence (1804), a document of immense value not just to Haitians but to all the world's citizens. With its revolutionary banner of "*Liberté ou la morte!*" (Liberty or death!) atop an extraordinary proclamation of Haitian nationhood, the charter affirms the unwavering spirit of a nation rising from the ashes of a brutalizing enslavement. In more ways than one, this document and the doleful circumstances preceding its discovery are emblematic of the triumphs and tragedies of Caribbean peoples. As an endpoint for the complex story our contributors tell—a story whose key instances and thematic strands we will preview in the balance of this introduction—the moment is nevertheless arbitrary, as is our choice to begin this discussion with a familiar figure, the Enlightenment philosopher John Locke.

Writing at the end of the 17th century, when European notions of "America" were still largely centered on the Caribbean region, Locke once remarked that "in the beginning all of the world was America." Implying—much like Michel de Montaigne before him—that the New World exemplified what the Old World had once been in primordial times, Locke (1963, 343) resorted to a rhetoric strangely at odds with what must have been his own experience. As an investor in the Royal African Company, and architect of the laws that enshrined slavery in the colonial charter of what became the Carolinas, Locke ought to have known better: the social worlds taking shape in the Caribbean at the time of his writing were anything but Edenic commonwealths. They were violent social experiments organized on strikingly novel principles, though the precise nature of what was unprecedented about them may not have been immediately apparent to contemporary metropolitan observers such as Locke.

Still, during Locke's own lifetime, not only Barbados—the first successful British outpost in what formerly had been Spanish overseas dominion—but Jamaica, wrested from Spain in 1655, and the western third of Hispaniola, ceded to France in 1697, came to exemplify a type of society the world had never seen before. To be sure, earlier land-based empires such as Rome had engaged in massive attempts at social and economic reorganization of conquered spaces. Yet nothing resembling the near-complete destruction of previous societies in the Caribbean and their replacement by new and unprecedented political, economic, and cultural orders had ever been envisioned or achieved elsewhere before. This is not to say that the developments out of which the Caribbean emerged as the geohistorical region we recognize today were the product of prior design rather than historical default. Rather, their beginnings were at least partly a result of the unforeseen demographic disaster that unfolded in the Antilles within two generations after Columbus's first landfall.

Thus, while concurrent and subsequent European colonial ventures in Mesoamerica, Asia, and western central Africa built upon and were in turn shaped by significant persistence in the political structures, economy, and culture of large indigenous population bases, no such continuities occurred in the Caribbean. Nor were there any concerted or sustained attempts to export European settler populations. England and France did initially deploy metropolitan surplus laborers in various schemes centered on temporary bondage, but none of these early experiments were to last. Consequently, the systems of European domination emerging in the Caribbean were characterized more by rupture and innovation than by the transfer and gradual modification of Old World institutions, as happened in British North America.

Although the earliest Spanish attempts at establishing control over Native American populations in the Antilles were informed by legal and political precepts born of Iberia's centuries-long Christian reconquest (Seed 1995), the actual forms of colonial rule and exploitation that took shape in the islands soon acquired characteristics that were largely new. As described in this volume by Reinaldo Funes Monzote in chapter 5 and Jalil Sued-Badillo in chapter 6, for example, the local workforce originally targeted for mining and plantations gave out early as Amerindian societies disintegrated under the impact of Spanish violence and disease, thus rendering older Iberian methods of labor extraction impracticable. Slavery, too, was initially introduced as a traditional, legally circumscribed institutional mechanism for binding labor to the land, but it quickly expanded in scale and scope. While small-scale slave raiding had characterized the frontiers of Christian and Muslim Iberia for centuries, Spanish colonizers on the larger Antilles were already conducting commercial slaving expeditions against the natives of the Lesser Antilles and the Central and South American mainland by the mid-16th century.

New sources and methods for procuring captive labor on the African continent, combined with the rapidly increasing brutality of exploitation and degradation of the enslaved, transformed slavery from an economically and socially marginal institution in early modern Iberia into a lasting determinant of Caribbean social orders. This transition to a colonial and racial form of slavery occurred principally in the Caribbean. Since slavery as a legally recognized institution had disappeared from most of northwestern Europe by the end of the medieval era, the colonies founded by England and France in the second quarter of the 17th century initially adopted a system of bonded or indentured European laborers rather than large-scale, inheritable bondage. As Hilary McD. Beckles suggests in chapter 13, many novice sugar planters preferred the powers over labor that indentured servitude provided. But expedience and cost soon overrode those preferences, and once enslaved Africans replaced indentured Europeans in these colonies later in the century, the transformation was swift and deadly. As emerging Caribbean plantation economies became incubators of what the historian Philip Curtin (1969, 3) influentially defined as the South Atlantic System—"a complex economic organism centered on the production in the Americas of tropical commodities for consumption in Europe, and grown by the labor of Africans"—a truly horrific social experiment began to unfold.

Colonial control by the great European powers was integral to the South Atlantic System. Conquering the native Caribbean peoples and forcing them to work, exploiting the islands' deposits of valuable minerals, producing high-value agricultural staples, and, when it became necessary, importing millions of enslaved workers from Africa were all enterprises requiring the overseas deployment of organized, institutionalized force on an unprecedented scale. As the Spanish, English, French, and Dutch sought to obtain wealth and geopolitical influence, only the military and related commanding devices of colonial states could muster the necessary force and legitimacy. State power, disguised at first by private capital when the first European colonists arrived in the Caribbean, invariably expanded in scope over time.

By the latter part of the 17th century, as Josep M. Fradera explains in chapter 10, the four main Caribbean empires had established a stable foothold in the region. During the 18th century they spent decades at war with one another and wasted thousands of lives competing fiercely for wealth and territory. Despite these intense rivalries, all four empires survived (albeit two of them, the Spanish and the French, with a diminished territorial footprint) until the late 19th century, when Spain was forced to bow out for good. The three remaining empires sputtered into the second half of the 20th century, eventually joined by another aspiring imperial power, the United States, which by 1898 had replaced Spain in dominating Cuba and Puerto Rico. This "new empire" (LaFeber 1963) began to impose its own hegemony on the Caribbean as its older competitors turned their backs on the region. When the de-colonization struggles of the mid-20th century washed away most of the existing empires elsewhere in the world, the Netherlands, France, and the United States came up with putatively noncolonial formulas to continue exerting influence in the Caribbean. In this effort they were supported by local actors who openly preferred a revamped colonial dependence to outright independence.

Because of this long history of colonial domination, the Caribbean is rightly considered the oldest theater of overseas European expansion. The extended duration of the region's colonial experiences and the depth of the colonial imprint on its society and culture dwarf those forged in African or Asian colonies during the age of high imperialism (ca. 1850–1914). Whereas in those latter regions, with very few exceptions, colonial arrangements lasted less than a century, in the Caribbean most societies were built from scratch at least 350 years ago (and some more than 500 years ago), all within strictures dictated by a mercantile, colonial capitalism. Put in even starker terms, except for Haiti, which violently overthrew French colonial rule after little more than a century, all of the Caribbean nations that gained independence in the course of the 19th or 20th centuries had endured at least three centuries of colonial domination.

Moreover, few other colonial settings were as dramatically affected by European agency—demographically, politically, and culturally—as the insular Caribbean. The drama of the Spanish conquest of the Aztec and Inca states notwithstanding, the success of Iberian colonialism on the American mainland rested heavily on the mobilization of large indigenous populations, often with the significant collaboration of subjugated native elites. Though mainland Spanish America received its share of European settlers and African slaves, Amerindians (and, increasingly, mestizos) predominated demographically throughout the colonial era. Likewise, Europeans rarely managed to gain more than coastal footholds in Asia until the late 18th century, and in Africa not until the second half of the 19th.

In the Caribbean, however, the demographic collapse of the indigenous population led to the near-complete repopulation of the islands by enslaved Africans transported to the region as a rightless and degraded workforce for emerging plantation enterprises, which increasingly provided the raison d'être for colonies in which sugar, coffee, tobacco, indigo, cocoa, or other tropical staples shaped the course of political and economic development. To be sure, communities of Native Caribbean descent persist today in Dominica, St. Vincent, and other islands, and in Puerto Rico and its diaspora a neo-Taino movement that aims to attain federal recognition has recently taken hold. Likewise, as Aisha Khan points out in chapter 27, the size of populations locally identified as "white" (or "Asian") varies greatly from island to island. Yet there is no question that the Caribbean region as a whole is demographically the most highly "Africanized" part of the New World.

Contemporary historians of the transatlantic slave trade tend to agree that the Antilles absorbed about 45% of the upwards of 10 million enslaved Africans who survived the violence of capture in Africa and the ordeal of the Middle Passage (Eltis 2001). But the sheer extent of the moral catastrophe entailed in the transplantation of Africans to the Caribbean becomes clearer in comparative terms. The French Windward Islands (Martinique, Guadeloupe, St. Lucia, and Grenada), whose combined landmass of 1,483 square miles is about equal to that of the state of Rhode Island, imported more than 300,000 slaves between the early 17th century and the ending of the trade in the mid-19th century, while the entire British mainland of North America imported some 389,000 over a comparable period. Even more dramatically, French Saint-Domingue, slightly larger than Maryland, is estimated to have received upwards of 770,000 enslaved Africans between its formal cession to France in 1697 and the outbreak of the Haitian Revolution in 1791, a vast majority of them arriving in the decades immediately preceding this event—yet no more than 450,000 of them were still alive when the revolution put a decisive end to slave importation into the colony. Still, the French islands were far from exceptional in this regard. British Jamaica imported more than a million enslaved Africans between 1655 and 1807, yet released a mere 310,000 of them and their descendants into freedom once emancipation arrived in the 1830s.

While historical demographers and historians of the slave trade will continue to debate and refine these numbers, what they indicate is unambiguously clear: never before in human history had the allure of wealth and a transcontinental political economy geared toward its accumulation engendered as vast and deadly a system of agro-industrial exploitation as took shape in the Caribbean, especially after northern European competitors began wresting island after island from Spain's pioneering, but ultimately faltering, economic and political control. Although different islands (and in some cases different regions of the larger islands and mainland zones) experienced the operation of the South Atlantic System to varying degrees and within different timeframes, even areas unsuitable for plantation agriculture were drawn into its orbit—if only as garrison colonies, as staging grounds for centuries-long inter-imperial rivalries, as provisioning zones for sugar islands, or as entrepôts for the slave trade and the shipment of sugar and other plantation crops.

As Marx clearly saw but—given his misunderstanding of slavery as an archaic mode of production—could not adequately conceptualize, and as Eric Williams demonstrated in his pathbreaking monograph *Capitalism and Slavery* (1944), it was this system that endowed mercantilist Europe with the capital that seeded its industrial revolution and so, in contemporary economists' parlance, ensured its lasting "competitive advantage" over the rest of the world. It was this system, too, that, in the words of another distinguished Caribbean intellectual, Guyanese historian Walter Rodney (1972), led to Europe's active "underdevelopment" of Africa. And, as the Trinidadian activist, historian, and essayist C. L. R. James (1963) argued, it made the Caribbean an initial focus and lasting fulcrum of what we today might understand as the modern global capitalist system.

All three qualifiers in this term—"modern," "capitalist," and "global"—merit emphasis, as all three represent major forces in and characteristics of Caribbean history and social life. Indeed, it is not an overstatement to assert that modernity, capitalism, and the collection of factors that many of us glibly and anachronistically subsume under the label "globalization" (Mintz 1996; Cooper 2009) first asserted themselves in the post-Columbian Caribbean. As the Cuban scholar Fernando Ortiz put it in 1940, in a marvelously erudite essay on the "contrapuntal" forces exerted by tobacco and sugar in shaping the history and culture of his native island, sugar had always been capitalism's favorite child (Ortiz 1991a). Ortiz was not the first to perceive this connection, but he was responsible for exposing how the fate of the region was shaped by—and in turn helped shape—the global transition from mercantile to industrial capitalism, from European nation-states' groping attempts to establish commercial empires to the emergence of modern imperialism and neocolonial forms of dependency.

Yet it would be misleading to understand the origins and development of the South Atlantic System only in terms of large-scale agriculture and the coercive labor systems on which it depended. Those who were most victimized by colonial capitalism continually resisted it and adapted to it. The narratives of Caribbean history contained in this book are thus full of contrasts and ironies for which Ortiz's musical metaphor of "contrapuntal" forces still provides an arresting and analytically fruitful image. Counterpoints of seemingly opposed processes and antagonistic forces, jarring dissonances alternating with unforeseen harmonies—these, rather than fictions of consonant, linear development, guide the historical interpretations favored in this volume.

The horrors of the Middle Passage, for instance, led to the formation of "fictive kinship" bonds among enslaved passengers. These connections eventually permitted the elaboration of new familial ties to replace those broken by capture and forced shipment. Such novel moral bonds, in turn, enabled the growth of multigenerational traditions that flourished in the small and always imperiled spaces of autonomy the plantation regime afforded the enslaved. As shown by Philip Morgan in chapter 16 and Jean Besson in chapter 21, the ensuing processes of creolization—creation of new cultures out of fragmented ways of life that had originated across the Atlantic—drew upon these new, re-created kinship ties and also upon numerous other adaptations made necessary by enslavement. If, as Jamaican sociologist Orlando Patterson (1982) noted, slavery was a kind of "social death," it did prompt new forms of "social life" in the New World generally and the Caribbean specifically.

Among these forms was an assortment of communities elaborated in opposition to legal enslavement. Although the slave system attempted to tie bondsmen down to areas controlled by masters or their surrogates, control that absolute was almost universally unattainable, as Isaac Curtis makes plain in chapter 9. Especially in territories with large, forested hinterlands or secluded mountain ranges, slaves escaped continually and in large numbers. While most sought refuge in locations too difficult to reach, others fled into the circuits of interisland navigation, becoming "maritime maroons," pirates, or privateers. Hispaniola in the 16th century was the first to experience these forms of marronage on a large scale, but it would be in 18th-century Jamaica and especially Suriname that the phenomenon of grand marronage reached its greatest extent in the Caribbean. Once far from the masters' grasp, many maroon communities survived for generations (some, in fact, to the present day) as social formations adapted both to the difficult natural environment and to the tension-filled relationship with colonial power. Other such communities did not fare as well, and as the outside world encroached upon their autonomous spaces, their members became integrated into the larger society.

Flight of one sort or another was one way in which Caribbean peoples confronted the power of slaveholding elites and the colonial state. But there were others, none more prevalent than the compulsion toward peasanthood. Soon after the earliest European intrusions in the 16th and 17th centuries, the Spanish islands saw the emergence of a multiracial peasantry, relatively tolerant of interracial unions, primarily in spaces left unoccupied by a declining plantation system. The Puerto Rican sociologist Angel Quintero-Rivera (1990) persuasively argues that these peasantries were united primarily by their counter-plantation, antigovernment ethic; they sought to escape as far as possible from institutions of church and state that for the ruling elites marked the boundaries of "civilization."

Later, when the plantation system took off in the British, French, and Dutch spheres, a "slave economy" developed and prospered there, partly for the masters' benefit and partly for the slaves' own as they sought to diversify and enrich their diet by producing subsistence crops on provision grounds granted to them by the planters and selling the excess produce. In many 18th-century Caribbean plantation societies, such proto-peasant activities fostered the growth of urban markets dominated by female slave marketeers, who in much of the Anglophone Caribbean were called *higglers*. Over time the provision-ground and marketing systems tended to become part of a sort of informal social contract: a "happy coalition of interests" between planters and slaves, as the 18th-century Jamaican planter-historian Bryan Edwards once called it. These institutions not only allowed enslaved workers to supplement their food rations and accumulate cash but, more important, they became a fulcrum of creole cultures deeply grounded in rules that governed communal possession of the land. After emancipation, the peasantries that had emerged on these islands elaborated creatively upon the cultures forged by the proto-peasants, redefining what it meant to live in freedom while remaining within the grasp of a colonial economy dominated by the plantation—a grasp so potent that it would not be loosened until well into the 20th century.

Caribbean history, then, involved multiple adaptations to the insular colonial environment beyond those spun from the plantation's cloth. Another sharp counterpoint arose between the urban landscapes of various colonial powers. Despite the Spanish colonies' meager population, cities such as Havana, Santiago, Santo Domingo, and San Juan were significantly denser urban conglomerates than primal cities in the British Caribbean such as Kingston or Bridgetown. In the Spanish colonies a simplified, militarized, yet aristocratic form that mirrored peninsular Spain's urban society took shape—one that stood in stark opposition to, and in some cases was quite disconnected from, the rustic lives that the inhabitants of the hinterland led beyond the massive walls and fortresses surrounding the cities. As argued by Francisco A. Scarano in chapter 11, Havana stood out among these cities both for its size and for the mercantile logic that made it a truly Atlantic entrepôt. In the British islands, by contrast, rural plantations concentrated both population and wealth, while the urban zones were not just administrative centers but "bridges" between the wealth produced by slaves on plantations and the trading circuits of the Atlantic world.

Yet another set of contrasts concerns the relation of the social and cultural formations emerging in the Caribbean and what many of us today consider "global modernity." Although the Caribbean was one of the birthplaces of a capitalist world order, some of the novel social arrangements that arose from the ruins of Native American societies hardly yield to retrospective explanations based on today's notions of capitalist development and rational modernization. Take here, for example, the haphazard and often far from successful European experiments in reproducing Old World institutions and cultural forms in societies characterized by extreme volatility and—in the case of full-blown slave societies—held together by naked force and endemic violence. From early Spanish reports about the immorality and spirit of insubordination among the conquistadors and first settlers to the writings of missionaries, planter-historians, and travelers in the 18th and early 19th centuries, there runs a thread of complaint not only about the disloyalty and insolence of the white lower classes, but about the ostentation, consumptive excess, sexual depravity, virulent racism, and political unreliability of the planter elites and the shocking violence they routinely unleashed to frighten their slaves into submission.

Or think of the quiet emergence of the multiracial peasantries, subsisting in regions untouched or abandoned by plantation development, engaged in a variety of small-scale agricultural pursuits as well as in contraband trade, exchange with the settlements of runaway slaves, and outright piracy. These surface in the historical record only rarely—mostly when colonial authorities sought to bring them under control—but where they survived for significant periods of time, as during the long stretch of economic stagnation in the Hispanic Greater Antilles, they left their mark on regional cultural formations. Then there were the desperate attempts of enslaved Africans to revive the diverse social and cultural forms—religious beliefs, kinship systems, political structures, aesthetic preferences, and the like—that they carried across the Atlantic in what rarely amounted to more than individual memories. Rather than survivals of a timeless African past, today's Afro-Caribbean cultures might better be seen as new traditions that grew out of a brutal experience of New World modernization (Palmié 2002). And then there were the contributions of the late waves of Chinese and South Asian contract laborers, arriving mostly after the formal end of slavery, to the multiracial, hyperstratified, linguistically and culturally heterogeneous social cauldrons that had emerged in the Caribbean.

Historical and ethnographic research continues to cast new light on these Caribbean social and cultural formations, which at a minimum raise questions about the overlapping boundaries of "peoples," "territories," "languages," and "cultures." They also force us to reconsider the very notions of "tradition" and "modernity." Europeans and North Americans have tended to elide the role this peculiar string of islands and associated mainland regions has played in the making of their own modern histories, despite the decisive role that imperial rivalries over Caribbean colonies played in the emergence of European nation-states, and that the sufferings of enslaved Amerindians, Africans, and even unfree Europeans played in generating the wealth that underwrote much of Europe's global ascendancy. Indeed, the forms and principles of Caribbean social life, as they unfolded historically, not only enabled but in many ways anticipated processes of modernization in the European core itself. This is what C. L. R. James (1963, 392) meant when he famously argued that

> the sugar plantation has been the most civilizing as well as the most demoralizing influence in West Indian history. When three centuries ago the slaves came to the West Indies, they entered directly into the large-scale agriculture of the sugar plantation, which was a modern system. It further required the slaves to live together in a social relation far closer than any proletariat of the time. The cane when reaped had to be rapidly transported to what was factory production. The product was shipped abroad for sale. Even the cloth the slaves wore and the food they ate was imported. The Negroes, therefore, from the very start lived a life that was in its essence a modern life.

In part, this was so because the highly rationalized "factories in the field" of Caribbean agro-industrial export economies, which employed slave labor alongside advanced mechanized processing technology, anticipated the extensive division of labor and time discipline of Europe's so-called Industrial Revolution by at least a century. Adam Smith, who marveled at the productivity enabled by the minute division of labor in a British pin factory, likely would have been astounded by the sheer scale of organizational complexity achieved in contemporary Jamaican sugar mills. But the industrial character of Caribbean plantation production was only one aspect of a larger constellation of forces that imparted to Caribbean societies what anthropologist Sidney W. Mintz calls a "precocious" modernity, which had to do "not only with the organization of industry, but with the effects of such organization upon the labor force" (Mintz 1996, 295).

Of course, the slaves' experience of alienation as anonymous and interchangeable factors in a violent system of production was dramatically different from that of English peasants who were driven off their lands and into industrial wage labor in early 19th-century England. And it also differed dramatically from the experience of Puerto Rican peasants driven from their customary tenures under 19th-century vagrancy laws, or that of South Asian contract laborers in Trinidad or Guyana. But it again anticipated the radical break with traditional social relationships and ways of life that is so often associated with processes of modernization.

Out of such experiences of modernization, we would argue, the traditions we now understand as Caribbean cultures emerged. Yoked together under conditions rarely of their own choosing, the people who understand themselves today as natives of the Caribbean became such only through processes of massive cultural transformation that we have come to understand as creolization. Few have characterized this process more eloquently than Ortiz (1991a, 88) when, speaking of Cuba, he notes that "since the sixteenth century all its peoples and cultures, invading it whether by free will or by force [have been] all exogenous and all torn from their origins, traumatized by uprooting and the rude transplantation to a new culture in the process of creation." Ortiz's point, of course, is that this "new culture" was created by such processes, and by the people whose lives were drawn into their orbit. "There were no human factors more important for [the evolution of] Cuban-ness," he continues, "than these ongoing, radical, and contrasting transmigrations of geographic, economic, and social scope of its settlers; than this perennially tran-sitory character of objectives, and this life always uprooted from the land it inhab-ited, always maladjusted to the sustaining society. People, economies, cultures, and ambitions—all were foreign, provisional, changing, birds of passage over the land." And yet elsewhere Ortiz (1991b compares Cuba to one of its national dishes—the "ajiaco criollo," a stew to which new ingredients continue to be added during the process of cooking—emphasizing that this ongoing dialectical synthesis of human, social, economic, and cultural factors generated a unique sense of peoplehood on which, or so he hoped, a truly Cuban national project might come to rest.

For Ortiz this was no vain hope, since in Cuba nationalist traditions had already grown deep roots. As Robert Whitney shows in chapter 24, the Cubans' (and, one might add, the Puerto Ricans') search for nationhood was inspired foremost by a sense of shared culture and identity, tied to but separate from the collective of re-gional identities loosely subsumed under the Spanish flag. Over the course of the 19th century a mostly inchoate idea of the nation had given voice to a variety of class positions devised alternatively by elite and popular actors: from annexation to the United States, favored early on by a racist minority, to a socially inclusive, democratic, and racially blind *Cuba libre*, an idea that aroused key Afro-Cuban and broadly popular participation during the wars of independence (1868–98). All of these forms of nationalism were catalysts of important political movements and decisions during the the 19th century, culminating in a prolonged and bloody in-surgency against Spain that put an end to the old colonialism but ushered a new form of outside domination: a neocolonial republic under the United States, cov-ered by Luis Martínez-Fernández in chapter 25 and by Brenda Gayle Plummer in chapter 28. At that time in the Caribbean, only Haiti and the Dominican Republic had attained the status of republics, and the latter more by historical default than by autonomous design.

If the struggle for separate nationhood developed relatively early in the Hispanic colonies and Haiti, it was much slower in coming elsewhere in the Caribbean. Not until the crisis of the 1930s, as indicated by O. Nigel Bolland in chapter 31 and Anne S. Macpherson in chapter 32, did movements seeking to eliminate colonial rule emerge strongly in the British and French, let alone Dutch, West Indies. Even then, anticolonial and nationalist intentions were not always at the fore, as they vied for primacy and often clashed with labor-inspired agendas. The emergence of Caribbean nationalism was thus a long, uneven, and in many ways tragic process. And it again must be viewed in relation to the rise and transformation of global regimes of modernity.

It is no accident that the oldest nongovernmental organization active today, Anti-Slavery International, has its roots in the British mobilization against the transatlantic slave trade and slavery in the West Indies in the second half of the 18th century—a time when single Caribbean island colonies were still perceived as being worth fighting intercontinental wars over. Although abolitionism represented the first modern transnational, humanitarian social movement, it involved its own hypocrisies and ironies—evident, as shown by Diana Paton in chapter 19, in the variously frustrated attempts, enacted under the pretence of civilizing missions, to prepare future ex-slaves for existence as a docile agro-industrial working class. Likewise, the patently racist undertones of metropolitan abolitionist activity in the Caribbean and its near-seamless ideological convergence with imperialist ventures on the African continent give us some clues as to the "unthinkability" of Caribbean political self-determination. But the reverberations in Europe and the slaveholding Americas of the founding of Haiti—the first black nation-state, and the first state in the Western hemisphere to effectively abolish slavery—make the connections between a belated European humanitarianism and a staunch refusal to acknowledge the capacity of non-white people for self-rule even more palpable.

There is no doubt that if the Caribbean region engendered a single event of world historical proportions, it was the Haitian Revolution, which is treated in chapter 39 by Laurent Dubois. And yet, as anthropologist Michel-Rolph Trouillot (1995) has written, even for the most liberal European thinkers of the time, the Haitian Revolution remained a monstrous aberration in the course of history as they had come to envision it. Although Friedrich Wilhelm Gottfried Hegel was certainly aware of the events in Saint-Domingue, for example, he conveniently chose to ignore them, instead flatly denying Africans the capacity for historical action in his *Lectures on the Philosophy of History* as late as 1820 (Buck-Morss 2000). If, as Williams (1944) famously argued, it was not racism that gave birth to slavery, but slavery that gave birth to racism, then by the time Jean-Jacques Dessalines, Henri Christophe, and Jean-Pierre Boyer defeated Napoleon's troops in 1804 this had become a moot point: for both pragmatic and ideological reasons, few European nation-states were willing to acknowledge Haiti's sovereign independence. France, its former metropole, eventually did so only after imposing a massive indemnity that would cripple Haiti's economy for the rest of the 19th century and, along with other factors, would pave the way for the growth of predatory merchant elites who, together with their international partners and investors, soon began to control the state—thus foreshadowing the fate of many non-Western nation-states that gained independence in the aftermath of World War II.

At the same time, Caribbean societies not drawn into the orbit of the emergent financial and political hegemony of the United States by the end of the 19th century had begun what increasingly looked like a curious process of demodernization. Having once devoured the lives of hundreds of thousands of enslaved Africans, most of the islands in the British Caribbean had by the end of the 19th century turned into increasingly impoverished exporters of labor. When, in 1865, the end of the US Civil War coincided with the revocation of Jamaica's colonial self-rule in the aftermath of a violently quashed peasant revolt in Morant Bay (described by Gad Heuman in chapter 23 and Elizabeth Cooper in chapter 26), it was becoming clear that the region's relationship to the world economy—and thus to world history—had radically changed. "The 'modernization' stopped," writes Mintz (1996, 296). "As the Caribbean's definition as a key world economic region declined, what had once been modern soon seemed archaic."

While the United States, which had been investing in the Cuban sugar industry since the 1820s, had remained lukewarm about Cuba's first war of national independence (1868–78), it rose to the occasion in 1898, just when a multiracial Cuban insurgent army had brought Spain to the point of capitulation. Establishing neocolonial rule in Cuba and de jure colonial control over Puerto Rico, American capital was to effectively determine the region's political situation for much of the 20th century. The United States invaded Cuba in 1906 and aborted its 1933 social revolution. It occupied Haiti for close to two decades beginning in 1915, and the Dominican Republic shortly thereafter and again in 1964, as detailed in chapter 37 by Pedro L. San Miguel. It imposed a crippling economic blockade on Cuba beginning in 1961, overthrew Grenada's New Jewel Movement government in 1983, and, after having sponsored the Duvalier family's dictatorial rule for close to three decades between 1957 and 1986, reluctantly intervened in Haiti once more in 2000 to reinstate an elected president whose overthrow in 1994 it had condoned, if not abetted.

Perhaps the most striking challenge to the US-dominated order emanated from Cuba, where the youthful Fidel Castro Ruz's ragtag guerrilla army overthrew the dictator Fulgencio Batista in 1959 and installed a Soviet-backed government in America's very backyard. The failed invasion attempt by Cuban exiles supported by the Kennedy administration in 1961 and the global crisis occasioned by Soviet stationing of nuclear missiles on Cuban soil the following year brought the island nation and its socialist revolution to worldwide attention. Its achievements in education, health care, and land reform have been a lasting inspiration to intellectuals throughout Latin America and the so-called Third World, though much of that success was owed to Soviet economic backing. Once the USSR disintegrated at the turn of the 1990s, the dire consequences increasingly eroded what was left of the revolutionary generation's charisma, especially among younger Cubans who had grown accustomed to the benefits of the revolution while chafing under the impact of economic failure and the ongoing US embargo. And along with that embargo, the United States continued to maintain its controversial extraterritorial (and largely extralegal) military base turned suspected-terrorist holding camp in Guantanamo, which it had acquired on the terms of a now seemingly indefinite lease in the course of ratifying Cuba's first republican constitution in 1902.

Despite the unparalleled duration of their history of colonization, the sheer brutality of the systems of domination unleashed against them, and the racist discourses that belatedly came to rationalize their oppression, Caribbean people fought back. They did so first in deeds, then in words—and this in itself is eloquent testimony to a spirit of resistance in a region whose inhabitants were denied their humanity before they acquired a vocabulary to contest iniquitous characterizations of themselves. The attack on racism began in earnest with Amerindian and African slave rebellions and the abolitionist movement, and it heated up as locally-based Caribbean figures joined the struggle against the slave trade and slavery, against worldwide racism, in defense of Haiti, and for Spanish Caribbean liberation. One such figure was Ramón Emeterio Betances, the Puerto Rican physician, abolitionist, and separatist leader who advocated Haiti's inclusion in plans for an Antillean Federation. While in exile in Haiti in 1869, Betances befriended the Haitian intellectual Anténor Firmin, who, as Winston James writes in chapter 30, penned one of the signal antiracist books of the 19th century. Betances's writings on Haiti and on race underscore the connection that existed between the revolutionary Spanish-Caribbean separatists and the antiracist struggles of the age—including, of course, the antislavery struggle itself, until emancipation finally came to Cuba in 1886.

In the heat of the Cuban insurgency against Spain, numerous other intellectuals helped elaborate an inclusive ideology to go along with their conception of national liberation. None of them was more significant than José Martí: poet, journalist, revolutionary leader, and, later, iconic figure of the struggle for Cuban nationhood. Realizing that racist divisions in Cuban society could spell doom for a separatist insurrection, Martí wrote of his vision of a "raceless Cuba," where the sacrifices of war would wash away past sins of slavery. His ideas resonated far and wide, and came to signify an important milestone in the development of Caribbean antiracist thought. It may not be surprising that the first genuinely political black movement—the Cuban Partido Independiente de Color, founded by disgruntled veterans of the second war of independence and brutally crushed by the Cuban state in 1912—explicitly harked back to Martí's founding myth of Cuba as a raceless nation.

With the official dawn of American rule at the turn of the 20th century, Carib-

bean intellectuals began to reorient their attacks upon racism and imperial domina-
tion toward the ideological, economic, and political influence of the United States.
Perhaps unsurprisingly, the Jamaican Marcus Garvey's United Negro Improvement
Association, founded in 1914, garnered as much support in the Jim Crow–ridden
United States as it did in various regions of the Caribbean and the British Empire.
Spreading rapidly along the travel routes of labor migrants from Kingston and
Bridgetown to the United Fruit enclave economies in Cuba and Central America,
and on to British colonial West Africa, Liberia, and Sierra Leone and the mining
camps of South Africa, Rhodesia, and Tanganyika, Garveyism represented the first
truly global movement organized by nonwhite people.

Though of lesser scale and scope, the négritude movement, inspired by Haiti's
Jean Price-Mars and characterized by insistence on racial difference and pride, soon
found its echo in the Cuban literary, musical, and pictorial "afronegrismo" movement that celebrated that nation's African heritage as what one member called an
"antidote to Wall Street." It also resonated in the Harlem Renaissance, one of whose
major figures, Claude MacKay, was of Caribbean origin, and whose perhaps most
distinguished poet, Langston Hughes, was in close contact with Cuban and Haitian
writers such as Nicolás Guillén and Jacques Roumain. And it reverberated across
the Atlantic—for example, in the thought and writing of African intellectuals like
Léopold Senghor, who openly acknowledged his debt to Caribbean intellectual
comrades-in-arms such as the Martinican poet and politician Aimée Cesaire.

Though many Caribbean intellectuals and artists were influential architects
of postcolonial nationhood, and inaugurated lasting attacks against the pervasive
racist stereotypes burdening the nonwhite world, their ideas were sometimes taken
up more eagerly abroad than in their home societies. Their ideological target often
had been a politically and culturally conservative elite invested not only in the
"pigmentocracy" that centuries of European rule had helped to install, but also in
the denigration of forms of popular culture created by the black lower classes. Price-
Mars thus excoriated his elite Haitian compatriots for their pretensions to Frenchness, their defensive rejection of the nation's African-derived cultural traditions,
and their disdain for the Kreyol-speaking peasant majority.

Yet the manner in which elements of Afro-Caribbean folk cultures were belatedly
drawn into elite national projects was often suspect, as when François Duvalier harnessed the tradition of vodou to the consolidation of his dictatorial rule by, for example, using a network of *hungans* (ritual specialists) to neutralize political dissent.
Only after Bob Marley had catapulted a musical style, reggae—based on a fusion of
Nyabingi rhythms with North American soul music and Rastafari-informed lyrics—
to international attention did Jamaica's political elite reluctantly acknowledge the
contribution of the Rastafari religious movement to the island's national culture,
while continuing to marginalize its adherents. Similar contradictions plague revolu-

tionary Cuba's selective promotion of its African-derived religious traditions; Trinidad's institutionalization of Orisha Family Day as a national holiday; and Guyana's legalization of obeah, a locally varying set of ritual practices that are still penalized in much of the rest of the Anglophone Caribbean. While such gestures may indeed be beneficial to practitioners of these previously stigmatized lower-class cultural traditions, it is often unclear to what extent their origin lies in genuine acceptance as opposed to populist political maneuvering, the desire to appease international human rights organizations, or efforts to promote cultural tourism.

International cruise ships have now replaced the Spanish galleons that once carried the agents of violent cultural change to Caribbean shores. Along with tourism, offshore finance and assembly industries and the international drug trade, discussed by Anthony P. Maingot and Robert Goddard in chapters 35 and 38, have become economic mainstays of the region as it enters another figuration of the global capitalist world system that originally gave birth to the Caribbean as a recognizable political and economic entity. Yet the Caribbean region never truly was a world apart, the primordial garden envisioned by John Locke. Ever since it entered European purview, it has been a primary site of world history and the processes we now call globalization. Here, then, is another Caribbean counterpoint. Drawn largely from the margins of the Old World and dragged to the the New World by violence or the often unfulfilled promise of riches, the people who became native to the Caribbean, having absorbed the remnants of its aboriginal population, were never far from the pulse of global history.

It is not only that riches drawn from "the Indies" helped propel Europe to global ascendancy, or that the Haitian Revolution shook imperial Europe and the slaveholding Americas to their very core. Even when the Caribbean went into decline as a site of hyperprofitable commodity production, the "grand experiment" of emancipation in many ways foreshadowed the global transformations out of which what we today, anachronistically, continue to call the Third World emerged more than a century later. Likewise, a region that once served as a prime staging ground for the development of racist ideologies justifying global white supremacy also proved to be a seedbed for globally influential antiracist movements. And though it was once regarded as a fruitless ground for ethnographic fieldwork aimed at reconstructing precontact cultures, the Caribbean has belatedly, and not uncontroversially, been recognized as a site whose processes of creolization previewed the kind of "modernity" (or perhaps "postmodernity") that Westerners themselves seem to be experiencing today (Trouillot 1992; Mintz 1996; Palmié 2006).

At the same time, however, Caribbean populations have experienced near-global dispersion, as Christine M. Du Bois shows in chapter 39. Such migrancy has a long history, beginning as soon as Caribbean peoples were granted legal personhood—that is, at emancipation, and sometimes even earlier. Extraregional connections have played a role in the affairs of the Caribbean ever since, enabling local forms of historical agency just as the stranglehold of the South Atlantic System had once constrained it. From the activities of prerevolutionary Haitian agitators, such as Vincent Ogé in Paris, to the Cuban *separatista* diaspora in New York and Tampa, Marcus Garvey's meteoric success in the United States, and Eric Williams's scholarly work at Oxford University, Caribbean historical figures have long sought to influence the fate of their native region from abroad.

If anything, this trend has intensified over the years. Caribbean diasporas in London, Paris, Brooklyn, Toronto, and Montreal today constitute not migrant populations displaced from their homelands, but key nodes within a densely interconnected Caribbean global network. Since the 1960s, Cubans have transformed Miami into a highly self-conscious Cuban "capital" in exile, fiercely antagonistic to the nation's official capital, Havana; Haiti's former president Jean-Bertrand Aristide once campaigned with an explicit appeal to Haiti's "fifth department"—that is, its diasporic population; all former French colonies except Haiti are now formally part of the European Union; and large parts of Suriname's maroon populations have resided in suburbs of Amsterdam and Rotterdam since the civil war of the 1980s. And given that more Puerto Ricans and people of Puerto Rican descent live in major urban centers of the continental United States than on the island itself, it is not an exaggeration to say that Puerto Rico's territorial politics are decided as much by its diaspora as by its resident population.

Nonetheless, the Caribbean homelands of these migrant populations and their foreign-born descendants are just that: homelands, which have attained that status, as both real and imagined communities, over centuries of bitter and often iniquitous history.

WORKS CITED

Buck-Morss, Susan. 2000. "Hegel and Haiti." *Critical Inquiry* 26:821–65.

Cooper, Frederick. 2009. "Space, Time and History: The Conceptual Limits of Globalization." In *Empirical Futures: Anthropologists and Historians Engage the Work of Sidney W. Mintz,* ed. George Baca, Aisha Khan, and Stephan Palmié, 31–57. Chapel Hill: University of North Carolina Press.

Eltis, David. 2001. "The Volume and Structure of the Transatlantic Slave Trade: A Reassessment." *William and Mary Quarterly,* 3rd Series 58, 1:17–46.

James, C. L. R. 1963. *The Black Jacobins: Toussaint L'Ouverture and the San Domingo Revolution.* New York: Random House.

Knight, Franklin W. 1978. *The Caribbean: The Genesis of a Fragmented Nationalism.* New York: Oxford University Press.

LaFeber, Walter. 1963. *The New Empire: An Interpretation of American Expansion, 1860–1898*. Ithaca, NY: Cornell University Press.

Locke, John. 1963. *Two Treatises of Government*. Cambridge: Cambridge University Press.

Mintz, Sidney. 1966. "The Caribbean as a Socio-Cultural Area." *Journal of World History* 9, 4:912–37.

———. 1996. "Enduring Substances, Trying Theories: The Caribbean Region as Oikumenê." *Journal of the Royal Anthropological Institute* 2: 289–311.

Ortiz, Fernando. 1991a. *Contrapunteo cubano del tabaco y el azúcar*. La Habana: Editorial Ciencias Sociales.

———. 1991b. *Estudios etnosociológicos*. La Habana: Editorial Ciencias Sociales.

Palmié, Stephan. 2002. *Wizards and Scientists: Explorations in Afro-Cuban Modernity and Tradition*. Durham, NC: Duke University Press.

———. 2006. "Creolization and its Discontents." *Annual Review of Anthropology* 35:433–56.

Patterson, Orlando. 1982. *Slavery and Social Death: A Comparative Study*. Cambridge, MA: Harvard University Press.

Quintero-Rivera, Angel G. 1990. "La música puertorriqueña y la contra-cultura democrática: Espontaneidad libertaria de la herencia cimarrona." *Folklore Americano* 49:135–67.

Rodney, Walter. 1972. *How Europe Underdeveloped Africa*. London: Bogle-L'Ouverture Publications.

Seed, Patricia. 1995. *Ceremonies of Possession: Europe's Conquest in the New World, 1492–1640*. Cambridge: Cambridge University Press.

Trouillot, Michel-Rolph. 1992. "The Caribbean Region: An Open Frontier in Anthropological Theory." *Annual Review of Anthropology* 21:19–42.

———. 1995. *Silencing the Past: Power and the Production of History*. Boston: Beacon Press.

Williams, Eric. 1944. *Capitalism and Slavery*. Chapel Hill: University of North Carolina Press.

PART 1

The Caribbean Stage

1

Geographies of Opportunity, Geographies of Constraint

The Caribbean region's diverse physical environments and land-scapes have acted both as a constraint on and an opportunity for human endeavor. Some of its territories are rugged and mountainous while others have subdued landscapes, undulating lowland plains, and gentle hills. Mountain environments constrained the pace of conversion to plantation economies, but at the same time offered opportunities for refuge and resistance by oppressed peoples. Hurricanes and tropical storms, earthquakes and volcanoes also litter Caribbean history and have been as violent and unpredictable as the region's turbulent colonial history.

The region's strategic location was critical to its historical development. Opportunities for territorial expansion and mercantile profit beckoned Spain and later British, French, and Dutch colonial powers. In the days of sugar, slavery, and sailing ships, the North Atlantic trade routes connected the West Indian colonies to Europe and Africa. Later, trade connections were forged between the United States, Cuba, and other Caribbean territories. Following the

25

opening of the Panama Canal in 1914, the Caribbean Sea acquired greater strategic significance as an international transport conduit in an increasingly globalized and interconnected world.

The Physical Setting

The Caribbean region, defined broadly, includes the islands within and adjacent to the Caribbean Sea, as well as the coastal areas of South and Central America that share a common cultural and economic history, notably Belize, Guyana, Suriname, and French Guiana. There are three main island groups: the Greater Antilles, the Lesser Antilles, and the Bahamas and Turks and Caicos archipelagos. Another line of islands fringes the north coast of South America and includes Aruba, Bonaire, and Curaçao, while Trinidad and Tobago lie to the south of the Lesser Antilles and the three Cayman Islands are located west of the Greater Antilles.

The total land area of the Caribbean islands is relatively small: some 91,000 square miles, roughly the size of the United Kingdom. Cuba is by far the largest island, and its 42,803 square miles represents nearly half the total (insular) land area. At the other end of the scale, Barbados covers 166 square miles and Aruba only 77. Most of the islands are sovereign states, but the Cayman Islands, Montserrat, and Anguilla are among the last colonies in the world. While its political status remains disputed, Puerto Rico is technically an internally self-governing territory of the United States, and Martinique and Guadeloupe are overseas *départements* of France. Several countries are territorially fragmented, like the twin-island Republic of Trinidad and Tobago, while the Bahamas' national territory comprises more than 700 islands, ranging in size from Andros to tiny uninhabited cays. The mainland countries of Guyana and Suriname (83,000 and 63,039 square miles, respectively) are much larger than any of the islands.

The geological evolution of the Caribbean Basin is the key to understanding the geographical distribution and relative sizes of the various island groupings. The theory of plate tectonics explains that the Earth's crust is composed of interlocking plates in constant motion relative to each other, and the Caribbean Plate is one small piece of this global jigsaw (fig. 1.1). The Caribbean Plate is moving eastward relative to the North and South American Plates, and is colliding with the North American Plate on its eastern margin. The plates' speed of movement is infinitesimal, only 0.3 to 0.6 inches per year, but inexorably the North American Plate is being forced under the Caribbean Plate. Geologists call this process *subduction* because crustal material is forced to descend into the Earth's mantle, where it mixes with magma. Inside the mantle, this super-

Figure 1.1 The Caribbean Plate and surrounding plates.

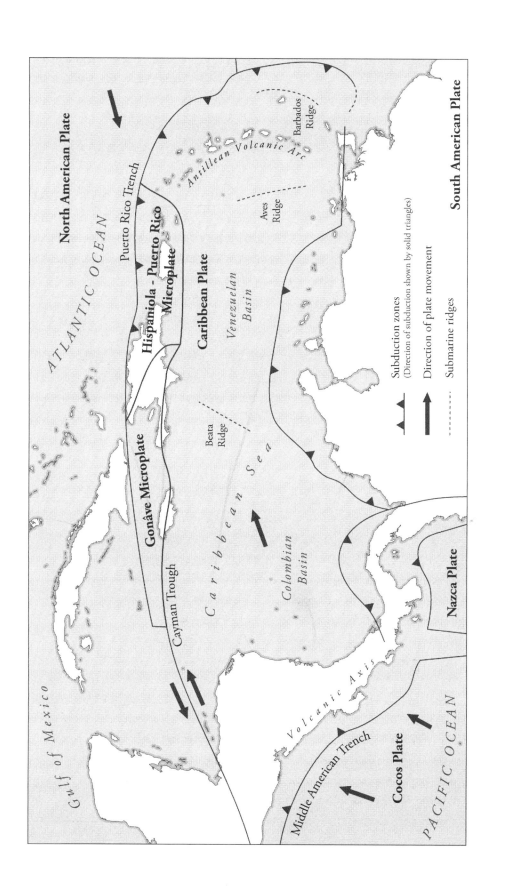

North American Plate

ATLANTIC OCEAN

Puerto Rico Trench

Hispaniola - Puerto Rico Microplate

Caribbean Plate

Gulf of Mexico

Gonâve Microplate

Cayman Trough

Beata Ridge

Caribbean Sea

Colombian Basin

Venezuelan Basin

Aves Ridge

Antillean Volcanic Arc

Barbados Ridge

South American Plate

Volcanic Axis

Middle American Trench

Cocos Plate

PACIFIC OCEAN

Nazca Plate

Subduction zones
(Direction of subduction shown by solid triangles)

Direction of plate movement

Submarine ridges

heated material eventually rises through vents in the Earth's crust and erupts onto the ocean floor, creating a submarine volcano. Over millions of years, such volcanoes grow in size and eventually appear above sea level as volcanic islands. Because subduction occurs along the entire plate boundary, a chain of volcanic islands is formed: a landform feature termed a *volcanic island arc*.

The islands of the Lesser Antilles consist of two volcanic arcs, an inner arc and an older outer arc. The inner arc, known as the Volcanic Caribbees, comprises the islands of Saba, St. Eustatius, St. Kitts, Nevis, Montserrat, western Guadeloupe, Dominica, Martinique, St. Lucia, St. Vincent and the Grenadines, and Grenada. These rugged, mountainous islands have 25 dormant and potentially active volcanoes, nine of which are on the island of Dominica, and they include the highest peaks in the eastern Caribbean, Soufriere (4,813 ft.) on Guadeloupe and Morne Diablotins (4,747 ft.) on Dominica. The scenically beautiful Pitons in St. Lucia are examples of extinct volcanic plugs. The process of volcanic island formation is being monitored carefully in the Grenadines, where a submarine volcano called Kick-'em-Jenny will one day emerge above sea level to form a new Caribbean island.

There have been 17 volcanic eruptions in the islands' historical record. Unfortunately the andesitic volcanoes typical of the eastern Caribbean, formed when two plates rub against each other, are capable of extremely violent and explosive eruptions. The worst volcanic historical disaster occurred in 1902 on Martinique. At the climax of a series of eruptions by Mount Pelée, a *pyroclastic flow*, a cloud of superheated gases and ash, raced down the volcano's flanks and annihilated the town of St. Pierre in less than two minutes. Nearly 30,000 people were either incinerated or asphyxiated. There were only two survivors, one of whom was Auguste Ciparis, incarcerated in the town dungeon on a charge of murder.

The geologically older outer arc, the Limestone Caribbees, is the second chain of islands including Anguilla, St. Maarten, St. Bartholomew, Barbuda, Antigua, eastern Guadeloupe, La Desirade, and Marie Galante. The volcanoes that created these islands are long extinct. Their land surfaces were weathered and eroded long ago, then submerged under warm tropical seas, where limestone formed. Later they were raised above sea level again, so that today these islands are flat with low-lying hills.

The Lesser Antilles are more commonly subdivided into the Leeward and Windward Islands, a nomenclature that has nothing to do with their geology. It may be attributed to Columbus, who sailed westward through the Dominica passage—between Guadeloupe and Dominica—during his second voyage, to shelter from a hurricane in the lee of the northern Lesser Antilles. Two early English sugar colonies were established in the Leeward Islands group. Antigua is a relatively flat island—one of the Limestone Caribbees—whose forests were quickly cleared for sugar plantations. St. Kitts, geologically part of the Volcanic Caribbees, has fertile volcanic soils on the coastal plains surrounding Mount Liamuiga, which provided opportunities for early planters to grow sugarcane.

Barbados is a relatively flat island like Antigua. Its forests, too, were quickly cleared for agriculture; its fertile, clayey soils were rich in lime and provided ideal conditions for the cultivation of sugarcane. The geological origin of Barbados, however, is different from that of other islands in the eastern Caribbean. Barbados lies on what geologists call an *accretionary prism* or *wedge*, created when part of the North Atlantic Plate buckled and crumpled as it slid under the Caribbean Plate over millions of years. Thick limestone and other sedimentary rocks formed in shallow seas over this deformation in the crust. Then further tectonic activity thrust the land above sea level, creating a mainly limestone coraline island with a series of parallel coral reef terraces that step downward toward the sea.

The Greater Antilles are larger, more mountainous, and more geologically complex than the Lesser Antilles. They are located along the northern boundary of the Caribbean Plate and include Cuba, Jamaica, Hispaniola, and Puerto Rico. The oldest rocks were once part of an ancient volcanic island arc, formed more than 100 million years ago, which disappeared under tropical seas and were overlain with sandstones and limestone. About 10 to 4 million years ago, the islands of the Greater Antilles were formed during a period of violent tectonic activity and mountain building that thrust the older rocks up above sea level again.

Jamaica, Hispaniola, and Puerto Rico are thus composed of various sedimentary, igneous, and metamorphic rocks that have been folded, faulted, and fractured. In places they have been sculpted into mountain blocks, plateaus, and steep escarpments. The islands are topographically similar, with central upland mountain ranges circumscribed by flatter coastal plains, the accessibility and good soils of which provided opportunities for human settlement and plantation agriculture. The highest peaks are Pico Duarte (10,417 ft.) in the Dominican Republic's Cordillera Central, and Jamaica's Blue Mountain (7,405 ft.). Many mountain ranges in Hispaniola, Puerto Rico, and eastern Jamaica are rugged, inaccessible, and deeply dissected by streams and rivers, producing spectacular, steep-sided, forested river valleys.

Only the southeastern portion of Cuba lies on the Caribbean Plate, so the geology of most of the island is different from that of the rest of the Greater Antilles and is reflected in a different topography. Cuba's mountain ranges are fairly isolated, such as the Sierra Guaniguanico in the west, famous for its tobacco, and the Sierra Maestra in the east. Most of Cuba is dominated by lowland limestone plains with fertile soils, ideal for the cultivation of sugarcane.

The location of the Greater Antilles along the northern boundary of the Caribbean Plate is significant. The Caribbean Plate is sliding very slowly past the North Atlantic Plate, and in an opposite direction. The movement is jerky and intermittent, and when slippage occurs, tremendous pressures released deep inside the

Earth's crust cause devastating shallow-zone earthquakes, so called because their point of origin, or focus, is less than 45 miles below the Earth's surface. Northern sections of the Caribbean Plate are fragmented into two small microplates, and it was slippage along the southern boundary of the Gonâve microplate that caused the January 2010 earthquake in Haiti. Measured at 7.0 on the Richter scale, with an epicenter only 15 miles from Port-au-Prince, it was not the largest-magnitude quake recorded in the region, but it caused loss of life and economic and social disruption on a scale unprecedented in Caribbean history.

The combined effects of these microplate movements along the northern plate boundary mean that the most devastating earthquakes in Caribbean history have occurred in the Greater Antilles. Puerto Rico suffered major earthquakes in 1670, 1787, 1867, and 1918. In Haiti, earthquakes destroyed Port-au-Prince twice in the 19th century and Cap Haitien in 1842. The famous 1692 earthquake in Jamaica killed more than 2,000 people and destroyed the pirate town of Port Royal, which had acquired a reputation as "the richest and wickedest city in Christendom" (Black 1988, 17). A large part of the town disappeared under the sea as a result of a submarine landslide. Aptly illustrating the theme of constraint and opportunity, most of the survivors abandoned Port Royal for the nearby Liguanea Plain, where they founded Kingston, one of the world's largest natural harbors and today a major transshipment center and container port.

Limestone regions are ubiquitous throughout the Greater Antilles. There are extensive limestone plateaus in northwest Haiti and Puerto Rico, And limestone uplands in central Jamaica are overlain with valuable bauxite deposits. These uplands have many common and distinctive landform features, including karst towers and cockpits and extensive underground cave systems created by the chemical weathering of limestone rocks. Large inland valleys in limestone areas are called *poljes*, and their alluvial soils are ideal for sugarcane. Impenetrable rugged limestone terrains once provided refuge for various groups who were in conflict with authorities. The spectacular Cockpit Country in Jamaica sheltered maroon communities that, from their remote and inaccessible villages, raided English plantations until the signing of a 1739 peace treaty. More recently, limestone caves in the Sierra Maestra provided refuge for Cuban rebels before the 1959 revolution. On Barbados and Puerto Rico, limestone caves are a major tourist attraction. The Bahamas and the Turks and Caicos Islands are archipelagos formed on stable and tectonically inactive low-lying limestone platforms where the combination of a shallow sea floor and warm tropical seas has created physical environments rich in exploitable marine resources and ideal for water sports.

Trinidad is geologically similar to the adjacent South American mainland. Its Northern Range was a separate island millions of years ago, but Trinidad was connected to mainland South America during the last Ice Age. Further south, Guyana,

Suriname, and French Guiana are low-lying littorals on the South American continent. Their coastal zones comprise mudflats and mangroves, with huge sluggish rivers draining from the continental interior. The coastal zones were the main areas of human settlement, and in colonial British Guiana, Dutch engineers constructed elaborate systems for water control. The large interiors of all three countries are still relatively uninhabited, and almost 80% of Guyana is still pristine tropical rain forest, its conditions very similar to those that existed at the time of Columbus's voyages.

Climate, Winds, and Ocean Currents

The Caribbean islands have a tropical maritime climate with humid, warm conditions throughout the year. The diurnal temperature range at sea level in summer, 34° C (93° F) in daytime to 20° C (68° F) at night, is greater than the seasonal temperature range—that is, the difference between the average daily temperatures of 28° C (82° F) in August and 25° C (77° F) in January. There are distinct wet and dry seasons, the timing of which varies slightly across the region. In Jamaica, for example, the wettest months are September and October and the driest are January and February, but there is a short rainy period around May and June. Climate and weather conditions are strongly influenced by the region's location in the path of the northeast trade winds. These winds originate in the Atlantic Ocean, blowing predominantly east to west—rather than from the northeast, as their name suggests—from a permanent high-pressure zone known as the Azores-Bermuda anticyclone. They blow all year, and their consistency and reliability were very important in the days of sailing ships (fig. 1.2).

This combination of rainfall, topography, and island size gives the Greater Antilles a mosaic of local climates. The rainfall is generally heaviest to the east and in mountain areas. In Jamaica, for example, the annual rainfall in the Blue Mountains is over 200 inches, whereas much of the central part of the island receives between 50 and 75 inches. There are also drier regions with low rainfall, known as rain shadow areas, in the lee of mountain ranges. In the Dominican Republic, for example, the Enriquillo depression is an east-west-trending valley with arid semi-desert conditions, places that lie below sea level, and a large salt lake.

There are also marked differences in rainfall patterns on the Windward Islands, where central mountains ensure that the eastern (windward) sides are wetter than the more sheltered western (leeward) sides. In the eastern Caribbean, the more tranquil weather conditions on leeward coasts provided opportunities to establish sheltered ports, and many of the region's capital towns, such as Kingstown (St. Vincent), Castries (St. Lucia), and Forte-de-France (Martinique), are notably located on the western sides of their islands.

The Caribbean islands are of course affected by the North Atlantic hurricane

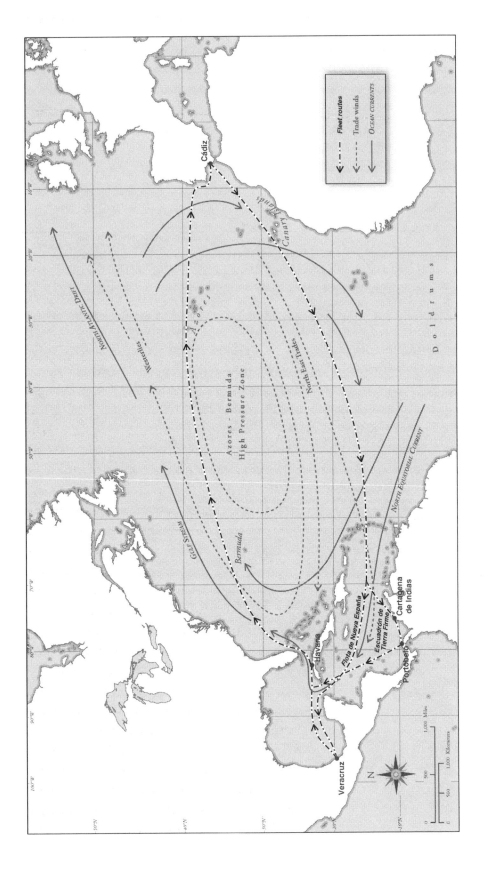

season. The word "hurricane" is derived from the Taino word *hurakan* (devil wind). Hurricanes and tropical storms are intense, low-pressure weather systems that begin as tropical disturbances and intensify through various stages with awesome destructive power. Ferocious winds spiral outward from the eye of a storm in a counterclockwise direction, at wind speeds ranging from 74 to more than 155 miles per hour. Only the island of Trinidad and the continental lands of Guyana, Suriname, and French Guiana lie outside the paths of these weather systems. The storms generally move from east to west, though their movement is not entirely predictable and depends on many meteorological factors. The hurricane season runs from June through November, with a peak frequency in the first two weeks of September. Storm systems tend to form in the Atlantic and move into the Caribbean Basin, but early- and late-season storms can begin within the basin itself. Hurricanes can strike the islands and Central America, but many curve northward and move into the Gulf of Mexico or hit Florida and the Carolinas.

The first recorded hurricane in Caribbean history was logged during Columbus's second voyage, in June 1495. In those days, hurricanes were more a threat to shipping than to human populations—for example, scattering and capsizing the French fleet in 1565 and the Dutch fleet in 1640. When the Great Hurricane of 1831 slammed into Barbados on October 10 of that year, however, at least 27,500 deaths were reported, including 1,500 slaves—the highest number of fatalities ever recorded from a hurricane in the region. By comparison, Hurricane Mitch, the most catastrophic Atlantic hurricane in modern times in terms of loss of life, killed 18,000 people in Honduras and Nicaragua in 1998.

Ocean currents have also played an important part in the region's history. Gyres are wind-driven ocean currents that, on a global scale, proscribe huge circular patterns around subtropical high-pressure cells. In the Northern Hemisphere the rotation of ocean currents is clockwise; the circulation of the North Atlantic gyre is shown in fig. 1.2. Ocean currents move at different speeds, but the Gulf Stream has a velocity of 1.8 to 2.5 miles per hour and is one of the fastest in the world.

The directions of ocean currents and surface winds were important in the days of sail. From Columbus's epic voyages to the notorious triangular trade, the North Atlantic system of winds and ocean currents was used effectively by navigators of sailing ships. The routes of the Spanish treasure fleet's annual voyages aptly illustrate the opportune synchronization of wind, ocean currents, and human endeavor. The fleets sailed from Spain down the coast of Africa to the Canary Islands, then westward, catching the northeast trades. In the Caribbean the fleet divided into the Escuadrón de Tierra Firme and the Flota de Nueva España, following the routes de-

Figure 1.2 Trade winds and ocean currents in the northern Atlantic Ocean greatly aided navigation between Europe and the Caribbean, as in the routes of Spanish treasure fleets shown here.

picted in fig. 1.2, to collect their booty. The ships later rendezvoused in Havana before making the perilous journey home, which took them through the Florida straits (making use of the Gulf Stream) before they set a course for the Azores and then back to Cádiz. The directions of the wind and ocean currents were critical at all segments of these annual voyages.

Population and Demography

The size of the region's indigenous population at the time of European contact is not known. Spanish chroniclers estimated the population at 1 million, but modern anthropologists argue that the numbers were much higher, between 6 and 12 million, with large populations on Hispaniola, Puerto Rico, and Jamaica. Tragically, these peoples and their societies were decimated within a few decades of contact, by Old World diseases, slave labor, emigration, and suicide. However, recent mitochondrial DNA studies of present populations have revealed a high Native American contribution, which suggests extensive sexual encounters between Spanish men and native women during the conquest period. Several thousand descendants of the Caribs still live on the island of Dominica, while "Black Caribs," people of mixed Carib, African, and Taino descent, live in northern St. Vincent. The mountainous volcanic island of St. Vincent was so successfully defended by the Caribs that it was one of the last of the Lesser Antilles to be colonized. After their defeat by the British, several thousand Black Caribs were deported in 1797 to an island off the coast of Honduras. Their descendants eventually settled on the Caribbean coast of Central America between Belize and Nicaragua, where they created a distinctive Garifuna culture.

The insular nature of the Caribbean region is significant because islands provided opportunities for colonial powers to establish defensible colonies during periods of intense European rivalry and warfare. Neighboring islands belonging to different colonial powers had little contact with each other, so despite their common histories, islands acquired some of the distinctive cultural traits of their colonists' mother countries, especially with respect to language and styles of governance—a legacy that has contributed to the cultural diversity of the region today.

Caribbean populations increased significantly under slavery, when more than four million people were brought from Africa, dramatically shaping the future ethnic composition of the population. A second important wave of immigration took place in the decades after emancipation, when large numbers of indentured laborers were brought from Asia to alleviate labor shortages on the plantations. Between 1835 and 1917, almost 700,000 workers arrived from British India and another 150,000 came from China, primarily into Trinidad and British Guiana, while approximately 50,000 from the Dutch East Indies (mainly Java) settled in Suriname.

After completing their indentured service, many laborers stayed on, encouraged by land grants and prospects for economic advancement, further enriching the cultural diversity of Caribbean societies. Today, people of East Indian descent form the largest ethnic group in Trinidad and Guyana (formerly British Guiana). Tens of thousands of Western Europeans (mostly Spaniards) also arrived in the Hispanophone Caribbean during the 19th and 20th centuries.

By 1960 the Caribbean population had reached 17 million, and it has since more than doubled to 40 million. Cuba, the largest island, has 11 million people, and the Greater Antilles together account for more than 90% of the region's total. In terms of language groupings, about 64% of the people live in the Spanish-speaking countries (Cuba, the Dominican Republic, and Puerto Rico) and 22% live in French-speaking territories (mainly Haiti). Only about 6 million people live in English-speaking countries, two-thirds of whom live in either Jamaica (2.7 million) or Trinidad and Tobago (1.4 million). Islands such as Antigua, St. Lucia, St. Vincent, and Grenada have populations between 100,000 and 200,000, while St. Kitts and Nevis has only 40,000.

Not surprisingly, population densities are high by international standards, with an average of 66 people per square mile. However, as with other demographic statistics, there is considerable variability from island to island. The highest population densities are in Barbados (1,663 per square mile), Aruba (1,479), and Puerto Rico (1,115), while the lowest are in the Bahamas (60) and the Turks and Caicos Islands (127). The population densities are even lower in continental French Guiana (3), Suriname (7), and Guyana (10) because their populations are geographically concentrated in the lowland coastal areas, while the interior rainforests and savannas are relatively unpopulated.

Recent improvements in health care have significantly reduced child morbidity and mortality, and birth rates and death rates now compare favorably with those in industrialized countries. As of 2007, the birth rate for the region was 19 per 1,000 residents, the death rate was a low 8 per 1,000 residents, the infant mortality rate was 32 (deaths of children under age one per 1,000 live births), and life expectancy was 71 years. These averages are distorted by atypical data from Haiti, where the birth rate was 29, the death rate 11, infant mortality 57, and life expectancy only 58. For most islands the proportion of people under age 15 ranged between 25% and 30%, which is more typical of Asian than African countries, and higher than in the industrialized world. Again Haiti was an exception at 39% while Martinique, Barbados, and Puerto Rico had values closer to 20%. The average rate of natural increase of the region's population was 1.1, much lower than in some developing regions, but again Haiti and the Dominican Republic had much higher rates. Cuba, Puerto Rico, Barbados, and Trinidad and Tobago had lower rates of natural increase.

Urbanization and Migration

The Caribbean is one of the most urbanized regions in the world, and the level of urbanization has increased significantly during the last 50 years. In 1960, less than 40% of the population lived in cities, but today 62% is defined as urban. The official statistics for Guadeloupe and Martinique imply that virtually their entire populations live in an urban areas, while in the Bahamas and Puerto Rico the rates are as high as 90%. An important feature of Caribbean countries is that each capital town or city is much larger than the second largest urban center in its country. Puerto Rico, Trinidad and Tobago, Antigua, Martinique, and Jamaica each have more than 30% of their national population living in the largest urban center. This trend is called *urban primacy*.

Caribbean cities are generally much smaller than capitals elsewhere in the developing world. The largest, Port-au-Prince in Haiti, has an estimated population between 2.5 and 3 million people, closely followed by Havana and Santo Domingo, each around 2.1 million. The largest city in the English-speaking Caribbean is Kingston, with a population of 800,000. Because Caribbean islands are among the world's smallest sovereign states, seats of government, civil service, and port facilities may be located in capital towns that can barely be classified as urban centers by world standards. For example, Basseterre, capital of St. Kitts and Nevis, has a population of 15,000, while Charlestown, the largest settlement on Nevis, has a population of only 1,500.

Urban growth, as elsewhere in the developing world, is the result of both rural-urban migration and demographic increase. Towns and tourist areas offer more attractive employment opportunities than agriculture, especially for young people, and have better social services, educational opportunities, infrastructure, and housing. Rapid, unplanned, and uncontrolled urban growth has characterized Caribbean towns and cities since the 1960s and has resulted in poor housing in inner cities and squatter settlement in unoccupied areas, often in hazard-prone locations. Infrastructure development is unable to keep pace with rapid urbanization, and the flood of new and secondhand cars from Japan and Korea since the onset of trade liberalization in the early 1990s has contributed significantly to urban congestion. Another feature of urbanization has been rapid suburban development, especially upscale housing for the affluent middle classes, which has spread to the hills overlooking the old colonial towns and contributed to urban sprawl. The general visual impression of modern Caribbean towns and cities is one of haphazard, unplanned, and overcrowded urban development, in sharp contrast to the neat, precise gridiron street patterns laid out when the original colonial towns were founded. Indeed, old street patterns and colonial facades can still be discerned in the decaying urban fabric of historic downtown areas.

Caribbean island populations would be much larger but for overseas migration. The decision to emigrate reflects a mix of push (constraining) factors at home and pull (opportunistic) factors abroad. Depressed economic conditions and lack of livelihood opportunities are the usual driving forces. However, a major natural disaster can trigger a sudden exodus of people. A good example is Montserrat, where the Soufriere Hills volcano began erupting in 1995. Loss of life was minimal, but more than 8,000 of the island's 12,000 people left in the immediate aftermath of the eruptions, which rendered two-thirds of the island uninhabitable. The island's capital town, Plymouth, was buried under repeated pyroclastic flows and ultimately abandoned, and a new capital town and airport have been constructed in the tiny area relatively unaffected by the eruptions.

Migration as a response to negative economic conditions began immediately when Caribbean people were no longer enslaved. They left the plantations and settled the relatively unoccupied interiors of the larger mountainous islands as independent farmers, or moved to capital towns and cities to try their luck in paid employment. Around the same time, the interisland schooners plying their trade in the eastern Caribbean began to carry the first interisland migrants, initiating the intra-Caribbean migrations that continue today.

The first major international migration involved 5,000 Jamaicans who helped construct a railway across the Isthmus of Panama between 1848 and 1855. Jamaica's large labor force and proximity to Central America were important factors in the early migrations. Generally, between the 1880s and 1920s, Caribbean plantation economies were severely depressed, and overseas employment provided economic opportunities for an impoverished and disenfranchised population. Over the next 40 years, West Indians were attracted to construction projects and agricultural work in many countries bordering the Caribbean Sea. The failed efforts by the French to construct the Panama Canal from 1881 to 1888 attracted West Indian laborers, as did new banana plantations in Central America in the 1880s and construction of the Panama Canal between 1904 and 1914. More than 121,000 Jamaicans worked on Cuban sugar plantations between 1902 and 1932. In each of these examples, descendants of the migrants who stayed have added to a country's ethnic mix. After World War II, migration from the Caribbean to Britain, France, and the Netherlands became significant, as did migration from Puerto Rico to the continental United States. Since the 1970s, the United States, Canada, and Europe have attracted tens of thousands of migrants from all parts of the region, so that today vibrant Caribbean communities exist in many European, Canadian, and American cities.

The intimate relationship between the physical environment and the human population that has characterized the last 500 years of Caribbean history is critically important to the region's prospects for sustainable economic development. The United Nations defines Caribbean islands as small island developing states (SIDS) and considers them a special case. Small islands have economic development problems markedly different from those of larger, continental developing countries. The constraints include limited land space, limited amounts of good arable land, exposure to natural hazards, high population densities, small internal markets, reliance on imported manufactured goods, high transportation costs, and expensive infrastructure. Limited or absent mineral resources are also a severe constraint. Of small island nations in the Caribbean, the only ones with exploitable economic reserves are Trinidad and Tobago (oil and natural gas), Cuba (oil and copper), the Dominican Republic (gold), and Jamaica and Guyana (bauxite).

Thus, many Caribbean countries have opted to take advantage of their tropical island environment and proximity to North American markets to develop tourism. This classifies them as service economies, not industrial or agricultural economies. Indeed, the future of traditional export agriculture in the Caribbean is uncertain. The region once held a comparative advantage for tropical produce by virtue of its cheap labor, tropical climate, good soils, and favorable terrain—but it was trapped in colonial dependency. Today, in an era of neoliberalism, it is difficult for traditional Caribbean export crops to compete with cheaper produce from larger tropical countries. The region as a whole is peripheral to the world economy, and many of the countries are economically marginalized at a time when the forces of trade liberalization and globalization are quite unforgiving. Thus, economic circumstances still limit opportunities for most Caribbean people, and migration is an agenda item for many, though the flourishing tourist industry clearly demonstrates how people of the region continue to adapt to a changing world and use their cultural resources in innovative ways.

WORK CITED

Black, C. 1988. *Port Royal*. Kingston: Institute of Jamaica Publications.

2

Contemporary Caribbean Ecologies

DUNCAN McGREGOR

The Weight of History

The history of European horticulture in the Americas dates back to the second voyage of Christopher Columbus in 1493, which brought a variety of Old World seeds and cuttings to the Caribbean. As colonization increased and spread, Europeans introduced a wide variety of plants and animals to the region (along with diseases to which Native Americans had little or no resistance, such as smallpox). In this sense, early colonization enriched Caribbean ecology to a certain extent. Sugarcane, which was later to play an important part in ecological degradation, was among the successful introductions. On the other hand, wheat, a staple of the colonizers' diet, did not grow well in the Caribbean climate, which was hotter and wetter than that of Europe. Domesticated animals were also introduced by Columbus in 1493 and generally adapted well to the new environment.

The plantation era that followed was characterized by widespread ecological degradation, through the progressive depletion of both flora and fauna. Thus, the roots of Caribbean environmental degradation lie in the history of the plantation economies and the colonial legacy. Resource exploitation at the expense of the environment was widespread then and it continues today, extending beyond the boundaries of agriculture to urbanization, extractive industries, and tourism.

The early foundations of plantation agriculture were probably laid in the early 16th century when sugar mills were imported from the Canary Islands and established on lands to the west of Santo Domingo, in the part of Hispaniola that is now the Dominican Republic. But ecological degradation began almost immediately, as *conuco* farmland (land fertilized with organic crop and household residues, often in mounds, and used to grow manioc) was abandoned by the indigenous population and used as rough pasture for hogs and cattle (Watts 1987, 117). Soil compaction induced by the animals' trampling rapidly led to loss of topsoil, and a degraded vegetation of shrubs and native grasses took over the abandoned *conuco* land. On higher ground, Old World quadrupeds adapted well to the forests and multiplied wildly.

Throughout the 16th century and into the 17th, as the Spanish increasingly faced northwestern European attempts to establish colonial possessions in the region, plantation agriculture took over in some parts of the Caribbean, especially the British islands. St. Kitts and Barbados appear to have been the first islands settled as permanent, crop-growing colonies in the West Indies. The introduction of tobacco, and subsequently sugarcane, to Barbados and St. Kitts around 1640 initiated large-scale clearance of native vegetation throughout the Caribbean basin. Only isolated pockets of natural forest remained in Barbados by 1665. This rapid deforestation was mirrored in many of the other islands where plantation crops of tobacco, sugarcane, and cotton were established, and worked by slave labor. Overpopulation also became a factor contributing to relatively intense cultivation for export and domestic markets, degrading soil resources in the process (Richardson 1992).

Plantation owners often set aside parcels of land, known as provision grounds, where estate slaves could grow their own food. This land, usually about half an acre per slave family, was judged unsuitable for plantation crops. In Haiti and Jamaica, the crops grown on provision grounds might have included familiar African crops such as guinea yam and okra; Native American crops including maize (corn), sweet potatoes, potatoes, and tomatoes; European vegetables such as cabbage and carrots; and even Southeast Asian food trees such as breadfruit (Mintz 2007). A variety of fruit-bearing trees including citrus, avocado, mango, coconut palm, papaya, soursop, and ackee were also cultivated, particularly around the house plots. These multistory assemblages of plants were also common in many of the eastern Caribbean islands (Berleant-Schiller and Pulsipher 1986).

Aiding the transition from predominantly plantation agriculture to a more mixed situation in which domestic agriculture was also important, plantation owners allowed slaves relative freedom of choice in the crops they grew on the provision grounds. In Jamaica, slaves were also permitted to sell their surplus produce as early as 1711, thus laying the foundation for a system in which both free men and women and slaves could buy and sell food (Mintz 2007, 197). The higgler system—in which an individual, usually a woman, buys small amounts of produce from farmers and transports them to urban markets to resell them there—remains a major plank of the Jamaican domestic food market system today.

In the 1830s and 1840s, British and French slave emancipation exacerbated environmental deterioration. Denied access to the best land, which was still held by plantation owners, and often to their provision grounds, former slaves who wished to farm were forced onto lands characterized by poorer soils, often on steeply sloping hillsides or in lowland marshlands. There they persisted with deleterious plantation practices such as fire clearance (setting fire to felled timber and bush to clear the land for planting) and clean weeding (regular removal of weeds from among the developing crops), both of which accelerated soil erosion by removing root structures from already precarious hillsides (Barker and McGregor 1988). The former slaves generally abandoned sugarcane to plant various crops that they could eat or sell, and this also helped accelerate erosion.

Although examples of land degradation were ubiquitous throughout the cultivated areas of the colonized islands, possibly the worst cases occurred in Haiti. Because it achieved independence in 1804, earlier than other Caribbean lands, Haiti experienced relative isolation within and beyond the region until the US occupation began in 1915. This isolation slowed social and cultural change, effectively entrenching a traditional peasant way of life throughout rural Haiti. Economic stagnation followed, with an ever-growing dichotomy between poor rural cultivators and a small but powerful elite. Extreme rural poverty remains the norm in Haiti today, with most land held in small, steeply sloping plots of low productivity. Continuing governmental instability, poor communications and access to markets, excessive taxation, and limited credit facilities are among the problems that continue to beset the Haitian agricultural sector (Mintz 2007).

The earthquake of January 2010 amplified Haiti's problems and severely set back its agricultural production, which had actually increased by 15% in 2009, due principally to aid programs supervised by the United Nations Food and Agriculture Organization (FAO). Earthquake damage to irrigation works devastated the bean and maize crops that were almost ready for harvest, while breakdowns in the supply of seeds and fertilizers affected preparations for the main planting season (March to May). Work on restoring Haiti's forests was suspended.

Ecological Degradation in the Modern Era

Possibly the most significant agricultural land-use change in the Caribbean in recent decades has been the decline of the sugar industry. Although sugar still occupies an estimated 30% of agricultural land, its importance on the export balance sheet continues to decline. In 1961 Caribbean sugar accounted for 20% of world production; today, that number has declined to less than 4%. The general contribution of agriculture to Caribbean nations' GDP is also in decline; for example, in St. Kitts and Nevis it fell from 40% of GDP in 1964 to less than 6% by the end of the century (Potter et al. 2004). Abandoned sugarcane lands are not necessarily taken up by other forms of agriculture. At one location near San Fernando in Trinidad and Tobago, for example, the ruling People's National Movement (PNM) has annexed former sugarcane lands for "affordable" housing, considered locally to have been preferentially allocated to PNM supporters.

But new agricultural land has more or less continually been created through processes of deforestation. In recent decades, annual rates of deforestation have been the subject of much debate, despite the availability of satellite imagery and aerial photography. One expert has estimated them at about 1.5% in the eastern Caribbean (Eyre 1998). His estimates for Jamaica have been as high as 5.3% per annum (Eyre 1987, 1996), but a more recent figure of 0.1% per annum for the period 1989–98, based on a thorough analysis of remotely sensed data, seems more realistic (Evelyn and Camirand 2003). Where the abandonment of agriculture has occurred at a fast pace, as in Puerto Rico, an interesting contrary trend has taken hold. Reforestation is now occurring at relatively high rates there, although experts believe that it is not extensive or coherent enough to undo the centuries-old damage brought by destructive agricultural practices (Rudel, Pérez-Lugo, and Zichal 2000).

Haiti is perhaps the worst example of deforestation in the region, where estimates of the extent of surviving original forest range from 2% to less than 1%. Though Haiti's deforestation has been accomplished largely in the quest for new land for agriculture, forested land elsewhere in the Caribbean has been lost to housing. Trinidad's Northern Range has recently suffered significant encroachment for both agriculture and housing.

What is certain, however, is the clear linkage between deforestation, for whatever reason, and increasing soil erosion. This pattern particularly affects hillside farming systems, which experience high rates of soil erosion and widespread land degradation throughout the Caribbean. In the case of St. Lucia, soil losses from intensely cultivated agricultural watersheds can be 20 times higher than those from adjacent forest.

Caribbean hillside farming systems are characterized by small and fragmented holdings, short or absent fallow periods, fire clearance, and clean weeding. With the exception of Barbados, plot fragmentation is the norm in the Caribbean (Potter et al. 2004, 127). The use of fragmented plots may reflect a positive choice by farmers to use parcels of land in different environmental circumstances, such as differences over relatively short distances in rainfall, temperature, soil quality, and slope angle. This is in effect a risk-spreading strategy, reducing potential losses to pests and diseases or to natural events such as erosion or landsliding.

Although there have been multiple soil-erosion control schemes since the middle of

the last century, few of these have proved effective over the longer term. There are many reasons why these schemes have largely failed, including lack of continuation funding, application of inappropriate technology, and breakdown of integrated systems of structures and waterways. In the case of Haiti, a lack of capital and widespread absence of land tenure hinder development of rural agriculture. But the basic physical limitations of slope, soil, and climate remain major constraints on hillside agriculture (fig. 2.1).

Figure 2.1 Degraded hillside agriculture, Upper Yallahs Valley, Jamaica. Photo by Duncan McGregor.

A further reason for the lack of success with soil-erosion control schemes lies in their relative failure to incorporate and make appropriate use of indigenous technical knowledge. Kitchen gardens and food forests are two such potentially useful adaptations. Kitchen gardens reflected the planting by slaves of small areas around their dwellings with crops, trees, and other plants from which they obtained food, drinks, and medicines. A food forest, which may include a kitchen garden, is a multistory assemblage of food trees. It may be around the house or some distance from it. It may be large, up to several acres in size. Not only are kitchen gardens and food forests risk-reducing strategies—in that different foods will be produced at different times of the year, and mixed crops are more resistant to pests and diseases than mono-crops—but they also reduce soil erosion significantly. These are in effect traditional agroforestry techniques that have long been recognized as potential solutions to the sustainability problems of Caribbean hillside farming (fig. 2.2).

Figure 2.2 Food forest, upper St. Andrew, Jamaica. Photo by Duncan McGregor.

Such agroforestry systems have long been in use in Haiti. According to one observer, home courtyard gardens there may incorporate coffee, cassava, plantain, castor bean, mango, avocado, and citrus plants (McClintock 2004). Live fences are used to protect fields and gardens. Initiatives in Haiti have included extensive provision of free seedlings to more than 200,000 farmers through a United States Agency for International Development (USAID) agroforestry outreach project in the late 1980s. Yet the soil conservation strategies that persist today are often focused on long-standing indigenous practices such as building contour residue barriers, vegetating gullies, and hoeing weeds into contour ridges before planting.

Island population densities in the Caribbean are often high, and relatively dense settlement on rural hillsides remains common. However, younger people have been abandoning hillside agriculture for decades, leaving behind an aging farming population. There is no easy solution to this problem, though governments have attempted to introduce alternative livelihood strategies, as in the promotion of agroforestry in Haiti. Meanwhile, soil nutrient depletion and accelerated erosion continue to increase in some countries. Agriculture has thus become an extractive industry, one that is unsustainable in the long term in its present form unless significantly reconstructed by governments and aid agencies alike.

The Constraints of the Small Island Setting

One characteristic of small island developing states (SIDS)—the designation given to many Caribbean islands by the United Nations—is that the relationships between people and their environments are much more immediate and dramatic than those in most continental areas. Deforestation in the uplands leads directly to accelerated soil erosion. Sediment is transferred rapidly through the catchment—particularly on islands dominated by steeply sloping land with a relatively narrow coastal fringe, such as St. Lucia and Dominica—to offshore regions, where it will settle on and damage fringing reefs. Hurricanes or flash floods can have disastrous effects on an island economy. A hurricane may hit an entire island with its destructive winds and rains.

Small islands are characterized by limited physical size of land area, difficult topography, and limited renewable and nonrenewable resources. Watershed degradation leads not only to increased levels of soil erosion but also to a progressively deteriorating water supply. This problem is particularly acute in the limited coastal zone, where overabstraction of groundwater (for irrigation, industry, or urban or tourist development) causes aquifers to become depleted and invaded by sea water.

This physical vulnerability transmits itself to economic vulnerability in the Caribbean SIDS. Centuries of outward-looking plantation agriculture have led to an unhealthy dependence on undiversified agriculture, which is subject to world trade and economic fluctuations and hampered by the cost of transporting raw, processed, or manufactured materials to market. The domestic food system has historically been based on agriculturally marginal farming. Despite opportunities provided more recently by tourism, small farmers struggle to provide a decent standard of living for their families in marginal physical circumstances and, now, in the face of global trade liberalization and a flood of cheap food imports into the region.

Caribbean SIDS are net importers of food. Radical trade imbalances exist for staple foods: for example, statistics from the FAO show that several islands, including Antigua and Barbuda, Jamaica, Trinidad and Tobago, Barbados, Dominica, and Grenada, import more than 90% of their cereals. Not only have food imports increased progressively in recent decades, but exports of agricultural commodities such as sugar and bananas have decreased due to external market changes and the reduction of traditional preferential trade arrangements. This trend represents a significant challenge for the Caribbean SIDS, despite the World Trade Organization's 2004 Doha Framework Agreement, which asserts that the trade-related issues of SIDS should be addressed.

Ecological Sustainability, Industry, and Tourism

Extractive industries and tourism have become significant threats to the ecological sustainability of the Caribbean in recent decades. Excluding agriculture, extractive industries are of significance in only a few territories. Cuba has exploitable reserves of petroleum and nickel. Bauxite mining is a significant industry in the Dominican Republic, Jamaica, Suriname, and Guyana—though at present only the Jamaican industry could be described as thriving—while Trinidad and Tobago has considerable petroleum reserves. Some gold is also mined in Guyana, the Dominican Republic, Suriname, and Haiti, although these reserves are not large on a world scale. Sand mining should perhaps be added to this list, as the demands for fabricated tourist beaches have risen throughout the insular Caribbean in recent decades.

Although Trinidad and Tobago's petrochemical industry is extractive, the oil and gas resources are mostly offshore and the impact on land is relatively restricted. There are, however, persistent reports that the Gulf of Paria has been polluted by the effluents from Trinidad's Point Lisas natural-gas–supplied industries. Significant expansion of Cuba's petrochemicals industry may be expected, as recent estimates of reserves of oil (ranging from a US Geological Survey estimate of 9 billion barrels to Cuba's CUPET estimate of 20 billion barrels) indicate significant extractive potential off Cuba's northern shores.

Bauxite mining is probably the region's most environmentally damaging extractive industry, due to the opencast nature of bauxite mining. Further, the profits of such mining in the English-speaking Caribbean have accrued to European and North American corporations rather than being reinvested locally (Richardson 1992). In Jamaica, significant pressure has been brought to bear on bauxite mining companies to clean up their act and to restore mined-out land to agriculture. However, toxic red mud lakes, the waste disposal from alumina processing, have polluted groundwater aquifers and will remain hazardous for decades.

Agriculture has more recently become less important to the islands' economic well-being than tourism. Tourism is now the major industry in many islands in terms of economic value, although agriculture remains the main livelihood of many and is still the major land user. The corresponding growth in service-sector industries has been dramatic. For example, the economy of Antigua depended entirely on sugar exports until that industry collapsed in the 1960s, with the last factory closing in the 1970s. Antigua then turned to tourism and offshore banking, thus exchanging one unhealthy dependence for another.

As with agriculture, however, the development of tourism and tourist infrastructure have taken place without due note of environmental issues, including ecology. The direct effects of tourism have fallen largely in the coastal zone, where agricultural land use has frequently been squeezed out by rising rents and land prices. Although this chapter focuses largely on terrestrial ecology, marine ecology has also suffered greatly under tourism (Conway 2004; Pattullo 2005).

The resulting problems are legion. Development is relentless, and leaders have been reluctant to learn the lessons of eroded beaches, polluted waters, inappropriate garbage and sewage disposal, destroyed mangroves, and blighted coral reefs. With those in power frequently benefiting directly from development, environmental legislation has been quietly bypassed. Objections by environmentalists have frequently been set aside and in many cases discredited. There is now, however, a growing awareness that neither mass tourism nor elite "all-inclusive" resorts are environmentally sustainable as they stand.

Ecotourism, with its focus on environmental protection, is cited by many as the way out of the economic dilemma presented by traditional forms of tourism. Islands such as Cuba and Dominica and continental states such as Belize and Guyana have espoused ecotourism in recent years. Belize and Guyana are looking to develop their rain forests as ecotourist resources. Despite a lack of white sand beaches, Dominica is also developing its natural rainforest resources to encourage ecotourists. Belize and Dominica are now on the cruise ship circuit, which is proving to be a mixed blessing.

Part of the problem has been the perception that the natural landscape or seascape is a resource to be exploited. Yet until recently, relatively little attention has been given to the question of how to "value" such a resource, or how to weigh the costs to the environment and local traditional livelihoods against the benefits to be gained by exploitation. One such evaluation technique assesses the impact that recreational use of natural resources has on the services provided to tourists by terrestrial and marine ecosystems (Thomas-Hope and Jardine-Comrie 2007). These services include the absorption of liquid waste (sewage and waste water) and the sequestration of carbon dioxide. Analysis shows, for example, that the replacement cost of fresh water currently used by Jamaica's hotels is approximately 80 times more than the amount paid in utilities to the National Water Commission. Evaluating the environmental costs of tourism is a complex task, yet it is a nettle that must be grasped if tourism in the Caribbean SIDS is to be environmentally sustainable into the future.

Of course, tourism also provides an opportunity for local farmers. Although agricultural production has generally declined in the insular Caribbean since 1960, there has also been a shift to nontraditional crops such as lettuce, cucumbers, and tomatoes to supply the growing tourist industry. Although the picture is variable, islands where tourism is a significant component of the economy—such as Barbados, Jamaica, St. Lucia, Guadeloupe, and Martinique—have experienced significant growth in many nontraditional and some traditional crops. The pattern is not uniform: for example, Puerto Rico's production of many crops appears to have dropped significantly despite the island's large tourism sector (Conway 2004). But statistics can sometimes be misleading in a region where individual, high-magnitude climatic events can have a devastating effect on island agriculture in a particular year.

Examples of particularly damaging hurricanes in recent decades include Gilbert (Jamaica, 1988), Hugo (Guadeloupe, Montserrat, and Puerto Rico, 1989), Luis (Barbuda and the Leewards, 1995), Georges (Puerto Rico and Hispaniola, 1998), Ivan (principally Grenada, but also Haiti and Jamaica, 2004), and Dennis (Haiti and Cuba, 2005). Haiti was hit in 2008 by a series of hurricanes and tropical storms in close succession (Fay, Gustav, Hanna, and Ike) and then by the devastating earthquake of January 2010; each time, agriculture there suffered greatly. The volcanic eruptions in Montserrat since 1995 represent yet another case in which natural events drastically affect agricultural production and the tourist sector alike.

As tourism and its infrastructure expand, it is not inevitable that agriculture will suffer. Tourist infrastructure is principally developed in the coastal zone, where agricultural lands may be marginal. Also, tourism can influence agriculture positively by offering alternative off-farm employment opportunities, raising land sale values, offering incentives to farmers to produce high-value and high-quality food for tourist hotels and resorts, and creating aesthetic uses for rural land (such as ecotourism).

One positive agricultural by-product of tourism has been expanding exports of fresh and processed tropical food products. This exploitation of niche markets can be illustrated by the success of Walkerswood Caribbean Foods, a producer of pepper sauce, "jerk" seasoning, mango chutney, and other Jamaican sauces in St. Anne Parish, Jamaica. The rural community of Walkerswood has benefited from increased farm incomes and employment opportunities through the setting up of a local food processing factory, while Jamaica has benefited through new sources of foreign exchange, which reached more than £1 million (US$1.3 million) in 2008.

Tourism can thus be seen, in its demand for high-quality food, as a stimulus to domestic agriculture. Farmers are adept at exploiting opportunities, and their store of indigenous technical knowledge enables them to adapt to changing environmental and market circumstances. In southern St. Elizabeth Parish, Jamaica, for example, farmers have adapted to low annual rainfall totals (around 800 mm, or 31 in., annually) to produce a wide range of crops (carrots, scallions, watermelons and other melons, sweet peppers, and tomatoes) for both the domestic and tourist markets (McGregor et al. 2009). They do this through ingenious use of mulches and improvised irrigation systems. These farmers have had to contend with successive droughts in the early parts of each year and tropical storms and hurricanes through the main growing season from August to November. They have also contended with competition from imported foods, since as little as 40% of the food consumed in large all-inclusive hotels is grown locally in Jamaica (Pennicook 2006).

Pressures on farmers are both external and internal. Agricultural development programs were rolled back by the Jamaican government in the 1980s under conditions of neoliberal agricultural reforms. The onset of global trade liberalization policies not only prejudiced the long-standing preferential marketing arrangements with the European Union, but also led to significant increases in cheap food imports through significant decreases in import duties (Rhiney 2009).

Farmers face a multitude of problems in supplying the tourism industry, including a reliance on purveyors who may or may not have appropriate transport and offer them a fair price. Farmers' cooperatives have been tried in Jamaica, with variable success in supplying hotels and restaurants. A growing concern for farmers is the increasing tendency for purveyors to purchase imported food instead of domestically grown crops for onward sale. Thus both natural and human events contribute to the considerable uncertainty facing small farmers who produce for the domestic market.

Caribbean Ecologies in Summary and Prospect

Caribbean ecologies have undergone a remarkable transition since 1492, with natural vegetation being replaced to a great extent by the managed vegetation of plantation and domestic agriculture. Significant interchange of flora and fauna, and of pests and diseases, has taken place, principally but not exclusively between the Old World and the New World. Widespread deforestation, reaching its peak in Haiti, and replacement of natural forest with agriculture have led to basin-wide accelerated soil erosion and more or less ubiquitous degradation of soil status through overuse and misuse. Population pressure on resources and the social and economic pressures associated with a globalizing world have driven deforestation and degradation alike. Despite the aspirations of environmentalists, Caribbean ecologies cannot substantially revert to their pre-Columbian status.

Nor indeed is the pace of change likely to slow down in the forthcoming decades. Prospects for Caribbean ecologies are not encouraging. Pressure on resources is relatively high in these densely populated islands, yet further intensification of land use is likely. Paradoxically, rural populations are in decline, with people moving out of domestic agriculture and either into city life or out of the islands entirely. Domestic agriculture is almost universally depressed throughout the basin. Farmers with progressively more degraded soils struggle to maintain output to feed ever-growing populations. External globalization pressures also come into play, including trade liberalization, which increases avenues for food imports into the region and prejudices traditional food export markets.

Against this background of human activity must be set the ongoing climate changes induced by global warming, itself now understood as almost certainly human-induced. Basin-wide temperature rises are combining with stormier hurricane seasons, more severe early-season droughts, and emerging evidence of declining rainfall throughout much of the basin.

Thus, agricultural systems that are already marginal in either human or physical terms may become yet more marginal in the near future. People are adaptable and innovative in the face of change, whether its causes are natural or human, but there are limits. For example, the farmers in St. Elizabeth Parish, Jamaica, appear to be progressively stepping back from agriculture as a consequence of deepening drought and rising prices for mulching materials and irrigation water.

On a more positive note, Caribbean peoples are becoming progressively more aware of the need to conserve what little original vegetation exists, and of the necessity to use land sustainably in the future. Environmental pressure groups are springing up throughout the islands, and groups and individuals are now capitalizing on the influx of project-oriented, environmentally related funds available from international sources. For example, the Global Environmental Facility (GEF) Small Grants program ostensibly focuses on biodiversity and climate change, but in practice facilitates the implementation of many locally based, sustainable livelihood strategies. It is perhaps through such initiatives that the continued clearance of native Caribbean ecologies may at last be halted. Provision of sustainable human land-based livelihoods that do not further impinge on native ecologies will undoubtedly help to attain this goal.

WORKS CITED

Barker, David, and Duncan F. M. McGregor. 1988. "Land Degradation in the Yallahs Basin, Jamaica: Historical Notes and Contemporary Perspectives." *Geography* 73, 116–24.

Berleant-Schiller, Riva, and Lydia D. Pulsipher. 1986. "Subsistence Cultivation in the Caribbean." *New West Indian Guide* 60 (1–2), 1–40.

Conway, Dennis. 2004. "Tourism, Environmental Conservation and Management and Local Agriculture in the Eastern Caribbean." In David T. Duval, ed., *Tourism in the Caribbean: Trends, Development, Prospects*, 187–204. London: Routledge.

Evelyn, Owen B., and Roland Camirand. 2003. "Forest Cover and Deforestation in Jamaica: An Analysis of Forest Cover Estimates over Time." *International Forestry Review* 5, 354–63.

Eyre, L. Alan. 1987. "Jamaica: Test Case for Tropical Deforestation." *Ambio* 16, 338–43.

———. 1996. "The Tropical Rainforests of Jamaica." *Jamaica Journal* 26, 26–37.

———. 1998. "The Tropical Rainforests of the Eastern Caribbean: Present Status and Conservation." *Caribbean Geography* 9, 101–20.

McClintock, Nathan C. 2004. *Agroforestry and Sustainable Resource Conservation in Haiti: A Case Study*. Partners in Progress. Available at http://www.piphaiti.org/overview_of_Haiti2.html.

McGregor, Duncan F. M., Donovan Campbell, and David Barker. 2009. "Environmental Change and Caribbean Food Security: Recent Hazard Impacts and Domestic Food Production in Jamaica." In Duncan F. M. McGregor, David Dodman, and David Barker, eds., *Global Change and Caribbean Vulnerability: Environment, Economy and Society at Risk?* 197–217. Kingston: University of the West Indies Press.

Mintz, Sidney W. 2007. *Caribbean Transformations*. New Brunswick, NJ: Transaction Publishers.

Pattullo, Polly. 2005. *Last Resorts: The Cost of Tourism in the Caribbean*. London: Cassell.

Pennicook, Paul. 2006. "The All-Inclusive Concept: Improving Benefits to the Jamaican Economy." In K. Hall and R. Holding, eds., *Tourism: The Driver of Change in the Jamaican Economy?* 31–38. Kingston: Ian Randle Publishers.

Potter, Robert B., David Barker, Dennis Conway, and Thomas Klak. 2004. *The Contemporary Caribbean*. Harlow, UK, and New York: Pearson/Prentice Hall.

Rhiney, Kevon. 2009. "Defining the Link? Globalization, Tourism and the Jamaican Food Supply Network." In Duncan F. M. McGregor, David Dodman, and David Barker, eds., *Global Change and Caribbean Vulnerability: Environment, Economy and Society at Risk?*, 237–58. Kingston: University of the West Indies Press.

Richardson, Bonham C. 1992. *The Caribbean in the Wider World, 1492–1992*. Cambridge: Cambridge University Press.

Rudel, T. K., M. Pérez-Lugo, and H. Zichal. 2000. "When Fields Revert to Forest: Development and Spontaneous Reforestation in Post-War Puerto Rico." *The Professional Geographer* 52, 386–97.

Thomas-Hope, Elizabeth, and Adonna Jardine-Comrie. 2007. "Valuation of Environmental Resources for Tourism in Small Island Developing States: Implications for Planning in Jamaica." *International Development Planning Review* 29, 93–112.

Watts, David. 1987. *The West Indies: Patterns of Development, Culture, and Environmental Change Since 1492*. Cambridge: Cambridge University Press.

3

The Earliest Settlers   L. ANTONIO CURET

At the time Europeans arrived, the Caribbean was characterized by diverse and vibrant native communities occupying almost every island of the archipelago. These groups represented multiple languages, cultural traditions, and environmental adaptations produced by long and complex historical processes. Traditionally, Caribbean historiography has simplified this picture by homogenizing these groups into broad cultural types and describing the ancient history of the region as a simple sequence of cultures that emerged either through cultural evolution or the immigration of new groups. Furthermore, the chronologies have been full of gaps, neglecting certain islands and periods.

In the past few decades, however, archaeologists and ethnohistorians have made great strides in advancing our knowledge of the region's ancient history. These advances have resulted from a new cadre of scholars asking new questions, employing novel theoretical frameworks, and relying on new methods and techniques. This chapter reviews the current state of knowledge about the indigenous groups of the Caribbean islands in precolonial times, from more or less 5000 BCE to about 1500 CE.

Naming Indigenous Peoples

After Columbus's arrival, Europeans began differentiating native Caribbean groups on the basis of their experiences with them and the accounts they received from the indigenous peoples. They created a relatively simplistic classificatory system that scholars of the Caribbean have often adopted, expanded, and perpetuated without questioning the validity of the categorizations or clearly defining the terms.

Taino, for example, is a term widely used by scholars to name the groups that inhabited most of the Greater Antilles at the time of contact. Contrary to common belief, however, this term was never used by early Europeans or the natives as a cultural or "ethnic" label. Europeans apparently first heard the word *taíno* during Columbus's second voyage in 1493, when they landed on Guadeloupe. There they encountered Amerindians from the Greater Antilles who supposedly had been captured by so-called Caribs and used the word *taíno* to describe themselves. Since *taíno* means "good" or "noble" in local Arawakan languages, they seem to have used the term not as an ethnic label or ethonym but as an adjective to differentiate themselves from their captors.

Since the late 19th century, scholars from different disciplines have variously used the term Taino to refer to a cultural, biological, and/or linguistic population that inhabited much of the region. Today, most Caribbean archaeologists agree that Taino refers to more than a single culture and includes several distinctive but historically related sociocultural groups that occupied most of Hispaniola, Puerto Rico, Jamaica, Cuba, the Bahamas, and the northern Lesser Antilles. Put another way, Taino refers to a widespread set of Antillean cultural practices and norms shared by several or more localized cultures in the Greater Antilles and beyond.

Another term commonly used as an ethnic designation by Caribbean scholars is *Carib*. Unlike Taino, the terms *Carib*, *Caribe*, and *Caniba* were used by inhabitants of the Bahamas and the Greater Antilles to refer to groups living to the east and south of the Greater Antilles. According to native interlocutors, the Caribs raided the Greater Antilles and Bahamas, looting villages and stealing women and children, and they had the custom of eating some of their prisoners (the word *cannibal* has its origin in the term *Caniba*). While there is some debate about whether the native informants were referring to spiritual entities, mythological beings, or real people, Europeans used the term *Carib* to refer first to the indigenous groups of the Lesser Antilles and later to any group in the Americas that resisted Spanish conquest and colonization. Given these ambiguities, it is perhaps not surprising that the Caribs have been difficult to identify archaeologically with any specific group and its artifacts. Today the term *Carib* is principally used to name a South American language family, and recently the designation *Island Carib* was introduced to distinguish the Carib-speaking groups of the Lesser Antilles from those on the mainland.

In addition to Tainos and Caribs, early Europeans also reported the presence in the Caribbean of cave-dwelling hunting and gathering groups called *Guanahata-beyes* by local natives. These groups inhabited the western tip of Cuba and possibly also the peninsula of Guacayarima in southwestern Hispaniola. Some documentary evidence suggests that they were linguistically different from their Taino neighbors. Traditionally, they have been considered "leftover" populations of the first inhabitants of the islands in Archaic times. Recently, however, some scholars have argued that many of the Guanahatabeyes may instead have been renegade Tainos who lived in marginal areas to escape from European colonizers. Cuban archaeologists relate many sites consisting mostly of stone and shell artifacts, which are characteristic of hunters and gatherers, to the historic Guanahatabeyes. Still, the archaeological data strongly suggest that the case of the Guanahatabeyes is much more complicated than the scenario presented in European historical documentation.

Finally, *Ciboney* is another term present in the chronicles and used by scholars to refer to certain ethnic groups that occupied western Cuba and the Bahamas. The sources describe the Ciboneyes as remnants of the original populations of the islands who were pushed out by later migrations. In the early 1500s, Spanish priest Bartolomé de Las Casas noted, "they seem to have no sin . . . they were simple and extremely good people, without any vice and most blessed . . . they were peaceful, benign, naked" (Las Casas 1951, 507, 515; my translation).

Although many scholars use the terms *Guanahatabey* and *Ciboney* interchangeably with *Archaic* to refer to the initial populations of the islands, such usage is based on weak assumptions and tenuous connections between archaeological and ethnohistorical data. In this chapter, the term *Archaic* is used to designate people associated with specific assemblages of archaeological artifacts, especially those appearing to reflect early hunters and gatherers. Most likely, however, the Archaic people encompassed a variety of ethnic groups or cultures.

Archaeology and the Chronology of the Ancient Caribbean

Archaeology is not only the best way, but sometimes the only way to study ancient history. Analysis of archaeological sites and artifacts can reveal historical trends and culture change over long periods of time. The following discussion of the ancient history of the Caribbean as it is presently understood relies mostly on such information, complemented occasionally with documentary sources closer to the 16th century.

Since the 1930s, studies on the cultural chronology of the Caribbean have been dominated by the work of archaeologist Irving Rouse, who devised a classificatory system to identify groups of people based on the characteristics of the assembled artifacts they left behind. His system is hierarchical and has three main levels: style, series, and subseries. At each level, names are based on key archaeological sites associated with specific groups. Regional sequences of groups can be represented as charts or matrices, with the horizontal axis representing geographical distribution and the vertical axis representing time. Rouse's chart for the Caribbean, with some modifications, is shown in fig. 3.1. For the sake of simplicity, only series and subseries classifications (names ending in *oid* and *an*, respectively) are used in this chapter.

The First Islanders: The Archaic Cultures

The earliest evidence of humans in the Caribbean dates to between 5000 and 4000 BCE. This evidence comes from both ends of the island chain—Trinidad in the southeast and Cuba/Hispaniola in the northwest—and suggests that more than one migration wave may have occurred. The evidence from Trinidad was probably produced by migrant groups from northeastern South America, given the similarities between stone artifacts found in both regions. On the other end, some scholars believe that early assemblages from Cuba and Hispaniola resemble those from Central America, especially from the Yucatan Peninsula.

Later Archaic sites have been found in most of the Lesser and Greater Antilles, with dates ranging between 3000 BCE and 300 BCE in the Lesser Antilles, between 2500 BCE and 100 CE in Puerto Rico, and between 4000 BCE and the time of contact in Cuba. No evidence for any of these traditions has been found in the Bahamas or Jamaica, however. Based on archaeological remains, it seems that these early groups were hunters, fishermen, and gatherers, and most of the material culture available for their identification consists of stone and shell artifacts. The relatively small size of most of these sites has led many researchers to describe these groups as having been organized into small, highly mobile bands that followed the availability of wild resources and did not possess ceramics or cultivate any of their food. But such characterizations have recently been questioned on the basis of reports of burial caves, sophisticated technology for the production of stone tools, highly elaborated ceremonial or high-status artifacts, relatively large sites, and a certain degree of sedentism (permanent residence in one place). Further investigations have shown the presence in some of these assemblages of early ceramics and of cultivars—including exotic ones of continental origin, such as avocados—indicating that these people were actively involved in food production. All this evidence strongly suggests that some Archaic societies were more diverse and elaborate than once believed, and that they were similar to many "complex" hunting and gathering societies in other parts of the world.

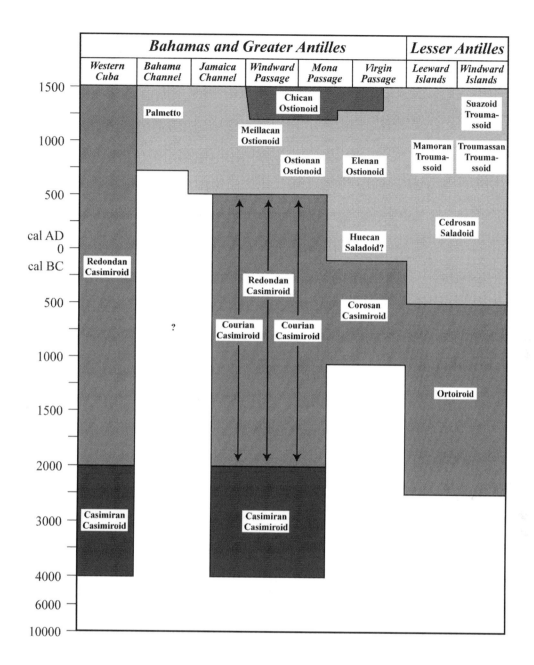

Figure 3.1 Irving Rouse's classification system of Caribbean peoples.

The end point of this Archaic period varies from place to place. In many cases the conclusion of this phase is marked by the arrival of agricultural, ceramic-making groups known as Saladoid, from the Orinoco basin in Venezuela. However, evidence of the presence of ceramics and cultivation in some of the assemblages from these cultures strongly suggests that the end of the Archaics in some regions was produced by local culture change rather than influx of new populations. Furthermore, hunting-fishing-gathering groups (for example, the Guanahatabeyes and Ciboneyes) seem to have persisted in Hispaniola and Cuba.

More Migrations: The Early Ceramic Age

Sometime around 500 BCE, the archeological record suggests, new groups began to arrive in some parts of the eastern Caribbean from South America. Traditionally this population movement was thought to be a migration wave of one people who used the Lesser Antilles as stepping-stones until reaching Puerto Rico several centuries later. Recent discoveries, however, strongly suggest that two cultural groups migrated almost simultaneously.

Around 500 BCE the Saladoid people began migrating from the coast of Venezuela to the Lesser Antilles. They moved through the Lesser Antilles relatively quickly, some reaching areas of Puerto Rico earlier than 300–400 BCE. With the exception of one or two sites in eastern Hispaniola, the evidence suggests that the interisland migration of Saladoid people stopped in Puerto Rico. The most salient characteristic of Saladoid material culture is its ceramics. Saladoid pottery is probably the most elaborate in the ancient Caribbean, demonstrating the highest level of craftsmanship. Other materials associated with the Saladoids include small stone, shell, and mother of pearl amulets and exotic, semiprecious stones of South and Central American origin.

Ironically, despite the abundance of studies on the Saladoid, knowledge about their social organization remains incomplete and superficial. With few exceptions, most discussion of the subject has concentrated on the northern Caribbean, especially Puerto Rico, while little is known about the Saladoid of the Lesser Antilles or of the continent. On the basis of the settlement data and the size of a few houses, it appears that most Saladoid people seemed to prefer living in sizable, multifamily structures in relatively large villages. Communal clusters of burials in the central clearings or plazas of several sites in Puerto Rico have been interpreted as an indication of lineal descent groups that acted as economically corporate groups (in which economic resources such as land are owned communally, in this case by kinship groups such as lineages or clans). The centralized location of these burial clusters and the corporate nature of society have also been interpreted as evidence of the communal orientation of the Puerto Rican Saladoids. It has even been speculated that the Saladoid kinship system was matrilineal.

Many researchers have concluded that the Saladoid people were egalitarian. Others see evidence of specialization and social stratification in the elaborate decorations and high quality of craftsmanship in the pottery and lapidary, but there is little independent evidence to support this assessment. It also has been suggested that the widespread use of symbols in artifacts of domestic and personal use indicates relatively "equal" access to symbolism and, to a certain degree, to the supernatural. This evidence, combined with mortuary and household data, tends to support the idea of weak social stratification in Saladoid societies.

In the 1970s, archaeologists Luis Chanlatte Baik and Yvonne Narganes Stordes called into question the long-standing assumption that Saladoid people were the first and only Ceramic Age people to migrate from South America to the Caribbean islands. At the La Hueca complex on the island of Vieques, southeast of Puerto Rico, Chanlatte Baik found early Saladoid deposits located next to deposits containing distinctly different types of ceramics and lapidary artifacts.

Explanations for this new type of assemblage have been diverse. Some scholars have argued that the pottery is from a Saladoid culture, while others suggest the arrival of a new cultural tradition. This debate, which has dominated many aspects of Caribbean archaeology for the past few decades, remains unresolved. Other sites similar to the La Hueca complex have since been investigated. In Puerto Rico, the southeastern site of Punta Candelero includes separate La Hueca and Saladoid deposits. Moreover, similar ceramics have been found in some of the Lesser Antilles (St. Maarten, Guadeloupe, Martinique), but they are normally located in Saladoid deposits. Most of the studies have concentrated on the artifacts, and to date very little evidence of houses or burials has been unearthed. Thus the social organization of La Hueca culture remains unknown, just as the question of its origins is unresolved.

The Creolization of the Ancient Caribbean

The end of the Saladoid/La Hueca period is marked by strong cultural processes of diversification and regionalization in the Caribbean islands. At first glance the cultural changes seem to be similar throughout the islands, where the highly elaborate and decorated ceramics of the Saladoid are gradually replaced by more mundane pottery. These shifts in pottery were accompanied by other cultural changes, such as decreased production of lapidary artifacts and changes in settlement patterns and demographics. Also during this period there was a resumption of the "movement" of agricultural and ceramic practices from Puerto Rico to Hispaniola, the Bahamas, Jamaica, and parts of Cuba. The timing of these changes varies from island to island.

In the Greater Antilles and the Virgin Islands between 600 and 900 CE, the Saladoids were followed by the Ostionoids, who included the Elenan, Ostionan, and Meillacan subseries. This period is generally characterized by a decline in the aesthetics and craftsmanship of ceramic styles. There are more and larger sites in the Greater Antilles from this period, and centralized distribution of settlements appeared in several islands. There is also some evidence for the intensification of agricultural production and for changes in mortuary practices and household units. Furthermore, ball courts, plazas, and ceremonial centers began to be built during this time, especially in Puerto Rico. Possible interregional networks of interaction have been identified in parts of Cuba, suggesting some supraregional form of sociopolitical organization.

All these changes have been interpreted as evidence for the development of institutionalized social inequality and the beginning of the cacicazgo (chiefdom) system. Yet some of the archaeological data from Puerto Rico suggest that the power of emerging elites during this period was unstable, relying on ceremonies that emphasized social and communal cohesiveness rather than the sanctity of a leader. In Cuba and Hispaniola, the Meillacan and Ostionan subseries are considered "transitional" between Archaic societies and the late pre-Hispanic groups (Chican Ostionoid), and also between egalitarian and hierarchical societies. Toward the end of this period (around 1200 CE), many sites in Puerto Rico—especially some with monumental architecture—were abandoned, possibly indicating a realignment of the social and political landscape.

During the Ostionoid era, some of the islands, such as the Bahamian archipelago and probably Jamaica, were colonized for the first time. The earliest dates for these first settlements fall between 600 and 700 CE. The material associated with the early dates suggests that, contrary to previous suppositions, the archipelago was colonized by several migrations originating from both Cuba and Hispaniola. However, some of the islands may have been visited long before colonization.

The lack of comprehensive research on many of the Lesser Antilles has produced relatively large gaps in the understanding of their cultural history. Recent regional and site studies, however, have begun to produce a complex picture of inter- and intraisland cultural and social interaction. Different islands or groups of islands apparently developed different cultural traditions depending on their geographic position and their sphere of interaction within the Lesser Antilles and with other larger regions. Generally speaking, for example, the Leeward Islands close to Puerto Rico were strongly influenced by post-Saladoid groups from the Greater Antilles, while the islands near the continent were more culturally influenced by Venezuelan and Guyanan groups.

In general, the Lesser Antilles of this period were culturally and perhaps politically more diverse than in earlier times. The presence of some forms of interaction between groups of islands has been interpreted as evidence of social and trade networks, alliances, or even some form of supraisland political units. According to some researchers, one or more new forms of leadership may have developed, such as war leaders or chiefs who controlled the networks.

The Late Precolonial Period

To sum up, the ancient history of the Caribbean begins with early inhabitants consisting of hunting-gathering groups, probably from multiple origins. Later, groups from South America with ceramic and horticultural skills began to migrate to the Lesser Antilles and Puerto Rico, possibly interacting biologically, socially, and culturally with the previous Archaic populations. Although it is poorly understood, this interaction was probably intense and continuous, leading eventually to a process of creolization and an increase in cultural diversity throughout the Caribbean archipelago and even within single islands. Many of these processes and cultural characteristics were also present in late pre-Columbian times.

Archaeologically, the Greater Antilles in this era encompassed multiple cultural groups, including the Chican and Meillacan subseries of the Ostionoids. On the basis of ceramic evidence, it appears that the Chicans occupied the Virgin Islands, Puerto Rico, the southern and eastern parts of Hispaniola, and at least the eastern tip of Cuba, while Meillacans were more prevalent in the northern and western parts of Hispaniola, in some regions of Cuba, in Jamaica, and in some islands of the Bahamian archipelago. The Taino have been associated through their artifacts with the Chican people. Depending on the region, the Chican and Meillacan presence can be dated to between 800 and 1500 CE.

Many aspects of material culture in the Greater Antilles became increasingly sophisticated in this period. Larger, more numerous, and more elaborate ball courts, plazas, and ceremonial centers continued to be built in Puerto Rico. Some monumental architecture is also present in Hispaniola, Cuba, and the Virgin Islands. Religious, ceremonial, and high-status objects increased in size and elaboration. In some cases, gold ornaments are present.

At the time of contact with Europeans, Hispaniola had several powerful chiefdoms. According to early European accounts, the island was divided into five provinces, each one covering more than 1,000 square kilometers and ruled by a single paramount chief. However, it is also possible that other smaller polities coexisted in Hispaniola at the same time, presenting a wide variety of political structures and interactions. While no substantive data is available on population, the archaeological record and the evidence included in the ethnohistoric documents seem to indicate that Hispaniola was densely populated. It is also clear that a number of "ethnic" groups coexisted in this island until the time of contact.

Several researchers have argued that in this period Puerto Rico was also divided

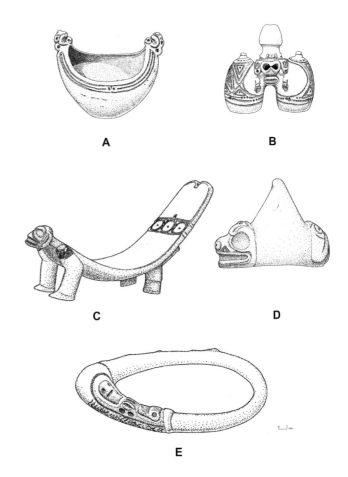

Figure 3.2 Taino (Chican Ostionoid) pottery and ceremonial objects: A–B, pottery from Hispaniola; C, ceremonial seat, or *duho*, from Hispaniola; D, three-pointed idol, or *zemi*, from Puerto Rico; E, stone collar or belt from Puerto Rico. Drawings by Jill Seagard. Source: Field Museum of Natural History.

among several paramount chiefdoms. However, considering that most of the cacicazgos mentioned in the chronicles tended to be located either near rivers or in intermontane valleys and that ball courts and plazas are widely distributed, Puerto Rico seems to have been divided instead into competing polities smaller than a paramount chiefdom. The island also seems to have suffered a noticeable population decrease at this time.

Meanwhile, Cuba continued to have both horticultural and hunting-gathering groups. While no clear archaeological boundaries are observable between the two types of groups, settlements of the former tend to concentrate on the eastern part of the island and settlements of the latter on the western side. Several researchers have reported the presence of a variety of site sizes, including regional centers, suggesting the presence of hierarchical societies. Other studies have found less socially and politically differentiated patterns that indicate the presence of diverse sociopolitical organizations. A number of possible ball courts and plazas have been reported in eastern Cuba. The "cemetery" at the Chorro de Maíta site has presented strong evidence for social stratification in the form of rare offerings including several pieces of gold jewelry resembling Colombian styles. The Spanish chronicles mention several cacicazgos present in eastern Cuba at the time of contact, including one whose leaders and some of their followers allegedly migrated from western Hispaniola shortly after the Spanish conquest began. Nevertheless, none of these groups seem to have been of the necessary size or hierarchical organization for a paramount chiefdom as observed in Hispaniola.

Unfortunately, little is known about the cultural and social history of Jamaica at this time. Some of the early chronicles and ceremonial objects found recently in caves suggest the presence of elaborate religious practices and political units. But the lack of long-term archaeological research has limited understanding of the dynamics and processes that took place in this island.

Although historical documents dating from the period of Columbus's first voyage described the populations of the Lesser Antilles as ethnically different from those of the Greater Antilles—branding the former with the name of Caribs—the ethnohistoric and archaeological evidence presents a more diverse cultural picture. As in the previous period, for example, the southern Lesser Antilles continued to interact more with the South American continent and the northern Lesser Antilles more with the Greater Antilles, especially Puerto Rico. In addition, there is some evidence indicating interisland networks and alliances. Later European documents from the 18th century report the presence of leaders who controlled trade, alliances, and war parties. It is not clear, however, whether this type of leadership was present before 1492 or whether it developed as a consequence of interaction with the Spanish colonies in the Greater Antilles.

Recent Research and New Directions in Caribbean Archaeology

Caribbean archaeology continues to contribute to the understanding of the region, and it has recently experienced an exciting period of development, with an influx of new ideas, theories, and paradigms. Two themes in particular serve as examples of how much the discipline has advanced, and also indicate new directions it has taken. The first theme concerns interregional interaction between the islands and different parts of the continent, especially what has been called the Isthmo-Colombian area. The second relates to the development and use of new methodology, particularly in the area of archaeometry, or the application of techniques from the natural sciences in archaeology.

Long-Distance Interaction

Most of the explanations and discussions of the ancient history of the Caribbean so far presented assume that once groups migrated to the islands, all social and cultural changes, processes, and dynamics occurred almost in isolation or with little influence from continental ones. In other words, the cultural groups that inhabited the Caribbean archipelago have been considered to have been not only geographically but also socially isolated from the surrounding landmasses. It used to be assumed that because of the South American origin of most of the Caribbean groups, and the facility of island-to-island travel from Venezuela to the Greater Antilles, long-distance interaction was more probable with South America than with other continental regions such as Central America, Mesoamerica, and North America.

Recent research, however, has questioned many of these traditional assumptions. Chemical analyses have demonstrated the exotic nature of different types of artifacts, especially green stones and gold, and determined that the most likely source of the raw material of several green objects from Antigua and Puerto Rico is the Motagua fault zone in Guatemala. Although no researchers claim that there was necessarily a direct movement of this raw material from Guatemala to the Caribbean, at least one suggests that it could have arrived directly from Lower Central America (perhaps Costa Rica).

Other evidence of possible direct contact with continental areas besides South America includes stylistic similarities of many ritual or status objects. For example, ethnohistorians have proposed the presence of spheres of interactions between the Greater Antilles and Lower Central America, on the basis of the importance of "black" wood artifacts for religious and status purposes in both regions. Some scholars have pointed out the strong similarities between the "condors" made of green stone of the La Hueca complex and the "long-beak birds" common in Costa Rica and neighboring regions. Moreover, while only a few precolonial gold objects have been unearthed in the islands, most can be traced with some degree of certainty to the Colombia-Panama gold-smelting regions, mainly on the basis of chemical and stylistic similarities.

Not all evidence is restricted to ornamental or religious objects, however. Edge-grinder cobble tools, common in the Archaic sites of Puerto Rico and other islands, are not present in the Archaic assemblages of the Lesser Antilles and Venezuela, but are prevalent in Panamanian sites of the same age. The suggestion of a possible Archaic connection between Panama and Puerto Rico is also strengthened by the cultivars and wild botanical products found in both regions but not necessarily present in intermediate areas (Venezuela and Lesser Antilles). These cultivars and wild resources include maize, sweet potatoes, tannia, beans (*Leguminosae/Fabaceae*), yam, zamia (*Zamia portorricencis*), jackbeans (*habas; Canavalia* sp.), achira (*gruya; Canna* sp.), yellow sapote (*Poutevia campechiana*), sapodilla (*Manilkara zapota*), and avocado (*Persea americana*).

Strong evidence exists for these and other island-continent connections. Interaction between the islands, especially the Greater Antilles, and the Isthmo-

Colombian region has major consequences for understanding the past, and points to cultural and social dynamics previously not taken into consideration. In many ways, these suggestions may well change the prevailing view of the ancient history of the Caribbean. The presence of similar artifacts, cultivars, and other resources in Archaic assemblages of Puerto Rico and Hispaniola and in Panama from the same period should in particular change the view of the early migration and first colonizers of the islands. Success in colonizing a new environment, marriage patterns, and population and social structures could differ considerably, depending on whether the migration involved a single cultural group or several groups from different regions.

Similarly, attempts to study social and political changes that eventually led to the development of chiefdoms or cacicazgos now have to include possible "international" relationships. This interaction may have included a process of transculturation in which groups influenced each other through the exchange of objects and information. Moreover, since objects and knowledge obtained from geographically faraway places are often considered to have esoteric powers, emerging or well-established elites may have manipulated and monopolized access to such interaction to increase, justify, and maintain their prestige, status, and power.

In short, contrary to traditional reconstructions, recent research has suggested that the ancient people of the Caribbean may have been interacting with continental areas other than northeastern South America. Recognizing the presence of long-distance interaction will oblige scholars to rethink the study of the Caribbean from the perspective of "isolated" social groups, and to take into consideration that the social, economic, political, religious, and cultural dynamics within the different groups involved may have been heavily influenced by foreign artifacts, knowledge, and social relationships.

New Methodology

Another exciting aspect of today's Caribbean archaeology is the application of many different analytical techniques, especially those borrowed from the natural sciences, to gain new insights into the ancient history and peoples of the region. To take just one prominent example, archaeologists have recently made great advancements in their techniques for reconstructing ancient diets.

The easiest and most common type of archaeological diet reconstruction used to be the study of faunal remains, such as bones and shells. However, this began to change in the 1980s and 1990s with the systematic study of macrobotanical remains, such as wood (in the form of charcoal), seeds, and nuts. After a slow beginning, the collection of soil samples for the recovery of botanical remains has become routine in most archaeological projects in the region. Results of macrobotanical research have provided Caribbean archaeologists with a more complete view of the diet of ancient people. For example, some of the continental species of plants mentioned earlier in this chapter were identified first through their macrobotanical remains. These include avocado, yellow sapote, and sapodilla.

Some of these studies have also shed light on aspects of social behavior and interaction between humans and the environment. In the late precolonial site of En Bas Saline in Haiti, for example, Lee Newsom was able to identify differences in the consumption of certain botanical foods by comparing remains found in a possible elite context with those from the rest of the site (Newsom and Wing 2004). She has also analyzed the evidence of both edible and nonedible plants to investigate how indigenous groups used them and managed their environment. Among other discoveries, she confirmed the use of cojoba (*Anadatera peregrina*) as a hallucinogen for religious rituals, tobacco seeds as a stimulant, evening primrose for medicinal and hallucinogenic purposes, mangrove tree for firewood, and a variety of hardwood trees for house construction.

Another approach that has changed perspectives on how people relate to botanical resources is starch grain analysis. One problem with the study of macrobotanical remains is that, at least in tropical areas, the items that have survived for centuries in a volatile climate may not be representative of the distribution and proportion of plants in precolonial times. But starch grains tend to be more resilient and to better survive the passage of time, meaning that their presence in archaeological samples better reflects pre-Columbian reality. Through the extraction and analysis of starch grains from artifacts, archaeologist Jaime Pagán-Jiménez has been able to reconstruct the indigenous diet in a more complete manner. For example, he has been able to record the presence of maize, zamia, manioc, yams, and other products that rarely survive enough to be identified through macrobotanical remains. Some of these plants have also been added to the growing list of introduced species on the islands (Pagán-Jiménez 2007). Because the samples for this type of analysis come directly from the surface of artifacts, starch grain studies have also advanced knowledge of the function of many artifacts. One of these has been the edge-grinder cobble, which starch grain analysis has confirmed was used as a grinder for food. The identification of grains on the surfaces of griddles or *burenes* has also demonstrated that they were used not only for the preparation of manioc bread, as traditionally thought, but also to cook a variety of botanical products.

Another method that is being used in the Caribbean for the reconstruction of diet is the analysis of stable isotopes in human remains. This type of analysis can determine some general details of the diet, such as the amount of meat, the proportion of terrestrial versus marine animals, and the proportion of maize, tropical grasses, and cacti versus other types of plants consumed. While other methods study diets indirectly through whatever is left of the resources consumed, stable isotope analysis measures only what people consumed and was incorporated into their bodies. Furthermore, macrobotanical and starch grain analyses concentrate on "bulk" samples without knowledge of how many people or which ones consumed the different resources. Stable isotope analysis, on the other hand, studies what individual people consumed. This last advantage allows the study of differential access to food resources within a community. Finally, stable isotope analysis can measure the intake of both botanical and faunal resources, while most of the other methods tend to concentrate on only one or the other.

The combined evidence of all these types of studies has begun to provide a more complete and accurate view of the pre-Hispanic diet. The studies have shown that indigenous people in the Caribbean were consuming maize or possibly other tropical grasses, such as amaranth, in higher proportions than was once thought. And in at least one case, stable isotope analysis has suggested that river fauna, whose remains are not well represented in the archaeological record, may have been an important component of the diet of ancient people from Puerto Rico.

The Caribbean Basin has a long, complex, and dynamic history that began thousands of years before the arrival of Europeans. During all this time, social processes such as migrations, culture change, development of social stratification, colonization, and transculturation combined to create a broad diversity of cultural and social expressions similar to the diversity observable in the region today. The archaeological record is one way to learn about the history of these processes, particularly that of the period before the first European documents. It offers ample evidence that the Caribbean has always been an arena of interaction, integration, contestation, and amalgamation, leading to the emergence throughout the archipelago of truly "creole" cultures.

WORKS CITED

Las Casas, Bartolomé de. 1951. *Historia de las Indias*. Fondo de Cultura Económica, Mexico City.

Newsom, Lee A., and Elizabeth S. Wing. 2004. *On Land and Sea: Native American Uses of Biological Resources in the West Indies*. Tuscaloosa: University of Alabama Press.

Pagán-Jiménez, Jaime R. 2007. *De antiguos pueblos y culturas botánicas en el Puerto Rico indígena: El archipiélago borincano y la llegada de los primeros pobladores agroceramistas*. BAR International Series No. 1687. Oxford: British Archeological Reports.

4

Old World Precedents WILLIAM D. PHILLIPS JR.

Sugar and Slavery in the Mediterranean

Sugar and slavery, key components that helped shape the colonial
Caribbean, were present in the medieval Mediterranean world in
both Muslim and Christian areas. Elements that contributed to the
development of the plantation complex in the early modern Caribbean and elsewhere in the Americas had long Mediterranean histories: the use of slaves, slave trade, sugar cultivation and refining,
merchant capitalism, and marketing networks.

Sugar in the Islamic World

The Muslims first introduced sugarcane growing and refining to
the Mediterranean after they found the crop under cultivation and
production in Khuzistan in Mesopotamia, just north of the Persian Gulf. When the Muslims conquered the region in the seventh
and eighth centuries, they established a labor force imported from
East Africa to work in the cane fields, thus foreshadowing the links
between sugar production and black slavery. Still, in the Islamic

world and the Christian Mediterranean, free labor predominated in sugar production.

From Khuzistan, sugar refining spread to Baghdad, which lasted as a refining center until the end of the Middle Ages. Egypt was the next step along sugar's westward march; the first sugar plantations were established there in the early eighth century. From Egypt, the Muslims spread sugarcane to Yemen and to the lands around the Mediterranean: Syria, Sicily, southern Morocco, and southern Spain. In ancient and early medieval times, the Mediterranean had not known sugar; sweetening came from honey and fruit juices. Honey remained a luxury because its supply was limited and could never be expanded much. Sugarcane was entirely different, its growth limited only by the availability of suitable land and labor.

By the 10th century, sugar production was thriving in several places in the Islamic world, and cane sugar traded widely in the Muslim markets and afield to the Byzantine Empire and the Christian West. Because of the special requirements of successful sugarcane production, it was mainly large landholders who could afford the necessary investment. The intensive nature of the industry has been a feature of cane sugar production ever since.

Egyptian sugar processes became famous throughout the world. The Egyptians probably invented the manufacture of cube or *misri* (Egyptian) sugar. They had long used two minerals, natron (sodium carbonate) and alum (aluminum potassium sulfate), for the refining of honey, and around the 11th century they began to refine cane sugar with the same minerals.

The first written evidence of sugarcane in Spain appears in the 10th century, even though Muslims conquered most of the Iberian peninsula early in the eighth century and, from the time of the emir 'Abd al-Raḥmān I in the mid-eighth, were introducing and acclimating new crops in palace gardens in southern Spain. The *Calendar of Córdoba* first mentions sugarcane around the year 961, but this source may reflect conditions in Egypt more accurately than in Spain, or may be referring to all territory under Cordoban control rather than Córdoba itself. Certainly in Muslim times, sugar was grown in a wide stretch of southern Iberian territory, from the wetlands of the lower Guadalquivir south of Seville to warm coastal valleys along the Mediterranean coast from Málaga to Almería and occasionally as far north as Castellón. Arab geographers mentioned that sugar was grown in the Vega de Granada, but this is virtually the only mention of it inland.

Sugarcane and the other tropical crops the Muslims introduced to semiarid Spain required heavy irrigation. Iberian Muslims employed a variety of irrigation techniques, most of them of Middle Eastern origin, including canals along rivers, underground water conduits, spring-fed gardens, and norias: devices with belts of buckets bringing water to the surface. By the 12th century, sugarcane refining was documented in the peninsula, with machinery originally developed for milling and pressing olives likely adapted to the needs of sugar manufacture. The entire industrial complex for processing the canes and making sugar centered on a mill, which could be a water mill (*ingenio*) but most often was an animal-powered mill (*trapig* or *trapiche*). A 12th-century account described the process:

> Regarding the manner of making sugar from the canes, when the canes are mature in January, they are cut into small pieces, and, in order to obtain the juice, these, well pressed or chipped in the mill, are squeezed in wine presses or similar places in the mill. Their juice is placed in a clean cauldron to boil on the fire, and left until it clarifies; afterward it is brought back to a boil until part remains; and clay forms filled with it are placed to solidify in the shade and also the sugar is taken from there; and the residue of the cane after the pressing is kept for the horses as it is a very enjoyable food for them, with which they get fat (González Tascón and Pérez 1990, 104–5).

During Islamic times, sugar was a luxury product, used extensively in pharmacology and medicine and as a significant component of cuisine. Muslim physicians, following Galen's approach, used it to balance the four humors. Honey and sugar, usually dissolved in water, were used to treat disorders of the respiratory, urinary, and digestive systems. A 15th-century Egyptian allegorical tale showed the personification of sugar leaving the ranks of the army of medicine and joining the army of the foods, reflecting the increasing availability of cane sugar. Sweets, including candy and sweet baked goods and other confections, were popular throughout the Muslim world. Equally important was the common use of sugar, along with fruits and other sweeteners, in meat dishes and vegetable recipes throughout medieval Christian as well as Islamic lands. In modern times the cuisine of Europe has tended to shed such recipes and to confine sweetened foods to the dessert course, whereas in North Africa main courses of meats and vegetables sweetened with sugar and fruits have remained popular.

Egyptian sugar production prospered in the 13th and 14th centuries, with sugar exported to the commercial centers of Italy, France, and Spain. Yet at the same time, the sugar industry in the Near East began to fall victim to the same forces that were causing an overall decline in the economy of the Islamic world, including deforestation and the Christian advance in maritime power and trade. Sugar factories began to close around the middle of the 14th century, and that process accelerated in the 15th. Cairo had 66 sugar mills in 1325; by the first years of the next century, nearly half had been abandoned.

The Impact of the Crusades

Part of the decline in Egyptian sugar production was attributable to internal changes in the Islamic economy. Another factor was increasing sugar production by

Europeans, who from the time of the Crusades in the 12th and 13th centuries had begun to develop sugar plantations and refining centers. The crusaders found sugar-cane under cultivation and production in the areas they conquered. The chronicler Fulcher of Chartres, who participated in the First Crusade, reported the hardships caused by limited food supplies for that army and went on to say that

> in those cultivated fields through which we passed during our march there were certain ripe plants which the common folk called "honey-cane" and which were very much like reeds. The name is compounded from "cane" and "honey," whence the expression "wood honey," I think, because the latter is skillfully made from these canes. In our hunger we chewed them all day because of the taste of honey. However, this helped but little (Fulcher of Chartes 1969, 130).

After they reached Jerusalem and conquered it in 1099, the crusaders maintained the cultivation of sugarcane in the states they established. This afforded them im-mediate revenues and, more important in the long run, created additional demand in the West, as returning crusaders and pilgrims took home samples of cane sugar and thus helped to spread the taste for it. William of Tyre, in his late-12th-century description of the irrigation projects around Tyre, also mentioned sugar.

> All the country round about derives immense benefits from these waters. Not only do they supply gardens and delightful orchards planted with fruit trees, but they irrigate the sugar cane also. From this latter crop sugar (zachara) is made, a most precious product, very necessary for the use and health of mankind, which is carried by merchants to the most remote countries of the world (William of Tyre 1943, 2:6).

Sugar plantations were controlled by the king of Jerusalem, by corporate groups such as the military orders and the Italian cities, and by individuals.

Sugar production, dependent as it was upon water for irrigation and for mo-tive power to turn the cane-crushing mills, was concentrated in those places where water was readily available. The main centers were coastal—Sidon, Acre, and Tyre, with the latter most important—and inland in Galilee and the Jordan Valley. Sugar production in the region predated the Crusades, but it soon expanded under Chris-tian rule and with the employment of local Muslim labor under sharecropping ar-rangements.

Although their existence was precarious toward the last, the Christian states continued to produce sugar for their own use and for export. When the Muslims drove the last of the Christian rulers from Palestine in 1291, the refugees spread the intensive cultivation and processing of sugar westward to Mediterranean islands and mainland areas held by Christians. In some of these regions, sugar had been grown by Muslims since the eighth or ninth century, but only in the later Middle Ages did it come to be exploited more fully.

The fall of the crusader states in the Levant did not mark the end of commerce in sugar between Muslims and Christians. Even though sugar from the Christian-held Mediterranean islands soon began to be exported to Europe, Damascus and Tripoli in Syria and Alexandria and other Egyptian ports continued to provide Western merchants with Muslim-produced sugar and other goods.

Among the first islands that the Christians exploited for sugar production was Cyprus. Sugarcane had probably been grown on the island since being introduced by the Muslims in the seventh century, but only after the crusader states had fallen did it became important in the island's economy. Famagusta, the principal city, became the nexus of Christian trade in the region. The first recorded export of sugar from Cyprus dates from 1301, when a Genoese merchant in Pisa purchased 10 chests of the commodity. Sugarcane in Cyprus was grown in irrigated fields, and rival producers feuded over water rights. Although some slaves were used in Cypriot sugar production, especially on the royal estates, the bulk of the labor was non-slave and included Greek and Syrian immigrants given special political status by the Venetians. The Syrians were often skilled sugar workers, brought in especially for their expertise. In 1494 an Italian visitor reported that some 400 workers were engaged in sugar production at Piskopi.

Other islands in the eastern Mediterranean also produced sugar. Crete was in Byzantine hands until the early 13th century, when the Catalan count of Monserrat conquered it in the aftermath of the Fourth Crusade. Shortly afterward the Venetians bought Crete and, in the 15th century, fostered sugar production there.

Sicily was probably the most important Mediterranean center for sugar in the late Middle Ages. Sugarcane had been introduced shortly after the Muslims conquered the island in 878, and by the end of the ninth century Sicilian sugar was being sold in North Africa. Palermo was in the main region of sugar production, and one observer wrote that "the banks of the streams around Palermo, from their sources to their mouths, are bordered by low-lying fields, upon which the Persian reed is grown" (Deere 1949–50, 1:76). In the 11th century the Normans took Sicily from the Muslims, their conquest motivated in part by sugar. No doubt because of the destruction accompanying the conquest and the inexperience of the new estate and mill managers, the Sicilian sugar industry declined during the Norman period, although Hugh Falcandus in the late 12th century could describe the

great extension of wonderful reeds which are called by the inhabitants honey canes, from the sweetness of the juice they contain. The juice of these canes, when it has been boiled with care and to the right extent, converts itself into a kind of honey; if on the other hand it is subjected to a more complete and perfect boiling, it becomes condensed into the substance of sugar (Deerr 1949–50, 1:77).

The reign of the Holy Roman Emperor Frederick II (king of Sicily 1197–1250) marked a temporary revival. Consistently sponsoring enlightened reforms for the economy of Sicily, Frederick was particularly interested in sugar production. He had the fields hedged to prevent damage to the cane, and once during an infestation of caterpillars he mobilized the population and assigned a daily quota for the hand collection of the pests. In 1239 he had two experts in sugar refining sent from Tyre to Sicily to examine the industry there and recommend improvements.

After Frederick's death, Sicily underwent more than a century and a half of disordered political conditions, leading to the expulsion of the Muslims from the island and the decline of the sugar industry. Early in the 15th century the situation began to reverse, and during the reign of the Aragonese king Alfonso V (1416–58) the Sicilian sugar industry reached a peak, aided by studies of proper irrigation of the fields undertaken by the University of Palermo.

It has often been asserted that the famous three-roller sugar mill, so characteristic of the New World plantations, came into use in Sicily during Alfonso V's reign. This is almost assuredly not the case: the new mill did not appear until after the discovery of America. Still, the support of the island's rulers did help sugar reach new heights in Sicily in the 15th century. An indication of its importance there was the designation of one of the entries into the city of Syracuse as the Porta degli Zuccheri, or the gate of the sugars (or sugar workers). Also, in 1446, one of Syracuse's streets was named Cannamella, honey cane.

Sugar production also spread to the Italian mainland, although it never became important there. Some sugar was produced in the kingdom of Naples, and around 1550 Ferdinand de' Medici introduced it unsuccessfully near Florence.

Sugar could be produced readily in southern Spain, but attempts to spread its cultivation northward were relatively limited until the late Middle Ages. King James II of Aragon (1291–1327) undertook to grow sugar in Valencia on Spain's eastern Mediterranean coast by securing plantings from Sicily together with a Muslim slave skilled in sugar techniques. Still, the first production was not mentioned until the 1380s. In 1433 the cathedral chapter of Valencia attempted to secure the right to collect a tithe on sugar production, and in the process the canons provided an important account of the growth of production in Valencia. They reported that since the 1380s and 1390s both Christian and Muslim farmers had planted sugarcane as a secondary crop and sold it in its raw state as a delicacy for children and adults. In the second decade of the 15th century, planting increased and grain gave way to cane in many places. In 1407 the Valencian government gave financial aid to Nicolau Santafé, a sugar expert, to set himself up in Valencia. The first evidence of a mill in that city dates from 1417, when the master potter Thahin Aburrazach contracted to move to Burriana and make ceramic forms and vessels needed for the mill. By the 1430s numerous mills were in full operation. This expansion in Valencia took place just at the time when eastern Mediterranean sugar production was faltering and commerce there was being threatened by the expansion of the Ottomans.

In these circumstances, Valencian sugar drew the attention of a large German merchant house, the Ravensburger Handelsgesellschaft. By 1420 the company had agents and warehouses in Valencia and exported Valencian products, including sugar. The production and export of Valencian sugar generally increased in the first half of the 15th century, and by 1460 Ravensburger's profits were great enough to encourage its directors to enter the production side. They acquired land along the river Alcoy near Gandía and built a mill and refinery managed by *maestre* Santafé, probably the son of Nicolau de Santafé. The manufacturing complex prospered at first, and the quality of sugar produced there was extremely high. But in the 1470s a lawsuit slowed production, coinciding with the company's loss of some of its markets, difficulties in transportation, and competition from Madeiran sugar. The company's directors sold the facility in 1477 and a few years later rejected a proposal to reopen it.

Methods of Sugar Production

Most labor for the Mediterranean sugar industry—on both the Christian and Muslim sides of the sea—was free. Although here and there some slaves may have been used, they were the exception. The close identification of sugarcane and slave labor came later, in the islands of the Atlantic.

The methods of growing and refining sugarcane remained more or less constant in the Mediterranean and Atlantic growing regions, despite differences in scale. Cane was planted from cuttings of mature stock, not from seed. The "setts," as these roughly foot-long cuttings were called, needed a slightly acid soil, and cane did best with a rainfall of some 60 to 70 inches per year. because few if any Mediterranean lands had that much rain, irrigation projects were necessary to increase the water supply to the setts, which were planted at the bottom of the furrows of the plowed fields to receive the maximal amount of water. When the plants reached maturity, the long stalks were cut back near the ground, leaving the bottom (or ratoon) in the ground to produce the next crop.

The next stage was the transportation of the cane from the field to the mill, carried on the backs of draft animals, in carts, or by humans. At the mill it was cut into appropriate lengths and crushed to extract the juice for refining. The fresh juice contained a small percentage of foreign matter that had to be removed if the sugar were to attain its pure form. Boiling the juice with an additive made the separation of the pure sugar easier. In the late Middle Ages natron and potash were commonly used as clarifying additives, as the juice was boiled in successive stages until it was ready to be dried in loaf-shaped molds of pyramidal or cone shape. In the 14th century the Italian Francesco Balducci Pegolotti, in his famous manual of commerce *La pratica della mercatura*, described the varieties of sugar on the market. The best was *mecchera*, in pyramidal shape, white and dense. Next in order came *caffetino*, shaped like a cone with a rounded top; then *bambillonia*, *musciatto*, and *domaschino*, the least preferred. Powdered sugar was pressed into the form of a loaf, but it usually turned to dust during transport. Perfectly transparent candy sugar was also produced and sold.

Sugar found a ready market as European demand constantly expanded. Eventually the Mediterranean producers could not keep up with that demand. By the late 15th century, sugar from the new colonial areas, particularly from Madeira, began to enter the market, often at substantially lower prices than those of the Iberian producers. This foreshadowed the series of sugar booms that followed sugar's introduction into semitropical and tropical areas in the Caribbean and on the American mainland. Sugar production declined but did continue in the Iberian peninsula long after competition from Atlantic production began.

Sugarcane agriculture in the Mediterranean basin was a marginal operation at best. Originally a tropical crop, sugarcane needs warm growing conditions throughout the year as well as abundant water. Neither of these conditions obtained in Spain, one of the most northerly regions where sugar has ever been grown commercially. In the Mediterranean basin, coastal regions escape freezing temperatures during most years, but the winters are cool and they prevent the cane from reaching its optimal growing conditions. Water proved to be a problem as well. The warm summer months, when the cane demands ample water, are just the time when rainfall is most sparse. The fields must nestle along the streams and in the deltas of major rivers (of which there are few), where irrigation can bring the water to the canes. Cane produced in the Mediterranean has a low sugar content, and consequently it could not compete successfully with sugar from tropical or semitropical regions with more favorable growing conditions. An additional problem was a chronic lack of firewood for the sugar refineries. The question of the timing and extent of deforestation in the Mediterranean is still open, but by the late 15th century a lack of firewood for boiling cane juice clearly hindered Iberian sugar production and likely that of other Mediterranean regions. In the 15th century the Spaniards and the Portuguese established sugar growing and refining on the Atlantic islands off the west coast of Africa, where temperatures were typically warmer than in the Mediterranean lands and where water, by rainfall or irrigation, was more available.

Expansion into the Atlantic

The story of sugar's expansion into the Atlantic unfolded slowly. As Europeans made their first tentative excursions into the Atlantic in the 13th and 14th centuries, they brought back little more than geographical knowledge of two groups of islands: the Canaries, and Madeira and its companion Porto Santo. By 1339 a portolan sailing chart produced in Catalonia had accurately identified them. At first, Portuguese and Castilian ships put in at the islands for easily obtainable items such as wood and the red dye "dragon's blood" (the resin of the dragon tree), and sailing masters used the islands occasionally as pirate bases. The Portuguese crown was not very interested in the islands until 1417, when the Castilians visited Madeira with a large force. Faced with potentially serious Castilian competition, King John I of Portugal sent out an expedition of some 100 men to Madeira and Porto Santo to establish permanent settlement. The leaders were two Portuguese, João Goncalves Zarco and Tristão Vaz Teixeira, and an Italian, Bartolomeo Perestrello (whose daughter later married Christopher Columbus). Zarco, with greater authority, worked out the division of the islands, allocating himself one-half of Madeira, while Teixeira got the remaining half of Madeira and Perestrello the much dryer Porto Santo. Each was to be lord of his territory with the right to parcel out lands to the other settlers. In 1433 King Duarte made his brother Prince Henry lord of the Madeiras for his lifetime. Henry in turn made the threefold division permanent by creating captaincies and awarding them to the three lords on a hereditary basis.

The agricultural exploitation of the islands was first based on mixed farming and grazing, but sugar soon became important. Madeira was uninhabited and fertile, and even though the first experiments with sugar were successful, the phenomenal growth of the industry happened only after careful and extensive preparation. The island had a dense cover of vegetation that had to be cleared before cultivation or even pasturing of animals was possible. The simple expedient of burning was adopted, and great fires rapidly did the work of years. Some of the settlers reportedly had to flee into the sea or rivers to escape clearing fires that had spread beyond their control, but in the wake of the burning, a fertilizing layer of ash covered the soil. Next, irrigation canals and terracing had to be constructed. That took more time, and settlers likely brought in technicians skilled in irrigation to direct the construction along with slaves from the Canaries for the labor. By 1450 these efforts were completed, and Madeira began to produce profits. The emerging sugar industry on Madeira received a boost in 1452 with the construction of the first water-powered sugar mill.

From the mid-15th century, the Portuguese took slaves to work on Madeira: Moroccans and Berbers, black Africans, and Canary Islanders. The number of slaves who could be profitably employed was limited because the Madeiran sugar establishments were still relatively small in comparison to the later Caribbean and Brazilian plantations. Because of population growth in Portugal itself in the 16th century, many free Portuguese laborers migrated to Madeira, further lessening the demand for slaves. There were even proposals to export some of the slaves already there. In the 15th century, Madeira was a precursor of the future American colonial areas, but by the early 16th century its development had transformed it into a replica of metropolitan Portugal.

The Portuguese established sugar production on other Atlantic islands, but none rivaled the early profits of Madeira. In the Azores sugar production met with little success because of the unfavorable climate; there grain and dyestuffs were always more important, and slaves were few in number. Portuguese agriculture in the arid Cape Verde Islands concentrated on cereals and fruits and was complemented by cattle raising. São Tomé, which became a crucial entrepôt for the transatlantic slave trade, experienced a sugar boom in the 16th century and can also be seen as a prototype of the sugar islands of the Caribbean.

With sugar production and trade prospering, shiploads of sugar were delivered to the large European markets: Lisbon, Seville, Antwerp, and cities of the Mediterranean. Although most of the plantations and mills were in the hands of Portuguese, the bulk of the export trade was controlled by foreigners, many of them Italians resident in Portugal. Columbus traded in Madeiran sugar early in his career and lived on the neighboring island of Porto Santo for a time in the 1470s. The European demand for sugar was strong, and the lower costs of Madeiran sugar caused heavy competition for the longer-established Mediterranean producers.

The Portuguese were not the only Europeans who were developing the Atlantic islands during this time. In the early 15th century, Castile began sponsoring conquests in the Canaries, and by the end of the century it had secured control of all the islands. Unlike the other Atlantic islands, the Canaries had a native population who were likely akin to the Berbers. Foreshadowing events in the Americas, the Spaniards subdued the islanders and enslaved those who resisted. Of these, a number were exported to Europe or Madeira, while others were employed on Canarian sugar plantations.

The island population was relatively small to begin with, and its numbers fell due to epidemic disease after the European incursion. Members of indigenous groups whose leaders had signed treaties could not be enslaved legally, unlike members of the non-treaty groups, and those who were enslaved frequently attained manumission. In the early years of the 16th century, the Canarian slave trade to Europe ceased as the islanders increasingly assimilated European culture and intermarried with the colonists. Since native workers never filled the labor needs of the Canaries, the islands witnessed an influx of other workers, including a number of free

Castilian and Portuguese settlers. Wealthier settlers brought their own slaves with them from the peninsula. Portuguese slave traders brought in blacks from West Africa, and Castilian mariners raided the coast for North Africans, Berbers, and other slaves. Following the first Spanish contact with the Americas, a few American Indians were sold in the Canaries, but the Spanish crown soon outlawed the slave trade in Indians.

These sugar establishments on Madeira and in the Canary Islands turned out to have some important features of the Caribbean plantations that would emerge in the 16th century, including elements both agricultural (growing the cane) and industrial (refining the sugar), the use of slave labor, and the export of a product to be sold in the growing markets of Europe. The significant difference between the sugar establishments on the Atlantic islands and the later plantations of the Caribbean was size; the former had smaller plots of land and fewer laborers. Those Atlantic islands provided a link between Mediterranean sugar production and the plantation system that was to dominate New World slavery and society into the 19th century.

Madeira and the Canaries formed the staging area from which sugar cultivation and refining would reach Hispaniola, the island where sugarcane was first planted in the Caribbean. Columbus, knowledgeable in the Portuguese sugar trade, had ships of his second transatlantic voyage stop in Madeira for additional supplies. These included refined sugar as a medicinal store and cuttings of sugarcane, which were later planted at Columbus's ill-fated settlement of La Isabela on the north shore of Hispaniola. The first canes grew but failed to establish permanent sugar production. Only in the first decade and-a-half of the 16th century did successful sugar plantings and newly introduced sugar mills on Hispaniola establish the foundations for the fateful beginning of the colonial plantation complex in the Americas.

WORKS CITED

Deerr, Noël. 1949–50. *The History of Sugar*. 2 vols. London: Chapman and Hall.

Fulcher of Chartres. 1969. *A History of the Expedition to Jerusalem, 1095–1125*. Trans. Frances Rita Ryan, ed. Harold S. Fink. Knoxville: University of Tennessee Press.

González Tascón, Ignacio, and Joaquín Fernández Pérez. 1990. "El azúcar en el viejo mundo: El impacto en su elaboración." In Antonio Malpica, ed., *La caña de azúcar en tiempos de los grandes descubrimientos (1450–1550): Actas del Primer Seminario International, Motril, 25–28 de septiembre 1989*. Motril: Junta de Andalucía and Ayuntamiento de Motril.

William of Tyre. 1943. *A History of Deeds Done beyond the Sea*. 2 vols. Trans. and ed. Emily Atwater Babcock and A. C. Krey. New York: Columbia University Press.

PART 2

The Making of a Colonial Sphere

5

The Columbian Moment

REINALDO FUNES
MONZOTE

Politics, Ideology, and Biohistory

Few events in human history have been as momentous as the arrival of Christopher Columbus and his companions in the Caribbean in 1492. More than 10,000 years earlier, the pathways across
the Bering Strait, by which *Homo sapiens* first arrived on the
present-day American continent, had closed. Columbus was not
the first European to reestablish the intercontinental connection;
besides the sporadic Viking presence in Greenland and in the territory northeast of the North American–Atlantic mountain range
between the 9th and 15th centuries, there was probably also inad-
vertent contact. Still, the report of Columbus's discovery, delivered
upon his return to Europe, is what irrefutably triggered the genuine
encounter between ancient civilizations that had evolved in complete isolation (Crosby 1986).

The Caribbean islands were the first setting for the rapid demographic and ecological changes that followed the European irrup-
tion in the Americas and the intense "Columbian exchange"

Figure 5.1 Christopher Columbus's arrival on Hispaniola in
1492. Engraving from Theodore
de Bry, *Americae pars quarta*
(1594). Source: The John Carter
Brown Library.

between the Old and New Worlds that ensued. As indicated by
his insistence that he had landed in Asia, Columbus himself
does not seem to have been conscious of the true magnitude
of his achievement. Whatever the case, and without ignoring
Columbus's intuition and determination, this achievement
can only be adequately explained from within its historical
European context.

Columbus and His Project

Beginning in the 14th century, navigators from Genoa, Portugal, and the maritime
kingdoms of Aragon traveled to islands in the Azores, Canary, and Madeira archi-
pelagoes. The boats used for these incursions were basic, oar-powered craft that employed sails to catch tailwinds and crosswinds. The appearance of ships and caravels
with rigging that combined Latin triangular sails and cross sails permitted dependence on wind power alone and made possible longer journeys with less risk. Also

contributing to this navigational advancement were portolan charts, which allowed sailors to determine their route without direct geographic observation.

The Portuguese were the vanguard in this European expansion into the Atlantic: in 1418 they carried out an expedition to Porto Santo, in the Azores, and two years later they began exploration of the African littoral and identified Madeira. In 1442 Portuguese ships reached the Cape Verde archipelago; in 1452 they discovered Flores and Corvo, islands further removed from the Portuguese mainland than the Azores. In 1472 they entered the Gulf of Guinea, after which began their use of the so-called *volta de Mina*, a favorite return route to Lisbon aided by trade winds. In 1488 they navigated beyond the Cape of Good Hope and returned to the Atlantic.

Christopher Columbus was born in 1451 or 1452 in Genoa, an important commercial and financial center in medieval and Renaissance Europe. From his youth Columbus was dedicated to the sailor's life, one means of social mobility for those not destined for high society through inheritance. In 1477 he moved from Genoa to Lisbon, and his marriage in 1478 or 1479 brought him into a Portuguese family of aristocratic antecedent: his father-in-law possessed the fief of Porto Santo. Presumably, this affinity helped shape Columbus's ambitions as a discoverer and allowed him to become acquainted with the geographic literature of the age.

Time spent in Portugal also allowed Columbus to become familiar with the latest findings on the northeast trade wind current between the Iberian Peninsula and the Canaries, the eastern trade winds in the Atlantic's central tropics, and the return current to the north of the Azores. During these years, he transformed himself from mercantile agent to learned geographer, albeit self-taught (Fernández-Armesto 1991). Several objectives inspired him: the discovery of new islands, the search for the antipodes (the opposite side of the earth), and the reaching of Asia by westward navigation.

The Atlantic discoveries of the 14th and 15th centuries had stimulated such speculation among the learned. Maps from the period situated imaginary islands according to ancient and medieval legends, such as those of Brazil, which had been the objective of voyages organized from Bristol at the end of the 15th century, and of "Antilia" or the "islands of the Seven Cities," which the Portuguese as well as the Flemish aspired to reach from their departure point in the Azores. This intense speculation coincided with the 15th-century rediscovery of Ptolemy's second-century geographic compendium, which featured an image of the world as a perfect sphere with a continuous landmass from Europe to Asia and an intervening ocean whose torrid zone contained unknown lands and inhabitants.

Among the works studied by Columbus was Pierre D'Ailly's 1480 edited compendium *Imago Mundi*, which dealt with themes such as the navigability of all oceans, the inhabitability of all climates, and the existence of the antipodes, together with descriptions of the riches of the Orient. Columbus also knew the theory of a circumscribed Atlantic, developed and charted in 1474 by Italian cosmographer Paolo dal Pozzo Toscanelli, who indicated distances of 5,000 nautical miles between the Canaries and Cathay (China) and 3,000 nautical miles between the Canaries and Cipango (Japan), a possible stopover. Columbus's estimation of these distances was even shorter, an erroneous calculation that worked to his advantage in a time when sea voyages did not usually exceed 800 miles. A similar understanding of the earth was shared by cosmographers in Nuremburg, as illustrated by a globe crafted in 1492 by Martin Behaim. In addition, Marco Polo's accounts offered reports of thousands of islands off the coasts of Asia, and of the great distance from Cipango to Cathay, though there is no consensus on the date Columbus consulted Polo's writings. The primary source of Columbus's convictions might even have been the eyewitness testimony of navigators who had inadvertently reached unchartered lands in the western Atlantic (Manzano 1989).

But in the search for patronage among Europe's principal monarchies—both in financial terms and as a safeguard against potential competitors—the discovery of new islands or the antipodes was secondary to the promise of finding a new route to Asia. This goal corresponded perfectly with the interests of the Spanish monarchy, from which Columbus finally gained the backing to make his longed-for voyage a reality.

The Spain of the Catholic Monarchs

On several occasions (most significantly between 1484 and 1485) Columbus attempted to secure support for his explorations from Portugal, and he also pointedly solicited England and France. But the bulk of his efforts after 1486 focused on Spain. This was no accident, despite the Portuguese having greater credentials as explorers of the Atlantic.

The union of the crowns of Castile and Aragon in 1479 was the first step in the formation of the modern Spanish state, and it stimulated a rivalry with Portugal that influenced the course of events leading up to the Columbian encounter. As a result of Portugal's war against Ferdinand and Isabella over the crown of Castile (1474–79), frequent permission was granted Castilian subjects to carry out contraband trade and piracy along the African coast. At the same time, Genovese citizens in Seville and Cádiz showed interest in investing in the Atlantic enterprise as the potential for sugar production in Madeira and the Canary Islands became evident—trade in which Columbus later intervened. Thus industry, commerce, and navigation met in a moment of prosperity that led to the search for new trade routes and exotic markets and provided the necessary capital for these undertakings.

The 1480 Treaty of Alcaçovas delimited Portuguese and Spanish spheres of influence. The treaty recognized Portuguese possession of the Azores, Madeira, and

Cape Verde and exclusive rights of navigation toward Guinea. In return, the Portuguese had to accept Spanish sovereignty over the Canaries, though not until 1489 did the Spanish overcome native Guanche resistance there. This partition, endorsed by papal bull, would provide Columbus with an intermediate stopover in the westward journey to Asia, and the bulk of his companions were veterans of the campaigns against the Guanches.

In 1482 the Spanish war of reconquest began against the kingdom of Granada, the only territory the Muslims retained on the Iberian Peninsula. This undertaking created an urgent demand for new gold sources, especially with African mines in Portuguese hands. Around 1489 Columbus renewed his lobbying of the Spanish crown with the increased backing of an influential group that constituted the crown prince's inner circle. From within the monastery of La Rábida, Columbus received the crucial support of friars Juan Pérez and Antonio Marchena, the latter the only astronomer of the court who gave any credit to Columbus's geographic speculations.

In 1492, at the request of the Catholic Monarchs, Columbus traveled to the recently conquered Granada to present his plan once again. Though it was focused on the idea of reaching Asia, court experts reiterated their rejection of the plan, seemingly due to the level of compensation Columbus demanded should the venture prove successful. Nevertheless, the crown finally assented. On April 17 the Capitulations of Santa Fe were signed, wherein Columbus was granted such demands as the title of admiral and viceroy of all islands and lands discovered. On April 30 the monarchs made these titles lifelong and hereditary, and granted Columbus the use of the honorific *Don*. They also signed a letter for presentation to Asian monarchs affirming these credentials. With royal approval and financial backing, the expedition was mounted, with between 90 and 120 men aboard three small caravels setting out to the uncharted ocean. On August 3 they weighed anchor at Palos de Moguer and within a week they arrived in the Canaries, leaving a month later from La Gomera. After navigating for a little over a month, Columbus and his companions made landfall on October 12, 1492, marking the beginning of the historic encounter between two worlds.

Occupation of the Caribbean Islands and Indigenous Depopulation

The first contact of these Europeans with the New World was confined to a portion of the Caribbean: a few islands in the Bahamas archipelago, part of the northeast of Cuba, and the north of Hispaniola, which Columbus identified as the Antilles. The speculations of European geography and cartography permeated his perception of this encounter and his understanding of the new territories. Very soon (on October 17), the terms *Indians*, to identify natives, and *the Indies*, to signal the expedition's arrival in Asian lands, appeared in his diary.

The floral vitality and variety of the New World surprised Columbus, as did the quantity and diversity of fish and fowl. In contrast, he commented on the scarcity of quadrupeds, "Neither sheep nor goats nor any other animal did we see"—a clear contrast to the abundance of domesticated animals in the Old World. To Columbus the climate seemed excellent and promised prodigious riches. As the days passed, he increasingly began to compare the animals, plants, and fruits to those of Europe and to name them accordingly. The act of discovery covered the terrain with imported toponyms. After his first expressions of surprise at the Caribbean environment, Columbus began to see Hispaniola's natural environment as equal or superior to that of Castile (Gerbi 1978, 32–33).

Columbus's perception may have been influenced by the finding of gold on Hispaniola, the first evidence of potential economic benefits. Likewise, it was not long before he saw the natives, described as peaceful, docile "people of love and without greed," as potential slaves in the service of the conquistadors. With samples of gold and other souvenirs—such as parrots, chiles, maize, yams, and 10 natives—he departed for Spain on January 16, 1493. His arrival in Lisbon on March 5 was made possible by the fortuitous discovery of favorable winds and was immediately turned into a grand event. In April, the admiral presented himself before the Catholic Monarchs in Barcelona. Peter Martyr, who was present, wrote that the Genovese explorer had returned from the antipodes with news of many precious things—particularly gold—which those regions generated by their nature (Sauer 1966). To give an idea of the reception of this news throughout Europe, it suffices to note that Columbus's first letter went through nine printings in 1493. In May of the same year, Pope Alexander VI responded to a request from the Spanish monarchs with a bull that officially recognized their possession of the discovered lands in exchange for the conversion of their inhabitants to the Catholic faith. The bull also marked the line of demarcation between Spanish and Portuguese territories in the Atlantic.

During the admiral's three remaining voyages to the New World, all within Caribbean space, his search for gold turned into an obsession. This explains his tendency to deviate toward the south, in consonance with the ancient belief that gold was created by warm temperatures and silver by cold. His second voyage was carried out between the end of September 1493 and June 1496. From the Canaries it took his crew 21 days to reach the arch of the Lesser Antilles, which extends northward to Puerto Rico and Hispaniola. They also reconnoitered the southern coasts of Cuba and Jamaica. The third voyage was carried out from May 1498 to November 1500 and it reached the continental coast of South America at the mouth of the Orinoco. The fourth voyage, between May 1502 and November 1504, included exploring the Central American coast from Honduras to Panama.

At the beginning of 1499, the Spanish crown ceased exclusive recognition of

Figure 5.2 A hurricane strikes Hispaniola, capsizing a ship and causing Spanish soldiers and native people to flee. Engraving from Theodore de Bry, *Americae pars quarta* (1594). Source: The John Carter Brown Library.

Columbus and his relatives in matters of the Indies, designated a new governor for Hispaniola, and began to grant licenses for independent expeditions concentrated on the South American coast. These were headed by Andalusian sailors previously under the admiral's command. Little by little, the initial narrow interest in the Caribbean began to give way before visions of immense continental territories with fabulous riches. Colonization extended to Puerto Rico in 1508, to Jamaica in 1509, and to Cuba in 1511. The remaining, smaller islands barely received attention except for raids in search of slaves.

There has been much debate, without any consensus, over the total population of the Caribbean islands in 1492. The case most extensively covered is that of Hispaniola, where contemporary documentation is abundant. Among the most utilized sources is the work of Bartolomé de Las Casas, dismissed by some due to its denunciation of Indian mistreatment. Las Casas's estimate was that in 1493 between three and four million natives lived on Hispaniola, but that the population rapidly fell to a little more than a million—a figure he proposed on the basis of a census of adults ordered after the abrupt demographic decline around 1495. Other studies based on demographic and ecological projections coincide with Las Casas's figures or in some cases double his count. Such calculations are based on the perception of a healthy population with a long life span—one that is free of epidemics, wars, and famines; has more births than deaths; and has women bearing between three and five children. The lower estimates, in contrast, place the number of inhabitants on Hispaniola in 1492 between 400,000 and just 100,000.

The same sort of variation exists for the rest of the islands. The predominant understanding is that Jamaica and Puerto Rico were the most populous and that Cuba had uneven population concentrations throughout its territory. Evaluations of the entire population of the Antilles are rare, but they show similar tendencies: the lowest estimations range between 450,000 and 550,000 and the highest between five and six million. This great contrast is due to differing methodologies and perhaps to the academic affiliations or political motivations of contemporary scholars. But consensus does exist on the dramatic drop of the aboriginal population of the Antilles prior to the European occupation of the mainland.

The causes of the drop were multiple: massacres, slavery, the extreme cruelty of the colonizers, suicides, famines due to the abandonment of subsistence crops, loss of the will to live. One fundamental cause of death was the diseases of European origin against which natives had no immunological defenses. The case of Hispaniola receives a good deal of attention because demographic collapse began on a continental scale after a well-documented epidemic of smallpox spread from the island in December 1518, when only 10,000 of its indigenous inhabitants remained alive. Controlling for these numbers, scholars typically use the example of Hispaniola to highlight causes of mortality other than disease.

Nevertheless, there is evidence that several diseases were introduced from the second of Columbus's voyages on. One of these pathogens, identified by some authors as swine flu, caused high mortality among the close to 1,500 Spanish who had relocated to Hispaniola. Its impact on the indigenous population is more difficult to gauge but may have been much greater, as the disease combined with other illnesses that seem to have arrived on the same voyage, such as influenza, typhoid, meningitis, smallpox, and malaria (Cook 2002).

The various waves of Eurasian and African diseases decimated the New World's native population because it had not undergone the ancient exchange of microbes and germs that had occurred on the other side of the Atlantic. In the Caribbean, indigenous demographic collapse was almost total, and it advanced in correspondence with the forceful occupation of territories and accompanying raids in search of a labor force. By the middle of the 16th century there were only a few representatives of indigenous groups remaining in the Greater Antilles, together with a few remnants in areas of the Lesser Antilles that were unoccupied by Europeans. The spread of diseases from the New World among Europeans was significantly less, although it may have begun earlier with outbreaks of syphilis.

Among the epidemics coming from the Old World, none had more lasting effect than yellow fever (or "the black vomit"). Originating in tropical West Africa, this was one of the deadliest diseases in the tropics and occasionally in cities of temperate zones of the Atlantic from the 17th to the 20th century. Among its principal areas of impact were the Caribbean islands during the height of the slave-labor based sugar plantation. The conditions created by the environment and the systematic exploitation of human labor facilitated yellow fever's spread, as sugar plantations and factories replaced native forests. Until the end of the 19th century the precise means of its transmission remained unknown; it turned out to be the female of the mosquito species *Aedes aegypti* (a hypothesis advanced by the Cuban doctor Carlos Finlay in 1881).

Deforestation created greater proximity between mosquito and human populations and reduced the number of possible natural predators for mosquitoes, while the new sugar-producing landscape offered an ideal medium for mosquito reproduction, from clay vessels that were used for the crystallization of syrups to the growing human presence—in particular, African slaves. These slaves, coming from regions where mosquito-borne diseases were common, enjoyed a higher level of immunity to yellow fever, and in time the same occurred with creoles, who were able to acquire immunities during childhood and survive. The course the illness took was contrary to those of other epidemics from the Old World in that the first infected were adults coming from Europe to participate in military engagements or colonial administration. Thus would yellow fever become a key element of geopolitics in the Caribbean area, and a relative brake on European immigration to lowland tropical America.

Beginnings of the Columbian Exchange of Animals and Plants

With the arrival of the conquistadors came other more visible elements of their biota, such as cultivated plants and domesticated animals, fruits of the Old World's Neolithic agricultural revolutions (Crosby 1977, 1986). The 17 ships of Columbus's second voyage not only brought Spanish subjects to occupy the new territories (as well as pathogenic viruses), but also carried plants and animals that formed an indissoluble part of the Spaniards' subsistence and farming culture. The former included seeds of wheat, garbanzo, onion, radish, melons, grapes, some unidentified vegetables and fruits (including citrus), and sugarcane; the latter horses, cattle (adults and calves), pigs, sheep, and goats.

It seems that acclimatization was somewhat slower with plants than with animals. Some plants, such as garden produce, grew much more rapidly than in

Europe; but other crops failed, such as wheat, grapevines, and olive trees. In addition to differences in climate, adaptation was made difficult by the conquistadores' refusal to become farmers instead of recipients of exploited indigenous labor in the search for gold. Old World animals, on the other hand, showed an amazing capacity to reproduce in their new setting. The quick decision to introduce these animals may have been motivated by Columbus's surprise at the scarcity of quadrupeds on the islands. For example, in a letter to the Spanish monarchs from January 1494, the admiral attributed his men's illnesses to the lack of fresh meat and pleaded that they be sent beasts for food and labor, "for there are no animals here that are valuable and helpful to man." A few years later Fernández de Oviedo would describe a very different panorama: "Since the arrival of the first cows . . . there are already so many that the ships return full of hides," and there was even left "in the pastures wasted meat, for [all] the hides [are] taken to Spain" (Gerbi 1978, 335). Pigs adapted equally well on all the islands and would be raised in free range within their forests. Horses were soon born in the Caribbean and were of great service to the conquistadores of the mainland.

The multiplication of European animals such as dogs, cats, and rats—under feral conditions and in the absence of natural predators—had a great impact on native fauna and undergrowth and damaged small indigenous subsistence plots (*conucos*). In several islands of the Lesser Antilles, a process similar to the proliferation of European cattle occurred, above all with pigs. After the exhaustion of gold sources, cattle ranching was the predominant activity on the larger islands, aided by high demand for leather in Europe. The importance of leather in the 16th century is comparable only to that of sugar at the apex of cane plantations on Hispaniola and, in smaller measure, Puerto Rico from the second decade of the century to the 1580s. In Caribbean lands, sugar production grew faster than it had in previous locations. Experience and technical knowledge in the cultivation and processing of sugarcane were transplanted by financiers and merchants with interests in Madeira and the Canaries. Nonetheless, agro-industrial production in the new territories differed in the use of African slaves as the predominant source of labor.

The introduction of plants to the Caribbean, particularly those from the Mediterranean area, continued throughout the 16th century and included carrots, cabbage, garlic, eggplant, lettuce, and cauliflower around 1509; rice after 1512; and the banana tree in 1516. The latter came from the Canaries and was called *guineo* on some islands, due to its origins in the African zone of the same name. The Asian coconut, so common in present-day Caribbean landscapes, had reached Pacific American coasts in pre-Columbian times but appears not to have reached the Caribbean before 1525. Ginger, also either from Asia or the Atlantic islands, arrived around the middle of the 16th century and gradually replaced diminishing sugar production on Hispaniola. In the centuries that followed, other plants arrived and gained great importance in the area, such as mango, brought by the Portuguese to the Bahía region in 1700 and mentioned in Puerto Rico after 1740, and breadfruit, brought by the English as food for slaves toward the end of the 18th century. Less has been written on African plants such as the yam, present since 1510, and one variety of African rice. But from the beginning these crops traveled in slave ships and were cultivated on subsistence plots (Carney 2001). Africa also became an important source of grasses for cattle pasturage, such as Guinea grass, and it contributed animals such as the fowl that was given the same "guinea" appellation.

Before 1492 some plants of the Columbian exchange—such as coffee, plantain, and tamarind—were propagated from their centers of domestication throughout Asia, the Middle East, or Africa, while others—such as cotton—already existed in different varieties on both sides of the Atlantic. Flora domesticated by Amerindian cultures became highly significant in the agriculture, eating habits, and other customs of the Old World: the long list includes maize; *solacenae* such as potato, tomato, and tobacco; and pineapple. Of those foods that were staples in pre-Columbian Caribbean societies, the most important contributions were high-producing tubers such as yucca and *boniato*, or sweet potato (Sauer 1966), which became part of the colonizers' diet and crossed the Atlantic to become important food sources in sub-Saharan Africa.

When Europeans arrived, the Caribbean islands had a wide range of fruit-bearing plants that produced papaya, guava, mamey, soursop, cherimoya, and pineapple (though not all of these were present on every island), as well as oleaginous plants such as the peanut, and condiment sources such as chiles. Spanish colonization accelerated the influx of other plants domesticated on the American mainland but not previously present in the Antilles, such as sapote, avocado, and tomato from Mesoamerica and cashew from Brazil (Vega 1997). From the mid-18th century, botanical gardens on islands dominated by the British, French, or Dutch—and, a little later, in the Spanish Antilles—played an increasingly important role in the intercontinental spread of flora.

The wealth of timber in the Antilles was a fundamental resource in the colonization process owing to the abundance of excellent woods. These included varieties both precious and used in construction, including cedar, mahogany, and bulletwood; dyewood trees such as brazilwood and fustic; and other woods of great utility such as various palm trees, particularly the royal palm. The ratio of forest to savannah on the larger islands has been the subject of long debate among botanists, geographers, and historians, but there is no disagreement on the fact that forests were predominant throughout the Antillean archipelago—which is not to say that they were in a virgin state (Denevan 1992). Yet despite the practice of irrigated agriculture for small subsistence plots, and hunting and fishing as a complement to diet, aboriginal communities of the Antilles lived "largely in harmony with their physical and biological environment, so preserving its innate resource potential" (Watts 1987). The depopulation of the islands after 1492 may have resulted in the appearance of expanding reforestation in areas that previously had been cleared for subsistence farming. But soon, promotion of commercial crops such as sugar, tobacco, or, later, coffee would provide the origins of the greater environmental transformations through human intervention that were registered in the Caribbean.

The Columbian Moment: A Brief Balance

The implications of the Columbian moment were not the same for all parties involved. To speak of the "encounter" of cultures in the Antilles can be misleading if the near-absolute disappearance of the indigenous inhabitants is taken into account. More than an encounter, it was a cultural and biological erasure, despite vestiges of the native population that remained through cultural and biological hybridization (*mestizaje*), a few words, toponyms, foods, and crops. The later introduction of African slaves on a massive scale, together with other minor migrations and colonies of European origin, formed the racial and cultural diversity of the newer inhabitants. Plants and animals from Eurasia and Africa made their mark on the Caribbean landscape, which saw its biodiversity diminished in favor of some few species of high commercial value, or due to invasive plants spread unintentionally.

Conversely, for Europe the New World meant an increase in wealth and power through the possession of a territory several times larger than itself as a source of raw materials, food, and merchandise for its industries and, moreover, as a place to which excess European population could be sent. On intellectual and spiritual levels, Europe's mental horizons expanded as a good number of old assumptions about geography, history, theology, nature, and humankind were challenged. For Spain, dominion in America and the invocation of a civilizing mission helped lay the foundations for an era of hegemony that endured until the mid-17th century. This marked the birth of the first great transoceanic empires, whose price was a high level of social conformity and submission to metropolitan authority (Elliot 1970).

With the colonization of the New World, the scope of conflicts between European states extended beyond their immediate geographic space. The Caribbean was one of the principal settings for these conflicts through the actions of corsairs, pirates, and buccaneers during the 16th and 17th centuries, contributing to the undermining of Spanish power. In the end, Spain's weakening opened the door to forcible occupation of several territories in the Lesser and Greater Antilles by the English, French, Dutch, and Danish. From the middle of the 17th century, a new phase of plantation slavery began in these areas, which would be fundamental to the processes of wealth accumulation and to the birth of Europe's industrial era, which was achieved in exchange for great human and environmental tragedy in the Caribbean islands.

Translation by Zachary J. Chase

WORKS CITED

Carney, Judith A. 2001. "African Rice in the Columbian Exchange," *The Journal of African History* 42, no. 3: 337–96.

Cook, Noble David. 2002. "Sickness, Starvation, and Death in Early Hispaniola," *Journal of Interdisciplinary History* 32, no. 3 (Winter): 349–86.

Crosby, Alfred W. 1977. *The Columbian Exchange: Biological and Cultural Consequences of 1492.* Westport, CT: Greenwood Press.

———. 1986. *Ecological Imperialism: The Biological Expansion of Europe, 900–1900.* Cambridge: Cambridge University Press.

Denevan, William M. 1992. "The Pristine Myth: The Landscape of the Americas in 1492," *Annals of the Association of American Geographers* 82, no. 3 (September): 369–95.

Elliot, John H. 1970. *The Old World and the New, 1492–1650.* Cambridge: Cambridge University Press.

Fernández-Armesto, Felipe. 1991. *Columbus.* Oxford: Oxford University Press.

Gerbi, Antonelo. 1978. *La naturaleza de las indias nuevas: De Cristóbal Colón a Gonzalo Fernández de Oviedo,* traducción de Antonio Alatorre. México, DF: Fondo de Cultura Económica.

Manzano Manzano, Juan. 1989. *Colón y su secreto: El predescubrimiento.* 3rd ed. Madrid: Ediciones Cultura Hispánica.

McNeill, John. 2008. *Epidemics and Geopolitics in the American Tropics, 1640–1920.* New York: Cambridge University Press.

Sauer, Carl O. 1966. *The Early Spanish Main.* Berkeley: University of California Press.

Vega, Bernardo. 1997. *Las frutas de los taínos.* Santo Domingo: Fundación Cultural Dominicana.

Watts, David. 1987. *The West Indies: Patterns of Development, Culture and Environmental Change since 1492.* Cambridge: Cambridge University Press.

6

From Tainos to Africans in the Caribbean
JALIL SUED-BADILLO

Labor, Migration, and Resistance

Until fairly recently, historians have based their research concerning the native societies and cultures of the Caribbean on two major types of sources—contemporary chronicles and histories, and Spanish administrative documents. While both are still considered invaluable fonts of data, their very nature is deeply problematic—a situation that has shaped traditional portrayals of Amerindian life in the precontact and immediate postcontact periods.

Chronicles have long been considered the starting point for Amerindian history and culture. Beginning with the writings of Christopher Columbus himself, this category of sources comprises wide-ranging observations made by contemporary travelers and other writers. But information from these sources is decidedly partial, contradictory, and problematic, particularly in regard to the native Tainos.

Of equal importance are the voluminous writings of the first "historians of the Indies," who recorded the process of conquest and colonization. One of the earliest, Peter Martyr, author of *De orbe novo* (in two volumes, the first published in 1511), never set foot in America but wrote from a privileged position at the Spanish court with access to important reports. In contrast, Gonzalo Fernández de Oviedo, author of the *General and Natural History of the Indies* (in five volumes, the first of which appeared in 1535), lived most of his life on Hispaniola, served important official positions, and wrote as a champion of Spanish colonial rule. Friar Bartolomé de las Casas, the most prolific of these historians, is best known for his brief *Account of the Destruction of the Indies* (1552), but less so for his major published works *History of the Indies* (1875) and *Apologetic History of the Indies* (1909). Although he was a witness to much of what he wrote about, he drafted much of it late in life, in constant struggle with his memory.

Of particular interest is *An Account of the Antiquities of the Indians*, a brief but significant account of some religious beliefs of the Tainos in Hispaniola, written by Friar Ramón Pané in 1494. This very first "ethnographic" report drafted on American soil has had an erratic history. The Taino *caciques* (chiefs) were interviewed through interpreters, and the work itself was published in an Italian translation only in 1571. Even aside from the great confusion admitted by Pané in the organization of his early notes, or the different versions of key Amerindian names and place names in each subsequent translation or transcription, the reliability of this work is obviously questionable.

The same can be said of all the other chronicles. They were not systematic studies, and they were often based on casual observations. Many are riddled with cultural biases, exaggerations, omissions and, worse yet, contradictions. This becomes obvious when, for example, comparing Oviedo's work with that of Las Casas. These authors were at opposite ends of the political spectrum of their times, yet no serious historian can do without them.

Far more important than the writings of early chroniclers and travelers are the Spanish administrative archives—primarily the Archivo General de Indias in Seville, which remains the most important source of information on Spain's colonial empire. Containing extensive but rigorous records of everyday affairs, judicial documents, official and private correspondence, reports, testimonies, policy papers, census records, and other facts and figures, its holdings include invaluable data on Amerindian cultures, particularly those on Hispaniola. But, like the chronicles, these documents were created by Spanish officials with at best an imperfect understanding of the people whose lives they were documenting, and often with patently ideological motives.

Only recently have archaeologists and ethnohistorians begun to reconstruct Amerindian societies from a perspective aimed to approach that of the natives themselves. Although contemporary knowledge of the Caribbean as it existed in 1492 is becoming more sophisticated and interdisciplinary, it is still one-sided at best.

The Tainos

Historians do not know what the native populations of the Caribbean named themselves. The designation *Taino* is a modern label now applied to a variety of ethnic groups coexisting in the Caribbean archipelago at the end of the 15th century. The term, recorded first off the coast of Haiti and later in Guadeloupe as hearsay, is said to have meant "good or noble Indians," but this meaning has not been linguistically confirmed. The application of this term to the original inhabitants of the Greater Antilles has been a recent practice by historians and archaeologists, mainly those in the Spanish-speaking Caribbean; their North American counterparts have usually preferred the term *Arawak*, also a modern label. Whatever its origin, the collective term at least acknowledges that, in spite of their diversity, the people of the Caribbean region had more characteristics in common than differences.

The islands had been inhabited for more than 7,000 years, having been populated initially in several waves of migration from South and Central America. The last of these migrations occurred from 500 BCE to 300 CE, bringing horticulturalists and proficient pottery makers from Amazonian and Andean backgrounds. They introduced lasting cultural essentials such as language (Arawak), religious symbolism, family structure, economic strategies and products, animals, and metallurgy and pottery making, all to be further developed on the islands. The term *Taino* has been reserved for the people of the last stage before the European conquest and limited to the regions where more social and cultural complexity was achieved; their predecessors are referred to in the archaeological literature as *pre-Tainos*. By the middle of the first millennium CE, pre-Tainos were establishing a new cultural scenario reflecting their progress in adapting to the insular environment and its challenges. The ethnic fusion of the new continental horticulturalists with the original and poorly understood "Archaic" population of the islands transformed the latter's cultures and ushered in new social formations.

Perhaps the most conspicuous center for this process of transculturation, as the Cuban scholar Fernando Ortiz was to call it, was the island of Borinquén (today's Puerto Rico). The smallest of the Greater Antilles, Borinquén was the foremost boundary of the last wave of continental migrations to the insular Caribbean. Its territory proved suitable for slowing down migratory expansion and allowing for the effective integration of newcomers with natives. Borinquén thus experienced ethnic admixtures more comprehensively than other islands, and produced the formative social configurations for the future Taino culture. Migration and other forms of influence from Borinquén toward the Greater and Lesser Antilles acted as a cultural vector and induced a basic cultural uniformity throughout the archipelago.

Two islands were the prime centers of Taino social complexity in the Caribbean:

Haiti-Quisqueya (today's Hispaniola, including Haiti and the Dominican Republic), whose sphere of cultural influence also included eastern Cuba and Jamaica, and Borinquén, whose social formation extended into eastern Quisqueya and the Lesser Antilles as far back as Guadalupe. The diffusion of pre-Taino cultural traits from Borinquén, probably beginning around 400 CE, was made possible by the emergence of a chiefdom-like political formation on that island. This regional form of government, transcending smaller tribal boundaries, first appeared in the southern coastal valleys of the island, slowly spreading to the mountainous interior and outward to the neighboring islands.

This type of social arrangement is often considered a forerunner to state formation and has been extensively discussed by modern anthropologists, but its operation remains elusive. Agreement seems to exist that among the Tainos and others like them, a chiefdom was a thickly populated region with multiple communities that were organized politically and hierarchically and subordinated to a center. Such political formations are considered to have been geographically expansionist and war-prone while zealous of their formal frontiers; their paramount chiefs are also considered to have acted as high priests, with religion more than force as the basis of their authority. Such chiefs, known as *caciques*, were polygamous (as attested to by most chroniclers) and highly respected figures who mainly acceded to their positions through inheritance. The governed communities paid tribute mainly in the form of services rendered to the chiefs in agricultural labor, occasional ceremonial constructions, and conscription in case of war. But the chiefs did not control productive activities. They had neither standing armies nor permanent bureaucracies, and close family members acted as occasional administrators, envoys, and key allies.

Kinship structure was matrilineal—that is, the succession to inheritance and rank ran through the mother's side in an arrangement that permitted women to participate in public activities and assume political status as *cacicas*. In Puerto Rico, 12 cacicas have been identified in the historical sources. In Hispaniola, dozens are listed in census reports dating from the early years of colonial occupation, and Anacaona, sister of a former high provincial chief from Jaragua, inherited the rank and ruled over a large number of vassal polities. The participation of women in the political and religious realm makes the Tainos heirs to an ancient and conspicuous Andean practice traceable from Peru to the Antilles and abundantly observed and recorded in the 16th century (Sued-Badillo 1985, 2007).

In Puerto Rico, only one chiefdom governing about two-thirds of the island appears to have existed in 1492. Its central enclave, known as Cayabo, was in the modern southern region of Ponce, and the reigning family bore the name of Agüeybana. The rest of the island apparently remained in the hands of local tribal chiefs, who sought Spanish protection from the lead chiefdom's encroachment. In His-

Figure 6.1 A cacique on the island of Cuba leads his people in negotiations with Columbus. Engraving by Benjamin West and Francesco Bartolozzi (1794). Source: The John Carter Brown Library.

paniola, most of the island was divided among five large polities—Jaragua, Maguá, Maguana, Marién, and Cayacoa or Higüey—while some of its more isolated regions remained locally independent. In the principal islands, then, the chiefdoms apparently had not yet realized the formation of a political status, which would have implied a much wider and more effective integration beyond the immediate region. A permanent bureaucracy and army, a religion with temples and priests engaging in practices beyond traditional shamanic ceremonies, and forced regular tributes on production and on services (beyond occasional ones) were all things that did not yet exist.

In the absence of formal social classes, public inequalities and an elite structure beyond nuclear kinship were beginning to develop in Haiti and Borinquén, and the fabrication and circulation of sumptuary goods were likely controlled by the caciques for prestige and social status. But a state system organized to control and exploit the general population existed only in parts of Mexico and Peru. In Cuba and Jamaica there is evidence not even of chiefdoms, but only of a still-dominant "tribal" (or kinship-based) social structure and a very limited political geography. Most Spanish observers concurred that Hispaniola had a population of more than a million inhabitants by 1492. Along with Puerto Rico—perhaps the more densely populated of the two principal islands—it harbored the Tainos' most impressive material and artistic expressions, which validated their political significance.

But the Tainos' main social achievements came in their effective and ingenious management of their environment. Tropical lands are not paradisiacal; the welfare of their inhabitants depends on their ability to utilize diverse resources efficiently. The Tainos had evolved from horticulture or food gardening to intensive and diversified agriculture with strategies including raised fields, mound planting (*conucos*), crop rotation, water canals, fish traps, and slash-and-burn techniques, and they went on to exploit varied ecological niches for different crops, like mangroves and reefs (Newsom and Wing 2004). In Puerto Rico the Spanish observed a Taino preference for cultivation on hillsides, contrary to practices in Hispaniola. The result was a rich and diverse production of staple foods, grains, and vegetables that, coupled with successful hunting and fishing, provided a balanced caloric intake, definitely superior to that of most Europeans.

The Tainos also had varied animal assets, both wild and domesticated. Marine species came to the island mangroves or estuaries and were caught in fish traps for consumption over time. Domesticated animals included guinea pigs, bush rats (*hutías*), dogs, and doves and other exotic birds. Edible wild resources included crabs, shellfish, iguanas, seals, manatees, land and sea turtles, and birds. The forests supplied rich woods for construction and fuel, resins, medicines, fruits, seeds, fibers, narcotics, dyes, and a long list of other resources. Of complementary importance, the islands were rich in all types of rocks: chert and quartz, granite, marble, jadeite, jasper, and a fair share of semiprecious stones. This permitted a long tradition of superb stonework, including unsurpassable religious icons, petroglyphs, and numerous stone artifacts.

The Tainos substantially modified their environment, making the land and sea work for them. In contrast, lack of prior experience in tropical environments greatly limited Spanish agricultural colonization of the islands. Many of Iberia's main native farming techniques and products were not reproduced for decades, and some foods—like wheat, olives, and grapes—would not be introduced successfully for centuries, thus allowing the survival of many Taino food products and even their planting techniques. Taino root crops, as well as cultigens such as maize, to-bacco, peanuts, native fruits and herbs, drugs, and beverages, are still common in the modern Caribbean. The Taino world has been an intrinsic part of Caribbean historic memory and modern national identities—if not biologically, then certainly culturally and spiritually. Today it represents the world before colonialism, a kind of idealized, mythical past suggesting that if life was better in the past, it can also be better in the future.

The Encounter

Beginning with the conquest of the Caribbean islands, European expansion to the New World was one of the first chapters of modern colonialism. The Tainos were fated to be among the first Amerinidans to be conquered and directly exploited by a distant and culturally distinct power. The political and economic forces responsible for this major thrust naturally transcended the microcosm of Columbus's life and Castilian politics. They encompassed a massive transformation of the Old World itself. In only 60 years after 1492, Europe shifted from a multiplicity of small war-ring kingdoms into a handful of strong monarchies building competitive nation-states and expanding frontiers. Commercial cities dominated the seas and estab-lished ties with hitherto unthinkable partners. The fragmentation of Christianity, the intense rivalry with the emerging Ottoman Empire, population growth, recur-rent agricultural crises, and the need for currency to compete commercially—all these factors were involved in the forces in Europe that took Columbus to the land of the Tainos in 1492.

It is no exaggeration to say that the fate of the New World was sealed by the few golden trinkets Columbus found on the necks and ears of the first Amerindians encountered in the Lucayan islands—not because of any unique Spanish obsession with gold, as Black Legend advocates traditionally argued, but because gold and silver were the Old World's commercial lubricants at a time when trade was reshap-ing economic and political geography. In the 15th century, precious minerals were as important as crude oil is today. The same interest groups that drove Columbus and others to explore far and wide were motivated by an accepted bimetallic mone-tary system (gold and silver) that permitted trade among the most diverse econo-mies. Europe lacked gold deposits, and depended for them on unreliable inter-mediaries. The kingdoms of the Spanish Peninsula, notably Castile, had a notably disorganized monetary system supported by too little gold.

Prior to Columbus's voyages, Castile had been bracing to conquer territories in North Africa to obtain the precious mineral then filtering from the interior of that continent into the hands of Italians, Arabs, and Portuguese merchants. The Catholic Monarchs had devoted much effort to monetary reforms and economic enterprises that could assure them a more competitive position. So, when Columbus returned and informed the monarchs of new lands—greatly exaggerating the first amounts of gold found—their response was immediate and positive. A mere nine months after the first voyage, Columbus returned to the islands in command of 17 ships carrying a variegated crew of nearly 1,500 passengers.

The promise of gold determined the fate of the new lands. Ethnic groups were classified according to the mineral importance of their lands and their disposition to collaborate with exploration ventures or hinder them. If lands were labeled as "useless"—that is, with no tangible assets to be obtained—their populations could be removed by force to places where labor was needed. Such were the cases of Jamaica, Aruba, Curaçao and Bonaire, the Bahamas, and large stretches of the Venezuelan coast during the early 16th century. The prior cultural identities of native communities perished under these coerced migrations. The most notorious case of such identity theft was that of the "Caribs," a label that came to be used to criminalize different groups throughout the Caribbean and on the American mainland in order to legally justify violent measures against them.

Beginning in the first years of the 16th century, Hispaniola, Puerto Rico, and Cuba became primary mining centers, their native populations coerced into exploration, porterage, clearing and constructing, extraction, and smelting and shipping of ore. The costs of conquest and exploitation were nearly unmanageable for a poor and distant Catholic kingdom with a weak agricultural tradition that was primarily oriented toward livestock. Although the earlier Spanish conquest of the Canary Islands had set a limited precedent, no kingdom in Spain possessed significant experience with tropical environments or large forced-labor enterprises. Consequently, agriculture and animal husbandry were initially neglected, and food and tools came primarily as cheap imports from Seville—salted sardines, wine, oil—sold at highly inflated prices in the Caribbean.

Some time later, interisland trade slowly began to provide substitutes for some imports. Cassava replaced wheat bread, lard supplanted oil, and local fishing and animal husbandry—mainly swine—supplanted salted meat products. Iberian diets reflected in the early import trade of the islands did not replicate the variegated foodways of the large, ethnically mixed Andalusian population. Instead, the traditionally sober diet of Christians in the countryside of central and northern Spain—which lacked grains like rice, contained very little meat, and rejected spicy products—was imposed on the insular populations, to their despair and considerable suffering.

Meanwhile, the high cost of metal implements led to the practice of forcing Amerindian workers to till, dig, and labor with their own stone tools, greatly increasing their hardship—a practice denounced by Las Casas and his followers. Finally, the *encomienda* system, which distributed natives as workers among the colonizers, removed them from their traditional food collecting and agricultural activities. When they returned from the mines to their villages nine or ten months later, they had no food available. Rest periods were times of widespread famine. At least during the conquest period, natives also seem to have rejected Spanish salted meat products, and there is no evidence that they raised or consumed animals brought by the Europeans.

After 1508, coinciding with the conquest of Puerto Rico—the second island after Hispaniola to be occupied—private merchants were allowed to trade with the colony, and the encomiendas (also known as *repartimientos*), a system of Indian labor allocation, in essence transferred the administration and care of the natives (including in the spiritual realm) to the private sector. These encomiendas effectively signaled the monarchy's admission of its inability to assume full responsibility for colonial enterprises. With the subsequent conquest of other islands, the task of organizing the economic exploitation of the new territories fell to an ill-equipped assortment of persons and groups, including soldiers of fortune, clergymen, artisans, merchants, part-time urban laborers, and overseers of leading administrators, locally and abroad. The monarchy reduced its required share of benefits to the famous *quinto real* (royal fifth, or 20% of gold minted) and withdrew from directly participating in mining.

Much attention has been given to the study of the encomienda system in the Antilles without rooting it in mining, the primary economic activity of the period. However, subtle differences in its implementation on the different islands were entirely irrelevant to the fate of the natives: all the mining islands experienced significant population decline. When the islands inhabited principally by Tainos were afflicted around 1518–20 by smallpox epidemics, apparently brought into the Caribbean by the first direct slave shipments from Africa, their populations had already dramatically diminished. The census of 1514 on Hispaniola gave ample proof of this, as did the intensity of the slave raids sent from the mining islands to seek replacements.

As the underfed and overworked natives perished, armadas were sent to loot and capture slaves in the region in a way much like the earlier practice of pillage and plunder throughout the Mediterranean. Between 1510 and 1542, tens of thousands of enslaved natives were violently extracted from the Guianas to the region of present-day Colombia, and also from Costa Rica to Florida. The legal excuse covering most of these expeditions was the capture of "Caribs" (a name etymologically equivalent to "cannibals"), who supposedly were a menace to "peaceful" natives and had proven reluctant to accept Christianity. Indians who had resisted relations with the Spaniards were also labeled "Caribs." Slaves were even brought from Mexico in exchange for cattle raised on the islands.

The amount of gold extracted from Hispaniola, Puerto Rico, and Cuba—in that order of importance—and legally exported to Spain between 1500 and 1550 has been estimated at 50 to 60 tons, and it probably represented one-fifth of all the gold shipped from the Spanish empire during the 16th century. But as the first colonial venture of their kind, the islands suffered from metropolitan inexperience, lack of capital, and absence of the infrastructure necessary for mining activities, which Mexico and Peru would both possess decades later. Lack of mining implements, experienced technicians, and roads, along with poor logistics, plagued the mining experience on the islands. Of equal importance was the lack of labor legislation and work regulations that only later were put into practice on the continent. The wealth extracted from the Taino islands by Taino hands, in a relatively short period under such brutal conditions, explains the truly genocidal population decline in the region, openly admitted by Charles V in 1526 when he blamed the repartimiento/encomienda system for its share in that human tragedy and tentatively barred its implementation in Mexico.

Gold mining remained the primary economic activity in the major Taino islands until past the mid-16th century, when it was overshadowed by gold and silver mining in Peru, Colombia, and Mexico. This economic phase lasted much longer than was once believed by historians, who assumed, for example, that with the conquest of Mexico the new territory immediately opened up its mineral wealth. Mexican ores were discovered and exploited only decades after the fall of Tenochtitlan, so that initial conquest did not displace the insular Caribbean as the main gold producer. Nor did the conquest in Central America, from Panama to Guatemala, yield profitable colonies until the second half of that century. Instead, during the initial phase, much of this geographic expanse became rewarding for Amerindian slavers who aimed to supply the labor needs of mining industries in the insular Caribbean. During the late 1530s, Colombia and Peru began to reorient this human traffic away from the islands, forcing gold miners and sugar planters to take recourse in African slavery.

Establishing the factual chronology of conquest and colonization permits a more realistic and holistic understanding of these events and their consequences. Taino societies were subjected to a massive alteration of their existence and culture for nearly half a century. They were victims of forms of violence ranging from forced labor to population displacements; of deliberate dismemberment of communal structures and warfare; and of the often overstated factors of disease, hunger, deprivation, and mistreatment. Their tragedy was not the result of unavoidable forces of nature at play. Dramatic human consequences can come about from natural causes, such as ecological changes triggering population displacements, epidemics, and the like. But the Taino tragedy was the result of an organized economic venture, planned and executed quite consciously by its continental planners, who deliberately took the human costs involved into consideration. The Taino people did not succumb on contact with the first colonizers; their physical and cultural constitution was not as frail as has often been claimed. They perished under the onslaught and callous demands of an internationally ramified economic system, which, while still evolving, was nevertheless proving its capacity to conquer and subdue people and extract significant material benefits. The Tainos were thus the first victims of the social experiment of modern capitalism, and the native Caribbean was where the dynamics between "core" and "peripheral" regions of what became the capitalistic world system were first effectively experienced.

This first capitalistic enterprise in the Antilles was not limited to mining operations, but also generated complementary activities and a well-knit economic network. Pearls were extracted from the fringe islands of the eastern Caribbean—Cubagua, Margarita, and Coche—to which hundreds of Tainos were forcefully removed. The traffic in slaves became an economic enterprise of its own, intermingling dozens of ethnic groups while depopulating vast coastal regions in Venezuela, the Lesser Antilles, the Bahamas, Guyana, Panama, and Nicaragua. Ponce de León's "discovery" of Florida was accomplished during a slaving expedition in which the governor of Cuba, Velázquez, also participated. The need for local food supplies forced large contingents of Tainos to spend their very short periods of rest away from the mines in agricultural tasks or animal husbandry, both of which were very profitable activities for the white elite. Salted fish was traded on the Venezuelan coast, along with slaves. Wooden plates (*bateas*) used to pan gold in the rivers were handmade by natives in Hispaniola and sold in Puerto Rico. Jamaican Tainos ended up on other islands. And of course, an extremely rewarding commerce that involved the coming and going of dozens of ships every year to the Antilles to supply the growing number of colonizers was maintained through Andalusian intermediaries. This was an activity that produced important customs taxes (*almojarifazgo*) for the crown and a large array of goods for the settlers.

Blacks and Gold

Tainos and other Amerindian slaves brought from different parts of the Caribbean region also participated in the first labor-intensive sugar plantations created in Hispaniola around 1520 and in Puerto Rico in the 1540s. The traditional view that mining labor was limited to Amerindians and sugar labor to black slaves is far from correct. Blacks began their ordeal in the Caribbean by working in the mines, and natives lasted long enough to be forced into plantation agriculture, another economic venue that proved as profitable in Europe's progressive accumulation of wealth as it was painful for its coerced labor forces in the New World. By the 1560s, more than 50 sugar mills in Hispaniola and Puerto Rico exported more sugar to Andalusia than did their much larger Mexican counterparts. Being closer to Seville,

Figure 6.2 Slaves mining for gold under the watch of Spanish soldiers. Engraving from *Americae pars quinta* (1595). Source: The John Carter Brown Library.

the islands had a competitive advantage which permitted them to satisfy the demand for sugar in the only legal market in Spain. Aside from this geographical advantage, their greater importance as sugar exporters can be explained only by the intensity of the productive operations that rested on the backs of Africans and Indians.

Although Tainos helped the Spaniards locate the gold-producing regions and became the primary workforce in them, the general logistics associated with placer mining were strained by the Spaniards' inability to communicate effectively with the natives. This factor, more than any other, probably prompted the early introduction of black slaves from the Iberian Peninsula. Being fully assimilated into Christian culture, and fluent in the colonizer's language—many of them having been born in Castile or Portugal—these *ladino* slaves became an important asset in the new colonial scenario. Together with the ladinos also came free blacks (*libertos*), who were not socially different from other poor Spanish Christians migrating to the new frontier in search of a better life. The libertos fared quite well, but for the black slaves life on the islands was a nightmare. Toiling in a harsh tropical environment far from home proved tragic for them.

As early as 1503, ladino slaves were reported to have run away in Hispaniola and were described as exerting a negative influence on the native inhabitants. And in 1514, the first of several ladino uprisings occurred quite unexpectedly in Puerto Rico, where gold production was reaching very high levels. Probably a strong hurricane that year was a precipitating factor. In any case, the event clearly represented the first black slave uprising in the New World. In 1521 another one occurred in Hispaniola, and thus began a tradition of resistance throughout the slaveholding Americas.

Slave labor of the scale and intensity organized in the first Caribbean colonies had no counterpart or antecedents in Europe. Mining and sugar making were both labor-intensive, a fact that imposed a distinctly new style of slavery throughout the Americas—more ruthless, more demanding, and insensitive. The Antilles had not been its first laboratory. The practice of using African slaves to produce sugar in large quantities had originated on Atlantic islands such as Madeira or São Tomé, but the Caribbean islands were where this economic combination acquired much of its historic force and social characteristics.

Modern plantation systems began to take shape in the Spanish Antilles during the 16th century based on enslaved Indians and Africans, who often were intermingled in an ethnic cauldron of hitherto unknown proportions. By 1560, for example, Hispaniola and Puerto Rico had a combined African slave population of some 45,000, not including clandestine groups of Amerindians of various origins. Such numbers of enslaved workers, applied primarily to operations like mining or sugar, were not to be found elsewhere in the hemisphere during that century.

Indians and black slaves—who began to arrive directly from Africa in 1518, according to very exact Spanish documentation—formed a variety of relationships with each other. Some ladinos and enslaved Africans sided with the Tainos and other ethnic groups against the Spaniards; some allied themselves with conquistadors against the Indians. Their life expectancy was terribly short. Few enslaved Africans were able to form families or survive long enough to transform their wretched existence into lasting forms of collective life. Given the high death toll in the mining camps and sugar fields, African slaves were constantly replenished in a vicious transcontinental economic cycle. Nonetheless, personal names of noted maroons (escapees) were always heard throughout the islands, and strong clues about the survival of many black runaways among the "Caribs" (surviving and regrouping Amerindians) of the Lesser Antilles are being uncovered. Only small groups of Creole or mulatto slaves were able to survive, but while they eventually came to constitute an important segment of Caribbean colonial societies during the late 16th century, that process was painfully slow. The overall creolization of Caribbean societies had to wait until almost a century after the conquest, when the dynamic export economies of the larger islands had collapsed and the large cattle ranches (*hatos*) that sprang up throughout the Spanish Greater Antilles significantly attenuated slavery's importance and established a less harsh and demanding life for the enslaved.

Resistance to Conquest

The myth of the easy conquest of the Caribbean islands, the submissive character of their inhabitants, their hospitable nature, and their dire need for protection against invading barbarians bent on devouring their victims has persisted to this day. This colonial version of the events and relations between the European invaders and the Tainos has become entangled with latter-day historical and anthropological accounts to a degree where it has gained widespread acceptance, both abroad and in the Caribbean itself. Yet the original facts of the European-Amerindian encounter have long been distorted and deformed for ideological reasons. This is so because that same period witnessed the forging of the colonial justifications for the conquest of America itself, and the emergence of political discourses used to legitimize European rule in the New World.

The Greater Antilles were the first battleground in the European conquest of the Americas. Many lives were lost in military encounters that lasted for decades. Resistance began with the burning of Columbus's first settlement in Hispaniola, La Navidad, and the killing of all 39 of its residents by warriors of the chief Caonabo in 1492. Most provinces in every island have their tales of local heroic caciques and brave or desperate deeds in defense of their homelands. After Caonabo, the epic figures in Hispaniola are Guarionex, Cotubanama, Guarocuya, Mayobanex, and Enriquillo. In Puerto Rico, where official commemorations have traditionally downplayed Amerindian symbols, popular recognition of local caciques represents an almost intuitive respect for the precolonial past, thus challenging official discourses. For more than 200 years, poets and political dissidents have kept alive a strong sense of admiration for the warring caciques Agüeybana el Bravo, Urayoán, Guarionex, Comerío, Humacao, and others. And long-overlooked, newly discovered documents from the Archivo de Indias in Seville attest to the intense resistance in Borinquén and a high toll of lives on both sides, with evidence of the burning of the first Spanish towns of La Aguada (1511), Caparra (1513), and Santiago (1513), followed by relentless guerilla warfare which, as on the other islands, lasted until the 1530s. In Cuba, meanwhile, Hatuey and Guama have long been recognized as national figures.

Chronicles and administrative documents, furthermore, confirm the conquest's policy of violence, followed from the outset, against the reluctant caciques. Be-

ginning with Columbus's reaction to Caonabo's rebellion in Hispaniola and the subsequent enslavement and shipment to Spain of several thousand Tainos, some native victims of Spanish reprisals were even condemned to row in the infamous galleys of the Mediterranean.

Figure 6.3 Spanish conquistadors burning a resistant native at the stake. Engraving based on an account by Friar Bartolomé de las Casas (1620). Source: The John Carter Brown Library.

Events such as these reveal the falseness of the image of the Tainos' supposedly docile character and their incapacity to defend their lands—a trait applied to Puerto Ricans in colonial discourse to this very day. But the violent nature of the "encounter" also reveals and dramatizes the intolerance and bigotry of the conquistadores toward culturally different groups, their historical record of hostility to cultural dissidence, and their turbulent religious experience with non-Christians. It dramatizes the limitation of material resources at the onset of their historic entrance to the New World and their inclination to treachery and deceit.

Las Casas denounced the early practice in Hispaniola of killing local chiefs to provoke uprisings that justified punitive and enslaving measures. In 1500, Governor Nicolás de Ovando planned and executed the death of more than 80 caciques

Figure 6.4 Natives committing suicide to escape Spanish brutality. Engraving from Theodoro de Bry, *Americae pars quarta* (1594). Source: The John Carter Brown Library.

in the kingdom of Jaragua (Haiti) who had been assembled by the high chieftainess Anacaona to welcome him, in a deceitful move to reduce Anacaona as a potential threat to the conquest of the island. The event has gone down in history as the Massacre of Jaragua. Anacaona herself was publicly hanged some weeks later. Reports of subsequent strategic slaughter to instantly subdue rebellious natives on other islands are associated with the locations where the events took place: Higüey in Hispaniola, Caonao in Cuba, Daguao and Vieques in Puerto Rico. In 1513, 17 caciques from Puerto Rico were abducted and shipped to Hispaniola without confirmation of their ever having reached the destination. Reports indicate that the practice of killing local chiefs was also carried out in Jamaica.

But resistance to conquest followed many paths and involved different events. Every island reported suicides, escapes, and violent behavior. Many women chose to kill their offspring or resort to abortion rather than see their children live as slaves. In Cuba, the chief Anaya hanged himself and his teenage daughter when he was unable to rescue her from a privileged settler. Collective suicide is also reported to have taken place in Cuba. In Puerto Rico, many Tainos escaped to the neighboring "Carib islands," shattering the myth of their traditional enmity with the inhabitants of those islands. In Cuba and Hispaniola *ranchos de indios alzados*, or maroon camps, were reported as early as the 1520s. The first *cimarrones*, a term generally associated with runaway blacks, were actually Taino escapees. But resistance also took nonviolent forms. Refusal to accept the Christian faith was constantly cited by clergymen. And in secret, the outlawed ancestral religions were kept alive.

WORKS CITED

Newsom, Lee A., and Elizabeth S. Wing. 2004. *On Land and Sea: Native American Uses of Biological Resources in the West Indies.* Tuscaloosa, AL: University of Alabama Press.

Sued-Badillo, Jalil. 1985. "Las cacicas indoantillanas." *Revista del Instituto de Cultura Puertorriquena* 87, enero a mayo.

Sued-Badillo, Jalil. 2007. "¿Guadalupe: Caribe o taína? La isla de Guadalupe y su cuestionable identidad Caribe en la época precolonial. Una revisión etnohistórica y arqueológica." *Caribbean Studies* 35, no. 1.

7

Negotiations of Conquest   LYNNE A. GUITAR

When Christopher Columbus and a mixed crew of mostly Spaniards entered the Caribbean Sea in October 1492, landing first on
the island they named San Salvador, then Cuba, followed by Hispaniola, they encountered peoples and cultures unlike any they
had known. Initially, they negotiated with and through the native
rulers, as they would have done with any monarch. But as the
number of "Indians" (an obvious misnomer; Columbus believed
he had reached Asia) declined drastically and the number of Spaniards and mestizos in the Caribbean increased, these delicately
negotiated relationships began to break down. Yet, on Hispaniola
from the initial "encounter era" through the 1520s, the occupiers'
violence toward the native population was accompanied by subtle
and complex Spanish-Indian negotiations. These negotiations of
conquest, articulated with constant violence, forged important
patterns and set key precedents for the balance of Spain's Caribbean conquests, as well as for the occupation and settlement of
continental areas.

European Arrival on Hispaniola

"In appearance it is all very intensely cultivated," Columbus wrote about the island of Hispaniola on December 9, 1492, calling its fields "the most beautiful in the world" (Columbus 1991, 213–15). The Tainos of the Greater Antilles dominated not only Hispaniola, but also Puerto Rico, the Virgin Islands, southeastern Cuba, the Turks and Caicos, the Bahamas, and Jamaica. There were several different indigenous peoples in the Greater Antilles, but the Tainos were dominant, hence the conquistadores called all the islands' peoples by that name. The Tainos had a highly developed socioeconomic system and advanced agricultural techniques that provided a reliable food base for hundreds of permanent villages, some which were larger than many European cities of that era. These were organized into an overlapping series of *cacicazgos* (chiefdoms) under the authority of at least three ascending levels of *caciques* (chiefs). They had ritual and medical specialists, a rich heritage of oral history and mythology, and an intricate sense of art expressed in weavings, ceramics, and exquisite carvings in wood, stone, shell, and bone. Religious beliefs and traditions were interwoven into every aspect of their lives.

Columbus initially gave the Tainos the highest praise imaginable, comparing them favorably to Europeans. He wrote effusively about the richness of "king" Guacanagaríx, the prestige accorded to him, and the many people he commanded. Columbus treated Guacanagaríx with the same deference he would have paid any foreign monarch, entertaining him aboard his flagship, giving him expensive clothes and other high-status gifts—and receiving gold-decorated objects in exchange.

Had the relationship between Europeans and Tainos remained strictly one of trade, the results of the encounter might have been more favorable for the Indians, who soon realized that the newcomers did not share their ideology about the mutual respect and extensive obligations inherent in gift exchanges. They also soon understood the relative values of the objects Spaniards offered in exchange for food and gold, for they were accomplished traders, with a complex web of intra- and inter-island networks.

Columbus returned to Hispaniola in 1493 with 17 ships carrying some 1,500 conquistadores who were not as impressed as Columbus, particularly once they discovered that the Indians had massacred the 39 men left behind to collect gold. The faction supporting Columbus immediately clashed with the bulk of the Spaniards, who were supposedly under his command but resented him because he was a foreigner, not born to the nobility, and a poor administrator. Whereas Columbus planned to establish a trading fort on the northern shore of the island, the Spaniards' principal goals—developed through eight long centuries of reconquest against the Moors in Iberia—were conversion of "the heathens" to Christianity and personal enrichment through conquest, settlement, and permanent domination of the entire region.

Military squadrons under Columbus's command built Fort Santo Tomás, the first of a chain of forts to protect the route between the gold-bearing mountains and the first Spanish town, La Isabela. Soldiers foraged throughout the interior, seeking food, gold, and women. Taino complaints about the

Figure 7.1 Columbus and "king" Guacanagaríx. Painting entitled *Primer uso de la moneda*, by Juan Medina (contemporary).

indiscriminate taking of women escalated. Captain Alonso de Ojeda cut off the ears of a Taino nobleman allegedly caught stealing—a concept that must have

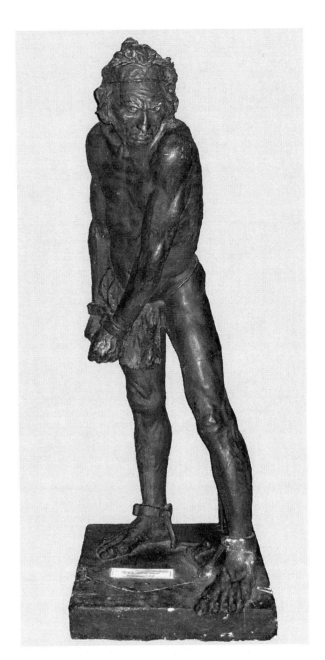

Figure 7.2 *Caonabó in Chains* by Abelardo Rodríguez Udaneta, in the Museum of Dominican Man, Santo Domingo. Photo by Lynne A. Guitar.

been nearly incomprehensible to the Tainos, given that, as several Spanish chroniclers reported, they held all property in common (although the nobles among them had apparently begun to accumulate personal possessions along with increased power and authority, as indicated by increasingly ornate burial rituals). Still, their caciques had not given Spaniards authority to punish anyone. Then Ojeda captured Caonabó, the second most powerful cacique on the island, and accused him of ordering the massacre of the men Columbus had left behind in

1492. That was the final straw for the "pacific" Tainos, who rose up in unison to fight the Spaniards.

The First Spanish-Indian War

In March 1495, Columbus and his brother Bartolomé led an all-out war to "pacify" the Tainos with the help of their ally Guacanagaríx and his approximately 3,000 warriors. Guacanagaríx appears to have been a minor cacique intent on gaining prestige and power by allying with the newcomers. His actions set the precedent for later tactics on the part of conquistadores, including Hernán Cortés, whose cultivation of similar alliances on the mainland helped them to achieve their astonishing successes. This war lasted 10 long months, but its legendary version, written by Spaniards, barely mentions the contribution of indigenous allies and makes victory sound like the work of a day, attributed to the miraculous intervention of the Our Lady of Mercy at the Battle of Santo Cerro. This Spanish tendency to take all the credit for victories, leaving their indigenous allies out of the conquest histories, would also continue on the mainland.

Indigenous peoples had a concept of war very different from that of the Spaniards. The Tainos had been dominant for so long in the Greater Antilles that most arguments were settled by *batey*, a ballgame: combatants chose teams and played, and the winning team won the argument. When warfare was necessary, the idea was to prove to the enemy that you were stronger.

Tainos showed up in force at the Battle of Santo Cerro: all the major caciques and thousands of warriors came armed with spears, dart throwers, and war clubs, yelling blood-curdling screams to show their ferocity. Despite Taino losses to Spanish cannon shots, harquebuses, and steel swords wielded by mounted knights, by the end of the first day of battle Guacanagaríx's warriors had run away and the Spaniards had retreated to their wooden palisade. The Tainos believed they had shown them the futility of trying to wage war against their united forces, so they went home. Fighting to the death was not the indigenous way. No terms of capitulation were required; who had won and who had lost was plain to see, so both sides were expected to return to their families, and to their daily lives.

The Spaniards, however, believed *they* had won, for the following morning there were no enemies to be seen. Ten months later, after negotiating a settlement with Guarionex, the principal cacique of the region, the Spaniards really did win. In the aftermath, Columbus levied a quarterly tribute of one gold-filled hawk's bell on each Taino over age 14, to be collected by the caciques. Later, he agreed to accept food and cotton textiles in tribute, for the Tainos were unable to supply so much gold. Columbus punished the "rebel" Indians by selling some into slavery in Spain and forcing others to work under the direction of his captains.

Mistreatment and Denigration of the Indians

Columbus left his brother Bartolomé in charge of the island in March 1496, with Francisco Roldán as chief justice. Roldán and his men rebelled and went to Jaraguá, the richest and most densely populated of the cacicazgos on Hispaniola, where they married noble *indias* in order to gain the natives' labor services. They had discovered that even the lowliest-born Spaniard could "marry" a native woman of high social standing and henceforth live the life of an indigenous nobleman. Columbus was compelled to approve these illegal alliances when he returned to the island in August 1498, for the process resembled the way Spanish conquistadores in Iberia were elevated in status by conquering and settling as lords of formerly Moorish regions. (Among the soldiers who began the American process of *mestizaje* by fathering children with indigenous women on Hispaniola were *ladinos*—Africans who had been born in Iberia or had adopted Christian customs and the Castilian language, had been baptized Catholic, and had taken Spanish names.)

Queen Isabella of Spain officially authorized forced Taino labor on December 20, 1503, supposedly for the laborers' own good. Her decree led to the *encomienda* system, wherein indigenous peoples were "commended" to the care of a Spaniard, their *encomendero*, who was obliged by royal contract to feed and clothe his Indians (though he did not buy and could not sell them). The encomendero also had to ensure that they were taught the Christian faith and "civilized" ways. In return, theoretically, the commended Indians would gratefully perform whatever labor their encomendero demanded of them. The queen's original *cédula*, directed to Governor Nicolás de Ovando, read:

> Because the King and I gave you instructions that the Indians of La Española were free, and they, abusing their liberty, go about as vagabonds without wanting to be indoctrinated [in the Catholic faith] nor to work on the land nor in the mines, which has harmed the Spanish residents: so that . . . they may be more easily converted, and furthermore help to cultivate and to obtain metals, we order you our governor to compel them and oblige the said Indians to converse with the Spaniards, to work on their buildings, on their agricultural lands, and in the mines, paying them a just salary assessed by you (Marté 1981, 52–53).

Numerous complaints arose in the following years about the encomienda system and its handling by the island's various governors—Columbus, Francisco de Bobadilla, Ovando, and Diego Colón (Columbus's elder son and legal heir). Spaniards charged these leaders with granting Taino laborers at will to those who supported them, and with revoking them just as arbitrarily. The uncertainty of not knowing how long they would be able to reap the rewards of the Taino labor tribute contributed to the encomenderos' mistreatment of the Indians under their care. They attempted to get the most labor out of the natives as quickly as possible at the least cost. The idea was to get rich quickly and then return to Spain, where they could live as proper Spanish noblemen—much preferable to living as noblemen among the Tainos.

Perhaps as justification for their exploitation, Spaniards began to refer to the Tainos in their letters and reports as "primitives" and "barbarians," because their beliefs, values, and customs were so different from those of the Europeans. Instead of finding the natives ripe for conversion because they were "without religion," as Columbus had initially described them, Spaniards claimed that the Tainos practiced demon worship. They also began to use the Tainos' lack of interest in profit, surplus, and savings as proof of Indian irrationality and, thus, lack of humanity. Glowing descriptions of the Taino lands as "intensively cultivated" changed to disparaging descriptions of them as disorganized because the multiple cultigens were not planted in neat rows and segregated fields, but were instead intercropped in ecologically highly efficient garden plots (*conucos*), a method found among Caribbean peasantries to this day. And although the Taino diet was not only well balanced but also responsible for keeping the Spaniards alive (imported supplies rotted, and Spanish staples did not grow well in the tropical climate), Spaniards began describing the Tainos as weak and sickly because their food base was "cassava bread and water," not good red meat and wine. This "weakness" was often invoked as the cause of their rapid population decline.

Opponents of the encomienda system, led by the Dominican Order of Friars on Hispaniola, believed that exploitation and mistreatment by encomenderos was the primary cause of the precipitous decline of the Tainos. The encomienda system was worse than slavery, declared Bartolomé de Las Casas and other Dominican friars. Slaves had some protection from mistreatment through the Siete Partidas, Spanish laws regulating relations between master and slave that were compiled in the 13th century by King Alfonso the Wise. "I am the voice crying out in the wilderness . . . Are these not human beings?" Fray Antonio de Montesino, a Dominican friar, pleaded in defense of the Indians in his famous advent sermon of 1511, demanding that the encomienda system be abolished.

At that time, however, the Spanish crown was not in a position to repeal the system, despite eloquent pleas for a replacement that would bring the Indians peaceably to Christianity. Not only were too many politically powerful Spaniards deeply invested in the encomienda system, but too much of the royal income was directly dependent on gold extracted by Tainos on Hispaniola who were held in King Ferdinand's name and managed by overseers. Yet the Spanish crown dominated the new lands and the new people by decree of the pope, whose 1493 bull had granted said dominion so that the peoples of the new lands could be taught the holy Catholic

Figure 7.3 Statue of Fray Antonio de Montesino at entrance to Río Ozama, Santo Domingo. Photo by Lynne A. Guitar.

doctrine and converted to the true faith. Caught between two cross-purposes, the crown attempted to refine and regulate the encomienda system via the Laws of Burgos (1512), to protect commended Indians with their own specified rights. In this way the crown hoped to eliminate any basis for papal complaint.

The Laws of Burgos

Grants of encomienda on Hispaniola were not permanent. The average length of time that individual Spaniards held Indians was three years. The encomenderos did not own the Indians who were commended to their care, so they could not legally sell or rent them out. The Spanish crown could and did remove Indians from the control of encomenderos who abused them or otherwise defied the growing multitude of regulations—and from the control of those who were not politically powerful or persuasive enough to avoid the consequences. The Indians were then commended to other Spaniards, who were likely to be grateful for the favor. The crown reaped additional profits because the new encomendero paid an annual fee of one gold peso per head for his Indians.

The threat of removal curbed some but not all of the system's abuses, especially as the encomiendas were gradually concentrated into ever fewer but more politically powerful hands. In a *cédula* dated February 22, 1512, the crown attempted to limit the number of Indians that any encomendero could have to 300, but the number of times this order had to be reissued over the next few years is evidence that it was not followed. In an attempt to appease the Dominican friars (including Las Casas) and their supporters, a series of laws and instructions was promulgated to effect improvements, leading up to the Laws of Burgos, which were implemented on December 27, 1512, and amended on July 28, 1513.

These laws and instructions clearly identified the natives of Hispaniola as "vassals of the crown." Among the first of the 24 articles in the Laws of Burgos was the requirement that the encomenderos teach the Indians the basic tenets of the Catholic faith and how to live a Christian lifestyle. This meant, among other things, ensuring that the Indians each had only one wife and that they were paid wages, albeit the standard wage was only one to one and-a-half gold pesos annually (a single large nail cost one peso at the time, a linen shirt one and-a-half). Furthermore, the Laws provided that commended Indians, even those who worked for Spaniards in the gold mines, could legally be forced to work for only a portion of the year, which varied over time from five to nine months. Initially the commended Indians lived the balance of the year in their own towns, so that they could care for their crops and celebrate their traditional ceremonies. The laws specified that Indians were to be provided with minimum allowances of red meat and not to be used as beasts of burden, beaten, whipped, or addressed as "dog . . . nor by any name other than their own." Special provisions provided protection for women, especially pregnant women, for orphans, and for all children under age 14. The existence of these provisions obviously suggests that the Tainos *were* being subjected to just such indignities. And like Isabella's 1503 writ, in their final form the Laws of Burgos acknowledged that the Indians "must be subject to coercion" in matters of both work and religion for their own good.

Taino Negotiations within the Encomienda System

Why did most Tainos submit to the encomienda system? The fierce wars between the Tainos and Spaniards that began in 1495, most particularly the campaigns in 1503–5 against Jaraguá and Higüey during Ovando's first years as governor, demonstrate how the Spaniards could dominate by violence and force. But the Spaniards did not have to impose the encomienda system upon the Tainos by violent means. As the chronicler Pedro Mártir de Anglería noted: "Although [the Tainos] submit to this restraint with impatience, they do put up with it" (Martyr 1970, 182).

The explanation is complicated but revealing, for the encomienda system on His-paniola appears to have been negotiated through the island's caciques. This does not necessarily imply collaboration or collusion, but it does imply adaptation and flexibility on the part of the caciques—and the Spaniards. During the initial decade and-a-half of the conquest period, Spaniards generally recognized the authority, prestige, and privileges of the caciques and other *nitaínos* (noblemen) and acknowl-edged that nitaínos were lords over a lower class called *naborías* (workers).

Evidently, at least some Spaniards were voluntarily accepted by marriage into the nitaínos' families, a traditional way in which Tainos incorporated outsiders and strengthened their socioeconomic ties to them. Sometimes a *guaitiao* (kin through Taino ritual name exchange) was integrated into the family in the same way. Thus, the paramount cacique Guarionex "had been pleased" to give one of his sisters to the Taino who was baptized Diego de Colón (the same name as Columbus's younger brother and elder son). "Guarionex had hoped by these means to establish a more intimate friendship with the Admiral" (Martyr 1970, 106), for Diego de Colón was Columbus's personal servant and interpreter.

On the surface, at least, both Spaniards and Tainos conceived of name changes and name exchanges as a way of establishing fictive kinship—the Spaniards through baptism and godparentage, the Tainos through guaitiao. Unfortunately, these fictive kinship relationships did not succeed in maintaining amity among all the partici-pants, for neither the Spaniards nor the Tainos fully understood the other's tradi-tions. Violations were inevitable among peoples with such disparate customs and beliefs: Guarionex revolted against Spanish rule (no doubt his Spanish "kin" vio-lated traditional rules of reciprocity), and Columbus hunted him down during the 1495 war of pacification in the Cibao.

Despite intercultural misunderstandings, noble Tainos like Guacanagaríx and Guarionex appear to have negotiated alliances with Spaniards in an attempt to gain social prestige and economic-political advantages for themselves and their people, and to better observe and evaluate the strangers and their ways. As more and more Spaniards arrived—and stayed—the Tainos had to reevaluate, adjust, and adapt their traditions, and reconsider their previous negotiations.

The Spaniards also evaluated, adjusted, adapted, and renegotiated. Early in the colonization of the Caribbean, the Spanish crown and its representatives recognized the power and authority of the regions' caciques, negotiating through the traditional leaders in the same way that the crown attempted to negotiate and deal diplomati-cally with any foreign state. The crown knew that the Tainos had a well-established tribute system—which included labor tribute—and it tapped into this tradition through the encomienda system. The royal cédulas granting encomiendas did so through the caciques, and it was generally understood that laborers who served the Spaniards "voluntarily" through their caciques were to be treated better than the slaves who were drawn in increasingly large numbers from populations defined as "rebellious subjects" and were soon traded from one Spanish territory to the other. The crown consistently ordered that caciques be the best treated of all Indians, although there is some indication that it feared their power and attempted to regulate and control it, just as it attempted to curb the power of Spanish noblemen.

The Taino caciques and cacicas of Hispaniola who appear to have been acting as agents of Christian values and as middlemen for their Spanish encomenderos by providing mine workers, agriculturalists, fishermen, construction workers, and domestic servants from among their naborías no doubt did so because it seemed to be a natural extension of their traditional privileges and prestige. As heirs to the position of cacique became ladinoized (that is, as they became proficient in Castilian, were baptized and catechized, and adopted other European ways), they likely acted as more traditional middlemen, perhaps truly believing it to be in the best interests of their remaining people to cooperate with the Spaniards.

Taino Resistance

Sometimes, however, caciques did resist the orders of their encomenderos, as exemplified by the cacica Isabel de Azua and her 25 to 75 workers. Around 1512, Isabel apparently fell in love with a Mallorcan named Pere Martín and chose to work with him rather than obey her encomendero, Juan de Serralonga. As late as 1544, Serralonga's heirs were still fighting the courts to recover Serralonga's heritable goods, claims that included monetary recompense for the commended Indians that Serralonga had lost.

Relationships between Spaniards and native women appear to have repeatedly created resistance to the orders of encomenderos, complicated by the fact that the Spanish crown understood that it could position its own people among the nitaínos through intermarriage. This was, after all, a traditional method in both European and Taino politics; hence the crown did not punish—and instead encouraged—those Spaniards who went to Indian villages to marry *indias*, particularly cacicas.

The Taino must have become torn between the loyalty and tribute they owed to their encomendero and the loyalty and tribute they owed to their cacique and his or her family members. No doubt, as the case of Isabel de Azua shows, the labor demands of a Spaniard who had married into a nitaíno family took priority over the demands of a crown-appointed encomendero. As the encomienda system became more formalized, however, and as more Spanish women arrived in the New World, the crown became less interested in intermarriage and began insisting that Spaniards married to Tainas move to Spanish towns. The requirement written into the preamble of the Laws of Burgos that Tainos were to be relocated into new *pueblos* (villages), where they could emulate their Spanish encomenderos so as not to backslide into their habits of "idleness and vice," was another problematic element of the increasingly formalized encomienda system.

Royal instructions given to Nicolás de Ovando on March 20, 1503, illustrate how the crown sought to modify the Tainos' lifestyle and integrate the Indians into Christian society. Ovando was instructed to see that each Taino male lived in a house with only one wife and their children, surrounded by their own things—in other words, polygamy was to be excised, as were extended families and community property. Tainos were to be properly dressed, to not go about "naked," and to be discouraged from "painting themselves." Of course, their "superstitious rites" were to be suppressed. Ovando was ordered to see that a church was built in each Taino town and a chaplain maintained there to celebrate the Mass and teach Catholic doctrine (the inhabitants of the native pueblo were to pay a tithe of 10% to cover the expenses of their religious conversion). And Ovando was ordered to "reduce" together into new pueblos—called *reducciones*—the survivors of several pueblos where many Indians had died or run away. Officially, the motive for moving the Tainos to reducciones was one of Christian charity and goodwill. Most scholars concur, however, that the true motive was to concentrate workers closer to the gold mines in order to increase profits for the royal coffers and crown patrons.

The caciques fiercely resisted moving to new towns. Their power and authority were connected to geographic locales. Their myths and ceremonies suggest that the land of their birth had sacred connotations, that it bound them to their *cemíes* (the Tainos' spirit guides and protectors) and vice versa. Leaving their cacicazgos to move to other locales presented multiple difficulties. This is evident in the way that Ovando was unable to begin complying with the crown's orders until he had first "pacified" the Tainos of Jaraguá and Higüey by having his armies assassinate the native caciques along with most of their family members and counselors. Between 1503 and 1505, Ovando's men thus "reduced" many of the remaining Tainos into seven rural towns.

The plazas and central roads, the houses and churches, and even the fields of the new towns were built using Indian labor, supervised by Spaniards. As Las Casas describes it: "The Spaniards began to behave as though they were the natural rulers, and as though the Indians were their subjects and vassals; or, rather, their chattel slaves" (Parry and Keith 1984, 2: 271).

Indigenous Slavery

There were not many slaves of any kind on Hispaniola in the first decades of its colonization, because of the readily available supply of indigenous laborers. Beginning in 1504, the crown decreed that those Tainos who resisted being thrust into encomiendas or reducciones could justifiably be enslaved (Marté 1981, 53). On

April 30, 1508, a royal cédula was issued permitting the enslavement of any Indian who fled from Spanish dominion, not just those who resisted by fighting; a law that would spread across the Caribbean and mainland colonies.

The chronicler Mártir de Anglería provides extensive detail on the depopulation of the Lucayas (today's Bahamas), which the Spaniards called "useless" islands because they had no gold. The Lucayans were shipped to Hispaniola to supplement the dwindling native population. They were not commended to Spaniards, but neither were they slaves. They were brought to Hispaniola as naborías, unattached to any particular cacique, and therefore were neither protected from exploitation, as commended Indians were by the Laws of Burgos, nor protected by the laws for slaves. The arrival of the Lucayans, distant kin of the Tainos, probably did not unduly destabilize the fragile balance that apparently was maintained between Hispaniola's caciques and Spanish encomenderos. Not so the arrival of the Tainos' enemies, the Caribs (as the Spaniards called natives of the southern Caribbean who resisted their encroachment).

Spaniards brought hundreds of enslaved Caribs to Hispaniola, and also enslaved them to work in the Lesser Antilles. Their capture and enslavement was considered "just" because of the abominable nature of their alleged protein base: other humans. Their cannibalism seemed to be confirmed when in Carib villages explorers like Columbus and Amerigo Vespucci discovered skulls and other human remains, which more likely were the sacred remains of ancestors. (For centuries there have been intense debates about the Carib diet, and the term "cannibal" has "Carib" as its etymological base, but current scholarly consensus is that Caribs did not practice cannibalism.) At first, licenses to hunt down and sell "Caribs/cannibals" were restricted to a few rich merchants, but in late 1511 the field was opened wide. Royal provisions conceded rights to residents of both Hispaniola and Puerto Rico to go to other islands and the mainland to make war against Indians so classified, capture them, and take them as slaves, as long as they were not sold outside the Indies.

The horrors of imputed cannibalism gave Spaniards a legal excuse for capturing other Indians, too, under the cover of *rescate*, which generally meant "rescue" or "ransom" and referred to those Indians whom Caribs had supposedly captured and taken to their villages as slaves, as wives, or for what were alleged to be "fattening pens." Many licenses of rescate were issued, for the concept appealed to the Christian missionary ideology of conquest and settlement: far better to be forced into servitude under a Christian master than to serve, or be consumed by, cannibalistic heathens.

In 1512, Queen Juana publicly approved of the "war" against the Caribs in light of all the harm they had done to the new colonies on the island of San Juan Bautista (Puerto Rico). Besides, it was generally agreed that Caribs were stronger, and thus better workers, than Tainos—even though, to the Spaniards, one Indian looked like another. A royal provision dated July 25, 1511, thus ordered that Indians brought from elsewhere to Hispaniola were to be branded on the legs "in the manner prescribed by the Admiral [Diego Colón] and the other officials, so that they can be known" and distinguished from the indigenous Tainos.

The demand for indigenous slaves on Hispaniola was a response to the dwindling Taino population. The crown was particularly worried about having enough workers for the gold mines, but it also was increasingly worried about justifying indigenous enslavement. In an attempt to placate Las Casas and the other Dominican friars' pleas for justice on the Indians' behalf, a legal document and procedure called the Requirement was created upon royal request by a committee of scholars, theologians, and jurists led by Dr. Juan López de Palacios Rubios. From 1513 on, each Spanish expedition had to read the Requirement aloud to every newly encountered group of natives. The document was long and complex—and, of course, totally incomprehensible to the natives, who did not understand Castilian, let alone the underlying political and religious legalities which required them "to submit immediately and voluntarily to the authority of Their Catholic Majesties or be subjected to enslavement," which would be their own fault for not complying with the Requirement.

Breakdown of Negotiations between Indigenous Leaders and Spaniards

The numerical decline of Hispaniola's indigenous peoples—from disease, malnutrition, and exploitation, as well as through exportation to Spain and other Spanish colonies—coupled with the arrival of massive numbers of Indians who were not Tainos must have been very unsettling to the native caciques. The new indigenous peoples, principally slaves owned by Spaniards, had no tradition of subservience to Hispaniola's nitaínos, nor did they work through the caciques as commended Tainos did. More important to the Caribbean's subsequent history is that the influx of Indian slaves affected the way in which Spaniards began to perceive *all* Indians.

The delicately negotiated balance represented by the encomienda system as it first developed on Hispaniola was breaking down by the second decade of the 16th century. This system, whereby the Taino caciques, as the traditional leaders of their people, organized and sent out work parties for their Spanish encomenderos in exchange for special rights and privileges, ceased to function. The new generation of Spaniards who came to the island, and the "old settlers" who had lived through the initial wars of conquest and pacification, began to take Indian compliance to forced servitude for granted.

As early as Diego Colón's arrival as governor and viceroy in 1509, the Spaniards were becoming less willing to negotiate with and defer to the Taino caciques. And the Tainos' sociopolitical infrastructure had been all but destroyed within the first two decades of their encounter with Spaniards. The Spanish chroniclers, however, mistook the Tainos' political disintegration for a complete social, cultural, economic, and political capitulation. That perception proved to be mistaken, as evidenced by a 15-year rebellion that was begun in 1519 by the cacique Enriquillo, and whose termination would necessitate the very first peace treaty negotiated between an Amerindian chief and a European monarch.

Meanwhile, Spaniards in the Caribbean turned their diplomatic efforts inward, becoming ever more deeply embroiled in internal politics as they scrabbled over the remaining "peaceful" Indians in the Greater Antilles, attempted less successfully to exploit Caribs as laborers in the Lesser Antilles, and in general continued trying to gain as much land and personal wealth as possible—just as the original Spanish conquistadors had done in 1493. In the process, they came to value the indigenous peoples of the Caribbean and their cultures less and less, and to denigrate them more and more. It was, unfortunately, just one more of the patterns of conquest that were negotiated on Hispaniola, and which spread throughout the rest of the Spanish Caribbean and mainland colonies.

WORKS CITED

Columbus, Christopher. 1991. *The Diario of Christopher Columbus's First Voyage to America, 1492–1493, Abstracted by Fray Bartolomé de las Casas*, trans. and ed. Oliver Dunn and James E. Kelley, Jr. Norman, OK: University of Oklahoma Press.

Marté, Roberto, comp. 1981. *Santo Domingo en los manuscritos de Juan Bautista Muñoz*. Santo Domingo: Ediciones Fundación García-Arévalo.

Martyr D'Anghiera, Peter. 1970. *De Orbe Novo: The Eight Decades of Peter Martyr D'Anghiera*, trans. Francis Augustus MacNutt. New York: Burt Franklin.

Parry, John H., and Robert J. Keith, eds. 1984. *New Iberian Worlds: A Documentary History of the Discovery and Settlement of Latin America to the Early Seventeenth Century*. New York: Times Books.

8

Toward Sugar and Slavery
STEPHAN PALMIÉ

Slavery and plantation agriculture have long and complex histories in the Old World, effectively linking the history of the Caribbean to that of medieval Europe. Although the institution of slavery had virtually disappeared in large parts of central and northern Europe by the time of Columbus's voyages, it had survived on the violent frontiers generated by the Christian reconquest of Al-Andalus, and it remained legally regulated by codes ultimately rooted in Roman law. When Spain instituted slavery in its first New World possessions in the Caribbean, it essentially transferred a long extant, legally recognized institution of bondage to new frontier situations that opened up in the Americas.

No such clear institutional transfer obtained in the case of the British, French, Dutch, or Danish, who by the 17th century had begun to wrest the Lesser Antilles from Spain and to establish perhaps the first economically sustainable plantation colonies in the Caribbean. At least in the British case, the very word "plantation" offers a clue to the continuities between Old and New World histories of violent expansion, for it entered the English language during the Tudor period, in the context of the English conquest of Ireland. When the English broke up the previous social and political structures of the Celtic Irish, installed themselves as lords of the land, and pressed their new subjects into agricultural service, they called the result "planting." To the 16th-century English, planting meant improving the land—in the sense not just of planting crops, but of implanting a social order they thought superior to what had been there before. The phrase speaks to migration and agriculture, but also to political domination. This is the sense in which Francis Bacon used it in his "Essay on Plantations" in 1625. Some 30 years later, Thomas Hobbes was even more precise in referring to a plantation as "numbers of men sent out from the commonwealth, under a conductor, or governor, to inhabit a foreign country, either formerly void of inhabitants, or made void then by war."

The plantation was thus not simply a type of agricultural enterprise, but a political institution deployed in organizing colonial social space. It also welded a model of political domination to one of economic enterprise. As sociologist Edgar Thompson (1935) argued, at least since Tudor times, planting had come to signify "a form of migration and settlement which was organized, controlled, and given direction by capital; and it looked to a profitable return from capital." Planting meant colonizing, but in a rather specific sense: it involved capital investment and the anticipation of profit. A plantation colony is one established not for military purposes, or as a place where individuals from overpopulated areas migrate to gain access to land (although it may come to serve such purposes as well). It is a planned enterprise geared toward generating return on capital by transplanting people who are expected to produce commercially valuable crops in a colonized territory.

This is what the British charter companies so important in the colonization of North America were about: their goal was to transplant people for profit. It just so happened that the settlers in Virginia found the right kind of crop (tobacco), whereas those in New England did not—which is part of the reason why the term "Plymouth plantation" sounds quaint to us. The Puritans certainly "planted," and quite violently so; but the result was something rather different from a plantation colony as generally understood today. The intriguing historical semantics of the English term "plantation" notwithstanding, the forms of violent, agriculturally based settler colonialism it implied did not set the precedent for the institution that would leave its indelible imprint on the history of the Caribbean: the agro-industrial complex of the slave labor–based sugar plantation and its tri-continental economic articulation that linked New World colonial production sites with markets for commodified human labor from Africa and networks of capital, credit, distribution, and consumption in Europe. The origins of the institution arguably lie in the very first phase of Spanish colonialism in the Caribbean.

Iberian Beginnings: A Prelude in the Eastern Atlantic

When the British started "planting" in the New World, they were latecomers by more than a century. The original Spanish colonizers had not intended to turn the Caribbean into a place where profits would be reaped from agriculturally based forms of settler colonialism. When Columbus was looking for a sea route to Asia, he was seeking not colonization in any modern sense, but trade. After the fall of Constantinople in 1453, Muslims had blocked Christian access to the old land routes along which gold, spices (including sugar), incense, silk, and other exotic luxury goods had previously traveled to medieval Europe; Columbus's unintentional discovery had been motivated by the desire to find a maritime solution to this problem.

Even so, during Columbus's lifetime, establishing trading posts in the West Indies on the model of Portuguese *feitorias* in West Africa proved to be an illusory project. Gold mining provided the initial economic platform for Iberian ventures in the Caribbean, but once the mineral deposits gave way, the region offered little other merchandise valued by Europeans that natives produced systematically in a large enough quantity to make commercial sense. Nor did the far-flung trade networks characteristic of Africa exist in the era of the first Spanish contacts. However, there already existed a second model of organizing overseas enterprises at the time of Columbus's voyages, and he knew about it from firsthand experience: that of the sugar plantation, operated by unfree and usually ethnically alien labor.

Europeans first systematically grew sugar on large agricultural estates in the Norman crusader states in Palestine and Syria. There, sugar production reached its apogee in the 12th century but broke down after the Islamic reconquest in 1187. Sugar then moved westward across the Christian Mediterranean via Cyprus, Crete, and Sicily. It likewise spread within the Muslim world, reaching the Islamic part of the Iberian Peninsula well before the end of the Christian reconquest. In the course of this movement, sugar production acquired a number of specific organizational features—conspicuously, the utilization of enslaved labor.

It is unclear to what extent early sugar plantations in the eastern Mediterranean relied on legal arrangements granting owners wide-ranging rights over enslaved workers (of various provenance), or whether they merely extracted labor from native peasant populations. However, captive Muslims worked as slaves on the Iberian peninsula and in Sicily, where they were joined by quite a number of Africans. More important, Christian Iberians used a combination of large-scale slavery and sugar cultivation in their first overseas colonial ventures on the Atlantic islands of Madeira, the Canaries, Cabo Verde, and São Tomé. These islands off the coast of Africa became a sort of laboratory for New World plantation colonialism.

Three basic characteristics of sugar cultivation gave the Iberian experiments in plantation colonization on these islands a specific cast right from the start: a need for large tracts of fertile, well-irrigated land; a seasonal need for large labor forces; and a need for complex, expensive machinery to process the cane and refine the sugar. Madeira, for example, had the right climate but was uninhabited when the Portuguese first settled there in 1420. Sugarcane was introduced in 1435, and soon after, the Portuguese found a solution to the labor problem by introducing large numbers of enslaved Guanches, the original inhabitants of the Canary Islands who had been violently subjugated in the course of a Spanish conquest. Toward the end of the 15th century, the Guanches, who may have numbered as many as 100,000, had been severely decimated, and were being increasingly replaced by African slaves whom the Portuguese acquired in the feitorias they had begun to establish in coastal West and Central Africa beginning in the 1480s.

By then, Madeira had become the first large-scale exporter of sugar and a genuine slave-based plantation society. The next step came with the transformation of the depopulated Canary Islands into a similar enterprise at the hands of the Spanish and the development of São Tomé, Principe, and Annobón, three islands in the gulf of Guinea, into plantation colonies. These islands reached their maximum output and profitability in the first half of the 16th century. At that point, however, the emerging slave-based plantation system had already taken root in New World.

The Rise and Decline of Spanish Plantation Colonialism in the Caribbean

The transplantation of this system was, of course, not the work of any single person. Still, Columbus's career neatly symbolizes the transition. Of probable Genovese origin, Columbus early on had been familiar with the trans-Mediterranean trade, including sugar shipped westward from the Levant. He began his maritime career aboard Portuguese ships and learned to navigate the Atlantic in the context of Portuguese slaving ventures on the African coast. He transported sugar from Madeira to Genoa and eventually married the daughter of one of the original colonizers of that group of islands. On his first voyage of discovery Columbus described the inhabitants of Hispaniola as remarkably similar to the Guanches, and of potential value as slaves. On his second voyage, he not only took sugarcane from the Canary Islands to the New World, but also took royal authorization for planting, building mills, and extracting labor from the natives.

In 1503 sugar syrup was first produced on Hispaniola. That same year, Governor Nicolás de Ovando asked the Spanish crown to recall the authorization for introducing African slaves: so many of them had already fled and joined the natives that Ovando worried about a military threat to the fledgling colonial enterprise. However, the crown did not heed his advice. Since the treaty of Tordesillas (1494) had excluded Spain from direct trade with Africa, in 1517 the Spanish crown resorted to a system of exclusive licenses (*asientos*) granted to foreign contractors to introduce specified numbers of slaves into its New World possessions. Although the asiento system would prove to be notoriously inefficient during its more than 250 years' duration, by 1540 it had begun to replace a first generation of *ladino* (i.e., Hispanophone) slaves shipped directly from Spain with Africans enslaved on the continent itself. It thus set in motion the demographic, and in many ways, cultural "Africanization" of the Antilles—a process that would only come to an end in the last third of the 19th century, when the by then illegal transatlantic slave trade finally came to a halt.

In 1517 the first shipment of Caribbean sugar reached Seville, and by the 1530s there were 34 sugar mills in operation on Hispaniola. The largest of these, not incidentally, belonged to Columbus's son Diego. At that time the indigenous population had declined to a fragment of its original size. In contrast, as the chronicler Oviedo reported, by then there were so many Africans on the island "as a result of the sugar factories, that the land seems an effigy or an image of Ethiopia itself." By mid-century, when this demographic transition reached its apex on Hispaniola, perhaps 5,000 to 6,000 Spaniards were facing a veritable army of more than 25,000 enslaved Africans. As Sidney Mintz (1966, 918) wistfully put it, the Spanish in the Caribbean had transformed themselves from guests into hosts by exterminating the indigenous population and replacing it with an extraneous, racially alien labor force violently—as well as profitably—extracted from another continent.

Oviedo also provided a vivid characterization of the early Caribbean sugar industry that illustrates the amazingly modern character of what the Spanish called "ingenios"—the agro-industrial complex, comprising both the cane fields and the sugar mill proper. "Each of the important and well equipped ingenios," Oviedo writes:

in addition to the great expense and value of the building or factory in which the sugar is made, and another large building in which it is refined and stored, often requires an investment of ten or twelve thousand gold ducats before it is complete and ready for operation. And if I should say fifteen thousand ducats, I should not be exaggerating, for they require at least eighty or one hundred Negroes working all the time, and even one hundred and twenty to be well supplied; and close by a good herd of cattle to feed the workers; aside from the expense of trained workers and foremen for making the sugar, and carts to haul the cane to the mill and to bring in wood, and people to make bread and cultivate and irrigate the canefields, and other things that must be done and continual expenditure of money (Oviedo 1959[1546], I: 107).

Figure 8.1 Slaves work in an early sugar mill on Hispaniola, gathering, grinding, and boiling the sugarcane. Engraving from *Americae pars quinta* (1595). Source: The John Carter Brown Library.

Here, in a nutshell, is what Caribbean sugar plantation slavery was all about: enormous investments, huge labor forces, a virtually industrial degree of division of labor, and a highly sophisticated infrastructure for transport and processing. Nothing comparable to the size of work forces, massive capitalization, and extensive division of labor and mechanization that characterized Caribbean sugar plantations during Oviedo's time existed in Europe, and it would take more than two centuries before the Industrial Revolution would generate production sites in the metropoles comparable to those that existed in Europe's Caribbean colonies as early as the mid-16th century. What Oviedo fails to mention is the violence, whether merely threatened or actually unleashed upon the enslaved, that was a necessary component in the management and enforcement of labor discipline in such peculiarly "modern" and certainly "protocapitalistic" agro-industrial enterprises.

Three hundred years later, this system would reach its highest point of development in the vast *ingenios* of mid-19th-century Cuba. These boasted an acreage under cultivation that Oviedo would not have dreamed of, slave labor forces of up to 800 workers, steam-driven sugar mills, railroad freight connections to major port cities, and forms of "scientific management" that were at least as sophisticated as those employed in contemporaneous European or North American industrial enterprises.

However, the three centuries between Oviedo's early ingenios on Hispaniola and the last great slave-operated Cuban sugar plantations in the 19th century do not represent a period of continuous progress. Spanish sugar plantations on the Greater Antilles began to flounder and decline before the end of the 16th century. The reasons for this decline have long been subject to controversy, and there surely is no single cause for Spain's failure to turn its Caribbean possessions into plantation colonies exhibiting "sustained growth." What certainly played a significant role was that Spanish interest in the Caribbean declined after the conquest of mainland America and the discovery of precious metal deposits in Mexico and Peru. After the 1530s, the island colonies faced a serious population decline due to emigration to mainland America. Of at least equal importance, however, was Spain's rigidly centralized commercial policy, which never quite enabled would-be planters in the early Spanish Caribbean to lay their hands on sufficient capital and slaves to sell their product profitably enough to sustain growth. Finally, it has been argued that at mid-century the Spanish and wider European markets for sugar—which was an extreme luxury at the time—were not yet elastic enough to absorb a steady amount of relatively high-priced Caribbean sugar. This situation really only began to change when Portuguese planters in Brazil succeeded in depressing sugar prices, thus setting New World sugar production on the path towards an economy of scale.

The result was that the Spanish islands partly reverted to a kind of peasant economy wherein small-scale cultivators engaged in highly diverse forms of agricultural production and exchange—often with Spain's enemies. Locations where Spain's early experiments with plantation agriculture collapsed after an initial boom period illustrated the beginnings of a historical pattern that was to become characteristic for much of the Caribbean: a systematic contradiction between agro-industrial plantations based on unfree labor, and the growth of peasantries that tended to thrive when and where the plantation sector went into contraction.

French and British Beginnings

At least since the 1560s, other European powers had tried to gain entry into the Spanish colonial world. Initially they did so not to colonize, but to sack the Spanish treasure fleet. Spurred by myths of El Dorado, Sir Walter Raleigh repeatedly tried to set up colonies on the American mainland, in the Guianas and in Virginia. But the main focus of 16th-century British, French, and Dutch naval activities in the Caribbean was contraband trade and plunder.

As a result, the Caribbean Sea in the second half of the 16th and into the early 17th century became a maritime frontier zone swarming with vessels whose crews engaged in open piracy, their activities often endorsed by European rulers. This situation was closely linked to the phrase "beyond the line," which goes back to the

Treaty of Cateau-Cambrésis between Spain and France (1559). This treaty stipulated that the maritime region west of the prime meridian in the mid-Atlantic and south of the Tropic of Cancer would be exempted from European treaty law. Since military aggression on the high seas was rapidly increasing, the treaty's goal was to avoid the escalation of overseas naval conflicts into full-scale wars on European soil by allowing European states formally at peace to fight each other beyond this "line of amity."

What this meant was that once a ship crossed the line, its crew and captain were on their own. Any foreign vessel could prey on them, even though their country of origin and allegiance may have been at peace with that vessel's nation of origin. This situation also made settling New World territory a dangerous enterprise. Spain obviously had no intention of enabling foreigners to establish a foothold on islands from which they could attack their fleet. As early as 1555, Dutch pirates sacked Havana; in 1586 Sir Francis Drake devastated Santo Domingo, and in 1596 he wiped out the Spanish settlement Nombre de Dios on the Isthmus of Panama. Although the Spanish could not keep England and France out of their waters, they at least tried to keep them from establishing territorial bases of operations.

Even when the British, French, and Dutch began their first colonial ventures in the Americas, they did not dare confront Spain directly. Rather than attacking the Spanish garrisons on the Greater Antilles, they began "planting" on much less attractive islands of the southern wing of the Caribbean archipelago, particularly in the Leeward group. The Spanish had never effectively colonized these islands, finding them too inhospitable—either on account of geography, or because of the presence of large and hostile Native American populations. Due to wind and current conditions, the southern Caribbean was also fairly safe from Spanish reprisals. Spanish naval forces wanting to attack these islands from their northern bases on the mainland, Cuba, or Hispaniola had to tack against the wind and prevailing northerly currents for too long to effectively mount a surprise attack on northern European settlers.

The beachhead for non-Spanish colonization in the Caribbean eventually became a tiny, mountainous island in the northern part of the Lesser Antilles: St. Christopher—known today as St. Kitts—which was originally settled as an uneasy Anglo-French joint venture in 1624. The next steps were Barbados, colonized by the British in 1627, Nevis in 1628, San Andrés and Providencia in 1629, and Montserrat and Antigua in 1632. In 1635 the French established themselves in Guadeloupe and Martinique, while the Dutch made Curaçao their base of operations in 1634 and from there gradually took possession of neighboring Bonaire and Aruba, as well as Saba and St. Eustatius.

Some of these islands were little more than barren rock piles. Others, such as Antigua, were flat and fertile but lacked water; still others, such as Montserrat, were so rugged in terrain that plantation agriculture never took hold. A crucial exception was the largest of them all: Barbados. And it was here that the northern European variant of the slave-based sugar plantation complex first emerged. It was also in Barbados that this complex first went through a characteristic developmental cycle that was to set a precedent for most future colonial enterprises in the insular Caribbean—a development that forever changed the meaning of the term "plantation" and its cognates in modern European languages.

The "Sugar Revolution" in Barbados

Initially, the character of British settlement in Barbados resembled the first successful British colonial experiments on the North American mainland. As in Virginia, the first group of Barbadian colonists had been sent out by a charter company that intended to "plant" them there in the sense discussed above. Little is known about the first years in Barbados, but it seems as if the colony almost failed. As in Virginia, the British policy was to give out land grants to settlers and to employ the labor of indentured servants (Barbados had no indigenous population). The first commercial crops in Barbados were tobacco and, to a lesser extent, cotton—largely because the Barbadians tried to emulate the tobacco-driven success story Virginia had experienced in the 1620s. But tobacco cultivation in Barbados turned out to be a failure. Although the European tobacco market remained good until the late 1630s, the Barbadian product was considered vastly inferior to that of Virginia.

Nevertheless, in the 1630s the population of Barbados grew rapidly. As in Virginia, a majority of its inhabitants arrived as servants hoping to acquire land after the expiration of their term. Quite a large number of them, however, came involuntarily: they had been rounded up in British cities as vagrants, criminals, or seditious agitators and sentenced to "transportation." This practice of deporting surplus populations from the metropole became so common that the phrase "to Barbados someone" (meaning to spirit away innocent people to servitude in the Caribbean) entered the lexicon of everyday English speech at the time. Many of the Irish defeated by Cromwell, followers of dissident sects, and royalists sentenced by Parliament during the English Civil War likewise found themselves aboard ships bound for the West Indies.

Temporary servitude was not uncommon in England at the time. As in the North American mainland colonies, most settlers to Barbados were attracted by the promise of eventually acquiring freehold status, but the margin of opportunity gradually shrunk as wealthier planters increased their holdings through purchase. Land available to ex-servants or free newcomers to Barbados virtually ran out at the end of the 1630s, and, unlike in Virginia, there was nowhere else to go. Also unlike the situation in England, where servants and apprentices enjoyed a certain amount of legal

Figure 8.2 English tobacco planters and slaves in Barbados. Engraving from Carel Allard, *Orbis habitabilis oppida et vestitus* (ca. 1680). Source: Library of Congress.

protection, was that Barbadian masters exercised almost un-restrained control over their servants and often abused them in ways entirely unprecedented in the motherland. As early as 1634, white servants rebelled on Barbados: and, as in the case of Bacon's Rebellion in Virginia (1675), there are good indications that these servants, particularly the Irish, repeatedly tried to join forces with similarly maltreated Africans.

Nevertheless, by the end of the 1630s, Barbados still had not developed into a genuine plantation society. Although demographic data for this period are notoriously unreliable, toward the end of the 1630s the island had a population of almost 6,000; of these, some 760 held land—a proportion comparable to that in the European countryside, which is especially noteworthy because Barbadian landholdings still greatly varied in size. Some of the larger planters held tracts of several thousand acres, but the majority of freeholders farmed small parcels between 10 and 50 acres each. This situation changed drastically in the 1640s. Within less than a decade, most members of the white yeomanry on Barbados were squeezed off their land: servants were replaced by African slaves, and the social

Figure 8.3 Map of Barbados with plantations and roads. Engraving from Richard Ligon, *A True & Exact History of the Island of Barbadoes* (1657). Source: The John Carter Brown Library.

organization of the island irreversibly switched from that of a society with slaves to that of a society organized around the legal institution of slavery.

The reason for this dramatic transformation was sugar. Understanding the Barbadian "sugar revolution" requires stepping back to look at the development of sugar planting in the Americas after the decline of the early Spanish experiments. Both figuratively and literally, sugar arrived in Barbados from Brazil and aboard Dutch ships. It took hold there not because of British metropolitan intentions, but in spite of them.

Discovered by the Portuguese in 1500, Brazil became the site where the Portuguese first managed to reinstall the sugar plantation complex they and the Spanish had pioneered on the Atlantic islands off the coast of Africa, and to achieve its continuity and growth. By 1526 Brazil was exporting sugar, and in the early 17th century its output superseded not only that of earlier Atlantic outposts but also that of the rapidly declining Spanish-Caribbean sugar industry. Part of the reason for this success was that the Portuguese straddled both shores of the Atlantic. Most of the slaves, on whose labor the early Brazilian sugar industry depended, came from the Portuguese colony in Angola, the civil war-ridden neighboring kingdom of Kongo, or the Portuguese factories in the Bight of Benin and Cape Verde (which drew on Senegambian sources). As a result, Portuguese planters in Brazil did not face a problem their Spanish colleagues in the Caribbean would unsuccessfully struggle with for another two centuries: the highly restrictive and inefficiently organized asiento system by which Spain provisioned its New World colonies with African slave labor. While Spanish plantations floundered after the turn of the 17th century, the same period marked the beginning of a boom in Brazil. If the British and French in the Caribbean were looking for a model for hyperprofitable overseas agricultural enterprises, by that time it would not have been Hispaniola or Cuba but the northeastern Brazilian province of Pernambuco.

But what about the Dutch? Like other northern European nations, the Dutch initially began to prey upon the Spanish fleet in the second half of the 16th century. Like the British and French, they also perceived the advantages of piratical raids on the Spanish mainland colonies. By the early 17th century, however, the new Dutch West India Company, founded in 1621, embarked on a different course of action. Its novel approach was not merely to skim off profits by raiding Iberian colonies or preying upon the homeward-bound fleet, but to take over the very source: fully developed colonial enterprises.

Aware of the advantages the Portuguese enjoyed by maintaining a connection between Angola and northeastern Brazil, the Dutch seized control of both places at once. Between about 1630 and 1650 they achieved three distinct but interrelated goals: they subjected both regions to a rigorous scheme of capitalistic development, pumping in the requisite cash and credit for building up the plantation infrastruc-

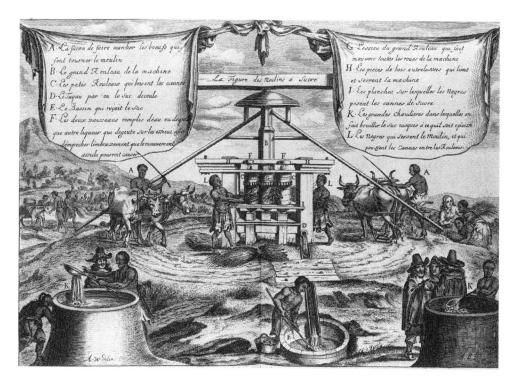

La Figure des Moulins a Sucre

A· *La façon de faire marcher les boeufs qui font tourner le moulin*
B· *Le grand Rouleau de la machine*
C· *Les petis Rouleaux qui brisent les cannes*
D· *Le Tuyau par ou le suc decoule*
E· *Le Bassin qui reçoit le suc*
F· *Les deux vaisseaux remplis d'eau ou de que autre liqueur qui degoute sur les essieux, afin d'empescher l'embrasement que le mouvement assidu pourroit causer*

G· *L'essieu du grand Rouleau qui fait mouvoir toutes les roues de la machine*
H· *Les pieces de bois entrelassees qui lient et serrent la machine*
I· *Les planches sur lesquelles les Negres posent les cannes de Sucre*
K· *Les grandes chaudieres dans lesquelles on fait bouillir le suc jusques à ce qu'il soit epaissi*
L· *Les Negres qui servent le moulin, et qui poussent les Cannes entre les Rouleaux*

ture of Brazil; they continued their role as major maritime architects of legal and illegal commercial links between the Caribbean colonies of various nations; and they turned Amsterdam—which already was the center of finance and banking in northern Europe—into one of the major international European markets for sugar. In contrast to the Portuguese, the Dutch apparently had no strong interest in monopolizing sugar production. In their view, profit lay in offering credit and taking over commercial shipping and distribution.

Figure 8.4 Sugar mill with vertical rollers powered by oxen. Engraving from Charles de Rochefort, *Histoire naturelle et morale des iles Antilles de l'Amerique* (1665). Source: The John Carter Brown Library.

While the importance of the Dutch introduction of sugarcane to Barbados in 1637 is open to question, the crucial role of Dutch merchants in providing financial backing with which British settlers built the first sugar mills on that island is beyond dispute. Dutch planters and sugar masters also taught the British Barbadians what they came to call the "method of Pernambuco"—which included not only the know-how of planting, milling, and processing cane, but also the rudiments of a legal code regulating slavery. Dutch ships, finally, linked Barbados's emerging plantation economy both to the supply of African labor provided by the Atlantic slave trade and to the effective and profitable distribution networks in the Netherlands. Although the extent of Dutch involvement has lately become the subject of debate among historians, it may be safe to say that within little more

Figure 8.5 Drax Hall, built by English planters in Barbados in the 1650s (photo 1972 by Jerome Handler). Image NW0084, www.slaveryimages.org, Virginia Foundation for the Humanities and University of Virginia Library.

than the decade between 1640 and 1650, the Dutch helped to transform Barbados from a slaveholding society with a large yeoman population engaged in fairly diversified economic pursuits into a slave society solidly based on sugar monoculture.

These developments were due in no small measure to a fortuitous Atlantic conjuncture. For the "sugar revolution" in Barbados occurred at a time when English metropolitan control over the island faltered. What allowed the Barbadians to engage in such principally illegal dealings with the Dutch was the colonial result of the turmoil in the metropole incited by the English Civil War. As the eminent historian of that war, Christopher Hill (1986), put it, between 1641 and 1650, Barbados virtually became an independent state, or at least approached a state of home rule. As a consequence, the emerging planter elite began to control legislative and executive matters in a manner unprecedented in any New World colony. Only when the British Parliament sent the fleet in the fall of 1651 did the Barbadians finally resubmit to imperial control. They arguably did so, however, because they had become too afraid of their own slaves and rebellious servants to risk giving out arms to them—a situation foreshadowing the agonizing decisions the Jamaican planter elite made when the protest of the 13 North American colonies against British commercial legislation began to escalate into a full-scale colonial war more than a century later.

Still, the intervening period had allowed the Barbadian planter elite enough autonomy to achieve three major objectives: first, to engineer the crucial economic takeoff with the help of Dutch capital and distribution networks; second, to forge a brutal slave code—first properly codified in 1661, but developed in the 1640s—that allowed masters almost unlimited power to exploit their human chattel; and third, to begin a process of concentration of landholding that effectively pushed small freeholders off the island.

The Demographic and Socioeconomic Consequences of Sugar

Demographic figures illustrate the extent of the resulting transition. In the mid-1640s, Barbados had upward of 30,000 white inhabitants, of which about a third were landowners and another third servants. Already at that time, the slave population numbered about 6,000. By 1680 the white population of Barbados had shrunk to less than 20,000, and the number of landowners to about 3,000. Of these, almost 1,200 owned fewer than 10 acres and no slaves, about 1,000 had fewer than 30 acres and up to 20 slaves, and another 190 planters owned up to 100 acres and 60 slaves. The crucial group, however, consisted of 175 large and very powerful planters, each of whom owned upward of 100 acres and more than 60 slaves. Collectively, these planters owned more than half of the island's land and more than half of its unfree population—a figure approaching optimum allocation of land to labor, given the technological capacities of sugar mills at the time.

As successful sugar planters bought up land from failing tobacco planters and small cultivators, land concentration in the hands of a few spelled the dispossession of small freeholders. By the 1670s, Barbados had become the richest and most populous of all British colonies in the Americas, but it was marked by a steady stream of emigrants: people pushed to the wall by an "overmighty" planter gentry. "Twelve thousand good men formerly proprietors have gone off," a report stated in 1667, "wormed out of their small settlements by their more suttle and greedy neighbors." At the same time, the inflow of servants rapidly declined. Barbados was no land of opportunity anymore. For poor white settlers, it had become a trap. Not surprisingly, those who saw an opportunity to escape from the island before slipping into servitude took it. As servants and luckless poor yeomen fled Barbados, the number of African slaves exploded. By 1680, the number of indentured servants had fallen to less than 2,400, and the number of slaves surpassed 46,000. Before the end of the 17th century, Barbados would import another 60,000 Africans.

By 1680, Barbados was the most valuable British possession in the New World. Its sugar exports to England were worth more than the exports of all British North

American mainland colonies combined. The Barbadian planter elite were among the richest men in the Americas. Profits reaped from sugar induced a veritable frenzy. By the late 17th century so much of the land was taken up by cane that the island's population had become unable to feed itself, importing the better part of their food from elsewhere, particularly North America. In this respect, late-17th-century Barbados was a mercantilist's dream come true.

In the emerging British overseas empire, full-fledged mercantilist schemes first took hold with the Navigation Acts of 1650, 1651, and 1660, which severely curtailed colonists' rights to trade with foreign nationals and led to protests in Barbados similar to those in the North American colonies. But mercantilism prevailed in Barbados, and for a time the island was living proof of its utility. Given Barbados's highly overspecialized economy, toward the end of the 17th century sugar and its by-products (molasses and rum) accounted for 95% of all its exports. At the same time, Barbados imported all of its manufactured goods from England—from the machinery needed to refine sugar to the crockery Barbadians ate from. Finally, since the island no longer produced any other agricultural goods to speak of, Barbados imported huge quantities of grain, salt beef, dried cod, and timber from the British colonies on the North American mainland.

Although the Barbadians continued to trade surreptitiously with other nations, they set the precedent, and seemingly provided proof, for the profitability of a full-fledged mercantilistic colonial economic system. They also set a precedent for a type of colonial society fully based on slave labor and the systematic legal oppression, economic exploitation, and social debasement of black people. Along with the sugar-producing provinces of northern Brazil, Barbados first exemplified the workings of what the historian Philip Curtin (1969, 3) called the South Atlantic System, defined as "a complex economic organism based on the production in the Americas of tropical staples for consumption in Europe, and grown by the labor of Africans." It was one of the several birthplaces of the modern Atlantic world, and perhaps of capitalist modernity more generally. And it foreshadowed a history that would, with significant variations, repeat itself throughout the insular Caribbean.

Oversimplifying matters, this historical pattern can be summarized as follows. In its earliest stages it included a labor force transition from servants to slaves, for which Barbados established a model, and which the earliest French colonies of Martinique and Guadeloupe would also develop in the late 17th century. On these islands, too, the plantation and an exploding African slave labor force would displace earlier European settler populations. But parts of the model established by Barbados also set the course for later slave colonies such as British Jamaica and French Saint-Domingue, neither of which ever went through a prolonged "yeoman phase" of small-scale diversified agriculture. To be sure, indentured servants and engagés worked in Jamaica and Saint-Domingue after the British and French took possession of them in 1655 and 1697 respectively. But in both cases, slavery and the plantation were dominant institutions right from the start.

Importantly, the "modular" nature of the transition to sugar and slavery in Barbados also irrevocably linked the further history of the Caribbean to that of West Africa. The Barbadian precedent made clear just how much money lay not only in producing sugar but in procuring the enslaved manpower demanded by burgeoning plantation economies. And just as various European nations came to vie with each other over the possession of Caribbean plantation colonies, so they competed with each other over who would have the largest share of the international slave trade—increasingly displacing the Portuguese who, until the middle of the 17th century, still had held a monopoly over the export of slaves from Africa.

WORKS CITED

Curtin, Philip D. 1969. *The Atlantic Slave Trade: A Census.* Madison: University of Wisconsin Press.

Hill, Christopher. 1986. "Radical Pirates?" In *The Collected Essays of Christopher Hill*, vol. III, 161–87. Amherst: University of Massachusetts Press.

Mintz, Sidney W. 1966. "The Caribbean as a Socio-Cultural Area." *Journal of World History* 9, 4: 912–37.

Oviedo y Valdés, Gonzalo Fernandez de. 1959 [1546]. *Historia general y natural de las Indias.* Biblioteca de autores españoles, vols. 117–21. Madrid: Ediciones Atlas.

Thompson, Edgar T. 1935. "Population Expansion and the Plantation System." *American Journal of Sociology* 41:314–26.

9

Masterless People

ISAAC CURTIS

Maroons, Pirates, and Commoners

In the 16th century, the wealth of the Caribbean region and of the New World more broadly was generated largely by indigenous and African workers, and the riches they produced were transported by sea with the labor of sailors drawn from Spain's developing port cities. These intercontinental movements of people and commodities changed over time as the Dutch, French, English, and Danish played an increasingly active role. The combined labor of sailors and slaves made possible not only the luxury consumption of Europe's ruling classes but also the economic development, territorial wars, and voyages of conquest that continually reestablished their dominance of their own and other societies. At the same time the world was becoming smaller, as greater numbers of people from ever more distant regions were brought together in ways previously unimaginable. But while this was initially a world envisioned by the masters of the Caribbean and Atlantic economies, it also became a world for those who would have no masters at all.

Maroon Societies

The history of rebel slaves in the Caribbean was as old as slavery itself. In 1502, Governor Nicolás de Ovando arrived in Hispaniola to establish a permanent Spanish settlement. His fleet of 30 ships carried a cross-section of Spanish society, including African slaves. Among them was an unnamed man who wasted no time in escaping from his Spanish masters after arriving in the New World. He joined the indigenous communities that survived in the island's mountainous interior and became the first African maroon in the Americas (Price 1996, 1).

The English term "maroons" came from the Spanish *cimarrones*, which designated communities of "Indian" slaves who abandoned their work and formed mountain strongholds with the other survivors of genocide and slavery. As African women and men restocked the understaffed mines and estates of Spanish colonial masters, those who followed in the footsteps of their Taino forebears came to be known by the same name. Within a few decades, the word came to mean African slaves who fled their masters.

Resistance to slavery began in Africa and slowed the spread of African slavery in the Americas. Even as European slavers expanded the trade in the late 17th and 18th centuries to meet the surging needs of Caribbean sugar production, they met with resistance up and down the West African coast. Skilled mariners like the Kru kept Europeans off their shores and even assisted in the shipboard revolts of those already captured and taken to sea (Rediker 2004). The peoples of coastal Upper Guinea adopted a range of strategies to resist enslavement that prefigured the settlement strategies and defensive fortifications used by maroons in the Americas (Diouf 2003, 155–60; Price 1996, 220). As the Atlantic slave trade reached deeper into Africa, it drew more people with a wider range of ideas and experiences into this struggle. The resistance of groups that never left African soil sprang from the same well of ideas and reflected a common intellectual tradition (Diouf 2003, 62–78, 142–44; Searing 2002). Maroons and rebel slaves throughout the Caribbean invoked these and other traditions in their struggle for freedom (Campbell 1988, 4). African knowledge of the Caribbean itself also developed very early, with a 17th-century slave ship sailor reporting that Africans had "a more dreadful apprehension of Barbadoes than we can have of hell" (Heuman 1986, 17–18).

As important as African traditions were, however, it was the experience of slavery itself that drove thousands of enslaved women and men to attempt the flight to freedom. Regardless of their roots, these great masses of people were brought face to face with the production-oriented logic of plantation society, which placed them within ever more industrial and densely populated settings. To remain within the confines of such a society was to accept a world in which the act of whipping alone had "a thousand refinements" (James 1963, 12–13; Price 1996, 88). Hands were shackled to feet and feet to blocks of wood, to prevent escape. Tin masks were secured over the faces of field slaves to prevent them from eating the sugarcane that they lived and died to produce. All manner of tortures were employed to enforce discipline and punish insubordination, and no parts of the body were off limits to mutilation.

For most of the enslaved, the path to freedom was shaped by their skills, their local geography, their degree of independence, and, most important, their relationships with their fellow slaves. Whether brought from Africa or acquired in the New World, skills such as experience in coastal navigation could provide the means for achieving freedom. For example, the Danish islands of St. Thomas, St. Croix, and St. Jan had virtually no viable interior retreats in which rebel slaves could establish defensible communities, and the deforestation that came with the rapid expansion of sugar plantations removed what little tree cover might have provided shelter to runaways. With few other options, the enslaved women and men of the Danish islands used skills acquired on turtle fishing expeditions to navigate their way to a better life in adjacent islands. These "maritime maroons" depended on connections with urban slaves and free blacks in port cities like Charlotte Amalie to help ensure relatively easy access to idle seacraft (Hall 1985). Solidarity, manifested in networks of communication and reciprocity, was thus the foundation of all marronage. In a world of masters and slaves, those who sought to live on different terms would come to depend on such connections.

While many maroon communities would also develop connections to colonial society, others were relatively independent and autonomous and offered new opportunities to escaped slaves. When one escaped slave arrived at a forest hideout in French Guiana in 1747, he found a vibrant economy based on subsistence agriculture (Price 1996, 312–19). Newly arrived runaways were given garden plots that they cleared and planted, and they were provided for by the community until their crops were ready to eat. They planted manioc, millet, rice, sweet potatoes, yams, sugarcane, and bananas as well as cotton, from which they made their clothes.

More well-established maroon communities might acquire goods by hijacking trade caravans or even by trading with nearby towns. In fact, such connections with the colonial economy were increasingly the norm over time. For special ceremonial occasions, some maroons dressed in fine Spanish silks. Members of a maroon community in French Guiana stored their more utilitarian attire and other small goods in *pagarats*, double-plaited woven baskets first made by indigenous Caribs, which could be waterproofed with leaves and stacked, hung, or nested. In addition to the various foods produced on the garden plots, the maroons fished and hunted wild pig, deer, and jaguar. Similar practices prevailed in the early years of maroons and buccaneers on Jamaica, where the abundant livestock was described by an abbot in 1611 as "common to all" (Carey 1997, 68).

In spite of the communal agriculture and traditions of mutual aid, masterless-ness was far from absolute within maroon societies, as is suggested by the place of women in their social order. Almost all maroon communities were dispropor-tionately male, and the polygamous arrangements imposed by military strongmen exacerbated the skewed gender ratio (Price 1996, 19). A half-dozen women from the settlement in French Guiana eventually asked to be returned to their mas-ters, arguing that they were kept in place "by force and threat of violence" (Price 1996, 318). Things seem to have been more equitable among the cimarrons of 16th-century Panama. Though they routinely kidnapped slave women from Spanish settlements to balance their numbers, historical records suggest that life for women remained far better in maroon communities than within slave society (Pike 2007, 251–54).

Although the incomplete and fragmentary historical records documenting maroon societies are inevitably more dense for the authoritarian and militaristic settlements most familiar to Europeans, the world the maroons made stands out as remarkably egalitarian for its day. Evidence of democratic elections survives for maroon officials in Jamaica, Cuba, and Panama (Price 1996, 41, 51, 260). Two sepa-rate slave plots in the 1690s threatened to overthrow the governments of Carta-gena and Barbados and to elect an African king (Thornton 1998, 301–2). Security concerns and isolation did leave relatively hierarchical structures in place in many maroon societies, but even this changed over time (Price 1996, 19–22). One influ-ence in that democratization may have been the other masterless peoples of the Ca-ribbean, people who escaped similar conditions and formed their own alternative societies outside the bounds of colonial control.

Pirate Societies

The deep-sea sailing ships that crisscrossed the Atlantic from the time of Columbus until the Industrial Revolution have rightly been called "the most complex machine[s] of the epoch" (Perez-Mallaína 1998, 63). They held together the inter-national economy centered on the Caribbean. The silver mines and sugar planta-tions that formed the basis of European empires, not to mention the large and ever-expanding number of African slaves who labored in them, were made possible by these vessels and by the maritime workers who made them move. Like the mines and plantations of the terrestrial world, each ship was a factory, an enclosure in which a small number of officers could successfully discipline and exploit the labor of large crews.

Like slaves, sailors recoiled against their working conditions. Justice was often applied arbitrarily: when in 1572 General Cristóbal de Eraso put some of his crew in stocks for using the Lord's name in vain, they protested that it was insult upon injury, "especially on a ship that is already jail enough by itself" (Perez-Mallaína 1998, 129). There was also the matter of wages. Sixteenth-century Spanish sailors made only slightly more than day laborers in urban Spain, while working under much more dangerous conditions. English sailors fared little better. Their wages were generally low, delinquency and fraud in payment were common, and slumps in trade could leave thousands unemployed and cut salaries in half in a matter of just a few years (Rediker 2004, 43, 23).

One alternative was the pirate ship. To understand what it meant to be a pirate, it helps to remember what it meant to be a maroon. In a world of masters and slaves, the maroon was neither. Masters and slaves were interlocked parts of the same system. Maroons could not have existed without that system—indeed, marronage arose out of and in direct response to it—but what defined a maroon community was its potential to transcend the dialectic between master and slave. In practice these societies took various forms, with varying degrees of engagement with the plantation system and varying degrees of masterlessness in their internal structure, but at the most fundamental level a maroon society existed in opposition to the world of masters and slaves. Pirates emerged from a similarly stratified society, each ship a wooden world contingent upon the domination of the captain over his crew. Although the world of captains and crews was destined to continue, pirates began to challenge the foundation of that system in the 17th-century Caribbean.

The first genuine pirates of the Caribbean were the buccaneers, and the first buccaneers were in fact maroons. The 1620 journal of a French sailor records an encounter on the coast of Hispaniola with two men, a "*marron*" and a "*nègre*," huddled around a campfire with a wooden grill that the two called by its indigenous name, *boucan*. The two men described how they and others subsisted by poaching Spanish livestock and living in common in the unoccupied northwestern section of the island. Their lifestyle appealed to men who were trapped for so much of their lives on ships and subjected to the whims of high seas and violent captains. When the French ship set sail a few days later, six of its crew had gone missing, swelling the ranks of these men of the boucan, the buccaneers (Moreau 2006, 58–59).

Conflicts within and between imperial powers presented new threats and new opportunities for the buccaneers. Many took to the sea as privateers—pirates in the service of whatever state would temporarily license their activities. At the same time, the Caribbean was increasingly becoming a nexus for the outcasts of societies on both sides of the Atlantic. Peasant uprisings and urban rebellions across Europe brought migrants to the Caribbean from regions known for widespread banditry and vagabondage. When the English Revolution ended in 1660, many of the rebels—who had sought protection for their common lands, overthrow of the monarchy, and an end to African slavery—fled across the sea and took to buccaneering (Linebaugh and Rediker 2000, 104–42; Hill 1986). Meanwhile, French rebels had intermixed with the outcasts of other nations in Caribbean pirate havens such as Port Royal, Jamaica, whose governor protested that the island "subsisted in disorder" and that there was no one "who does not believe himself to be beyond the officers of the King" (Pennell 2001, 169–94).

Piracy was an especially attractive opportunity for the unfree, black and white alike. Creoles and experienced seafarers made particularly adept pirates. Conservative estimates suggest that black and mulatto sailors comprised at least one-quarter of all pirates in the 17th and 18th centuries. Men of color were frequently elected to lead pirate crews and some, like Francisco Fernando of Jamaica, were successful enough to retire as rich men (Pennell 2001, 199–201). Pirate ships were tightly knit communities, and solidarity among the ranks extended across racial lines. When pirate John Cornelius was discovered planning to abandon the black sailors on his ship, a majority of the crew mutinied and elected a new captain (Defoe 1724, 604–5).

A significant number of buccaneers were Irish, usually escaped indentured servants who had been deported to the West Indies—"Barbadoesed"—after the Cromwellian conquest of 1649–53. The plantation experience frequently brought them into common cause with fellow slaves, with whom they led multiple rebellions in the 17th century (Hill 1986). When called upon to help fight the maroons of Jamaica, Irish militiamen joined regiments of free blacks in mass desertions (Campbell 1988, 85–86).

Though women were much less common among pirates than among maroons, they enjoyed greater freedom on the seas. At a 1721 trial in Jamaica, two pirates headed for the gallows—Anne Bonny and Mary Read—were discovered to be pregnant. They had been captured in the midst of a spirited defense of their ship in which only one male crew member assisted them, and they were held in high regard by their fellow crew members: "No Person amongst them was more resolute, or ready to board or undertake any Thing that was hazardous" (Defoe 1724, 156).

Pirates faced an even more difficult flight to freedom than maroons—they first had to get hold of a ship. For most of the 17th century, they could simply join state-sanctioned privateering expeditions. By the early 18th century, however, peace between European powers and distaste for the unpredictable and independent character of the buccaneers meant that outright piracy was the only option. Read first decided to "go on the account" after pirates boarded a Dutch vessel she had been sailing in the Caribbean. Though she briefly retired from the sea and "liv'd quietly on Shore," she returned to piracy after signing onto an English privateering vessel, where she promptly helped lead a mutiny (Defoe 1724, 155–56). Her story represents the experience of most pirates, almost all of whom joined in one of these two ways.

In the 18th century about one in every five pirates was a mutineer, and roughly half of all mutinies ended in the decision to turn pirate. Such mutinies were par-

Figure 9.1 Pirates Ann Bonny and Mary Read. Engraving by B. Cole (1724).

ticularly common on slave ships, which represented the convergence of slavery, colonialism, and maritime labor—the defining institutions of the Atlantic world. In less dramatic fashion, most new recruits were those who, once given the choice, elected to pursue a life of liberty beneath a black flag in place of the poverty and brutality of traditional seafaring in the service of capital and state. These could include not only the crews but also slaves who, though they were sometimes captured as prizes and at other times put to work in subordinate positions, were often released and sometimes joined their liberators as equals. Even when they did not join the crew, slaves were often freed, armed, and left to do justice on their former masters (Rediker 2004, 46–47, 138; Pennell 2001, 183–84, 199–202).

Although the most widely recognized image of piracy is that of a ship flying the infamous black flag, many did not sail under the "Jolly Roger." It came into widespread use only in periods of peace between the European powers, particularly after the 1713 Treaty of Utrecht left thousands of sailors out of work with few other options but to turn pirate on their own behalf (Rediker 2004, 53, 24, 164). Still, the politics of the pirate ship were always concerned more with democracy and equality than with nationalism, and the use of flags or state sanction for their activities could mask the underlying commonalities that united pirates.

Much more important than the colors under which pirates sailed was the way in which they organized their lives. Based on the practices of the early buccaneers, pirates in the 17th and early 18th centuries "'distributed justice,' elected their officers, divided their loot equally, . . . limited the authority of the captain, resisted many of the practices of the capitalist merchant shipping industry, and maintained a multicultural, multiracial, and multinational social order" (Rediker 2004, 16–17, 65). Whether at sea or in port, a pirate could expect to spend most of his days "being daily regal'd with Musick, Drinking, and the Gaiety and Diversions of his Companions" (Defoe 1724 [1999], 244). These rejections of cultural conservatism, political oppression, and economic exploitation resemble the aspirations of maroon societies, and for good reason.

Connections

In 1722 the French Dominican priest Jean-Baptiste Labat wrote that the people of the Caribbean were "all together, in the same boat, sailing on the same uncertain sea." He had lived in the Caribbean for more than a decade at the turn of the century, even sailed among the buccaneers, and he knew well the region and its people. His statement holds most true for the masterless people of the Caribbean— the maroons, pirates, and other commoners who pursued alternative ways of life in an age when capitalism, colonialism, and slavery were prevalent. Beyond sharing common interests and some common values, many masterless communities were actually connected by their opposition to the encroaching imperial powers. Yet conflicts often existed within and between these communities, and the growth of the plantation complex and the expansion of imperial control further complicated this situation. The connections among masterless communities, as well as their diverse relationships to the colonial economy, shaped the course of Caribbean history well into the 18th century.

Among the most important groups in the masterless Caribbean were indigenous commoners—communities of people generally organized on principles of mutual aid, rather than private accumulation, that existed both before and after the conquest period. Though the Cuna of Panama and Colombia had been a relatively hierarchical society before the conquest, they responded to the Spanish invasion by leveling their social order, abandoning metalworking, and organizing their society on principles of subsistence and reciprocity. They welcomed runaway slaves from the Spanish territories and made common cause with the buccaneers, with whom they traded food and supplies for firearms to wage war on the Spanish empire (Wolf 1982, 155–56).

Connections among masterless people had existed since the beginning of colonization; indeed, the solidarity of indigenous commoners with sailors and slaves is implied in the very terms *boucanier* and *cimarrón*. These connections also extended to Spanish commoners who resisted royal officials. Ovando's 1502 mission to Hispaniola carried troops to suppress a rebellion in which Spanish and indigenous laborers had united to halt production in the mines. After coaxing the indigenous leaders into a building with offerings of peace, the Spanish officials burned them alive, hanged their wives, and put 50 Spanish strikers to the sword. And when the Spanish first attempted to put down the *cimarrones* of Panama in 1556, they could find no Spaniards willing to enlist in the effort.

The solidarity among maroons, pirates, and commoners shaped their lives in numerous ways. Conscious of their common lot, pirates routinely referred to their trade as "a marooning life" and gave their ships names like the *Maroon* and the *Murrone Galley*, or referred to them as "maroon periaguas [piraguas, or canoes]" (Rediker 2004, 56, 192n8; Pennell 2001, 202). Even today, a visible artifact of this solidarity survives in the Jamaican practice of jerking meat over a boucan, originally an indigenous tradition that was preserved and passed on to the Jamaican maroons through their exchanges with buccaneers (Carey 1997, 66–76).

Decline

Just as maroon and pirate societies did not exist in isolation from one another, neither did they exist in isolation from the colonial projects of the various empires. By their very nature, both maroons and pirates had arisen out of the colonial economies. The enslavement of Africans gave rise to maroon communities, and the intolerable conditions of seafaring labor generated mutinous crews and pirates. The expansion and intensification of production with slave labor drove more and more slaves to flee their masters, while increases in commerce made piracy more tempting than ever. By the end of the period, these contradictions were forced to a resolution: the economic development of the Caribbean in the 17th century, made possible in part by the actions of maroons and pirates, eventually required the eradication of those same communities.

Buccaneers, active in the small island of Tortuga since at least 1630, played a key role in handing the island decisively to the French in 1640. The island quickly became a hub of pirate activity, both sanctioned and unsanctioned. Further outposts were established on Hispaniola at Port Margot, Port de Paix, and Petit-Goâve, from which the buccaneers expanded their depredations against the Spanish and extended the zone of French control in the western half of the island (Haring 1910, 58–66; Camus 1997). Jamaica itself was conquered only with the combined assistance of maroons and buccaneers. The maroons of Jamaica, who first fled the plantations in large numbers after the English invasion of 1655, were the decisive force in ultimately driving the Spanish from the island. Too racist to acknowledge the contribution of the maroons, the 18th-century historian Edward Long nevertheless conceded in his 1774 account that "it is to the buccaneers that we owe the possession of Jamaica" (Campbell 1988, 14–34). Throughout the mid-17th century, the establishment of non-Spanish colonies in the Caribbean depended in large part on the labor of buccaneers.

Maroons and pirates continued to play important, albeit different, roles in the development of colonies once they were established. To develop large plantations effectively, however, the English had to address the issue of marronage. Though some hostilities continued after the earliest Jamaican maroon treaties of 1663 and 1670, a pair of treaties in March and June 1739 ensured the position of the planters. These treaties were driven almost exclusively by concern for economic development; they regulated the crops and livestock maroons could raise, the areas they could settle, the distances they could travel, and the terms on which they could trade with other colonists (Campbell 1988, 127–63). In their new and more integrated role in the plantation economy, Jamaican maroon communities became a major source of food on the island and even produced some finished goods, such as processed tobacco, that were outside the concern of the large planters (Campbell 1988, 133, 192). Equally significant was the requirement that the maroons turn over runaway slaves who had recently joined them and help suppress rebellions and catch fugitives in the future. By employing maroons in enforcing the boundaries of the plantation, Jamaican planters eliminated the logical base of future maroon support while establishing more complete control over their own work force. The connection between containing maroons and developing sugar plantations was most blatant in islands like Martinique and Guadeloupe, where the bounty for returning runaway slaves was paid in sugar (Price 1996, 113).

The relationship of buccaneers to the colonial economy was even closer than that of the most complicit maroons. Where maroon communities by their very nature existed at a certain distance from colonial society, pirates operated precisely along the most active trade routes and required friendly ports in which to unload their prizes. In the case of Jamaica, piracy was the initial economic base of the colony, and the revenues it generated provided start-up capital that contributed to the development of large-scale capitalist agriculture based on slave labor (Zahedieh 1986). The economic development of western Hispaniola, controlled by the French, was also founded on piracy based out of ports like Petit-Goave and nearby Tortuga (Camus 1997, 75). After Spain formally ceded the territory to France in 1697, the colony of Saint-Domingue went on to become the world center of sugar production in the 18th century. In addition to enriching the local merchants in sympathetic ports, some pirates themselves became quite wealthy. The Frenchman Montauban was one of a number of pirates in the 1690s who enriched themselves first by raiding Spanish commerce and then by investing the profits in sugar plantations (Moreau 2006, 138–40). Alexander Exquemelin, the most famous chronicler of the buccaneers, records that provisions for wounded pirates were made in terms of either money or slaves (Exquemelin 1684, 83–84).

All of this has led some recent scholars to suggest that pirates were in fact prototypical capitalists driven by the values of the market economy and the logic of the invisible hand (Moreau 2006, 127–48; Leeson 2007). Of course not all pirates opposed slavery; not all maroons did either. Pirates operated in a world that was increasingly organized along capitalist lines, but they organized the pirate ship in a very different fashion. They depended for their survival on a network of communal economies, and the pirate ship itself was one of them. When their democratic and egalitarian values were violated, as when Welsh pirate Henry Morgan refused to promise an equal share to all members of a 1665 expedition out of Jamaica, the overwhelming majority of the crews mutinied or deserted (Haring 1910, 129). Also, many pirates had experienced slavery or indenture directly (Rediker 2004, 63–64). If there is some debate among historians about the place of pirates in plantation society, there was no such debate among contemporary planters—in their view, both pirates and maroons were fundamentally incompatible with the imperatives of capitalist plantation slavery.

Maroons and pirates were united, if not by opposition to colonial society, then by opposition from it. Where piracy had once been encouraged, it was now suppressed. Where maroon societies had once been tolerated, they were now subdued or contained. Some, like the pirate-investor Montauban, were able to cash in and rejoin society. Others switched sides, like former maroons who became slave-catchers, or erstwhile buccaneers who enlisted as pirate hunters. Still others faded into the forests and hills of uninhabited areas, returning to hunting and gathering for subsistence, smuggling dyewoods off the coast of Brazil, or panning for salt in the plains of Saint-Domingue and Venezuela. Most often, however, their lives ended violently. At least one-tenth of pirates were executed, and when accounting for other casualties, the number rises to at least one-quarter and perhaps one-half (Rediker 2004, 163). Piracy was largely driven from the Caribbean by 1726, and of the maroon communities that survived the 18th century, only in Jamaica and Suriname do they still recognizably persist. The successful development and expansion of plantation slavery thus depended not only on technological and agricultural advancements, but also on the initial complicity and ultimate suppression of these masterless people who tried to make history on their own terms.

Legacy

In the age of masterlessness, the Caribbean was a place where women and men from all corners of the Atlantic brought together a wide range of ideas and experiences to challenge their masters and prove that another world was possible. The eventual suppression of their efforts in the Caribbean meant the relocation, not the disappearance, of their struggles. The following years witnessed a worldwide dissemination of those values back to Europe and to Africa. The Trelawny Town maroons of Jamaica were deported to Nova Scotia and then Sierra Leone after a year-long rebellion that ended in 1796 (Campbell 1988, 11, 209–49). The former Martinican slave Abraham Samuel went pirating in the Indian Ocean, Arabian Sea, and Persian Gulf before arriving in Madagascar, where he was declared heir to the throne of an African kingdom (Ritchie 1986, 84–85). Samuel was just one of many pirates who shifted their bases of operation to the coasts of Africa, mixing in with the local population and attacking the slave trade or raiding the commerce between Europe and Asia. One gang of pirates settled among the Kru of West Africa, a maritime people who had successfully fought the slave trade on both sides of the Atlantic. As the popular press spread word of their exploits, Caribbean pirates became a presence in literature and the arts. The famous painting of the French Revolution, Delacroix's *Liberty Leading the People*, appears to be based closely on an image that appears on the cover of a volume of stories about Anne Bonny and Mary Read (Rediker 2004, 55–56, 121–26).

Ideas of liberty flowed both ways across the Atlantic, and over time it became increasingly difficult to tell which intellectual currents flowed from which shores. The Jamaican-born Robert Wedderburn, the mulatto son of a slave, traced the English conquest of that island to the defeat of the radicals in the English Revolution. Wedderburn himself moved to England in 1778 but always took inspiration from the maroon freedom struggle. In his correspondence with his half-sister, the maroon Elizabeth Campbell, Wedderburn invoked the oral history of the maroons in letters that convinced her to free her own slaves and redistribute her property. In her replies from Jamaica, Campbell relayed stories of how the freed slaves of the island "are singing all day at work about Thomas Spence," the English radical democrat and advocate of communal land ownership. The sailor William "Black" Davidson, a fellow Jamaican mulatto expatriate in Britain and also an adherent of Spence, protected a pirate flag bearing the inscription "Let us die like Men and not be sold like Slaves" at an 1819 labor demonstration in London (Linebaugh and Rediker 2000, 287–326). Such stories were commonplace in an era when radical ideas, first brought together in the Caribbean, were recirculating around the world.

This legacy was felt in the Caribbean itself. In key moments, rebel slaves went beyond merely escaping colonial society to transforming it. The anticolonial movements that swept Spanish America in the 19th century began in Venezuela in 1810, where maroons were among the first to join in the struggle (Price 1996, 73). In *The General in His Labyrinth*, contemporary novelist Gabriel García Marquez envisions Simón Bolívar himself marching across the countryside carrying a pirate flag, "the skull and crossbones superimposed on a motto in letters of blood: 'Liberty or Death.'" Without a doubt, however, the greatest standard bearer of the masterless legacy was French Saint-Domingue, where in 1791 the slaves rose up against their masters and put the torch to their plantations. They continued their struggle for more than a decade, overthrowing both slavery and colonialism, and established the independent republic of Haiti on New Year's Day 1804. Seeking to convey the fears of planters across the region, the Spanish consul in Philadelphia immediately likened the rebels to "some second buccaneers . . . that will try to light the revolutionary fire in our islands if all of their movements are not surveyed." Though the fears of pan-Caribbean revolution were not realized, Haiti survives as a testament to the women and men who struggled in their own way for freedom in the centuries before and since. The boucan, the central flame around which the earliest maroons, pirates, and indigenous commoners had gathered, was a metaphor for masterlessness not soon forgotten.

WORKS CITED

Campbell, Mavis C. 1988. *The Maroons of Jamaica, 1655–1796: A History of Resistance, Collaboration, and Betrayal.* Granby, MA: Bergin & Garvey.

Camus, Michel Christian. 1997. *L'Ile de la Tortue au coeur de la Flibuste caraibe.* Paris: L'Harmattan.

Carey, Bev. 1997. *The Maroon Story: The Authentic and Original History of the Maroons in the History of Jamaica, 1490–1880.* Gordon Town, Jamaica: Agouti Press.

Defoe, Daniel. 1724 [1999]. *A General History of the Pyrates.* Edited by Manuel Schonhorn. New York: Dover Publications.

Diouf, Sylviane A., ed. 2003. *Fighting the Slave Trade: West African Strategies.* Athens: Ohio University Press.

Exquemelin, A. O. 1684 [1993]. *The Buccaneers of America.* Edited by Robert C. Ritchie. Annapolis, MD: Naval Institute Press.

Hall, N. A. T. 1985. "Maritime Maroons: 'Grand Marronage' from the Danish West Indies." *William and Mary Quarterly* 3rd. ser., 42, no. 4 (October): 476–98.

Haring, Clarence Henry. 1910. *The Buccaneers in the West Indies in the XVII Century.* London: Methuen.

Heuman, Gad J., ed. 1986. *Out of the House of Bondage: Runaways, Resistance and Marronage in Africa and the New World.* London: Cass.

Hill, Christopher. 1986. *The Collected Essays of Christopher Hill,* vol. 3. Brighton: Harvester Press.

James, C. L. R. 1963. *The Black Jacobins: Toussaint L'Ouverture and the San Domingo Revolution.* 2nd ed. New York: Vintage Books.

Leeson, Peter T. 2007. "An-arrgh-chy: The Law and Economics of Pirate Organization." *Journal of Political Economy* 115, no. 6: 1049–94.

Linebaugh, Peter, and Marcus Rediker. 2000. *The Many-Headed Hydra: Sailors, Slaves, Commoners, and the Hidden History of the Revolutionary Atlantic.* Boston: Beacon Press.

Moreau, Jean-Pierre. 2006. *Pirates: Flibuste et piraterie dans la Caraïbe et les mers du sud, 1522–1725.* Paris: Tallandier.

Pennell, C. R., ed. 2001. *Bandits at Sea: A Pirates Reader*. New York: New York University Press.

Perez-Mallaína, Pablo E. 1998. *Spain's Men of the Sea: Daily Life on the Indies Fleets in the Sixteenth Century*. Baltimore: Johns Hopkins University Press.

Pike, Ruth. 2007. "Black Rebels: The Cimarrons of Sixteenth-Century Panama." *The Americas* 64, no. 2 (October): 243–66.

Price, Richard, ed. 1996. *Maroon Societies: Rebel Slave Communities in the Americas*. 3rd ed. Baltimore, MD: Johns Hopkins University Press.

Rediker, Marcus. 2004. *Villains of All Nations: Atlantic Pirates in the Golden Age*. Boston: Beacon Press.

Ritchie, Robert. 1986. *Captain Kidd and the War against the Pirates*. Cambridge, MA: Harvard University Press.

Searing, James F. 2002. "'No Kings, No Lords, No Slaves': Ethnicity and Religion among the Sereer-Safèn of Western Bawol (Senegal), 1700–1914." *Journal of African History* 43: 407–29.

Thornton, John. 1998. *Africa and Africans in the Making of the Atlantic World, 1400–1800*. 2nd ed. New York: Cambridge University Press.

Wolf, Eric R. 1982. *Europe and the People without History*. Berkeley: University of California Press.

Zahedieh, Nuala. 1986. "The Merchants of Port Royal, Jamaica, and the Spanish Contraband Trade, 1655–1692." *William and Mary Quarterly* 43, no. 4 (October): 570–93.

PART **3**

Colonial Designs in Flux

10

The Caribbean between Empires

JOSEP M. FRADERA

Colonists, Pirates, and Slaves

Following the Europeans' arrival, the Caribbean was for centuries a laboratory of far-reaching social and political change. Few places in the world have witnessed so much destruction and political competition. What existed in 1492 hardly survived a century later, and the islands of 1700 did not look very much like those of 1600. The changes that ushered the region into modernity almost destroyed its native societies: between 1492 and 1530, the population of the Antilles was decimated, coming close to extinction.

From that well of violence against the Indians emerged the behaviors that would orient the evolution of unusual colonial societies. Among these was the need to ensure the subsistence of the sailors, *conquistadores,* and colonists transplanted to the Antilles. The Spaniards quickly realized that the high incidence of illness and mortality among these groups stemmed from a chronic scarcity of food, which in turn resulted from the destruction of indigenous agriculture and the perpetual failure of regular provisioning from Spain. The agricultural disaster of the first years had arisen from the disruption of local forms of subsistence—the multi-crop *conucos* (Indian culti-vation grounds) as well as the hunting and fishing activities from which settlers obtained protein—with serious consequences for both the native population and the invaders. The food crisis also resulted from the compulsory transfer of many Indians from agricultural work to alluvial gold extraction. During the early years of experimentation on Hispaniola, all efforts to rationalize labor by distributing the natives among the conquerors via *repartimientos*, and to balance their work between agriculture and mining, failed. The third factor to bear upon colonization was the Spaniards' subjection of the indigenous leaders, or *caciques*. Native leadership was destroyed, dominated, or co-opted with impressive determination. During the occupation of the Vega Real in Hispaniola, the struggle with local chiefs—the most famous of whom was Guarionex—became a test run for the conquerors' strate-gies of dominion. Although the Indians were numerically superior, the Spaniards compensated with aggressively deployed firearms (*arcabuces*), horses, and mastiffs trained to dismember the adversary.

The occupation of Hispaniola, an island that became the epicenter of the Carib-bean, was one facet of Spanish dominion; another was the spread of colonization throughout the region. The discovery and early settlement of new areas, from New-foundland to the Río de la Plata, proceeded at a dizzying rate, with a particular focus on the coast of today's Venezuela and Colombia, Panamá, and the Darién, and the territories of modern-day Honduras and Belize. The objective was twofold: the dis-covery of new areas for expansion, and the capture of slaves to fill the islands' grow-ing population vacuum. The latter strategy responded to the rapid exploration and partial colonization of the remaining Greater Antilles. The search for labor seemed unstoppable, taking the Spaniards to Panama between 1502 and 1511, to Puerto Rico in 1508, to Cuba in 1511, and to Florida—all the way to present-day Georgia (Cape Fear)—from 1513 until the end of the decade.

Agricultural Experiments, Early Slavery, and Imperial Defense

By 1530 the islands were severely depleted of their original inhabitants. The Euro-pean population had also diminished, due to a relative lack of opportunities, the decline of gold mining, and the opening of other attractions on the continent. Also during the 1530s, Spain's rivals—France in particular—began interfering in territo-ries belonging to it under the Treaty of Tordesillas (1494). All these factors gradually altered the forms of territorial occupation, changed the population composition, and generated new economic activities, although they did not impede the drain of colonists toward the continent or the decline of many existing urban centers.

The new colonization strategies began to materialize in the 1520s. The first was linked to the only product on the islands besides gold that had acquired positive economic value: tobacco. Amerindians' consumption of tobacco was widely de-scribed in treatises by Bartolomé de Las Casas and Gonzalo Fernández de Oviedo, among other chroniclers and apologists of the Spanish colonial enterprise. Ship-ments of tobacco to the Iberian Peninsula began almost immediately, attracting the attention of merchants and sailors from Europe and Asia, and particularly from their countries' royal courts. Nevertheless, during the first half of the 16th century, tobacco consumption was limited mainly to sailors on transatlantic routes, which is perhaps why significant changes in the organization of its production would not come until the next century.

The introduction of sugarcane saved the Spanish Caribbean from ruin. This plant of Old World origin was brought to Hispaniola by Columbus on his second voyage, together with other seeds and plants. Unlike tobacco, which could be cultivated on small, dispersed plots, sugarcane depended for its profitability on intensive culti-vation and large-scale processing, and so demanded a significant initial investment of capital. The size of that investment depended essentially on the kind of mill used to press the cane, so a distinction arose between units employing animal force and those using hydraulic energy. Soon the incipient sugar industry was receiving royal concessions in the form of credits, discounts on tithes and tariffs, and judicial relief from debt-induced embargoes.

Adequate labor supplies were necessary for the sugar industry to consolidate, yet Indian labor had begun to be phased out by the 1520s, when a modest sugar economy had taken shape in Hispaniola and Puerto Rico. Although enslaved Afri-cans had been introduced at the beginning of the 16th century, they did not arrive on a regular basis until the second decade. The slave trade was initially unregulated, but in 1513 a licensing system was established to prevent the Portuguese from smug-gling Africans. The number of enslaved workers on Hispaniola grew to some 25,000 in 1550, while the European settler population stood at only 5,000.

Another factor in the transformation of the Spanish Caribbean was its conver-sion into an indispensable base for transatlantic navigation, as official regulation of naval traffic increased between the American continents and Seville, the only port authorized to trade with the colonies. While the continental possessions be-came the core of the empire, the Caribbean declined to the periphery. The empire as a whole was regulated to ensure a constant flow of precious metals from the American colonies: silver and gold were produced mainly in Alto Perú (present-day Bolivia) and New Spain (present-day Mexico)—for European markets. The idea was to reach some price equilibrium between the precious metals sent to Seville and the European goods sent in exchange. This regulation, effectively enforced since the 1530s, reached its peak by the end of the 16th century and lasted until the so-called Bourbon reforms of the late 18th century. The Caribbean possessions were crucial to this system more for strategic than for economic reasons: they were a central part of the chain linking the Spanish peninsula and its distant possessions in the American continents.

The regulations concerning American trade and settlement were established through two institutions. The first was the Casa de Contratación (a sort of chamber of commerce), which since the time of American discoveries had assembled both merchants and royal officers to deal with regulations and tariffs. The second and more important institution was the Consejo de Indias (Board of the Indies), which counseled the king in all matters related to trade, justice, and politics in his overseas dominions. Although northern European countries generally preferred to form private companies to trade and organize emigration to the Caribbean and mainland America, the Spanish monarchy from the beginning controlled all matters concerning its huge overseas possessions.

Formalizing a system of secure maritime routes in the Antilles required facing up to significant challenges. The incursions of French and English pirates, for example, became a growing problem after the 1520s. Preventing their interference with the passage of registered vessels required, first, a system of fortified cities, the most important of which were San Juan de Puerto Rico and San Cristóbal de la Habana, on the islands, as well as Cartagena de Indias, Veracruz, and Portobelo on the continent. An organized fleet system—with annual departures of the merchant marine authorized by the royal maritime authority, along with tariff obligations to meet the growing costs of protection—was not fully realized until the final decades of the 16th century. Before then, navigation between Spanish and American ports took place in a more flexible manner, involving naval departures called "loose registers," single ships authorized to leave Spain without waiting for the rest of the fleet. Until the disastrous Dutch seizure of the 1628 fleet, the regular and secure arrival of Spanish ships at Seville demonstrated that Spain's defenses of its colonial navigation had been quite effective.

Another strategic imperative consisted of reinforcing the Spanish presence on the islands, a requirement that seemed unattainable in light of their depopulation. Only the main ports, like Santo Domingo and (later) Havana, were attractive as passenger destinations. Some smaller cities founded during the gold rush and the initial apportioning of land had been abandoned after 1530. The depopulation was even greater in many rural areas, some of which were literally deserted. Little by little, expeditions to the smaller islands were dropped, with the exception of Trinidad and the Venezuelan coast, which drew occasional explorations for pearls or brazilwood. This neglect allowed the Lesser Antilles to provide refuge to scattered Amerindian societies that survived the disastrous smallpox epidemic of 1518–19, and to fugitive slave communities. Only in the second half of the 16th century did a remote world of small farmers and ranchers emerge in the interior of the Greater Antilles, consisting of the remnants of old settlers, Indians, and blacks, to whom were added Spanish immigrants, primarily from the Canary Islands and Andalusia. This new peasant adaptation was driven by the demand for food in cities through which the fleets passed, but it also thrived on smuggling by sailors and pirates from other countries. A lucrative business of leather exports also arose with the proliferation of wild cattle, the origin of the herds that would dominate the landscapes of Cuba and Hispaniola for centuries to come.

Trade, Plunder, and Settlement

In 1523, the French corsair Jean Fleury sacked the Spanish fleet transporting part of the Aztec treasure that Hernán Cortés had sent to Emperor Charles I of Spain. During the next decade pirates and corsairs, buccaneers and filibusters would acquire a mythic prestige as their attacks on Spanish interests became more common and successful. These attacks had a fundamental objective: to capture the precious metals being transported by Spanish ships. Because corsairs enjoyed state protection, these incidents often sparked conflicts between states. In practice, however, there was no real distinction between their activities and simple piracy. Diplomacy could not prevent this disappearance of the boundary between war and peace. Consequently, the militarization of commerce and the fortification of the ports sustained by it increased the Spanish monarchy's military expenditures. In addition, it was impossible to keep ships from rival countries away from islands that were in utter disarray, and whose only opportunity to adequately supply themselves was by illicit means. Thus, many enslaved Africans arrived on board Portuguese, English, and French ships and were exchanged for skins, tobacco, sugar, and other island products that had been exported to those countries without passing through the monopolistic funnel of the licensed Spanish ports.

It is important to distinguish different phases of engagement between the Spanish world and sailors and merchants from rival countries. From the 1530s, when the French began to take Spain's fleets and Caribbean settlements hostage, the activity of corsairs, pirates, and buccaneers was limited to combined operations of commerce and capture, without any pretense of permanent settlement. The 1560s saw a notable expansion of these activities, dominated by expeditions organized in northern Europe, to the detriment of the "illicit" commerce with Spanish enclaves. Between 1530 and 1570, French pirates were the main scourge of the Spanish possessions. They systematically attacked Spanish ships and looted important towns and cities in Puerto Rico and Hispaniola. The increase in piracy and privateering among the English was linked to the famous disaster of San Juan de Ulúa (1568), in which John Hawkins (with Francis Drake) lost most of his ships and crew; until that point, their expeditions had concentrated on illicit trafficking. The 1580s were dominated by the war between the Spanish and English monarchies, which motivated the 1588 fiasco of the Invincible Armada and the intensification of pirate activity throughout the Caribbean. In those years, the attacks on Spanish ships were systematic and devastating. In turn, the attacks on Spanish port cities such as Cartagena de Indias and San Juan de Puerto Rico became less fruitful, as the Spanish monarchy invested in fortifying them.

These patterns of conflict resulted by 1620 in a kind of spatial separation between imperial zones of influence. Spain surrendered protection of the Guianas and the Leeward Islands; all of the western Caribbean, with the exception of the Bahamas, remained under its control, but the east was opened to occupation by potential rivals. Foreign occupation inevitably ensued. Nevertheless, colonization succeeded only when the geopolitical conflict between empires took an essential strategic turn, moved by the financial and naval interests of the northern European countries. Its most tangible aspect was the unprecedented willingness of these occupiers to establish themselves on the basis of new models of colonization that relied less on predatory attacks on Spanish wealth.

Finding an economic foundation that would guarantee continuing settlement in the region was the key. On that point, French and English tactics were significantly different from those of the Dutch. The Dutch—who arrived late to the Caribbean, but had established the world's preeminent merchant marine—were focused on trading, legally or illegally, with everybody. This strategy required becoming business partners in transatlantic trade and engaging the inhabitants of both the Spanish possessions and the smaller French and English enclaves in the Lesser Antilles, a pattern that intensified when the Portuguese finally drove them out of northeastern Brazil in 1654. As part of this strategy, the Dutch established ongoing contracts with the Spanish for the transport of slaves, salt, and other merchandise to American ports or, from those, to Europe. These transactions apparently did not challenge Spanish sovereignty, as they were conducted on the high seas or from the Canary Islands.

The Dutch sustained these semi-legal forms of commerce by using Curaçao as a base for illicit trade with the islands and the Venezuelan coast. Meanwhile, the West Indian Company (WIC) occupied a set of small possessions, including Saba, St. Eustatius, St. Maarten, Aruba, and Bonaire; the almost depopulated Tobago (between 1628 and 1678); and Suriname, the only Dutch possession that would later become a plantation economy (from 1667). In Curaçao, a group of Spanish and Portuguese Jews with the necessary linguistic skills and good connections in the Atlantic became decisive actors. This model procured for Amsterdam an enormous quantity of precious metals during the middle decades of the 17th century, although in the long term it proved too fragile to resist competition from other countries. Its weakest point lay in the suspicion with which the British and French governments viewed the close commercial connections between their colonial subjects and their Dutch competitors.

Imperial domination in the Caribbean, institutionalized by Oliver Cromwell (1599–1658) in England and Jean-Baptiste Colbert (1619–1683) in France, restricted as much as possible the commercial freedom of the Caribbean colonies, while preventing Holland's access to metropolitan markets through mercantilist measures. This was the logic behind the English Navigation Acts of 1651 and 1660 and the commercial *exclusif* imposed by Louis XIV during the same period in France. Caribbean colonists of all nations resisted these measures, recognizing the importance that the Dutch navy had acquired, for example, in the slave trade, which was one of its principal activities. Between 1674 and 1709, Dutch vessels brought 80,000 enslaved Africans to the islands, just as the sugar revolution was stepping up the demand for labor.

Both in the Caribbean and in North America, the French and English responses focused on organizing associations devoted to cultivation, with sufficient autonomy to adapt and survive in an imperial crossroads. The growing population required a steady supply of food, which Antillean buccaneers and pirates could not satisfy. In the French islands, intensified farming of local products—such as manioc, potatoes, or other root vegetables—forced confrontations with local Indians. Still, under the leadership of Pierre Belain d'Esnambuc, the French established the modest settlement of Saint-Cristophe in 1625 on an island shared with the English, who named it St. Christopher (later St. Kitts). On a greater scale, they occupied Martinique and Guadalupe in 1635, followed soon afterward by the small surrounding islands of Marie Galante, La Désirade, Les Saintes, Dominica, and Grenada. During this expansion the Compagnie des Isles de l'Amérique (1635) was formed to consolidate French interests in the region. Meanwhile, English settlers founded Barbados in 1627 and subsequently established themselves in Nevis, Antigua, and Montserrat.

If food production was a necessary condition for the northern European presence in the Antilles, it was not a sufficient one. At a minimum, attracting new colonists and viable financing for slaves ultimately depended on the capacity to sell some commodity in metropolitan markets. Only native tobacco offered such a possibility. Its potential had already been demonstrated in the Chesapeake region (now Virginia), with seeds carried from Bermuda by John Rolfe. Later, the modest export capacity of the primary islands would be augmented by cotton, ginger, and indigo.

But if establishing a commercial crop in the Caribbean was the key to the consolidation of Spain's longtime adversaries, the logistics of transportation to a good port were not so simple. Developing an agricultural colony implied, first, acquiring rights from the corresponding monarchy, the ultimate proprietor of overseas territories. Those who established charter companies then had to recruit sufficient voluntary or indentured settlers to proceed with the distribution of land. Next, the investors responsible for the new settlements had to ensure the provision of sufficient food, farming equipment, arms, and maritime transport until the colony could sustain itself. Without recourse to private capital, such resources were generally only available through effective state involvement, such as that of the French minister Colbert, who sponsored the Compagnie des Indes Occidentales (1664) as part of an ambitious scheme of colonial politics. Once these requirements were met, the proprietors of the companies decided how to direct the colonizing process and, in the case of the English, elected the first governors of each of the new overseas possessions.

Paradoxically, sugar was a late addition to colonial efforts on the French, English, and Dutch islands. It first caught the attention of colonists in Barbados at the end of the 1630s, but attracted the interest of British importers only decades later. Much of the available knowledge about sugarcane processing at first rested in Dutch hands, thanks to their contact with the Portuguese of northeastern Brazil. Although the historical details of this episode are unclear, the transfer of technology to the English seems to have occurred in Barbados during the 1640s, when local growers were desperately looking for alternate crops for export. From there, sugar cultivation expanded to other English as well as French islands.

As the Spanish had discovered a century and a half earlier, establishing a sugar industry required significant investments. The plantations were large and demanded a great deal of fixed capital and labor. Between 1670 and 1700, the number of enslaved Africans in Martinique expanded from 7,000 to 15,000, while Saint-Christophe possessed about 12,000 at the end of that period. Nevertheless, the figure of 30,000 slaves living in the French Antilles was dwarfed by the estimate of 100,000 slaves living in the British Caribbean. Sugar was the unquestioned engine of this social transformation. The financial and organizational demands of the industry gave rise to a planter class that was very different from the growers of the prior century, who had combined food production with cash cropping. The success of the sugar plantations, with their spectacular increase in disposable income, would plunge the Caribbean into a chronic dependency on food imports.

A Politically Fragmented Caribbean

Two variables subsequently fostered the emergence of a new political geography in the Caribbean: the local dynamics of population substitution and economic transformation, and the relentless struggle between rival empires in the region. Once European colonization had stabilized, the most noteworthy developments were the French and English conquests of one of the Greater Antilles and portions of another.

The French occupation of western Hispaniola occurred first. Some modest French settlement had already appeared there in the 1620s, but without political support from the faraway metropolis. To supplement their activities against the

Spanish, a later generation of buccaneers and filibusters began some subsistence farming and planted the first tobacco fields. Part of this motley group had been expelled from Martinique and Guadeloupe under pressure from the expanding sugar plantations. However, commercial cultivation of any scale did not appear in the French-occupied portions of Hispaniola until the final decades of the 17th century. First came indigo and later—in 1685—the first documented plantation of sugarcane.

The ensuing economic and social transformation, which implied the introduction of slavery, coincided with the Spanish recognition of French sovereignty over that territory in 1697. Although France had sought to establish royal authority there through its financial and military arm, the Compagnie de Saint-Domingue, the multihued colonial world was little accustomed to political constrictions, and even the most effective control on the part of the royal officials did little to diminish French attacks from Saint-Domingue on the Spanish colonies in the Caribbean and on the mainland (Veracruz and Campeche). These attacks were part of a more complex commercial relationship with the Spanish world that combined piracy with the slave trade (through *asientos*, or royal contracts) and extensive smuggling. The capital amassed via these channels was vital for the expansion of indigo and sugar cultivation on the western third of Hispaniola. But in 1698, when the planters and slaves of St. Croix were displaced en masse to the recently legalized French colony of Saint-Domingue, a more complex society began to take shape in that colonial frontier. Open war and pirate attacks diminished in importance, replaced by the construction of more stable societies under the protection of international treaties. By 1715, some 7,000 white colonists and 30,000 slaves of African origin were living on the French part of the island.

The British takeover of Jamaica provides the second important case of a rival incursion into Spanish Caribbean space. In 1654, Cromwell sent a fleet to conquer Jamaica as part of his "Western design." That conquest was a decisive step in the consolidation of the British presence in the Caribbean and the conversion of the region into the economic core of its Atlantic empire. But the revolutionary Puritans did not intend to colonize Jamaica in the style of Barbados and the other Lesser Antilles. Their military strategy contained two fundamental motivations: to weaken the commercial position of the Dutch and to strike a decisive blow upon a crippled Spain's hegemony in the western Caribbean. Indeed, the capture of Jamaica formed part of an ambitious plan to harass the Spanish through piracy, smuggling, and the control of key maritime routes—the same objective cherished a century earlier by the generation of Hawkins and Drake. Nevertheless, the British would have to wait another century to see definitive results, following the Seven Years' War (1756–63).

Within the framework of this plan, Jamaica quickly turned into a refuge for pirates. Port Royal, in particular, enjoyed mythical fame throughout the world as a base of pirate operations, though a powerful earthquake destroyed it in 1692. Of all the pirates plying the waters of the western Caribbean and using Port Royal as their base, Henry Morgan was the most famous, thanks to his looting of Puerto Prín- cipe, Portobelo, Maracaibo, and Panama between 1668 and 1671. Between 1688 and 1690 an attempt by a Scottish company to establish itself in the isthmus of Darien (present-day Panama) ended in failure. For the most part, then, Spanish military strength was still robust enough to expel unwelcome intruders.

But while the occupation of Jamaica was decidedly a military fact, the establish- ment of a colonial society proved to be problematic. Only at the end of the 17th century did an agricultural community begin to take shape there, as expeditionary soldiers were replaced by immigrants from the Lesser Antilles and New England. This conspicuous group of rural landowners posed enormous difficulties when the time came to impose a government under imperial British rule. A delicate balance had to be maintained between a local elected assembly and a governor named in London, along with an elective council formed via co-optation. Conflicts between the imperial government and local interests impeded the stabilization of that gov- ernment formula until 1728, when a satisfactory solution was finally found to the sticky question of colonial finances.

The Treaty of Madrid (1670) attempted to move matters between Spain and Great Britain in a less bellicose direction. Nevertheless, martial hostilities through- out the Spanish system had consequences far beyond the conflicts themselves. For reasons both external and internal, the Spanish proved unable to reestablish the previous order in the final decades of the 17th century. Beginning in 1680, their system of fleets and galleons ceased to function; it would not operate smoothly again until after the War of Spanish Succession (1701–1713), and then only within a changed economic and political context. This change meant that supplies to American consumers were falling increasingly into the hands of foreign contraband traders. Among the most serious disruptions in the transoceanic system of naviga- tion, the vacuum opened by French smugglers (in particular Bretons of Saint-Malo) along the Pacific coast was certainly unprecedented. The conflicts between the European powers continued without truce into the final stretch of the 17th century, and Spain became immersed in them.

France's war against the so-called Grand Alliance (England, Spain, Holland, and the Holy Roman Empire), which culminated in the Treaty of Ryswick in 1797, helped consolidate the new balance of forces in the Caribbean region. The treaty affirmed England's right to establish itself and conduct commerce throughout the Lesser Antilles, all the way to the northern coast of Trinidad—a key possession for control of the black market with northern South America. It also established the border between the French and Spanish on Hispaniola, a problematic question that would reappear in the 1770s and 1790s. Spain withdrew to the remaining Greater

Antilles and allowed its rivals to stabilize their colonies in the rest of the Caribbean, from the British Bahamas to Dutch Curaçao, French Saint-Domingue, and British Jamaica. Coerced into accepting its rivals' capacity to settle and conduct business in areas not yet occupied by Europeans, Spain's pretensions of regional hegemony came to an end. But despite the conflicts and treaties that seemed to continue without respite through the 18th century, a new situation had become manifest by the end of the 17th. Areas of interest had been delimited, and international compromises that affirmed the power of the imperial states to defend that order had been agreed to. In consequence, the space for uncontrolled occupation and piracy had diminished appreciably.

When new hostilities broke out between France and Great Britain during the War of Spanish Succession, they only deepened this new order by temporarily suspending Spain's ability to control its imperial space. The Treaty of Utrecht (1713) ended the war with a victory for the French candidate to the Spanish throne, and it forced Spain to compensate Great Britain with extraordinarily generous concessions in colonial commerce. This in turn earned for Great Britain—or more precisely, for its Royal African Company—the *asiento de negros*, a monopoly over the Spanish colonial slave trade, for the next 30 years, during which it would be allowed to import 4,800 Africans annually into Spanish America. In addition, Britain gained the right to a special commercial permit, formalized in 1716, by which the South Sea Company was authorized to introduce 500 tons of merchandise into protected American markets once a year. Both concessions were mortal blows to the exclusive monopoly over transatlantic navigation that Spain had defended since the 16th century at the cost of remaining at the periphery of the slaving outposts along the African coast. They also implied direct and legal contact between the traders and officials of the British navy and the *criollo* buyers of the Spanish American dominions—something that had previously happened only in the years immediately preceding and during the war, when the Spanish forces were at their weakest.

Spanish authorities greatly feared the risk of trade deregulation, but it took them more than a decade to formally respond to these concessions. Checked by other reform projects, their plan to resurrect the fleet system and control commerce—the well-known *proyecto de flotas y galeones* (fleet and galleons plan), prepared by José Patiño—was finally made known in 1720. An effort to regain the effectiveness lost during the 1600s, this plan included a reconsideration of the tariffs that burdened trade so that they would not clash with the international compromises entered into by the monarchy during the war years.

By the beginning of the 18th century, the Caribbean had thus been divided into distinct areas of European influence and had become one of the preferred—and permanent—theaters of conflict between empires. This pattern was eloquently demonstrated by the War of Jenkins' Ear (1739–48) and the Seven Years' War (1756–

63) even before North American independence further altered the political map in the 1770s. The plantation economy and slavery on a grand scale extended these trends even further in time. When Saint-Domingue's crisis in 1791 brought echoes of the French Revolution to the region, it revealed a terrible disjunction between European and Caribbean societies. In a very succinct and dramatic way, it presaged a march toward total collapse, given the inherent contradictions of a model of growth that could be sustained only through omnipresent violence over hundreds of thousands of slaves who performed the vast majority of labor in the colony.

Translation by Lisa M. Simeone

11

Imperial Decline, Colonial Adaptation

FRANCISCO A. SCARANO

The Spanish Islands during the Long 17th Century

In the late 16th century, irruptions by France and Britain into the Caribbean region put an end to Spain's hegemony. Stretched by an empire too vast to administer effectively, its sea power challenged and compromised, this once-dominant power hunkered down, using its Caribbean islands' small populations and meager resources to advance its defensive goals. Foremost among them was protecting its New World wealth from foreign aggressors, ensuring that its silver-laden fleets made their way safely back to the Iberian Peninsula. Thus, after the 1570s, a "bunker mentality" of sorts permeated Spain's Caribbean officials and subjects, doubtless encouraged by Spain's turn toward an overtly militaristic posture in the region.

The effects of these changes on the Spanish islands were profound. With the important exception of western Cuba, by the early years of the 17th century the Spanish Caribbean population had fallen to critically low levels, commercial traffic with the metropole had slowed down, and high-value agricultural activities such as sugar production had given way to lower-value economic enterprises such as subsistence farming, logging, ginger production, and cattle hunting. A local peasantry adapted to the new conditions had emerged as a prominent rural social type. The era of imperial declension (ca. 1580 to 1700, here called the "long 17th century") had played a major role in shaping local peasant traditions and fashioning the distinctive cultural expressions that would distinguish Spanish Caribbean cultures for centuri

nuye
-mineral-rich + dense populated regions overshadowed disease-ridden mineral-depleted + hurricane-prone
-Spain's rivalries incr. shaped the regions destiny

Backgr

Along w … Greater Antilles (Hispaniola … inal nucleus of Spain's New W … the 1490s to the 1510s marked … mericas. In the 1530s, howeve … gradually fell into imperial d … nerica and the Andes. ✱These h … ntually overshadowed the dise … ands. Once the latter's gold de … ained after a phase of intense … ducers of agricultural exports—primarily sugar—and to make their territories a destination for tens of thousands of enslaved Africans.

For a long time after the eclipse of the sugar economy and the emergence of the "bulwark colonies" at the end of the 16th century, Spain's rivalries in the Caribbean increasingly shaped the region's destiny. England, France, and Holland took turns placing Spain on the defensive and, in the case of the first two countries, overtaking large portions of its insular Caribbean territories, with the English occupation of Jamaica in 1655 and the unavoidable concession of Saint-Domingue (the western third of Hispaniola) to France in 1697. After 1580 the paramount imperative for Spain remained the defense of its principal colonies in order to protect vital trade routes—the silver trail—from foreign intrusion. While such efforts would meet with limited success, they helped frame the conditions that forced Spanish Caribbean settlers to adapt and forge distinctive societies and cultures.

In the broad sweep of Spanish Caribbean history between 1580 and 1700, then, the themes of imperial decline and cultural adaptation are like two sides of a coin. Such decline stemmed in part from Spain's economic, demographic, and military disaster which began under Philip II, foretold by the defeat of the Invincible Armada in 1588. More fundamentally, it was an expression of a basic realignment that occurred in European capitalism as the economies of the Low Countries and England—and, to a lesser extent, France—began to outpace those of the Italian city-states, Spain, and Portugal. The epicenter of the European economy, now fed by the wealth of the Atlantic (including ~~~~~~ ~~~~~~ from the Mediterranean to Europe's northwest.

In the Spanish Caribbean, imperia ~~~~~~~~~~ By the mid-17th century, the Caribb ~~~~~~~~ had existed before. These borders v ~~~~~~~~ sides of the frontiers laid down by E ~~~~~~~~ prohibitions to interact with their ~~~~~~~~ settlements, now fairly isolated fr ~~~~~~~~ came more racially mixed as they ~~~~~~~~ ant peasantry. These conditions o ~~~~~~~~ adaptations that blended artifacts ~~~~~~~~ Amerindian, African, and Europe ~~~~~~~~ gave rise to the vibrant Cuban, D ~~~~~~~~ servable to this day.

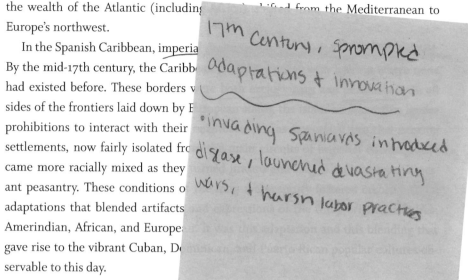

17th Century, prompted adaptations + innovation

°invading Spaniards introduced disease, launched devastating wars, + harsh labor practices

Vagaries of Decline

By 1580, after more than eight decades of European colonization, the physical and human landscapes of the Greater Antilles had been profoundly transformed. The invading Spaniards had introduced diseases, launched devastating wars, and devised harsh labor practices that disrupted indigenous societies. As a result, the aboriginal population, though not exterminated as many have claimed, was nonetheless decimated. At the same time the introduction of new animals, plants, and pathogens from Europe, Africa, and Asia profoundly altered insular landscapes and ecologies. The four settled and politically organized Spanish Caribbean islands saw the most far-reaching changes attendant on this "Columbian exchange" (Crosby 1973). Accounts from the middle decades of the 16th century describe hundreds of thousands of wild animals roaming freely across these mostly wooded, mountainous territories. A small settler group largely comprising enslaved Africans and the mulatto and mestizo offspring of unions between Africans, Indians, and Europeans organized expeditions, called *monterías*, to hunt down these animals for their hides, which were a much sought-after commodity in Europe.

At the beginning of the long 17th century, an aggregate of several dozen sugar-cane mills called *ingenios* still operated on the four islands. The epicenter of this activity was the city of Santo Domingo, the southern capital of Hispaniola. In neighboring Puerto Rico, the majority of ingenios were located along river valleys close to San Juan, where transportation costs were lower. In western Cuba, the area around Havana was only then beginning to see the development of sugar ingenios that supplied the growing port city with a key dietary staple. Elsewhere in Cuba, the eastern cities of Santiago and Bayamo contained a small number of sugar mills, as did the more dense Spanish settlements in Jamaica. Enslaved Africans, by now the predominant laborers in sugar, had become a population majority on all four of these islands.

The decline of the sugar complex after 1580 did not uniformly spell demographic doom. Santo Domingo, Puerto Rico, and Spanish Jamaica likely saw a flat population curve for some time after the turn of the 17th century, although the proportion of enslaved persons declined with time. Any upward movement in the population was usually followed by a smallpox epidemic or other catastrophe, like an earthquake or a hurricane, which increased mortality and shrunk the overall number yet again. Santo Domingo and Puerto Rico likely saw their lowest population numbers during the last third of the 17th century. In Cuba, however, the curve was noticeably different: the year 1540 may have witnessed its lowest population total after the European invasion. Cuba experienced a gradual recovery thereafter, most par-tic_____ around Havana, a city that steadily expanded and eventually be-ca_____tern regions of Cuba settled ea_____graphic stagnation followed b_____as fate of the coastal city of S_____mo, which had Cuba's most s_____the conquest. By 1700 these _____not numbers that challenged _____arge enough to suggest that in _____significant population growth

> *handwritten note:*
> – *countryside = most sig.*
> – *early settlers had established certain kinds of farms + ranches*
> ↳ *economic lives built*

_____life in the Caribbean, the coun-_____mic and cultural developments took place during the long 17th century. Even as the plan to export high-value staples came up short in the late 16th century, the colonists still looked to the land for subsistence. For this purpose they relied on agrarian units created during the conquest. While the early settlers had established certain kinds of farms and ranches with the intention of supplementing the cash economy, many of their descendants built their economic lives around these farm types. The agrarian regime they created was the crucible of the new creole cultures clearly in evidence by the late 1500s.

To feed the colonists and produce goods for export, the Spanish crown and its insular representatives had distributed huge extensions of land among leading individuals and families soon after the conquest. Those whose social status fell short of that of the conquistadores had received smaller grants that sometimes were farther away from markets or port cities, but were of significant size nonetheless. Although population densities were minimal, by the 1550s the most desirable lands had been deeded to the colonists (often only with usufruct rights) according to formulas that privileged peninsula-born Spaniards and other white settlers. The largest grants had been for *hatos*—immense, unfenced circular farms dedicated to cattle grazing. These hatos occupied a leading role in the colonial venture, since animal husbandry had been associated with aristocracy in medieval Spain. By the late 16th century, the hundreds of hatos on the islands created a peculiar landscape full of circular and often overlapping farms (see figure 11.1). Although the colonists at first had considered these farms to be accessories to the sugar ingenios, by the 1600s they were the backbone of the rural economy, supplying meat to the population, providing hides for export, and generating goods that were coveted by foreign smugglers, such as cattle, hides, tallow, and timber. Jamaica marked an important exception to this trend, however. Most of the hatos the Spaniards had carved in the southern half of the island, commercially connected to nearby Cartagena and faraway Spain in an earlier period, later fell victim to labor shortages. By the early 1600s, many had been abandoned and Spanish Jamaicans had gone back to the practice of hunting cattle "the whole year . . . killing cows and bulls only to get hides and the fat, leaving the meat wasted" (Otto 1986, 119n18).

Interspersed among the hatos were smaller, enclosed cattle farms called *corrales*. Although much smaller than the hatos, they were not necessarily less productive, as experience showed that it was better to raise cattle and other animals in contained areas rather than on the open range. On the corrales, the colonists also grew pigs and smaller animals, such as goats and sheep. Further down this scale of farming units were thousands of *estancias* and *conucos* (the Taino name for a manioc field), smaller farms dedicated to raising crops, from manioc and various other starchy root vegetables to maize, rice, beans, plantains, bananas, citrus fruits, pineapples, and other staples. In terms of ownership and modes of operation, the estancias and conucos were diverse. Some, usually in the vicinity of major cities and towns, belonged to members of patrician families who ma[...] other commercial farm, with enslaved Africans ar[...] most of the labor. But in locations farther from urb[...] self-contained units focused on satisfying the fami[...] consisted primarily of family members and only r[...] focused on subsistence farming, *estancieros* occasio[...] for imports introduced clandestinely by foreigners.[...]

An already wide gulf between city and countr[...] the 17th century. As foreigners and Caribs threate[...] carrying out repeated attacks on virtually all coas[...] ish monarchy spent millions of pesos beefing up [...]

Figure 11.1 Map of Cuban *hatos* and *corrales*. 20th-century drawing based on 17th-century information. Source: Ricardo V. Rousset, *Historia de Cuba* (Harama, 1918).

complex array of forts, tunnels, sentinels, and ramparts built by enslaved Africans and paid for with subsidies (*situados*) from the Mexican viceroyalty (see figure 11.2). The cities' enclosure within enormous walls and the attendant development of a mindset among city dwellers that saw danger lurking outside the urban perimeter ("for the Dutchman will carry me away," as a contemporary Puerto Rican axiom put it) opened a breach between the casual folkways of rural inhabitants and the regimented customs of the city, which were more attuned to those of Spain. Not only did European-descended groups see fit to affirm their privileged origins now

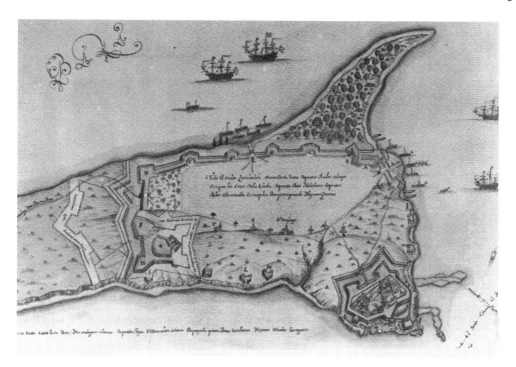

Figure 11.2 Plan of San Juan, Puerto Rico, in 1673, showing the defensive walls around the urban perimeter. Drawing by Luis Venegas Osorio (1678).

more than ever, but they were often surrounded by scores of soldiers whose very presence guaranteed those privileges. In fact, transient troops stationed in these outposts often made up the single largest social grouping in a particular town, and their habits of consumption and entertainment gave the walled-in cities the flavor of military compounds surrounded by people eager to cater to their needs. Civilians and soldiers needed each other.

Beyond the *murallas* or walls, a different set of developments marked the countryside's evolution. As life there concentrated almost exclusively on hatos, corrales, and estancias or conucos, the sharp social distinctions of the early colonial period partially broke down, giving way to more fluid interactions across the boundaries of race and class. The institution of slavery, for one, became less attractive as a means to extract and purvey labor. The extensively run hatos and the subsistence activities prevalent elsewhere relied preferentially on free workers; slaves were too expensive, and in any case were ill-suited to the labor processes of those largely precapitalistic enterprises. Thus, while Spain had made the Caribbean islands the epicenter of its African slave imports in the middle decades of the 16th century, by the 17th century the bulk of this trade had moved to the city of Cartagena, which became the most important slave entrepôt in Spanish America. But African slaves were not the only ones whose numbers dwindled; the number of Spaniards who arrived via the regular immigration channels also declined, though soldiers and sailors were the exception.

As immigration from the Old World diminished, higher proportions of the inhabitants were born and raised in the colonies. These folks bore the appellation of *criollos* or creoles, a word used indiscriminately to signify both enslaved and free people born in the New World. A stepped-up rate of manumission, an increased free population of color, and a higher proportion of free to enslaved people of African descent were among the other consequences of these trends. Naturally, under these conditions a more casual attitude toward racial difference emerged, along with a higher rate of sexual unions across racial lines and higher numbers of mixed offspring. Consonant with this, many native-born people of the Spanish Caribbean became more sharply aware that the largely creole cultures around them—amalgams of African, Taino, and European beliefs, practices, and traditions—were fundamentally distinct from their own original cultural roots. In the Spanish Caribbean's long 17th century, then, the variegated creole population began to develop a sense of itself as an ethnic community separate from those of the Spanish metropole and the population's other constituent groups, native or imported.

Far from the fortified cities and relatively isolated from the imperial state and the Catholic church, its stalwart ally, communities throughout the Spanish Caribbean engaged in numerous forms of unsanctioned behavior. The church preached against *matrimonios desiguales*—or marriages between racial non-equals—to no avail. Disobedience also took many other forms. Enslaved persons fled to isolated, mountainous areas, and from their maroon communities (*palenques*) they harassed people living in non-nucleated settlements as well as in villages and towns. Cattle ranchers who resented laws that forced them to bring a fixed number of head each year to city markets, to be sold at prices fixed by the local governments, underreported their herds or sold their animals through illegal channels. Most important, rural denizens violated commercial exclusivism—the prohibition against trading with non-Spaniards without a special permit—and freely exchanged with foreigners the "land's bounty," along with some of the cash that arrived to sustain the military. European goods obtained through contraband were often cheaper and of better quality than those bought only irregularly from Spain. Contraband relations expanded during the second half of the 17th century. In fact, smuggling became so commonplace that it was carried out not only in remote locations but in plain sight of government and Church officials, often with these high-ranking officers involved in it or at the top of the contraband pyramid themselves.

Spanish policies to thwart contraband produced awkward results—indeed, the opposite of what was intended. As more foreigners filled the sea lanes around the Spanish-held islands in the late 16th and early 17th century, for instance, and the issue of contraband relations with them became increasingly sensitive, officials adopted policies that reduced, rather than protected or augmented, the effective radius of colonization. The most dramatic example of this came between 1603 and 1605 on Hispaniola. In this underpopulated colony's northern and northwestern stretches, known as the Banda Norte, colonists had frequent contacts with French, English, and Portuguese corsairs, to whom they sold most of their cattle and from whom they obtained valuable goods. These exchanges were so beneficial that some residents of the southern city of Santo Domingo moved their herds to the Banda Norte just to sell them to foreigners. Concerned about a hemorrhage of the colony's resources, in 1603 authorities in Madrid approved a plan hatched by Baltasar López de Castro to remove all Spanish subjects and their herds from the Banda Norte and concentrate them closer to Santo Domingo, the capital city. The forced resettlement was carried out in 1605–6 under Governor Antonio de Osorio. Most people protested, and some rebelled. A lot of cattle escaped into the wilderness instead of being safely transported south, and ultimately the ruinous policy did not discourage the foreigners' presence or contain contraband. On the contrary, the coerced removal of settlers, many of whom were free people of African or mixed-race descent, left a huge flank of the colony, north and west, open to foreign penetration and eventual colonization, first by multiethnic groups of buccaneers and later by French settlers. It also failed miserably to stimulate greater exports through Santo Domingo. More than any other set of policies and events in the colonial Caribbean, then, the failed reconcentration on Hispaniola in 1605—aptly remembered as *las devastaciones de Osorio*, or Osorio's devastations—symbolized Spain's utter failure to contain contraband and thwart foreign interloping and settlement.

Havana and San Juan: A Caribbean Counterpoint

As large stretches of the Greater Antilles were falling into general decline and had begun to look inward, giving rise to the peculiar creole cultures one associates today with the Hispanophone Caribbean, one city—Havana—was experiencing unparalleled growth and prosperity. In effect, one of the few Spanish Caribbean success stories of the long 17th century was Havana's conversion into a major maritime outpost, a dynamic, multicultural center where goods and people from distant lands built an emerging mercantile capitalism. With this change, the economic and demographic epicenter of the Spanish Caribbean moved decisively from the old colonial capital of Santo Domingo to western Cuba. Havana's growth, laggard at best until about 1590, would be unstoppable after that year. Historians have often remarked how, in economic prowess and cultural achievement, western Cuba became more like a continent than an island. By the end of the 18th century, Havana, this capital of "continental Cuba," was the third most populous city in the Americas and a crucial link connecting the main elements of Spain's dispersed overseas empire. The demographic and economic growth that fueled its ascent began around the middle of the 16th century and continued in spurts throughout the long 17th century.

Historian Alejandro de la Fuente and his collaborators (2009) have narrated in great detail the story of Havana's emergence as the most important of Spain's Caribbean maritime cities, initially rivaled in importance only by Cartagena. Beginning in the second half of the 16th century, Havana emerged as the crossroads of three key trading circuits in the Spanish Atlantic: the transatlantic trade, the intercolonial trade between various ports in the Spanish circum-Caribbean region, and the intra-colonial trade connecting various Cuban ports with the island's principal commercial hub. The first of these trading circuits funneled large amounts of silver from the continental colonies and some American staples such as sugar, tobacco, indigo, and hides toward Europe in exchange for manufactures, foodstuffs, wine, and enslaved Africans. The second circuit, the intercolonial, grew in importance as Spain's fleet system of transatlantic navigation (the so-called Carrera de Indias) became more developed. It connected the more marginal ports in the Caribbean, usually bypassed by Spanish ships, with the Atlantic routes. The third circuit, to and from the Cuban interior, linked Havana to the outside world as both supplier and market. Because the forces that made up Cuba's great maritime city were so far-flung and diverse, and because the people who built the city also hailed from diverse corners of the Atlantic world, referring to Havana as one of the few "Atlantic communities" seems justified.

The three mercantile systems that converged in Havana interconnected with each other in the city's harbor, a large, deep, well-protected port capable of accommodating dozens of vessels at a time. It was one of the two or three best harbors in the Caribbean and, considering its proximity to the Gulf Stream, easily the best located. During the second half of the 16th century, Havana's window to the sea would be made virtually impregnable by the construction of three forts (one at each side of the bay's entrance, and one closer to the main docks) as well as an underwater chain at the harbor's entrance to interrupt traffic whenever necessary. This defensive complex was highly successful and—as the English corsair Francis Drake found in 1586—could be so formidable that it discouraged even the most daring aggressors from attacking the city.

The intersection of key vectors of commerce, navigation, and migration at the city's doorsteps gave Havana an unequalled economic vitality while promoting demographic growth and social diversity. The city's free population grew from about 38 *vecinos* or heads of households (implying a total free population of approximately 250 persons) in 1558 to 60 vecinos (400 persons) in 1570 and 500 to 600 vecinos (3,500 to 4,000 persons) in the first decade of the 17th century—and, again, to a total population of 27,000 by 1700. The city's population would eventually include a large contingent of enslaved Africans, although during the early stages of this cycle the enslaved population of the city grew rather slowly, and its African population, at first, was not as significant as in rural areas of the Caribbean where slaves were put to work on sugar plantations. By the 1590s, however, the transatlantic slave trade began supplying the city with several thousand additional Africans per decade, a number that seems to have remained fairly steady at the beginning of the next century. In addition to the African population, much of it enslaved, the city boasted an array of European immigrants (many from Spain, of course, but some also from Portugal). Most Spanish settlers came from Andalusia, the Canary Islands, and Castile—a pattern of immigration that still mirrored the earliest waves of settlers in the Caribbean after the conquest.

As an Atlantic city, Havana gradually became a Spanish Caribbean anomaly in several ways. First, it became a thriving port that drew strength from Spain's increasing presence as a precious-metal producer in the European system at a time when other port cities in the region were becoming more inward-looking and less cosmopolitan. It also bred a social order more hierarchical than those of smaller cities: Havana's elite was ethnically more diverse, economically more dynamic, and in its business orientation more akin to other Atlantic hubs like Seville, Cartagena, and Veracruz. As its prosperity grew, Havana's elite drew more resources from the agriculturally rich hinterland, from which it obtained goods, including sugar, that later were sold via Atlantic networks. Local fortunes grew enough in the 17th century so that some *habanero* families purchased titles of nobility and imitated in the Caribbean the lavish lifestyles of the Spanish aristocracy. The *habanero* elite stood at the pinnacle of a society profoundly stratified by class, status, and race—a socio-racial hierarchy that in its well defined and protected social spaces was not quite replicated in any other Spanish Caribbean city.

If, in its vitality amid the relative poverty of the 17th-century Spanish Caribbean, Havana occupied one extreme, San Juan stood at the opposite end of the spectrum. A heavily fortified bastion governed by military men, it was the only port in Puerto Rico authorized to engage in direct trade with the metropole. When contacts with the mother country were frequent, as in the final quarter of the 16th century, this arrangement had worked relatively well. After 1625 or so, however, the monopoly trading system collapsed and Puerto Rico was thrust essentially to the margins of Spain's Atlantic trading circuits. Between 1651 and 1675, reportedly only nine ships left Seville, the Spanish peninsula's single designated port for colonial trade, for San Juan. As commercial relations with Spain came to a virtual halt, the colonists in Puerto Rico were forced to rely on contraband. These contacts, illegal but commonplace, drew them into a web of trade relations that was centered in the Danish and British islands to the east and south. Thus, contrary to Havana, the Atlantic port city par excellence, San Juan had become a regional port city where life centered on the contraband relations that thrived at the imperial margins and in proximity to foreign colonies.

Still, this poor, underpopulated city on the eastern edges of the Spanish empire, surrounded by impressive walls and guarded by a massive fort (San Felipe del Morro) at the entrance to the bay, was racially stratified and hierarchical in ways reminiscent of Havana, although it was less residentially and socially segregated. Whites (whether rich or poor), free people of African descent, and enslaved persons cohabited in many of the *barrios* into which the city's small footprint was divided. San Juan's landholding and commercial elites were clearly poorer than those of Havana or even Santo Domingo, although many foreign observers remarked on their aristocratic aspirations and claims to racial purity. In 1673, when a census counted 1,794 persons older than 10 years of age, not including soldiers, an unusually high number (820, or 46%) were classified as white, 662 (or 37%) were enslaved blacks, and 312 (or 17%) were free blacks or people of mixed descent. This made for a large white population, one observes, but still a majority of nonwhites. Perhaps because of the emigration of men, the immigration of women, or a combination of both trends, women outnumbered men in San Juan two to one, a proportion that was steady across the three socioracial groupings. This pattern stands in sharp contrast to those of other Caribbean cities, both Spanish and British, where males predominated, but it conforms to a pattern found in 18th-century New Orleans, where the putative greater "polish" of foreign men squeezed local men out of the "marriage market" and may have led them to emigrate (Stark 2008). The excess of women over men in San Juan also reflected the military character of the city, which, like Havana in an earlier era, provided ample employment to women in the service economy.

Conclusion

In 1701, European powers went to war over the question of who would succeed the feeble Charles II of Spain. In the Spanish Caribbean colonies, the monarchy's subjects found themselves in a drastically changed regional context. During the 17th century, Spain's leading rivals had been busy colonizing the Lesser Antilles, the western third of Hispaniola, and the island of Jamaica, thus weakening the Catholic country's one-time stranglehold over the region. But Cuba, two-thirds of Hispaniola, and Puerto Rico remained firmly in Spanish hands, and despite the relative weakness they had endured during the past century, these colonies were now poised to slowly begin recovering and even prospering again. Beyond the security afforded by Spanish fortresses, soldiers, and weapons, the colonies' sources of strength now included an array of creole cultures deeply rooted in the violence, negotiations, compromises, and intimacy that had taken place between the native populations and several immigrant groups of African and European origin. Those creole cultures were found both in urban and rural milieus, but it would be from the latter that their most distinct and lasting features would emerge. The Dominican *monteros* and *campesinos*, the Puerto Rican *jíbaros*, and the Cuban *guajiros* and *vegueros*—creole cultural types that for two centuries or more would be held up as prototypes or symbols of those countries' respective ethnic communities—all emerged from the unsettled conditions prevalent between 1580 and 1700. For a period long regarded by historians as a "blank slate" (Gelpí Baíz 2000)—a little-understood middle period of the islands' history—the emergence and lasting influence of these social types is a powerful reminder that the Spanish Caribbean's long 17th century was far from uneventful.

WORKS CITED

Crosby, Alfred W. 1973. *The Columbian Exchange: Biological and Cultural Consequences of 1492.* Westport, CT: Praeger.

De la Fuente, Alejandro, with César García del Pino and Bernardo Iglesias Delgado. 2009. *Havana and the Atlantic in the Sixteenth Century.* Chapel Hill: University of North Carolina Press.

Gelpí Baíz, Elsa. 2000. *Siglo en blanco: Estudio de la economía azucarera en el Puerto Rico del siglo XVI (1540–1612).* San Juan: Editorial de la Universidad de Puerto Rico.

Marrero, Leví. 1975. *Cuba: Economía y sociedad*, vol. 3. Madrid: Playor.

Otto, John S. 1986. "The Origins of Cattle-Ranching in Colonial South Carolina, 1670–1715." *South Carolina Historical Magazine* 87, no. 2 (April):117–24.

Stark, David M. 2008. "'There Is No City Here, but a Desert': The Contours of City Life in 1673 San Juan." *Journal of Caribbean History* 42, no. 2: 255–89.

12

The Atlantic Framework of 17th-Century Colonization

ALISON GAMES

By the turn of the 17th century, Spain's European rivals had a mixed record in their efforts to dislodge the Spanish from the Caribbean. For all the aborted French, Dutch, and English settlements on the circum-Caribbean mainland and pirate bases nestled along well-protected coasts, Spain still held sway in the Americas and the Caribbean. But in the 1620s, Spain's rivals began to expel the Spanish from territory they had long claimed and often occupied in the western Atlantic, and the Caribbean was central to that process. The English took St. Christopher (1624), Barbados (1627), Nevis (1628), Providence (1630), Antigua (1632), Montserrat (1632), and Jamaica (1655) while the French claimed portions of the Spanish colony of Santo Domingo (1641), Saint-Christophe (1625), Guadeloupe (1635), and Martinique (1635). The Dutch focused less on land than on commerce, but they, too, established permanent claims to St. Martin (1631), Curaçao (1634), St. Eustatius (1635), and Saba (1640) in addition to Aruba and Bonaire (1634). Some of these islands (like Jamaica) were wrested from Spanish control, while others had been unclaimed or abandoned by Spain, and were either bereft of human occupation (like Barbados) or settled by Carib Indians who, despite initial violent resistance to European invasions, were ultimately restricted to Dominica and St. Vincent by 1660. And some, such as St. Martin and St. Kitts, were shared, in one of the distinctive features of settlement in the region.

All of this European activity was part of multipronged global efforts by Spain's rivals to challenge Iberian hegemony on the North American mainland, on the coast of central Africa, in the Indian Ocean, and in the Caribbean itself. This chapter explores the Atlantic context that explains how and why northern Europeans were able to succeed in settling the Caribbean starting in the 1620s, and it concludes by addressing the Atlantic context of the Caribbean region's major transitions in the 1650s and 1660s. If European affairs shaped the initial settlement of the Caribbean and redefined its geopolitics, the Caribbean had by the mid-17th century become more tightly enmeshed in a web that included Africa and the American mainland.

Northern European ascendancy in the 17th-century Caribbean was primarily a story of Spanish weakness. Where previously Spain had had the financial reserves to build fortifications and staff them with sufficient armies to fend off rivals, and also to destroy interlopers who dared settle in Spanish territory (as the French had attempted in Florida in the 1560s), the general economic crisis that hit Europe in the early 1600s especially weakened Spain. Forced to prioritize defense spending, Spain focused its energies on its many wars in Europe, leaving Caribbean defenses to flag (Klooster 1997). At the same time England, the Netherlands, and France each enjoyed a brief interlude of internal peace, with the period's vicious religious wars over for a while. These three nations were even at peace with Spain—although, significantly, they did not recognize Spain's exclusive right to the West Indies, the region "beyond the line" or outside the boundaries of European treaties.

The United Provinces, which were not immediately affected by the economic crisis, were in an especially advantageous position, and in the early 1600s they made aggressive inroads in Brazil (seizing Pernambuco and Recife in 1630 from the Portuguese), in North America (establishing their first settlement in New Netherland in 1624), and on the African coast (seizing Elmina from the Portuguese in 1637). They were highly motivated to strike against the Spanish. In 1566, the Dutch had revolted against the Spanish Habsburgs who controlled the Netherlands. The rebellion merged with religious grievances in this age of deeply contested religious affiliations; the northern provinces tended to be Protestant, the southern provinces Catholic. The Caribbean figured in this mix at first in an indirect way. As the Dutch cast about for ways to critique their Spanish rulers, they drew on the writings of the Dominican friar, Bartolomé de las Casas, whose *Short Account of the Destruction of the Indies* described Spain's conquest of the Caribbean in brutal and graphic detail. First published in Spanish in Seville in 1562, the book was reissued in Dutch in Antwerp in 1578, and several editions in other languages soon followed. Tales of Spanish inhumanity in the Caribbean stood in for Spanish atrocities in the Netherlands; the ordeal of the Tainos represented the sufferings of the Dutch. Political and religious motivations joined to fuel Dutch attacks on Spain—at home, where the Dutch Republic emerged from the northern provinces, and in the Caribbean, where Dutch mariners and merchants dominated shipping and seized islands in the formerly Spanish sea. No constituency opposed peace with Spain more vigorously than the merchants who ran the Dutch West India Company (chartered in 1621) and regarded commerce and themselves as instruments of war.

Domestic affairs took a slightly different form in England, where the period from 1580 to 1640 was characterized by dramatic population growth (by some 40%). Increased population put strains on rents and food prices, which were exacerbated in some regions by the collapse of England's textile industries. One consequence of these intertwined demographic and economic pressures was increased migration, as men and some women traveled the kingdom and beyond in search of employment. These people made England's overseas growth possible by providing manpower for ships, armies, trading posts, agricultural settlements, colonies, and fisheries precisely at the moment of Spanish weakness.

Of those English who migrated west across the Atlantic in the 17th century, approximately 200,000—more than half—ventured to the Caribbean rather than to the American mainland. French migrants were even more likely than the English to choose the Caribbean, although they were also much less likely than the English to leave home in the first place. In 1645, some 8,500 French lived in the Caribbean, while New France (Canada) contained only about 300. Recruits were also available in both England and France because of domestic turmoil in mid-century. The wave of protests and rebellions in France known as the Fronde (1648–53) and civil war and revolution in England (1642–60) generated waves of political and economic refugees, many of whom found their way to the Caribbean, while others were forcibly deported there after being on the losing side of civil conflicts. Dutch migration, in contrast, was negligible. Curaçao contained some 600 men in the 1660s after 25 years of settlement, while New Netherland boasted several thousand. For the Dutch, a major global power in the 17th century, commercial enterprises in the East Indies always attracted more investment and manpower than did the small holdings in the West Indies.

A final crucial context that shaped rivals' aspirations for Caribbean land and resources lay in European consumer tastes. By the early 17th century Europeans craved tobacco, which was first introduced by Iberians. Although reviled by some critics (King James I of England deplored it as a "noxious weed"), the crop's alleged medicinal benefits helped overcome opposition, and smoking became a popular pastime. According to the Spanish doctor Nicolás Monardes in 1565, tobacco possessed no fewer than 20 medicinal uses. It could cure gout, snake bite, gas, headaches, chest pains, skin diseases, and asthma (Norton 2008, 115–16). Europeans sought to meet the soaring demand for this marvelous and addictive substance through new arable land in the Caribbean. The crop was planted, with varying degrees of success, on most of the islands occupied by the French and English, and marketed in Europe. The substance was popular in Africa, too, and it emerged as an important trade good, as did the Dutch- and English-made pipes in which people smoked it. Another more pedestrian European consumer good also encouraged Caribbean incursions: herring. According to a Dutch adage, the herring fisheries were "the mother of all commerce" (Goslinga 1971, 116), and they boomed in the 17th century. Herring required salt for preservation, and after the Dutch lost access to Spanish salt sources, they found their way to the Caribbean, where they mined salt first at Punta de Araya (off the Venezuelan coast) and later at Bonaire, St. Martin, and Tortuga.

Although in many respects northern Europeans sought to emulate Spanish economic success in their own Caribbean exploits, they had to find solace in salt mines and tobacco crops instead of the silver mines they coveted. They also pursued their goals very differently. In their American and Caribbean conquests and settlements, the Spanish and Portuguese had created a variety of public institutions controlled directly by the crown. In contrast, the French, English, and Dutch relied on private companies to carry out their commercial and colonial efforts. These companies had a range of powers, including the right to wage war, establish armies, sue for peace, and make commercial treaties. The West India Company controlled Dutch activities in the Atlantic after 1621 and placed the responsibility for developing and populating new territory in the hands of patrons: private individuals who held titles to colonies in a quasi-feudal system. In 1626 the French minister, Cardinal Richelieu, approved of—and invested in—a company with plans to colonize Saint-Christophe, and he formed two other companies in 1627 with monopoly rights over foreign trade. The Company of the Islands of America (1635) organized the colonization of Martinique, Guadeloupe, and some other Caribbean islands. The English crown suffered financial constraints similar to those of the Dutch and French, and English investment proceeded under the auspices of men such as the Earl of Carlisle, who secured patents from the crown for rights to claim and settle islands. Private men and companies, not European governments, carried most of the risk for overseas enterprises in the first half of the century.

New settlements were characterized by their mixed economies and agricultural experimentation, an appropriate reflection of the Caribbean's incredibly varied ecosystems, with rainfall, soil, and topography varying dramatically from one island to another and even within a single island. Europeans hunted, planted, and plundered in the territory the French claimed on the northern coast of Hispaniola. Saint-Domingue, as the French called this colony, was not recognized by the Span-

Figure 12.1 Slaves curing tobacco. Engraving from Jean Baptiste du Tertre, *Histoire generale des Antilles habitués par les François* (1667). Source: The John Carter Brown Library.

ish until 1697 in the Treaty of Ryswick. Elsewhere, Europeans cultivated cotton, indigo, and tobacco in search of profitable and viable export crops before many islands switched to sugar cultivation. Island economies were always characterized by volatility; invasions and wars disrupted and destroyed plantations, as did the hurricanes and, in some places, volcanoes that defined the region. Life was unpredictable, mortality was high, newcomers were more likely to face early death than quick wealth, and in many places a frenzied pace reflected this awareness that life was likely to be all too short.

Given the economic aspirations of investors, it is no surprise that the majority of Europeans who ventured to the French and English islands in the Caribbean were bonded laborers—indentured servants (for the English) and engagés (for the French). Those who worked in French settlements generally served three-year contracts, while English servants labored under contracts lasting from four to seven years. In return for passage to the colonies, they sold their labor to the highest bidder, normally with no choice in the matter, and during their term of service they could be sold like livestock or passed down as part of an estate like any other movable good.

The abundant supply of servants kept their price low and perhaps contributed to their masters' brutality. "If the Masters be cruel," Englishman Richard Ligon recalled, "the Servants have very wearisome and miserable lives" (Ligon 1673, 44). Some of the worst cases made it to local courts. One servant in Barbados named John Baddam complained in 1640 to the island's council that he had been tortured by his two masters. They had hanged Baddam up by his hands and placed lit matches between his fingers. As a result, several of his joints no longer functioned, and he was at risk of losing his right hand. The council sided with Baddam, condemning what the councilors characterized as inhumane and un-Christian torture; it freed the abused servant immediately, arrested and fined his masters, and arranged for his medical care. Alexander Exquemelin, a French indentured servant on Tortuga in the 1660s, lamented the bad luck that had put him in the employment of "the wickedest rogue in the whole island." Deprived of adequate nutrition, Exquemelin endured "intense hunger" and sickness until finally his master sold him off to a new owner. As luck would have it, the new owner restored Exquemelin to health, provided him with food and clothing, and allowed him to buy himself on credit after one year's service (Exquemelin 1969, 34). Such were the quirks of fate that could shape a servant's life.

Escape for those who sought to flee was always hindered by their island residence, but desperate and enterprising men tried nonetheless. Tortuga and the rugged coast of Saint-Domingue proved to be favorite sanctuaries for escaped engagés. Those who could neither escape their servitude nor endure their treatment occasionally engaged in overt resistance. Barbados experienced one such plot in the 1640s. Servants there planned a massive uprising, intending to murder their masters, free themselves, and govern the colony. After the plot was revealed by a servant who had a change of heart, repression was brutal. Authorities executed 18 servants.

With freedom for those lucky enough to achieve it came the possibility of land and the promise of "freedom dues," which might range from a new shirt to farm implements that enabled the freeman to launch his own career. Freedom from service gave men the opportunity to establish themselves as independent farmers, laborers, or craftsmen in the agricultural economies of the region. Some servants completed their indenture without credit or resources sufficient to establish themselves, and signed on for another period of service for their masters. So Thomas Hubbard did in Barbados after he became free after five years of service in 1640; he agreed to work another year in return for 120 pounds of cotton, one hammock, and one pig. Some newly freed servants joined together in partnerships (called *matelotage* on the French islands and mateship among the English), sharing a single dwelling, working the land together, and dividing the profits. Matelotage was common in Saint-Domingue by mid-century. There, men spent part of the year hunting cattle, processing hides, and curing meat to trade at fairs on Tortuga, where they swapped their wares for tobacco, alcohol, and muskets (Lane 1998, 98). Barbados land deeds reflect similar patterns in the 1640s; in contrast to the hunting culture of Saint-Domingue, Barbados mates shared dwellings and combined forces to gain enough credit and capital to establish themselves as farmers.

These mateships point to some of the varied forms families took in the male-dominated islands. On Providence Island, an English colony inhabited almost exclusively in the 1630s by male laborers (English, Africans, and a few Native Americans from North America) and their masters, the governor, Philip Bell, was ordered by his employers in London to "distribute all the Inhabitants into several families whereof one shalbe the Chiefe." As the number of enslaved Africans grew on places such as Providence, family patterns altered to accommodate them. Worried about the possible threat posed by enslaved Africans in English households, the Providence Company ordered that each family should adhere to a ratio of two English for every African (Games 1999, 96–97).

As the Providence example suggests, enslaved Africans and Indians labored alongside European bondsmen. Ligon asserted that on Barbados enslaved Africans were treated better than indentured Europeans, but a close reading of his account reveals this comparison to have been shaped by his assumptions about the fragile nature of English bodies: slaves had less food, fewer clothes, and poorer shelter than did European servants. Barbados had no indigenous inhabitants when the English claimed the island for themselves, but by the 1650s some Indians worked there as slaves. On St. Eustatius, Dutch colonists adopted tobacco cultivation soon after conquering the island, but European laborers were not interested in working in the fields. The Dutch turned to Indian laborers, but those were also soon in short supply, so the Dutch then raided other islands and the mainland for slaves.

European and African populations in the Caribbean grew quickly, almost exclusively through migration rather than natural increase. If the numbers are often vague, two patterns are clear. First, the white population in the islands was predominantly young and male until the late 17th century. Second, the population came to be dominated by enslaved Africans by the end of the century, first on the English islands and then on the French. The population of the French islands was 19% black by 1650 but 36% by 1660 (Boucher 2008, 115). By 1655 the population of Barbados contained some 20,000 Africans and 23,000 Europeans; 18 years later, the slave population outnumbered the European population, 33,184 to 21,309 (Dunn 1973, 87). Enslaved Africans came from a variety of ethnic groups, as did Europeans—especially on the English and Dutch islands.

Although most European migrants traveled as indentured laborers, there were some free migrants as well. Some were ambitious men eager to improve their economic condition: Tom Verney hoped in 1639 that his time in Barbados would "be an engagement for mee for my new lead-life," promising both prosperity and personal redemption for past failures (Games 1999, 80). Some were men of the cloth. The presence of Caribs on French-occupied islands not only hindered French settlement but also inspired the French to send Catholic missionaries to proselytize. Jews found haven in Suriname, Curaçao, Barbados, and Jamaica. English Catholics, forbidden to practice their faith openly at home and banned from holding public office, inhabited all of the English colonies in the Caribbean. French Huguenots made their way to the islands, too, where many governors tolerated their presence. If for many the 17th-century Caribbean was a place of violence, premature death, and avarice, for others the islands offered relative sanctuary—whether prompted by indifference or acceptance from neighbors—from some of the religious and political violence of the era.

European affairs continued to punctuate Caribbean life in the middle of the 17th century, defining mature colonial settlements just as they had facilitated their creation. Other regions of the Atlantic also began to shape the Caribbean. Trading ties thickened connections to the American mainland, Europe, and Africa. One overpopulated Caribbean colony, Barbados, even spawned a supply colony on the American mainland, Carolina. Africans became a larger presence in the region, dominating some islands and posing strategic challenges and opportunities for residents and invaders. Several regional transitions illustrate these new intersections.

The first transition involved sugar, another commodity of growing popularity in Europe. Tobacco may have sparked interest in Caribbean land in the 1620s, but sugar wrought an even greater frenzy. It took hold gradually in the English and especially the French Caribbean, primarily because sugarcane cultivation and processing required a large capital investment in equipment and labor, one well beyond the reach of most European planters, many of whom also lacked expertise in processing cane. In 1654 came a crucial turning point in the Caribbean, sparked by events outside the region: the Dutch, after nine years of struggle with the Portuguese, finally abandoned Brazil, where they had learned the complicated and costly techniques of sugar cultivation and, more important, of transforming sugar into rum and molasses. As Dutch merchants, planters, and investors dispersed into the Caribbean, they brought those techniques with them. While some English settlers had already begun to experiment with sugar on Barbados, the infusion of Dutch capital contributed to the "sugar revolution," in which sugar monoculture replaced other crops and enslaved Africans replaced European indentured laborers.

Sugar wrought major environmental transformations wherever it took hold, and those changes assisted the *Aedes aegypti* mosquito, which had crossed the Atlantic from Africa in slaving vessels. As Europeans cleared land for sugarcane, they felled

trees, removing bird habitats and facilitating the survival of
insects the birds had once consumed. Sugar processing also
required clay pots, which stood empty much of the year, collecting rainwater that enabled mosquitoes to flourish. *A. aegypti* is the vector for yellow fever, and it is no accident that
the Caribbean's first yellow fever epidemic started in Barbados
in 1647, in the wake of sugar's introduction to the island. In
that first epidemic, as much as one-third of the island's population may have died.

Figure 12.2 Pots used for processing sugar, which also bred
mosquitoes. Engraving from
Jean Baptiste du Tertre, *Histoire
generale des Antilles habitées
par les François* (1667). Source:
The John Carter Brown Library.

Yellow fever also undermined the siege tactics of European
armies in the Caribbean after 1650. Here the attackers died in
high numbers and the defenders won the day, a trend that made it almost impossible for the Spanish to reclaim their Caribbean islands, or for other attackers to
displace rivals. The explanation for this failure of long-standing European military
practice lay in a complex combination of factors all shaped by the Atlantic context
of the region: heightened European demand for sugar, the *A. aegypti* mosquito, the

environmental transformation of sugar plantations, and fresh European blood for the mosquito to consume (McNeill 2004).

A second turning point in the Caribbean came in 1655, when English conquest made Jamaica the last major island to change hands in this period, ending an era of frontier settlement and introducing a new era of plantation settlement. The conquest also revealed shifting relations between England, on the rise in the Western Hemisphere, and the Dutch. In 1667 the Dutch had conquered Suriname, but this turned out to be what the historian Wim Klooster characterizes as "the last convulsions of Dutch Atlantic ambitions" (Klooster 1997, 58). In the end the Dutch were left with their six Caribbean islands.

What had happened to the Dutch? They had made themselves indispensable—and wealthy—through the carrying trade, which was especially vital in the French (and to a lesser extent the English) islands. But both the French and English began to exert more control over their island colonies in the 1650s and especially the 1660s—surveying the land, requiring censuses of island inhabitants and property, and taking direct control of colonial governance. The French chartered a new company in 1664, the Compagnie des Indes occidentals françaises (French West India Company), which assumed responsibility for adjudicating affairs in the Caribbean. Seeking greater control over colonial trade, both the French and the English moved against the dominance of Dutch shipping. In 1651 and 1660 the English passed navigation acts that required goods to travel on English ships, and in 1664 the French crown banned trade with the Dutch, despite fervent colonial opposition.

Although these laws dislodged the Dutch from the official carrying trade with these islands, illegal trade continued to flourish. More important, in 1662 the Dutch secured a new asiento, or trading contract, from the Spanish crown that gave them license to trade slaves in Spanish America—a trade made easier for them by the growing number of trading posts in Africa and an enterprise that signaled the tightening of connections between the Caribbean, Africa, and the American mainland. The Spanish colonies of Santo Domingo and Puerto Rico were increasingly important in this trade, and Curaçao (and later St. Eustatius) emerged as its lucrative center. Despite formal trade prohibitions, the Dutch also supplied the French colonies of Martinique, Guadeloupe, and Saint-Domingue. Thus the Dutch continued to generate great wealth through legal and extralegal commerce and especially the slave trade.

Shifting European politics and economies in the early 17th century had also precipitated important transformations for the Caribs of the Lesser Antilles, who had long traded with Europeans passing through the region. Their trade goods were so well known that when Sir Henry Colt traveled through the Caribbean in 1631, he was especially eager to purchase a hammock at Dominica, where the "people are thought to have the best" (Harlow 1924, 77). But Caribs were unprepared for the permanent occupations envisioned by Europeans in the 1620s. The English and French on St. Christopher learned this lesson soon after their arrival in 1625, when they were surrounded by a fleet comprised of some 400 or 500 Caribs. "We bade them be gone," remembered Captain John Smith, "but they would not," and so a battle ensued (Harlow 1924, xix). Carib threats forced the Europeans to post a constant guard for almost a year, and other efforts to settle and occupy the land came to a temporary halt.

As Europeans flooded the region, islands quickly became overpopulated in terms of the arable land and economic opportunities available, resulting in new diasporas with their own consequences for Caribs. After 1628, English tobacco farmers claimed the unoccupied islands of Nevis, Montserrat, and Antigua, and were opposed in their efforts by the Caribs, who were more successful in preventing English settlement at Barbuda after 1632. Further dispersals in the 1630s, 1640s, and 1650s by the Dutch, French, and English to the Windward Islands of Tobago (where the Caribs destroyed an English settlement in 1639), Grenada, St. Lucia, Marie Galante, and St. Martin met with continued resistance. Overt war between the French and Caribs erupted in 1654 and lasted for five years. The wars brought the French and English into alliance in 1659, and by 1660 the region was at peace. In that year, a settlement restricted Caribs to St. Vincent and Dominica and ended their protracted wars of resistance against European incursions.

Finally, the Caribbean continued to be embroiled in the numerous European conflicts of this period. The Treaty of Westphalia in 1648 put a temporary end to the hostilities that had consumed Europe for the first half of the century, but soon two former allies, the English and the Dutch, launched a series of three wars (1652–54, 1665–67, and 1672–74). In the second of these wars the French were involved as allies of the Dutch, though from 1672 to 1678 the French and Dutch fought each other in the Indies. In the context of these European conflicts, the three nations frequently attacked the Caribbean holdings of their rivals.

But these wars were never simple extensions of European conflicts, because of the complex assortment of people who had come to inhabit the Caribbean by the 1660s—free and unfree, European, African, Indian, Protestant, and Catholic. Caribs continued to affect colonial affairs just as they had shaped initial settlements. Samuel Winthrop, an English colonist on Antigua, described the French attack that took place there in October of 1666. The French, accompanied by their Carib allies, burned property and killed residents as they worked their way across the island until the English finally sought peace. The English feared the Caribs—scorned by Winthrop as the "cruell Indian"—more than the French, and Winthrop alleged that after the French departed, the Caribs stayed behind, raping and murdering for five days and claiming, Winthrop reported indignantly, "liberty to do soe" (Winthrop [1667], 355–57).

Combat de la Pointe de Sable.

Figure 12.3 Warfare between the French and the English on St. Christopher. Engraving from Jean Baptiste du Tertre, *Histoire generale des Antilles habitées par les François* (1667). Source: The John Carter Brown Library.

Divided loyalties characterized warfare in the region, often to the benefit of invaders. Indentured servants and slaves sometimes allied themselves with intruders. When the French attacked the English island of Montserrat, for example, they found the Irish Catholic indentured servants who were the majority of the island's population—and whose kingdom had suffered terribly under English rule—eager to assist them, and the French were victorious (Akenson 1997, 85–86). Attackers came to rely on assistance from discontented laborers. When the Spanish attacked Providence in 1640, they loitered offshore in their ships, hoping to get news of island conditions from the runaway servants and slaves who had fled the island in boats and canoes. Wars also provided opportunities for unfree laborers to escape, as Winthrop's slaves did in 1666 while the French seized his home and property. The laborers whose toil generated profits for European planters and investors posed daily threats to the survival of those enterprises, and European wars vividly exposed that tension.

The transformation of the Caribbean between 1620 and the 1660s was remarkable. Islands that had long been abandoned by the Spanish were claimed and settled by Dutch, French, and English settlers in an age of diminishing Spanish power and transformed European geopolitics. These European invaders displaced Caribs, and confined them to only two islands. Forced African migrants joined Europeans in ever larger numbers. Tobacco and sugar generated wealth for investors and pleasure for distant consumers. Northern Europeans planted themselves around the Caribbean in an outgrowth of European conflicts, while European and, increasingly, African and American events continued to shape the region, embedding it in dense webs of connection to the world beyond.

WORKS CITED

Akenson, Donald Harman. 1997. *If the Irish Ran the World: Montserrat, 1630–1730.* Montreal and Kingston: McGill–Queen's University Press.

Boucher, Philip P. 2008. *France and the American Tropics to 1700: Tropics of Discontent?* Baltimore: Johns Hopkins University Press.

Dunn, Richard S. 1973. *Sugar and Slaves: The Rise of the Planter Class in the English West Indies, 1624–1713.* New York: Norton.

Exquemelin, Alexander. 1969. *The Buccaneers of America.* Trans. by Alexis Brown. Baltimore: Penguin Books.

Games, Alison. 1999. *Migration and the Origins of the English Atlantic World.* Cambridge, MA: Harvard University Press.

Goslinga, Cornelis Ch. 1971. *The Dutch in the Caribbean and on the Wild Coast, 1580–1680.* Gainesville: University of Florida Press.

Harlow, V. T., ed. 1924. *Colonising Expeditions to the West Indies and Guiana, 1623–1667.* London: Hakluyt Society.

Klooster, Wim. 1997. "Winds of Change: Colonization, Commerce, and Consolidation in the Seventeenth-Century Atlantic World." *De Halve Maen* 70, no. 3: 53–58.

Lane, Kris E. 1998. *Pillaging the Empire: Piracy in the Americas 1500–1750.* Armonk, NY: M. E. Sharpe.

Ligon, Richard. 1673. *A True and Exact History of the Island of Barbados.* London.

McNeill, J. R. 2004. "Yellow Jack and Geopolitics: Environment, Epidemics, and the Struggles for Empire in the American Tropics, 1650–1825." *OAH Magazine of History* 18, no. 3: 9–13.

Norton, Marcy. 2008. *Sacred Gifts, Profane Pleasures: A History of Tobacco and Chocolate in the Atlantic World.* Ithaca, NY: Cornell University Press.

Winthrop, Samuel. 1667. "Samuel Winthrop to John Winthrop Jr., [April 1667]," *Collections of the Massachusetts Historical Society* 5th series, vol. 8: 255–58.

13

Servants and Slaves during the 17th-Century Sugar Revolution

HILARY McD. BECKLES

There was nothing unthinking about it: European colonists in the Caribbean who invested heavily in enslaved Africans did so strategically, after detailed market assessments and considerable social reflection. At the outset they imagined a mixed-labor regime with enslaved natives at the core, supplemented by workers imported from back home. Enslaved Africans would be a welcome addition if they could be procured at reasonable rates.

The Spanish implemented this model in the Greater Antilles during the 16th century. In the 17th century it provided an attractive template for the colonizing efforts of the English and French in the eastern Caribbean. The newcomers modified and standardized the arrangement in order to meet the peculiar needs of time and place. To promote clarity and certainty in labor relations on the first plantations, for example, English officials at Barbados in 1636 established guidelines for colonists: voluntary contracted workers from "back home" would serve between five and seven years, and those deported by the state, ten years. The few "negroes and

205

Indians" would "serve for life unless a contract was made before to the contrary" (Dunn 1972, 228). Yet the core plan for the labor regime remained intact.

Local labor supplies in the Caribbean, however, proved numerically inadequate and politically unsuitable; enslaved Africans were not readily available and their prices were prohibitive. Trapped between commercial marginalization from the transatlantic slave trade and persistent, damaging military aggression from the indigenous population, English and French colonists did what the market and political environment dictated: they "turned to Europe for bonded labor, as the Spaniards before them had done" (Williams 1970, 95). In order to stimulate the supply of European labor without creating for themselves any major legal, social, or political crises, they turned to the most familiar and acceptable labor system: indentured servitude, a widely respected and legitimate institution. The English referred to workers indentured, or contracted, as servants; the French called them engagés. These workers were expected to serve employers for a fixed term of years in return for passage to the colony—an opportunity to improve upon their material and social condition.

Initially, these servants were promised at the end of their contracts a "freedom due" in the form of a small parcel of land, generally no more than 10 acres. This practice was quickly abandoned, and replaced with the granting of a fixed amount of money or its commodity equivalent. In this way it was easily devalued and generally manipulated. Conceptually, the freedom due was meant to distinguish indentured servants from enslaved Africans. It was promoted by desperate, labor-starved, first-generation planters as a post-employment asset to lure workers to the colonies. It promised them a path to ensure their participation in the colonial dream.

By the mid-17th century, changed social and economic conditions in the infant colonies and new imperial thinking about colonial development determined that the approved labor model was unsustainable and needed to be rethought. This led to a revised strategy of gradually moving enslaved Africans from the labor system's periphery to its center, thus displacing the masses of indentured servants and pushing aside the few enslaved natives. In 1645, George Downing in Barbados wrote to John Winthrop, governor of Massachusetts, to explain the revised model: If a planter could obtain a good supply of servants to clear the land, lay out the field, and plant the soil, he could "in a short time . . . with good husbandry" be able "to procure negroes out of the increase." Here was the generic labor formula that would shape the future and underpin what became the "sugar revolution" (Sheridan 1974, 67–69).

The island colonies were transformed by investors growing rich through a sugar industry that deepened its dependence on labor of the enslaved Africans. Barbados gave birth to the new dispensation, and earned the distinction as the first slave society in the Americas. It was not the first to rely entirely on thousands of imported enslaved Africans; that legacy belonged to Santo Domingo and Brazil. But it was the first to close its frontier, deprive servants of access to commercial land and social mobility, and institutionalize slavery as the basis of all economic production and civil society reproduction. In the French Antilles, Guadeloupe and Martinique were similarly transformed, though at a slower pace. Other islands planned to duplicate this experience and succeeded to varying degrees.

Barbados emerged, furthermore, as the first English Caribbean headquarters of the Atlantic slave-based sugar plantation complex. In so doing, it attained a reputation as the "richest little spot in the New World." The Lesser Antilles replaced the Spanish Greater Antilles as the primary site of colonial enrichment. "Sugar and African enslavement" became a Caribbean brand that set the Lesser Antilles apart from the rest of colonial North America.

The Transition to African Enslaved Labor

In explaining the 17th-century remaking of the island colonies, scholars have faced many enigmas, but none as persistent as the planters' choice to build social structures and economic enterprises upon the large-scale enslavement of Africans. The sugar industry was already associated with enslaved African labor in the islands of the eastern Atlantic and with enslaved Europeans in the Mediterranean. But the coming together of the sugar industry and the plantation in the islands of the western Atlantic—that is, the Caribbean—is said to have launched the first transition from a predominantly white to a predominantly black labor system.

The term "sugar revolution" has been used for decades to describe the transformations brought about by sugar, slavery, and plantations. According to historian Stuart B. Schwartz, as the sugar plantation complex moved westward into the Caribbean, it brought with it traditions of "close attention to economies of scale" and "the institution of regimented gang labor for slaves." In all locales, he concludes, "the result of the process was a rapid transformation of the regions, often from white or indigenous to black population, from small farms to large plantations, from sparse to intensive settlement, and from small farmers and free workers to slaves" (Schwartz 2004, 2–8).

More recently, this transformation of Caribbean economy and society toward the mid-17th century has become the object of scrutiny and revision by a host of scholars, who have questioned its timing and the assumption of a direct causal relationship between the rise of sugar and black slavery.

In the 1630s and 1640s the English established viable settlements at Barbados, Antigua, and Nevis; the French at Martinique and Guadeloupe. They agreed to share the island of St. Kitts as a strategy to survive native (Carib) hostilities. The English added Jamaica to their network in 1655; the French took in Saint-Domingue (later Haiti) in 1697. In these colonies successful investments were made in the cultivation of many commodities for export, notably cotton, indigo, hardwoods, tobacco, and finally sugarcane and coffee. It was the sugarcane, however, that stimulated economic activities and the massive importation of indentured labor from Europe and enslaved labor from Africa. "Sugar and slavery" thus became the investor's dream in the 17th-century Caribbean. Why and how this occurred, however, remain contentious. General statements that suggest the simultaneous emergence of "sugar and slavery" have come under attack. More resistant have been detailed case studies that suggested the complexity and diversity of the transition.

Comparative studies have served to effectively situate the Caribbean transition to slave labor within the wider Atlantic context so accurately outlined by David Brion Davis when he stated that "the Africanization of large parts of the New World was not the result of concentrated planning, racial destiny, or imminent historical design, but of innumerable local and pragmatic choices made in four continents" (Menard 2006, 31). Davis's reminder helps put to rest as myth the climatic theory of Caribbean slavery, which posits that white workers failed on the tropical sugar plantations for physiological reasons while black workers were successful for reasons of their race and color.

The earliest Caribbean historian to dismiss the climatic theory was Eric Williams. His pioneering work provides a compelling case for the triumph of market forces over all other considerations in explaining the 17th-century transition. Given the opportunity, Williams suggests, sugar planters especially, driven by profit motives in the high-risk colonial environment, preferred enslaved workers above all others. He concludes that "indentured servants were temporary chattels," though he does not agree with Daniel Defoe, who suggested that in the West Indies the "white servant was a slave" (Williams 1944, 17–18).

Since Williams, Caribbean scholars of "transitions to slavery" have generally embraced economic choice over other arguments. Critics and skeptics alike have focused on the power of racial paradigms and political philosophy in shaping decisions with respect to labor. Of primary concern to these scholars has been the general European acceptance of slavery in the first place. Their tendency, not always explicit, has been to minimize the importance of relative cost and to attach greater significance to European value systems in which racial and cultural outsiders were earmarked for special kinds of negative discrimination—slavery being the most common expression.

Empirical data from the cane fields, however, speak to details of the transition in the French and English colonies. Robert Louis Stein argues that the introduction of commercial sugarcane planting to the French West Indies was the "most significant single event" to occur during the 17th century. It was linked, he says, to the arrival of Dutch and Jewish settlers from Brazil, who were the driving force behind "sugar and slavery" there, as well as to the development of the regional market in enslaved Africans (Stein 1979, 9–11).

The sugar sector in Brazil initially depended upon coerced indigenous labor, Portuguese wage and contract workers, and a few enslaved Africans and free mulattos. In 1580, when the colony dominated the European sugar market, fewer than 10% of all workers were enslaved Africans. By 1600, this number had risen to near 40%, and by the early 1640s, when English and French colonists entered the market, it was up to 90%. At the same time, white and free mulatto workers were being displaced in the technical, skilled, and supervisory jobs. By 1650, the century-long transition was complete.

French colonists before 1640 relied upon engagés to meet most of their labor needs, but that soon changed. Dutch commercial capacity was the catalyst. The Dutch provided capital, sugar-making technologies, and access to the African slave market and offered training in large-scale slave management. The effect was immediate: "Within a few years," notes Stein, "the economies and societies of the French Islands were changed beyond recognition." There had been a few enslaved Africans in the French Antilles before the commercial advent of sugarcane, but their number increased when the sugar plantation system took hold (Stein 1979, 7).

On Guadeloupe, for example, the enslaved African population rose from 3,000 in 1656 to 80,000 in 1700, while the French population, which included more than 40 percent engagés, remained at about 12,000 during the same period. The shortage of engagés was beyond the capacity of planters to resolve. Financially secure colonists led the way in looking to the African slave trade to resolve their labor problems. Those with access to credit made large purchases and quickly shifted the composition of plantation labor.

What transpired in the French islands also took place with greater intensity in the English islands. Barbados, St. Kitts, and Antigua led the way. Large- and small-scale cotton and tobacco enterprises were converted into sugar plantations. The process was enabled by Dutch finance, technology transfers, and slave trading. After 1650 the white servant population in Barbados decreased rapidly, while the enslaved African population doubled between 1645 and 1650, reaching 40,000 in 1665. By 1700 there were fewer than 2,000 servants, down from a 1650 level of near 15,000. The black population rose from 20,000 to 41,970 between 1655 and 1712.

In the period up to 1660, indentured labor remained more economical than enslaved African labor, hence its continued use and general adoption on the sugar plantations. The transition to enslaved labor began despite the higher per capita costs of enslaved Africans. The growing efficiency of the slave trade made it possible for Africans to be used as satisfactory, economical substitutes for servants when necessary. But only after the mid-1660s, when adverse forces affected the servant market, drastically reducing supply and pushing up costs, did enslaved African labor gain a clear cost advantage over servant labor. The acceleration of the displacement process during the 1650s merely suggests that planters had correctly perceived these trends and were able to absorb, in the short term, the higher marginal costs incurred by enslaved African labor because of the large profits generated by sugar production. Significant increases in the purchase price of indentured labor and in related operating costs, coupled with intense competition in the sugar industry, gradually reduced planters' profits and encouraged them to seek alternative sources of labor.

A New Regime of Slavery

The transition to enslaved African labor, however, did not represent a fundamental adoption of a qualitatively different labor system. It was essentially a move along a continuum of further labor subjection. Low profit levels in the tobacco and cotton economies had threatened not only investments but also the future of West Indian colonization. Capital investment in labor was second only to investment in land, and planters developed and implemented property conceptions of all workers. Consequently, servants were subject to what became a new regime of slavery.

Williams's assertion that these servants were not slaves but rather "temporary chattel" because the definition of slavery entails lifelong bondage is well known. Yet more recent scholars have not seriously explored his assertion or analyzed this creolized labor institution. To some extent this inertia, or reluctance, has to do with the unfamiliarity of the evidence produced by servants themselves, especially where it details their daily life on the plantations. The Williams thesis has had a determining impact on working definitions of slavery and has contributed to the subservience of other experiences to the criterion of "time." Other criteria, unfortunately, have been weighed far less. Also, the gruesome standard of treatment meted out to Africans has become the New World benchmark, suggesting the existence of only one form of slavery on the plantations. While it is important to be clear about what constitutes enslavement, it does not help matters to focus on legal criteria at the expense of the lived experience of workers.

No scholar has argued that indentured servants caught in the sugar regime were converted into chattel slaves. The concept of "proto-slavery" has been used as a qualifier, suggesting that in "Old World" contexts the term "slavery" would have been applied to these same people. Yet while servants and enslaved Africans both experienced the forms of hyper-exploitation and practical rightlessness that characterized slavery in the Old World, the unprecedented brutality imposed upon enslaved Africans in the Caribbean transformed Old World concepts of slavery such that the innovative institution of white enslavement paled comparatively in significance.

Both forms of slavery, however, were associated with the chattel principle and with real estate status, as well as with owners' extensive legal authority over the body. That the enslaved African in an English colony could be murdered in cold blood by an owner whose punishment under law was a nominal cash fine also suggests the importance of criteria other than lifelong bondage in determining what was slavery. The system of indentured servitude practiced on the plantation did not fit within the traditional terms and conditions of the institution. As a type of chattel slavery, it became specifically associated with legally enforceable property rights in persons.

Servants and servant traders, in addition to planters, understood the significance of the chattel status. Richard Povey, a prominent 1650s merchant, wrote of the servant trade to Barbados: "The ship owners who transport these persons made a gainful business of it. . . . Many consider the charge of the passage and disbursement as a debt which entitled them to claim a sort of property in the bodies of their passengers and to dispose of them amongst the planters." One such servant reported that on arrival in Barbados he was accounted for as the "goods" of Mr. Noell, who had shipped him "without name or individuality." Another well-known servant trader, Mr. Cole of Bristol, was described as a "merchant that deals in slaves and the souls of men" (Beckles 1989, 59–60).

Richard Ligon arrived at Barbados in 1647 and during his three years' residence recorded his observations of servant life. He reported that indentured servants and enslaved Africans worked in the same gangs in the cane fields from 6 a.m. to 6 p.m. with a break from 11 a.m. to 1 p.m. Unaccustomed to being driven by brutal overseers, and unwilling to accept enslavement, they were in persistent rebellion. Ligon described the suppression of the 1647 servant revolt, the first of many acts of rebellion on the island. When servants refused to work, he wrote, "they are beaten by the overseer: if they resist, then their time is doubled. I have seen an overseer beat a servant with a cane about the head till the blood has followed for a fault that is not worth the speaking of and yet he must have patience, or worst will follow. Truly, I have seen such cruelty there done to servants, as I did not think one Christian could have done to another" (Ligon 1657, 44).

Servants who documented their experiences confirmed much of what was reported by Ligon. Typical is the assessment of Henrich von Uchteritz, a German indentured servant "sold" in Barbados in 1652. Von Uchteritz used the "time" criterion to distinguish between himself and the enslaved Africans among whom he worked, but he indicated that the difference was more form than content. Taken from a London prison where he was serving time as a political captive, he had his sentence changed to 10 years' servitude in Barbados. Shipped out in a consignment of 1,300 other prisoners, he was "sold for eight hundred pounds of sugar" to a sugar planter who had on his estate 300 "Christians," "negroes," and "Indian slaves." His work was the same as that of the others. "I had to sweep the plantation yard the first day," he wrote, and "on another day I fed the pigs, and thereafter I had to do the kind of work usually performed by the slaves" (Von Uchteritz 1970, 92–93).

Sugar planters were prepared to enslave labor from any source; neither race nor color was a deciding issue. They were driven by market forces and social factors to create from traditional indentured servitude a new, more relevant labor institution. Barbados quickly acquired a reputation for the rapid expansion of African enslavement and the development of white slavery. In this its planters felt justified despite the unconvincing tears of parliamentarians, since, as Henry Whistler noted on his visit to Barbados in 1655, the "Illand is the Dunghill wharone England doth cast forth its rubidg: Rodgs and hors and such like peopel are those which are gennerally Broght heare."

News of a white slave market in Barbados spread to its trading partners. Soon it was receiving white persons from other colonies and countries for sale as slaves. In 1640, for example, an agent brought a cargo of Frenchmen, presumably engagés, to Barbados to be sold as slaves. The cargo consisted of "200 freight" and was sold for 900 pounds of cotton per head. Three years later the Dutch governor of Brazil sent a consignment of 50 Portuguese political prisoners to be "sold as slaves." The governor of Barbados considered their knowledge of sugar production a special asset and ordered them freed.

Servants were bought and sold, taxed as property, mortgaged, used as collateral, transferred, and alienated as chattel in much the same way as enslaved Africans. The deeds, inventories, and wills of the colonies show this explicitly. Ligon notes that "'tis an ordinary thing here, to sell . . . servants to one another . . . and in exchange receive any commodity that are on the island" (Beckles 1989, 73). When the servants revolted, reprisals from the colonial government took the same form as in cases of enslaved Africans.

Planters were concerned with the diminishing market value of labor assets, and made detailed comparative calculations. With respect to enslaved Africans, historian Robin Blackburn noted, they were "thinking of only five or eight years ahead, given Caribbean mortality rates" (Blackburn 1997, 331). In 1645 as the sugar revolution took shape, George Downing, an English merchant investor in Barbados, stated that "six or eight or nine years service" from a servant "would do very well" (Beckles 1986, 9). When comparative cost data are assessed, the advantages of slave over servant only became evident during the late 1660s.

From the planter's perspective, however, the primary advantages of one form of labor over the other were the ability to establish and maintain a rigid regime of discipline consistent with production routines, and to maintain social control and authority for the sake of reliability. Historical sociologist Dale Tomich has argued, for example, that African enslavement was quickly established in the French Antilles not so much because of any cost advantage, but because with enslaved Africans sugar planters were able to implement better control arrangements and settle more satisfactorily their major concern about the regularity and efficiency of labor (Tomich 1990, 1–14).

Efforts were made in the English and French colonies to hold African slaves and European servants to similar standards of work discipline and social control. Planters were more successful with enslaved Africans, even in the face of persistent resistance, because they had more freedom to violently crush black rebellion without public expressions of concern. As the French priest and longtime Caribbean resident Jean-Baptiste Labat showed, planters used laws to extract from insubordinate servants longer terms of service, and while they were also not reluctant to use military methods to ensure discipline, reports of such events often resonated in France. There was no imperial objection, and rarely a discussion, when Africans were put to death for the crime of rebellion.

The colonial planter, then, was not alone in making the important decisions that accelerated the transition to enslaved labor. Imperial governments and colonial officials facilitated the process with policies and postures that made it rational and more attractive for investors to choose African over European labor wherever necessary and possible. Furthermore, they enabled colonists to maintain two distinct labor cultures in the same colony, one slave-based and one free, in the face of economic factors that suggest the overwhelming market advantage of using enslaved labor.

In Pursuit of Profits

Sugar planters operated within the context of imperial economic policies, as well as the sociocultural and political sensibilities of European nation-building projects. It was an age of aggressive nationalism that centered notions of ethnic solidarity in the face of competition from outsiders. But as profit-seeking entrepreneurs, sugar planters were neither imprisoned by nor immune to metropolitan thinking. Some spoke of the inevitability of slave labor in the colonies while considering slavery a vile system with no place in civilized society.

Planter supporters in the metropolitan judiciaries of France and England keenly invented and endorsed legal systems for African enslavement in the colonies while seeking to keep it illegitimate at home. Imperial politicians welcomed opportunities to "export" convicts, vagrants, the troublesome unemployed poor, and some political prisoners, and turned a blind eye to their enslavement, but they were not willing to accept a definition of them as "slaves."

Europe could not have provided the millions of workers required for the colonial enterprise, because the issue of labor availability is not simply a question of the physical existence of workers. The supply of labor is determined as much by psychological, cultural, and social conditions as by wages and material rewards. It would have required nothing short of a meltdown in the quality of social living for the poor of England and France to promote successful mass emigration to colonies, and for workers to accept a sociolegal status beneath that to which they had been accustomed. This did not occur, and neither the English nor French state was sufficiently strong and confident, or politically willing, to enforce mass involuntary emigration.

As the 17th century drew to a close, English and French colonists were no longer able to justify investments in indentured servitude, even as temporary chattel, on economic grounds. They were, however, able to promote the institution on social and political grounds. The policy decision to pull white women from field gangs because they were better placed to serve the colonial enterprise in the field of reproduction exemplifies the significance of social forces in determining the shape of the labor system. Importantly, it shows that the planters' efforts to reinvent servitude as slavery received some pushback for social and political purposes. In addition, there was the matter of sustaining militia regiments to assist in the suppression of enslaved Africans. To these ends colonial governments, rather than planters, sought to ramp up the demand for male servants.

Given the harshness of Caribbean work and epidemiological environments, for many servants the plantation experience amounted to lifelong enslavement. The legal requirement of fixed-time servitude and the social reality of lifelong labor were offset by mortality trends and management policy. To suggest, as one scholar does, that it "was, of course, inconceivable that any of the [white] labor pools mentioned (convicts, prisoners of war, or vagrants) could have been converted into chattel slaves" is to ignore what was taking place on the ground in the colonies (Eltis 2000, 70).

The conversion of servitude into slavery was conceived by planters of cotton, tobacco, and sugar. If these planters failed at this conversion, it was not because of weak managerial resolve, but because of the multiple internal and external forces that militated against them, including servants' unrelenting ambition to participate in colonialism as independent wealth makers.

From the beginning, those Barbadian planters who received large grants of land calculated the benefits of importing African labor to work them. Pre-sugar Barbadian planters, such as James Drax, were directly involved in sponsoring slave voyages to the African coast; the Drax family later became sugar barons in Barbados and Jamaica. Other English merchants with investment interests in Barbados were known slave traders. The Earl of Warwick, who claimed in 1629 that Barbados was granted him by the monarch, and Maurice Thompson, a large landowner, were involved in the supply of enslaved Africans directly to Barbados before the "sugar revolution."

The contrast with smaller landholders is sharp. Before the Brazilian political crisis of 1645 wrecked that country's sugar industry, the Dutch West India Company was selling slaves on easy terms to creditable planters in Barbados and Guadeloupe. Strapped for cash and alienated from credit, the "small holders did not take to sugar," says Blackburn, "because it was a new and unfamiliar crop, and because it could not be harvested for at least eighteen months after the first planting" (Blackburn 1997, 231). They did not attract Dutch or English credit, had no access to core funding for slave purchase, and thus remained in the servant market. In this way they drove the demand for servants despite the potential availability of slaves.

"Slavery and cotton," then, was as established in Barbados and Guadeloupe in 1640 as would be "sugar and servitude" in 1650 and "sugar and slavery" in 1660. Between 1645 and 1650, the midpoint of the transition, the mixed-labor regime was at its peak. As big investors in cotton production, planters with financial access did two things that prepared them for sugar: they consolidated small plantations into large ones, and they made substantive purchases of enslaved Africans. Economies of scale in cotton production enabled many of these planters to access larger external credit instruments that enabled the expansion of both the servant trade and the slave trade. In addition, the planters sped up the land consolidation process that facilitated the sugar industry.

These investors became industry leaders who championed the charge into sugar production and plantation expansion after 1645. In effect, they were deepening rather than creating the reliance upon enslaved Africans. Capital was scarce and expensive; risks were high. In pursuit of profits, planters fully exploited whatever labor was within their reach. Alongside "sugar and black slavery" there was "sugar and white slavery." Plantation agriculture before, during, and after the sugar revolution generally meant disciplined, coerced labor—and, as Williams so aptly concluded, "at times that labor has been slave, at other times nominally free; at times black, at other times white or brown or yellow" (Williams 1944, 29).

WORKS CITED

Beckles, Hilary McD. 1986. "Blackmen in White Skins: The Formation of a Proletariat in West Indian Slave Society." *The Journal of Imperial and Commonwealth History* 15:5–21.

———. 1989. *White Servitude and Black Slavery in Barbados, 1627–1715.* Knoxville: University of Tennessee Press.

Blackburn, Robin. 1997. *The Making of New World Slavery: From the Baroque to the Modern Times, 1492–1800.* London and New York: Verso.

Dunn, Richard. 1972. *Sugar and Slaves: The Rise of the Planter Class in the English West Indies, 1624–1713.* Chapel Hill: University of North Carolina Press.

Eltis, David. 2000. *The Rise of African Slavery in the Americas.* New York: Cambridge University Press.

Ligon, Richard. 1657. *A True & Exact History of the Island of Barbadoes.* London: Humphrey Moseley.

Menard, Russell R. 2006. *Sweet Negotiations: Sugar, Slavery, and Plantation Agriculture in Early Barbados.* Charlottesville: University of Virginia Press.

Schwartz, Stuart D., ed. 2004. *Tropical Babylons: Sugar and the Making of the Atlantic World, 1450–1680.* Chapel Hill: University of North Carolina Press.

Sheridan, Richard. 1974. *Sugar and Slavery: An Economic History of the British West Indies, 1623–1775.* Kingston, Jamaica: University of the West Indies Press.

Stein, Robert Louis. 1979. *The French Slave Trade in the Eighteenth Century: An Old Regime Business.* Madison: University of Wisconsin Press.

Tomich, Dale. 1990. *Slavery in the Circuit of Sugar: Martinique in the World Economy, 1830–1848.* Baltimore: Johns Hopkins University Press.

Von Uchteritz, Heinrich. 1970. "A German Indentured Servant in Barbados in 1652: The Account of Heinrich Von Uchteritz." *Journal of the Barbados Museum and Historical Society* 3:92–93.

Williams, Eric. 1944. *Capitalism and Slavery.* Chapel Hill: University of North Carolina Press.

———. 1970. *From Columbus to Castro: The History of the Caribbean, 1492–1969.* New York: Vintage.

14

The French and Dutch Caribbean, 1600–1800

PHILIP BOUCHER

Recent historians of the Caribbean have highlighted the social and economic diversity of the colonial era prior to 1800. The popular image of that period as one of "King Sugar" reflects the domination of sugar plantations in Barbados after 1650, Martinique and Guadeloupe from the 1670s, Antigua from the 1680s, Jamaica and Saint-Domingue (now Haiti) after 1700, Suriname from the 1720s, and Cuba in the 19th century. The somewhat exaggerated focus on sugar derives from the fact that the British islands were largely sugar monocultures, and North American students of the pre-1800 Caribbean have paid most attention to those islands. The societies of the colonial British Leeward Islands and Jamaica, especially during the 18th century, were dominated by sugar and the sugar planter elites in a way not found elsewhere in the Caribbean. This chapter comparing the evolution of the Dutch and French Caribbean emphasizes their deviation from the British "model" of the plantation complex, but also points to differences in their develop-

Figure 14.1 Indigo processing plant, including pools for processing the indigo and drying sheds. Engraving from Jean Baptiste Labat, *Nouveau voyage aux isles de l'Amerique* (1742). Source: The John Carter Brown Library.

ment. Historians of the Spanish Caribbean before 1800 may well be sympathetic to a more complex depiction of colonial Caribbean society.

Sugar cultivation, to be sure, did play a major role during the brief Dutch possession of northeastern Brazil from 1630 to 1654, as well as in the economic development of French Martinique and Guadeloupe in the latter third of the 17th century, and of French Saint-Domingue and Dutch Suriname during the 18th century. However, other crops occupied French and Dutch colonists. Tobacco was the first cash crop in the French colonies, and it remained important in Saint-Domingue until the 1690s. From the 1640s, indigo and cotton were important in different islands at different times; from the 1720s, coffee assumed enormous importance in Martinique and Saint-Domingue as well as in Dutch Suriname and Berbice in northern South America. None of these alternative crops required as much capital and slave labor as did sugar, so more modest planters could enter into their production. The average coffee plantation in Saint-Domingue deployed 33 slaves, as compared to the hundreds on large sugar estates. Saint-Domingue exported seven million pounds of coffee in 1755 and fifteen million in 1764 (Garrigus 2006, 173). In 1789 it counted 793 sugar planters (the elite of the island), 787 cotton producers, 3,171 indigo manufacturers, and 3,117 coffee producers (*Voyage aux Iles d'Amérique*, 1992, 197). Martinique and Guadeloupe coffee and indigo makers outnumbered sugar barons about four to one. Around 1750, adult slaves working on sugar plantations constituted just 40% of the total slave population.

By 1770 French planters outproduced their British counterparts in sugar, molasses, coffee, cotton, cacao, and indigo. Antillean commodities constituted half of France's reexports by 1750. Between the 1750s and 1790s, the value of commerce between France and Saint-Domingue tripled; most of the tropical commodities were reexported to European markets. By the 1780s France's tropical American empire was the envy of Europe.

Unlike the English and the French, the Dutch established two important island commercial entrepôts, with only marginal acreage devoted to agricultural or pastoral enterprises. In the 17th century, Curaçao emerged as an economic powerhouse based on legal and illegal commerce, not least the slave trade to Spanish America. St. Eustatius in the northern Leeward Islands became prominent in the 18th century. Thus planter elites did not dominate Curaçao's capital Willemstadt or the town of St. Eustatius, as they did Suriname's capital of Paramaribo, and Cap Français in Saint-Domingue. Another social factor in Dutch colonies that was largely absent from the French Caribbean was the presence of mainly Sephardic Jews in Curaçao and in Suriname, where they actually outnumbered the Dutch. Although a significant Jewish community had existed in the French islands during the middle decades of the 17th century, Louis XIV's policies led to their exodus. Thus, greater economic and religious diversity characterized the Dutch Caribbean (Klooster 1997, 73–75).

Although the Dutch and French colonies shared some similarities with the English sugar islands, they also differed in significant ways. In turn, French and Dutch colonization in the Caribbean also differed significantly from each other.

The Frontier Era: From the 1620s to 1667

During the frontier era, both the French and Dutch put down roots in Caribbean islands and in northern South America. Friendly relations in Europe, due to common hostility to Spain, led to generally amicable French-Dutch interactions in the greater Caribbean. From their initial base in half of St. Christopher (now St. Kitts), first settled in 1625, French colonists and unprepared emigrants from France occupied Martinique and Guadeloupe, relatively large islands of the Lesser Antilles. In the western Caribbean, French buccaneers joined people of various nationalities, including Dutchmen, in establishing outposts at the turtle-shaped island of Tortuga and the nearby coast of northwest Hispaniola (now Haiti). This motley crew of desperadoes hunted wild pigs and cattle for leather and smoked meat, both for their own consumption and for trade with passing ships. These buccaneers occasionally took to the sea in small boats to attack ships of any nationality. By the 1660s the French faction dominated the northwest coast of Hispaniola. Still, it would take the French authorities two generations to transform these proud ruffians into marginally lawful colonists.

The Dutch were somewhat less active in establishing colonies in this period. The Dutch Republic had by far the highest living standard in Europe; its huge merchant and fishing fleet and its prosperous manufactures soaked up all available labor in that country, so resort to a dangerous overseas migration held little appeal. Dutch activities in the Caribbean thus focused on establishing trading posts. For example, the Van Pere family established a post at Berbice in Guyana for trade with the indigenous peoples in dyewood, hammocks, medicinal plants, and other products. Even after the Dutch captured the world's most productive sugar area in Brazil in 1630, their migrants there were primarily agents of the Dutch West India Company, which had been founded in 1621. Portuguese planters and farmers, along with their aboriginal and West African slaves, continued to produce the sugar that now found its way to Amsterdam and to the cities of the southwestern Dutch province of Zealand.

In these same decades the Dutch captured Curaçao (1634), off the coast of modern Venezuela, along with the less valuable islands of Aruba and Bonaire. The almost impregnable harbor of Curaçao, adjacent to the capital, Willemstadt, made that island ideal for access to the rich trade of Spanish America. In return for Spanish silver, cacao, and indigo, Curaçao merchants supplied slaves and manufactured goods desired so ardently by Spanish colonists that official sanctions against the trade proved ineffective (Goslinga 1971, 353). Willemstadt merchants were also delighted to trade with English and French colonists. To the northeast of Curaçao, the Leeward Islands of St. Maarten (from 1648 shared with the French, who call it St. Martin), St. Eustatius, and Saba also came under Dutch control.

During the frontier era chartered companies, such as the old Dutch West India Company (1621–74) and various French trading entities, governed these territories with varying success. Because the French companies were undercapitalized, French colonial trade fell into Dutch hands. In 1664 the French West India Company was founded to remedy this situation, and it slowly managed to direct the flow of French colonial goods to the motherland. When it suffered bankruptcy in 1672–74, Louis XIV took direct control of the French Caribbean.

Colonial Conflicts and Economic Transition, 1667–1720

A second era for the French and Dutch Caribbean began in 1667 and ended about 1720. Louis XIV confronted the Dutch Republic in a series of wars that had dramatic consequences for the greater Caribbean. In 1667 at the conclusion of the Treaty of Breda, which ended the Second Anglo-Dutch War, the Dutch surrendered New Amsterdam (today's New York City) to England for Suriname, which gradually evolved into the richest Dutch plantation colony. Due to treaty obligations, Louis XIV had grudgingly supported his Dutch allies in this war, but in 1672 he attacked them. The isolated republic appeared doomed.

The defensive position of the Dutch in Europe was not mirrored in the Caribbean. Although Louis moved as quickly as possible to build a navy, he could not systematically commit resources to the Caribbean. Between 1673 and 1678 almost constant warfare between the French and Dutch eventually determined the fate of islands like Tobago, which would remain French for some time thereafter, and Curaçao, which over the next four decades would attain its heights as a bustling Dutch trade center.

After the 1670s, Dutch military power in the Caribbean no longer threatened Dutch enemies. In the later wars of Louis's reign, the Dutch allied with England against the French. Dutch possessions on the northern coast of South America suffered from French naval squadrons and corsairs, which forced significant ransoms of slaves and cash. Suriname and Berbice paid the price of painfully slow development as a result. Meanwhile the French Windward colonies, once again left to fend for themselves, were damaged by English assaults but survived intact—except, that is, for St. Christopher and St. Croix, whose inhabitants migrated to Saint-Domingue, where they would help make up for population losses due to Spanish and English invasions.

The War of Spanish Succession (1701–13) had lasting repercussions for the French Caribbean. The accession of Louis XIV's grandson to the Spanish throne as Philip V was the direct cause of the war. England and the Dutch might have tolerated this connection between the French and Spanish royal houses, but then Philip awarded a French syndicate the highly prized contract (asiento) to supply Spanish America with slaves, and this facilitated the smuggling of manufactured goods. England and the Dutch could not stomach the potential loss of their illegal but lucrative trade with the Spanish American empire. At the end of the war, however, Spain changed course and granted Britain permission to introduce slaves into the Spanish American colonies for 30 years under the terms of a new asiento.

During this second period, the major French islands—Guadeloupe and especially Martinique—made the transition to being plantation societies, though at a significantly slower pace than contemporary English Barbados. The French slave

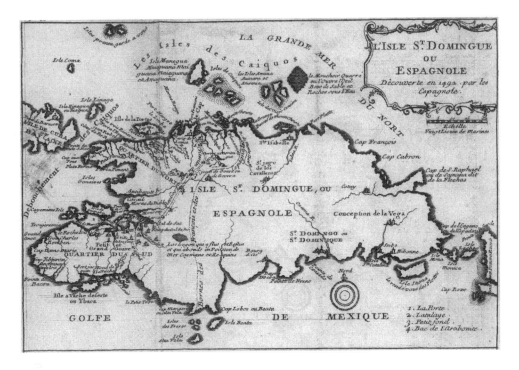

Figure 14.2 Map of Hispaniola. Engraving from Jean Baptiste Labat, *Nouveau voyage aux isles de l'Amerique* (1722). Source: The John Carter Brown Library.

trade was negligible before 1715, so shortages of slaves impeded the French colonies' "progress." Dutch and English smugglers supplied some slaves, and corsairs out of St. Pierre, the commercial capital of Martinique, stole others. Meanwhile, a burgeoning slave trade supplied Barbados—and later the English Leeward Islands, especially Antigua, as well as much larger Jamaica—with adequate forced labor. Louis's wars after 1689 significantly impeded growth in the French Windward Islands—especially in Martinique, where slaves numbered about 16,000 in 1715, the same as they had in 1700 (Pritchard 2004, 424).

Saint-Domingue profited greatly from the 1698 French capture of Spanish Cartagena in South America, which yielded a booty including hundreds of slaves who were then deployed to stake out sugar plantations. Four years later, the War of Spanish Succession opened new opportunities for Saint-Domingue. The English had far too many problems in the European theater to launch attacks in the western Caribbean. With Spain and France now locked in a Bourbon family alliance, Saint-Domingue's colonists obtained access to Spanish Santo Domingo's cattle, which were so important because most sugar mills used them to crush the cane. Spanish silver pesos helped French colonists buy slaves, and the Dutch at Curaçao, technically the enemy, were happy to sell slaves to the French. English merchants also had few scruples about trading with the enemy. Dramatic results ensued. In 1701 about 9,000 slaves worked at Saint-Domingue; in 1715, some 35,000 toiled there (Pritchard 2004, 424). No longer were planters obliged to supplement their incomes with dangerous buccaneering activities.

Plantations, Enslavement, and Revolution, 1720–90

The third era comprises the decades between about 1720 and the beginning of the French Revolution (ca. 1790), which brought turmoil and indeed revolution to some Caribbean islands. During this period, the titanic struggles between the British and French empires allowed the Dutch to largely avoid confrontations in the greater Caribbean, which as a whole saw phenomenal growth, albeit at the expense of the brutal treatment of exploding numbers of African slaves. Years of peace between 1715 and 1744 were beneficial to French colonists at Martinique, Guadeloupe, and Saint-Domingue, to merchants of Curaçao and planters of Suriname, and to the Dutch settlements of Essequibo and Berbice in the Guyanas. The subsequent four years of war had little impact in the Caribbean. In 1746 the Dutch established a new colony at Demerara in Guyana.

Peace and prosperity certainly did not reign during the Seven Years' War (1756–63). For the first time the British navy not only dominated the seas but successfully assaulted Guadeloupe (1758) and Martinique (1761). Planter elites on these islands, having lost the military skills and will of their ancestors, put up minimal resistance. From their perspective, the silver lining in this cloud was that the British poured slaves into these islands. The number of slaves at Guadeloupe, for example, doubled from roughly 42,000 in 1750 to 84,000 in 1772; in Saint-Domingue, the number grew from 148,000 to 261,000 during the same period (Peabody 2002, 75).

For 15 years after 1763, the French and Dutch colonies were generally prosperous, but mercantile St. Eustatius, under Dutch rule, astonished contemporaries. That colony welcomed all comers, including North Americans who were increasingly involved in the triangular trade.

In 1778 France signed an alliance with the American rebels against Britain, and this had large consequences for the Caribbean. The Dutch did not formally join the alliance, but their promotion of an anti-British neutrality pact and their loans to the Americans enraged the British. Both the French and the Dutch paid a price. In 1782, a year after the French Caribbean fleet combined with a Franco-American land force to humiliate the British at Yorktown, the Royal Navy under Admiral George Brydges Rodney annihilated the French fleet. The same Rodney assaulted, captured, and utterly battered St. Eustatius in the fourth Anglo-Dutch War (1782–84; Goslinga 1985, 149–51). In these years, Britain also conquered Demerara. No doubt these victories eased British pain over the loss of the North American colonies.

Peace after 1783–84 promised to restore prosperity in the French and Dutch Caribbean. After a half-century of slow growth, drainage and irrigation projects led to an increase in the number of plantations in Suriname—from about 100 to 400—by the later 1780s. On a much smaller scale, the same was true for Berbice, Essequibo, and Demerara. The boom at Saint-Domingue was even more startling, with 480,000 slaves working in often horrific conditions by 1791. All these societies, however, writhed with the rising social tensions always inherent in slave societies. The revolution that broke out in France in 1789 was a catalyst of revolution in the Caribbean. In 1791 slave rebellions erupted in the north of Saint-Domingue, and the French colonies faced enormous turmoil and even extinction.

Economic and Social Evolution of the Colonies

The dominance of Caribbean society by large plantations was a slow process and not an inevitable one. Planters never dominated Curaçao, St. Eustatius, or the smaller Dutch and French islands (St. Martin/St. Maarten, St. Lucia, Tortuga, Saba, Aruba, Bonaire, Tobago). Curaçao in 1750 had some 4,000 Europeans and 13,000 slaves; St. Eustatius at the same date had only 420 Europeans and 1,200 slaves (Knight 2007, 48). Since most slaves worked in the urban areas, these were not plantation islands like some of the larger colonies.

Small tobacco operations, husbandry, provision farms, salt works, and other small-scale economic activities dominated all island economies prior to the emergence of sugar, indigo, cotton, and coffee production in some of them. Sugar was crucial at Martinique and Guadeloupe by the 1680s, but not to the extent that it would be by the 1750s. In relatively parallel fashion, Suriname and Saint-Domingue emerged as near-mature plantation societies by the 1720s, but their heyday awaited another generation.

Although the Island Caribs of the Lesser Antilles and the Arawaks of the Greater Antilles had already significantly transformed island ecologies, the European intrusion had even harsher environmental impact. Profitable trees such as logwood and mahogany fell to European iron axes, seasonal hunts decimated sea turtle populations, Spanish-introduced cattle and hogs trampled island flora before hungry colonists hunted them to near extinction by 1700. In this era, masters who bemoaned the money spent to feed slaves encouraged them to hunt and fish, because for hungry slaves everything was good to eat: snakes, rats, land crabs, parrots, the rabbit-like agouti, and much else were fair game. The expansion of sugarcane cultivation near the end of the frontier era meant the clearance of land wherever water was accessible. Dutch and French engineers drained swamps and built irrigation ditches. By the 1720s, the introduction and rapid expansion of coffee plantations led to the initial exploitation of uplands in Martinique, Saint-Domingue, and the interior of Suri-

name. Only the sea fish stocks remained relatively untouched because of low market demand: the hot, humid climate made their preservation difficult. Larger, more heavily-forested colonies such as Suriname and Saint-Domingue suffered slower ecological damage than did St. Christopher, Martinique, or Curaçao.

Figure 14.3 European turtle hunters amid a scene of Caribbean biological abundance. Engraving from Jean Baptiste Du Tertre, *Histoire generale des Antilles habitués par les François* (1667). Source: The John Carter Brown Library.

Prior to the triumph of the plantation regime, certain features characterized society in the French and Dutch Caribbean. For one, West African slaves did not overwhelm the European population, in part because they were either unavailable or too costly for farmers in this era. Less affluent whites, even former indentured servants, could find a niche in society, and with few colonists able to achieve great wealth, absentee ownership was not a serious problem. Finally, both colonists and slaves were more likely to produce creole, that is American-born, offspring. These factors tended to promote relatively less harsh master-slave relations than in the mature plantation era. No exact dates or criteria can determine the precise moment of transition to the plantation regime, but historians agree that when the slave population outnumbered freemen by 3, 5, 10, 20—or, as in the case of late 18th-century Suriname, more than 20—to 1, the pre-plantation era was over.

Classic plantation societies emerged primarily in the 18th-century Dutch and French Caribbean. Population changes indicate the scope of the transformation. Martinique in 1700 had 6,774 whites, 15,266 slaves, and 533 people of color; in 1730 the numbers were 12,558, 47,866, and 1,424, respectively. In 1700 Saint-Domingue, which would become the Caribbean's largest plantation colony by the late 18th century, had 4,560 whites, 9,082 slaves, and an unknown number of people of color; in 1730 the numbers were 10,449, 79,545, and perhaps 2,000, respectively (Pritchard 2004, 424). By 1791, Saint-Domingue's European population had grown to almost 31,000, but slaves numbered 480,000 and free blacks and people of color numbered more than 27,000, an unusually high number in a slave society (Peabody 2002, 75). Yet the fact that at least 700,000 African slaves had been imported into Saint-Domingue before 1789 offers a stark demonstration of high slave mortality rates there.

The population development of Suriname differed from that of Saint-Domingue in both the low number and the slow growth of the European population. In 1700 there were but 745 whites and 8,926 slaves; thus blacks already outnumbered Europeans by well more than 10 to 1. No French colony at that time had more than a 2-to-1 imbalance. In 1744 Suriname had 1,217 whites and 25,135 slaves, roughly 1 to 21; by 1754 the numbers were 1,441 and 33,423 (1 to 23). In 1787 at least 90% of Suriname's 63,000 people were slaves. The fact that at least 108,000 slaves were imported to the colony from 1735 to 1787 again testifies to their disproportionately high mortality rates (Postma 1990, 185, 212–13). In contrast, the size of Suriname's European population is attributable to the paucity of Dutch migration, the damage sustained during wars, the failure of Europeans to reproduce, and the colonists' strong urge to get rich quickly and return to the motherland before disease, slave rebels, or maroons terminated such hopes.

Newly arrived slaves from Africa constituted a significant majority of the slave population in both Saint-Domingue and Suriname. The consequences of African predominance in both societies were manifold and transformative. Geographical factors made it possible for slaves to risk running away to found or join maroon communities, and slaves from Africa were more likely to flee than were creole slaves who had never known any other life and who were more likely to have local family ties, although the latter had a better chance of success, given their local knowledge. The inability of Dutch troops to suppress such communities before succumbing to various tropical diseases or maroon ambushes themselves meant that by the 1750s, colonial authorities had to recognize some maroon settlements. Martinique and Guadeloupe, with their more stable creole slave communities and limited hiding places, were not as heavily beset with the maroon threat.

After 1715, the major French islands and Suriname had easier access to the slave trade. Monopoly of the trade by chartered companies had largely ended in France, and after 1730 the New Dutch West India Company (which in 1674 replaced the first, defunct West India Company) had to accommodate private Dutch traders—for a fee, of course. With the exception of about eight years during the Seven Years' War and the American Revolution, planters feared less the wholesale destruction of some previous wars. For the French islands, the British capture of Guadeloupe (1758–63) and Martinique (1762–63) accelerated the evolution of the plantation regime.

Governments and merchant capitalists became increasingly aware of the significance of colonial wealth to the national economy, which prevented neither group from exploiting and alienating colonial planters. Sugar works—and to a lesser extent indigo, coffee, and cotton production—required enormous capital. Capital expenses in machinery, and especially in human labor, strained planter finances. To fund their indulgent life style, an all too human response to a precarious existence characterized by such natural disasters as hurricanes and by early mortality due to disease, planters had to mortgage their lands heavily to retain access to credit. The result often was foreclosures and an increase in absentee ownership. To be sure, the now infamous planter lifestyle played out more intensely in the no-holds-barred colonies of Suriname and Saint-Domingue. Eighteenth-century Martinique and Guadeloupe suffered less from absentee ownership, from extravagant imbalances of free and slave populations, or from significant maroon communities. Although social extravagances and severe treatment of slaves were hardly absent from the French Windward Islands or from Curaçao, they paled in comparison to what existed in Suriname and Saint-Domingue.

The laws governing master-slave relations in the Dutch and French Caribbean were somewhat different—on paper. Dutch governors and colonial councils largely took an ad hoc approach that concentrated on punishing specific slave "crimes" as they occurred. The laws of Curaçao and St. Eustatius were not as starkly rigid as those of Suriname or the Guianese colonies of Essequibo, Berbice, and Demerara, all of which had significant imbalances between European and African populations. For example, punishment for running away was lighter in the island colonies. To be sure, at the height of the maroon scare at Suriname in the 1750s, a reforming governor partially succeeded in implementing measures that temporarily reduced the harshness of slave punishments, much to the masters' dissatisfaction. In none of the Dutch colonies was there a formal effort to convert slaves, although Catholic and Moravian missionaries were sometimes allowed to pursue their activity. Civil marriage of slaves was strongly discouraged, and slave families had no protection from masters selling a father, mother, or child.

In 1763 Berbice suffered a major slave rebellion that nearly succeeded. There, unlike in Suriname, slaves had little hope of establishing maroon communities because the Dutch bribed the indigenous population to shut off escape routes into the jungle. Isolated in a sea of African slaves, mostly newly arrived Berbice planters were notoriously harsh as well as uninterested in militia service—a deadly combination. A mysterious epidemic had reduced their numbers in the 1750s. Led by the creole slaves Coffy and Accarra, the 1763 rebellion nearly drove the Dutch into the sea. Re-

Figure 14.4 Slaves preparing flour from cassava or manioc root. Engraving from Jean Baptiste Labat, *Nouveau voyage aux isles de l'Amerique* (1742). Source: The John Carter Brown Library.

inforcements from other Dutch colonies and division among the slave rebels doomed the revolt, with horrific consequences for those slaves who survived. About half the plantations lay in ruins after this cataclysm.

French authorities attempted to regulate master-slave relations to promote "rational" management of slaves for the long-term benefit of plantation owners and the mother country. The infamous Code Noir (Black Code) of 1685 required Christianization of slaves, encouraged marriage and discouraged separation of family members, provided specific rations of food and clothing, tolerated slaves achieving manumission (freedom), and prohibited masters from using "excessive" force when punishing slaves. Because of changing views in 18th-century France, including the emergence of harsh racism related to growing imbalances between free and enslaved peoples and to mounting colonial pressure, the more "humanitarian" aspects of the Code Noir suffered degradation as the century of "Enlightenment" un-folded. Local sovereign councils, dominated by large planters, interpreted the code according to their own interests. The understaffed colonial church could do little to protect the exploding slave population, and when the Jesuits attempted to do so, they faced strong resistance from colonial authorities and ultimately expulsion (1762–63).

The French colonies avoided slave rebellions on the scale of that in Berbice and maroon conflicts of the intensity of those in Suriname and Jamaica, although maroon communities existed in Saint-Domingue during most of the 18th cen-tury. Why? Masters in Saint-Domingue matched those in Suriname and Berbice for harshness. Perhaps in Saint-Domingue the far larger number of whites and free people of color, many of whom owned slaves and imitated European racial attitudes, made slaves less sanguine about outright rebellion. This is not to say, however, that they accepted the system or that they did not conspire to promote rebellion, as is shown by the discovery in Saint-Domingue of an apparent slave conspiracy led by a charismatic spiritual leader named François Mackandal in 1757—a clear antecedent to the conflagration that was the Haitian Revolution, begun in 1791.

At first glance, relations between the mother countries and the colonies appear very different in the French and Dutch cases. After all, the Dutch political system was federal and largely decentralized, whereas France was the paragon of royal ab-solutism. The Dutch States-General exercised only a loose control of colonial proj-ects in the greater Caribbean, but when pressured by powerful interests they could force changes. For example, in the early 1730s the States-General forced the Dutch West India Company to abandon its slave trade monopoly. The company, however, appointed the colonial governors, and to facilitate its interests in the slave trade the company maintained warehouses and agents in the Caribbean both before and after 1730. Governors ruled the colonies with the help of councils whose members were nominated by the colonists. Invariably, wealthy men, merchants, and planters dominated these councils, and governors who refused to acknowledge their inter-ests had a rough time.

The French governmental structure appears much more centralized. The king—advised by the secretary of state for the navy—appointed colonial governors and, unlike the British, paid their salaries. Officials known as intendants were in charge of civil and judicial affairs. Both governor and intendant worked at the king's plea-sure. The major islands each had at least one sovereign council composed of wealthy men commissioned by the king upon the advice of his colonial officials. These coun-cils implemented the orders of the king and his officials, and handled most judicial cases. In practice, royal officials could not without consequences ignore the advice and interests of the most influential island planters. Temporarily successful rebel-lions at Martinique and Saint-Domingue between 1717 and 1723 demonstrated that the colonial wishes of the emerging planter elite could not be blithely ignored.

Especially during the 18th century, French planters, increasingly resentful of metropolitan creditors and of royal intrusions that inhibited their desperate drive for profit and social honors, demanded greater autonomy and respect. They understood their own dependence on the king for protection against the British and against slave rebellion, and for elevation to noble status. Further stoking resentment was the disdain of royal officials and visitors from France who laughed at the social pretensions of the planter elite, even when in some cases accepting their rich daughters as wives. Especially in Saint-Domingue, the growth of absentee ownership from the 1740s and the emergence of a large, impoverished white group (*petits blancs*) aggravated tensions within the European community. After 1763, both governmental officials and white elites created racial barriers to stop the economic power and social "pretensions" of a burgeoning class of free and often wealthy people of color. Nevertheless, the numbers of that class exploded, reaching some 40% of the free population in 1789—a telling commentary on the effectiveness of royal legislation. Such social anxieties and frustration led in 1789–91 to political tumult among and between the white people and the free people of color, which in turn opened the way for the slave rebellion that ended French rule in its "Pearl of the Indies."

WORKS CITED

Garrigus, John. 2006. *Before Haiti: Race and Citizenship in French Saint-Domingue.* New York: Palgrave MacMillan.

Goslinga, Cornelis Ch. 1971. *The Dutch in the Caribbean and on the Wild Coast, 1580–1680.* Gainesville: University of Florida Press.

———. 1985. *The Dutch in the Caribbean and in the Guianas, 1680–1791.* Assenl Maastnicht, the Netherlands: Van Gorcum.

Klooster, Winn. 1997. *The Dutch in the Americas, 1600–1800.* Providence: John Carter Brown Library.

Knight, Franklin, ed. 2007. *The Slave Societies of the Caribbean.* Vol. 3 of the *General History of the Caribbean.* New York: Palgrave MacMillan.

Peabody, Sue. 2002. "'A Dangerous Zeal': Catholic Missions to Slaves in the French Antilles, 1635–1800." *French Historical Studies* 25, no. 1: 53–90.

Postma, Johannes. 1990. *The Dutch in the Atlantic Slave Trade, 1600–1815.* Cambridge: Cambridge University Press.

Pritchard, James. 2004. *In Search of Empire: The French in the Americas, 1670–1730.* Cambridge: Cambridge University Press.

Voyage aux Iles d'Amérique. 1992. Catalog of an exposition organized by the French National Archives, Paris.

15

Slaves and Tropical Commodities

The Caribbean in the South Atlantic System

SELWYN H. H. CARRINGTON

RONALD C. NOEL

In the 18th century, the Caribbean represented a crucial link in the South Atlantic System, in which European traders transferred what they considered goods of limited value to the African continent in exchange for captives, who in turn were transported to the Caribbean. While the British initially believed that such goods—household utensils and substandard guns, for example—were of marginal importance to their domestic economy, they served as units of exchange in Africa, and the proceeds from this kind of commerce eventually contributed to the growth and prosperity of a number of European industrial cities where industries such as metallurgy and shipbuilding benefited significantly from the African trade. Meanwhile, goods taken to Africa were used to secure a supply of captives to be sold to planters as labor to provide tropical commodities for the European and American markets. Those commodities—most notably, sugar—were transported to European metropolitan centers for domestic consumption, and the surpluses were traded in European markets to complete the transfer process.

Trade was conducted within the context of mercantilism, which informed the structure of the political economy. British leaders did not want their colonies to compete with domestic industries. They planned to specialize domestically in the production of high-value-added manufactured goods for consumers and to import low-value-added raw materials from the colonies. In this context, "value added" meant roughly "the greater value of output of a productive process than (hopefully) the inputs necessary to its production" (Scott 1997–2001). This chapter provides a general introductory discussion on the concept of value-added linkages in the South Atlantic System, the trade and exploitation of African labor, and the sugar economy and diversification of the commodities produced in the Caribbean. The main referents will be Great Britain, its supply outposts in Africa, and its Caribbean colonies.

The South Atlantic System must be examined in the context of both intrinsic and extrinsic value-added linkages. The process began when British goods were exchanged for African captives, who were thus transformed from mere human cargoes to enslaved chattel. They worked in bondage within a plantation system that obtained intrinsic value-added benefits which could be exploited at the next stage in the Atlantic. Some of these benefits included the demand for human labor power in the Caribbean; the metallurgical and agricultural skills that Africans possessed; immunity to tropical diseases, which enhanced their survival rates in the new environment; and, in spite of rapid depreciation, labor that was relatively cheap to maintain in the Caribbean and thus extremely attractive in the political economy as a whole.

The enslaved also added extrinsic value through the transformative capabilities of their labor to produce commodities that were subsequently used or processed by Europeans; that is, their labor became the base of all output. In terms of the specific kinds of agricultural commodities their labor produced, they added value to the land. Moreover, their ability to replicate this production continuously brought a level of reliability and assurance to the economic system. These characteristics of the international trade in enslaved Africans underscore the extent to which Europeans depopulated the African continent for their own enrichment.

Europeans and the Transatlantic Trade in Enslaved Africans

What to call the human beings trafficked from the African continent has always been a difficult question, but as recommended by a 2007 conference sponsored by UNESCO, they will be referred to here as "captured" or "enslaved" Africans rather than "slaves." This usage emphasizes that the Middle Passage was only one segment in a whole series of dehumanizing experiences that Africans endured in the "New World." Beginning in the early 16th century, captives from various parts of Africa left the Atlantic side of the continent to serve the interests of traders and planters in the Americas and the Caribbean. From the moment of captivity, enslaved Africans were stripped of their identities. European predators exhibited little regard for the humanity of millions of people who were extracted from their African homelands and transported to the West in one of the worst forms of labor migration and capitalist exploitation ever. Of these, untold millions died before they arrived in the Americas.

The New World portion of the transatlantic trade in Africans commenced soon after the invasion of the Americas and the foundation of colonies. The Portuguese were faced with a great demand for labor in their colony of Brazil and in the Spanish empire, for which they held the asiento (a license to sell Africans to Spanish merchants). Portuguese traders initially looked for captives on the Senegal and Gambia rivers, on the Gold Coast, at Benin, in the Niger Delta, on the islands of Fernando Po and São Tomé, and in the Congo at Cabenda, Luanda, and Loango. The trade in Africans to the Caribbean began in the 16th century, only a couple of decades after the Spanish colonized Hispaniola. The first wave of African laborers came into the Caribbean as replacements for the decimated populations of Taino and Kalinago (Carib) people throughout the region.

The establishment of the slave trade created intense commercial activity among the four major European powers involved: the Dutch, British, French, and Portuguese. Even though Spain possessed most of the insular Caribbean area in the heyday of the African trade, it did not control territories in Africa. For the greater part of the history of this trade, Spain remained a customer relying on the asiento. Portuguese merchants were the first to hold the asiento, but when Portugal revolted against Spain in 1640, it lost that right. The Dutch then controlled the supply of Africans to Spanish territories until 1702, when the asiento passed to the French. In 1713 the Treaty of Utrecht gave it to the British-owned South Sea Company, which was given a 30-year right with an annual import of 4,800 Africans. Britain held the asiento until the War of Jenkins' Ear in 1739.

British involvement in the African trade reportedly began with Sir John Hawkins in 1562. In 1660, British merchants formed their first joint stock company for trading in Africa. For more than 200 years they took measures to enhance the trade, given its importance to their economy. In 1662 Charles II established an exclusive African company that proved unsuccessful; in 1672 he created another such company with a thousand-year charter.

In 1689 Caribbean planters complained about the exorbitant prices of the enslaved Africans sold by the Royal African Company (Moya Pons 2007). The price of captives in Barbados and Jamaica had increased from an average of £12–14 a few years earlier to a high of £20. The company argued that it was constrained by high maintenance costs in Africa. Moreover, a shortage of captives in the Caribbean encouraged many merchants and absentee planters to make use of independent traders, who paid the company a fee of 10% on the value of their trade from 1698 onward. The trade flourished, and independent traders prospered. In the first decade of the 10% rule, nearly 90,000 captives were taken to Jamaica, Barbados, and Antigua through independent traders. Between 1680 and 1708, by comparison, the Royal African Company transported approximately 64,000 captives to the colonies.

The British government ended the company's monopoly in 1698 and the 10% rule in 1712. Since all merchants now had permission to trade in captives, the shortage in the British colonies came to an end. Most of the traders functioned from Liverpool, London, and Bristol and to a lesser degree from Lancaster and Manchester. The Royal African Company terminated its operations around 1752, and the independent merchants formed a loose association called the Company of Merchants Trading to Africa. Like the former company, they maintained forts on the African coast, whose upkeep was now financed by the British Parliament.

By the time the British crown and Parliament sought to take control of the trade to Africa, other European countries had become firmly established in this venture. The French and Dutch were probably the first to charter joint-stock companies. The Dutch had been involved in the trade since the early days of the Portuguese, and in 1621 they formed the Dutch West India Company. Capturing Brazil involved the Dutch more significantly in the trade, and by 1642 they gained a monopoly by systematically capturing all the Portuguese trading bases on the Gold Coast, as well as in Arguin, Goree, and Angola. Dutch preeminence in the trade was enhanced with the settlement of Curaçao and other Caribbean territories, which became significant entrepôts for the Caribbean end of the African trade. In addition, investors in Amsterdam, Zealand, and elsewhere underwrote investments in other national joint stock companies such as the Danish West India Company, the Swedish African Company, and the Brandenburg African Company. The role of the Dutch as suppliers diminished after the 1650s with the passage of mercantilist legislation and with the ability of the European nations to supply their own Caribbean islands with captives.

In 1645 Louis XIII approved legislation allowing the French Company of the West Indies, chartered in 1664, to import African captives into the French West Indies. A decade later the company collapsed and was replaced by the Company of Senegal, which carried out its activities in the Senegambia region. The French Guinea Company, which was established in 1685 and won the asiento in 1701–2, lost its contract to the British in 1713. Yet the expansion of the French Caribbean sugar industry increased the growth of the French share of the trade in the 18th century. The economic "golden age" of the French sugar islands began after the Seven Years' War; the demand for African labor there attained new heights, and measures were taken to ensure a steady supply of captives. From 1763 onward, French traders operating in Africa had strong motives to exert pressure to eliminate the British and Dutch as suppliers to the French islands, especially Saint-Domingue.

The decade of the 1780s witnessed the peak of the French captive trade, which was halted by the revolution in Saint-Domingue in 1791 and the abolition of slavery there in 1794. The trade was reopened to some French colonies in 1802, but it never attained its earlier levels. Estimates placed the number of Africans imported into the French islands at an annual average of 15,000 in the period before the American Revolution. Another estimate for the years 1774 and 1776 placed the average number at 16,000. For the eight trading years of the 1780s, the annual average reached an astounding 36,000 or more Africans. French estimates for Saint-Domingue alone were 37,000 in 1785, 31,000 in 1787, and 30,100 in 1788. It is estimated that in 1791 Saint-Domingue's enslaved community numbered 480,000.

The transition to enslavement was very difficult for the captives. Many of the slaving vessels picked up shipments of captives from various points on the coast of Africa, creating an abundance of African ethnicities on the different islands. On Dominica alone there were captives from Old and New Calabar, Gambia, Cape Mount, Angola, Bonny, Cameroon, and Anamaboo (Anomabu), among others. These names refer to the regions from which the Africans were acquired for shipment, not their specific ethnic groups. In fact, the African ethnic groups identified today may not have existed as such during the period of the African trade. It was only after the need to differentiate among groups of Africans under slavery that planters developed stereotypical notions of African ethnicities.

Such ideas often had very little basis in how the captives themselves may have identified, and tended to function more like "brand names" in the context of the slave trade. Planters thus often expressed preference for certain of these "ethnicities," but their preferences varied—not only regionally, but over time. The users of African enslaved labor wanted to ensure that they had purchased the best stock of human labor. Some planters, for example, preferred slaves categorized as "Mandingoes" because of their appearance, while others shunned them for allegedly being haughty and disobedient. In the British and French Caribbean, people classified as "Ebo" (exported from the Bight of Biafra) acquired a reputation for being prone to kill themselves, while no such image became attached to Africans from this region in the Hispanic islands. A group that particularly captivated the minds of British Caribbean planters were the "Koromantyn" (Coromantees/Coromantin) or Gold Coast Africans, who belonged to Akan-speaking linguistic groups and were considered arrogant and rebellious (Long 1970). Indeed, "Koromantyns" led several rebellions in the Caribbean, though of course there is no way to directly relate this fact to any characteristics of the societies and cultures in Africa from which they had come. Nor is it clear who these "Koromantyn" rebel leaders really were, since many Africans in the West Indies came to call themselves "Koromantyns" because the name created fear in the minds of white society.

Mortality rates in the trade were very high, beginning at the moment of capture in the African interior. Traveling in coffles, the captives passed through inhospitable terrain to coastal entrepôts. The long journey, which could take months, led to the loss of captives as a result of exposure, fatigue, starvation, thirst, and suicide. Those who survived and were selected—based on age, health, and ethnic or regional origin—for exportation were often stockpiled in barracoons (coastal slave barracks) or aboard slave ships for lengthy periods because of various circumstances that delayed their voyage across the Atlantic. Those who were ultimately rejected for enslavement became displaced, in a form of forced relocation, and many died.

The journey through the Middle Passage took several weeks. It is well accepted that very many captives died during the Middle Passage; only the rate of such mortality is in dispute. Just as historians cannot agree on exactly how many Africans were forcibly removed from their homes and shipped overseas, they cannot identify the total number who died during the Middle Passage. An average figure might put the loss at about 35%. This percentage includes those people who did not survive the period of adjustment ("seasoning," as it was called) or who died young on plantations. It does not include those who died before leaving Africa—a figure that was shockingly high. In 1789 the British parliamentarian William Wilberforce gave an overall mortality figure of 50%, which formed part of the emerging numbers game. However, mortality varied over time, with higher numbers obtaining during the earlier years.

It has been argued by apologist historians of enslavement that even if there was a lack of humanity, planters were still encouraged by "motives of self-interest" to provide for the health, welfare, and long life of their enslaved workers (Sheridan 1973). Although some individual plantation records show evidence of this, the greater proportion of data does not support it as the norm. The sad reality was that the enslaved population was not self-renewing. Using the findings of 15 notable English and French authors, Williams Dickson came to the conclusion in 1814 that field slaves did not live longer than 7 years and the overall population of enslaved people did not survive beyond 15 years. Dickson estimated that the rate at which enslaved people died was more than twice that of normal human mortality (Sheridan 1973). Thus, even at the time, there was a perception that West Indian planters purchased Africans for the purpose of working them to death.

In most colonies, enslaved Africans and their descendants worked in the fields from sunrise to sunset, under the burning rays of the sun and at times in the pouring rain. Under these conditions, they worked in gangs in constant fear of the whip that exploded on their backs at the slightest sign of relaxation. In one phase of the gang system of organized work, Africans dug holes for sugarcane. Individuals were required to dig on average of 120 holes per day in previously plowed land but only 90 in unplowed fields. This activity was considered one of the hardest and most deadly on the plantations. The death toll was highest among women of all ages and among children. The former had difficulty becoming pregnant, while the latter developed spinal injuries. Ultimately, the African populations in the Caribbean reproduced at unnaturally low rates, a direct result of the severe stress of plantation life as designed by European planters.

The Greater Enterprise

But enslavement of Africans was just the first step in a much larger and more lucrative enterprise. Their agricultural output had to be exported in ships. The ships had to be built and the crews found. Port facilities had to be developed to accommodate the ships, and firms established to manage sailings. Insurance companies became involved in securing the freight against the risk of peril at sea. Each step required the establishment of a discrete industry. Thus, the shipbuilding industry required designers, carpenters, blacksmiths, industrial tailors, and ammunition experts; it also needed wood, iron, tools, technique, and suitable locations. Shipping companies required bookkeepers, accountants, clerks, managers, and crews. Insurance companies required underwriters, claims adjusters, actuaries, and clerks. From these needs a growing body of knowledge developed based on repetition and practical reasoning, which in turn influenced the character of the education system needed to train the people used by these industries. The tremendous flow of output by enslaved Africans in the Caribbean thus added value in both financial gain and social knowledge, both of which translated into the employment of European managerial talent in diverse ways.

The extrinsic value-added phenomenon also involved the secondary stage of the production process: processing the raw materials imported from the Caribbean and converting them into other goods. In normal times, this was the point at which value was added to African labor. Throughout the colonial period in the West Indies, all cultivated crops served key purposes in the homeland economies. Indigo was produced for coloring clothing, and cochineal was used as a red food colorant, but these were both minor exports. Tobacco was cultivated and processed into cigars. Cocoa beans were transformed into chocolate beverages, candies, cakes, and pastries. Coffee was used for hot beverages on both sides of the Atlantic. All items provided personal satisfaction to those who enjoyed their consumption, as well as economic benefits to those who engaged in their production and transformation. It is not unreasonable to suggest that they helped diversify household and industrial recipes used by Europeans.

But it was sugar, the major Caribbean export, that exponentially increased the value-added phenomenon and fundamentally transformed the industrial landscape of the West Indies. Sugarcane monopolized the vast amount of land allocated to agriculture. This crop yielded not only crystalline sugar, in a primary form called muscovado, but also two important by-products, molasses and rum. The appetite for sugar in northern Europe expanded in the 18th century, especially in England. Its success depended on the fact that so many household, industrial, and pharmaceutical recipes and formulations required it as an ingredient. Additional refining improved the quality even further, for both marketing and aesthetic reasons. This was an important value-added stage because it stimulated other branches of industrial activity in Britain.

As sugarcane spread in the latter half of the 17th century, the mercantilist system, with its requirement that colonies trade exclusively with their metropoles, grew in significance for Britain and France. Although the Caribbean colonies underwent some agricultural diversification in this period, partly in response to the food demands of a growing population, in reality all other agriculture and animal husbandry had now become distant seconds to sugar and its by-products. Consequently, by the 18th century the region's political economy had been reoriented toward sugar production for export, based on the labor of enslaved Africans.

The political culture of the Caribbean planters and merchants and their agents adjusted to this shift. This group had originally obtained its political will through shrewd deployment of capital. Its members exerted a great deal of influence over the local governors, legislatures, and judicial systems, since colonial laws favored this oligopolistic group. The legislatures did not act *on behalf of* the establishment; they *were* the establishment. The whole framework of creole society in the British Caribbean was built to fulfill the demands and wishes of this group, which experienced the value-added phenomenon by virtue of being the wealthiest and most respectable people in the colonies.

This group's benefits extended to Britain. Members bought their way into the British Parliament in the 18th century and were influential there until the Reform Act of 1832. Therefore, prior to that time they were in a strategic position to shape colonial policy. Their objective was to obtain an abundance of revenue for planters, merchants, and other stakeholders but not for the masses, who were in various forms of servitude. The crown in turn earned revenues in the form of taxes and duties, which were supposed to reflect its role as custodian of the people. It was through this crude model of agriculture and commerce that many hoped to achieve a personal fortune from the commercial capitalism operating in the Caribbean.

But this political economy contained highly strategic conflicts of interest, because planters legislated for their own benefit and not for efficiencies that would have benefited laborers if free market conditions had prevailed. By far, most laborers in the Caribbean were enslaved persons who had been obtained at a relatively low cost. While their nominal cost was a factor cost of production, their purchase and maintenance costs were lower than their long-term value as assets. Even in the eyes of shrewd planters, the need to use enslaved labor was governed by the expectation that the value of output would surpass the value of costs. This logic helped drive the demand for enslaved labor. Moreover, in many instances the lands owned by the planters had been acquired for less than their real market value, and the savings were most probably used to acquire still more land and enslaved labor. In this context, those who controlled the means of production, distribution, and exchange were able to obtain wealth and exercise political power directly and at a relatively low cost.

In *The Wealth of Nations* (1776), Adam Smith, a political economist and vanguard of the industrial bourgeoisie, questioned the extent to which this value-added benefit remained intact when notions of efficiency were raised. He argued that it was the masters' lust for power that drove the need for enslaved labor, which was actually more expensive than free hired labor (Williams 1994). Smith also believed in the self-regulating dynamics of the marketplace. His ideas about mercantilism, which he saw as too restrictive, were very influential in Britain. By the late 18th century, there was a growing momentum toward a self-regulating market system, one that would cater both to the interests of the emerging industrialists and to the welfare of those who would have to consume the output they helped to make in factories. Moreover, the commercial capitalism that informed the political economy of the metropole was now breaking away from its traditional reliance on chattel to one in which wage labor and mechanization would coexist in a new, more efficient capitalist industrial paradigm. The budding Industrial Revolution gave legitimacy to this perspective. Technological advances demanded a new relationship between labor and the state in the colonies and between labor and the industrialists in the metropoles. The industrialists were poised to crush the hegemony of the landed gentry, and in this new political economy, planters began to appear obsolete.

Sugar and the Diversification of Commodities

From the beginning of the settlement of the region, Caribbean economies were organized toward satisfying and meeting the demands of external markets. The small domestic market played only a minor role in determining the quantity of goods produced. In fact, these were and had been free capitalist economies inhibited mainly by market forces. Karl Marx qualified this early notion of capitalism by suggesting that the settlers behaved "like people who, driven by motives of bourgeois production, wanted to produce commodities." Plantations were therefore units of "commercial speculation where a capitalist mode of production exists, if only in the formal sense." The enslaved populations were used in businesses operated by capitalists. Marx also noted that regarding plantation owners as capitalists was "based on their existence as anomalies within a world market based on free labor" (Mintz 1986). During the 18th century, these economies were organized in a system of near monoculture of sugarcane and its relevant by-products as the chief earner of foreign revenue (Thompson 2002).

But even as the sugar economy reached its peak in the British and French Caribbean, signs of trouble and diversification began to appear. The colonies of the Greater Antilles, such as Jamaica and Saint-Domingue, arrived at their optimum sugar production potential in the 1750s. Sugar products represented 93% of Barbados's exports by 1770 and more than 97% of the Leeward Islands' exports. Jamaica was the largest producer of sugar in the British empire from 1750 until the 1830s; by 1774 it had a population of about 18,000 whites who were in charge of over 193,000 enslaved Africans, with 755 sugar plantations producing an output of 50,000 tons of sugar (Moya Pons 2007, Sheridan 1973). But the American Revolution affected the British Caribbean economically by isolating the colonies from their metropolitan markets (Williams 1984). Again, enslaved Africans suffered the consequences: from 1780 to 1787, as many as 15,000 of them may have died as a result of famine in Jamaica, with additional casualties on other islands.

In French Saint-Domingue, a number of sugar estates were established in the coastal areas during the 1720s and 1730s. By the 1740s these estates produced more sugar than all of the British islands combined. Between 1766 and 1770 their average annual sugar production was 61,300 tons. Saint-Domingue's white population increased from 4,336 in 1681 to 32,650 in 1775, while the number of enslaved Africans grew from 2,312 to 249,098. By the 1770s, the colony's total production outstripped that of the British islands; with a healthy coffee sector experiencing unprecedented prosperity, it had become the Caribbean's most prosperous economy (Carrington 2010). Major irrigation projects such as reservoirs, diversion dams, levees, aqueducts, and canals were undertaken to make the island the world's leading supplier of sugar until the beginning of the Haitian Revolution in 1791.

In spite of this concentration in sugar production, economic diversification was an option pursued throughout the region after the middle of the 18th century. Coffee, cocoa, and the livestock industry emerged and flourished in Jamaica, St. Vincent, Dominica, Grenada, and Tobago. In the 18th century Jamaica and Saint-Domingue stood out as producers of multiple secondary crops, which by the end of slavery would emerge as significant cash and revenue earners. Jamaica contained about four times the total acreage of the remaining British sugar colonies, and its physical features, soil fertility (especially in the many extensive valleys), and varying climatic conditions made its estimated 2,350,000 acres of cultivable land well suited to the growth of several species of tropical products and to the rearing of cattle. Moreover, the island contained more than 16 major harbors and numerous bays or roads with good anchorage (Long 1970). Throughout the century, Jamaica exported a number of items apart from sugar, including coffee, cocoa, lignum vitae, ebony, fustick, ginger, and pimento. Coffee emerged as an important tropical commodity to rival sugar toward the end of the century.

But no British West Indian island was large enough to establish a true equilibrium between tropical commodity production and subsistence agriculture. As early as 1720, Jamaica's assembly adopted schemes to populate the island with small immigrant planters. In 1736, 30,000 acres of land in the Manchioneal and Norman Valley regions were designated for distribution to new settlers, with 50-acre lots going to heads of families and their wives, 20 acres to each child, and 10 acres for every enslaved African, up to a maximum of 300 acres per family. These attempts were designed to develop a proto-peasant economy because the labor force would still be under servitude until 1838 (Mintz 1985); full peasantry came after that date. It is important to point out that the idea of peasantry in the West Indies was not the same as what obtained in Europe, where the quantity of land per peasant was higher: about 15 acres, as opposed to two to five acres in the West Indies.

The Caribbean colony with the most diversified economy in the 18th century was ultimately Saint-Domingue. It has generally been held that the French colonies refrained from developing monocultural economies during this period even though sugar was the primary tropical commodity produced on the island. The products it exported to France, apart from sugar, included many of the crops grown in Jamaica. Martinique, Guadeloupe, and St. Lucia—the smaller French dependencies—exported the same commodities.

Conclusion

Eighteenth-century Caribbean colonies existed for the sole benefit of the European metropolitan economies. Restricted by the doctrine of mercantilism, they had a strong tendency toward oligopoly in their political framework, with a European minority—to whom the majority of profits from commodity production flowed—in control. In spite of the colonies' consistent production of tropical commodities, governments and their planter allies imposed limitations on their economic potential. Enslaved labor was heavily favored over waged labor because back in the metropoles it was seen as an expedient and seemingly inexhaustible "human resource." The inhumane treatment of enslaved Africans did not elicit moral outrage from the planters and merchants; instead, it was justified as an economic virtue.

In addition, the colonial relationship placed limitations on economic innovation. The growing momentum of industrial capitalism challenged the efficiency of this archaic system, furthering instead a less restrictive trading environment—"free trade," as it was called in the British sphere—and fostering the emancipation of enslaved workers. Thus, the political economy governing commercial capitalism was forced to change in order to accommodate to the new philosophy underpinning a triumphant industrial capitalism. The implications for this new world order would be more clearly grasped in the 19th century.

WORKS CITED

Carrington, Selwyn H. H. 2010. "Statistics for the Study of Caribbean History 1650–1850." Manuscript.

Harris, Joseph. 1998. *Africans and Their History.* New York: Meridian.

Long, Edward. [1774]1970. *The History of Jamaica.* 3 vols. London: F. Cass.

Mintz, Sidney W. 1985. "From Plantations to Peasantries in the Caribbean." In *Caribbean Contours,* ed. Sidney W. Mintz and Sally Price, 127–54. Baltimore: Johns Hopkins University Press.

———. 1986. *Sweetness and Power: The Place of Sugar in Modern History.* New York: Penguin Books.

Moya Pons, Frank. 2007. *History of the Caribbean: Plantations, Trade, and War in the Atlantic World.* Princeton, NJ: Markus Wiener Publishers.

Scott, Carole E. 1997–2000. "America's Colonial Period: Understanding the Colonial Period through Economic Theory." http://freepages.history.rootsweb.ancestry.com/~cescott/colonial .html.

Sheridan, Richard. 1973. *The Development of the Plantations to 1750: An Era of West Indian Prosperity, 1750–1775.* Barbados: Caribbean University Press.

Thompson, Alvin O. 2002. *Unprofitable Servants: Crown Slaves in Berbice, Guyana, 1803–1831.* Barbados: University of the West Indies Press.

Williams, Eric. 1984. *From Columbus to Castro: The History of the Caribbean 1492–1969.* New York: Vintage Books.

———. 1994. *Capitalism and Slavery.* Chapel Hill: University of North Carolina Press.

PART 4

Capitalism, Slavery, and Revolution

16

Slave Cultures

PHILIP MORGAN

Systems of Domination and Forms of Resistance

The Caribbean received more enslaved Africans than any other
region in the New World. Slavery took a highly exploitative form
in the region, yet enslaved Africans and their descendants there
created some of the most vibrant cultures anywhere in the Americas. One of the paradoxes of slave life in the Caribbean is therefore
the harshness of its material conditions coupled with the resilience
of its sociocultural forms.

The Caribbean gave rise to a bewildering variety of slave cultures. There were imperial variants: slave culture in the Spanish
sector differed from that in the Dutch, British, French, and Danish
sectors. There were great differences between the slave cultures of
big and small islands, lowlands and highlands, terrestrial and maritime worlds, sugar-dominated and diversified economies, urban
and rural settings. Spatial variations were complicated by tempo-
ral changes. Slave life differed in the early and mature stages of
a society's development, in frontier and settled phases of growth,

from slave-owning societies to slave societies, from eras of consolidation to ages of revolution and emancipation.

Slave cultures were also shaped by a complicated array of factors: the timing, magnitude, and coastal origins of the African slave trade; birth and death rates of enslaved Africans; demographic proportions of whites, blacks, and people of mixed racial ancestry; gender ratios; the type and intensity of the work performed by slaves; the constraints set by the masters' power and institutions; religious structures; and imperial frameworks—just to mention some of the most important variables.

Slave Trade

Between 1500 and 1870, the Caribbean region (construed as the islands and associated mainland rim) was the destination of about 5.75 million Africans, about 46% of all captives involved in the transatlantic slave trade. Four years after the first black slaves came from Seville in 1501, 17 African slaves arrived in Hispaniola to work in its copper mines and 100 or so in its gold mines. In 1525, 213 captives from São Tomé landed in Santo Domingo, marking probably the first slave voyage from Africa to the Americas. For the next century Africans continued to arrive in small numbers (perhaps 7,000 total) in the Spanish Caribbean islands. Not until the second quarter of the 17th century did a significant number (about 27,000) arrive in the British Caribbean. The 18th century was the high point of the trade, accounting for two-thirds of all Africans shipped to the Caribbean, although Cuba received most of its slaves (710,000) in the 19th century. The British Caribbean received the most Africans—almost 2.8 million—with the French next at 1.3 million, the Spanish about 1 million, the Dutch about 500,000, and the Danish just 130,000. About 15% to 20% of Africans arriving in the Caribbean were subsequently traded within the Americas.

The origins of these Africans varied. Overall, West-Central Africa supplied the most slaves—about 1.6 million. After 1595 Angola became the leading source of slaves for Spanish America; later it contributed about one-third of Africans brought into Cuba. The next most important region was the Bight of Biafra, which supplied about 1.3 million slaves, while the Gold Coast supplied just over a million, mostly to the British West Indies. The Bight of Benin exported just under a million, over a third of them to the French West Indies. The three regions of Upper Guinea—Senegambia (500,000), Sierra Leone (300,000), and the Windward Coast (300,000)—were minor suppliers despite being geographically the closest to the Caribbean. South East Africa sent fewer than 200,000.

Particular islands drew on specific regions of Africa for considerable periods of time. Before 1725, about three-quarters of Africans in Jamaica came from the Gold Coast and the Bight of Benin, accounting for the early prominence of so-called

"Coromantees" from the former coastal region and Adja-speakers from the latter on the island; later, however, Jamaica received most of its Africans from the Bight of Biafra. In the first quarter of the 18th century, 60% of African arrivals in Saint-Domingue were from the Bight of Benin; by the third quarter of the century, 60% came from West-Central Africa. Overall, about half of Saint-Domingue's Africans came from Angola and the Congo. When the slave trade into Cuba began in earnest in the late 18th century, about a third of its Africans were from the Gold Coast. Thereafter, West-Central Africa and the Bight of Biafra predominated.

Slave Populations

The scale of the demographic disaster among Caribbean slave populations was staggering. By 1790 about 3.5 million Africans had arrived in the Caribbean, but the slave population, then at its peak, stood at only 1.5 million. This number represented a doubling of the population since 1750—primarily due to the remarkable intensification of the Atlantic slave trade and the constant infusions from Africa, since the existing slave population failed to self-reproduce. Annual rates of natural decrease in this population were about −5 or −6% in the late 17th century, gradually improving to about −1% in the early 19th. Throughout the 18th century, rates averaged about −2%, although they worsened in the latter half of the century as the numbers of Africans rose markedly, and they were always higher in the British and Dutch Caribbean than in the Danish and French Caribbean—a difference probably best explained by the greater British and Dutch focus on sugar.

The Spanish Caribbean—where slave populations were growing naturally by the 18th century, if not before—represented an obvious exception to these trends. In the first half of that century, the slave populations grew about as fast on these islands as on the North American mainland; later in the century, as the number of African arrivals rose significantly, the rate of natural increase dropped to less than 1%, but the continued positive rate was nevertheless a striking achievement in larger Caribbean terms. Births exceeded deaths not only in Cuba, Santo Domingo, and Puerto Rico during the pre-plantation era but also in Barbados and Antigua during the late slave era. Possibly the sugar economies on these two British islands became less onerous by this period and their slave populations, increasingly comprised of creoles, with more equal sex ratios, began to grow naturally. Other smaller islands where sugar production never took hold, such as the Bahamas, also had slave populations growing by natural increase.

As abolition of the slave trade made itself felt—first in the Danish islands, and then in the British, French, Dutch, and finally Spanish—the African proportion of the slave population declined. African arrivals represented about 45% of Jamaica's slave population in 1807, but only 25% in 1832. A classic divide in any slave society occurs when a majority of its population comprises not forced immigrants but the native-born. This transition happened earliest in the Spanish Caribbean, during the 17th century. Of major Caribbean slave societies, Barbados was the first to exhibit a creole majority by about the 1760s. Jamaica followed by the turn of the century. Even with the staggering influx of Africans just before its revolution, Saint-Domingue's slave population was then about 40% creole. Cuba followed an inverse trajectory: it went from a creole majority by the early 18th century to an African majority a century or so later.

Slaves in most mature Caribbean territories constituted demographic majorities, except in the Spanish Caribbean, where whites and free coloreds almost always outnumbered slaves. In 1750 slaves represented from 85% to 88% of populations in the British, French, Dutch, and Danish territories, but only 15% in the three Spanish Caribbean islands. By 1830, the proportion of slaves rose to 31% in the Spanish Caribbean but dropped everywhere else—to 81% in the British Caribbean, 80% in the French (not counting newly free Haiti), 73% in the Dutch, and 65% in the Danish. The major reason for these declining proportions was marked growth in the numbers of free persons of color. In 1830, almost two-thirds of the region's free persons of color resided in the Spanish Caribbean, a percentage that would decline as emancipation spread across the Caribbean.

African Influences and Creolization

How much of African culture was lost in transit or retained in some fashion is a contentious and complex issue. Few scholars would now argue that the Middle Passage was so traumatic that it stripped Africans of all their cultural assets. Conversely, few would claim that large elements of any one African culture could survive intact in the New World. No group—certainly not an enslaved one—can transfer its way of life from one locale to another. Much inevitably was jettisoned in the transition. But while the loss was great, the opportunity to reformulate and reinterpret elements of homeland cultures in new settings remained. Some merging, blending, and combining was inevitable, but precisely how this happened and to what extent is subject to debate.

New African ethnicities undoubtedly came into being in the diaspora. "Coromantee" in the British Caribbean and "Caramenty" in the French were new ethnic terms acknowledging the African port city of Kormantin that came to be applied rather indiscriminately to any slaves from the Gold Coast. Similarly, "Mina" referred to persons brought from the Gold Coast generally (Costa da Mina in Portuguese), not just from the port Elmina, and it encompassed speakers of many distinct African languages. Africans in the Biafran interior would not have understood themselves as "Igbo," but so labeled at the coast by their captors, many embraced the term. Only through the process of enslavement—and its profound sense of alienation and dis-location—did these Africans develop the need to form new patterns of identifica-tion. The process was predicated on loss, but also on the forging of new bonds both at the coast and aboard slave trade vessels.

In some places and times, African ethnicities clearly played vital roles, as in the "Amina" slave revolt of 1733 on the Danish island of St. John. The participants in this revolt were former members of the Gold Coast state of Akwamu, which had been in the forefront of slave-raiding and selling. In 1728, opposition to Akwamu from its conquered provinces led to its destruction, and large numbers of slave-trading Akwamu became slaves themselves. In launching their rebellion on St. John, they aimed to recreate elements of their Akwamu state. Not surprisingly, fellow Africans who had once been victims of Akwamu failed to join the revolt. This was an "ethnic" revolt, not a pan-African coalition.

Perhaps a more typical process was extensive inter-African syncretism. Even when Africans from one region dominated in a particular Caribbean territory, they came from different locales and interacted with other Africans from other regions. This process happened among the Saramakas, one of the many maroon peoples of Suriname and French Guiana. Different African ethnic groups certainly contributed beliefs, knowledge, and rituals to the larger collectivity; no single group dominated. Compared to other African American societies, Saramakas built their culture fairly autonomously, drawing little from Europeans and Native Americans. Intermarriage among Africans of different origins was common, and by the mid–18th century most maroons were native-born. Thus, anthropologist Richard Price notes, early Saramaka society "was far closer to Saramaka today, in terms of cultural develop-ment, than it was to Africa." Saramakas are one of the African American diaspora's most creolized people (Price 2006, 140).

Plantation slaves in Suriname and many other parts of the Caribbean undoubt-edly maintained African practices and identities more strongly than did maroons. In 1750, for example, about three-quarters of Suriname plantation slaves were African-born, more than half having left Africa only within the previous decade. Constant infusions of Africans kept memories and practices of the homelands alive. Nevertheless, even the slave population of early 19th-century Trinidad, nearly two-thirds of which came from Africa, exhibited rapid inter-African syncretism, in part because the Africans were drawn from territories extending from Senegambia to Mozambique, in part because the island was demographically urban, and in part because slaveholdings were small. Consequently, few Africans found conjugal part-ners of their own ethnic group or region, and ethnic identity dissolved rapidly due to extensive intermarriage.

African influences also depended on timing. Although the Adja-Fon from the Bight of Benin ultimately represented a minority of Africans in Saint-Domingue,

Figure 16.1 A spiritual healer in Suriname attempts to heal her client of an illness. Lithograph by Pierre Jacques Benoit and Jean-Baptiste Madou (1839). Source: The John Carter Brown Library.

they arrived in large numbers in the first quarter of the 18th century. In other words, they constituted a charter group, creating many of the cultural norms and contributing the major deities, the ceremonies, and most of the African vocabulary to Haitian vodou. Later, as the Kongo region increasingly became the major supplier of slaves to the island, vodou began to incorporate various Kongo rituals.

If Haitian vodou owed much to first-comers, Cuban Santería derived heavily from latecomers. One of its major components was the worship of Yoruba deities known as orisha, yet not until the fall of the Oyo empire (1835) did extremely large numbers of Yoruba end up in Cuba, where they became known as Lucumí. Along with Yoruba-derived forms of worship, Santería incorporated notions deriving from West-Central African *minkisi* cults—hardly surprising, since 135,000 "Congos" flooded into Cuba in the last 15 years of the slave trade. Urban environments in western Cuba also became crucial to Santería's development, offering slaves a less regimented existence than in rural areas. Urban slaves and freed people created Afro-Cuban *cabildos*, or lodges, and mutual aid societies. By the end of the 18th century, 21 cabildos existed in Havana alone. One or more Lucumí cabildos—neo-African ethnic formations—provided the crucible out of which Santería emerged.

This process of cultural adaptation and transformation in which all Africans were engaged—which involved continuities and discontinuities, gains and losses, inventions and borrowings—usually goes by the name *creolization*. As to whether Africans reproduced at least part of their homeland cultures or largely adopted the customs of their host societies, the best answer would be that they did both, depending on many local circumstances. Slaves frequently accepted European institutions and civic and religious rituals, insinuating themselves into various social frameworks or niches—whether fraternities, festival cycles, or churches—and reworking them to their own ends. In other words, Africans selectively appropriated aspects of new cultures even as they remained faithful to aspects of their homeland cultures.

Ultimately, Africans in the Caribbean had to adapt to survive. They had no time for debates about cultural purity or precise roots, nor any necessary commitment to the societies from which they had come. They were denied much of their various cultural heritage and the institutions that socially anchored and maintained them. And even what they brought was sometimes ruthlessly jettisoned because it was no longer applicable or relevant to their new situations. Slaves had to be forward-looking. No wonder, as anthropologist Sidney Mintz puts it, when we think of the history of the people of African descent, "we are speaking of mangled pasts." For that reason, he continues, "It is not the precise historical origins of a word, a meaning, a phrase, an instrument, or a rhythm that matters, so much as the creative genius of the users, molding older cultural substances into new and unfamiliar patterns, without regard for 'purity' or 'pedigree'" (Mintz 1970, 9; Mintz 1974, 17).

Slave Economies

Perhaps the two greatest determinants of the slaves' economic lives were whether they grew sugar and whether they were primarily responsible for growing their own provisions. Perhaps as many as 8 of 10 Africans arriving in the region came initially to work on sugar plantations, which always employed the most slaves. Yet while sugar was the great consumer of labor, many slaves in the Caribbean worked at other jobs and with other crops. Moreover, slaves worked to provide not only for their masters but for themselves. The precise balance between sugar and non-sugar and master's and slave's economies varied greatly by place and time.

Few other regions in the world were more exclusively committed to a single economic activity than the Caribbean. Some islands were little more than vast sugar plantations. By the early 19th century, 9 in 10 enslaved workers in Nevis, Montserrat, and Tobago toiled on sugar estates, as well as three-quarters of enslaved workers on Guadeloupe and two-thirds on Martinique. Over time, sugar began displacing alternative export crops such as tobacco, indigo, and cotton, which required less capital. Nevertheless, in some places, especially after 1750, cotton, cacao, indigo, and particularly coffee became more prominent, although the overall trend was not away from but toward sugar monoculture. Cuba is the last great example of an island turning to full-scale sugar production late in its history.

Sugar involved labor far more onerous than that required by any other crop. Working in gangs, overseen by a driver with whip at hand, toiling in shifts at harvest time, sugar slaves experienced a draconian labor regime. Perhaps 90% of all 18th-century Caribbean slaves worked on sugar estates—probably one of the highest labor participation rates anywhere in the world. Women soon comprised the majority of most gangs, since they usually outlived men and skilled jobs were denied them. The one advantage of working on a sugar plantation was the opportunity to develop a craft—sugar plantations usually had twice as many skilled personnel as did coffee or cotton plantations—but such jobs were the preserve of men.

The large islands of the Greater Antilles generally encompassed a wider range of economic activities than did their smaller counterparts. Slaves on Hispaniola, Puerto Rico, and Cuba raised cattle for their hides; grew ginger, cacao, and tobacco; and raised provisions even after these islands turned intensively to sugar cultivation. Jamaica, Britain's largest sugar island, was always quite diversified. In the late 18th century, the proportion of Jamaica's slaves on sugar estates was about 60% and declining. Saint-Domingue, too, was notable for its large number of cotton, coffee, and indigo plantations. Coffee plantations, which tended to become important on mountainous islands, often were smaller and more diverse than sugar estates, provided less occupational variety, and were usually more isolated and healthier because of their highland locations.

Although sugar was the archetypal slave crop, many Caribbean slaves worked at other activities. A few marginal colonies grew no sugar at all. In British Honduras and Belize, most slaves were woodcutters. In the Cayman Islands, Anguilla, and Barbuda, a majority of slaves lived on small, diversified agricultural holdings. On the Turks and Caicos and on Bonaire, many slaves raked salt. On the Bahamas, cotton cultivation was important for some decades, and fishing and shipping occupied a significant minority of slaves. Indeed, on islands known for their entrepôts, such as St. Eustatius and St. Thomas, most slaves worked at sea or on the docks. Even in a monocultural economy such as Barbados, about 1 in 10 slaves produced cotton, provisions, ginger, arrowroot, and aloes. Slaves built forts, churches, and other essential public buildings as well as private dwellings.

By the late 18th century, the proportion of urban slaves ranged from about 1 in 20 on French Saint-Domingue (where they congregated in three large towns) to 4 in 10 on Danish St. Thomas (where they resided in Charlotte Amalie). In between these extremes, about 1 in 10 slaves lived in towns on most British islands, and 1 in 5 on the Spanish and Dutch islands. By the early 17th century, Havana had about 10,000 residents, half of whom were slaves; almost two centuries later, its population had

grown to 41,000, but now only about one-quarter were slaves. Unlike most of their plantation counterparts, urban slaves were often outnumbered by whites and freed people, and they lived in extremely small units under the close watch of resident masters. Women usually outnumbered men, and slaves of mixed racial ancestry were often prominent. Most urban slaves worked as domestics, but hawkers, higglers, and transport workers were numerous in towns, and roughly twice as many skilled tradespeople, fishermen, and general laborers lived in urban as in rural settings. Slaves who hired their own time were a notable feature of urban life.

Figure 16.2 An urban market in Saint-Domingue, 1770s. Engraved print of painting by Agostino Brunias (1804). Image NW0009, www.slaveryimages .org, Virginia Foundation for the Humanities and the University of Virginia Library.

The internal economy of slaves varied greatly. On marginal islands such as Barbuda and Great Exuma in the Bahamas, which did not grow sugar, slaves were virtual peasants, farming extensive provision grounds, owning livestock, and spending a good deal of time hunting and fishing. Somewhat less advantaged were slaves with access to provision grounds on larger sugar islands such as Jamaica and Saint-Domingue, where they could at least sell their produce in the large urban markets. Slaves' economic opportunities were least extensive on small islands such as Antigua or Barbados, where they were permitted, at best, small garden plots.

The impact of the slaves' economy was double-edged. Drawbacks included the lack of time slaves often had to tend their provision grounds; the distance separating slave huts from outlying grounds; the pressures on aged, infirm, and young slaves; the exposure to environmental threats of hurricanes and droughts; and the poorer health, lower life expectancy, and lower fertility associated with provision ground systems (as opposed to ration systems). Benefits included the variety of the slaves' horticultural repertoires, the material advantages accruing from selling and bartering produce, and the firm foundation that independent production and marketing gave to the slaves' domestic, religious, and community life. Before long, slaves engaging in "proto-peasant" activities came to dominate the Sunday markets, and whites came to depend on them for fruits, vegetables, and meat. The trade-off was greater autonomy for greater exposure to risk.

Slave Societies and Cultural Forms

Caribbean slavery created brutal and volatile societies beset by constant tensions and power struggles. They were the first societies in the Americas to develop elaborate slave codes, which commonly prohibited and suppressed unauthorized movement, large congregations, possession of guns and other weapons, sounding of horns and drums, and secret ritual practices. French and particularly Spanish laws provided minimal protections to slaves, but control and repression were primary concerns. Terror was at the core of the institution of slavery: slave owners depended above all on local militias and imperial troops for their safety. The punishment for actual or threatened violence against whites was severe. Special slave-trial courts existed in many colonies to provide summary and expeditious "justice." Occasionally redress was possible: some colonies had an official to hear slave complaints, and legislation governing slaves tended to become somewhat less terroristic over time. The murder of a slave by a white man, for example, generally became a crime, but mandated amelioration was always limited by the sheer fact of planter power.

Everywhere custom was as important as law in shaping the slave experience. Slavery by definition involved highly personal mechanisms of coercion; the whip, rather than the law, was the institution's indispensable and ubiquitous instrument. On the plantation or in the household, the master and his delegates used various methods of physical coercion without recourse to, and usually unchecked by, external authorities. Brutality and sadism were widespread, but newly settled places and those with stark black majorities, where masters felt most isolated and insecure, gained the worst reputations. Paternalism was not a governing ideal in the Caribbean. In some colonies (most notably the British and French), many masters were absentees, distanced from their slaves. The ideals, practices, and power of white planters and their managers determined much of the context of slave life.

The masters hoped that rewards would offset punishments. Over time, allowances and privileges became entrenched in both custom and law. Granting slaves half-days or full days to tend their provision plots became commonplace, and allowing them to attend extraordinary social functions such as funerals became standard practice. Masters also generally granted slaves time off during the Christian holidays. Christmas, in particular, became a time for permissiveness and even social inversion—a black Saturnalia. Special gratuities became routine: an extra allowance of food here, some tobacco there, a ration of rum for completing the harvest, cash payments for Sunday work. Favors and indulgences were disproportionately allocated to concubines, domestics, drivers, and tradesmen.

Although masters and slaves were locked into an intimate interdependence, blacks were not just objects of white action, but subjects who regulated social relationships among themselves. Masters obviously subjected slaves' familial aspirations to enormous stress. Owners generally recognized only the mother-child tie; bought mostly men, who then had difficulty finding wives; separated slave families by sale and transfer; and committed sexual assaults on slave women. Notions of instability, promiscuity, casual mating, and inherent disorganization in slave family life are commonly overdrawn: slave families were often remarkably resilient, kinship bonds could be strong, and parent-child affection was real. Nevertheless, in slave populations dominated by Africans, family life was extremely tenuous. At least half of African slaves lived with friends or other solitaries, not with relatives. They often practiced forms of "fictive kinship," particularly toward shipmates, who looked upon one another's children as their own. When they formed families, they probably saw the unfamiliar two-parent form as an essential building block toward the extended or polygamous family types that were common in their homelands.

As populations creolized, their kinship networks grew more elaborate, and family life often centered less on the household than on networks of relationships involving various relatives and spouses. Marriage among slaves generally gained more support in Catholic than in Protestant countries, due to legal strictures, but size of estate and stage of colonial development were critical determinants of slave family life. Thus, on smaller slaveholdings the dominant unit was composed of mother and children, while on larger plantations the nuclear family was more prevalent. Similarly, the proportion of slaves living in two-parent households was always much lower in frontier regions than in long-settled areas. The notion of slaves as being stripped of kin, the mother the only recognizable family figure, is a caricature.

Language was another case in point. Although Africans for a time continued speaking their native languages, most slaves—and some masters—came to speak creole languages, each of which derived much of its vocabulary from a European language but owed much of its phonology and syntax to a prior West African creole or pidgin and, beyond that, to various West African languages. In the early modern Caribbean, scores of identifiable creole languages arose. The one exception was the Spanish Caribbean, where most slaves learned the masters' language. This trend resulted from the unusual demographic situation in the major Spanish islands, where slaves were heavily outnumbered by free peoples for so long; from the incorporative stance of the Spanish; and from the absence of Spanish-based contact languages along the West African coast.

Much as a broad spectrum of linguistic forms existed among slaves, a continuous scale of musical expression, ranging in inspiration from Europe to Africa, also unfolded. At one end of the spectrum were, for example, slaves who became integral members of military bands or street players in urban settings. At the other extreme were Africans who danced their ethnic dances to their own homeland musical accompaniments—banjos, balafos, harps, lutes, gourd rattles, or various kinds of drums. In the Caribbean some musical styles were ethnically identifiable, even if most involved some degree of syncretism. Black music developed in ways akin to the formation of creole languages. A basic musical aesthetic, which emphasized the importance of music and dance in everyday life and the role of rhythm and percussion in musical style, survived the Middle Passage. Even complex musical instruments made the crossing, although more notable is how slaves adapted traditional instruments, invented new ones, and borrowed Euro-American ones. These adaptations, inventions, and borrowings were interpreted and reinterpreted according to aesthetic principles drawn from African musical traditions. Slaves retained the inner meanings of traditional modes of behavior while adopting new outer forms. In musical terms, the key elements of the inner structure were complex rhythms, percussive qualities, syncopation, and antiphonal patterns.

Black religious expression also spanned a large continuum. Some Africans, particularly those from Upper Guinea, were Muslims; others from Kongo had been exposed to Catholicism. But overall, an extraordinary diversity of religious forms coexisted with certain widely shared basic principles. Most Africans drew no neat distinction between the sacred and the profane, shared assumptions about the nature of causality, believed in both a high god and many lesser gods, and thought the dead played an active role in the lives of the living. In the Caribbean, because of enforced coexistence with other African groups and the serious, everyday problems of dealing with harsh taskmasters, slaves turned in large measure to magical practices—the most common term for which, in the Anglophone Caribbean, became *obi* (or *obia* or *obeah*). The slaves' religious worldview featured strong beliefs concerning the power of ancestors, elaborate funeral rites, and diverse ritual practices to invoke natural or ancestral spirits—which became part of Haitian vodou, Cuban Santería, Trinidadian *Shango*, Jamaican *Myal*, and Afro-Surinamese *Winti*.

Over time, slaves began accepting Christianity on their terms. The Catholic clergy in Spanish and French territories were officially committed to converting slaves—and certainly made greater initial inroads than did Protestants—but by the 18th century other groups such as the Moravians, Baptists, and Methodists were increasingly successful in gaining members among slaves. The Moravians, for example, established the earliest Afro-Protestant congregation in the Americas (in 1736 on St. Thomas) and by the 1780s had thousands of converts in the Danish and British West Indies and in Suriname.

Slave Resistance

List all the plots and rebellions mounted by Caribbean slaves, and resistance appears structurally endemic; recall the bitter fact that the vicious system of Caribbean slavery lasted for hundreds of years and was dynamically expansive until the very end of the 19th century, and Caribbean slavery seems much less brittle. Jamaica experienced a serious slave revolt about once a decade, none more consequential than the island-wide insurrection of 1760 that resulted in the deaths of 90 whites and 400 blacks, with another 600 deported. Yet Barbadian slaves never mounted a serious slave rebellion until 1816, and even that claimed few white lives. The greatest slave revolt in history—that of Saint-Domingue in 1791—was of monumental significance, but before it, that island's slaves had no great reputation for rebelliousness. Furthermore, ambivalence marked that signal event, as it did slave resistance in general. The only successful slave rebellion in the history of the Americas served as a beacon of liberty, but 12 years of unremitting warfare destroyed this most valuable of all plantation colonies, thereby encouraging masters to launch a huge expansion of slavery in other parts of the Caribbean.

Slave rebellions and conspiracies varied over time. There were clusters of incidents: insurrections and insurrection panics peaked in the 1680s, 1730s to early 1740s, 1770s, and 1790s. Other periods saw few or no revolts. Some events seem connected to spikes in the arrivals of Africans, times of warfare, and troop movements, but mechanistic explanations will not wholly account for incidents driven by group psychology and interactions among many individuals. Shifts in composition and goals tended to occur: from events inspired primarily by Africans to events dominated by creoles, from attempts to secure freedom from slavery and restore a lost social order to attempts to overthrow slavery itself, from acts of rage to forms of industrial strife. Such neat descriptions of the transformations are too schematic, but still the revolutionary era marked an important transition. The circulation of revolutionary ideas broadened horizons: some slaves drew inspiration from Haiti while others saw the possibility of sympathy from the emerging antislavery movement. The three great slave revolts in the early 19th-century British Caribbean— Barbados in 1816, Demerara in 1823, and Jamaica in 1831–32—are most notable for their self-restraint and awareness of metropolitan debates. Rebelling against the system from within, the argument goes, caused abolition to be hastened from without.

Slave resistance was always more than collective violence. It encompassed flight, sabotage, and individual murders. Most plantations experienced a few desertions each year; arson occurred occasionally; tool-breaking, cruelty to animals, and crop destruction were everyday problems; and every now and again enraged slaves killed overseers or masters. But none of these actions threatened the economic viability of the institution. Furthermore, the cook who poisoned the master's food had first to get the job. Slaves who plotted in the marketplace had first to produce for the market. The slave who ran away was often the one who possessed a skill, had some mobility, and could perhaps pass as free in town. There was no simple unilinear gradient from accommodation to resistance.

Maroons, the ultimate symbol of resistance, were also forced to accommodate. Small groups of maroons existed in various colonies—usually ones with mountainous interiors—but only in Suriname and Jamaica were they self-sustaining. Even there, their numbers were never large—about 1,000 in Jamaica and 6,000 in Suriname during the 18th century. Maroons waged wars against colonial governments, often for decades, forcing them in some cases to recognize their free and separate existence. Post-treaty maroons, however, often proved to be effective allies, tracking down slave runaways and rebels, adopting the military hierarchy of the establishment, living in an uneasy symbiosis with their white neighbors, and seeking arms, tools, pots, and cloth as well as employment.

Slaves were found on both sides of most disputes. In the early years of many settlements, slaves were often used as soldiers, but as their numbers grew, opposition arose to arming them. However, in emergencies—for example, local rebellions or foreign invasions—those thought to be loyal were periodically placed under arms. Moreover, slaves continued to be used as auxiliaries and pioneers, free blacks and coloreds became an important part of the militia, and the Anglo-French Wars of 1793–1815 brought an extraordinary intensification of the practice of arming slaves. Winning the allegiance of slaves became an imperative for the governments of Spain, Britain, and France during the Haitian Revolution. In 1795 the effectiveness of black troops and shortage of white manpower led the British to form black regiments. Eventually they raised 12 regiments by recruiting 30,000 slaves, but they were always careful to enlist captives from Africa, whom they thought they could more easily control.

Most resistance was not destructive of the institution. By carving out some independence for themselves and forcing whites to recognize their humanity, slaves opposed the dehumanization inherent in their status and demonstrated their autonomy. Such assertions of will eased the torments of slavery, gave slaves a reason for living, and made them less likely to sacrifice everything in what seemed like a futile, invariably suicidal attempt to overthrow the institution. For this reason, the distinction between resistance (drawing on sources outside the system) and opposition (working from within the system) is useful.

Figure 16.3 Stick fighting between English and French slaves in Dominica. Print of painting by Agostino Brunias (ca. 1779). Image Bilby-3, www.slaveryimages.org, Virginia Foundation for the Humanities and the University of Virginia Library.

Conclusion

The history of Caribbean slave cultures abounds in paradoxes. Most slaves in the region lived short and oppressed lives, worked most of the time, grew one of the most onerous crops imaginable, formed fragile families, and suffered great brutality. Arguably, then, slave culture ought to have reached its most impoverished form here. Yet Caribbean slaves also invented creole languages, developed distinctive musical styles, created rich religious systems, and established elaborate domestic economies, thereby opposing the dehumanization involved in slavery. Similarly, African ethnicity, itself a creation of the diaspora, was a useful resource upon which many slaves could draw, yet inter-African syncretism and creolization were the dominant trends in Caribbean slave life.

Finally, in the only such occurrence in history, slaves on Saint-Domingue overthrew the institution, thereby revealing that black liberation was possible and inspiring several conspiracies, revolts, and assertions of black pride throughout the Americas. But if this massive slave insurrection was like the dropping of the atomic bomb—a nightmare for slaveholders which signified that the world would never be the same—planters in Cuba, Jamaica, Trinidad, and many other places nonetheless sought more Africans immediately. The destruction of slavery in the world's most profitable colony provided a huge boost to plantation slavery elsewhere. Furthermore, if Haiti was unforgettable, it was also unrepeatable; no other revolt could follow its model. The story of slave life in the Caribbean is depressing and uplifting in about equal measure.

WORKS CITED

Mintz, Sidney W. 1970. Foreword to *Afro-American Anthropology: Contemporary Perspectives,* ed. Norman E. Whitten, Jr. and John F. Szwed, 1–16. New York: Free Press.

———. 1974. *Caribbean Transformations.* Baltimore: Johns Hopkins University Press.

Price, Richard. 2006. "On the Miracle of Creolization." In *Afro-Atlantic Dialogues: Anthropology in the Diaspora,* ed. Kevin A. Yelvington, 115–47. Sante Fe: School of American Research Press.

17

Rivalry, War, and Imperial Reform in the 18th-Century Caribbean

DOUGLAS HAMILTON

Between 1702 and 1783, the great European powers fought four major wars lasting 37 years as they struggled for preeminence. Even the periods of peace were short and uneasy. For Britain, France, and Spain (and to a lesser extent the Netherlands), rivalry overseas was an integral part of the European power struggle. Over the course of the 18th century, the increasingly global nature of European conflicts afforded vast navies and colonial possessions ever greater significance. In this power struggle, no overseas region was more important than the Caribbean. Its geographical location in the western Atlantic gave the Caribbean a strategic significance as the "key to the Indies," while its growing commerce based on slave-produced commodities made it a crucial theater for struggles between Britain, France, and Spain.

As the rivalries of the 17th-century Caribbean intensified in the 18th, they were heightened by a transformation in the nature of imperial activity. There was a movement away from the economic nationalism of closed markets and national chartered companies towards an increasingly important independent merchant class. The great strength of Spanish mercantilism, underpinned by bullion shipments from Spanish America, was initially challenged aggressively and often illegally by its rivals, and ultimately overtaken by the emergence of the new, more open and commercially driven Caribbean empires of Britain, France, and the Netherlands.

Four Major Wars

After the Treaty of Ryswick ended the Nine Years' War in 1697, merchants and colonists from the major European powers sought to use the return to peace to reestablish their normal trading patterns but were hampered by continuing diplomatic difficulties between the imperial rivals. Peace in Europe largely rested on a balance of power in which no single country or group of countries was able to establish a significant advantage over the rest. When the Spanish succession came into the hands of the French Bourbon dynasty in 1702, however, the balance of power in Europe was upset. The shift had important implications in the Caribbean because it increased the potential for collaboration between the French and the Spanish, not least in providing French shipping with greater access to protected Spanish markets. An early effect was the transfer of the asiento, or the right to trade enslaved Africans and commodities into Spanish America, from Portugal to France (Pares 1963, 10). The threats to England caused by this closer alliance between France and Spain, and by France's recognition of the right of the exiled Stuart claimant to the English crown, pushed it towards war.

Conflict in the Caribbean during the War of Spanish Succession (1701–13) focused especially on attacks on the hugely valuable Spanish fleet bringing bullion to Europe. This "institutionalised looting" by British vessels (Kennedy 2004, 84) was mirrored by raids on British islands and shipping by French buccaneers based in Martinique and Saint-Domingue and by the French navy. Colonists in all islands were terribly aware of the threat of attack to their homes and their trade. The Jamaica garrison was strengthened by the arrival of 3,000 regular soldiers, but the Leeward Islands in particular were vulnerable to hostile forces. Strikingly, these raiders seized enslaved Africans when they attacked: in 1706 more than 3,000 slaves were taken from Nevis to Martinique after an attack by the French (Sheridan 1998, 400). That slaves were regarded as a valuable spoil of war was a clear sign of their importance to the Caribbean colonies. As well as being lucrative for the buccaneers, captured slaves provided new labor for plantations in French colonies while simultaneously depriving British estates of it. This plunder also highlights how the rivalry between Britain and France in the Caribbean differed from the nations' individual rivalries with Spain. Both Britain and France tried to infiltrate the

Spanish trade system, which was focused primarily on mainland America. But as historian Richard Pares pointed out many years ago, the rivalry between Britain and France was not just mercantile but centered on two rival groups of plantation colonies that competed strategically, economically, and commercially (Pares 1963, 179). As a result, in future wars between France and Britain, the capture of enemy colonies, as well as the interruption of trade, became increasingly important.

Although effects of the War of Spanish Succession were felt keenly in the Caribbean, the war's outcome was largely determined by strategy in the European theater. Yet as the century wore on, and as the Caribbean became increasingly important for the European powers (and especially for Britain and France), the colonial elements of European wars became ever more significant.

The Treaty of Utrecht (1713), which marked the conclusion of the War of Spanish Succession, had important implications for the Caribbean region. Complete British control over the island of St. Kitts—previously divided with France—was secured, and a series of new land grants were made to British settlers. In 1713 Spain controlled Cuba, Puerto Rico, Santo Domingo, Tobago, and Trinidad, among other territories; the French occupied Saint-Domingue, Martinique, Guadeloupe, St. Lucia, Dominica, and St. Vincent; meanwhile British territory was concentrated in Jamaica, Barbados, and the Leeward Islands. The British also took over from France the right to supply slaves and a restricted quantity of legitimate trade goods to Spanish America through the asiento. The Spanish, like the British with their Navigation Acts, regarded their colonial spaces as closed to non-nationals. The riches of Spanish America had long attracted smugglers and privateers, but the asiento provided the British with a key and legitimate breakthrough into Spanish colonial markets. The asiento was initially confined to one chartered company, the South Sea Company, but at the same time individual merchants continued and extended their illicit trades from ports like Kingston or Bridgetown. The Spanish, in an attempt to keep these interlopers out, deployed its *guarda costas* (naval squadrons) throughout the Caribbean. The British government made no attempt to limit the activities of its traders, and the guarda costas continued to harry British shipping and often failed to distinguish between contraband and legitimate traders.

These Spanish actions raised a growing clamor among British merchants at home, which placed the prime minister, Robert Walpole, under severe pressure. Walpole was anxious to avoid another costly war with Spain (and, in all probability, with France) and he resisted the calls for action for a time. Throughout the 1730s, however, Spanish seizures and British reprisals continued. In 1738 a British captain, Robert Jenkins, gave evidence to a House of Commons committee at which he displayed his ear, which he claimed had been severed when a guarda costa boarded his ship seven years earlier. Whatever the veracity of his claim, it sparked outrage among the British public. Walpole was no longer able to withstand the pressure for war and, after a series of tit-for-tat maneuvers, the so-called War of Jenkins' Ear was declared in October 1739.

This war, which later exacerbated tensions in Europe and led into the continental War of the Austrian Succession, had its roots in the colonies and arose out of intense commercial rivalry for the riches of the Americas. The British, employing their increasingly powerful Royal Navy, went quickly on the offensive. Under Admiral Edward Vernon, a British squadron attacked Portobelo on Panama's Caribbean coast. In Britain it was portrayed as a glorious victory for the heroic Vernon, even though its effects were greater for Spain than for Britain. The loss of Portobelo forced Spain, for the first time, to rethink the way it shipped commodities. Rather than focusing its activities in fleets sailing from a few key ports, it began to use more ships at a wider variety of locations.

For the British, the victory at Portobelo inspired a series of other dramatic attacks on Spanish territory. Vernon, buoyed by his early success, led an ill-fated assault on the Spanish stronghold of Cartagena de Indias. Similar attacks on Havana and in Florida were also rebuffed. The war's major Caribbean engagements, intended by Britain to bring down Spanish America, had no long-lasting strategic effect. Much more damaging to both sides were the constant attacks by naval vessels and privateers on merchant shipping. In Europe, too, the war, which lasted until 1748, was indecisive. The Treaty of Aix-la-Chapelle ushered in an uneasy truce which lasted until a renewed outbreak of hostilities that were to have a seismic effect on the 18th-century Caribbean.

The next major conflagration erupted in North America, where the French and Indian War broke out in 1754. The Seven Years' War in Europe followed from it in 1756 and quickly drew in colonial disputes around the world. Indeed, the global nature of the conflict, which stretched from India to Europe and the Americas, qualifies it to be called the first truly world war. Unlike the rivalries of the early century, in which colonial conflicts were adjuncts of the European struggles, the Seven Years' War was profoundly influenced by the demands of empire. France, realizing that it lacked the colonial population base and naval power to defeat Britain in the colonies or at sea, deliberately attempted to draw Britain into a ruinously expensive conflict on the European continent while continuing to attack overseas where possible. France hoped to defeat the British empire by quickly exhausting Britain in Europe. In the early years of the war this strategy appeared well founded, as Britain lost Minorca in 1756 around the same time the East India Company station at Calcutta was taken by the Nawab of Bengal. In 1757, France and Austria had Britain's European allies on the brink of collapse, and these setbacks, along with French North American victories at Fort William Henry and Ticonderoga (1758), represented a serious crisis for Britain.

Remarkably, however, the tide turned for Britain in 1759 with some astonishing victories. In strategic terms the most important of these were the crushing defeats of the French navy off western Europe at Quiberon Bay and Lagos, which effectively ended any threat of invasion and severely curtailed the French capacity to support its colonies. Control over the Western Approaches to Europe blocked the French navy in and enabled the British navy to pursue its goals overseas with greater impunity.

In the Caribbean, the British capture and occupation of Guadeloupe in 1759 presaged the seizing of further territory from France, and victory at Montreal in 1760 confirmed the French loss of power in North America. By early 1761 the British seized Dominica, Grenada, St. Vincent, and Tobago. In 1762 Britain used its considerable naval might to launch attacks on other islands in the Caribbean, including Martinique and the strategically important island of St. Lucia. From St. Lucia, the Royal Navy could keep watch over the French fleet stationed at Martinique. The capture of St. Lucia was regarded as highly significant by the British, and the island's location made it a key element in British strategy in later Caribbean conflicts.

Despite the apparent hopelessness of the French situation, the duc de Choiseul continued to believe the British could be defeated. He turned to France's Bourbon ally, Spain, for additional support in the Family Compact of 1761. Spain's entry into the war in January 1762 prompted an almost immediate response from Britain, and resulted in one of the war's (and indeed the century's) most spectacular assaults. In March 1762 forces left Britain to lay siege to, and then occupy, the city of Havana. The loss of this city was as great a defeat for Spain as it was a victory for Britain. Havana was one of the largest cities in the Americas. It had a population of some 35,000 people and boasted one of the finest harbors in the Americas (McNeill 1985, 38). It was a crucial node in the Spanish mercantile system and, as such, was heavily fortified. Indeed, the Spanish thought it impregnable. It was much prized by Britain, which had tried and failed to take it two decades earlier, and as soon as war with Spain was declared, the British began preparations for an attack. They surprised the Spanish, partly by attacking at all, and partly by approaching Havana along the Old Bahama Channel, which until then had been thought unsuitable for the largest fighting vessels, the ships of the line. Employing a fleet of more than 150 ships, including 22 ships of the line, and an army of more than 15,000 men, the British launched their assault in June 1762 and succeeded in taking Havana in August. The Spanish also surrendered 14 ships of the line, as well as other vessels that were trapped in the harbor.

Under the terms of the Peace of Paris (1763), which ended the war, the British returned Havana to Spain and Martinique, St. Lucia, and Guadeloupe to France, but retained their rivals' territory in North America (notably French Quebec and Spanish Florida). Britain also made significant gains in the Caribbean by taking four

Figure 17.1 British ship at the
entrance to Havana harbor.
Engraving by Elias Durnford
and Peter Canot (1768). Source:
The John Carter Brown Library.

of the Windward Islands: Dominica, Grenada, St. Vincent, and Tobago. Grenada, in particular, rapidly became a crucial colony for Britain as the second largest sugar producer in the British Caribbean. The terms of the peace were a matter of great controversy in Britain. Not everyone believed that concessions should have been made to France and Spain, in part because it was clear that Britain had emerged from the war triumphant. Above all, the war showed for the first time that British naval power was a reality rather than a national myth, and that an effective combination of navy and army operations could bear spectacular fruit in the Caribbean (Rodger 2004, 289–90).

In many ways, though, the Peace of Paris stored up problems for the next conflict. In Britain the great victory ushered in a sense of complacency. The might of the Royal Navy was not sustained after the war, as improvements to dockyard infrastructures and a ship rebuilding program were delayed. At the same time, and even as France and Spain were being defeated in 1762, the duc de Choiseul implemented plans to enhance the French navy, paid for by reforms in the country's finances. He was clear that continued cooperation between France and Spain was key. "I'm certain," he wrote, "that our best plan is to make peace, cost what it may, and then, in concert with the king of Spain, to work for the rehabilitation of our navy and colonies, in order that in a few years we may be able to wipe out our disgrace" (Christelow 1941, 523). Britain's strategy assumed that the Royal Navy needed to have greater strength than the navies of France and Spain combined. By the 1770s, it manifestly did not.

Furthermore, historians of the American Revolution often point to the legislation introduced by Britain in the aftermath of the Seven Years' War as key contributory factors in the secession of the 13 colonies in 1776. The imposition of limits on colonial settlement in the backcountry, the presence of British troops, and the series of new taxes (most notably the Stamp Act) were all parts of the British attempt to secure the boundaries of its North American territories, ensure relatively peaceful relations with Native Americans, and finance the costs of defending the colonies. At the same time, however, these measures were significant impositions on the colonists, and as such they formed part of the "long train of abuses and usurpations" which so irked them. Choiseul had thought France should wait five years before seeking revenge. In the event, the wait was longer, but the American Declaration of Independence in 1776 afforded France and Spain the ideal opportunity to exact vengeance for the Seven Years' War.

The outbreak of hostilities in 1775 marked the culmination of the century's gradual shift in the location of major wars. This was a colonial war that drew in European rivals, rather than a largely European war spilling overseas. The American Revolution was at once deeply shocking for Britain and a glorious opportunity for its rivals.

In the early years of the war, when Britain and the United States were sole adversaries, the Royal Navy was used largely as a troop carrier and protector of convoys in an attempt to limit the effects of American privateers on British shipping. Britain itself was not directly imperiled, and so no Western Squadron—so successfully used in Britain's two previous conflicts—was deployed to protect home waters. The stunning American victory at Saratoga in 1777 emboldened the French, who seized on this conflict as an opportunity to weaken their old rival. Fatally for Britain, the fact that the Western Squadron remained unemployed meant that the French fleet was free to operate across the Atlantic and to expand the war away from the American mainland.

The war went badly in the Caribbean, particularly after the intervention of French forces on the American side after 1778. British naval and army forces were severely stretched by a land war in North America and by a wide-ranging naval conflict all along the eastern seaboard of North America and the Caribbean. Increasingly, Britain was forced to concentrate its efforts, so while St. Lucia was seized from the French in 1778, Dominica fell to the French in 1778, and St. Vincent and Grenada in 1779, almost without resistance. By this time Spain had also entered the war. Despite the later notion of 18th-century British naval supremacy, Britain found itself facing superior naval forces—with devastating consequences.

Before the French intervention, Martinique had profited by trading supplies to the colonists in North America. After 1778 it was no longer a neutral port and much of the North American trade shifted to the Dutch entrepôt at St. Eustatius, which was a long-established free port. By early 1781, and before the formal Dutch declaration of war, Admiral George Brydges Rodney, commanding the British fleet in the Caribbean, decided to cut off that supply route by launching an assault on St. Eustatius. For nine months British forces engaged in indiscriminate plunder in contravention of the conventions of war between Europeans. This caused considerable controversy in Britain, and Rodney, concerned partly for his reputation and partly for his booty, concentrated on returning to Britain rather than watching over French Admiral de Grasse in Martinique. When de Grasse sailed northwards via Saint-Domingue, Rodney did not follow. De Grasse continued to the coast of the United States, where his fleet blockaded the Chesapeake. By sealing British forces in and preventing any aid from the Royal Navy from reaching them, the French navy played an important role in the Franco-American victory at Yorktown in October 1781, which effectively defeated British forces on the continent. In other words, this seismic event was influenced by events in the Caribbean (O'Shaughnessy 2000, 230–32).

Defeat for Britain in North America also meant that the combined fleets of France, Spain, and the Netherlands were now free to concentrate on the Caribbean. France quickly took St. Eustatius in November 1781, ending the British spree. The Dutch recaptured their lost colonies of Demerara, Berbice, and Essequibo. Faced by this combined threat, the British chose to defend St. Lucia and Jamaica. They had already lost their Windward Islands and were resigned to losing the Leewards as well. When St. Kitts fell to de Grasse, total French victory in the Caribbean seemed assured. Rodney remained much tarnished by events in St. Eustatius, but one decisive battle, the Battle of the Saints, at once rescued his reputation and thwarted French ambitions.

In April 1782, de Grasse led a fleet of some 30 ships of the line from its harbor at Martinique. Rodney's fleet, mustering 36 ships of the line, watched from nearby St. Lucia and tracked the movement of the French fleet. The French were heading for a rendezvous with a Spanish fleet and 15,000 soldiers to attack Jamaica with a force at least as strong that with which the British had taken Havana in 1762. Victory for the French and Spanish in Jamaica would at a stroke have annulled every previous British triumph at Quebec, Quiberon Bay, Havana, and elsewhere, and would have destroyed the British Empire in the Americas. The British and French fleets met off Les Saintes, a series of tiny islands between Guadeloupe and Dominica, on April 12. As the fleets met in line of battle, a gap appeared in the French line, which was then broken by Rodney, throwing the French into disarray. This was the first use of this tactic, which was later famously employed by Nelson at Trafalgar. It resulted in a great victory, with the French flagship, the *Ville de Paris*, seized by Rear Admiral Hood's *Barfleur*.

The Battle of the Saints was the final engagement of the war in the Caribbean. It was celebrated in Britain as the most important naval victory until Trafalgar in 1805, although in truth the Battle of the Saints probably remained more significant. The 1783 Treaty of Paris confirmed the independence of the United States but returned most Caribbean islands to their previous owners. Britain gave St. Lucia back to the French and surrendered Tobago to them, but it recovered Dominica, St. Vincent, and Grenada in the Windwards and St. Kitts, Nevis, and Montserrat in the Leewards, all of which had been lost in the disastrous years between 1778 and 1782.

The peace treaty ushered in a new era of prosperity in the Caribbean as the British and French islands and their trades recovered. Despite a growing clamor for the abolition of the slave trade, the future of planting in the Caribbean seemed secure. The loss of the American colonies had weakened the colonial lobby in London, but the Caribbean islands never countenanced declaring independence, and the governments of both Britain and France continued to regard the Caribbean as an important, loyal, and lucrative part of their imperial portfolios.

Effects of War

For all the powers, wars in the Caribbean were about defending the economic and commercial interests of their colonies and the prestige of their empires against the ambitions of their rivals. From being marginal to European conflicts at the beginning of the century, colonies became the principal causes and objects of European rivalry by the end. The shifting ownership of colonies, the threat of invasion, and the imperiling of lives and livelihoods all had serious consequences for residents in the Caribbean.

The arrival of a new power could have dramatic effects on a colony. In Havana, for example, the British victory in 1762 briefly offered new opportunities for British merchants. The opening of trade both allowed Cuba's greater integration with the wider Atlantic commercial world and acted as a catalyst for the more rapid transformation of Cuba's agricultural sector. Under Spanish rule, Havana's importance had lain in its role in the transshipment of American bullion to Europe. The Spanish had not yet turned Cuba over to sugar planting, so their demand for enslaved Africans was relatively small. In the year or so after August 1762, however, there was a sudden increase in the importation into Cuba of enslaved Africans, who were usually carried on British-owned slave ships. This was as yet only a temporary shift. But evidence from the slave trade suggests that despite an initial decline in the slave trade after the reversion to Spanish rule, by the late 1780s large-scale slave imports were normal in Cuba as the island increased its sugar production (Eltis et al. 1999).

The rush by British merchants to seize opportunities in newly acquired colonies was replicated across the Caribbean. In Guadeloupe and Martinique, British mer-

chant capital was quick to arrive. So great were these opportunities that merchants were among the loudest voices seeking the retention of captured islands, while planters—fearing increased competition with their produce in European markets—frequently petitioned for their return. Often, though, the occupying power allowed many of the existing structures to remain in place. Not all conquests were intended to be permanent, partly because captured territory could be a useful bargaining counter in future peace negotiations. In captured French and Spanish colonies, for example, the Catholic Church was allowed to continue.

On islands where the change in ownership was more longstanding, however, conflicts could arise between the new ruler and settlers and the older population. In Grenada, for example, British attempts to include the existing French landowners under their rule were so strongly opposed by British Protestant settlers that in the late 1760s and early 1770s the island's political and fiscal structures faced virtual paralysis (Hamilton 2005, 153–59).

Although invading powers tended to encourage colonies to continue functioning in wartime, the repeated conflicts had serious consequences for trade. Indeed, attacks on foreign shipping were endemic in the Caribbean, in both war and peace. Thousands of ships were taken by navies and privateers in the 18th-century wars. The Royal Navy seized more than 570 French merchant ships in the Caribbean as prizes in the Seven Years' War, while in 1776 and early 1777 alone, US privateers were estimated to have cost British ships the colossal sum of £1.8 million (O'Shaughnessy 2000, 164). Aside from the threat of being seized, merchants were confronted by rocketing insurance rates and a decline in the availability of credit, which was so important for Atlantic trade. As one large British company put it in spring 1778, "trade of every kind seems to be at a perfect stand owing to a most uncommonly great & general Scarcity of money over all three Kingdoms [of Britain], where it will terminate God knows, but we have never known the like before" (Hamilton 2005, 102).

Islands that were not overrun also faced enormous challenges as the great imperial rivalries played out around them. The hostile shipping that disrupted their export trades also affected their imports and resulted in severe shortages of supplies ranging from plantation stores to foodstuffs, most of which were imported. This was particularly a problem for the enslaved, whose rations were imported and who therefore faced starvation. For the planters, food shortages meant two predicaments: one was hunger, and the other was a perception of an increased risk of slave revolt. Uprisings by slaves and maroons were common in wartime, and this further undermined the security of the planters. Their frequent demands for greater military forces (of both army and navy) were a reflection of the risk of invasion and slave revolt. The presence of a naval squadron or military garrison could do much to calm colonists' nerves, and commanders might be thanked profusely for their mere presence. The planters of Jamaica erected a lavish memorial to Rodney in Spanish Town after the Battle of the Saints. Later, during the Napoleonic War, the merchants of Kingston commissioned and presented a silver tea kettle to Admiral Duckworth, just for being there, as an indication of how highly they valued the navy's presence.

By the late 1780s, the peoples of the Caribbean islands had rebuilt their trade and their plantations. Despite calls for its abolition, the slave trade boomed, and sugar became even more essential an item on European tables. The imperial rivalry remained, and despite the frequency of invasions and changes of ownership, the rivals' most important islands were the same in 1783 as they had been 70 years earlier (with the exception of Grenada, which had been transferred from France to Britain). The nature of the rivalry had changed, with a focus on the supply of imports and the facilitation of exports from a series of economic powerhouses, instead of on sniping by Britain and France at Spain. As the islands became more powerful, their position in the rivals' strategies also shifted, making them much more important in the Seven Years' War and the American Revolution than they had previously been. Yet, as throughout the century, peace in the 1780s was fleeting. When war erupted again in the 1790s, it did so in tandem with revolution, which spread from France to Saint-Domingue—soon to become Haiti—and into the British islands, often with disastrous consequences.

WORKS CITED

Christelow, Allan. 1941. "French Interest in the Spanish Empire during the Ministry of the Duc de Choiseul, 1759–1771." *Hispanic American Historical Review* 21 (4): 515–37.

Eltis, D., S. Behrendt, D. Richardson, and H. Klein. 1999. *The Trans-Atlantic Slave Trade: A Database on CD-ROM*. Cambridge: Cambridge University Press.

Hamilton, Douglas J. 2005. *Scotland, the Caribbean and the Atlantic World, 1750–1820*. Manchester, UK: Manchester University Press.

Kennedy, Paul. 2004. *The Rise and Fall of British Naval Mastery*. London: Penguin.

McNeill, John Robert. 1985. *Atlantic Empires of France and Spain: Louisbourg and Havana, 1700–1763*. Chapel Hill: University of North Carolina Press.

O'Shaughnessy, Andrew J. 2000. *An Empire Divided: The American Revolution and the British Caribbean*. Philadelphia: University of Pennsylvania Press.

Pares, Richard. 1963 [1936]. *War and Trade in the West Indies, 1739–63*. London: Frank Cass.

Rodger, N. A. M. 2004. *The Command of the Ocean: A Naval History of Britain, 1649–1815*. London: Penguin.

Sheridan, Richard B. 1998. "The Formation of Caribbean Plantation Society, 1689–1748." In *The Oxford History of the British Empire: The Eighteenth Century*, edited by P. J. Marshall. Oxford: Oxford University Press.

18

The Haitian Revolution LAURENT DUBOIS

At its height, the French colony of Saint-Domingue was the most profitable of all Caribbean plantation societies, outpacing even prosperous Jamaica in its production of sugar and coffee. For many planters and officials at the time, it seemed a model of success. But in the last decade of the 18th century Saint-Domingue became a model for something very different: first the disintegration and then the destruction of a plantation world, burnt quite literally to the ground. The enslaved—those who had faced brutal work regimes, the constant threat of punishment, and a devastating disease environment to make Saint-Domingue prosper—fought back, first winning their freedom and then, when that freedom was threatened, expelling the French for good. In place of the colony they created the new nation of Haiti, which was and remains a powerful and multivalent symbol of black resistance.

The Haitian Revolution emerged from the institution that defined much of Caribbean society and economy in the 18th century: the plantation. And the plantation weighed heavily on how the revolution unfolded and on what it ultimately produced. At once a radical break with the past and an ongoing effort to erase the burden of that past, the struggle for freedom in Haiti was epochal in scale and global in its ramifications. The Haitian Revolution transformed the very meaning of freedom, not just in the Caribbean but far beyond it, ushering in a new vision of human rights. It was in Haiti that the claim that every human being, irrespective of color or status, had the right to autonomy, dignity, and freedom was first fully realized and put to the test. In confronting and overcoming the slave system that dominated the Atlantic at the time, the revolutionaries in Haiti profoundly expanded the meaning and implication of human rights, going further than the American or French revolutionaries. The Haitian Revolution, then, is a vital part of the history of the Americas, of Europe, and indeed of global history—an event crucial to understanding the history of modern politics. A successful slave revolt that led first to general emancipation and citizenship, and then to the creation of an independent black nation-state in the Americas, it represents a signal moment in the history of ideas of universal rights.

However, the social transformation that many in Haiti dreamed of was never completed. The price of freedom was extremely high, in terms of both the carnage and devastation wrought by the war and the difficulties faced by Haiti to this day. The Haitian Revolution left a complex and in some ways paradoxical legacy. The most radical revolution of the Age of Revolution, it created a state undermined by internal conflicts and a society in which the struggle for true dignity and freedom would continue indefinitely. What happened in Haiti after 1804, of course, was only partly grounded in the revolution itself and must be explained within the larger Caribbean context of the 19th and 20th centuries. Within this context, Haiti was shaped by the same economic and political forces that shaped much of the rest of the region. At the same time, Haiti was always unique, bearing the history of a successful slave revolution—a history that powerfully shaped how Haitians perceived themselves and how they were perceived by others.

The Haitian Revolution was remarkable in its complexity. Although rarely included in histories of the French Revolution or of the history of the early American republic (at least until recently), it was deeply linked to both, shaping both and being shaped by them in return. In 1995 the Haitian scholar Michel-Rolph Trouillot famously argued that, for many in Europe and North America, the Haitian Revolution was and has long remained an "unthinkable" event, one that so deeply challenged assumptions about the nature of the world and humanity that it simply could not be assimilated into existing narratives and typologies. Since then, scholars have both built on Trouillot's claim and questioned it, pointing out, for instance, that while the Haitian Revolution was silenced in many contexts, it also echoed powerfully within many communities in the Americas as an example and inspiration for

the enslaved as well as for some abolitionists, and, of course, as a source of anxiety for slave masters. True, many historians in the 20th century may have forgotten or ignored the revolution: examples abound, such as its absence (pointed out
by Trouillot) from Eric Hobsbawm's classic book on the Age of Revolution, and its
omission from most histories of the French Revolution. Yet few of those who lived
in the Atlantic world when it took place could or did ignore it.

On the Slopes of the Volcano

At the beginning of the French Revolution, the French lawyer and representative
Honoré de Mirabeau—one of several prominent proponents of abolition, many of
them part of a group called the Société des Amis des Noirs—described the planters
of Saint-Domingue as "sleeping at the foot of Vesuvius." His comments would soon
ring prescient. Though planters would blame Mirabeau and other abolitionists for
having set off the volcano's explosion—after all, sleeping at the foot of a volcano
is not always deadly, just dangerous—the question of whether the planters could
have escaped the destruction of their colony has occupied historians for some time.
Other slaveholding societies did escape the fate of Saint-Domingue: Jamaica survived several decades longer as a plantation colony, the planters of the US South
prospered for another half-century, and slavery did not end in Cuba and Brazil until
1886 and 1888 respectively.

Nonetheless, in a sense all slave societies were volcanoes, steeped in violence,
strained by constant slave resistance, ready to explode. Few, however, actually did
explode. Neighboring Jamaica had a demographic composition very similar to that
of Saint-Domingue. There, too, a vast majority of slaves surrounded a small number
of masters and free people of African descent. Jamaica, furthermore, had a much
more intense history of rebellion during the 18th century, with maroon wars and
Tacky's Revolt both seriously threatening the stability of its society. Saint-Domingue
had also seen many rebellions, most famously during the 1750s, when a now legendary man named Makandal created a network of poisoners who terrorized the
masters. Like the maroons of Jamaica in the 1730s, a small maroon community in
the mountains along the border with Spanish Santo Domingo signed a peace treaty
with the French colonial government of Saint-Domingue in the 1780s. But as the
case of Jamaica shows, a history of resistance was not enough to create the foundation for a mass revolution of the enslaved. The eruption that took place in Haiti was
not inevitable. But it was the result both of the colony's internal structure and of the
larger historical conjuncture of the late 18th century.

Part of this conjuncture was demographic. During the second half of the 18th
century, the pace of slave imports into the colony was remarkable. In the decade

before the outbreak of the French Revolution alone, more than 30,000 people were annually brought from Africa to Saint-Domingue. Over the course of the century, the colony took in more than a million slaves from Africa. By the time the outbreak of the French and Haitian Revolutions brought the slave trade to Saint-Domingue to a halt, the enslaved population of the island stood at a mere 500,000—proof of both the horrendous death rates among the enslaved, due to disease and the brutal work regime, and the low birth rates, due mostly to the same reasons. Only a constant stream of imports sustained the laboring population, making Saint-Domingue *demographically* an African society. In 1789, not just the majority of slaves (two-thirds by contemporary accounts) but most the colony's population had been born in Africa. Although the people spoke a variety of African languages, there were forces limiting linguistic fragmentation: some of the disparate languages carried from Africa had commonalities, and by the mid-18th century a creole language had established itself so strongly that plays were written and performed in it. Likewise, African religious practices and beliefs not only survived but began to merge into a shared tradition. Many Africans also brought military experience, having served as soldiers in wars sometimes driven by the expansion of the slave trade, and having been captured in battle. Indeed, John Thornton (1991) has argued that the combat skills they learned in Africa, including the use of firearms, were put to use in a new war in the Americas.

The revolution came from the communities of the enslaved. Their thoughts, hopes, and actions made it what it was. Scholars have sometimes emphasized a cleavage between African-born and creole (that is, Caribbean-born) slaves, and there certainly were tensions and differences between the two groups. But firm distinctions between them are misleading. As Ira Berlin and others have argued, some African arrivals may have been relatively "creolized" already, having lived in cosmopolitan coastal areas or ports where cultural and social confrontations and exchanges echoed those taking place in the Caribbean. Many, especially those coming from the regions of West Central Africa, had been exposed to Catholicism, a tradition of religious practice that began with the arrival of Portuguese missionaries in the kingdom of Kongo in the late 15th century. Those born in Saint-Domingue to African parents, meanwhile, might well have maintained linkages, through practice, language, sentiment, and family histories, with the other side of the Atlantic. The religion that emerged in Saint-Domingue during the 18th century (eventually to be called vodou) represents a powerful system of thought that maintained connections with Africa and reflected on and refracted the experience of exile. Amid the brutalities of the plantation world, in the cane fields and sugar mills as well as in the thriving towns of Saint-Domingue, a remarkable process of cultural production unfolded over the course of the 18th century. It made possible the act of political imagination that became the Haitian Revolution.

Religious practices were part of a larger social world that by its very existence militated against the plantation order. Masters strove to reduce the enslaved to the status of laboring machines, their lives organized by the demands of plantation work. But the enslaved were human and they negotiated, pushed back against, and found ways to work around the insistence that they be nothing but embodied labor power. As in other slave societies, marronage (running away) was a fundamental part of daily life. What contemporaries and historians have called "petit marronage"—short-term flight from the plantation rather than permanent escape, which sometimes ended with capture and punishment and sometimes with a negotiated return—was particularly crucial in laying the foundation for revolution. For along with allowing slaves the mobility on Sundays to sell in local towns the produce grown in their garden plots, petit marronage made possible the creation of cross-plantation community and collusion. If the uprising of 1791 succeeded in Saint-Domingue, it was because its leaders were able to mobilize such cross-plantation networks in order to plan a massive, coordinated attack.

An Atlantic Revolution

The opportunity for attack came in 1791, and in an entirely unforeseen context: the French Revolution. How to understand the relationship between the French and Haitian Revolutions has intrigued and befuddled generations of historians. The most famous account, C. L. R. James's classic *The Black Jacobins* (1938), involves a rich meditation on this problem. James shows beautifully how the two revolutions shaped one another and how their histories illuminate one another. What his narrative suggests, and what subsequent historiography has urged readers to contemplate, is that ultimately it may be extremely difficult to figure out where one revolution ends and the other begins. The 1790s saw a French Atlantic revolution that played out on both sides of the ocean, and the currents of cause and effect were complex and varied but never unidirectional. In the Caribbean itself multiple revolutions were underway, for the French colonies of Martinique and Guadeloupe also saw upheaval and transformation. And the revolution that took place in Saint-Domingue really only became "Haitian" after 1802, when it aimed to create an independent nation. Before that, enslaved insurgents had actually won their freedom by arguing for, and eventually achieving, a closer legal and political connection between France and the colony of Saint-Domingue.

The revolution of 1789 in France shaped what happened in the Caribbean in many ways. First, and perhaps most important, it shook up the system of colonial governance and weakened its power, inviting protest and resistance. All social groups in Saint-Domingue saw an opportunity in the French Revolution. For many planters, who had long chafed under the commercial regulations of the *exclusif*, which required most trade in their plantation products to be with France, it was an opportunity to argue for greater economic freedom. For poorer whites in the colony, it was an opportunity to protest and fight against the social hierarchy that kept them marginalized and often landless. For free people of African descent, also called free people of color (*gens de couleur*) and often described in the literature as "mulattoes," though many were in fact not of mixed European and African ancestry, it was an opportunity to protest against decades of humiliating local legislation that constrained them politically and restricted them from practicing certain professions as well as controlling other aspects of their life, some as minute as the kind of clothes they could wear and the means of transportation they could use.

But if the French Revolution created an opening by undermining the central structure of authority and command in the colony, it also produced an outpouring of language and symbolism that could be powerfully mobilized. The 1789 Declaration of the Rights of Man thus produced a charter both immensely powerful and immensely vague in its articulation. Free people of color were particularly astute in harnessing the new language of rights to long-standing grievances about racial discrimination. Presenting themselves as wealthy, educated patriots, elite free people of color—led by figures such as Julien Raimond and Vincent Ogé, both wealthy men with substantial holdings in land and slaves—argued that they should have access to political rights alongside whites in the colonies. They allied themselves with the nascent abolitionist movement in France to take on the privilege of white planters, which they dubbed the "aristocracy of the skin." And they found that many were sympathetic to their arguments, which both drew on and buttressed the idea that a new era of equality was dawning in France.

They also ran into strenuous opposition. Despite having powerful allies—among them Mirabeau, the Marquis de Condorcet, and the Abbé Grégoire—the gens de couleur ultimately failed to make headway in the National Assembly in Paris. In 1790 an angry and disabused Ogé returned to Saint-Domingue, where he organized an armed uprising to demand political rights. Ogé and his men were defeated after a few engagements and he fled to Spanish Santo Domingo, from which he was extradited to be tortured and executed in Le Cap. His execution shocked many in France, turning the tide of opinion against French planters in the colony. It also left an impression among the enslaved, who would remember what had happened to Ogé a few years later when they negotiated with the French. Just as important, by the middle of 1790 the enslaved understood that they faced a major opportunity. Saint-Domingue's elites, including the free people of color, were divided, fighting each other openly, and lacking support or even understanding from a government in Paris that was itself in the midst of serious conflict and confrontation. In the summer of 1791, a group of enslaved organizers decided to strike.

Vodou and Revolution

The beginning of the Revolution, and the event often seen as the founding of Haiti itself, was the Bois-Caïman ceremony of August 1791. Although there has been debate about precisely when and where this event took place, the most careful study of the evidence (Geggus 2002) concludes that at least one and perhaps two religious ceremonies were organized before the great uprising of 1791. Plans were made, oaths taken, and inspiration gained from communication with deities, whose aid in the endeavor was seen as crucial by many. That the revolution was rooted in religious practice is no accident, for such practice enabled a diverse and fragmented slave population of disparate origins and experiences to find some common ground. Contemporary Haitian vodou carries the traces of the struggle of 18th-century slaves to retain ties to Africa and create new practices that could address the situation of plantation slavery. It also embodies the idea that diverse traditions could be incorporated into one system while retaining a certain autonomy, for the *lwa*, or gods, are organized into "nations" (in many cases into just two, Rada and Petwo, but sometimes more) that require their own rituals but still work together in a larger system of belief and practice.

Despite the oaths taken at the ceremony, a few rebels were discovered and the uprising seems to have been pushed to an earlier date. But it is hard to imagine that the insurgents could have had more success. In a simultaneous rising on the sugar plantations of Saint-Domingue's northern plain, the richest sugar-growing region in the colony, the insurgents rapidly turned cane fields and plantation houses to ash and smashed the sugar processing machinery. They killed most whites they encountered, sending the rest fleeing toward the capital in Le Cap. Soot and smoke covered the sky. At night the flames from the burning fields reached so high that according to one account a person could read by the light of the fires in the harbor of Le Cap. Had the uprising gone according to plan, the insurgents might actually have taken Le Cap, where most of the prominent planters had gathered for a meeting of the local assembly.

Nevertheless, the insurgents gained control of the plain and the mountains around Le Cap, turning plantations into military camps, recruiting new followers, finding weapons, and consolidating their territorial control. The French fought back, but to little avail. Despite counterattacks that anticipated characteristics of modern counterinsurgency campaigns—the French repeatedly slaughtered the old and infirm, along with women and children captured when they overran insurgent camps—the rebel army remained strong and grew steadily over the ensuing months. The insurgents also got help from the Spanish across the border in Santo Domingo, who began arming them in a bid to take over the valuable French colony.

Figure 18.1 Earliest known portrait of Toussaint Louverture, based on an oral description. Engraving by J. Barlow and Marcus Rainsford (1805). Source: The John Carter Brown Library.

From among their ranks came a series of brilliant and remarkable leaders—first Boukman, Jean-François, and Biassou, and later Jean-Jacques Dessalines, Henri Christophe, the African-born Sans Souci and Macaya, and most famously Toussaint Louverture.

Louverture was born a slave in the northern plain of Saint-Domingue. (He was originally named Bréda after the plantation where he was born, and took on the name Louverture at the beginning of the revolution.) He worked as a coachman on a plantation, but gained his freedom in the 1770s. For a time, Louverture rented and managed a coffee plantation, overseeing the work of the enslaved. He also briefly owned at least one slave himself. He seems to have joined the insurrection shortly after it began and worked his way up through the ranks. By 1792 he had begun to play a crucial role, working closely with the Spanish to obtain guns and ammunition. At that time the French leadership of the colony had passed to two civil commissioners of the revolutionary state, François Polverel and Léger Félicité Sonthonax, who had been sent with the mission to quell the insurrection. They brought a decree from the National Assembly, which, hearing news of the frightening insurrection, had at last agreed to give political rights to all free people of color, hoping that this would guarantee their support against the slave insurrection. It worked, but only in part, for as rapidly as the French commissioners gained allies among free people of color, they lost them among the planters, who were increasingly convinced that the revolutionary French government was determined to destroy slavery.

Some planters began negotiating with the British in Jamaica, hoping to secure a foreign occupation of the island to preserve slavery and their position of power. In September 1792, France transformed itself from a constitutional monarchy to a republic, and in January 1793 the king was executed. Soon, France was at war with all the monarchies of Europe, and Britain was eager to strike at its enemy's most important colony. Many royalist planters deeply distrusted the radicals in France, whom they believed (with some reason) were rabid abolitionists. These planters' increasing alienation from the new leadership in France set off the remarkable transformations that took place in the summer of 1793 in Saint-Domingue, when the slave insurrection achieved a significant victory that irrevocably changed colonial and French law and politics.

By the middle of 1793 the Spanish-supported insurgents seemed unstoppable. Sonthonax and Polverel were in a desperate situation: many whites on the island were vociferously attacking their authority and, in many cases, were eagerly awaiting the arrival of the British. In June, the antirepublican planter camp found a leader in a man named Galbaud, who had been imprisoned in the Le Cap harbor by Sonthonax and Polverel and who now mobilized sailors and royalists in an attempt to overthrow their regime. The decisive intervention of militias of free people of color, and notably of an African-born officer named Jean-Baptiste Belley, saved the commissioners from being captured. Desperate for support, they made a bold move: they offered the enslaved insurgents who were camped just outside of the city to join with them. In return they offered freedom and French citizenship.

A band of insurgents under the command of an African-born man named Jeannot accepted the offer, and they rushed down into the town, defeating Galbaud and his partisans. As the fighting went on, fires were set and looting began in the city; much of Le Cap was burned to the ground. Terrified residents flooded onto ships in the harbor, leaving—in many cases permanently—for North America, where they settled in Philadelphia, Charleston, New Orleans, and New York. Sonthonax and Polverel had won, but only partially. Some insurgents were on their side now, but many more still fought with the Spanish. In the next months insurgent demands expanded, some calling for an outright abolition of slavery.

Figure 18.2 Portrait of the
African-born Jean-Baptiste Belley, by French artist Anne-Louis
Girodet de Roussy-Trioson
(1797).

In August 1793, Sonthonax decreed slavery abolished in the Northern Province, while in subsequent months Polverel did the same in the other parts of the colony. It was a dramatic decision with profound implications. The commissioners had acted unilaterally and, with no encouragement or even indication of support from the National Convention in Paris, abolished slavery in France's largest slave colony. Five hundred thousand slaves were emancipated without a period of transition and with no indemnity given to planters, as there would be in later cases of emancipation. It was the first full emancipation in the Americas, and it was improvised on the ground in the Caribbean. It also represented the victory of the slave insurrection, which was transformed from a movement of people often characterized by the French as "brigands" into one embraced by the local French administration.

Some slave insurgents, including Louverture, remained aloof from the French. Louverture seems to have been awaiting confirmation that the decision would be approved by France. That happened in 1794, when a group of three representatives from Saint-Domingue, including Belley, spoke to the National Convention and explained what had happened in Saint-Domingue, arguing that the abolition of slavery had been both politically and militarily necessary. The National Convention, with little debate, ratified the decision taken in Saint-Domingue, declaring slavery abolished and all men, of all colors, citizens of France. Emancipation, furthermore, was to be extended to other French colonies.

Liberty was won by the slaves of Saint-Domingue, then, not by attacking French metropolitan authority but by pledging allegiance to it against planters who were resisting it. Slave rebellion thus found its ally in metropolitan colonial power. In the process, republican rights were expanded to those who had been excluded from all legal rights. After 1794, France and its colonies were united, in principle, under one set of laws understood as truly universal and applicable on both sides of the Atlantic. For a time, racial hierarchies were defeated by assimilationist universalism. Racially integrated armies defended French colonies against the British and even attacked British colonies in the eastern Caribbean, playing a crucial role in the global conflict between the two imperial powers.

Independence

The decision of the National Convention helped secure Louverture's alliance to France. His military astuteness had earned him the rank of general, but it was his political brilliance as a negotiator and charismatic leader that ultimately gained him the leadership role he secured for himself by the late 1790s. Appointed governor by the French General Etienne Laveaux, his steadfast ally from the mid-1790s on, Louverture took control of the colony's military and civil affairs. By 1801, when he declared himself governor-for-life, he had already been the colony's de facto leader for several years. Throughout the 1790s, he served France's military objectives effectively, turning against his former Spanish allies, whom he drove from the colony, and expelling the British, who had occupied parts of the island since 1794.

But enemy forces were only part of the problem facing Louverture. He also had to oversee a large-scale transition from slavery to freedom, the first of its kind in the Americas, with little support from the French metropole and no examples for how to proceed. He continued the policies set in place by Sonthonax and Polverel, which required former slaves to continue working on plantations in return for a wage—paid not in money, but as a portion of the sugar or coffee produced. He also introduced some forms of democracy on the plantation, where workers could now elect their managers and could also, under some conditions, move to other plantations. As time went on, however, Louverture increasingly used coercion to keep workers on plantations, using the army of formerly enslaved men he had built to police the plantations and suppress resistance among workers. For many ex-slaves, the situation was unsatisfactory if not outright unacceptable, and there was significant and sometimes violent resistance against Louverture as many crafted an alternative vision of the future: one in which they would become small-scale landowners growing food for themselves rather than for an export-oriented plantation economy.

Louverture's service was a tremendous boon to France, for by defeating the massive British invasion of Saint-Domingue he played a central role in France's broader military campaigns in the Caribbean. Unlike the British, the French did not need to send troops across the Atlantic to fight, since so many former slaves of their colonies served as soldiers. Louverture's economic policies also were quite successful in rebuilding the coffee economy to almost prerevolutionary levels, and also in partially rebuilding the sugar economy, even though much of the machinery required for sugar production had been destroyed during the insurrection of 1791–92. But Louverture was always wary of the French government, concerned that it might ultimately reverse its support for emancipation. And he was ready for that possibility. His powerful army served France, but it was also a counterweight to French authority.

In the late 1790s, just as Louverture had feared, the French government began a retreat from policies of emancipation. This retreat accelerated with the rise to consular power of Napoleon Bonaparte and the (ultimately short-lived) peace with the British in 1801. Urged on by advisors and unchecked by the French parliament, some of whose members had in previous years eloquently supported emancipation in the Caribbean, Bonaparte decided to crush Louverture and his regime and to reverse the effects of abolition. He reacquired Louisiana from the Spanish, largely so that it could serve as a source of wood and provisions for what he hoped would be a reborn slave plantation colony in Saint-Domingue. He also ordered his brother-in-law, General Charles V. E. Leclerc, to lead a vast expeditionary force, which with later reinforcements totaled at least as many as 50,000 soldiers and sailors, to bring Saint-Domingue back under French control.

French rulers sought to hide their intention to crush the black armies that had emerged in the Caribbean, but many in Saint-Domingue understood what was happening. From their arrival, the French troops faced serious resistance, which was led by Louverture and his generals, including Christophe and Dessalines. Leclerc's troops suffered heavy losses, but ultimately Louverture surrendered, though smaller bands of fighters continued to battle against the French. Fearing that Louverture would once again join the resistance, the French imprisoned and deported him to a fortress in the Jura Mountains, where he died in 1803. Meanwhile, Dessalines and Christophe fought for the French for several months. As resistance expanded—spurred on by news that the French had reestablished slavery in Guadeloupe—these generals eventually turned against the French once again. Dessalines became the leader of the resistance and, after securing the final defeat of the French troops—only a few thousand of whom remained alive after the spirited resistance and a devastating yellow-fever epidemic—declared independence on January 1, 1804. Dessalines's fiery declaration of independence and the choice of the name Haiti—used by the island's indigenous people who had been decimated by the Spanish centuries earlier—presented the victory of the revolution as an act of vengeance against years of oppression and slavery.

Isolated by France and a fearful United States in the early 19th century, Haiti's rulers ultimately made a deal in 1825 that allowed its ports to be opened up to trade with France. In return for diplomatic recognition, however, the Haitian government granted France the payment of a massive indemnity. Former slave and plantation owners from Saint-Domingue had for decades been lobbying the French government for compensation for the economic losses they had suffered during the revolution. Much of the capital lost had, of course, been invested in the very bodies of those who had now won their freedom. Thus, the "indemnity" levied in 1825 was literally a fine for revolution, to be collected from the descendants of those men and women who had gained their freedom through rebellion a few decades before. Unable to deliver the exorbitant sum of 150 million francs demanded by the French, the Haitian government borrowed money from French banks and spent the next century contributing a good portion of its revenues to service this debt.

Independent Haiti also faced other economic challenges. The colony's very raison d'etre had been to serve the economic needs of France. By the late 18th century, its environment had already been devastated—commentators at the time complained of the problems of deforestation (which economists and development experts are only too willing to blame nowadays on the peasantry's land use practices)—and the colony had been artificially populated through a slave trade that had sustained a highly industrialized plantation system. But the economic options available to Haiti in the international system—the production of sugar and coffee—depended on labor systems that, understandably enough, were anathema to many ex-slaves. Nevertheless, 19th-century Haiti saw an impressive expansion of the increasingly profitable coffee economy, which eventually reached levels that rivaled those of the colonial past. Sugar production, however, was never restored to its previous levels. Meanwhile, throughout the country many former slaves created new lives as small-scale peasants, farming and raising livestock for local markets.

The Haitian Revolution left a complex political legacy, shaping a political culture that brings a radical egalitarianism together with traditions of militarization and authoritarianism. Outside Haiti, the nation and the struggle that produced it were regularly evoked in the battle over slavery in the Atlantic world. While many who supported slavery presented Haiti as a nation destined to fail, others held it up as an example of successful resistance. Throughout the early 19th century, debates about slavery referred—sometimes openly, sometimes obliquely—to the Haitian experience. Abolitionists evoked it regularly, though often they were not sure quite how to deal with the fact that the one successful example of large-scale emancipation had been won through massive violence. Playwrights and novelists in France—notably Alphonse de Lamartine and Victor Hugo—wrote works of literature about it. The figure of Louverture, the political and military genius of the revolution, circulated as myth, and as proof of the absurdity of white supremacist ideologies. Most important, the example of successful revolution in Haiti was a constant presence within communities of African descent throughout the Atlantic world, both enslaved and free. For them the stories and images of slaves turned generals and emperors who led the revolution were a source of fascination and hope.

What is the legacy of the Haitian Revolution? For centuries, many parties have struggled with how to tell the story. These groups include French generals and officials who wrote contemporary accounts or memoirs; Louverture himself, as he struggled in prison to produce a memoir of his military actions; early Haitian historians, like Beaubrun Ardouin and Thomas Madiou; the French abolitionist Victor Schoelcher; the Martinican poet Aimé Césaire; the Trinidadian activist and intellectual C. L. R. James; the African-American artist Jacob Lawrence; generations of 20th-century historians in the Caribbean, the United States, and France; the American novelist Madison Smartt Bell; and even the American actor Danny Glover in a promised film. If it has always been tempting to explain the revolution with recourse to social and racial categories—poor and rich whites, "mulattoes" and blacks, creole planters and French administrations, creole and African-born slaves—the history itself disrupts such attempts. If there is anything that defines the Haitian Revolution, it is the fact that its course was always unpredictable, the results always exceeding what those involved might have thought possible not long before. The revolution disrupted old categories and created new ones; it was always shadowed by the past while also bursting forth into something new, perhaps unreachable, but certainly unknown.

Of course Haiti did not make its history exactly as it chose, and in the 19th and 20th centuries it has been subjected to enormous external pressures that have contained and shaped its politics and economy. The indemnity levied by France in 1825 had a crippling effect on the state's solvency and ultimately on the coffee economy. In the 19th century Haiti was already experiencing the debilitating cycle of debt that would shape life in many other postcolonial countries in the late 20th century. Within the country the revolution itself left a complicated political legacy, for it helped create a tradition of authoritarian military rule even as it produced a radical democratic political culture. Both traditions have coexisted and clashed ever since. So, too, have different economic models: one aimed at producing agricultural products or manufactures for export in the global economy, the other focused on local production through small landholding—a radical refusal of economic relations that to some felt too much like slavery. As Haiti begins its third century as a free country, the past still lurks in present crises, such as the disrupted attempts in 2004 to commemorate a Haitian Revolution that remains in many ways unfinished.

WORKS CITED

Geggus, David. 2002. *Haitian Revolutionary Studies*. Bloomington: Indiana University Press.

James, C. L. R. 1963. *The Black Jacobins: Toussaint Louverture and the San Domingo Revolution*. New York: Vintage.

Thornton, John. 1991. "African Soldiers in the Haitian Revolution," *Journal of Caribbean History* 25, nos. 1 and 2: 58–80.

Trouillot, Michel-Rolph. 1995. *Silencing the Past: Power and the Production of History*. Boston: Beacon Press.

19

The Abolition of Slavery in the Non-Hispanic Caribbean

DIANA PATON

After establishing, protecting, and supporting slavery for more than two centuries, the British, French, Danish, and Dutch imperial states took steps that led to its abolition over a 30-year period, from 1833 to 1863. The nature of these emancipation processes allowed each empire to claim the mantle of liberator of slaves. Such claims were sometimes made visible in images such as the one in figure 19.1, in which a representative of the French state bestows freedom on grateful, happy slaves. Images like this ignored the contribution of enslaved people to their own emancipation, as well as the European imperial states' very recent records of reinforcing and, in one case, reestablishing slavery. Despite these histories, the emancipation processes powerfully strengthened colonial rule in the non-Hispanic Caribbean, in contrast to events in Cuba and Puerto Rico, where the struggle to end slavery became intertwined with the struggle for independence from Spain.

The designers of emancipation in the non-Hispanic Caribbean hoped to end slavery through gradual reforms that would sustain

plantation economies while making minimal changes to the organization of class power and race privilege. In their visions of freedom, enslaved people would move out of slavery to become a rural working class without access to land. Liberals emphasized the morally improving character of wage labor, which they saw as inculcating values of thrift and aspiration, and of domestic patriarchy. In practice, the political action of enslaved people in the last years of slavery hastened emancipation processes almost everywhere, and their aspirations to become peasant farmers rather than wage workers, as well as their mobility around and beyond the Caribbean region, frequently frustrated plans for the continuation of the plantation economy.

In Saint-Domingue slavery was formally abolished in 1793, in the wake of the 1791 slave rebellion, as metropolitan administrators sought to attract rebels to the republican cause. On February 4, 1794, the revolutionary government in Paris declared slavery abolished throughout the empire with the Act of 16 Pluviose Year 2. In Martinique, planters evaded the act's implementation by acquiescing to occupation by British military forces, who ruled the island from 1794 to 1802. Guadeloupe was also occupied by the British in 1794 but retaken by French forces a few months later. The French enforced the Paris abolition decree, but also implemented an obligatory labor system and restrictions on the movement of former slaves. Similarly, General

Toussaint Louverture imposed labor requirements on all former slaves not engaged in active military duty in Saint-Domingue when he assumed territorial rule. French Guiana (Guyane) implemented the metropolitan abolition decree in 1794.

Except in Saint-Domingue, the revolutionary abolition of slavery proved short-lived. Under Napoleon, France no longer acted as an antislavery power, instead ordering slavery restored throughout the empire in 1802. In Guadeloupe, armed former slaves resisted the restoration of slavery under the military leadership of Louis Delgrès, but lost to the French forces' superior firepower. After their defeat, more than 10,000 people were executed or deported (Dubois 2004, 404). In both Guadeloupe and Guiana, slavery was reimposed on people who had experienced nearly eight years of declared free status. In Saint-Domingue, however, the confirmation that French forces aimed to restore slavery set off the final military campaigns of the revolution, culminating in the battles of Vertières, at which the French were decisively defeated. Haiti declared its independence in 1804.

Britain acquired additional colonies during the wars of the 1790s, most importantly the former Dutch colonies of Demerara, Essequibo, and Berbice (later British Guiana) as well as Trinidad, which it took from Spain. The British government soon abandoned its initial plans for the development of Trinidad as a showcase for tropical free-labor agriculture in favor of expanding the plantation slavery system that French planters had been developing since the 1780s. Trinidad and British Guiana, along with Mauritius in the Indian Ocean (acquired from France in 1810), became the new frontier for sugar slavery in the British Empire. Together, these colonies competed with Cuba to fill the gap left in the international sugar market by the overthrow of slavery in Haiti. Planters in these colonies, many of whom were French and Dutch as well as newly arrived British, rushed to import enslaved Africans in the first years of the 19th century, in anticipation of the likely ending of the slave trade. Despite the costs—paid largely in the lives and health of enslaved people who undertook the work—of clearing land previously unused for sugar, and, in Guiana, of protecting land below sea level from the ocean, planters in these areas had the advantage of being able to purchase the most up-to-date machinery. They also benefited from developing their plantations on land unaffected by the soil exhaustion experienced in many existing colonies. Nevertheless, planters in the older colonies of both Britain and France also expanded sugar production, attempting to grow their way out of debt. In Martinique, for instance, sugar expanded at the expense of coffee, as planters switched to the more profitable crop.

In 1807 Britain made the transatlantic slave trade to its colonies, but not slavery within those colonies, illegal. Many abolitionists hoped that cutting off the supply of African captives would in the long run erode slavery to the point where abolition became straightforward, but few at this stage proposed government intervention to end it. The population of most colonies declined between 1807 and the abolition of slavery in 1834 because of enslaved people's poor health and low fertility. With sugar production expanding, the pace of work for enslaved people intensified as fewer people labored to produce a larger crop. The result was an increase in struggle over the organization of work, the management of plantations, and time away from staple-crop production. Complaints like that of an enslaved man named Lewis, from Demerara, who reported to a fiscal (magistrate) that his overseer allowed him and the others in his gang no time to eat in the middle of the day, were common (Viotti da Costa 1994, 65–66).

The growth of antislavery feeling in Europe (especially Britain) combined with knowledge of the Haitian Revolution to produce a new awareness among enslaved people throughout the Caribbean that the ending of slavery was a political possibility. This sense was aided in the British colonies by the arrival of a significant number of missionaries from nonconformist Protestant denominations. The earliest missionaries were German Moravians who came to the Danish Virgin Islands in the 1730s; to Suriname, Jamaica, and Antigua in the 1750s; and to other colonies later in the 18th century. Methodists also established missions in Antigua in the 1750s and across the region by around 1800. They were soon joined in Jamaica by African American Baptists, including George Liele and Moses Baker, who both evacuated with the British after American independence. By the early 19th century, British missionary organizations including the Baptist Missionary Society, the Wesleyan Methodist Missionary Society, and the interdenominational London Missionary Society were all sending missionaries to the colonies.

These missionaries aimed to save the souls of slaves rather than help them to become free, and they accommodated themselves to the power of planters in order to be allowed to operate at all. Nevertheless, they remained outsiders in white society. They were paid significantly less than their Anglican equivalents and looked to each other, rather than to the planters, for support and sociability. Their presence produced a new political pole in societies previously made up almost exclusively of enslaved people and slaveholders. They helped develop a new type of community, organized outside the hierarchy of estates and frequently led by enslaved deacons and class leaders rather than white missionaries. Planters' efforts to control enslaved people's time, and in particular to prevent them from attending religious services held beyond the estates where they lived, led to ongoing conflict. Such conflict played an important role in two important rebellions during the last years of slavery.

After abolishing the slave trade, the British government took an increasingly active role in regulating slavery. The initial step was the introduction of slave registration laws, which required slaveholders to register the names and ages of their slaves and to report on births and deaths. The purpose was to attempt to prevent illegal importation of more enslaved Africans, on the assumption that this would lead slaveholders to improve the slaves' living conditions. First implemented in Trinidad in 1812, such laws were in force across the British colonies by 1820. Beginning in 1823, the British imperial state attempted to implement a program of "amelioration" of slavery, designed to rid the colonies of what were perceived as the worst excesses of the slave system. In the words of a resolution adopted by the House of Commons in 1824, "amelioration" was intended to lead to "a progressive improvement in the slave population, such as may prepare them for a participation in those civil rights and privileges which are enjoyed by other classes of his majesty's subjects" (Hansard House of Lords 1824). This resolution articulated a widely held belief that enslaved people in their current state were not "prepared" for freedom; they required instruction in morality and religion before they could live as free people.

The suggested "amelioration" measures included the promotion of religious instruction, a ban on the flogging of women and on the use of the whip in the fields, the prohibition of the separation of husbands from wives and of mothers (but not fathers) from children by sale, and the creation of a new state official known as the "protector of slaves" to hear complaints by slaves about their owners or managers. In addition, Christian slaves were to be permitted to give evidence in court, and Sunday markets, such as the Antiguan example depicted in figure 19.2, were to be prohibited. Undergirding this policy was the idea that enslaved people needed education in Christian principles. Such education would lead, advocates of amelioration asserted, to the transformation of degraded slaves into sober Christians and liberal acquisitive individuals, organized into stable patriarchal family units.

In Trinidad, where the local planter elite had little control over the law, the amelioration measures became law by imperial fiat. Elsewhere—either because the imperial government chose to try to persuade local colonial authorities to pass amelioration laws, or because colonial law was controlled by assemblies elected by free property-holding white men—the policy of imperial amelioration sparked an ongoing contest between representatives of the metropolitan and colonial states. Colonial legislators believed that implementing the full range of reforms would seriously undermine the authority of slaveholders and perhaps ultimately lead to the dismantling of slavery. Across the colonies, assemblies refused to pass new slave codes, or modified the suggestions of the Colonial Office when they did pass them. While many colonial assemblies agreed to abolish Sunday markets and to recognize enslaved people's property, not one agreed to the ban on flogging women.

The combination of the arrival of missionaries and the conflict over imperial amelioration reforms created a space that enslaved people used to expand their rights within the system of slavery. In the few colonies where protectors of slaves existed, slaves brought hundreds of complaints against masters and managers. Where the whip was no longer used in the fields or against women, planters complained that enslaved people took advantage of this situation, and they searched for alternative forms of discipline. Perhaps most significant, enslaved people used the amelioration

Figure 19.2 Sunday market at Antigua, with traders selling a range of produce to black, white, and mixed-race customers. Print by W. E. Beastall and G. Testolini (1806).

process to expand their semiautonomous economic activities, growing food crops on provision grounds and selling the surplus in regular markets, now usually held on Saturdays. This work, generally organized through family groups, would become the foundation of the post-slavery Caribbean peasantry.

Conflict between the local planter-controlled state and the imperial government sparked the three largest rebellions of the slavery period in the British-colonized Caribbean: in Barbados in 1816, Demerara in 1823, and Jamaica in 1831. In each case, rebellions were organized at a time when rumors were spreading rapidly in the context of British debates around slavery, amelioration, and abolition. In 1816, news about the proposed system of slave registration and the planters' opposition to it contributed to the first full-fledged slave rebellion to take place in Barbados, an event involving hundreds of enslaved people. In Demerara in 1823, knowledge of the debates over amelioration contributed to the belief of the rebellion's main leaders that slavery could be successfully overthrown, and to their ability to convince others to participate in the rebellion. In 1831, more than 10,000 enslaved people in western Jamaica took part in a rebellion that began after a series of meetings organized by planters

to protest against new British governmental moves towards imposing "amelioration" reforms, taken in the context of a renewed abolitionist campaign for immediate emancipation. The rebellion, like almost all Caribbean slave rebellions, involved the burning of many plantations, as shown in Adolph Duperly's painting of the firing of Montpelier plantation in St. James (figure 19.3).

Figure 19.3 Rebels burn Old Montpelier Estate, a large sugar plantation in western Jamaica, during the Jamaican Rebellion of 1831. Lithograph by Adolph Duperly (1833).

All these revolts also took place in the context of intensification of labor regimes and, especially in Demerara and Jamaica, conflict over religious worship. Their central leaders in Demerara and Jamaica—Jack Gladstone and Quamina in the former, Sam Sharpe in the latter—were literate, mobile, and creole and were deacons in missionary churches. The widespread oral circulation of information from newspapers was often crucial in motivating and organizing the revolts. Nanny Grigg, a literate woman who was one of the leaders of the 1816 Barbados rebellion, told others that she had read in newspapers that slaves were to be freed. According to the confession of another rebel, a man named Robert, "she said she had read it in the Newspapers and that her Master was very uneasy at it . . . the negroes were to be freed on Easter Monday, and the only way to get it was to fight for it, otherwise they would not get it; and the way they were to do, was to set fire, as that was the way they did in Saint Domingo" (quoted in Craton 1979). Robert's testimony indicates the significance of intertwined knowledge of the Haitian Revolution and of imperial-level debates about amelioration and emancipation in stimulating rebellion.

Each rebellion was suppressed by brutal force, implemented by British imperial military and naval units as well as by local militias, and followed up by judicial terror that left reminders of the planters' vengeance, in the form of the bodies of executed rebels, hung on gibbets across the areas where rebellion had taken place. Antislavery campaigners in Britain publicized the violent repression of the rebellions, contributing to a political atmosphere that ultimately turned against the slaveholders. (This is not to argue that a straightforward growth in compassion for slaves was responsible for the implementation of abolition; economic and ideological considerations were also important. The reasons for abolition remain disputed.) The publicity following the Jamaican rebellion made slavery an important issue in the British election of 1832. The impact of the rebellion and its suppression was heightened by the fact that this was the first election to take place after the passage of the 1832 Reform Act, which produced an expanded, although still minority, electorate. For the first time propertied men from industrial areas, who tended to favor abolition, could elect members of Parliament.

The Whig government that resumed power in 1833 followed through on the pledges of many MPs by passing the Act for the Abolition of Slavery that same year. The act led to the replacing of slavery from August 1, 1834, with a system known as "apprenticeship," which bound former slaves to their former masters for a projected four or six years ("non-praedial" [non-agricultural] apprentices were to become free after four years, while most were expected to have to wait six). The exceptions were Antigua and Bermuda, whose assemblies opted out of the apprenticeship system and moved instead to a contract-based system of labor, enforced by harsh vagrancy legislation. The act also compensated former slaveholders for the loss of their human property, setting aside £20 million of government funds for this purpose. It did not compensate those who had been enslaved.

The contradictions of the apprenticeship system led to substantial conflict between planters and state officials, between planters and apprentices, and between apprentices and state officials. Planters, no longer legally allowed to use direct violence to enforce labor discipline on their estates, turned to state-appointed magistrates to do the job for them, thus leading to increased use of colonial prisons and other state-authorized punishments and sparking abolitionist outrage. In 1838, under pressure from abolitionists to end apprenticeship outright, the British government passed legislation imposing greater imperial control on colonial administration of the system. In response, colonial legislatures, already concerned about the likely impact of the imminent freeing of the non-praedial apprentices, abolished apprenticeship entirely on August 1, 1838.

In the French colonies, slavery expanded after its restoration in 1802. Planters imported at least 50,000 new enslaved Africans in the 19th century. Officially, France agreed to abolish the slave trade to its colonies in 1815, but in practice significant number of captives arrived there every year until 1831. As a result, a higher proportion of the French colonial enslaved population was African-born than in the British colonies. As in the British colonies, enslaved people struggled over time and work discipline, but the absence of a mass abolitionist movement in France meant that there was less pressure on local elites to reform slavery. Substantial legal moves toward "amelioration" did not take place until the 1830s. Overall, the period from 1802 to 1830 was one of intense repression of slaves.

Free people of color also experienced harsh repression after 1802. The Napoleonic regime and colonial governments were keen to restore the discriminatory laws that had restricted the civil rights of free people of color prior to 1789, preventing them, for instance, from wearing particular types of clothing, receiving education, or using French names. The 1804 Napoleonic Civil Code was altered in the colonies to forbid marriage between whites and people of color and to prevent people of color from inheriting from whites. Nevertheless, the number of *gens de couleur* increased substantially during the last years of slavery, as the government lessened taxes on manumission. In Martinique, for instance, the population of free people of color rose from fewer than 10,000 in 1802 to approximately 36,000 in 1848, exceeding the number of whites by 1816 (Schloss 2009, 9, 73). White creole concern about the growing power of the gens de couleur led in 1824 to what became known as the Bissette affair. Cyrille Bissette, a prominent man of color, was prosecuted with six others for conspiracy on the grounds that he possessed and was suspected of authoring an anonymous pamphlet, *De la situation des gens de couleur libres aux Antilles Françaises*. Bissette was eventually exiled to France, where he became one of the most prominent and radical abolitionist leaders; hundreds of other gens de couleur were deported from Martinique. The Bissette affair attracted metropolitan publicity and contributed to turning French public opinion against the colonial planters, paralleling the impact in Britain of the repression of the rebellions in Demerara and Jamaica.

After the shift to a more liberal regime in France in 1830 (the July monarchy), the metropolitan government implemented limited reforms in and with regard to the colonies. These reforms included the final full suppression of the slave trade, increasing civil rights for free people of color, and the outlawing of whipping of women. Like the British government, French reformers understood the physical punishment of women to be particularly important and problematic because it entailed the exposure of women's bodies. Planters objected to these reforms, and in particular to what they saw as the erosion of the privileges of whiteness. Many of the reform laws were not fully implemented.

Although no armed uprising on the scale of the Jamaican and Demeraran rebellions took place in the French colonies during this period, there were significant conspiracies and rebellions in 1811, 1822, 1831, and 1833 in Martinique, some of them led by free people of color. The 1831 rebellion involved about 300 slaves, only slightly fewer than were involved in the Barbados rebellion of 1816. As had been the case with the 19th-century rebellions in the British colonies, political events in the metropole contributed to this uprising. Rebels reportedly marched to the tune of the revolutionary song *The Parisienne*, which was also sung by crowds in Paris during the 1830 revolution. White planters interpreted this as the result of the new July monarchy regime's alleged lenience toward slaves and its raising of aspirations for equality among free people of color.

Enslaved and free people in Martinique and Guadeloupe—adjacent to the British colonies of Dominica, St. Lucia, and Montserrat—were aware of the moves toward abolition taking place in the British Empire in the 1830s. After 1834, and especially after 1838, growing numbers of enslaved people from Martinique and Guadeloupe escaped by sea to the newly free territories. These escapes, along with the growth of a metropolitan abolitionist movement that was substantial in influence if still small by British standards, put increasing pressure on planters. By the 1830s French slaveholders were forced to accept that emancipation would one day take place, and they focused their political tactics on repeated deferrals of that day. Through the 1830s and early 1840s the planters and their allies resisted proposals for gradual emancipation. They managed, for instance, to defeat government proposals in 1847 for a gradual emancipation program along the lines of the one already implemented in much of the northern United States and Spanish America, which would have freed the children of enslaved women.

The most substantial reforms of this period were passed by the French government in 1845. These laws—known as the Mackau laws after their proposer, Martinican governor Ange-René Armand Mackau—facilitated self-purchase (*rachat*) by slaves and forbade the whipping of women. They limited the use of chains and the number of hours that enslaved people could work, and they authorized magistrates and colonial officials to visit plantations to check that the rules were being followed. Planters understood these laws as an attack on their rights and a move toward full abolition. In practice the reforms were carefully structured to prevent rapid change. The provisions for self-purchase, for instance, required that an enslaved person who bought his or her freedom serve a further five years for his or her former master; and the prices for self-purchase were high. An official in Guadeloupe noted the magistrates' limited use of their new powers, stating that "the magistrates are satisfied with the colonists and the colonists are satisfied with the magistrates. This reciprocity is certainly significant" (quoted in Blackburn 1988, 487). Yet if they had relatively small practical consequences, the Mackau laws were nonetheless a significant statement that in the long term, metropolitan France was no longer committed to protecting the interests of the creole plantocracy.

French emancipation, when it did come, was more sudden than that in the British Empire. It was precipitated by the revolution of February 1848, which overthrew the French monarchy, established universal male suffrage in metropolitan France, and began to implement a range of social reforms that favored the working class. In early March the new government gave the abolitionist leader Victor Schoelcher a mandate to implement the immediate ending of slavery. Schoelcher organized a commission that on April 27 issued a decree stating that all slaves would be freed within two months of its promulgation in each colony.

In practice, emancipation took place more quickly than Schoelcher's commission envisaged, because enslaved people took matters into their own hands. News of the February revolution and the appointment of the Schoelcher commission reached the French colonies by April. In Martinique plantation laborers collectively refused to work; many went to the island's largest town, Saint-Pierre, to demand the implementation of the new government's decision. For several days there was an uneasy standoff between slaves and the government's military and police forces which, after several deaths and the arrest of an enslaved man, escalated into an insurrection. The authorities conceded full emancipation on May 23, fearing that otherwise they would face an island-wide revolt. By the time the representative of the Schoelcher commission arrived on June 3, expecting to decree that slavery would be abolished on August 3, slavery in Martinique was already in the past. Similarly, the colonial government of Guadeloupe abolished slavery on May 27, before the arrival of the French commissioner on June 5. In French Guiana, emancipation took place as Schoelcher's commission had envisaged, on August 10, two months after the commissioner's arrival In the small eastern Caribbean island of St. Martin, which was divided into French and Dutch zones, slavery came to an end in the French zone according to the Schoelcher commission's proclamation. This effectively brought an end to slavery on the Dutch side of the island as well, although legally it was not abolished there until 1863.

In the Danish West Indies—made up of the Virgin Island territories of St. John, St. Croix, and St. Thomas—enslaved people also intervened to foreshorten a planned governmental process of abolition, which in Denmark's case was planned to take much longer than the French two-month delay. British abolition in the 1830s had led the Danish government to recognize that slavery would eventually have to end. In response, it implemented a series of reforms designed to shift colonial labor relations in the direction of wage labor while maintaining slavery. These reforms regulated the length of the work day, required the keeping of plantation record books for inspection, reduced slaveholders' powers to punish, and made Saturday a "free day" on which enslaved people would receive a wage if they did plantation work. In 1847 the government declared a "free birth" law and announced that full emancipation would take place by 1859, thus envisioning a longer period of transition than even the original British apprenticeship law.

Enslaved people were not prepared to wait a full 12 years for freedom. As had happened in the British and French colonies, rumors circulated that the Danish imperial government had already freed the slaves and that the local planters were withholding this freedom from them. Some enslaved people also drew inspiration when news reached them that slavery had been abolished in Martinique and Guadeloupe, and in July 1848 they organized a rebellion in St. Croix. Approximately 8,000 people went to the town of Frederiksted to demand freedom. Rather than use force to suppress the rebellion, the governor declared immediate emancipation, which was then generalized to St. John and St. Thomas as well (Hall 1992).

In the Dutch colonies of Aruba, Bonaire, Curaçao, St. Martin, and Suriname, slavery was not officially abolished until 1863, although it had informally ended in St. Martin in 1848. Of the 48,000 people who became free in 1863, more than 40,000 lived in Suriname. By the 1850s, with slavery no longer existing in the British, French, or Danish Caribbean, Dutch slaveholders were isolated. Enslaved people were aware that slavery was a dying system, and they pressured slaveholders for freedom and greater rights within the system of slavery. On Surinamese plantations they took increasing action to improve their conditions in the last years of slavery, with more than 60 incidents of striking or rioting occurring between 1848 and 1861—three times as many as during an equivalent period earlier in the 19th century (van Stipriaan 1995). As had been true across much of the Caribbean, the most contentious issue was time to work provision grounds. The Dutch government implemented amelioration reforms from 1851, and in 1863 introduced a period of "apprenticeship" that echoed the one established in the British colonies. Full emancipation did not come to the Dutch colonies until 1873.

Throughout the non-Hispanic Caribbean, the abolition of slavery was one step in a drawn-out process of struggle in which slaveholders, enslaved people, local state officials, imperial governments, and abolitionists in Europe all played important roles. These abolition processes differed in form, but in substance they shared certain features: they were officially implemented through decisions of imperial European governments, they sought to limit the degree of change in social relationships and to protect plantation economies, and they were accompanied by laws and policies that sought to shape the former slaves into a disciplined agricultural working class, committed to wage labor and to organizing family life through monogamous domesticity and male authority. In practice, emancipation was everywhere a response to the actions of enslaved people—whether directly, as in Martinique and St. Croix, or less directly, as in the British Caribbean and Suriname. Without this continual pressure, punctuated by rebellions, slavery surely would have lasted much longer than it did.

WORKS CITED

Blackburn, Robin. 1988. *The Overthrow of Colonial Slavery, 1776–1848*. London: Verso.

Craton, Michael. 1979. "Proto-Peasant Revolts? The Late Slave Rebellions in the British West Indies, 1816–1832." *Past and Present* 85, no. 1: 99–125.

Dubois, Laurent. 2004. *A Colony of Citizens: Revolution and Slave Emancipation in the French Caribbean, 1787–1804*. Chapel Hill: University of North Carolina Press.

Hall, Neville A. T. 1992. *Slave Society in the Danish West Indies: St. Thomas, St. John & St. Croix*. Edited by B. W. Higman. Mona, Jamaica: University of the West Indies Press.

Hansard, House of Lords Debates. March 16, 1824. "Amelioration of the Condition of the Slave Population of the West Indies," available online at http://hansard.millbanksystems.com/lords/ 1824/mar/16/amelioration-of-the-condition-oe-the (last accessed December 29, 2009).

Schloss, Rebecca Hartkopf. 2009. *Sweet Liberty: The Final Days of Slavery in Martinique*. Philadelphia: University of Pennsylvania Press.

Van Stipriaan, Alex. 1995. "Suriname and the Abolition of Slavery." In *Fifty Years Later: Antislavery, Capitalism and Modernity in the Dutch Orbit*, edited by Gert Oostindie. Leiden: KITLV Press, 117–41.

Viotti da Costa, Emilia. 1994. *Crowns of Glory, Tears of Blood: The Demerara Slave Rebellion of 1823*. New York: Oxford University Press.

20

Econocide? DALE TOMICH

From Abolition to Emancipation in the British and French Caribbean

Since its publication in 1944, Eric Williams's classic *Capitalism and Slavery* has remained an essential source for the study of Atlantic slavery, and a focus of scholarly controversy. A preeminent figure in 20th-century Caribbean history, Williams (1911–1981) was a distinguished scholar, the leader of the Trinidad and Tobago independence movement and that country's first prime minister, and a powerful advocate for the West Indian Federation. A work of engaged scholarship, *Capitalism and Slavery* directly challenged the prevailing historiographical canon by combining in a single account the development of industrial capitalism, colonial slavery, and abolitionism. Williams presents *Capitalism and Slavery* as "strictly an economic study of the role of Negro slavery and the slave trade in providing the capital which financed the Industrial Revolution in England and of mature industrial capitalism in destroying the slave system" (Williams 1994, ix).

In its simplest terms, Williams's argument is: "The capitalists

Figure 20.1 Eric Williams. Photograph (ca. 1954). Source: National Archives of Trinidad and Tobago.

had encouraged West Indian slavery and then helped to destroy it. When British capitalism depended on the West Indies, they ignored or defended it. When British capitalism found the West Indian monopoly a nuisance, they destroyed West Indian slavery as the first step in the destruction of West Indian monopoly" (169). Such sharp formulations have drawn the attention of both proponents and opponents, but they belie a more subtle and complex argument. Indeed, Williams poses the question of sugar and slavery in the British West Indies as an epochal historical transformation. In his interpretation, West Indian slavery, the colonial system, and mercantilist monopoly were inextricably linked. Taken together, they represented an obstacle to expanding industrial capitalism in Britain, and the new industrial interests progressively removed them in favor of free trade.

> The attack on the West Indians was more than an attack on slavery. It was an attack on monopoly. Their opponents were not only the humanitarians but the capitalists . . . The attack falls into three phases: the attack on the slave trade, the attack on slavery, the attack on the preferential sugar duties. The slave trade was abolished in 1807, slavery in 1833, and the sugar preference in 1846. The three events are inseparable (135, 136).

In seeking to systematically disclose the economic processes and interests that shaped the course of slavery and abolition in the British West Indies, Williams sharply distinguished economic factors in the abolition of slavery from moral and political factors. As important for understanding the reception of *Capitalism and Slavery* as his economic arguments is his critique of the abolitionists and the humanitarian account of abolitionism.

Although the quality of Williams's scholarship generally was recognized, initial reactions to the book were mixed. Black scholars were universally enthusiastic and saw it as a welcome new beginning for the study of slavery in the New World. In contrast, mainstream academic commentators expressed reservations about Williams's neglect of political and moral factors in his treatment of the abolitionists and the humanitarian argument for abolition, his exaggeration of the role of slavery in the establishment of modern capitalism, his single-minded economic determinism, his oversimplification, and the strident tone with which he treated those he criticized (Sheridan 1987, 319–21). These initial reactions set the parameters of the book's subsequent reception. The "Williams thesis" became an object of contention as much for his "economic interpretation of history" as for his substantive judgments on British motive and policy.

After a lull in debate during the 1950s, the 1960s saw a resurgence of interest in the book that continues today. This interest has largely been conditioned by two developments: first, the emergence of global anticolonial and antiracist movements, and second, a new style of economic history more attuned to the application of neoclassical economic theory to historical questions, quantification, and measurement than to the analysis of historical transformations of social relations. These developments have informed new historical paradigms and shaped the response to Williams's work in different ways.

Although some economic historians have been generally supportive of Williams or have challenged the arguments and data of his critics, most have been critical of his interpretations and their evidentiary base, and are often unsympathetic to his entire project. They are especially critical of his contention that the profits of the sugar and slave trades financed the Industrial Revolution. While most scholars have engaged Williams's economic arguments, others have attempted to recuperate the humanitarian interpretation of abolition, or to reconcile humanitarian and economic accounts of abolition. On the other hand, Williams's work has inspired new contributions to the debate from the Caribbean and Africa. These include mathematical models supporting the explanations of European development and African underdevelopment offered by Williams and others, studies of the slave trade's negative influence on Africa, and reexamination of the significance of slavery and the slave trade for the expansion of world trade and for British industrialization. Williams's work was also an important source for a distinctive structural account of

West Indian economic dependency, as well as for other dependency and world-economy approaches to political economy that emerged in the 1960s. Indeed, Williams's anticipation of dependency theory is in many ways responsible for his reception from the 1960s onward (Sheridan 1987, 323–39).

The debate over *Capitalism and Slavery* turned with the publication of Seymour Drescher's *Econocide* (1977). In the first monograph-length critique of Williams's interpretation of British abolition of the slave trade, Drescher took a new tack. Instead of arguing for the humanitarian causes of abolition, he argued against Williams's economic interpretation of it. Drescher's argument has gained wide acceptance, particularly in European and North American academic circles, largely because of his concern for empirical rigor, quantification, and measurement. While not offering an explicit economic history, he operates within an intellectual framework conditioned by the new economic history that developed after the 1950s.

Econocide presents a systematic empirical examination of the economic conditions that prevailed when the British slave trade was abolished in 1807. Contrary to Williams's "decline thesis," Drescher argues that "the British West Indies were absolutely and relatively far more valuable to Britain during the period of intense debate on the imperial slave trade (1788–1807) and on the world slave trade (1814–1820) than during the period when there had been no organized British pressure against the slave trade (1720–1775)." After 1773 the British West Indies accounted for a higher proportion of British trade, whether imports and exports are considered separately or in the aggregate. Further, they were Britain's most important non-European trading area from 1722 to 1822, and their share of British trade increased over that of their closest rivals between 1793 and 1812 (Drescher 1977, 16–17). Drescher also contends that the slave trade was analogous to West Indian trade generally: in value, tonnage, and volume, it peaked in the decade before abolition (71–76).

Thus, Drescher finds no correlation between either long-term or short-term economic trends and the abolition of the slave trade, concluding instead that "economic interests cannot account for either the timing, the occurrence, or the maintenance of the abolition of the slave trade between 1787 and 1820" (183). Hence, in Drescher's view, the economic motive for abolishing the slave trade must be disqualified. Indeed, he finds that abolition was achieved not by any definable interest group, but rather by a durable mass movement with a humanitarian ideology (183–85). Abolition of the slave trade was an act of "econocide" that set in motion a process of economic decline leading to the abolition of slavery itself in the 1830s.

Reconfiguring the Debate

Drescher's rejection of the "economic factor" and concern with ideology, politics, and social movements have reignited the materialist/idealist antinomy that has informed the debate from its inception, and have highlighted perhaps its most perplexing aspect. As scholars have amassed evidence to support or refute Williams's arguments, they have failed to move beyond the terms in which he initially posed the problem. However, resolution of his questions is not simply a matter of empirical demonstration. Each contribution to the debate is inflected by scholars' varied choices of conceptual frameworks, methodological procedures, and historical referents. More often than not, they fail to speak directly to one another, and the differences between them are not easily resolved. But the conceptual frameworks deployed in the debate expose its rich interpretive possibilities.

Williams's innovation—the source of his radical critique—is his treatment of colonial developments as being necessarily related to the metropolitan economy. He seeks to account for the West Indian contribution to British development, and for the British contribution to what would later be characterized as colonial underdevelopment. Williams's interpretation is shaped by his understanding of capitalism as a national phenomenon identified with the development in Britain of industry, wage labor, and the free market. Conversely, he construes slavery as a noncapitalist phenomenon and treats it as a property of the Caribbean. Thus, British capitalism and West Indian slavery are taken as given entities with distinct characteristics. They are brought into relationship through complex linkages of colonial domination, trade, imperial policy, ideology, and social movements. Though they interact with one another, each retains its distinctive character. British industrial capitalism appears as the single dynamic source of change acting on the increasingly backward, static, and archaic West Indian colonies. A unilinear process of industrialization and free trade in Britain produces a similarly unilinear sequence from abolition to emancipation in the West Indies.

But this formulation conflicts with Williams's broad historical conception of the Atlantic economy. By treating the Britain–West Indies complex as a closed analytical unit, he makes relations outside this sphere—including those with the French and Spanish empires and the United States—external to the fundamental relationship between the British metropole and the West Indian colonies. They enter into his account only insofar as they influence British industrialization or West Indian slavery, but are not themselves accounted for in his conceptual framework. Even as Williams proposes a broadly comprehensive historical interpretation, the world he describes extends beyond the limits of his explanatory framework, and the framework continuously excludes the full range of operative relations and processes.

Such conceptual fragmentation makes Williams vulnerable to his critics. Drescher and the modern economic historians seize upon trade as the economic link that conjoins these distinct and independent regions, and they reduce economy to the movement of prices and commodities. Such a perspective subtly disavows the broad historical conception that frames Williams's argument. Thus, Drescher focuses only on the abolition of the slave trade, and reinterprets Williams's conception of the relation of capitalism and slavery in terms of profitability. In his approach, market price determines relations and guides analysis. The social and political relations that constitute slavery, and indeed the market itself, have no price, and Drescher treats them as extra-economic factors. So long as slave-produced commodities are profitable in market terms, he regards the slave economy as viable and discerns no economic motive for abolishing the slave trade. Drescher's strategy is successful because it appears to undermine the initial step in Williams's causal sequence—the abolition of the slave trade. Once this "economic" link is severed, Williams's entire argument is dismembered.

Some historians have questioned whether Drescher's data actually support his case for a significant increase in the value of the West Indian colonies after 1773. However, the debate over empirical evidence does not adequately address conceptual issues. Supporters and critics of Williams interpret their data within the framework of an externally bounded, internally integrated British national economy. They measure the contribution of West Indian slavery to the British economy using trade statistics from a period in which the sugar colonies enjoyed a monopoly of the British domestic market. The value of the West Indian trade at the time of abolition is compared to its value before US independence. Its value in relation to foreign regions is measured by comparing trade of each of those regions with that of Britain. However, viewing Britain simply as the hub of diverse bilateral trading relations between apparently independent cases removes from consideration the multifaceted and multilateral relations among cases. The world economy appears as no more than the sum of independent and separable trade flows, rather than as a structured and interdependent network of relations. Such a formulation is particularly inadequate when the restructuring of the world market itself is at issue.

Contemporary conceptions of capitalism as an interrelated world economy offer a way of recuperating the potential of Williams's historical argument by rethinking his theoretical and methodological presuppositions. Instead of regarding slavery and industrial capital as distinct attributes of different societies, this perspective treats them as necessarily related parts of the same system. Similarly, it accounts for relationships outside the Britain–West Indies binary, and for the ways in which all the relevant parties influence one another.

Capitalism and the Crisis of British Colonial Slavery in the Atlantic Perspective

Williams's interpretation rests upon the indissoluble association of slavery and mercantile monopoly. However, mercantilism was at once an economic and a political policy—an instrument used not only for establishing control over colonies but also for political, diplomatic, military, and economic competition between rival European states. If political power opened the way for trade, the rationale for trade was to enhance the wealth and power of the state. Both the British mercantile system and the French *exclusif* asserted control over the sources of tropical production and attempted to dictate circuits of trade in order to increase metropolitan wealth. But they were also instruments of political and maritime power in the contest for dominance over the Atlantic and world economies.

Williams's account of West Indian decline begins with the impact of American independence on the mercantilist system. However, the significance of this event may be more fully grasped in relation to the dominant rivalry between Britain and France. The period 1764–83 was the classic age of the West Indian plantation economy. Sugar was the most valuable commodity in international trade, and the Caribbean "sugar islands" dominated world supply. Sugar production and the slave trade expanded dramatically throughout this period. The West Indies were at the heart of the colonial empires of both England and France, and they were of strategic importance to the Anglo-French rivalry on both sides of the Atlantic.

Within each mercantile empire, this period of economic expansion was marked by the ascendance of large islands—Jamaica in the British West Indies and Saint-Domingue in the French West Indies—as the preeminent centers of production, at the expense of smaller islands. Saint-Domingue played the strategic role in the competition between empires, becoming the world's leading producer not only of sugar but also of coffee, cotton, and indigo. It produced more wealth than all of the British West Indies combined, and its costs of production were much lower than those of its British rivals. Most French West Indian sugar was reexported rather than being consumed in France, and reexport of Saint-Domingue's produce brought French foreign trade to the level of Britain's. In contrast, British colonial sugar could not compete with cheaper French sugar in European markets, but because of mercantilist policy it had a monopoly of the British home market.

The 13 North American colonies became a destabilizing force for both the British and French mercantile systems as the West Indian colonies became dependent on the North Americans for foodstuffs, livestock, lumber, and other items essential to the plantation economies. Britain had to modify the metropolitan monopoly of the colonial market in order to accommodate the North American provisioning trade. France encouraged the Americans to trade provisions for rum to prevent competition with its domestic brandy. (The rum trade allowed ample opportunity for contraband.) This trade enabled the 13 North American colonies to build up their own shipping and commerce, including a slave trade. As their importance grew, they refused to extend credit to British planters and insisted on cash payments, which they used to buy cheaper goods in Saint-Domingue, thus draining currency from the British West Indies while increasing trade with Saint-Domingue. The expansion of the slave trade also destabilized mercantilist regulation of trade. The combined capacity of the British and American slave trade surpassed the capacity of the British West Indies to absorb slaves, and so both became significant suppliers to Britain's rivals. Thus, North American commerce undermined the colonial monopoly systems of both Britain and France by creating a pole of economic activity outside of each metropole.

The US achievement of independence in 1783 accelerated the destabilization of the British mercantile system and hurt its West Indian colonies. Britain closed its West Indian trade to the newly independent republic, cutting the sugar colonies off from this crucial source of supplies and raising their production costs. Meanwhile, the United States became increasingly involved in the international slave trade, and it began to trade more actively with Saint-Domingue and Cuba, reinforcing the productivity of the British West Indies' two main competitors. Indeed, increased commerce with the United States contributed to the rapid growth of the slave population and sugar production in Saint-Domingue between 1783 and 1791.

In Williams's interpretation, the second major turning point for West Indian slavery was the Haitian Revolution. What began in 1791 as a conflict between white and free colored elites over citizenship and the colony's status in the new French republic was transformed into a revolutionary struggle against colonialism and slavery by mass slave resistance. After a long and complex struggle, the successful revolution in Saint-Domingue and the creation of the independent republic of Haiti in 1804 overthrew slavery in Europe's most prosperous colony and marked a turning point for the politics of slavery and antislavery. It stirred hope and fear among groups throughout the Atlantic world and inspired diverse forms and combinations of resistance, reform, and repression that over time eroded the social and political conditions of slavery. Just as significantly, the Haitian Revolution destroyed the balance between empires and eroded the rationale for mercantilism in the Western Hemisphere. It resulted in the dramatic withdrawal of the world's largest sugar producer from the world market and removed Britain's chief rival for domination of the Atlantic. Defeat in Haiti crippled France's colonial system and ended its imperial ambitions in the Americas. After losing Haiti, Napoleon sold Louisiana—including the rich, slave-based cotton and sugar frontier of the Lower Mississippi Valley—to the United States. The combined effects of the Haitian Revolution and Britain's victory in the Napoleonic Wars led to destruction of the French navy and merchant marine and decline of the French port cities and left the United States as Britain's only potential challenger in the Atlantic.

Abolition of the Slave Trade

The creation of a new Atlantic division of labor and integrated world market was not simply the result of market forces, but was shaped by political forces of the Age of Revolution. Regardless of whether the abolitionists acted out of disinterested and humanitarian motives, the abolition of the slave trade was caught up in the politics and policies of the British state. With the defeat of France in 1815, Britain became the preeminent power in the world. It used its position as an island and a maritime power to reorganize and control the European state system from the outside, and mediated Europe's relation to the wider world through control of the sea. For Britain, maintaining political stability in Europe and avoiding entanglements on the continent was not an end in itself, but a means of securing the necessary conditions for overseas expansion. Commercial shipping and trade followed on naval supremacy, and new markets in the Atlantic and in the colonial territories of Asia provided outlets for British industry, commerce, and finance. In turn, enhanced maritime and economic power increased Britain's leverage over the European state system.

However, US independence and the Haitian Revolution signaled the collapse of the Atlantic mercantilist empires and the emergence of the Americas as a new political and economic space. Until the Age of Revolution, the Americas had been strategic elements in the European balance of power. After 1815 they became a fragmented mixture of colonies and sovereign states, increasingly detached from Europe. Britain's priority was to prevent the reestablishment of strong European colonial presences in the Americas and to integrate sovereign American states and national economies into a transnational political economic order under British hegemony.

Viewed in this light, Britain's unilateral, persistent, and vigorous pursuit of anti-slavery as state policy—which would not have been credible had it not abolished its own slave trade—can be interpreted as an effort to restructure the Atlantic economy in accordance with British interests. Abolition of the international slave trade was instrumental in weakening the European presence in the Atlantic and in preventing rival states from reestablishing closed colonial economies in the Americas. Further, as the countries of South America asserted their independence (with British encouragement), Britain sought to establish, through antislave trade treaties, a consensual international political-juridical order among sovereign states consistent with a transnational market economy. Finally, international agreement on abolition of the slave trade was a means to end US involvement in the legal and illegal slave traffic and to curb Britain's only commercial and maritime rival in the Atlantic.

In 1811, Britain declared participation in the slave trade an act of piracy. Its claim of the right to search any vessel suspected of slaving raised serious conflicts over national sovereignty and freedom of the seas. In particular, the United States jealously guarded its maritime sovereignty, and the American flag provided cover for slave traders wishing to avoid British suppression squadrons. Abolition of the international slave trade was included in the Treaty of Paris that ended the Napoleonic Wars in 1815, and it became a constant part of British diplomacy. Britain secured agreement at least in principle for the abolition of the slave trade from Spain in 1817, Brazil in 1827, France in 1830, and Portugal in 1842, although in practice the trade often continued after the treaties. By 1860, Cuba also agreed to end participation in the slave trade. Nonetheless, despite British efforts, the first half of the 19th century witnessed one of the largest cycles of slave importations in history.

The New Atlantic Order

Despite Drescher's claims, then, abolition of the British slave trade did not constitute "econocide," nor did it lead directly to economic decline and slave emancipation. Rather, world economic expansion under British hegemony eroded the position of the British West Indies. Yet it would be misleading to see British preeminence as the direct result of its industrial supremacy alone. Britain emerged from the period 1783–1815 not only as the world's only industrial country, but also as the center of world commerce and finance as well as its most powerful maritime nation. It pursued a strategy of free trade and informal empire in the Americas and colonial domination in Asia, above all in India. The impetus for free trade came from financial and commercial sectors, which saw an integrated transnational market economy as the means to enhance British financial, commercial, and maritime supremacy. Industrialists were reluctant participants in this project through the 1820s. The British cotton industry needed protection, especially from Indian textiles, and it only supported free trade after colonial domination transformed India into a consumer of British textiles.

The impact of these changes on Atlantic slave formations was not uniform. New zones of slave staple production arose, undermining old colonial structures, transforming the division of labor, and restructuring market relations even as the old zones intensified their output. The expansion of multilateral trade and the acceleration of commodity circulation benefited British commerce, finance, and shipping as well as British industry. However, with the economic downturn at the end of the 1820s, old slave zones declined, regardless of whether they had a slave trade, while new zones continued to expand, with or without slave imports.

The new slave zones in the US South and Cuba were representative of the emergent world market. The acquisition of West Florida and Louisiana, the invention of the cotton gin, and a vigorous internal slave trade opened the American South to cotton cultivation. The United States became the world's most important cotton producer and the primary supplier of raw material to the British cotton industry. British industrialization was inseparable from the creation of the new American slave cotton frontier. Cotton replaced sugar as the most valuable item in world trade. Unrestricted trade between the independent United States and Britain far surpassed commerce between the two before independence. Further, the cotton trade created a large balance of payments surplus that allowed the United States to become the major consumer of Cuban sugar. Thus, the cotton trade indirectly stimulated the Cuban sugar industry, and the United States developed important economic links with Cuba. Indeed, because of the strong American presence, Cuba was the one place where Britain could not undersell its competitors.

The emergence of Cuba redefined the terms of world sugar production in ways that shaped the crisis of sugar and slavery in the British and French West Indies. The Haitian Revolution opened the door for the dramatic growth of the Cuban sugar industry. In 1792, even as the slave insurrection in Saint-Domingue was in its early stages, Havana's elite saw an opportunity to dominate the world sugar market. They petitioned the Spanish crown for free trade in sugar and slaves and sought to systematically apply science and technology to sugar production. Under this program, the Cuban sugar industry progressed steadily. Cuban planters had to place their sugar in unprotected markets, and they labored under constant pressure to improve the productivity of their operations. By the end of the 1820s, Cuba emerged as the world's largest sugar producer, and its output doubled each decade until the 1860s.

This dramatic growth was possible because Cuba was a new zone of socioecological expansion. However, the island's fertile interior could not be fully exploited without cheap overland transportation. The construction of the railroad beginning in 1837 transformed Cuba's extensive territory from an obstacle to an advantage. The railroad not only allowed the geographical expansion of sugar production into new territory, but also facilitated the adoption of new technologies. Steam power, horizontal iron grinding mills, and later the vacuum pan and centrifuge transformed the refining process but required greater quantities of cane to be effective. With each innovation, Cuban planters founded more and larger plantations, established new economies of scale, incorporated new technologies, and organized labor in ways that were not possible in the old sugar colonies of the British and French Caribbean.

The changing global political economy condemned monopoly and slavery in the British West Indies. Those institutions no longer served a purpose for Britain and its empire. After the revolution in Saint-Domingue, the British West Indies increased their output. By the early 1820s Jamaica emerged, albeit briefly, as the world's largest sugar producer. However, even as they produced more, the West Indies were unable to compete with the flood of cheap sugar from the Americas and the Indian

Ocean. They became increasingly dependent on their monopoly of the home market, even as the justification for protection was being eroded.

After 1815, Britain carried the world's sugar to continental markets. This trade stimulated British commerce, shipping, and the sugar refining industry. However, the West Indian colonies produced more sugar than the home market could absorb. The high price and guaranteed market for British West Indian sugar impeded its reexportation. Britain sustained high prices in the domestic market, yet had to provide drawbacks to make West Indian sugar competitive in Europe.

Further, increased production created growing differentiation within the British West Indies. In the old colonies, output was increased without technically transforming production. Small islands such as Barbados offered few opportunities for further growth, and even Jamaica increased production only by extending cultivation to marginal lands and intensifying labor. The new additions to empire—British Guiana and Trinidad in the Caribbean, Mauritius in the Indian Ocean—were new sugar frontiers requiring capital and, above all, labor in order to compete in the emerging sugar economy. Monopoly of the home market subsidized the less efficient colonies, and arguably failed to stimulate the potentially more productive new ones. With the decline of world sugar prices in the 1830s, the old colonies contracted their production while the new colonies responded to the changing conditions despite shortages of labor and capital.

If British economic, political, and maritime supremacy and the changing world market undermined colonial monopoly and slavery in the British West Indies, they had the opposite effect in the French West Indies. Slavery was abolished by the French Republic in 1794 and restored by Napoleon in 1802. The colonies suffered from war, revolution, and foreign occupation. Those that remained after 1815 were virtually the only trading outlets available to France, and they were seen as vital to the recovery of its port cities, merchant marine, and navy. A colonial sugar boom was created under the auspices of the French state. Despite the anti–slave-trade clauses in the Treaty of Paris, France continued involvement in the trade until 1830 and established high tariffs to protect the colonies from cheap foreign sugar. In the colonies all available land and labor was devoted to sugar; secondary crops virtually disappeared. By the 1820s, the four small colonies of Martinique, Guadeloupe, French Guiana, and Reunion together produced more sugar than Saint-Domingue had at its height. However, after the end of the decade, they could no longer increase their output. They failed to supply the French market and required increasingly higher tariffs for protection from foreign competition. The high protective barrier allowed the revival of the French beet sugar industry, leaving the colonies with a dynamic and technologically advanced competitor in their own national market. Colonial interests had to fight a defensive battle to protect their position against beet sugar in the home market and to resist antislavery legislation.

In the context of deteriorating economic conditions, antislavery played out differently in the British and French West Indies. In Britain abolitionism effectively mobilized popular opinion against slavery, whereas in France an intellectual-political elite supported the idea of abolition but never determined how to accomplish it. In both the British and French colonies, diverse groups including abolitionists, missionaries, the metropolitan state, and even planters promoted regularization of slave provision grounds, internal markets, and family relations to ensure the reproduction of the slave population after the end of the slave trade and to ease the transition to free labor. Such measures increased opportunities for day-to-day slave negotiation and resistance that altered the character of social control and labor discipline. In the British colonies, this confluence of forces exploded in large-scale slave rebellion in Demerara (1823) and in Jamaica (1831). Slavery as an institution became less and less tenable.

In 1834 the British government abolished slavery, assigning former slaves to a five-year period of "apprenticeship" intended to secure the transition to free labor. Emancipation compelled West Indian planters to try to reorganize labor in ways consistent with the discipline of a competitive market. The old colonies, including Jamaica, failed to successfully adapt to the new conditions and were condemned to continuing economic, social, and political crises. Despite various difficulties, British Guiana, Trinidad, and Mauritius adapted to the new market conditions by means of indentured Asian labor. In the French colonies, slavery was abolished immediately upon the proclamation of the Second Republic in 1848, and former slaves were granted full citizenship rights. After emancipation, the position of the colonies continued to deteriorate despite the importation of indentured labor and other efforts to promote economic development.

Conclusion

For many, Drescher's *Econocide* effectively disproves "the Williams thesis." However, in seeking greater empirical precision and rigor, Drescher at once fragmented and narrowed the field of analysis. His argument rests upon a restricted technical conception of economy that differs from Williams's broader historical interpretation. It disrupts Williams's particular linkage between abolition of the slave trade, emancipation, and free trade. But viewed from the perspective of the capitalist world economy, it fails to offer a convincing account of abolition of the slave trade, much less slave emancipation.

Reinterpreting abolition and emancipation from the perspective of the capitalist world economy brings elements originally excluded by Williams into a more comprehensive explanatory framework, and also discloses a more complex and multifaceted relationship between capitalism and slavery. Such a reinterpretation is not inconsistent with Williams's arguments. Rather, it deepens and extends them. Indeed, *Capitalism and Slavery* remains an indispensable text because the creative tension between Williams's particular formulations and his broad historical conception continues to stimulate new questions and open new areas of investigation.

WORKS CITED

Drescher, Seymour M. 1977. *Econocide: British Slavery in the Era of Abolition*. Pittsburgh: University of Pittsburgh Press.

Sheridan, Richard. 1987. "Eric Williams and *Capitalism and Slavery*: A Biographical and Historiographical Essay." In *British Capitalism & Caribbean Slavery: The Legacy of Eric Williams*, edited by Barbara L. Solow and Stanley L. Engerman, 317–45. Cambridge: Cambridge University Press.

Williams, Eric. 1994 [1944]. *Capitalism and Slavery*. Chapel Hill: University of North Carolina Press.

21

Missionaries, Planters, and Slaves in the Age of Abolition

JEAN BESSON

Early and intense colonization, plantations, and slavery had a direct impact on the evolution of post-conquest Caribbean religions. The Europeans reinforced their colonial rule through the established churches: the Roman Catholic Church in the Spanish and French colonies, and mainly Protestantism in the British, Dutch, and Scandinavian territories. However, the effective Christianization of the slaves did not begin until the arrival of the Nonconformist missionaries from the late 18th century—such as the Moravians in the Danish West Indies, Dutch Guiana, and the British colonies of Antigua and Jamaica; the Methodists in Antigua, Jamaica, Montserrat, and Nevis in the British West Indies; and the Baptists in British Guiana and Jamaica. The systematic efforts by these missionary societies to Christianize the slaves reinforced colonialism in practice, for although the missionaries opposed the planters' religion, they did not aim to overthrow the plantation system. Yet the missionaries played a significant role in the movement to abolish slavery (Hall 1971; Olwig 1985, 1993; Besson 1989, 2002; Price 1990; Viotti da Costa 1994).

The slaves, however, did not passively absorb colonial mission Christianity, but appropriated and transformed it by drawing on their Afro-creole religions. This culture-building was part of a wider process of Caribbean creolization that lay at the heart of emergent slave cultures. Two leading scholars of the subject have argued that such Caribbean creolization involved slaves creating institutions "*within* the parameters of the masters' monopoly of power, but *separate from* the masters' institutions" (Mintz and Price 1992, 39). However, creolization involved an even more oppositional process of appropriating and overturning or reversing European institutions by Caribbean slaves and their descendants, as occurred in Afro-creole religions (Besson 2002, 2005). This chapter will illustrate these wider Caribbean themes by focusing on the case of Jamaica, the most profitable Protestant Caribbean slave-plantation colony in the late 18th century.

The Planters and the Slaves

Following the capture of Jamaica by the British from the Spanish in 1655, the island was transformed into a sugar and slave plantation society under British rule. By 1700 Jamaica was the world's leading sugar producer, and in the later 18th century it became a significant center of New World plantation slavery and the most important colony in the British Empire. In 18th-century Jamaica, the Anglican or Established Church was the only church allowed by law to function in the island, and as the official religion of the slave masters it supported slavery while completely neglecting the slaves' spiritual welfare. On the plantations, where the slaves were untouched by Christianity until the arrival of the Nonconformist missionaries in the late 18th century, the slaves forged a new Afro-Caribbean cosmology after the shattering of their African religions. This creative process drew on diverse but structurally similar African beliefs in witchcraft, medicine, ancestral cults, and a variety of gods and spirits, remolding them to oppose the slave plantation system. At the heart of this emerging worldview was the obeah-myal complex (Besson 1995b, 47, 56–57).

Integral to the obeah-myal complex was the belief in a dual spirit or soul (Besson 2002, 30–32). One spirit, the *duppy*, was believed to leave the body at death and, after remaining for a few days at the place of death or burial, to journey to join the ancestors. Elaborate funeral ritual was practiced to mark and effect this transition. Another spirit, the *shadow*, was thought to be buried with the corpse at death, but could be caught, harmed, and restored by obeah-myal men and women.

In his classic 1973 work *The Sociology of Slavery*, Orlando Patterson contrasted obeah and myal on the Jamaican slave plantations as being derived from West

African concepts of "bad" and "good" medicine. In this dichotomy, "obeah was essentially a type of sorcery which largely
involved harming others at the request of clients, by the use
of charms, poisons, and shadow catching. It was an individual
practice, performed by a professional who was paid by his clients. . . . Myalism, on the other hand, was obviously a form of
anti-witchcraft and anti-sorcery" (188). It was "organized more
as a kind of cult with a unique dance ritual" (188) that honored

Figure 21.1 Obeah-myal funeral
ritual, portrayed from a Euro-
centric perspective. Engraving
(19th century). Source: National
Library of Jamaica.

the African-derived minor deities of a spirit pantheon (rather than the distant Supreme Deity) and the departed ancestors who, it was believed, could possess the living. However, a later scholar of the subject, Mervyn Alleyne (1996, 84) observes that

> in Africa good and evil are not always clearly antithetical. This was even more true
> of Jamaica, where magic designed to harm members of the White ruling class and
> slaves loyal to them occupied that nebulous area between good and evil. Certainly
> the British viewed such magic as obeah. . . . But for Africans, resorting to the power
> of spirits in order to resist slavery was a positive expression of religion. Those writ-
> ers who reported that myal was hostile to obeah and undid obeah's evil work show
> clearly how Myalmen harnessed spiritual forces to resist slavery.

The nature of obeah and myalism has been the source of ongoing debate. One scholar has argued that the myal cult united the slaves in their resistance to slavery and European values, and was thought to protect their communities from internal and external harm (Schuler 1979a, 1979b, 1980). In this view, the shared body of myal ritual and belief also provided a mode of integration among slave plantation villages, although another study concluded that "essentially obeah was neither good nor bad: it could be used either way" (Curtin 1970, 29). Still another observer has questioned the widespread dichotomization of obeah and myalism, suggesting that obeah originally most often referred to morally neutral magical spiritual power that could be accessed through spirit possession or myal and used for protection and healing (Bilby 1993). Moreover, this morally neutral magical spiritual power (in some places still referred to as obeah) was and remains central to Afro-Jamaican religion. Even Patterson observed that "obeah in its myal form served certain important medicinal functions during slavery," thereby indicating the overlapping of myalism and obeah. Obeah was also important as a source of perceived protection in the context of slave rebellion (Patterson 1973, 191–92).

The Afro-Jamaican obeah-myal complex, with its elaborate mortuary ritual reflecting the perception of an active spirit world including ancestral kin, reinforced the evolving customary land transmission system, with its descent-based cemeteries created by the slaves. This system was an appropriation and overturning of a plantation institution in the context of the slaves' "proto-peasant" adaptation. The planters, who faced a problem in feeding the enslaved labor force, allocated marginal plantation land to both female and male slaves to grow their own food. However, the slaves appropriated and transformed the masters' provision-ground institution, creating surpluses for sale in marketplaces, transmitting customary land rights to descendants of both genders, and creating lineage burial grounds (Besson 2002, 26–32; Mintz 1989, 151–52, 180–213). These landholding descent groups had parallels with those in the African societies from which the slaves had come. However, the mode of descent and land transmission created by the slaves differed from the unilineal lineages common in West and Central Africa. In contrast to such restricted descent groups, which were traced through one gender only, the unrestricted Afro-creole cognatic, or nonunilineal, lineages reckoned through both genders maximized scarce land rights and kinship ties among the enslaved—who were not only legally denied land and kinship, but were also property themselves.

The creation of this customary system of land use and transmission, rooted in cognatic family lines and reinforced by obeah-myal rituals, beliefs, and kin-based cemeteries, was a central aspect of institution-building among the slaves. This system was created "*within* the parameters of the masters' monopoly of power" and was to some extent "*separate from* the masters' institutions" (Mintz and Price 1992, 39). However, the proto-peasant adaptation and its mode of land transmission appropriated aspects of the plantation system—which was the masters' central institution—while reversing the plantation principles of monoculture, legal freehold, the nuclear family, primogeniture, and chattel slavery. The dynamics of this creole institution-building were therefore not entirely "*separate from* the masters institutions," but entailed a direct engagement with, and overturning of, their Euro-creole styles of life (Besson 2002, 31–32).

The obeah-myal complex, which was closely tied to cognatic family lines, land transmission, and burial grounds in the slave communities, was initially more separate from the masters' institutions—namely, the planters' Anglican Christianity—than the slaves' Afro-creole kinship and land-tenure systems, for it was linked to slave rebellion and marronage (as well as with kin-based land transmission). In these contexts, the slaves sought to use obeah-myalism to resist the masters' domination by protecting themselves from the owners' "sorcery" of slavery (Schuler 1979a; Besson 2002, 32).

With the arrival of missionaries (many of them from Britain) in the late 18th and early 19th centuries, the slaves would hide their obeah-myal practices behind Nonconformist Christianity. In so doing, however, they not only would continue to oppose the planters and slavery but would also covertly transform the colonial religion of their missionary allies (through the control of Baptist Christianity by the obeah-myal cult in the Native Baptist variant) while attending the Baptist church. This strategy of engaging with and overturning colonial Baptist Christianity through both alliance and subversion continues in Jamaican free villages today, manifested in simultaneous adherence to the Revival cult (which evolved from obeah, myal, and Native Baptist Christianity) and to the orthodox Baptist church (Besson 2002, 32).

The Missionaries and the Slaves

In Jamaica, Britain's most profitable West Indian colony, the planters' Established Anglican Church had little impact on the slaves. Even after the passage of an act in 1816 to propagate the gospel among the enslaved, the impact of the Established Church on the slaves was largely superficial and ineffective. In the later 18th and early 19th centuries, however, the abolition movement and the religious revival in England led the Nonconformist churches to send missionaries to the island, and this missionary activity had more influence on the nonwhite population. The Established Church and most planters largely opposed the preaching of these missionaries, as it undermined the plantocracy's Anglican religion and slavery (Besson 2002, 32, 98–99).

The Moravians were the first English Nonconformist missionaries to arrive in Jamaica. They landed in 1754 in the parish of St. Elizabeth, where their proselytizing was focused on plantation slaves; they were followed by the Methodists in

1789 and the English Baptists in 1813. The Moravians had the least impact on the nonwhite population, while the Methodists became the stronghold of the free colored and free Negro group. The Baptists were the most successful in converting the slaves, as the Baptist faith had been introduced by black preachers at an even earlier date. Most prominent among these preachers were George Lisle (or Liele), an ex-slave from Virginia and Georgia, who went to Jamaica in 1784, and Moses Baker, another American ex-slave, who was baptized by Lisle in 1787. In 1788 Baker began preaching in the plantation parishes of St. James and Trelawny (Besson 2002, 98–99; Turner 1982; Patterson 1973, 209–11).

In 1813 the Baptist Missionary Society (BMS) in England dispatched its first missionary to Jamaica, the Reverend John Rowe, to reinforce the work of Lisle and Baker (Lisle had called on the BMS in response to the subversion of the Baptist faith by the slaves' obeah-myal beliefs and rituals). After he was met by Baker in St. James, Rowe took up residence in Falmouth, Trelawny. Following Rowe's death from yellow fever in 1816, a number of other Baptist missionaries went to Jamaica and established churches. Falmouth, however, remained without a Baptist minister until the Reverend Thomas Burchell formed the Falmouth Baptist Church in 1827. Burchell's assistant, James Mann, became the first pastor of this church, whose membership increased to about 600, and served until his death from malaria in 1830. By then he had organized two other Baptist churches in Trelawny, at Rio Bueno and Stewart Town (Besson 2002, 65, 99).

Mann was replaced in Falmouth in 1830 by the Reverend William Knibb, from Kettering, Northamptonshire. The appointment of Knibb, an outspoken opponent of the Established Church and slavery, was enthusiastically received by members of the congregation, the majority of whom were slaves from the surrounding Trelawny plantations. At the time of Knibb's arrival in Falmouth, there was no Baptist chapel or mission house in the parish, but he soon became involved in land purchase and building on behalf of the church at Falmouth, Rio Bueno, and Stewart Town. However, Knibb's work among the Trelawny slaves was interrupted by the "Christmas Rebellion" of 1831–32, a great slave revolt that also became known as the "Baptist War" (Besson 2002, 100).

To contextualize this slave uprising, which was the largest in the British West Indies and the most spectacular in Anglo-America, it is important to understand the relationship between the slaves and the Baptist missionaries, and the articulation of the obeah-myal complex with Baptist Christianity. The social significance of the Baptist church among the slaves in Jamaica was twofold. First, "the slave saw the Baptist missionaries as his allies against the planters in their fight for freedom" (Patterson 1973, 214). Second, the Baptist class-leader system (adopted from the Methodists and further appropriated by the slaves), whereby influential slaves became lay preachers for small groups of converts, opened up positions of leadership

among the slaves and facilitated the continuity of the obeah-myal complex (Besson 2002, 100).

The slaves therefore embraced the Baptist faith at a formal level and attended the Baptist churches while remaining committed to obeah and myal and interpreting Baptist Christianity through Afro-creole traditions (Schuler 1979a, 1979b). As a result, two variants of Baptist faith emerged: the "orthodox" form, taught by the missionaries and practiced by the slave

Figure 21.2 Interior of Knibb's Falmouth Baptist Chapel. Engraving (19th century). Source: National Library of Jamaica.

congregations in the churches, and the "Native" or "Black" Baptist form, controlled by obeah and myal and taught by black class leaders on the plantations. This latter variant played a central role in the 1831–32 slave revolt (Besson 2002, 100–102).

A combination of these various factors led to this rebellion being named the Baptist War. The revolt was widely thought to have been led by slave headmen (who were usually class leaders) from estates in the hinterland of Montego Bay, St. James Parish, and by a domestic slave named "Daddy" Sam Sharpe (or Tharp), who was a Native Baptist class leader in Burchell's congregation in Montego Bay. Moreover, the planters were convinced that the rebellion had been instigated by the Nonconformist and especially Baptist missionaries, although the missionaries denied any involvement.

Two days after Christmas 1831, a large number of slaves (estimates vary from 20,000 to 60,000) broke free, burning more than 150 estates. The revolt started "with the firing of Kensington estate, high above Montego Bay, on the night of

Tuesday, December 27, 1831" (Craton 1982, 293) and spread swiftly throughout the western parishes, including Trelawny and St. James. Martial law was declared, and the Falmouth Baptist Chapel was taken over as a barracks for the military-plantation regime. The rebellion, which lasted two weeks, was largely under control by mid-January 1832, and martial law was lifted on February 5. Only 14 whites died in the conflict, but several hundred slaves were either killed in action or executed—and a hundred more were flogged. The Native Baptist rebel slave leader, Sam Sharpe, was tried on April 19 and hanged on May 23, 1832, in front of the courthouse at Montego Bay in Charles Square. However, this rebellion would be a major factor leading to the abolition of slavery throughout the British Empire in 1834 and to the full emancipation of the slaves in the British West Indies on August 1, 1838.

In addition to reprisals taken against the slaves in this 1831–32 slave revolt, the planters took revenge on the Nonconformist missionaries, especially Knibb, who with Sharpe was regarded as a ringleader of the revolt. Knibb was arrested, imprisoned, and threatened with death. On his release he found that the Falmouth Baptist Chapel, along with 13 other Nonconformist chapels, had been totally destroyed by the Colonial Church Union (a planter-based organization) following the lifting of martial law.

After the rebellion the Jamaica Assembly appointed a committee to inquire into the causes of the revolt, and a deputation was sent to London in 1832 to represent the planters' case (Barrett 2000, 87). The missionaries also sent deputations to Britain in 1832, and the Baptist Church selected Knibb to report on conditions in the churches. In England Knibb contributed to the antislavery campaign, assisted by Burchell. Knibb and Burchell returned to Jamaica at the end of 1834 and continued to work for full emancipation of the slaves.

After political independence in Jamaica in 1962, Sharpe was made a national hero and Montego Bay's Charles Square was renamed Sam Sharpe Square. In 2007, the bicentenary of the parliamentary abolition of the British transatlantic slave trade, a marble monument was erected in Sam Sharpe Square on August 1 (Emancipation Day) in memory of those slaves who fought and died in what has been renamed the Emancipation War.

Abolition and Church-Founded Villages

The Nonconformist missionaries fought not only for abolition and emancipation, but also for a new society. After the abolition of slavery they became involved in negotiations for fair wages on behalf of the ex-slaves, and in establishing land settlements. The Baptists, especially Knibb, were at the forefront of these reforms. For example, through his wage negotiations with the absentee planter, Edward Barrett (owner of Oxford and Cambridge estates in Trelawny), Knibb effected the first wage

settlement on the island (Barrett 2000, 103). And with the
Baptist minister James Phillippo (who founded Jamaica's first
free village of Sligoville in the parish of St. Catherine between
1835 and 1838), Knibb initiated the island's church-founded
free-village system (Mintz 1989, 157–79; Besson 2002, 102–3).

The outcome of slave opposition and resistance and the
Nonconformist antislavery struggle, the free-village system
was triggered by post-emancipation state-planter legislation obstructing rights to
plantation house yards and provision grounds. Such free villages were often established through the purchase of ruined estates by the missionaries, who subdivided the land and sold it to ex-slaves in their congregations. Free villages emerged
throughout Jamaica, especially in the parish of Trelawny, and became the vanguard
of the flight from the British West Indian estates (Besson 1984, 1992, 1995a). In
other British West Indian colonies, where some land was available for peasant
settlement (though to a lesser extent than in Jamaica), the exodus from the plantations sometimes likewise occurred in alliance with the Nonconformist missionaries—for example in Antigua, Tobago, and St Kitts (Hall 1971; Henshall 1976, 39;
Besson 1992, 1995a).

However, as was evident in the case of the Baptists (and Methodists and Moravians) in Jamaica, the missionaries were not revolutionaries but reformers, and the

free villagers were their captive congregations. As the case of Jamaica also shows, the ex-slaves had a separate agenda for full freedom that would unfold within, appropriate, and transform the colonial mission model of free villages, just as the obeah-myal complex had appropriated orthodox Baptist Christianity and fueled the Baptist War (Besson 2002, 103). This agenda of Caribbean culture building, continued by the ex-slaves and their descendants to the present, would include the consolidation of Afro-creole kinship and land-tenure systems in the institution of family land, and the transformation of related obeah-myal beliefs and rituals in the Revival cult and Rastafarian movement in the 19th and 20th centuries (Besson 1995b, 2002; Chevannes 1994, 1995; Besson and Chevannes 1996). In the 21st century these Afro-creole institutions endure at the heart of the transnational Jamaican free villages that provide sites of identity for social relations that stretch into the Caribbean diaspora in North America and Europe (Besson 2002, 2005). Similar institutions of family land endure in other postcolonial Caribbean territories (Besson and Olwig 2005; Besson and Momsen 1987, 2007).

In Jamaica, the obeah-myal complex has persisted into the 21st century among the Accompong maroons in St. Elizabeth, where it was preserved and elaborated in marronage, and where it coexists with the former Presbyterian, now United, Church and is ascendant at the annual "Myal Play" (Besson 1997, 2005). However, ethnography from Trelawny free villages and related research suggests that whereas obeah-myal ideology has been retained at one level among Baptist free villagers, it was transformed at another level in the later slavery and post-emancipation eras through frequent interaction between slaves and free villagers on one hand and Baptist missionaries on the other (Besson 2002, 242–44). In this transformation, myal moved closer to Baptist Christianity and was aimed at eradicating obeah, which was seen as sorcery.

In the immediate aftermath of emancipation in 1838, Orthodox Baptist faith provided the formal religious focus as well as a means for acquiring land in Jamaican Baptist-founded free villages. At the same time, the Native Baptist variant, reinforced by a myalist revival from the 1820s to the 1850s (when Trelawny, with St. James, was the vanguard of the myal movement), formed "the core of a strong, self-confident counter-culture" against the persisting plantation system (Schuler 1980, 44). In the context of this revival, the relationship between obeah and myal became more complex—especially in the Baptist villages from around 1841. Myal shifted closer to Baptist Christianity, recognized "three grades of membership— Archangels, Angels, and Ministering Angelics," and rejected obeah as sorcery, as did the Baptist church (Schuler 1979b, 72). This development paralleled the anti-obeah view and legislation of the colonial state from the later 18th century, which is still evident in postcolonial Jamaica today. From this new stance, the myal movement evolved as an ideology aimed at eradicating the sorcery of post-emancipation hardships that were acute in Trelawny and St. James, including various epidemics and inequitable agrarian relations that the Baptist missionaries were unable to redress (Schuler 1979b, 70–74). This antisorcery activity was manifested in "clearing the land for Jesus Christ[, which] meant eradicating obeah through special public rituals which only Myalists could perform" (72). This contrast between myal and obeah consolidated around 1860 as one dimension of the Revival-Zion cult, and it persists today within this cult at the interface between the peasantry and plantations on one hand and tourism on the other in Trelawny and St. James, where similar public rituals continue to be held (Besson 2002, 242–43).

In 1860 an intense evangelical revival, known as the Great Revival, started in Ireland, swept through the Anglophone world, and arrived in Jamaica, where it began in the Moravian church, spread rapidly to Baptist and Wesleyan congregations, and "received overwhelming support from all the clergy, including the Anglican bishop" (Chevannes 1994, 20). Together, this Euro-Christian revival and the ongoing myalist revival generated a new Afro-Protestant religion, called "Revival," which both infused the Baptist faith with myalist beliefs and incorporated more elements of Baptist Christianity in opposition to obeah as sorcery. In 1861, however, the Great Revival "turned African," as historian Philip Curtin put it (1970, 171); that is, it was appropriated by the original obeah-myal ideology. In this way, two variants of Revivalism came to be distinguished: Revival-Zion (seen as nearer to Baptist Christianity and as opposing obeah) and Pukumina (closer to the original obeah-myal complex and regarded as practicing obeah). These two forms have been described as "important points in the continuum of religious differentiation created by the meeting of Myalism and Christianity" (Alleyne 1996, 96). Also known respectively as "the '60" and "the '61," these variants persisted in the 20th century. However, since the 1990s, Revival-Zion has become ascendant, with Pukumina being attributed by free villagers and urban folk either to other practitioners or to another time and place (Besson 2002, 243).

Obeah, in the sense of sorcery as portrayed by the Baptist Church and representing material hardship, is still explicitly opposed and "eradicated" in Trelawny by Revival-Zion meetings which are said to "cut and clear destruction"(as in the 19th-century myal movement). But simultaneously, obeah, in the original sense of a morally neutral magical-spiritual power that may be used for protection and healing, is still believed to be accessible through the "spirit possession" (the original meaning of myal) that is regularly enacted in this same Revival-Zion cult. Therefore, despite the distinction between the two variants of Revivalism and the apparent disappearance of Pukumina since the 1990s, belief in the morally neutral magical-spiritual power of obeah is retained and cocooned at the heart of Revival-Zion ideology. It is not only hidden behind the postcolonial symbol of the Baptist church, but also kept from view even at some Revival-Zion meetings. The case of the "Baptist" free villages of Jamaica therefore provides illustration of Afro-Protestant culture building, at the heart of the former British Caribbean, still ongoing in the 21st century (Besson 2002, 243–44).

WORKS CITED

Alleyne, Mervyn. 1996. *Africa: Roots of Jamaican Culture*. Chicago: Research Associates School Times Publications.

Barrett, Robert Assheton. 2000. *The Barretts of Jamaica*. Winfield, KS: Wedgestone Press.

Besson, Jean. 1984. "Land Tenure in the Free Villages of Trelawny, Jamaica." *Slavery & Abolition* 5 (1): 3–23.

———. 1992. "Freedom and Community: The British West Indies." In *The Meaning of Freedom: Economics, Politics, and Culture after Slavery*, ed. Frank McGlynn and Seymour Drescher, 183–219. Pittsburgh: University of Pittsburgh Press.

———. 1995a. "Land, Kinship and Community in the Post-Emancipation Caribbean: A Regional View of the Leewards." In *Small Islands, Large Questions: Society, Culture and Resistance in the Post-Emancipation Caribbean*, edited by Karen Fog Olwig, 73–99. London: Frank Cass.

———. 1995b. "Religion as Resistance in Jamaican Peasant Life: The Baptist Church, Revival Worldview and Rastafarian Movement." In *Rastafari and Other African-Caribbean Worldviews*, edited by Barry Chevannes, 43–76. London: Macmillan.

———. 1997. "Caribbean Common Tenures and Capitalism: The Accompong Maroons of Jamaica." In *Common Land in the Caribbean and Mesoamerica*, edited by Bill Maurer; pecial issue, *Plantation Society in the Americas* 4 (2 and 3): 201–32.

———. 2002. *Martha Brae's Two Histories: European Expansion and Caribbean Culture-Building in Jamaica*. Chapel Hill: University of North Carolina Press.

———. 2005. "Sacred Sites, Shifting Histories: Narratives of Belonging, Land and Globalisation in the Cockpit Country, Jamaica." In *Caribbean Narratives of Belonging*, edited by Jean Besson and Karen Fog Olwig, 17–43. Oxford: Macmillan.

Besson, Jean, ed. 1989. *Caribbean Reflections: The Life and Times of a Trinidad Scholar (1901–1986). An Oral History Narrated by William W. Besson*. London: Karia Press.

Besson, Jean, and Barry Chevannes. 1996. "The Continuity-Creativity Debate: The Case of Revival." *New West Indian Guide* 70 (3 and 4): 209–28.

Besson, Jean, and Janet Momsen, eds. 1987. *Land and Development in the Caribbean*. London: Macmillan.

———. 2007. *Caribbean Land and Development Revisited*. New York: Palgrave.

Besson, Jean, and Karen Fog Olwig, eds. 2005. *Caribbean Narratives of Belonging*. Oxford: Macmillan.

Bilby, Kenneth M. 1993. "The Strange Career of 'Obeah': Defining Magical Power in the West Indies." Paper presented to the general seminar, Institute for Global Studies in Culture, Power, and History, Johns Hopkins University, Fall 1993.

Chevannes, Barry. 1994. *Rastafari: Roots and Ideology*. Syracuse, NY: Syracuse University Press.

Chevannes, Barry, ed. 1995. *Rastafari and Other African-Caribbean Worldviews*. London: Macmillan.

Craton, Michael J. 1982. *Testing the Chains: Resistance to Slavery in the British West Indies*. Ithaca, NY: Cornell University Press.

Curtin, Philip. 1970. *Two Jamaicas: The Role of Ideas in a Tropical Colony 1830–1865*. New York: Atheneum.

Hall, Douglas. 1971. *Five of the Leewards 1834–1870*. Barbados: Caribbean Universities Press.

Henshall (Momsen), Janet D. 1976. "Post-Emancipation Rural Settlement in the Lesser Antilles." *Proceedings of the Association of American Geographers* 8:37–40.

Mintz, Sidney W. 1989. *Caribbean Transformations*. New York: Columbia University Press.

Mintz, Sidney W., and Richard Price. 1992. *The Birth of African-American Culture*. Boston: Beacon Press.

Olwig, Karen Fog. 1985. *Cultural Adaptation and Resistance on St John: Three Centuries of Afro-Caribbean Life*. Gainesville: University of Florida Press.

———. 1993. *Global Culture, Island Identity*. Philadelphia: Harwood.

Patterson, Orlando. 1973. *The Sociology of Slavery*. London: Granada.

Price, Richard. 1990. *Alabi's World*. Baltimore: Johns Hopkins University Press.

Schuler, Monica. 1979a. "Afro-American Slave Culture." In *Roots and Branches*, edited by Michael Craton, 121–55. Toronto: Pergamon Press.

———. 1979b. "Myalism and the African Religious Tradition in Jamaica." In *Africa and the Caribbean: The Legacies of a Link*, edited by Margaret E. Crahan and Franklin Knight, 65–79. Baltimore: Johns Hopkins University Press.

———. 1980. *"Alas, Alas, Kongo": A Social History of Indentured African Immigration into Jamaica, 1841–1865*. Baltimore: Johns Hopkins University Press.

Turner, Mary. 1982. *Slaves and Missionaries: The Disintegration of Jamaican Slave Society, 1787–1834*. Urbana: University of Illinois Press.

Viotti da Costa, Emilia. 1994. *Crowns of Glory, Tears of Blood: The Demerara Slave Rebellion of 1823*. New York: Oxford University Press.

PART 5

A Reordered World

22

A Second Slavery?

CHRISTOPHER SCHMIDT-
NOWARA

The 19th-Century Sugar Revolutions
in Cuba and Puerto Rico

Spain was the first European power to colonize the Caribbean and
the first to introduce African slaves and sugar plantations. Yet the
Spanish crown placed restrictions on the flow of African captives
to its American colonies, unlike the other European colonizers who
established themselves in the region beginning in the 17th century.
While Britain and France, and even smaller powers like the Netherlands and Denmark, constructed booming sugar islands worked
by hundreds of thousands of enslaved Africans, Spain maintained
quotas on the numbers of slaves that could be imported into its
Caribbean colonies, and farmed out the trade to foreign powers.
Between 1650 and 1800 the British Caribbean received slightly
more than two million African captives, the French Caribbean
slightly more than one million. In contrast, all of Spanish America
in the same period received 191,846 enslaved workers through the
transatlantic trade.

This situation changed radically at the end of the 18th century,
when the Spanish crown deregulated the African slave trade to

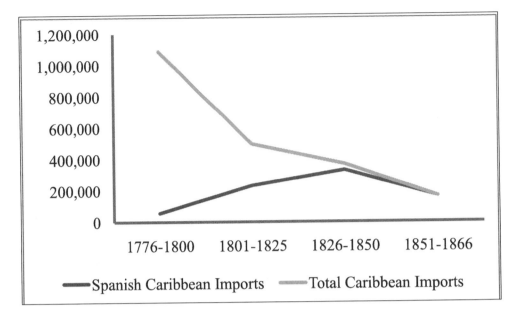

Figure 22.1 Slave imports into the Caribbean, 1776–1866. Source: Data from the table of estimates accessed on August 31, 2010, at slavevoyages.org.

Cuba, Puerto Rico, and its other Caribbean colonies just as the trade was being closed to the major British and French competitors. From the later 18th century until the suppression of the trade in 1867, the Spanish Caribbean received nearly 800,000 enslaved workers, most destined for work on Cuba's sugar plantations (see figure 22.1). This chapter will examine how these changes came about and how they affected colonial society in Cuba and Puerto Rico.

Slavery and Reform after the Seven Years' War

Spain's Caribbean colonies found themselves in a privileged but often dangerous position in the later 18th century. After the crushing defeat at the hands of the British in 1762, when Havana fell, the Bourbon monarchy undertook economic, fiscal, and military reforms that transformed Cuba and Puerto Rico. These islands served as laboratories for imperial restructuring, and as the front line of Spanish defense against ascendant British power. Most important, for the first time in the history of Spanish rule in the Americas, the crown would liberalize the traffic in African slaves, so that for a time after 1789 Havana planters would take part in a virtually free trade in servile labor. Later, Puerto Rico would also see its enslaved population and plantation belt grow after the crown granted the Cédula de Gracias in 1815, facilitating the influx of capital, technology, planters, and slaves. As the majority of the Spanish Indies fought for independence in the 1810s and 1820s, Cuba and

Puerto Rico underwent plantation booms that propelled them to the forefront of Caribbean sugar production while also reinforcing their colonial status.

How to reassert control over the colonies was a problem that vexed the Bourbon kings throughout the 18th century. The American empire was still rich in silver and other exports, but much of that wealth ended up in the hands of foreign merchants and rulers. Military and economic subordination to France and Britain forced the Spanish crown to recognize the cracks in the imperial façade. Bourbon reformers paid close attention to the Caribbean colonies as they sought to emulate aspects of French and British rule in the Americas. By the latter 1700s they recognized that Caribbean settlements such as Saint-Domingue and Jamaica were sources of significant wealth because of the free traffic in slaves and the export of tropical commodities. Though many Spanish and Spanish American institutions and interest groups remained committed to commercial exclusivism and the extraction of bullion as the cornerstone of the imperial economy, reformers and local elites in the Caribbean foresaw commercial wealth flowing into royal coffers from Cuba, Puerto Rico, Santo Domingo, Trinidad, and Louisiana.

The tipping point came during the Seven Years' War (1756–63), which revealed just how vulnerable the Spanish colonies were to British military power. The war was a global struggle between Britain and France for overseas preeminence. By its end, Britain had expelled France from Canada and ended French pretensions in North America. Spain figured in the war and peace only at the end of the conflict, entering it as an ally of France. Britain struck back immediately, capturing two nodal points of the Spanish colonial system: Havana and Manila. Spain regained those two ports in the peace, and also took control of Louisiana from France. However, the Spanish did make territorial concessions to Britain—including Florida, which placed the feared rival right in the Gulf of Mexico, close to Spain's Caribbean colonies and its richest possession, the Viceroyalty of New Spain, the great producer of silver in this era.

The fall of Havana pushed the Bourbon King Charles III (1759–88) and his advisers into undertaking major military, fiscal, and economic reforms in the Americas, beginning with the Caribbean. Spain needed more troops on the ground in the colonies, more fortifications in key sites such as Havana and San Juan, and more revenue with which to pay for these invigorated defenses. Here the question of the slave trade and slavery entered into the equation, leading the Spanish Crown ultimately to deregulate the slave traffic for the first time and commit to the kind of plantation agriculture heretofore found primarily in Brazil and the French and British Caribbean.

The Caribbean was the testing ground not only because of geopolitical considerations, but also because the colonies showed potential for considerable plantation-based wealth. Venezuela, for example, became the world's leading producer of cacao in the 18th century, while tobacco flourished in Cuba. Madrid hoped to encourage these stirrings of commercial agriculture, and to satisfy the constant demand for more slaves, by loosening its traditionally restrictive economic system. Puerto Rico and Cuba figured prominently in these plans. After the war, Bourbon officials toured the islands and concluded that these were potentially rich territories gone to waste after centuries of metropolitan indifference. They advocated reforms based in part on their observations of the much richer colonies that surrounded the Spanish Antilles, such as French Saint-Domingue and Danish St. Croix. If these islands could produce abundant exports, then so could Puerto Rico and the other Spanish possessions.

Field Marshal Alejandro O'Reilly traveled to both Cuba and Puerto Rico to inspect military preparedness. In his view, any upgrades to imperial defenses had to be founded on economic revival, which meant sugar and slavery. He pointed to the success of Danish St. Croix as an example of what could take place in Puerto Rico. France had ceded the island to Denmark in 1734. The Danish crown had established a chartered company to manage the new colony and had granted it important privileges and incentives to attract investment, including free entry of slaves carried by ships of any nationality. Towns and plantations had spread across the island, supported by an ample supply of servile labor. Without such reforms, Puerto Rico, one of Spain's oldest colonies, was a burden on the crown, and its inhabitants wallowed in poverty. A few years later the friar Iñigo Abbad y Lasierra penned an extensive study of Puerto Rico's history and conditions, and reached similar conclusions. Should the Spanish crown follow the example of the French and the British, "this island of Puerto Rico could with ease and without expense receive the population and cultivation that it needs" (Abbad y Lasierra 1776, 157–58).

Cuba, the largest and most populous of the Spanish Antilles, was the object of the most ambitious reforms. It was the cornerstone of Spain's imperial defenses, and Havana was a major port. The local planters and merchants were eager to invest heavily in the slave trade and plantation production in Havana's environs. In the last third of the century, Bourbon officials and the Havana elite reached a series of important compromises. In exchange for paying higher taxes, Cubans could trade with more Spanish ports and could use their own ships for carrying. Cubans would provide volunteer troops to the new disciplined militias that would complement the veteran troops already garrisoned on the island. Though this measure was expensive for local elites because they had to provide time and service to the militias and pay for equipment, it also provided significant benefits, including prestige and the right to enjoy the *fuero militar*, a bundle of legal and fiscal privileges and exemptions. This military reform reached deeply into Cuban and, later, other Spanish American societies. Creole elites formed the officer corps of the disciplined militias, but free people of color also served in their own units—usually divided between *morenos* and *pardos*.

These late 18th-century reforms seriously challenged vested interests in Spain. Under the Habsburgs, all colonial trade was routed through one port, initially Seville and later Cádiz. Bourbon officials were eager to weaken the power and privileges of the Cádiz merchants. They believed that deregulating trade would increase the monarchy's tax base and produce the revenues needed to bolster imperial defenses. In the deal worked out with Havana immediately after the Seven Years' War, Madrid opened trade far beyond Cádiz. Cuba (and other Caribbean colonies, like Puerto Rico and Margarita island) could now trade directly with ports around the Spanish periphery: Alicante, Málaga, Cartagena, Barcelona, Santander, Gijón, La Coruña, and Seville. The tilt toward colonial interests was clear: Havana's concerns now outweighed those of Cádiz.

This pact between Madrid and Havana also gave Cubans leverage for negotiating the opening of the slave trade. Over the course of the century, merchants and planters had sought to expand plantation agriculture on the island. However, the limitations of the *asiento*, the contract to provide slaves that the crown farmed out to foreign merchants, hindered their efforts. The terms of the asiento capped the number of slaves who could be legally introduced each year; it also fixed prices artificially high, thus making slave labor in Cuba expensive and scarce. Madrid raised the number of slaves that could be introduced into the island. It also adopted a policy known as *comercio libre de negros*, which permitted foreign merchants to enter Spanish American ports if they were also trafficking in slaves. But it was not until 1789 that Madrid, under intense lobbying from Havana in the person of the brilliant young planter and official Francisco Arango y Parreño, finally relented and lifted almost all restrictions on the slave trade between Africa and Cuba and the purchase of slaves from neighboring colonies like Jamaica. The stage was set for Cuba's ascendancy. From the late 18th century until the trade's suppression in 1867, the island would import almost 800,000 captives. Cuba would also remain firmly in the Spanish orbit even when most of Spanish America fought for independence in the 1810s and 1820s, in no small part because of slavery's centrality to the colonial economy.

The centrality of slavery and the slave trade in cementing Antillean loyalty to the Spanish crown is evident in the debates over the traffic that erupted after the overthrow of the Spanish monarchy, and also in the resistance to the French occupation of Spain that commenced in 1808. The political vacuum opened by the monarchy's demise soon led to wars for independence in much of Spanish America. Spaniards who resisted the French tried to counter unrest in the colonies by forming a provisional government in the southern city of Cádiz. In 1812 the Cádiz government drafted a constitution that sought to incorporate the colonies into the Spanish regime as equal provinces. One of the issues that came to the fore during this process was the abolition of the slave trade to the colonies. Opposition to the traffic in slaves, if not necessarily to slavery itself, was widespread in Spain and Spanish

America. The colonies that vied for independence in the 1810s and 1820s abolished the trade to their shores (some colonies did try to reopen it later, but were unable to do so in the face of British naval and diplomatic pressure). The Cádiz government briefly debated the suppression of the traffic. Peninsular and creole critics—such as Joseph Blanco White, Isidoro de Antillón, Juan Antonio Llorente, and Fray Servando Teresa de Mier—published antislavery tracts throughout the revolutionary era.

Denunciations of the slave traffic came soon after the French overthrow of the Bourbon monarchy. Most disturbingly for Antillean planters and merchants, the Cádiz government almost immediately entered the fray and in 1811 was poised to issue a decree banning the slave traffic. Deputies from both sides of the Atlantic, including the Mexican Miguel Guridi y Alcócer and the Spaniard Agustín de Argüelles, vigorously advocated the measure and spoke out against the brutality and inhumanity of the traffic. In the short run, the government relented in the face of Cuban opposition to a ban, and it suppressed further discussion. But a few years later, the restored monarch Fernando VII entered into a treaty with Britain in 1817 that called for the traffic's suppression by 1820.

Closing the traffic to Cuba was a major goal of the British government and of many Spanish liberals forced abroad after Fernando VII's restoration. In 1814, Joseph Blanco White from his London exile published an anti–slave-trade tract with assistance from the British Foreign Office. Basing his arguments on his familiarity with British antislavery, Blanco reserved especially harsh words for the Cuban planters who so vigorously defended the slave trade. He implored his Spanish readers to put themselves in the place of the Africans torn from their families and their homes. Having just freed themselves from the French occupation, he said, they must identify with captives victimized by warfare.

But the traffic's Cuban defenders were highly motivated and effective. They actively depicted the trade to the Antilles as a positive and necessary factor in the imperial economy. When they spoke, metropolitan political leaders listened and acquiesced even as they paid lip service to abolishing the traffic. During the revolution in neighboring Saint-Domingue in the 1790s, Cuban planters such as Arango y Parreño insisted that such a rebellion could never take place in a Spanish colony because venerable laws and customs distinguished slavery there from slavery in French and British settlements: "The French looked at the slaves as beasts, and the Spanish looked at them as men. . . . Our civil laws have balanced perfectly the two extremes, that is, the abuses of the owners and the development of insubordination and insolvency of the slave" (Tomich 2005, 74) Two decades later, in 1811, Arango y Parreño authored a petition on behalf of the municipality of Havana, intended to thwart the anti–slave-trade decree in the Cortes de Cádiz, in which he drew attention to "the great utility that all branches of our industry have received from dedicating the blacks to the service of all of our rural estates, and not to *some* of them, as those who seek to belittle us like to say." He argued that "the situation is such that without black slaves there would be no colonies"—an ominous warning to political and business leaders in the metropole, who responded by suppressing the Cortes decree and halting all further discussion of antislavery measures (Arango y Parreño 1952, 184–85). The Constitution of 1812 was mute on the issue of abolition.

In 1821, one of Cuba's representatives to the Spanish Cortes published a pamphlet critical of the 1817 treaty with Britain, arguing that slavery benefited both the planters and the slaves themselves: "I am not, let it be said, a defender of slavery," wrote Juan Bernardo O'Gavan, "but of *work*, without which there is no production, population, energy, wealth, or power; nor is there any means by which to perfect the intelligence of men and to keep them from falling into barbarism, brutality, disorder, and misery" (O'Gavan 1821, 4). In other words, not only was the traffic vital to the colony and to the metropole, it was also a means of civilizing barbarous Africans by carrying them to Cuba and forcing them to submit to the salutary labor of the plantation.

Arango y Parreño and O'Gavan's proslavery arguments carried the day in Madrid, overriding the efforts of abolitionists, both native and foreign. The slave traffic flowed unabated to Cuba despite the prevalence of antislavery sentiment in Spain and Spanish America and the formal commitment to suppress the trade. Puerto Rico, too, would tap into the traffic despite the 1817 treaty banning it. Spanish officials such as O'Reilly had encouraged the growth of a slave-based plantation economy since the late 18th century. But the sugar plantation took hold in the island only in the early 19th century, because of one of the few successes of the restored monarchy of Ferdinand VII: the granting of the Cédula de Gracias to Puerto Rico in 1815, setting the stage for the plantation takeoff. This provided a sharp contrast to Spanish actions in other colonies: war to the death in South America, reform and negotiation in the Antilles.

Slavery, Resistance, and Rebellion in the Caribbean Context

In Cuba, the deregulation of the slave traffic had commenced in the aftermath of the Seven Years' War and reached fruition by the early 1790s after extensive lobbying by Arango y Parreño and other planters. After the Spanish American revolutions, Spanish investors and merchants descended upon Cuba, now the focus of Spain's much reduced American empire. To the displeasure of creole elites who wanted to direct the local economy, Spanish immigrants came to dominate credit and slaving on the island. They also turned to planting, opening haciendas of vast scale and technological sophistication.

Puerto Rican creoles and immigrants from Europe and other parts of the Americas undertook the construction of a smaller but significant plantation economy centered on the production of sugar in coastal regions such as Ponce, Guayama, Mayagüez, and Arecibo. Like Cuban planters, they invested in steam-driven mills as early as the 1820s to boost production. But the high price of enslaved workers, driven up by the constant demand in Cuba, limited the prospects of the undercapitalized Puerto Rican *hacendados*.

In the 19th-century Spanish Caribbean, slavery was adapted to new conditions of production and consumption that permitted planters to open and operate acreage and mills on a greatly enlarged scale. One historian has called this system the "second slavery" in the Americas because of its unprecedented scale and technological sophistication (Tomich 2004). As European and US demand for sugar, coffee, and cotton boomed, planters and investors introduced steam-driven mills to extract and refine sugar, railways to carry their goods to port, and steamships to haul them across the Atlantic. Improved transportation and growing markets allowed planters to expand the frontiers of cultivation. The first Latin American railway, Cuba's 51-kilometer-long Havana-Güines line, connected the sugar frontier to the Atlantic world. Opened in 1837, the line became the foundation for a railway network that extended throughout the western and central sugar regions; it carried sugar to the mills for grinding and the finished product to ports for export. Large estates in the mid-19th century could produce two or three thousand tons of sugar annually, compared to three or four hundred a few decades earlier.

The greater size and capacity of the 19th-century plantation had a harsh impact on the lives of the enslaved. Planters bought more enslaved men and women, worked them harder, and policed their movements more closely. When the transatlantic traffic entered into crisis, planters turned to other sources. In Cuba, traffic in indentured Chinese workers from the 1840s to the 1870s brought more than 100,000 unfree laborers to the island; there was also a trade in indigenous workers from Yucatán in the 1860s. Puerto Rico lagged far behind Cuba in the scale of its plantation complex. Nonetheless, when faced with the virtual end of the traffic in slaves to the island in the 1840s, planters relied on the colonial state to coerce nominally free peasants into agricultural labor through a system known as the *libreta* (workbook).

As planters, slavers, and officials constructed robust plantation belts in Cuba and Puerto Rico by coupling cutting-edge technology with enslaved and other forms of coerced labor, they kept a wary eye on the changes taking place around them. The demise of slavery elsewhere in the Caribbean benefited the Spanish islands but also threatened their stability, shaping official and elite attitudes and policies. Cuba and Puerto Rico were surrounded by independent nations and colonies that the Spanish government and its local clients considered enemies and grave threats.

News and travelers from Saint-Domingue (later Haiti) always preoccupied Spanish officials. The movement between colonial Saint-Domingue and the Spanish Antilles was intense. Spain fought a proxy war in the colony when the great slave rebellion broke out in 1791. Defeated by Toussaint Louverture in 1795, Spain evacuated the island, bringing to Cuba and Puerto Rico refugees from both ends of the island, including planters with slaves and capital who set up shop in the Spanish colonies, as well as both Spanish and French soldiers. Among these soldiers were black officers, such as the general Jean François, who served the king of Spain but were unwelcome in these growing slave societies. Events in Haiti would legitimate harsh actions in Cuba and Puerto Rico by the colonial state until well into the 19th century.

Changes to the institution of slavery in the British Empire also echoed in the Spanish Antilles. The British government sought to terminate the slave trade to Cuba and Puerto Rico through bilateral treaties, naval patrols, and mixed courts in the Caribbean. Spanish governments signed treaties with Great Britain banning the trade in 1817, 1835, and 1845, though they consistently turned a blind eye toward the burgeoning contraband trade to both islands. In spite of this complicity, officials and planters feared that the Spanish government would capitulate to British demands, not only banning the trade but also freeing the thousands of slaves illegally imported into the colonies. They also worried about infiltration by abolitionist provocateurs.

Spanish American revolutionaries and their Antillean sympathizers threatened Spanish dominion. Though Spanish American governments were surely interested in the cause of Antillean independence, the threat of invasion was most useful to them as a bargaining chip with Spain. The metropole adopted measures to shield Cuba and Puerto Rico from the revolutions in South America and Mexico. These included control of the entry of information and travelers and the collection of intelligence from spies throughout the Caribbean, Europe, and the United States. Moreover, Spain used Cuba and Puerto Rico as jumping-off points and as relief for troops fighting elsewhere. Even well into the 1820s, after Britain had recognized Spanish American independence, Cuba was a base of operations for forces charged with the reconquest of Mexico.

The two islands did feel the influence of the independence wars. Exiled to the Caribbean, Venezuelan patriot Simon Bolívar openly called for Puerto Rican and Cuban independence in his 1815 "Jamaica Letter." Puerto Rico was an important base for Spain's efforts to quell the South American revolutions after 1814. In turn, the island was a magnet for North American privateers who flew the flags of revolutionary Buenos Aires, Venezuela, and Colombia as they devastated Spanish trade in the eastern Caribbean.

In the 1820s—when independence movements gained the upper hand against Spain in South America and Mexico—the creole José Francisco Lemus, son of a Spanish naval officer, plotted with Bolívar's agents to support a Colombian invasion of Cuba. He hoped that the disruption caused by an invasion would force the

Spanish captain-general to make a pact with the rebels and declare Cuban independence to preserve stability, as had happened in Mexico. But in 1823 the conspiracy was brought to light, and General Dionisio Vives vigorously arrested and exiled suspected supporters. Lemus escaped from his captivity in Sevilla and made his way to Mexico, from which he hoped to launch an invasion in 1825, but the Mexican government decided to withdraw its support, thwarting his plans for an independent "Cubanacán." Documents from the aborted rebellion indicate that it sought to overturn the institutions that bound the island to Spain—including slavery, though Lemus's proclamation was vague on that score: "Cubanacanos, . . . let us treat with tenderness the unfortunate slaves while the representatives of our homeland propose the means for their happy redemption without prejudicing private interests. They are the children of the same God" (Sevilla Soler 1986, 165).

More direct challenges to slavery and the colonial order were local, led by members of the free colored population in alliance with enslaved people. Despite the rapid and unprecedented growth of the slave traffic, there was strong continuity in many of the legal and religious aspects of slavery in Cuba and Puerto Rico. Throughout the 19th century, enslaved men and women took advantage of an important institution called *coartación*, which allowed them to purchase their freedom. Many demanded the right to change owners once they were *coartados* (enslaved people in the process of purchasing their freedom). Many also continued to gather in religious and military associations with long histories in the Caribbean. Free men of color served in *pardo* and *moreno* militia units. Slaves gathered in the *cabildos de nación*, associations based on African ethnic affiliations. The laws, customs, and forms of sociability that had developed over the centuries clashed with the new rigors of the plantation and the deregulated slave trade.

This tension between older and new forms of slavery came to a head in Cuba in 1812 when Spanish authorities uncovered, and then suppressed with great violence, an island-wide conspiracy of slaves and free people of color intended to abolish slavery. The accused leader of the aborted uprising was José Antonio Aponte, a free man of color who had served in the colonial militia, like his father and grandfather before him, and who belonged to a cabildo. The sociability protected in the militias and cabildos allowed conspirators, free and enslaved, to gather and plan and communicate with like-minded groups around the island. Though enslaved and free people lived under different circumstances and had different interests, both suffered increased discrimination and discipline during the plantation and slave traffic boom. Moreover, their common monarchical political imaginations—references to the king of Spain and to the king of Kongo were current in the conspiracy—allowed them to come together to fight against slavery. Caribbean influences were also apparent. Aponte recruited supporters to his cause by showing them his *libro de pinturas*—a book of paintings of revolutionary and monarchical figures which has never been recovered by historians, but is known through the voluminous testimony of Aponte and others. Among the book's portraits were those of the great Haitian generals Toussaint Louverture, Henri Christophe, and Jean-François as well as the leader of US independence, George Washington. Jean-François was well known in Cuba as Juan Francisco after his evacuation to the Spanish colony in 1795. The Aponte Rebellion, though suppressed by the colonial government, demonstrated that even where planters and slavers were most triumphant, they still had to contend with the diverse antislavery forces unleashed in the revolutionary era. Cuba and Puerto Rico would not be exempted.

In this context of regional rivalries and internal unrest, Spain clamped down on its Caribbean colonies even as Spanish political leaders consolidated constitutional government in the metropole during the 1830s. In Cuba and Puerto Rico they erected a regime based on extraordinary military rule, with the vague promise of drafting "special laws" for the so-called *provincias de ultramar* (overseas provinces). After the independence of the great majority of the American colonies, Spanish liberals were in no mood to make political compromises with creoles in Cuba and Puerto Rico. Justifying their decision to deny the colonies elected representation and constitutional rights by making reference to the threat of internal rebellions, invasion, and other forms of foreign subversion fomented by Haiti, Britain, and independent Spanish American states (and later the United States), Spanish political leaders gradually formulated a colonial regime characterized by "centralization of [military] command, absence of political representation, and degradation of the institutions of the late imperial period" (Fradera 2005, 326). Antillean elites were losing the leverage they had so effectively used since the late 18th century; the metropole repaid their loyalty with greater political control from Madrid and its proxies in Havana and San Juan. Nonetheless, despotic rule temporarily appeased some sectors of the colonial elite because of the economic trade-offs. With Spanish rule came the continuation of the slave trade in the face of British pressure, and a strong military presence for maintaining order in potentially unruly plantation societies. Indeed, the period of political repression coincided with a new stage of innovation of the sugar industry that would catapult Cuba to the fore of world production. Thus, in the short term this repressive regime was not completely devoid of legitimacy even as it faced opposition and resistance in the colonies and from its Caribbean and Spanish American neighbors.

Triumph and Crisis of the Second Slavery, 1830s–1860s

Slavery and political despotism proved durable, but not immutable, in Cuba and Puerto Rico. The plantation system of Puerto Rico was more vulnerable than that of Cuba. The slave trade faded to the smaller of the Antilles, so that from the 1840s onward the total slave population declined steadily. Planters clamored for other sources of coerced labor, while progressive critics of colonial society argued that the abolition of slavery was the most effective way for Puerto Rico to modernize its economy. These Puerto Rican critics—including the educator José Julián Acosta and the physician Ramón Emeterio Betances, the leading advocate of independence later in the century—would decisively shape the Spanish Abolitionist Society, founded in Madrid in 1865.

In western and central Cuba, in contrast, the plantation belt flourished between the 1830s and the 1860s, fed by a constant stream of unfree workers from Africa and China. The leading planters continued to introduce new sources of power and sophisticated processing technology that allowed them to increase productive capacity, though modernization was uneven (many mills were only partly mechanized, and others continued to rely on animal power). Among the innovations were huge steam-driven grinding mills and vacuum evaporators like the Derosne train, which allowed for greater yield from the sugarcane and more exact refining. Rails took cane to these modernized mills, and the size of the largest estates practically tripled. Meanwhile, the network of railroads also expanded, connecting deeper hinterlands around Matanzas and Cienfuegos to the Atlantic, which by this time was traversed by steam-powered ships. By the middle of the century, Cuba had become the world's dominant sugar producer.

Still, even at the height of their success, the Cuban planters faced serious domestic and foreign opposition. In the island another large-scale antislavery conspiracy took shape in the early 1840s, this time in apparent cooperation with British abolitionists and US agitators interested in annexing the island. As in 1812, the Spanish government responded with terrific violence against slaves and free blacks while suppressing what became known as the Conspiracy of La Escalera. Some Cubans in the 1840s and 1850s responded to US interest in annexing Cuba as a slave state, alarming Spanish officials, who increased the military presence on the island.

The Civil War in the United States had far-reaching consequences. Though Spain initially saw the war as an opportunity to extend its influence in the Caribbean by occupying Santo Domingo (1861–65), the defeat of the Confederacy and the emancipation of slaves put abolition and political reform squarely on the agenda in Spain and the Antilles. Under continued British pressure, the government agreed to suppress the slave trade to Cuba in 1867. In Madrid, a new abolitionist society openly discussed how to take the next step: the end of slavery in Cuba and Puerto Rico.

While abolitionists, planters, and politicians wrangled in Madrid, the decisive turning point took place in the colonies: defenders of Puerto Rican and Cuban independence launched uprisings in September and October of 1868. Though they did not realize their immediate aims, their initiatives decisively challenged the political, economic, and social status quo that had taken shape over the course of the past century. After 1868 Cubans, Puerto Ricans, and Spaniards dismantled the foundations of the second slavery and set the stage for new conflicts over work, wealth, freedom, and political rights.

WORKS CITED

Abbad y Lasierra, Fray Iñigo. 1970 [1776]. *Historia geográfica, civil y natural de la Isla de San Juan de Puerto Rico.* Río Piedras, PR: Editorial Universitaria.

Arango y Parreño, Francisco. 1952. "Representación de la Ciudad de la Habana . . ." In *Obras de Francisco de Arango y Parreño.* Havana: Dirección de Cultura, Ministero de Educación.

Fradera, Josep Maria. 2005. *Colonias para después de un imperio.* Barcelona: Edicions Bellaterra.

O'Gavan, Juan Bernardo. 1821. *Observaciónes sobre la suerte de los negros del África, considerados en su propia patria, y trasplantados a las Antillas Españolas: Y reclamación contra el tratado celebrado on los ingleses el año 1817.* Madrid: Imprenta del Universal.

Sevilla Soler, Ma. Rosario. 1986. *Las Antillas y la independencia de la América Española (1808–1826).* Sevilla: C.S.I.C.

Tomich, Dale. 2004. *Through the Prism of Slavery: Labor, Capital, and World Economy.* Lanham, MD: Rowan and Littlefield.

———. 2005. "The Wealth of Empire: Francisco Arango y Parreño, Political Economy, and the Second Slavery in Cuba." In *Interpreting Spanish Colonialism: Empires, Nations, and Legends,* edited by Christopher Schmidt-Nowara and John Nieto-Phillips, 55–85. Albuquerque: University of New Mexico Press.

23

Peasants, Immigrants, and Workers

GAD HEUMAN

The British and French Caribbean after Emancipation

The emancipation of slaves in the Caribbean was a complex process. Across the region, it took place at different times and in different ways. In the Anglophone Caribbean, emancipation occurred in 1838 and was preceded by a system of apprenticeship that severely curtailed the rights of former slaves. With the onset of full freedom, free people often sought to leave the estates where they had toiled their entire lives. Although emancipation occurred 10 years later in the French Caribbean, the process was similar. It was not simply a case of ex-slaves associating work on the plantations with slavery; their flight from the estates was also a response to the oppressive policies of the planters in the immediate aftermath of emancipation. But recently emancipated people were able to survive outside the plantation system, partly because they had behaved like a peasantry during slavery.

The Development of a "Proto-Peasantry"

From the earliest stages of plantation society, Caribbean planters often set aside land for their enslaved people to grow much of their own food. This had significant economic advantages for the planters: it meant that they could make great savings on feeding their slaves. Since the land planters provided for this purpose was often hilly or marginal, planters were making full use of their estates at very little cost to themselves.

While the economic advantages for the planters were apparent, there were also significant benefits for the enslaved population. Slaves could grow what they liked on their provision grounds, thereby varying their diet and improving their standard of living. In time, the enslaved produced surpluses on their land and developed a system of markets to sell and to trade their produce. This has been described as the "internal economy"; it was the slaves' own economy as opposed to that of their masters, which was directed at producing sugar and other commodities for export. In the process of creating the "internal economy," the enslaved were carving out areas of relative freedom within the institution of slavery. According to anthropologist Sidney Mintz, enslaved people were therefore behaving like a "proto-peasantry" (Mintz 1974, 184–94).

In time, customary practice meant that the planters were reluctant to interfere in the provision grounds of the enslaved. Planters therefore did not supervise the labor of the enslaved on the provision grounds. Moreover, while planters continued to own the land, it was the slaves who regarded it as theirs and were able to pass it on to their heirs. This practice could take surprising forms. For example, in Martinique a planter described having a problem with some manioc that enslaved people had planted in one of his cane fields, which he had left uncultivated for a year. When the planter decided to make use of the land for growing cane, he realized that he would have to buy the slaves' crop. But since the enslaved demanded too high a price, the planter had to wait until the slaves had harvested the manioc before planting his cane.

The slave markets that developed as a result of this "internal economy" were often very large: for example, 10,000 Jamaican slaves participated in the Kingston market at the end of the 18th century. The Saint-Domingue market was even bigger: there, 15,000 slaves were involved in the market at Cap Français, the capital of the colony. Interestingly, the enslaved did not just trade with each other in these markets; they also dealt with whites and free people of color. Indeed, masters as well as slaves came to depend on the markets for much of their food.

Although most slaves were unable to earn substantial amounts of money from their crops, some of the enslaved did have significant savings, which they accumulated from their activities as traders but also from payments for work beyond the stipulated hours for labor, such as on Sundays. Edward Long, the Jamaican historian and planter, knew of slaves whose estates were valued at between £50 and £200 (roughly US$2,500–$10,000 today) when they died. He also estimated that one-fifth of all the currency in Jamaica was in the hands of the enslaved in 1774. While most of this money would have consisted of small coins, it nonetheless testified to the significance of the "internal economy" and the slave markets.

It is therefore clear that the economic activities of the enslaved gave them some control of important aspects of their lives. They decided what they would grow in their grounds, they sold their produce in the slave-controlled markets, and they participated in the wider internal economy. The world of work for enslaved people was not limited to laboring for their masters; they also worked for themselves and their families and, in the process, gained an important measure of independence. This experience would prove to be highly significant in the aftermath of emancipation.

Apprenticeship and Emancipation

When slavery was abolished in the Caribbean, enslaved people were not freed immediately. Instead, in the British, Dutch, and Spanish Caribbean, systems of apprenticeship were adopted. These were envisioned as an intermediate stage between slavery and freedom that was intended, in part, to prepare the enslaved for full freedom. In most instances these systems were prematurely abandoned. Although it was expected to last for six years for the majority of the enslaved, apprenticeship in the Anglophone Caribbean ended two years early, in 1838.

Under the terms of apprenticeship, ex-slaves had to work for their former masters for up to 45 hours per week. This was unpaid compulsory labor, although apprentices were paid for any work outside of that time. From the perspective of British policymakers, the apprenticeship system was necessary to create a bridge between slavery and freedom. Officials did not believe that it was possible for slaves to be freed without a gradual transition to full freedom. However, enslaved people had very different views about what should happen at the moment of freedom.

Across the Caribbean, the enslaved resisted the idea of an apprenticeship system. The most serious resistance in the Anglophone Caribbean took place in St. Kitts, where the enslaved vowed across the island not to work without pay after the abolition of slavery on August 1, 1834. In addition to stopping work after that date, many apprentices fled from the estates. Faced with a strike of the apprentices, the authorities declared martial law and used imperial and local forces to round up the apprentices and force them back to work. Elsewhere in the Caribbean, there were similar reactions. In Trinidad, the apprentices also vowed to go on strike and shared many of the views of their counterparts in St. Kitts. For the Trinidad apprentices, it was clear that the king had freed them; in their view, it was their masters and the governor who were responsible for withholding their freedom. The apprentices blamed the local authorities rather than the Crown for their transition to apprenticeship.

The same was the case in Jamaica, where planters adopted a particularly harsh interpretation of apprenticeship. On that island, apprentices were unhappy not only about the terms of the new system, but also about the loss of many privileges they had enjoyed as slaves. For instance, mothers who had produced six children had been relieved of field work during slavery, but were forced to work in the fields during the apprenticeship period. Furthermore, the field cooks and nurses who had served the enslaved population were removed once slavery ended, and mothers were no longer allowed to nurse their children in the fields. Apprentices in the island responded by striking and by resisting the system, especially in the first few months after the end of slavery. But, as in St. Kitts, the authorities helped to put down this resistance and forced the apprentices back to work.

The response of the apprentices to the apprenticeship system reflected a deep-seated hostility to the continuation of compulsory labor. Apprentices could not understand how freedom could be equated with forced labor; moreover, as their activities as a proto-peasantry suggested, they believed they were fully prepared for freedom. On the other hand, planters were concerned about the implications of freedom; they sought to maintain the status quo and control of their labor force. Policymakers in Britain largely agreed with the planters: for them, it was critical to ensure the survival of the plantations. Officials equated the plantations with civilization, a view clearly not shared by the apprentices. The clash of these opposing viewpoints would create further difficulties at the moment of full freedom.

The Aftermath of Emancipation

With the onset of emancipation for the Anglophone Caribbean in 1838 and the French Caribbean 10 years later, planters took a variety of measures to ensure a continued labor supply on their estates. In the British West Indies, one method of accomplishing this end was the tenancy-at-will system, in which rents for the laborers' houses and grounds on the plantations were combined with their wages. The rents were often artificially high, and were sometimes even charged for each member of a family living in a house. Laborers' rents could therefore exceed their wages. The governor of Jamaica, Lionel Smith, was aware of this problem and reported some glaring examples of the practice. Smith knew of several cases in which freed laborers were paid five shillings a week but were charged eight shillings for rent, leaving the worker in debt to the plantation. Even when that was not the case, the intent was clear: the planters sought to use this system to force free people to work on the estates to pay for their housing and their provision grounds.

In Martinique and Guadeloupe, the planters adopted a different strategy, although the aim was similar. There, they imposed a head tax on each laborer, but the tax was significantly higher in the towns than in the countryside. With this differential tax, the planters sought to encourage ex-slaves to remain on the plantations. The colonial authorities also used taxes to discourage the production of ground provisions or crops other than sugar. In addition, a pass system was introduced in the French Caribbean to limit the movement of free laborers and keep them on the plantations.

Despite these measures, free people in the Caribbean left the plantations in significant numbers. Five years after the abolition of slavery in the French Caribbean, one-fifth of the ex-slaves had left the estates. In Jamaica, the figures were comparable: 60,000 people had established freeholds by 1845, seven years after emancipation. These freeholds were often small properties, which meant that many free people still needed to work part-time on the estates. Nonetheless, the flight of ex-slaves from the plantations demonstrated the desire of free people to farm the land and work for themselves.

In the Anglophone Caribbean, missionaries—especially Baptist missionaries—helped to establish free villages for the ex-slave population. Some of these villages had been set up during the apprenticeship period, but most were formed in the aftermath of emancipation. The villages often were often named after abolitionists such as Buxton and Wilberforce, reflecting the humanitarian impetus behind their establishment. Using funds raised in Britain, missionaries would buy land and sell it in small plots to the members of their churches.

While missionaries were crucial in the creation of the free village movement, ex-slaves also organized their own post-emancipation villages. Plantation headmen would group together to purchase land and then subdivide it appropriately. In one example in British Guiana, 63 people were involved in buying an estate, Northbrook, just after emancipation. Elsewhere in the colony, four headmen bought a plantation which they then divided among 70 people. Even in colonies such as Antigua, where there was not much land available for free villages, 27 such communities had been established by 1842.

The labor problem for planters arose not just from the movement of free people away from the plantations but also from the withdrawal of women from work on the estates. A significant proportion of free women left the plantations; this was important since women had made up the majority of the field labor force during slavery. The figures are striking: for example, on one estate in Jamaica, of the 137 women on the plantation just before emancipation, only 19 continued working two months later. Elsewhere on the island, women had made up roughly 60 percent of the labor force on the plantations in a western parish during the apprenticeship period; however, a few months after emancipation, this had gone down to just over 30 percent.

Rather than continue on the plantations, many women chose to work on their provision grounds and to market their produce. This choice made economic sense, as their pay on the plantations was significantly lower than that of men and they could earn more money working on their own account. It also gave women far more control of their lives, an important factor in light of the regimented and often harsh conditions on a plantation. Similarly, ex-slaves were very reluctant to have their children working on the plantations. It was already clear during the apprenticeship period that former slaves would refuse to allow their children to labor on the estates, despite financial inducements to do so. After emancipation, this pattern continued, with parents instead eager to have their children educated, wherever possible.

Post-Emancipation Resistance

Free people expected that emancipation would bring significant benefits to their lives. In addition to their freedom, ex-slaves believed that the crown would give them their houses and provision grounds. Many free people associated freedom with the possession of their homes; after all, they had built them and also worked on their provision grounds, often for several generations. In addition, free men and women expected to move around freely in the aftermath of emancipation. However, these expectations were quickly dashed. Officials soon made it clear that free people did not own their houses or their provision grounds, despite the length of time they had occupied them. Worse still for ex-slaves were the high rent charges imposed by many planters for their continued occupation of their homes. When coupled with low rates of pay, this situation led to serious problems between planters and laborers.

Free people reacted in a series of strikes, riots, and rebellions across the Caribbean. In the immediate aftermath of emancipation, many of them refused to continue working because of the low levels of pay that were being offered. In St. Lucia, for example, most of the free population went on strike: one report claimed that two-thirds of estate laborers were not willing to work on the plantations. Elsewhere in the region, there was a similar response on the part of the ex-slaves. In Grenada, a group of workers attacked constables who were seeking to eject a laborer from his house because he would not accept the wages on offer and also was not willing to leave his home. Free people believed that the queen had given them their houses, and they were determined to keep them. Similarly in Tobago, the lieutenant-governor of the island was worried about laborers striking across the island and acting together to resist low wages.

Some of these concerns were responsible for a number of riots in the post-emancipation period. Six years after emancipation, in 1844, the people of Dominica protested against the taking of a census, which for them was evidence that the authorities were intent on re-enslaving them. They attacked the enumerators carrying out the census and also targeted managers and estate property. Although the colonial authorities were able to suppress the riot, four people were killed in the process and several hundred arrested.

Many men and women in Dominica genuinely believed that they could be re-enslaved. They were aware that people had been freed and re-enslaved earlier in the century in the French Caribbean. A freed man, Saint Louis, expressed this view quite graphically (Chace 1989, 130):

> I think that our freedom can be taken away from us, because it was once done in another country near to us; it was the French who gave their people free, and afterwards made them slaves again; my parents told me so when I was quite a child, and I have remembered it ever since; what is done once can be done again, and we all know that liberty is good; I don't know but what the English will do like the French one of these days; it is only for the Queen to send a Gazette, and say "make them slaves again," and they will be all made slaves; if a man pays money, and does not get a receipt, he can be made to pay the money again; so it is with freedom; if we have been made free and have not paper to show for it, we can be made slaves again.

Similar concerns were expressed in Jamaica a decade after emancipation, when several disturbances broke out in that island. In 1848, the collapse of the protected sugar duties forced the planters to reduce wages on the estates by as much as 25%. For freed people, already faced with low wages, this was evidence that the planters were intent on re-enslaving them. This view was given added credibility by the continuing rumors of Jamaica becoming a slave state of the United States. The idea had been discussed just before the end of slavery in the early 1830s, as a response to abolitionist pressures to improve the condition of the enslaved population and ultimately abolish slavery. Blacks in Jamaica believed that August 1, 1848, the 10th anniversary of the emancipation, would be the date for their re-enslavement.

Low wages were an ongoing problem for free people after emancipation. When estates either cut existing wages or, as in the case of St. Vincent in 1862, significantly reduced the allowances of rum and sugar for their workers, problems ensued. For the laborers in St. Vincent, the cutbacks on their allowances were serious: they were equivalent to the wage reduction that Jamaican workers had faced in 1848. The result was similar: disturbances broke out on the island and ex-slaves attacked managers and plundered some of the plantation shops. These shops were a problem in themselves, since laborers were forced to buy goods from them, and their prices were often artificially inflated. As in the other post-emancipation riots, the authorities put down the disturbances, but four people were killed and many others arrested and imprisoned.

Figure 23.1 Paul Bogle. Photograph (ca. 1850).

Some of these factors were responsible for the most significant post-
emancipation disturbance in the Anglophone Caribbean, the Morant Bay Rebellion
in Jamaica. It broke out on October 11, 1865, when several hundred blacks marched
into Morant Bay, the principal town in the predominantly sugar-growing parish of
St. Thomas in the East. Led by a Baptist deacon, Paul Bogle, the crowd attacked the
police station, seeking to obtain weapons in its confrontation with the parish authorities. The crowd then marched to the courthouse, where the parish vestry was
meeting. Although the members of the vestry were defended by the local militia,
the crowd heavily outnumbered the authorities; in the ensuing melee, the crowd
killed 18 people.

There were local causes for the outbreak as well as more general ones. The mag-
istracy in St. Thomas in the east was dominated by members of the plantocracy; as
a result, planters were often judging cases involving their own employees. People
therefore believed that it was impossible to obtain justice in the parish. There was

an additional problem: the court fees were exorbitant and made it very difficult for free people to pursue cases in court. In response, the people in the parish established their own courts. These alternative courts issued fines and floggings; moreover, they were evidence of the people's dissatisfaction with the formal system of justice in the parish.

As elsewhere in the Caribbean, land was also a problem. Free people in Jamaica believed that the queen had given them their provision grounds along with their freedom. When planters imposed high rents on this land, they encountered resistance. One of the planters killed in the aftermath of the outbreak at Morant Bay, Augustus Hire, was targeted because he had sought to collect rent from people squatting on land. The land belonged to the estate Hire managed, and when he sought to organize a survey of the land, Hire and the surveyor were surrounded by a hostile crowd and a scuffle ensued. Hire sought to have the people involved brought before the courts; in fact, the case was due to be heard the week after Hire was murdered.

In the outbreak at Morant Bay, women played a significant role. They marched with the men from their villages to Morant Bay and were also involved in the initial confrontation between the militia and the crowd. Moreover, one of the women in the crowd was responsible for the suggestion to burn down the courthouse by initially setting fire to the neighboring schoolhouse. When some of the men wished to retreat from the town, women encouraged the men to continue their attack on the militia who were defending the courthouse.

As in other post-emancipation outbreaks, the authorities moved quickly to put down the Morant Bay Rebellion. The governor, Edward John Eyre, declared martial law in the eastern part of the island; he also called in the army, the militia, and the maroons to quell the rebellion. During the month-long period of martial law, the forces killed more than 400 blacks. This action was testimony to the fear among the whites and the people of color that blacks were intent on taking over the island. Eyre and his officials never doubted that this was the case, but a royal commission that investigated the rebellion could find no evidence of a planned insurrection of this magnitude.

In the French Caribbean, there was no comparable outbreak in the aftermath of emancipation, in part because emancipation was announced so suddenly. As a result of the 1848 revolution in France, Victor Schoelcher, the leader of the French antislavery movement, became part of the new government, occupying the position of undersecretary of state for the colonies. Though it was clear that the government intended to abolish slavery, news of the revolution led to a slave revolt in May 1848 in Martinique. The revolt forced the colonial authorities to abolish slavery even before the legislation freeing the slaves arrived in the colonies.

Planters in Martinique and Guadeloupe were therefore faced with an immediate problem: harvesting the 1848 sugar crop with a free labor force. The planters' solution was to turn to sharecropping schemes that would become more familiar in the American South after the Civil War. Under these terms, laborers received a portion of the proceeds from the sale of the crop, usually between a third and a half of the total. The former masters supplied the equipment and the land required to produce the crop, but they did not have to pay wages to their employees.

In the French Caribbean, there was a steep drop in the number of laborers on the plantations after emancipation. As in the Anglophone Caribbean, free people were concerned about being able to stay in their homes on the estates and continuing to work their provision grounds. The pattern of resistance in Guadeloupe and Martinique was therefore different: workers there were intent on controlling part of their time. For example, they sought to have Fridays for themselves, to maintain their provision grounds, and to market their crops. But when the colonial authorities decided to bring in a pass system, workers resisted. They even threatened to kill the mayor of a district in Guadeloupe. As elsewhere in the region, the authorities imposed more repressive labor codes and sought alternative sources of labor.

Immigration

In the face of the labor problems after emancipation, planters turned to a variety of schemes to import labor. One of the earliest of these involved liberated Africans: these were Africans who were on slave ships heading for the Americas that were intercepted by the British navy as part of the British campaign against the foreign slave trade. The enslaved Africans were taken to the nearest port that had a recognized international court to deal with them, most commonly Sierra Leone. Those intercepted further south were taken to the island of St. Helena, and those closer to the Americas taken to either Rio de Janeiro or Havana. The majority of liberated Africans were sent to Sierra Leone, where they were maintained by the British government for three months and then given a choice of whether to remain in the colony or to embark for the West Indies. Many chose to stay in Sierra Leone: some had heard rumors of the harsh working conditions on the sugar plantations of the Caribbean. However, thousands of liberated Africans did make the journey across the Atlantic. Between 1848 and 1850, 12,000 liberated Africans reached the West Indies and, overall in the quarter century after 1841, 36,000 arrived in the region. The overwhelming majority of the liberated Africans went to Trinidad, British Guiana, and Jamaica, but 16,000 were also sent to the French Caribbean. Though the numbers of liberated Africans arriving in the West Indies in any one year were not high, they were nonetheless significant.

For the planters, however, there were problems with the liberated Africans. The African immigrants often left the estates on which they were employed, looking for work outside of the plantations. To combat this problem, the liberated Africans were indentured, initially for one year and eventually for three years. More broadly, however, since these immigrants left the estates as soon as they could and often organized their own independent villages, they did not solve the labor problem for the planters. Instead, the planters turned to China and to India and to the larger pools of labor available there.

Chinese immigration to the British West Indies was concentrated in the period between 1859 and 1866. Most of the roughly 19,000 Chinese came from southeast China, and the overwhelming majority went to British Guiana, followed by Trinidad and to a lesser extent Jamaica. The Chinese came as indentured laborers, initially for five years, but there was no provision for a return passage to China at the end of their term of indenture. Moreover, women represented less than 15% of Chinese immigrants; many of them were not indentured and proved unwilling to work on the estates.

Planters generally regarded Chinese immigration as more problematic than Indian immigration. Costs were higher to bring in Chinese labor; moreover, Indian laborers were more plentiful and the recruitment system in India was better organized. Many planters also had a negative reaction to the Chinese, whom they believed to be prone to suicide and to drug taking and were often difficult to manage. Unlike the Indians, most of the Chinese did not remain on their plantations; once their indenture was over, many of them became peasant cultivators and then moved into rural and urban small retail businesses. This was especially the case in Trinidad, but by the 1880s, the Chinese had become a recognized small trading class across the British Caribbean.

The most significant source of labor for the West Indies in the aftermath of emancipation thus proved to be India. Nearly 250,000 Indians went to British Guiana, almost 150,000 to Trinidad, and more than 36,000 to Jamaica. There were also smaller numbers of Indians in the French Caribbean and the eastern Anglophone Caribbean islands. The Indians came to the West Indies in three phases: 1838–48, 1851–70, and post-1870, with the overwhelming majority of immigrants arriving after 1870. As a source of labor, India had significant advantages: it was largely British, and it was affected by periodic famines and high unemployment. Indians could therefore be attracted to work outside of India; hundreds of thousands of Indians traveled not only to the Caribbean but also to Southeast Asia, South Africa, and Mauritius during this period.

Like the Chinese, the Indians came as indentured laborers: in general, they were obligated to work in this capacity for five years. After they had completed their period of indenture, they were free to work for other employers but not entitled to a free passage back to India until after 10 years in the colony. The indenture system confined laborers to an employer and to a plantation; there were heavy penalties for violating the rules of the indenture. For example, in British Guiana between 1865 and 1870, roughly 6,000 to 7,000 cases a year were brought against Indian indentured laborers. These consisted primarily of claims that the laborers neglected or refused to work, were absent, or did not complete their tasks. Planters frequently resorted to the law to impose penal sanctions against the laborers; employers regarded this as one of the best methods of controlling their labor force on the plantations.

The planters also used the "pass-law" system for the same purpose. Under this system, immigrants were liable to be arrested if they were found outside their assigned estates without a pass. Inevitably, the pass system severely restricted the mobility of Indian indentured laborers. It also meant that immigrants found it difficult to ascertain wages rates on other estates or even to make complaints about their conditions to the appropriate immigration department. In either case, if they did not have a pass, the immigrants could be arrested and brought to court.

In addition to these limitations, indentured laborers were paid very poorly. The official rate in Trinidad after 1872 was just 25 cents per day, and many employers did not even provide that amount. Moreover, planters could reduce the pay of the Indian laborers by increasing the size of the task. Employers also deducted fines for supposed infractions that they imposed illegally on the workers, and some planters did not pay their workers for months at a time.

Despite these problems, Indian laborers made an enormous difference in the survival of the sugar plantations, especially in British Guiana and Trinidad. During the first phase of Indian immigration in the 1840s, sugar production rose significantly in these two colonies despite falling international prices. In the case of Trinidad, the crop harvested in 1852 was the largest ever produced in the island, while production costs were reduced by one-third. Indian laborers were also responsible for helping to defeat a strike led by black workers in British Guiana in 1848; the Indians continued to work on the estates, ensuring the failure of the strike.

The success of the Indians in helping to increase sugar production was not achieved easily. For example, there were serious difficulties among the Indian workers themselves: immigrants from north and south India did not speak the same language, and there were often frictions between them. Caste could also be a problem, as Brahmins were known to exploit Indians of lower castes. At the same time, such differences were less significant in the Caribbean than they had been in India. Work on the plantations had the effect of diminishing the significance of caste; headmen and skilled workers were generally chosen on the basis not of caste but rather of ability to do the work.

There was also discontent among the Indian laborers. At one level, this discontent became evident in the large number of Indian wives murdered by their husbands. Immigration officials even passed ordinances to protect Indian women from this type of violence. At a different level, Indian laborers were involved in a series of strikes and disturbances that reflected their dissatisfaction with conditions on the plantations. Some of the disturbances were collective outburst of protest rather than just involving workers on individual estates. In several outbreaks in British Guiana during the last half of the 19th century and the early years of the 20th, the government called in the armed forces to put down the unrest. The loss of life could be heavy: in one disturbance in 1913, 15 Indians were killed.

Yet in spite of all the difficulties associated with the indenture system, 70% of the Indians remained in the Caribbean permanently rather than returning to India. This was not the original intention: Indians came as transient laborers rather than as settlers. But they were able to envision significant economic and social possibilities for themselves and their families in the Caribbean. There were other factors as well that inhibited their return to India. Some had become involved in intercaste marriages, which would be unacceptable in many of their home villages. Others had not made enough money to return. Still others did go back to India, only to find that they preferred their new lives in the Caribbean, and they either reindentured themselves or paid for their own passages back to the region.

Once freed from their indentures, most Indians continued to work in agriculture. In Trinidad, many of them began to produce cocoa, while in British Guiana they were so successful in boosting rice production that it became one of the island's major exports. Many free Indians combined working part-time on the estates with working on their own account, often living in rural Indian communities. Well into the 20th century, the Indians remained a predominantly rural community working largely in agriculture.

Conclusion

The post-emancipation Caribbean witnessed a confrontation between former slaves and former masters. The enslaved had clear expectations about freedom: they expected to work for employers of their choice, to move around freely, and to reconstitute their families. They also believed that freedom meant more than the end of slavery; many expected to be given the houses they had built and the grounds they had worked. In many ways, the enslaved were more prepared for freedom than their masters: as a proto-peasantry, they had long experience of independent agricultural production and of marketing their produce.

The planters had very different ideas about the onset of freedom. Although forced to free their slaves, former masters sought to maintain the hierarchies and the value system that had grown up during slavery. The apprenticeship system in the Anglophone Caribbean was designed to aid this process. Moreover, the planters in both the Anglophone and the Francophone Caribbean passed legislation at the onset of full freedom that sought to restrict the mobility of their former slaves.

Meanwhile, to ensure the survival of their estates and their plantation labor force, the planters turned to alternative sources of labor. Indentured labor, especially from India, proved a salvation to many of them, ensuring their economic survival but also complicating Caribbean societies and cultures in the post-emancipation period.

Free people did not react passively to the actions of their former masters. Many of them left the plantations, some to establish independent free villages away from the estates. Others led protests of various kinds against the efforts to limit their freedom. They also objected to low wages, to the lack of impartial systems of justice, and even to the possibility of their being re-enslaved. In the end, the post-emancipation period involved different perceptions of freedom and different means of attaining it.

WORKS CITED

Chace, Russell E. Jr. 1989. "Protest in Post-Emancipation Dominica: The 'Guerre Negre' of 1844." *Journal of Caribbean History* 23: 118–41.

Mintz, Sidney W. 1974. *Caribbean Transformations*. Chicago: Aldine Publishing Co.

24

War and Nation Building

Cuban and Dominican Experiences

In the 19th century, the processes of nation-building in Cuba and the Dominican Republic were inseparable from the history of slavery and its abolition, though that history played itself out very differently in both nations. This chapter will focus on Cuba, with some comparative observations about war and national identity in the Dominican Republic. In Cuba, the relationship between war and nation-building forged a powerful—if divided and frustrated—popular nationalism, whereas Dominican nation-building was subject to the more diffuse influences of *caudillo* politics and, relative to Cuba, political and economic isolation.

Between 1868 and 1901, Cubans experienced two independence wars (1868–78 and 1895–98), the gradual abolition of slavery, the development of technologically advanced sugar production, and the transition from Spanish colony to a semi-independent republic under American hegemony. In contrast, in Santo Domingo the advocates for independence were victorious in 1844, and the former colony became the Dominican Republic; but Dominican identity was the product more of the country's antagonistic relationship with Haiti than of anticolonial struggle, as in Cuba. In Santo Domingo there were not so much wars for independence as wars against Haitian rule, especially between 1822 and 1844 when Haiti dominated the entire island. Considerable support for Haitian intervention existed among slaves and nonwhites, who favored the Haitians' abolitionist stance. Many whites, however, concluded that annexation by a foreign power—preferably the United States—or even recolonization by Spain was far preferable to rule by Haiti. Haitian intervention brought two decisive changes to Santo Domingo: first, slavery was abolished earlier there than in Cuba and as the result of external intervention, not internal revolution; second, conflicts with Haiti encouraged the formation of a discernable Dominican identity, even if many doubted the viability of independence. Dominican politics after 1844 was characterized by constant fighting among *caudillos* (charismatic but authoritarian leaders), and not until 1882 did anything resembling a national state emerge.

In the late 1820s Cuba was the world's largest sugar producer and Spain's most important colony. Sugar production was based on slavery, and by the 1840s Cuba was a full-fledged slave society. Between 1762 and 1860 its population increased from 150,000 to 1.3 million, including approximately 800,000 slaves who were imported during that period. In the 1850s blacks (both slave and free) nearly outnumbered whites, which provoked racist fears about the "Africanization of Cuba" and a Haitian-like slave revolution. In the 19th century, western and eastern Cuba were in many ways different societies. Slave-based agricultural production was not as important in eastern Cuba as in the west, and manumissions were relatively easier for slaves to obtain there. Only about 6% of the eastern population lived on sugar estates, whereas in the west the percentage was typically over 50%. Meanwhile, Spain tightened its grip on its wealthiest colony. Sugar planters paid high taxes on sugar production and high duties on exports. These policies resulted in higher sugar prices at a time when the sugar market was becoming more complex and competitive. Import duties on manufactured goods and machinery raised costs for Cuban planters and merchants, which further increased resentment against Spain. Still, prior to the 1860s, economic prosperity and fear of slave revolt ensured that most of the creole elite remained loyal to Spain.

In contrast, Santo Domingo had few large plantations, and its slave population was small. Most rural people had no title to their land. "Property" lines were usually ill-defined or determined by custom. Large amounts of land in the Dominican Republic—as in eastern Cuba—were occupied by escaped slaves, free blacks, and mulattos, and customary land tenure persisted well into the 20th century. For peasants in most of the Dominican Republic and eastern Cuba, access to land meant freedom, and they would defend both tenaciously.

The Cuban and Dominican struggles for nationhood, then, cannot be understood without taking into account the history of slavery and abolition. Freedom from slavery and freedom from colonialism were inseparable in the minds of many Cubans and Dominicans, no matter how much the political elites wanted to separate the two. Historians have pointed out that there was no single transition from slavery to freedom. Various labor systems emerged after slavery, but most of them could hardly be classified as "free." Rather, in most cases the transitions were from slavery to other forms of unfreedom. The historical evidence indicates that freedom is not an absolute category or a natural state; it is a social construct and has always been a contingent, and not a necessary, condition for workers or peasants not legally enslaved. Especially within the context of slave and post-emancipation societies, the historical meanings of freedom were often defined in the negative: to be "free" meant a person was not a slave, but what freedom looked like or meant without slavery was hard to imagine then and difficult to generalize about now. On the one hand, the day-to-day experiences of freedom for slaves or their descendants were shaped by localized struggles against those in power who tried to limit freedom based on a person's race, class, or gender; on the other hand, local conflicts shaped people's notions of race, class, and nation. What frequently began as local conflicts over land and freedom might—depending on political, economic, and military circumstances—merge with larger struggles against colonialism and for independence. And when local struggles merged with national movements, they brought with them popular notions about rights and freedom that clashed with those of the usually self-appointed white leaders of these movements.

In other words, just as there was no singular or inevitable transition from slavery to freedom, so there was no inevitable transition from colony to nation. Cuban and Dominican nationhood did not emerge out of a simple division between those who wanted independence and those who did not. If no one knew what freedom without slavery looked like, the political implications of citizenship and national independence after hundreds of years of colonialism were equally uncertain, especially in societies with deep racial and class tensions. There was more than one road to nationhood, and who should be included or excluded from "the nation" was highly contested. Political outcomes were uncertain in both Cuba and the Dominican Republic, and eventual independence was as much the result of bitter defeat and compromise as of a clear-cut victory by one side over the other. Depending on political circumstances, the option of independence was more appealing to some groups than it was to others, and a total break with Spain was not always a foregone conclusion. It was one thing for disgruntled planters or merchants to chafe at Spanish commercial policies, but quite another to sever ties with the imperial state that provided protection from slave revolts, rebellious free blacks, and the threat of anti-slavery conspiracies—both real and imagined—from Haiti. By the end of the 19th century, Cuban and Dominican nationalisms were divided along the lines of race and class: many whites (especially wealthier ones) developed a stronger sense of Hispanic-Cuban or Hispanic-Dominican identity that stressed the "civilizing" influence of Spanish culture on "barbaric" multiracial societies, while the subaltern nationalism of nonwhites was more egalitarian and reflected their long struggles for land, freedom, and equality.

Cuban and Dominican nation-building was profoundly influenced by the rise of American power in the region. Movements against Spanish colonialism were not necessarily movements for independence. For many people, the United States represented modernity and progress while Spain was backward and authoritarian. Plantation owners typically believed that it was their destiny to grow primary products and that geographical determinism, comparative advantage, and reliance upon black labor (whether slave or "free") were natural givens. This sentiment, especially before the American Civil War, convinced many elite Cubans and Dominicans that independence was impractical and that sooner or later both territories would join the United States. Of course not everyone felt this way, but the compelling, and later overwhelming, American presence in the Caribbean gave cause for great hope and deep anxiety for the future.

In the 1860s Cuba's relations with Spain changed dramatically. Tensions arose over an international economic crisis that combined with Madrid's more aggressive policies against Cuban contraband trade with the United States. At the same time, though slavery was secure in Cuba, both the US Civil War and abolitionist sentiment abroad forced many planters to conclude that slavery's days were numbered. Prior to 1865, Spain's weakness as a colonial power and Cuba's proximity to the United States fueled hopes for US annexation of the island, but after the South's defeat, US governments were too preoccupied with post–Civil War reconstruction to consider annexing a multiracial Cuba dominated by slavery. Many Cubans resigned themselves to Spanish rule. Others would not.

The 1860s proved decisive for the Dominican Republic as well. Since independence in 1844 two prominent caudillos, Pedro Santana and Buenaventura Báez, ruled the country through clientist networks. At mid-century there was no national state in the Dominican Republic. Báez and Santana were keenly aware of this reality, and to bring stability and prevent Haitian invasions, they looked for a foreign power to protect the young republic. Three countries showed some interest: France, the United States, and Spain. Báez preferred the French; Santana supported the United States. Ultimately, the French chose to retain good relations with Haiti over the less prosperous Dominican Republic, and they were also too deeply involved in Mexican internal politics to become entangled in another regional conflict. Meanwhile, with the start of the Civil War, any American interest in annexing the Dominican Republic disappeared. Finally, in 1861, in the only example of "voluntary" recolonization in the Americas, Santana agreed to annex the Dominican Republic to Spain. In theory, the Dominicans had considerable autonomy from Madrid; in reality, Spanish officials monopolized power and treated Dominicans with contempt. By 1864 even Santana, who was the captain general, had become disillusioned with Spanish rule, but he died before tensions could come to the fore. Meanwhile, guerrilla bands of mostly poor and nonwhite Dominicans pushed Spanish forces into the towns and capital city. This conflict, known as the War of Restoration, was fueled by popular concerns that Spain—and the Dominican elite—would reinstitute slavery. In 1865 Spain relinquished control and the country returned to *caudillo* rule.

In Spain civil war, *pronunciamientos*, and—in 1868—revolution undermined attempts at reform at home and abroad. Spanish industrialists, merchants, and bankers argued that the country's economic development required greater control over its remaining colonies. After all, they argued, Britain's industrialization would not have happened without protectionist policies and colonial slavery: why should Spain be denied the same opportunity to industrialize and modernize? By 1868 colonial policy toward Cuba, Puerto Rico, and the Philippines became more economically restrictive. Spanish attempts to stop the long-standing and thriving contraband trade between Cuba and the United States were especially resented by Cuban planters and merchants. Meanwhile, within Cuba, heightened slave and free black resistance, combined with an increasingly divided and disoriented elite, forced more people than ever to question colonialism and contemplate independence.

This was the background for Cuba's first war for independence between 1868 and 1878. Known as the Ten Years' War, the rebellion was initiated by disgruntled planters, merchants, slaves, former slaves, free blacks, and mulattos. Two weeks after a revolt against Spanish rule broke out in Puerto Rico (the Grito de Lares of September 23, 1868), Carlos Manuel de Céspedes, a sugar planter, slave owner, and regional political leader, organized the Grito de Yara (a call to arms) against Spanish rule in the eastern Cuban region of Manzanillo. For Céspedes and his allies, most of whom were also planters and merchants from the east, the struggle for Cuban independence was above all a fight for the political and economic liberty of the Cuban elite. Many of the rebel leaders were caught between their theoretical and moral desire to abolish slavery and the economic reality that Cuban wealth depended upon slave labor. While some believed that Cuba's continued dependence on slavery was the main reason why the island had not yet become independent, others could not envision Cuba without slavery. The rebel leaders were educated men; many had traveled to Europe and the United States, and some were Masons. They believed in the vague but powerful ideals of the Enlightenment, such as reason, historical progress, and human development. The examples of the American and French Revolutions, along with the liberal notions of citizenship and the "rights of man," guided much of their thinking.

Céspedes and most of the white leaders believed that slavery was an immoral institution that impeded human progress and should be abolished as soon as possible—but not immediately. They were reformists, not revolutionaries, and Spain's unwillingness to grant reforms—not a desire for radical change—forced Céspedes to rebel. Since Cuba's wealth depended upon sugar, and sugar production relied on slave labor, it would take time to find alternative forms of labor. Most planters doubted the reliability of free labor and feared that former slaves would exercise their freedom by refusing to work on plantations at all. Such a prospect would not only undermine the sugar economy but also raise the thorny political problem of how to compel "free" workers to remain on the plantations while still claiming to support free labor. Although many in the rebel leadership believed that slavery was immoral, they were equally convinced that its immediate abolition would lead to economic ruin and political chaos. One only had to look to the examples of Haiti and the southern United States to see the harm that immediate abolition did to once thriving plantation societies.

For these reasons, Céspedes advocated the gradual abolition of slavery. To allay the fears of planters, especially in the west, the rebel leadership encouraged the manumission of slaves but not abolition. This was hardly a radical proposal: the power of slave owners to free their slaves was a normal practice, and by leaving the issue of slaves' freedom up to their owners, Céspedes showed respect for private property. The white rebel leadership also discouraged commanders from incorporating slaves into their ranks; to do so would remove labor from the plantations and generate even greater political anxiety among planters and potential allies about the social composition and political direction of the war. Céspedes pleaded for slaves, free blacks, and mulattos to be patient and to have confidence that one day they would be free.

Many prominent white rebel leaders had grave misgivings about the ability of former slaves to be responsible and equal citizens in an independent Cuba. They believed it was unrealistic and even dangerous to encourage "culturally backward" slaves to think they could be free citizens. The practical problem for the rebel leadership, however, was that in the midst of an armed struggle against Spain, racist misgivings had to be muted in the interests of national unity. Nationalist discourse had to appear to transcend racial categories and include all Cubans within the same imagined community. But as the war continued, striking a balance between nationalist discourse and political practice proved difficult. On the one hand, most white leaders, as well as the wealthy landowners and merchants in the west, simply could not imagine being equal citizens with nonwhites. On the other hand, if the insurrection was to succeed, it needed slaves and nonwhite Cubans to fight. But the more people of color filled all ranks of the rebel army, the more demands for equal rights and immediate abolition came to the forefront. These tensions over the role, status, and political influence of nonwhites in the independence struggle would become a defining characteristic of Cuban politics for generations to come.

Indeed, planters' worst fears about the racial and social composition of the liberation army were confirmed within weeks of the Grito de Yara. Black and mulatto insurgents throughout the eastern portion of the island took their own initiative to attack sugar estates, requisition goods and property of plantation owners, and incorporate slaves into the military struggle. Some slaves voluntarily joined the fight against Spain, while others were seized by both sides and forced to supply or provision soldiers. Still others simply took advantage of the chaos of war to escape and survive the best they could away from the plantations and the fighting. Whatever the case, the large-scale incorporation of slaves into the struggle changed the political orientation of the independence movement, at least as far as the rank and file were concerned.

As early as December 1868, Céspedes realized that his appeals to slaves to have patience and wait for freedom were not enough to gain support. In an attempt to bring greater clarity to the issue of abolition, he decreed that the slaves of pro-independence planters could be declared free if their owners agreed, masters would be compensated for their loss, and slaves could be "lent" to insurgent forces as fighters or to help supply and maintain the troops. Many slaves rallied to this call because while such measures fell far short of immediate abolition, they offered opportunities to gain more freedom than in the past. It is important to remember that there was no predetermined political trajectory for those with slave ancestry. For some slaves, a world without slavery was impossible to imagine, and the most one could hope for was to carve out as much freedom as possible within the existing system. People's notions of freedom, racial identity, feasible alliances, and realistic possibilities and options were forged through the actual experiences of fighting and surviving in a war in which victory for either side was far from certain.

Still, for other participants and leaders within the independence movement, appeals for patience and patriotic unity were meaningless without the clear objective of immediate abolition and equal rights for all Cubans. In an attempt to respond to the growing antislavery sentiment within Spain and internationally, the Spanish government passed the Moret Law of 1870, which freed children born into slavery in Cuba and Puerto Rico. But this law did little to appease those fighting for immediate abolition. The political and military reality in Cuba was that the rebel army needed motivated fighters to confront the better equipped and more numerous—but not necessarily well trained—Spanish forces. When it became obvious that the war was going to last for an uncertain period, and as the need for more soldiers and supporters increased, the political motivation and morale of the rank and file became the decisive factor for victory. Since most fighters were poor and nonwhite, abstract patriotic slogans or vague promises about eventual freedom were not enough to convince large numbers of people to fight and sacrifice their lives. As the war continued, the moderate leaders of the rebellion were increasingly replaced by more charismatic and popular leaders, such as Máximo Gómez and Antonio Maceo, who refused to consider any compromise on the issues of immediate abolition and equal rights for all Cubans. Under their leadership, guerrilla bands of largely ex-slaves or free blacks proved to be the most effective fighters. This effectiveness was not due simply to their immunity from disease, knowledge of the people and terrain, and great mobility; their unambiguous opposition to slavery and demand for immediate abolition brought highly motivated fighters into the struggle.

After 10 years of war, however, it became clear that neither side could realistically win. In February 1878 the Pact of Zanjón was signed between Spain and moderate separatist leaders. Under this agreement Cuba was to have better representation in Madrid, slaves who fought for the rebels were to be freed, and leaders of the revolt could leave Cuba safely. These provisions fell far short of the goal of independence, but after a decade of war with no end in sight, the insurrection could no longer count on the sustained support of an exhausted population, even in the more rebellious east. Thus the Pact of Zanjón was more of a truce than a peace agreement.

None of the fundamental political and economic issues that caused the Ten Years' War were addressed by the pact. The east-west divide in Cuban society was stronger than ever, and despite efforts to extend the fighting throughout the entire country, military leaders were unable to sustain any political or military momentum in the west. The large-scale slave rebellions that leaders like Maceo and Gómez hoped would develop in the west did not transpire. Free people in the west, including mulatto peasants or poor farmers of Spanish origin, did not mobilize in large numbers for independence or for abolition. Western planters, no matter how much they resented colonial rule, were unwilling to sacrifice the economic certainty of slavery and the military security of the Spanish army for an uncertain future in a multiracial republic.

The rebel cause was also undermined by the refusal of the United States to support Cuban independence. Céspedes and many in the civilian leadership deeply admired the United States, which they hoped would intervene in support of their cause. Ultimately, however, the United States preferred to see a weak Spain rule Cuba than to intervene in a multiracial war that revolved around issues of slavery and its abolition. In the wake of the US Civil War and contentious debates about postwar Reconstruction, neither American politicians nor the American public were prepared to get involved in an international conflict that would only exacerbate a volatile domestic situation.

In the long run, Cuban nationalism after the Ten Years' War was more polarized along the lines of class and race than ever before. In the immediate aftermath of the war, autonomists believed the Pact of Zanjón would help strengthen Cuban identity

Figure 24.1 Heroes of the Cuban independence movement, including Máximo Gómez, Antonio Maceo, and José Martí. Lithograph by J. Weisenback (ca. 1896).

within the larger family of Hispanic nations. For them, the war only confirmed the "civilizing" influence of Hispanic culture as opposed to the "barbarian" and "uncivilized" cultural influence of blacks and mulattos. Paradoxically, the nationalism of many white Cubans was more Hispanic now than before the war began. Autonomists were strongly influenced by Spanish liberalism and federalism, and were convinced that Cubans could adapt to Spanish rule much as had Catalans, Galicians, Asturians, and Basques. Such optimism after Zanjón was fueled by the postwar reconstruction and Spanish migration to the island. The destruction of hundreds of older and technically backward sugar mills and estates, especially in eastern Cuba, opened the way for new money and technology for sugar production. Spanish merchants and bankers invested heavily in land and sugar mills, strengthening business and family ties between Cuba and Spain. This new investment was complimented by large numbers of Spaniards who migrated to Cuba: in a great irony, more Spaniards went to Cuba just before and after Spain lost the island in 1898 than during the entire colonial period. Between 1868 and 1898, more than 200,000 Spanish soldiers went to Cuba, and many remained there. Another 224,000 Spaniards immigrated to Cuba between 1878 and 1895, and by 1930, 800,000 Cuban residents were natives of Spain. While some emigrants eventually returned to Spain or left Cuba for other places, most stayed and maintained ties with Spanish family and friends. The initial optimism after Zanjón would soon fade as it became clear that Spain would not grant Cuba more autonomy, but in the 1880s Spain's control over Cuba seemed more secure than ever.

Yet if autonomists hoped that Cuba's economic and political future was more secure after 1878, many others could not reconcile themselves to peace without independence and immediate abolition. Zanjón had temporarily disoriented and divided the separatists, with some accepting defeat, others going into exile, and some intending to fight on. Most of the popular and intransigent rebel leaders, such as Máximo Gómez, the brothers Antonio and José Maceo, Flor Crombet, and Guillermo Moncada rejected the Pact of Zanjón because it symbolized the betrayal of everything they believed in. This sense of betrayal motivated Maceo, Moncada, and other leaders to launch what became known as the Guerra Chiquita (Little War) of 1879–80.

The Guerra Chiquita was significant for two reasons. Like the Ten Years' War, it was fought mostly in the east and its participants wanted Cuban independence; but unlike that earlier war, its leaders and followers were entirely people of color who were unwilling to compromise on the issue of immediate abolition. This predominantly black rebellion fueled racist fears among both pro- and anti-independence whites that a "race war" was about to break out—a sentiment that caused many whites to regard blacks as fearsome and capable fighters, but politically unreliable and unable to compromise when necessary. Following 10 years of inconclusive war, the Guerra Chiquita simply did not have enough support from an exhausted population to succeed. Still, the experience of mass mobilization and armed struggle transformed the political practice and discourse of Cuban nationalism for generations to come. Powerful and enduring national myths about Maceo, Gómez, and other figures became embedded in Cuban culture. And, as the 1880s came to a close, a new generation of Cubans would soon carry on the fight for independence. Cuban slavery ended in 1886, but the struggle for equal rights and access to land for former slaves and their descendants would continue. Yet before a new struggle for independence could be launched, political and economic circumstances had to be just right.

Meanwhile, in the Dominican Republic the situation was very different. After Santana's death in 1864, his rival Báez dominated the political scene until shortly before his death in 1884. But in a pattern similar to that which prevailed in Central American countries at the time, Dominican politics was characterized by violent conflicts among regional caudillos and frequent change of presidents. This unstable period ended in 1882 when one caudillo from the north, Ulises Heureaux, imposed a dictatorship over the country. Much like Porfirio Díaz in Mexico, Heureaux promised "order and progress" and, until his assassination in 1899, used authoritarian means to promote industry, transportation, and Spanish immigration.

In Cuba, conditions would not be right for a second war for independence until 1894. Economically, Cuban sugar had sharp competition from European beet sugar, which forced Cuba to become even more dependent on the American market. But in 1894 the United States withdrew earlier tariff concessions granted to Cuban sugar, and the subsequent decline in trade ruined hundreds of sugar producers, both large and small. Politically, a combination of elite disillusionment with Spain's unwillingness to grant reforms and the emergence of José Martí and the Partido Revolucionario Cubano (PRC) brought a tenuous unity to the independence movement.

The significance of Martí (1853–1895) to Cuban nation building is hard to overstate. Born to Spanish parents, he became a fervent advocate of independence in his youth. His political ideas are difficult to classify because he was inspired by Spanish and Mexican liberalism, republicanism, socialism, anarchism, and the German neo-Kantian philosopher, Karl Krause (1781–1832), who promoted ideas about the "perfectibility of man" and social harmony. After being imprisoned by Spanish authorities, Martí was exiled to Spain, Mexico, Guatemala, and the United States. He was a keen observer of politics in those countries and he became particularly worried the about the possibility of American annexation of Cuba. His humble manner and simple, clear way of speaking and writing appealed to nationalist Cubans from all classes. Although some older veterans of the independence movement such as Maceo and Gómez still mistrusted civilian exiles, by 1894 Martí, exiled in New York, was clearly the accepted spokesman for the independence movement. Such unity was fragile, and older veterans such as Maceo were too hardened from past betrayals to have blind faith in white civilian leaders, including Martí. But on February 24, 1895, Martí, Gómez, and Maceo met in the town of Montecristi in the Dominican Republic to write a manifesto promising a civilized independence war, racial unity, protection for private property, and a democratic nation for all Cubans.

The war that followed, however, was hardly civilized. Martí was killed early in the conflict, and despite the unity among pro-independence forces, internal divisions over strategy, tactics, and the place of nonwhites in leadership roles surfaced again. While western planters were more willing to support independence than in the first war, the sharp social and economic division between eastern and western Cuba remained. As in the first war, Gómez and Maceo were the national political and military leaders of the revolt, and they had widespread support among poor and nonwhite Cubans. But the second war had clearer objectives, especially in the areas of racial equality and land for the landless. At the same time, Spain's clear unwillingness to grant meaningful reforms drove more elite whites into the armed struggle than in the first war. By 1897 the liberation army and the Spanish were locked into a war of attrition, with Spain losing ground, but at a terrible cost to both sides.

This series of events set the scene for American intervention in 1898. The reasons for intervention were complex, but in the United States the rise of a populist nationalism, growing economic and military power, and racist cultural imperialism fueled anti-Spanish sentiment. What intervention would accomplish was a source of considerable debate among Americans: some supported Cuban independence, while others believed Cuba's multiracial population and "violent past" made it unfit for nationhood. Certainly one reason for intervention was US unwillingness to permit the existence of a democratic multiracial Cuba so close to its borders when southern states were implementing Jim Crow legislation. Cuban political opinion was split along the same lines. Despite grave concerns about American intentions, many Cubans hoped the United States would intervene, leave, and let them run their own affairs. Others hoped for American annexation. Both hopes were disappointed. After the Americans intervened in 1898, they quickly defeated the Spanish and marginalized the Cuban liberation army under Gómez. In 1901 the United States imposed the Platt Amendment on Cuba's first constitution. According to this amendment, the United States had the right to intervene in Cuban affairs if political order or American property were threatened. The choice for Cubans was semi-independence or no independence at all. After two devastating wars for independence, this was a bitter bill to swallow. The legacy of this intervention shaped Cuban nationalist politics for the next 60 years.

25

The Rise of the American Mediterranean, 1846–1905

LUIS
MARTÍNEZ-FERNÁNDEZ

Expansionism in its various manifestations—territorial, economic, and cultural—is one of the primary overarching themes in the history of the United States, both as a policy of its government and a cultural value of its people. The desire for unrestrained westward expansion was one of the motivations leading North American colonists to fight for independence from Great Britain, which in 1763 prohibited expansion beyond the boundaries of the original 13 colonies. While primarily facing west and focusing on continental expansion, early US political leaders viewed parts of the Caribbean, particularly Cuba, as a "natural" appendage to the United States. Not yet ready to pursue an offensive expansionist agenda, however, they maintained an official position that was best summarized by John Quincy Adams in 1823 as the "ripe apple" dictum—namely, that Cuba and other Caribbean territories would eventually fall, as if pulled by gravity, into the political orbit of the United States. The main pillar of postponed expansionism was, of course, the 1823

Monroe Doctrine, which guarded against any attempt at European recolonization of nations and territories in the American hemisphere.

While the Caribbean's apples slowly ripened, the United States embarked on a sustained process of continental westward expansion that culminated during the second half of the 1840s with the annexation of the Republic of Texas (1845), the formal acquisition of the disputed Oregon Territory (1846), and, most important, the wresting from Mexico of more than half of its national territory (1848). In a matter of 75 years, the original 13 British colonies had expanded into a vast trans-continental nation. Only the mighty Pacific Ocean limited further westward expansion.

The American Mediterranean as a Regional Dream, 1848–60

The incorporation of large extensions of land into the United States became intricately intertwined with the historically divisive issue of slavery and its expansion. Territorial aggrandizement became an increasingly polarizing issue that divided the nation along political party lines, and later along sectional lines, eventually leading to the breakup of the Union before the Civil War.

President James K. Polk, a southern Democrat and slave owner, desired to expand the institution of slavery to all newly acquired territories, but failed due to strong opposition from legislators representing non-slaveholding states. Just a few months after winning the Mexican-American War, Polk pursued further territorial expansion by seeking to purchase Cuba from Spain for $100 million, a move repudiated by both Spain and the Whig Party. This was the nation's first significant attempt to expand beyond its contiguous territories. The purchase offer responded to two convergent expansionist currents: the desire to liberate Cuba from Spanish control and establish free trade with the island, a growing market for US exports and chief supplier of sugar; and an emerging brand of southern agrarian expansionism, championed by planters seeking to acquire new lands and new sources of slaves.

Running on an anti-expansionist platform, Whig presidential candidate Zachary Taylor won the 1848 election. Given his administration's reluctance to support, let alone seek, further land acquisitions, expansionism during Taylor's presidency took the form of clandestine filibustering efforts. Between 1849 and 1851, three expeditions set forth with the object of liberating Cuba from Spain and annexing it to the United States. Organized under Cuban and North American leadership and commanded by Venezuelan-born General Narciso López, the filibuster forces consisted largely of Southern veterans of the Mexican-American War. Some envisioned that 7 new states could be carved out of Cuba and Puerto Rico and as many as 25 out of Mexico. This brand of expansionism peaked in 1853 under two colorful filibusterers: former Mississippi governor General John A. Quitman and Tennessee-born adventurer William Walker. Fearing the "Africanization" of Cuba if slavery were abolished, Cuban planters recruited Quitman to lead a massive invasion of the island. Their rationale was that annexation to the United States would guarantee the institution of slavery, which was being threatened by British abolitionist pressures on Spain. The invasion did not materialize, however, due to the Americans' mounting differences with the Cuban planters and to pressures from the administration of President Franklin Pierce, which sought to enforce neutrality laws. In the spring of 1854, Quitman disbanded his troop of 10,000.

Walker was perhaps the most famous Southern filibusterer of the period. Without any government support, he launched his first expansionist endeavor in 1853 along with 45 other adventurers, who temporarily gained control over portions of Baja California. Shortly thereafter, Walker established the basically fictional Republic of Lower California, declared himself its president, and legalized slavery as a way to attract Southern settlers. His most daring expansionist projects, however, took place in Nicaragua. In 1855 he secured authorization from the Nicaraguan government to bring a small army of US filibusters; within a few months he gained control over his host government and on July 12, 1856, officially became its president. Walker's decision to reestablish slavery in Nicaragua, and the threat his government posed to neighboring Central American countries as well as to Cornelius Vanderbilt's interests in a trans-isthmian canal and railroad project, forged a Central American coalition that deposed him within a year.

A new wave of official US expansionism, as opposed to private filibustering schemes, crested during the mid-1850s. Pierce, a Northern Democrat sympathetic to Southern expansionism, launched a multipronged expansionist agenda that envisioned the purchase of Cuba from Spain and the Gadsden strip from Mexico, the acquisition of land in the Samaná Peninsula of the Dominican Republic, and the annexation of Hawaii. Much of the fuel behind the new efforts to acquire Cuba stemmed from fear that British pressures and Spain's seeming incapacity to maintain social order would lead to a successful island-wide slave revolt. By that time in the United States, expansion had become an eminently sectional issue that faced much opposition in the North.

While failing to establish political sovereignty over Cuba, either by incorporating it as a territory or by turning it into a colony, the United States achieved a high degree of control over both Cuba and Puerto Rico by subordinating them economically. These Spanish colonies became dependent on the US market as the primary consumer of their sugar and other exports. During the period 1856–59, the United States stood as the single largest market for the two islands, absorbing 44% of Cuba's exports and 49% of Puerto Rico's. By contrast, Spain, the islands' de jure metropole, received only small proportions of its colonies' agricultural output. To a lesser extent, these islands also became dependent on the United States for a wide array of imports, from rice and coal to hand tools and steam engines. As early as 1851, the US consul at Havana declared Cuba a de facto economic dependency of the United States. Spain had gradually yielded commercial control over the region to the United States while retaining administrative, military, and fiscal sovereignty. Spain, the maxim says, administered the colonies of the United States.

The American Mediterranean Interrupted, 1861–65

After years of mounting tension and growing antagonism between the South and the North, the US political crisis exploded with the secession of several Southern states and the formation of the Confederate States of America. A bloody, four-year civil war ensued, bringing about major disruptions in almost every regard, including foreign relations and international commerce. The outbreak of the Civil War signaled the end of southern agrarian expansionism. Fighting for the survival of the Confederacy, Southern planters and politicians were in no position to engage in expansionist adventures beyond their borders. Not only did they suspend all plans of wresting Cuba from Spain, they also went out of their way to establish friendly relations with Spain and other European naval powers, whose diplomatic recognition and trade became critical for the Confederacy's survival.

European powers took advantage of the debilitated political and military state of the Union by infringing on the Monroe Doctrine. Spanish troops invaded the Dominican Republic in 1861 and reestablished colonial rule over it. In January 1862, French, Spanish, and British forces landed in Veracruz, ostensibly to collect debts from the Mexican government. Within a few months, Spanish and British troops withdrew, yielding to the imperial pretensions of Napoleon III, whose troops remained to establish Maximilian as Mexico's emperor.

In the realm of commerce and navigation, the United States endured a wartime setback that paralleled its political retrenchment from the Caribbean. The shift toward a war economy reduced US capacity to absorb the Hispanic Caribbean's sugar output, part of which was now redirected toward Europe. Likewise, the volume of US exports to Cuba and Puerto Rico fell, a drop that was neutralized by increased exports from Great Britain, France, and Spain.

The American Mediterranean as a National Project, 1866–93

The end of the US Civil War in 1865 led to the emergence of new forms of expansionism as well as the extension of foreign trade and navigation. In the war's immediate aftermath, the United States once again imposed the Monroe Doctrine. Accordingly, Spanish troops retreated from the Dominican Republic in 1865; a few months later, Maximilian's Mexican empire collapsed as US troops threatened to cross the border in support of republican forces fighting to reinstall the wandering president Benito Juárez. Likewise, the United States regained the commercial supremacy it had momentarily lost in Cuba and Puerto Rico, and established itself as the Dominican Republic's leading trading partner.

The Confederacy's defeat brought an end to the old Southern dream of a slave-based Caribbean empire. It also prompted the emergence of a new brand of expansionism that sought not to acquire Caribbean territories, but rather to establish commercial and naval dominance over the region. This new model responded to two basic forces. First, foodstuffs and manufactures were being produced beyond the capacity of the US market to absorb them. Second, the Civil War had underscored the importance of naval power, and particularly of securing coaling stations and navigation routes, to protect what historian Walter LaFeber termed the "New Empire" (LaFeber 1963).

This New Empire sought to turn territories into economic, rather than political or military, dependencies of the United States. Under such arrangements, the United States remained free from the entanglements, responsibilities, and expenses of direct rule while reaping economic benefits through the creation of what have been called "informal colonies." Needless to say, economic dominance often brought with it indirect political control.

The three most salient, interlocking components of the emerging New Empire in the Caribbean were Cuba, the Dominican Republic, and the isthmus of Central America. Cuba became an increasingly important market for US exports and the premier source of sugar for the US market. Its significance was obvious during the three depressions that hit the US economy in 1873–78, 1882–85, and 1893–97. Because of its specialization in sugar, Cuba became dependent on the importation of US food, manufactures, and other products. In 1890 while Spain, Cuba and Puerto Rico's de jure metropole, absorbed only 7% of those two islands' exports, the United States purchased 91%. Trade with the United States grew during the next few years, with Cuban exports reaching nearly $80 million in 1893.

Another manifestation of this dependence was Cuba's growing reliance on US technology, know-how, and capital. The McKinley tariff of 1890 and the Foster-Cánovas reciprocity treaty of 1891 opened wide the US market to duty-free Cuban sugar; likewise, US products entered Cuba without import duties. While appearing to favor Cuba, the dramatic reduction of tariffs created an economic trap for the island. When the United States replaced the McKinley tariff with the new Wilson-Gorman tariff in 1894 and terminated the reciprocity treaty with Spain, chaos broke out on the island, helping trigger the Cuban War of Independence (1895–98). By then, US residents had invested an estimated $5 million in Cuban landholdings and other businesses.

In the aftermath of the US Civil War, the Dominican Republic also became a target of US expansionism. Unlike Cuba, which remained a Spanish colony, the Dominican Republic was a vulnerable, indebted nation with a chronically unstable political system. Its vulnerability pushed some Dominican leaders to offer generous economic concessions to US and European interests. Between 1865 and 1867, US President Andrew Johnson's administration embarked on negotiations with Dominican president Buenaventura Báez to acquire land in the coveted Samaná Peninsula, either by establishing sovereignty over it or through a lease agreement. These efforts failed, as did parallel attempts to purchase the Danish Virgin Islands of St. Thomas, St. Croix, and St. John. The Ulysses S. Grant administration (1869–77) was even more aggressive in its desire to gain control over the Dominican Republic, or at the very least to obtain extensive land rights and mining concessions there. Grant's aspiration responded to two basic objectives: first, to establish ports for commerce and naval defensive stations, and second, to use the Dominican Republic as a place in which to relocate free blacks, mostly from Northern cities.

In 1869, a desperate Báez offered to sell the Dominican Republic to the United States for $1.5 million. This treaty was later rejected by the US Senate, with opposition led by anti-annexationist Senator Charles Sumner. Annexationist efforts revived soon thereafter, this time led by a private US corporation, the Samaná Bay Company. In 1873 the company successfully acquired a 100-year lease over the Samaná Peninsula in exchange for yearly payments of $150,000. A military coup toppled Báez a few months later, and the contract was rescinded. While unsuccessful in his bid to acquire territories in the Dominican Republic, Grant made a significant contribution to expansionism by adding the non-transfer clause to the Monroe Doctrine. If the Danish, for example, were to sell their Virgin Islands to another nation, that would now be considered a violation of the Monroe Doctrine and viewed as a threat to US security.

Beginning in 1882, President Ulises Heureaux ruled over the Dominican Republic with a heavy hand until his assassination in 1899. After decades of political turmoil, Heureaux's era brought relative stability and peace, restoring some faith among foreign lenders and investors in the republic's ability to fulfill its economic commitments and pay its debts. Much of the foreign investment came in the guise of generous concessions by the Dominican government: railroads, mines, harbor dredging, road building, utilities, even factories and sugar mills. European investors poured capital into the republic, while Dominican authorities also worked closely with, and favored, US economic interests, which in turn worked with the US government to gain indirect political power over the struggling republic.

These cases were early manifestations of what latter came to be known as "dollar diplomacy": in essence, the policy of the US government to use its diplomatic and, if need be, its military might to create conditions that allowed US financial and commercial interests to penetrate weaker countries, particularly in the Caribbean and Latin America. This cycle, in turn, benefited the US government, as US financial interests made loans and acquired foreign debt bonds, displacing European financial interests and thus expanding the political influence of the United States over nations such as the Dominican Republic.

During the last two decades of the 1800s, US capital poured into the Dominican Republic as that small nation embarked on a sugar-centered, export-oriented economic growth strategy. The investments went heavily toward the construction of a national infrastructure to support the export economy: roads, seaports, railroads, and the like. US capital flowed even more during the 1890s as investors in the San Domingo Improvement Company (SDIC) purchased Dominican bonds held by European investors. Because their citizens held such bonds, European nations had retained much influence over the Dominican government, to the point that in 1892 they took over the island nation's customs houses as a way to guarantee debt payment from tariff income. European influence waned, however, when the SDIC acquired the debt bonds as well as control over Dominican customs houses. Heureaux's successor, Juan Isidro Jiménez, expelled the SDIC in 1901 and returned control over the customs houses to European holders of Dominican debt.

The third major focus of US expansionism in this period was the isthmus of Central America. Following the construction of the Panamanian Railway and Vanderbilt's trans-isthmian transportation system, attention shifted toward a project to build a canal connecting the Atlantic and Pacific oceans. Such a waterway would facilitate and reduce the cost of shipping goods as well as the transport of Navy vessels to protect expanding US navigation routes and ports. A French company, the Compagnie Universelle du Canal Interocéanique, began construction of the Panama Canal in 1881. The project failed due to thousands of deaths among workers, mostly to malaria and yellow fever, and gross miscalculation of its budget. The French company finally went bankrupt in 1888. By then, the US government and the Maritime Canal Company had begun preliminary work on an alternate canal crossing Nicaragua. After French investors holding assets of the aborted Panama Canal project lobbied the US government to take on the work remaining on that canal, the Nicaraguan alternative was discarded.

The Quest for the American Mediterranean Reaches a Feverish Peak, 1895-98

During the 1890s—particularly the second half of the decade—US expansionism toward the Caribbean culminated in the military occupation of Cuba, Puerto Rico, and a few smaller islands under Spanish jurisdiction. This expansionist thrust responded to a combination of international and domestic factors, ranging from geopolitical realignments and economic developments, such as the rapidly growing production capabilities of the United States, to the diffusion of pro-expansion ideologies such as the desire to spread Anglo-Saxon religion, democracy, and civilization. The depression of 1893–96 was another significant factor. The growing productivity of US agrarian, mining, and industrial producers required the expansion of their markets beyond the already saturated domestic arena. The search for foreign markets thus became critical to the stabilization of the US economy. Moreover, the US public became increasingly irate at Spain due to its all-out war against Cuban independence fighters and civilians. Various news media helped spread—and in some instances, exaggerate—the atrocities taking place in Cuba.

The second half of the 1890s was also a propitious juncture for US expansionism because of geopolitical realignments among various European nations. Spain, by now generally perceived as the "sick man of Europe," was losing control over the remnants of its once-vast empire as Cubans (1895–98) and Filipinos (1896–97) engaged in massive, protracted, bloody insurrections for their independence. Germany began seeking coaling stations and naval bases in various parts of the Caribbean as well as the Pacific, including the Haitian islet Môle St. Nicholas and the Pacific island of Samoa. Meanwhile, the British, who had for decades been the strongest opponents to US expansionism, reversed their position in the light of German expansionist plans in the Caribbean and elsewhere. The ensuing rapprochement between the United States and Great Britain rested for the most part on ethnic and cultural bonds of shared Anglo-Saxonism. Great Britain's approval of US mediation in a territorial dispute between Venezuela and Great Britain (1895) and its acceptance of the dismantling of the British protectorate over the Mosquito Coast (1894) demonstrated its growing acknowledgment of the United States as the hegemonic power in the Caribbean.

With the ascendance of a new Republican administration under President William McKinley in 1897, conditions became increasingly favorable for a more bellicose brand of expansionism: the actual military occupation and administration of Caribbean and Pacific islands. This new expansionist era exploded during what is generally referred to as the Spanish-American War, a name that not only is historically inaccurate but also oversimplifies the conflagration and dismisses the fact that Cubans and Filipinos had been fighting Spain long before US troops entered the war. Some historians prefer the more accurate terms Spanish-Cuban-American War and Spanish-American-Cuban-Filipino War.

Conditions in Cuba had deteriorated dramatically during the mid-1890s. As the economic crisis brought on by the new US tariff deepened, Spanish colonial rule became increasingly brutal—arguably genocidal. In contrast, Puerto Rico remained loyal to Spain and, as a reward of sorts, was allowed to inaugurate a new autonomous form of government in the spring of 1898. Although on paper the Autonomic Charter satisfied many of the aspirations of Puerto Rico's liberals, its true reach was never tested: US troops invaded the island only six days after the autonomous government took office. The invading forces found virtually no armed Spanish opposition and were actually received festively by Puerto Rico's Creole population. Meanwhile, in Cuba, US and Cuban forces coordinated military efforts to defeat Spain, but Cuban patriots were alienated by US reluctance to include Cuban representatives in the peace negotiations.

The American Mediterranean as a Fait Accompli, 1899–1905

With Spain's formal cession of Puerto Rico, the Philippines, and Guam to the United States, the US military occupation of Cuba (1898–1902), and the formal annexation of Hawaii (1898), the United States became a de facto imperial power. Over the next few years, US government and business interests expanded their influence over other Caribbean islands and locations, establishing protectorates over Cuba, Panama, and the Dominican Republic and exercising "gunboat diplomacy" and treaty stipulations to avoid any threat of European intervention or expansionist ventures. Germany, in particular, became increasingly interested in establishing coaling stations or outright colonies at various locations in the Caribbean and the Pacific Ocean, and in 1899 it acquired from Spain the Mariana and Carolina Islands as well as Palau.

In 1898 Puerto Rico became the first formal US Caribbean colony. The island remained under military rule until 1900, when the Foraker Act created a civilian colonial form of government and declared Puerto Rico an unincorporated territory of the United States. The island's political elites, for the most part, responded positively to the US occupation and initially sought full integration into the nation through citizenship and statehood. But several military decrees soon alienated Puerto Rico's traditional reformist and autonomist elites. The Foraker Act, which failed to grant either US citizenship or statehood, turned out to be a great disillusionment.

The two-year period between the US invasion and the proclamation of the Foraker Act brought legal and constitutional changes with far-reaching economic and social consequences. Military decrees and new laws incorporated Puerto Rico into the US tariff and navigation system, established the rate of monetary exchange, and limited land ownership by individuals and corporations to 500 acres. Inclusion in the US tariff system penalized Puerto Rico's coffee sector, making its product too expensive for traditional European markets. Puerto Rican sugar, meanwhile, received preferential access to the US market: a 15% tariff at first, and no tariff after 1902. These new rules had an immediate impact on Puerto Rico's economy and commerce. Whereas in 1896 coffee had constituted 60% and sugar 26% of the island's exports, by 1901 coffee's proportion among all exports dropped to 20% while sugar's rose to 55%. During those early years of colonial domination, US capital also poured into construction, infrastructure, and utilities projects as well as into the sugar industry, most notably the Aguirre Corporation (1899) and the South Porto Rico Sugar Company (1899).

Postwar developments in neighboring Cuba differed markedly. Most saliently, while the United States retained Puerto Rico indefinitely as a formal colony, it withdrew its troops from Cuba in 1902 after forcing the island to accept the Platt Amendment to the Cuban constitution. Two major factors kept the United States from annexing Cuba: the Teller Amendment, a US Senate document that supported intervention in Cuba only if it was temporary, and the fact that Cuba's patriots would not accept the humiliation of coming under US rule after having fought for decades for their independence.

During the four-year occupation of Cuba, US military forces disarmed and disbanded the Cuban revolutionary army and worked diligently toward improving sanitation, particularly through the eradication of yellow fever and malaria. Political stability and a healthful environment were necessary preconditions for the establishment and prosperity of US corporations on Cuban soil. Although in Puerto Rico the Foraker Act specifically forbade the granting of concessions to US corporations during the military occupation (they were liberally dispensed afterward), in Cuba Generals John Brooke and Leonard Wood granted hundreds of generous concessions for railroad construction, mining, and utilities, and even made extensive land grants at bargain prices. During the military occupation, US corporations and entrepreneurs invested more than $30 million on the island. By 1902, US interests owned 10% of the land, controlled 90% of tobacco exports, owned 75% of ranch lands, and had a substantial hold over railroads, utilities, and other areas of the economy. Historian Louis A. Pérez, Jr. put it best: The Cubans "were the winners who had lost everything" (Pérez 1986, 85).

While the military occupation was meant to be short-lived, turning the island into a neocolonial protectorate remained a long-term aspiration, requiring legal and institutional guarantees for the United States to retain Cuba under its economic grip and to maintain the island's peace and political stability. The most notorious constitutional mechanism for establishing a protectorate over Cuba was the Platt Amendment, which Cubans were forced to accept as a requisite for the end of US occupation. The amendment's clauses severely curbed Cuba's independence by limiting its capacity to engage in foreign treaties or loan arrangements that might make the island vulnerable to foreign intervention. Another stipulation prohibited the cession of any portion of Cuban territory to foreign nations. Most humiliating of all was article 3, which allowed US military intervention if needed to restore order and stability on the island. Moreover, the Platt Amendment stipulated the sale or lease of portions of Cuban territory for the establishment of coaling stations or naval bases. This provision was formalized in 1903, when a treaty leased Guantánamo Bay and Bahía Honda to the United States in perpetuity. In that same year, the Reciprocity Treaty gave the United States a substantial advantage over Cuba's other trading partners. While it granted Cuban sugar a 20% discount in US import tariffs, it gave US imports to Cuba even more generous tariff discounts ranging from 20% to 40%.

During the same period two other circum-Caribbean nations, the Dominican Republic and Panama, were also reduced to the status of US protectorates. In the Dominican case the 20th century began chaotically, with political turmoil and severe financial problems. European warships were deployed to the Dominican Republic in 1900, 1903, and 1904 to intimidate the Dominicans into paying their debt to European bondholders and creditors. President Theodore Roosevelt responded by dispatching US troops to the embattled republic in 1903 and 1904. To avoid further European intervention, in 1904 Roosevelt appointed a US official to oversee tax collections in the struggling nation's customs houses; in the following year, this arrangement was further formalized when the United States took responsibility for collecting import and export taxes, retaining 55% of tariff revenues to pay the republic's creditors while turning over the remaining 45% to the Dominican government. A similar receivership status had been imposed on Haiti in 1903. This form of interventionism represented yet another stage in the expanding scope of the Monroe Doctrine. Known as the Roosevelt Corollary, the new doctrine established the US right to intervene anywhere in the hemisphere to stabilize political and financial crises that could lead to intervention by foreign nations.

The construction of a US–controlled canal in Panama became the centerpiece of Roosevelt's strategy for domination of the circum-Caribbean; he deemed it vital for the expansion of US commerce and the desired control of navigational routes in the Atlantic and Pacific Oceans. In 1902, French investors who still held bonds of the original canal project agreed to sell them to the US government. A major obstacle remained, however: Panama was a province of Colombia and any canal treaty had to be ratified by the Colombian senate. After Colombia's senators rejected the proposed agreement, the United States prodded Panamanians into a separatist revolt. With the support of US troops and battleships, the Panamanians became independent almost by default on November 3, 1903; a total of five shots were fired, and the death toll amounted to one person. In less than three months, the newly independent nation of Panama yielded what came to be known as the Panama Canal Zone to the United States in exchange for $10 million. The treaty was reached under scandalous circumstances: French lobbyist Philippe Bunau-Varilla appointed himself foreign relations secretary of the virtually fictitious infant Republic of Panama, and negotiated the cession of the Panama Canal Zone without ever consulting the Panamanians. In light of the US decision to pursue construction of the isthmian canal through Panama, Nicaragua's President José Santos Zelaya engaged in negotiations with Germany and Japan for the construction of another canal in Nicaragua. This was unacceptable for the US government, which proceeded to undermine Zelaya's rule and support his political opponents.

A major episode signaling the achievement of US hegemony over the Caribbean and the affirmation of the Roosevelt Corollary transpired between 1902 and 1905 in Venezuela. In 1902, British and German warships blockaded the Venezuelan coast in a show of force to collect debts owed to European companies and nationals. Unwilling to accept this sort of intervention, the United States threatened to go to war over the matter, forcing the European fleet to withdraw. Quite significantly, the British accepted the fact that the United States had become the American Mediterranean's hegemonic power. In the words of British Prime Minister Arthur J. Balfour (1903): "The Monroe Doctrine has no enemies in this country that I know of. We welcome any increase of the influence of the United States of America upon the Great Western Hemisphere" (Edington, 1905). Germany acquiesced as well, although reluctantly so—ending, for the time being, its aggressive policy of seeking territories in the Caribbean. When Theodore Roosevelt declared in 1904 that the United States now claimed "international police power" over the Western Hemisphere, the world accepted it as a matter of fact.

WORKS CITED

Edington, Thomas B. 1905. *The Monroe Doctrine.* Boston: Little, Brown, and Co.

LaFeber, Walter. 1963. *The New Empire: An Interpretation of American Expansion, 1860–1898.* Ithaca, NY: Cornell University Press.

Pérez, Louis A., Jr. 1986. *Cuba under the Platt Amendment, 1902–1934.* Pittsburgh: University of Pittsburgh Press.

26

The Conundrum of Race

ELIZABETH COOPER

Retooling Inequality

The transformation of Caribbean societies after the end of slavery took place over a long 19th century—from the Haitian Revolution of the 1790s until the dawn of the 20th century. Emancipation carried the possibility of new individual autonomy and political voice for slaves in the Caribbean. Yet while freedom and citizenship were the ultimate goals for slaves and abolitionists, many planters and politicians never considered them desirable or inevitable. The established planter interests in the Caribbean colonies and the European metropoles had reaped unprecedented profits from the transatlantic economy of plantation slavery, and they treated the 19th-century tides of abolition with great trepidation and often violent repression. At the same time, emerging sectors of the planter class and the urban bourgeoisie—including free people of African descent—found new chances for profits and political power in wage labor, innovations in sugar production, and new constituencies of freed people and immigrants. Indeed, the end of slavery in the Caribbean opened the immediate opportunity and challenge for all sectors of society to shape the space between the injustices of chattel slavery and the promises of modern freedom.

The development of the African slave trade and the South Atlantic System was intimately tied to the expansion of colonial plantation sugar production across the Caribbean region. During the 16th and 17th centuries, Spanish and French powers dominated Caribbean sugar production. In the late 18th century, the British colonies were at the center of the so-called triangular trade. By 1800 the British Caribbean sugar islands had reached their peak of production, slave importation, and profitability. In the mid-19th century the Spanish colonies, particularly Cuba, reemerged as the dominant sugar producers and slave importers in the Caribbean. The overwhelming importance of the Caribbean to the world economy was evidenced, in part, by the profits gained on the commodity markets of Antwerp and London and the rising levels of sugar consumption in rapidly industrializing Europe. By 1800, for example, sugar had become a necessity for the English working class; and a century later, sugar accounted for approximately one-fifth of calories in the English diet (Mintz 1985, 6). Plantation sugar production relied on a complex system of slave labor, cultivation organization, and time regimentation, and on new forms of capital and commodity exchange. The high level of abstraction and alienation that characterized Caribbean slavery has led anthropologist Sidney Mintz to call the Caribbean the first modern people and region.

The Haitian Revolution unequivocally exposed the contradictory yet deeply entangled relationship among modernity, European colonialism, and racial slavery in the Caribbean. By 1804 Haiti had achieved independence from French colonial rule, abolished slavery, and became the second independent nation in the hemisphere—the first in the Caribbean. Although national independence for Haiti—a black nation at the center of the Atlantic world economy—was widely perceived as an historical aberration (Trouillot 1995), the fundamental contradiction between Enlightenment philosophical principles and chattel slavery was not lost on Caribbean planters or colonial authorities, who deeply feared the spread of the Haitian Revolution. Neither was the importance of the political status of free people of African descent in Caribbean slave societies. In 1802 Governor Francis Seaforth of Barbados articulated the colonial "dilemma" in the following way: "There is . . . a third description of people from whom I am more suspicious of evil than from either the whites or the slaves, and yet whom I cannot bring myself to call free. I think unappropriated people would be a more proper denomination for them, for though not the property of other individuals they do not enjoy the shadow of any civil right" (Meditz and Hanratty 1987). Seaforth not only recognized the ideological and political dilemma free nonwhites posed to Caribbean slave society, but also foreshadowed the impending 19th-century contests over black economic and political power in a world without chattel slavery.

The withdrawal of Haiti from the world market left a gaping hole in sugar production and thus posed a dilemma: new demand and opportunity for profits from sugar production, with also greater dynamism for abolition. In 1807 both houses of the British Parliament passed legislation abolishing the slave trade. By far the largest importer of slaves at this time, Britain clearly intended to halt other colonial powers from trading in slaves. Spain, however, had just begun to redevelop sugar production in its Caribbean colonies, and Cuba would become the world's largest sugar producer by mid-century. Although Spain reluctantly signed a treaty with Britain in 1817 pledging to end participation in the slave trade, enforcement of anti–slave-trade legislation and treaties was lax and the illegal slave trade continued well into the century. Many planters and investors—particularly, but not solely, in the Spanish Caribbean—hoped the cessation of the slave trade and experiments in the use of indentured labor would postpone the total abolition of plantation slavery and, most important, maintain profits. In fashioning responses and obstacles to the emerging economic and social changes, the Caribbean plantocracy drew on contemporary European and North American scientific thought.

Some influential early-19th-century theories of human development purported that the basic dynamic of human society was degeneration. Every society in the world had degenerated since the origin of human life, but to differing degrees: whites less, blacks more. Variations in levels of degeneration ostensibly correlated to the different environments in which peoples lived—temperate climates ideal for and conducive to civilization, tropical climates dangerous (Gould 1996, 71). This belief was considered to be corroborated, in part, by the disproportionately high death toll among indigenous people and Africans in the Americas, and the decline in mortality from contagious diseases in European countries over the 19th century. Environmental forces were considered so strong that healthy and "civilized" persons were at risk of degeneration if they spent too much time in tropical climates or adapted their habits to those of "uncivilized peoples."

By the second half of the century, the work of Jean-Baptiste Lamarck and Charles Darwin on heritable traits and evolution began to circulate in the Atlantic world. Notions of "survival of the fittest" were translated into what became known as "social Darwinism," a pseudoscientific ideology based on the belief that the power structures within and among human societies could be explained by biological evolution. Different cultures and societies could thereby be set on an evolutionary continuum. Though social Darwinism conceived the thrust of human society in terms of progress rather than degeneration, racial hierarchies established in earlier theories of degeneration remained intact. Evolution never completely overtook degeneration as a paradigm. Rather, the two continued to interact over the course of the 19th and early 20th centuries.

New fields of study in physical anthropology and psychology—such as craniology (the study of the bones of the skull), phrenology (the study of personality through the shape of the skull), and physiognomy (the study of personality through facial features)—focused on explaining alleged differences in development between human populations. The American physician and naturalist Samuel George Morton and the French physician and physical anthropologist Paul Broca both asserted a correlation between brain size and intelligence, which, they argued, constituted evidence of intelligence hierarchies among population groups—within and among different societies. Broca invented a device for measuring the dimensions of skulls, called a "craniometer," to quantify these differences, and he inspired other scientists to take up similar research. The Italian criminologist and psychologist Cesare Lombroso argued that "deviant" social behavior was an inherited trait that was identifiable through one's physiognomy. These scientists were part of a larger intellectual trend proposing that data collection and statistical analysis would reveal the fundamental dynamics of the natural world and society. The application of the science of heredity and physical anthropology to social analysis led to explaining social differentiation—and, in particular, social inequalities—through hereditary traits that could be quantified through physical measurements and mental tests.

Contemporary public health scientists also dedicated themselves to collecting and analyzing statistics to determine the causes, and prevent the spread of, infectious diseases. Impoverished high-density urban neighborhoods characteristic of the Industrial Revolution produced conditions that facilitated the rapid spread of diseases such as cholera, typhoid, gonorrhea, and smallpox among Europe's poor and working classes. The revelation that environmental conditions increased the epidemiological rates of disease incidence transformed the outlook and purpose of social government. The science of public health and "social hygiene" became central to 19th-century policy. Not only was the physiological health of the population at stake, but also the moral health of society. Good habits and hygiene were considered the foundation of a healthy nation. Population control and sanitation became two pillars of most European governments' approach to public health. Groups considered particularly "dangerous," such as the destitute and prostitutes, as well as the sick were confined to new quarantine houses and "lock hospitals" until deemed fit and healthy enough to return to society. Alexandre Parent Duchatêlet's groundbreaking research on venereal disease and the lives of prostitutes led him to argue both for a national law to regulate prostitution and for investment in the public sewer system. Spanning the fields of psychology, phrenology, statistics, and medicine, Duchatêlet's work epitomized the belief that social progress and population control were interwoven.

Progress, following the logic of these new scientific movements, could be achieved through the manipulation of human reproduction and the reformation of "unfit" groups. The scientist Francis Galton advocated for selective breeding to shape and purify human society (Stepan 1991), and, like Lombroso, influenced policy makers and politicians of the day. William Gladstone, the former chancellor of the exchequer and prime minister of Britain, was familiar with and sympathetic to Galton's work, while Lombroso's research was used by sentencing and prison reform activists. Scientists would also proclaim their own political conclusions based on their research. The French naturalist Georges Cuvier explicitly argued that intelligence was hereditary and that Africans were the most "degraded race" and would "never arrive at regular government" (Gould 1996, 69).

The mixture of new ideas in hereditary biology, public health, psychology, and criminology had distinct ramifications for Caribbean societies in the era of abolition. When the British Parliament abolished slavery in the colonies in 1833, free brown Jamaicans—also known as "mulattoes"—had already achieved the right to vote three years earlier. Yet abolition did not immediately mean similar political rights for ex-slaves; those who supported the cause of abolition by no means unanimously favored granting them universal civil and social rights. Indeed, support for abolition could be coupled with plans to forcefully discipline and educate "primitive," "immature," and "undisciplined" black workers.

An "apprenticeship" system was devised by the Colonial Office, ostensibly to facilitate the transition to freedom throughout the British West Indies (except in Antigua and Barbados). Under this system, ex-slaves were to continue to work without wages for their former masters as "apprentices" for six years, during which time they would be civilized for modern life and citizenship. Planters and politicians in different colonies across the British West Indies were given significant leeway in implementing apprenticeship, but their shared fundamental goal was the end of slave labor without the loss of profits or productivity. Their racist rhetoric of laziness and immorality was based in part on firsthand knowledge that ex-slaves would often choose not to work for their former masters, or as plantation labor at all, preferring wherever possible to set themselves up as peasant producers. Casting ex-slaves as inherently immoral, antisocial, and lazy was critical to justifying the draconian measures taken to control the labor force and maintain profits without having to negotiate the terms and conditions of work and the standard of living of workers. Throughout the British colonies planters brutally overworked and punished their "apprentices," who in turn protested vehemently against the British authorities' version of freedom. Originally designed to last six years, apprenticeship collapsed in 1838 under pressure from popular protests in the colonies and abolitionists in Britain.

Spain finally began to enforce anti–slave-trade laws in mid-century, and by 1865 the transatlantic slave trade had become sporadic. In contrast to events in the British West Indies, however, the end of the slave trade and the abolition of slavery in the Spanish Caribbean colonies was part and parcel of a protracted anticolonial struggle. Indeed, the event considered to have sparked the first phase of the Cuban War for Independence—the Grito de Yara of 1868—came when the planter Carlos Manuel de Céspedes declared independence from Spain and freed the slaves who joined the rebellion. The connection between national liberation and slave emancipation was especially clear to Afro-Cubans, who joined the liberation cause in disproportionate numbers—many taking on high-ranking positions. Partly in response to the great numbers of free and enslaved Afro-Cubans who joined the anti-Spanish cause, Spain created an apprenticeship system known as the *patronato* immediately after the first phase of anti-colonial fighting. Though broadly similar to the British system, the patronato also extended the previously established rights to legal recourse and self-purchase to "apprentices." As in the British West Indies, however, the Spanish apprenticeship came to an early end in 1886 under immense pressure from anticolonial and antislavery forces.

Emancipation was ultimately framed by underlying political questions: who had legitimate claims to power and resources? And what forms of property, politics, and ideology would sustain these claims?

Given the alternatives of alienated and regimented plantation labor or a precarious life of debt peonage, ex-slaves in the Caribbean initially opted overwhelmingly to cultivate small plots of land or form rural free villages. Some freed people laid claim to the houses and grounds they had occupied under slavery, while others left the plantations to cultivate other lands. In the British Caribbean between 1838 and 1844, some 19,000 freed people left the plantations, bought land, and settled in free villages. In some cases when they lacked the capital to purchase land, they squatted on abandoned or uncultivated land, particularly in Jamaica (Mintz 1974, 160). Freed people cultivated crops such as rice, bananas, sugar, tobacco, cacao, and coffee, and ground provisions for sale in the market and for personal consumption. In stark contrast to the predictions of planters, freed people proved hard-working and entrepreneurial. However, this was not the sort of hard work or motivation from which planters could profit.

Not all ex-slaves decided to live as peasant or yeomen farmers. Those in the Spanish-speaking Caribbean tended to continue doing plantation agricultural work, individually or with labor gangs; to grow and sell sugarcane from leased small plots of land known as *colonos*; to work as part-time wage earners or in part-time sugar cultivation; or to emigrate from the sugar regions entirely (Scott 1993, 21). Many planters construed ex-slaves' decisions to work on plantations as evidence of their desire to remain with former masters. But from the perspective of the freed person, as the Guyanese historian and political leader Walter Rodney has noted, the question was: "What were the ramifications of leaving plantations or staying but bargaining for better standard of living?" (Rodney, 1981, 352). A savvy and sophisticated work force, freed people made strategic decisions about how best to manipulate the terms of labor, achieve the remuneration they knew they deserved, and find some form of human self-expression.

Planters, legislative assemblies, and magistrates across the Caribbean struggled to create and enforce legal procedures in response to the dynamism of the new peasantry and working class. On April 6, 1839, the police magistrate of St. Andrews Parish in Barbados addressed a meeting of free people thus: "Many of you have run away with the idea that you have a legal right to live in the cottages in which you resided before you were free . . . you are much deceived. Some of you, I am told, say when you are requested to work "here or there," at the bidding of the employer, that you will not, but will do this or that pleasing your own selves. Now this is decidedly wrong and rude" (*Barbados Mercury*, April 6, 1839).

Planters and government authorities crafted labor regimes and laws intended to control ex-slaves' movements and severely limit their economic options, particularly their access to land—including debt peonage, contract labor with penal sanctions, and regressive taxation aimed at forcing peasants to become wage laborers. Other forms of draconian population control, such as vagrancy laws and the violent repression of "primitive African" cultural practices and "witchcraft," were critical to justifying white planters' refusal to relinquish powers and privileges that had been garnered under slavery. These new laws were founded on the argument that black people in general were "unfit"—biologically, intellectually, and morally—to make sound individual or social judgments.

In addition to local laws and repressive tactics, planters and politicians who feared black majority rule and "racial degeneration" after slavery viewed the importation of immigrant labor to be both socially and economically advantageous. Though used sporadically prior to the 19th century, indentured labor increased significantly after abolition and continued into the early 20th century, particularly in the British colonial sphere. Also increasing was so-called spontaneous immigration from the destitute of Europe. Planters and governments across the Caribbean subsidized indentured or "contract" labor from colonial domains such as the Canary Islands, Mauritius, China, and the Indian subcontinent. Between 1838 and 1917, nearly half a million immigrants from British India came to work on British West Indian sugar plantations, the majority going to new sugar-producing zones with fertile lands. Guyana imported 240,000 workers; Trinidad, 145,000; Jamaica, 21,500; Grenada, 2,570; St. Vincent, 1,820; and St. Lucia, 1,550. In addition, between 1853 and 1879, British Guiana imported more than 14,000 Chinese workers, with a few going to some of the other colonies (Meditz and Hanratty 1987). In the Spanish colonies, private and governmental authorities contracted indentured Chinese labor and subsidized European immigration in an effort to create a labor surplus, push down wages, and "whiten" the island. Between 1898 and 1916 approximately 440,000 Spanish immigrants arrived in Cuba, a number that nearly doubled by 1930 (De la Fuente 2000)

The influx of immigrant workers constrained the strategies of ex-slaves to maximize their autonomy and their power to bargain with former masters. Many Afro-Caribbeans mobilized, protested, and withheld their own labor in opposition to the cynical use of immigrant labor to push wages down. At times protests and strikes took on a xenophobic and nationalistic character. Immigration also radically changed the urban landscape of Caribbean society. Immigrant shop owners and tradesmen competed with small businesses that historically had been controlled by free people of African descent—particularly in cities like Kingston and Havana, and also in the Spanish colonies more generally, which had always had higher rates of manumission and self-purchase. Though immigration and indentured labor were universally a force for change, their specific implications depended on the unique context of each Caribbean society. In British Guiana, for example, East Indian immigrants dominated agricultural work after emancipation, while in Jamaica they predominantly worked in or owned small businesses and other urban trades.

Afro-Caribbeans and immigrants were not just competitors, however. The cultural and social mixture that took place in post-emancipation Caribbean societies led to class and social distinctions that could not be readily made along "racial" lines. At the same time, growing economic pressure coupled with new limits placed on the political organization of black Caribbean people—including historically free people of African descent—created a common experience of racial oppression among Afro-Caribbeans and gave impetus to popular mobilization and formation of political parties.

Black men in post-emancipation Jamaica had the right to vote if they owned property worth six pounds, or paid thirty pounds in rent, or three pounds in direct taxes. Though the majority of Afro-Jamaicans were thereby excluded from voting, as many as 20,000 black small freeholders might have met the property qualification alone. The requirements for membership in the Jamaican Assembly were far more restrictive (Holt 1992, 216–17), yet a number of professional Jamaicans of African descent managed to get elected. The vast majority of Afro-Jamaican Assembly representatives formed a faction called the Town Party.

By the mid-1840s the Town Party began to pose a real challenge to planters in the Jamaican legislature. Town Party representatives consistently voted as a bloc and attended Assembly sessions more often than the planters (Holt 1992, 229). Rampant landlord absenteeism no doubt contributed to this process. Town Party members used their knowledge of everyday Jamaican realities to their political advantage. In response, planters instigated an election reform movement designed to undermine the predominantly Afro-Jamaican working class and freeholder constituencies of the Town Party. After much debate and repeated failed votes, an election bill was eventually passed in 1859 which introduced a new poll tax that reduced the number of freeholder registered voters from 60% of registered voters in 1858 to only 30% in 1860 (Holt 1992, 258).

By undermining Afro-Jamaican political power, planters cleared the way for further neglect of legislation and policy that might support Jamaica's working people. Indeed, black Jamaicans' lives worsened dramatically over the course of the early 1860s. In turn, peasants, workers and freeholders responded with a surge in attacks on property—especially plantation buildings and animals—and seizure of abandoned lands. This was true especially in the region of St. Thomas in the east, where sugar plantations with absentee landlords sat unproductive.

In 1865 the secretary of the Baptist Missionary Society, Edward Bean Underhill, wrote a letter to the British secretary of state for the colonies based on his travels and experiences in Jamaica during the 1850s and 1860s. He closely described the difficult circumstances of the majority of Jamaican people, and sharply criticized the Jamaican plantocracy for their focus on supporting plantations rather than building local markets and meeting working people's needs. Underhill also criticized high taxation and the restriction of the political rights of Afro-Jamaicans. Underhill's letter was published in the *Jamaican Guardian* on March 21, 1865 (Heuman 1994, 46). The Jamaican governor, Edward Eyre, responded by placing the blame for Jamaica's woes on peasant indolence and immorality. While sparking high-level debate about Jamaican society, the real power of Underhill's letter came from the space it opened for a range of political issues to be discussed and voiced at the grassroots level.

Town Party leaders, Baptist deacons, and others organized public meetings across the island to draft petitions, write letters, and mobilize protests. Among the leaders was George William Gordon, a major opponent of the Jamaican governor and an Afro-Jamaican Town Party representative to the Assembly. Gordon led a series of meetings in Kingston between May and June of 1865 in which he called upon all descendants of Africans in every Jamaican parish to form societies and hold public meetings. Key issues raised in these "Underhill" meetings included the planters' tendency to withhold wages, the prices of goods on the market, the taxes on selling goods, and ejections from lands. But these petitions fell on deaf ears in Britain, which was not prepared to take up the cause of Jamaican freeholders and laborers.

Having roused his parishioners for months toward a confrontation with magistrates and militiamen who enforced unjust laws against freeholders and peasants, Paul Bogle, a deacon of a Jamaican Native Baptist chapel and a close friend of Gordon, eventually led hundreds of peasant protesters on October 9, 1865, at Morant Bay in St. Thomas in the east. The rebellion spread quickly among both peasants and sugar workers. The colonial response was swift and brutal. Altogether, Governor Eyre ordered nearly 500 peasants executed, 600 brutally flogged, and 1,000 houses burned. Colonial authorities argued that the rebellion proved the failure of emancipation and Afro-Jamaicans' incapacity for self rule (Holt 1992, 299–307). Though the tide of public opinion in Britain turned against the Jamaican planter class after the Morant Bay rebellion, government officials sided with Governor Eyre. In December 1865 the Jamaica Assembly abolished itself, making way for crown colony government. The act was the final gesture of the old planter oligarchy, symbolizing that it did not wish to share political power in a democratic way.

As in Jamaica, freed people in post-emancipation Cuba had sought out accessible land to cultivate. Though the west of the island continued to be dominated by large sugar plantations, parts of eastern Cuba became increasingly controlled by peasants and small farmers. The intervention of the United States government at the final stages of Cuba's war for independence from Spain fundamentally shaped the development of post-emancipation Cuban society. US forces occupied the island from 1899 until 1902. During that occupation, the United States controlled all aspects of government and heavily influenced trade and investment in the island. Cuban peasants, in particular, found themselves under attack as US land purchases quadrupled between 1896 and 1911. Between 1899 and 1905, North American corporations and individual investors acquired 60% of Cuba's rural properties (De la Fuente 2000, 109).

US intervention helped undermine the Afro-Cubans' role in bringing about Cuban independence and their claims to power and authority in the new republic. The United States limited suffrage in Cuba to those over 21 and literate, with property valued more than US$250. Veterans of the war were officially exempt from these restrictions, though Afro-Cubans' veteran status was often called into question. In 1901 the US military governor, Leonard Wood, explicitly called for the "whitening" of Cuban society, and the occupation troops increasingly aimed at installing American-style forms of racial segregation. Although the American occupation officially ended in 1902, the United States retained the right to intervene in Cuban affairs through the Platt Amendment.

Universal male suffrage was finally instituted in Cuba by the first republican government, fulfilling the *independista* dream (espoused most notably by independence leaders José Martí and Antonio Maceo) of a transracial political brotherhood. However, the meanings of citizenship in the new Cuban Republic were not transparent, and they continued to be fiercely contested. Specifically, heated contests developed regarding Afro-Cuban political party organization and membership in the new government. Indeed, Afro-Cubans found themselves worse off in the new republic than during the war for independence, when many held public jobs and military positions.

In response to their increasing social and political marginalization, a group of veterans of the Cuban war of independence founded the Partido Independiente de Color (PIC) in Havana in 1908. This party was unique among Afro-Cuban civic organizations in its focus on the role of the state in administering justice and its emphasis on electoral representation for Afro-Cubans. The PIC platform demanded resources and rights from the state, such as education, health care, representation in the military, agrarian reform, and government leadership in negotiating worker-management conflicts. These demands were based on presumed rights and status in society, not on rights that had yet to be achieved (Bronfman 2004, 77). In what amounted to a direct attack on the PIC in 1909, the Cuban senate passed the Morúa Law, officially prohibiting political parties from organizing on the basis of race. Founded to help equalize social opportunity and political representation for all people, the PIC was silenced on the grounds that the Republic of Cuba was a "raceless" nation.

In 1912, three years after the party's prohibition, members of the PIC organized armed political protests across Cuba for the repeal of the Morúa Law. Most of these uprisings were stunted through mass arrests. In the eastern province of Oriente, however, the rebellion spread like wildfire. Protests broke out in May, and an estimated 10,000 workers and peasants participated, attacking mostly foreign and sugar property (Perez 1986, 533). US forces landed in the eastern part of the island in late May to aid the Cuban armed forces, who violently repressed the rebellion, massacring, according to estimates, between 2,000 and 6,000 Afro-Cuban peasants (Helg 2005, 189).

The PIC rebellion represented the coming together of the peasant class and a new political movement among urban liberal democratic Afro-Cubans. As historian Louis Perez Jr. has put it, "The causes of the rebellion were indeed racial and political. The sources of the rebellion, however, were social and economic" (Perez 1986, 5). The economic interests behind the rebellion's repression can be inferred in part from the fact that the percentage of Cuban sugar produced in US-owned mills increased from 15% in 1906—before the rebellion—to 75% by 1928 (Moore 1997, 27).

The Morant Bay Rebellion in Jamaica and the PIC uprising in Cuba proved critical turning points in the transformation of post-emancipation Jamaican and Cuban societies. The rebellions themselves reflected the political mobilization of a new Caribbean peasantry as well as a new political organization and consciousness on the part of Cubans and Jamaicans of African descent. Occurring only a few decades after emancipation, they were portrayed as signs of an impending "war of the races" rather than as outcomes of post-emancipation political and class conflict. In both cases, the official response to popular pressure for economic autonomy and political representation was wholesale slaughter of black protesters. This response, along with the political regimes imposed after the rebellions, signaled a reconfiguration of how race would be used to maintain white supremacy and colonial relations in societies no longer structured by chattel slavery.

Significant differences between the Jamaican and Cuban societies shaped the political outcomes of these rebellions. In Jamaica the ruling elites opted for a return to direct British rule rather than popular political representation. With periodic adjustments, crown colony government endured until the middle of the 20th century. In the Cuban case, emancipation had coincided with a successful 30-year war for independence from Spanish colonial rule, yet it was, as one observer has noted, "a most peculiar independence, . . . that transferred Cuba from the direct rule of one empire to the indirect rule of a new one" (Ferrer 1999, 1). In both societies, new racial discourses justified British and US claims of political immaturity among working men and women of African descent. At the same time, the Morant Bay and PIC rebellions exemplify how these same men and women recognized their common interests and struggles in a post-emancipation world and demanded their rights to social standing and political representation. As Walter Rodney would later observe, "Imperialism extinguished the rights of subjugated peoples to make their own autonomous history . . . Self-expression on the part of oppressed working people in that era therefore constitutes a definite historical achievement" (Rodney 1981, 222).

WORKS CITED

Bronfman, Alejandra. 2004. *Measures of Equality: Social Science, Citizenship, and Race in Cuba*. Chapel Hill: University of North Carolina Press.

De la Fuente, Alejandro. 2000. *A Nation for All: Race Inequality and Politics in Twentieth-Century Cuba*. Chapel Hill: University of North Carolina Press.

Ferrer, Ada. 1999. *Insurgent Cuba: Race, Nation, and Revolution, 1868–1898*. Chapel Hill: University of North Carolina Press.

Gould, Stephen Jay. 1996. *The Mismeasure of Man*. New York: Penguin Books.

Helg, Aline. 2005. "Race and Politics in Cuba." In *Contemporary Caribbean Cultures and Societies in a Global Context*, edited by Franklin W. Knight and Teresita Martinez-Vergne. Chapel Hill: University of North Carolina Press.

Heuman, Gad. 1994. *"The Killing Time": The Morant Bay Rebellion in Jamaica*. London: MacMillan Press.

Holt, Thomas. 1992. *The Problem of Freedom: Race, Labor, and Politics in Jamaica and Britain, 1832–1938*. Baltimore: Johns Hopkins University Press.

Meditz, Sandra W., and Dennis M. Hanratty, eds. 1987. *The Caribbean Islands: A Country Study*. Washington: GPO.

Mintz, Sidney. 1974. *Caribbean Transformations*. New York: Columbia University Press.

———. 1985. *Sweetness and Power: The Place of Sugar in Modern History*. New York: Penguin.

Moore, Robin Dale. 1997. *Nationalizing Blackness*. Pittsburgh: University of Pittsburgh Press.

Perez, Louis Jr. 1986. "Politics, Peasants, and People of Color: The 1912 'Race War' in Cuba Reconsidered." *Hispanic American Historical Review* 66, no. 3: 509–39.

Rodney, Walter. 1981. *A History of the Guyanese Working People, 1881–1905*. Baltimore: Johns Hopkins University Press.

Scott, Rebecca. 1993. "Former Slaves' Responses to Emancipation in Cuba." In *Caribbean Freedom: Economy and Society from Emancipation to the Present*, edited by Hilary Beckles and Verene Shepherd, 21–27. Kingston: Ian Randle Publishers.

Stepan, Nancy Leys. 1991. *The Hour of Eugenics: Race, Gender and Nation in Latin America*. Ithaca, NY: Cornell University Press.

Trouillot, Michel-Rolph. 1995. *Silencing the Past: Power and the Production of History*. Boston: Beacon Press.

27

Africa, Europe, and Asia in the Making of the 20th-Century Caribbean

AISHA KHAN

The Caribbean of today began to form half a millennium ago, impelled by European colonial expansion harnessed to nascent capitalism and centered on resource extraction and sugar plantations producing for a global market. Within 50 years of Columbus's landing, indigenous Caribbean populations had been dramatically reduced, largely due to disease and the harsh conditions of labor imposed by the Spanish colonizers. This diminution of indigenous peoples was accompanied by the addition of foreigners from the "Old World" of Europe, Africa, and later Asia—a socially engineered assemblage of disparate ethnolinguistic groups under conditions of coerced labor and massive wealth accumulation. The imported groups included indentured Europeans, enslaved Africans, and, later, indentured Africans and Asians.

The transformations of the plantation system had various effects on the racial and demographic composition of different colonial territories. For example, the Hispanophone Caribbean, particularly Cuba and Puerto Rico, was not significantly developed for the global sugar market until the 19th century (although by mid-century Cuba and Puerto Rico had emerged as the first and third largest producers of sugar in the hemisphere), and the proportion of European populations compared to non-European populations was far greater there than in the Francophone and Anglophone colonies.

Over the 19th century, slavery was gradually abolished in the Caribbean. Newly independent Haiti (formerly Saint-Domingue) abolished slavery in 1804, followed by the British West Indies in 1838, the French possessions in 1848, all Dutch territories by 1863, and Cuba in 1886. Emancipation presented plantation owners with a dilemma: ensuring sugar and other production at high levels without the benefit of enslaved labor, or with diminishing numbers of freed workers willing to engage in plantation labor under the conditions offered by the plantocracy. One strategy implemented by Britain and France was that of freeing Africans from the slave trade of other European colonizers (Dutch, Spanish, Portuguese) and then sending them to British and French Caribbean colonies as indentured laborers. Almost 40,000 Africans were thus sent to the British West Indies and approximately 16,000 to the French West Indies (Schuler 1980).

Another form of 19th-century indenture brought immigrant laborers from Asia into the region. Organized as either state projects or private enterprises, indenture schemes evolved over eight decades and changed the demographic, cultural, and social terrain of the Caribbean as irrevocably as African slavery had done earlier. Between 1890 and 1939, for example, the Dutch recruited almost 33,000 Javanese, primarily from Central Java and Batavia, for their Caribbean colony of Suriname. The two principal source regions of indentured labor, however, were India and China. Itself a British colony, India experienced indenture as a government-regulated industry, with laborers recruited primarily from the regions of Oudh, Bihar, and Uttar Pradesh and shipped out from the ports of Calcutta and Madras. Between 1838 and 1917, almost 400,000 Indians arrived in the British Caribbean, the majority in Guyana and Trinidad. Although China was never colonized, its political vulnerability allowed private interests to orchestrate indenture schemes, largely from Canton. Between 1840 and 1875, approximately 142,000 indentured Chinese arrived in Cuba (Helly 1993, 20); from 1853 until 1866 and in trickles thereafter, about 18,000 Chinese were indentured in the British West Indies (Look Lai 1993, 18). Later—beginning around 1890, and concentrated between 1910 and 1940—a second wave of Chinese immigrants, this time not under indenture, arrived in the Caribbean.

The relationships of Asian indentured laborers with the local populations they encountered have influenced the values, identities, and cultural practices of their respective societies. To one extent or another, all the Asian immigrants were initially viewed by the locals as labor competition. Particularly where they constitute

Figure 27.1 Newly arrived
Indian laborers in Trinidad.
Photograph (1897).

a large percentage of the population, Indians have been represented by local anti-indenture interests as "scab" labor, yet
historically they also have been pitted against Afro-Caribbean
workers. The tensions arising from perceived and actual labor
conflicts have left a monumental legacy of racial politics in
such contemporary societies as Guyana and Trinidad, where
Indians represent more than 40% of the population. Perhaps because of their relatively smaller numbers, Chinese and Javanese laborers have had less fraught relationships with established populations, especially with those in similar occupational
and class positions. In Cuba, for example, Chinese indentured laborers worked side
by side with enslaved Africans. Enmity between these two groups was encouraged
by colonial authorities as a divide-and-rule strategy, but tensions expressed in racial
terms did not significantly persist into the present, either in Cuba or in other parts
of the region. Once the Chinese found their economic niche primarily in the retail trades and shopkeeping, they no longer represented labor competition to other
populations.

Migrants to the Caribbean from the Levant—known as "Syrians," "Syrian-
Lebanese," or *árabes*—also began to arrive in the 1860s, increasing their numbers significantly by the 1890s. Most were Maronite Christians leaving Ottoman-occupied
regions. Lebanese immigrants came first, followed by Syrians and Palestinians. Although they spread out across the Caribbean (and into Latin America, where they

are also called *turcos*), certain communities predominated in particular countries. For example, of the three groups from the Levant, Lebanese comprise the largest population in Jamaica and the Dominican Republic, and Palestinians in Haiti (Nicholls 1980). These immigrants came as individuals, or sometimes in families, rather than in an organized migration arrangement; over the years, other family members followed. Although a few went into agricultural production, others became itinerant peddlers. Within a few generations these communities branched out into import-export trading, and today they comprise a large population of affluent and politically active citizens.

In addition to the transcontinental migrations, intraregional population movements have been crucial in contributing to the character of today's Caribbean. Although interisland labor migrations commenced soon after emancipation in the British West Indies, the late 19th century and first decades of the 20th saw the most dramatic population movements within the Caribbean basin. For example, between 1900 and 1914, some 60,000 Barbadians labored on the Panama Canal. Likewise, between 1917 and 1931, some 300,000 Jamaicans, Haitians, and other labor migrants from the region worked in Cuba on sugar plantations and in factories (De la Fuente 2001, 102), and several thousand more left the Leeward Islands to work in the US-owned sugar industry in the Dominican Republic (Conway 2003, 339). From the 1880s, Haitians crossed into the Dominican Republic to work on foreign-owned plantations as well as to farm smallholdings along the border. By 1935, Haitians in the Dominican Republic numbered perhaps 200,000—more than 10% of the national population (Andrews 2004, 140). Aside from the economic dimension of these population displacements, the resulting cultural and linguistic exchanges contributed significantly to the continuous formation of new social fabrics.

Interpreting "Creole" Societies

Four major languages are spoken in the Caribbean: Spanish, English, French, and Dutch. The 17 Caribbean countries that are predominantly Anglophone comprise more than 17% of the region's population, yet the total English-speaking population of the Caribbean is less than that of the Dominican Republic alone. These statistics clarify the demographic predominance of the Spanish-speaking countries of Cuba, Puerto Rico, and the Dominican Republic, which represent 61% of the Caribbean population. Of the 20% of Caribbean peoples who speak French or variations of French, three-quarters live in Haiti. The Dutch speakers of Suriname and the Netherlands Antilles represent another 2% (Knight 1995, 34). Other languages, spoken by fewer numbers of people, include Hindi and Javanese.

The languages of the European colonizers remain the official languages of formal Caribbean education and legal systems, but numerous African languages brought

by the slaves fused with European, Asian, and Amerinidian languages to create numerous "creole" languages, which are the spoken vernaculars of everyday life in
a number of Caribbean countries. Most Caribbean creole languages are young as
languages go, having existed for not more than two or three centuries. Today, however, there are growing written literatures in creole languages, and movements
to promote the languages to equal standing as vehicles of formal instruction and
communication. Among the most familiar examples is Haitian Kreyol, the spoken
language of approximately 12 million insular and diasporic Haitians, which along
with French has been an official language in Haiti since 1961. Other widely spoken creoles include Jamaican patois, which is spoken by about four million people
in and outside Jamaica, and the patois of Trinidad and Tobago, a historical legacy
primarily of French on Trinidadian English, which has been in decline since about
the mid-20th century. In Suriname, Sranan Tongo is the language of approximately
300,000 people; in Aruba, Bonaire, and Curaçao, Papiamento is spoken by more
than 350,000. And although the varieties of Spanish spoken in Cuba, Puerto Rico,
and the Dominican Republic share a number of linguistic properties, they also have
discernable differences based on geographic location and local histories.

As a region whose very foundations lie in multiple origins—assorted languages,
varied religions, diverse worldviews, contrasting cultural traditions—the Caribbean has long been represented by observers, local and international alike, as the
epitome of heterogeneity (Trouillot 1992; Glissant 1995). For more than a century,
the region has been the object of attempts to explain cultural change over time as
phenotypically and culturally heterogeneous peoples come into what is commonly
known as "culture contact" and undergo the cultural transformations that such contact engenders. The questions about how cultures retain or lose continuity across
vast geographical spaces (for example, after transatlantic migrations) and over extended periods of time (from the colonial period to the present), how the dynamics
of unequal power relations foster or challenge cultural assimilation in new environments, and how identities and worldviews are forged in the process remain central
to the study of Caribbean cultures. And certain concepts that have emerged from
this study—creole, creolization, *creolité*, survivals, retentions, transculturation, and
syncretism—have achieved much broader usage.

From its colonization, the Caribbean has represented newness, which Europeans
captured in the term "creole." When applied to the region, the Spanish word *criollo*
and the Portuguese word *crioulo* (derived from the verb *criar*, "to raise or bring up")
signified something or someone originating in Europe (or Africa) and reproducing
itself in the New World. Thus animals, plants, and people could all be designated
as creole. Creole people were the descendants of Europeans or Africans born in the
Caribbean, as well as the offspring of African and European parents. Inherent in the
idea of creole identity was an assumption that being born in the Caribbean or being

the "mixed" descendant of two racially differentiated parents meant losing one's ancestral cultural heritage.

Many of the earliest and most important social science studies of creole identity in the Caribbean were concerned specifically with Afro-Caribbean populations. They framed the question of cultural change over time in terms of the search for cultural heritage through "survivals" (or "retentions") and reinterpretations. Heralded in North America by anthropologists Melville and Frances Herskovits, this approach emphasized empirical evidence: the prevalence and intensity of survivals—as perceived by the Herskovitses in, for example, art forms, cuisine, technology, language, and religion—could prove cultural continuity between Africa and the Americas. As debates about African survivals progressed, however, the emphasis shifted from observable traits in the identification and study of cultural forms toward values, style, and systems of relationships.

While retaining an assumption that creole identity involves the loss of former cultural heritage in the process of forging new cultural adaptations, this shift brought greater interest in the variations of cultural forms and identities produced from dissimilar types. Thus the question of how new, creole types were produced became as much a focus of study as the types themselves. The creation of models to explain these processes emerged from different thinkers throughout the Hispanophone, Anglophone, and Francophone Caribbean. Among the most influential of these were Fernando Ortiz's early 20th-century model of *transculturación* based on Cuba, Edward Kamau Brathwaite's mid-20th-century model of creolization derived from Jamaica, and Jean Bernabe, Patrick Chamoiseau, and Raphael Confiant's (1993) late 20th-century model of *creolité* based on Martinique.

Ortiz coined the term "transculturation" as a way to interpret the multiplicity of histories, cultures, languages, religions, and worldviews that collectively form the Caribbean, and to express the various phases of the processes of transition from one culture to another. Ortiz saw these processes as entailing more than the simple and passive acquisition of, or submission to, other cultures, which he equated with "acculturation." Instead, transculturation involved the simultaneous loss or displacement of a preceding culture ("deculturation") as well as the resultant creation of new cultural phenomena ("neoculturation") (Ortiz 1995, 102–3). Parsing the concept into processes, or active elements, allows a highlighting of the ways in which subjugated peoples create their own versions of the dominant culture.

In the Anglophone Caribbean, Brathwaite's analysis of what he called the "creole society" of Jamaica emphasized the creation of new forms through the synthesis of existing ones. Arguing against understanding black and white populations as "separate nuclear units," Brathwaite saw them as being "contributory parts of a whole" that produce a uniquely Caribbean culture. Creolization here represents the potential for social integration and unity, where the "mixed" population serves "as a bridge, a kind of social cement" that integrates society (Brathwaite 1971, 307, 305). In calling for a renewed emphasis on creole identity and the literary value of the creole language, the most recent Francophone *creoliste* writers and activists celebrate the heterogeneous dimensions that together comprise the Caribbean or, in the words of Martinican poet and writer Edouard Glissant, constitute *Antillanité* (Caribbeanness). The *creoliste* position, along with those of other thinkers, points to the abiding debates about how to characterize and give meaning to the forms of diversity so apparent in the region.

Ideologies of Race, Color, and Class

From the earliest days of colonial rule, the Caribbean social and moral order was based on ranked gradations of "races" and "colors" represented by such physical attributes as skin color, hair texture, and facial features. These criteria were treated as literal descriptions of appearance, and their presumed fixed qualities formed a hierarchy of identities—from "white" at the top to "black" at the bottom, with various mixtures and gradations in between—supported by legal structures as well as social values and mores. Consequently, for much of Caribbean history, race and color also have connoted social position and class status. Yet the recognition of a vertical color continuum separates the Caribbean from the rigid binary racial logic of the United States.

Given the legacies of colonial rule and ideology, color and race are still commonly used in daily conversation as idioms for social organization. In Jamaica, for example, the color term "brown" (or "colored") serves as a category of racial identity but also connotes middle-class status. Color terms are necessarily relational; being "white" or "brown" or "black" necessarily means not being something else. In Haiti, *mulâtre* is an in-between term connoting a mixture of "black" and "white," flexible in its interpretation yet typically positioned above "black" and below "white." In the Dominican Republic, *indio* literally translates as "Indian," suggesting indigenous heritage, but its contemporary application signifies a lighter skin color (and perhaps straight hair)—someone not "black," yet also not "white." In Martinique, *beke* refers to French "white" slave owners and their descendants. "Trinidad white" and "French creole" have served as categories of racial identity in Trinidad, specifically distinguished from British, French, and Spanish "whites," who, in this racial accounting system, historically could claim to be "pure" white and, concomitantly, members of the upper classes. In Trinidad, the term "red" generally refers to a light-skinned individual of mixed "black" and "white" parentage (positioned toward the upper-status end), while in Barbados it is also a historical reference to "red legs" communities—poor whites who, from the days of the slave plantation, labored outdoors and hence were likely to get sunburned.

Mixedness can also refer to multiple combinations, not simply the amalgamation of "black" and "white." Thus, in the Francophone Caribbean, the term *marabou* refers to a black-white-Amerindian combination. In Trinidad the term "Spanish" should be interpreted as if in quotation marks, indicating a particular and fluctuating combination of local criteria, including area of origin (Venezuela, or certain locations in Trinidad with historical concentrations of Spaniards, Amerindians, and Venezuelan immigrant labor), skin color (some variation of "brown" or "red'), hair texture (not curly), and self-ascription (Khan 1993).

Notably, these terminologies are based on an African-European axis: the hierarchical color continuum does not lexically include South Asians or Chinese, or the mixed offspring of South Asian or Chinese and European parents. Though the term *achinado* is used in Cuba to index Chinese phenotypical features (as, for example, in *mulato achinado*), there is only one term, *dougla*—common in Guyana and Trinidad—indicating individuals of mixed South Asian and African descent. *Indio* (Amerindian) in the Hispanophone Caribbean and "Spanish" or "French creole" in Trinidad are not color terms per se, but are measured along the continuum of black and white ancestry. "Indian" (South Asian), "Chinese," and "Syrian-Lebanese" in the Anglophone Caribbean, "Hindustani" in the Dutch Caribbean, and *Hindou* in the Francophone Caribbean are common categories not amalgamated into the black-white lexicon.

Twentieth-century anticolonial movements encouraged Caribbean societies to project themselves as modern, sovereign democracies. Race and color were thus applied by political leaders to nationalist projects, with local perceptions of cultural, racial, and color heterogeneity representing the ideal of "unity in diversity": multicultural tolerance and harmony. In this mid-century nationalist narrative, evident throughout the region, evoking creolization became tantamount to celebrating the strengths of cultural heterogeneity. The claimed character of such "creole" societies as Trinidad, Guyana, Suriname, Jamaica, Belize, Cuba, Martinique, Curaçao, and French Guiana is a national identity in which culturally and racially distinct groups cooperatively coexist as united, independent nations. Claims about the strengths of diversity are deliberated across the region, and the discussion largely reflects debate about representation—that is, which constituent cultural-racial groups will be at the forefront of defining national identity and, by implication, national interests. The lack of any uniform local understanding of what constitutes "diversity" across the region complicates these claims and the narrative of harmony; each nation-state's self-perception is configured somewhat differently in terms of its cultural, religious, racial, and ethnic composition. Thus nationalist projects tackle the broad Caribbean theme of multiplicity in historically and ideologically particularistic ways. Whatever direction these discussions take, however, they show no indication of muting the salience of racial accounting and color categories in the region.

Gender and Kinship

Caribbean kinship forms have been shaped by the different governing structures and sociocultural character of European colonizers. In the British-influenced Commonwealth West Indies, for example, social welfare policy played a significant role in shaping family life, particularly during the period of high social unrest between the two world wars. Throughout the wider Caribbean, however, kinship is understood to have certain common patterns that transcend specific colonial identities. These patterns derive largely from two contexts that share certain region-wide similarities: slave plantation society, and class stratification systems that arose after emancipation. Because all the populations associated with slavery are African in origin, for example, kinship practices among Afro-Caribbeans have generally been distinguished in terms of social class positions rather than in terms of the ethnic, cultural, or racial differences that exist among these populations. Such differences come into play only when kinship practices are compared across the ethnoracially, culturally heterogeneous groups of the region, usually based on divisions among "African," "European," and "Asian" (or "East Indian") peoples.

In slave plantation societies, West African kinship forms met the constraints and agendas of European colonial rule. Although each colony had legal structures to control slaves' cultural practices, patterns of conjugality and religious worship largely remained outside the purview of the master's control. Over time, many forms of mating and cohabitation—from legal marriage to extra-residential unions, with a range of arrangements in between—became part of the social landscape. Such flexible diversity in domestic forms contributed significantly to the idea that the Caribbean consisted of, at best, fluidly adaptive social institutions and, at worst, unstable ones—in alleged contrast to European and North American society. Until the late 20th century many policy makers, scholars, and other observers assumed that among Afro-Caribbean peoples, corporate kinship groups were less important than dyadic ties between individuals. Today these assumptions are under more careful scrutiny, and the gender dynamics of Caribbean kinship are primarily understood as constructive responses to such shifting forces as migration, educational opportunity, and labor conditions.

In the context of post-emancipation society, the values and behaviors associated with different classes reflect a status hierarchy. According to a model first elaborated by anthropologist Peter Wilson (1973), Afro-Caribbean women are judged on their "respectability," which reflects bourgeois European colonial values, while Afro-Caribbean working-class men are judged on their "reputation," which reflects local or creole values and a disinclination to emulate European values and standards of behavior (nuclear families, wage employment, formal education, obedience to social and legal norms, self-control). Reputation is meant to convey an alternative system of status and prestige, one that emphasizes verbal dexterity, ease and mobility in the public sphere, sexual prowess, and lack of restraint in engaging in these behaviors. Although this model has been critiqued for its oversimplified binary opposition of gender roles—for example, Caribbean women engage in their own practices of "reputation"—it remains useful for understanding the ways in which gender in the Caribbean is culturally expressed and ideologically linked to class divisions.

Along with class differences, ethnocultural distinctions are significant in the formation and representation of Caribbean kinship practices. Like Afro-Caribbean peoples, Indo-Caribbeans who settled in the region were a diverse population. They came from various parts of the Indian subcontinent, spoke several languages (notably Hindi, Urdu, and a dialect called Bhojpuri), belonged to different religions (primarily Hinduism and Islam), and had a number of family and household arrangements. But Indo-Caribbean populations differed from their Afro-Caribbean and other neighbors in some key respects. Whereas plantocracies throughout the region discouraged enslaved Africans from practicing their cultural traditions, colonial authorities in the age of the indentured labor system were more flexible regarding Indian immigrants' activities. Practices and observances that were thought to hinder plantation production were curtailed, but cultural life was far freer than under slavery. Yet Hindu and Muslim marriages were not legalized in the Caribbean until the mid-20th century, presenting challenges for Indo-Caribbeans not faced by their neighbors who practiced Christianity or Afro-European religions. Moreover, marriages between Indo-Caribbeans reflected cultural traditions brought from the subcontinent—that is, they were often arranged, with families seeking potential mates for their children through the services of matchmakers from the community. This practice continues today, though less formally and much less frequently.

Cosmologies and Belief Systems

The basic distinction made between religions local to the Caribbean and those derived from outside the region raises an interesting question about the meaning of "indigenous." Because the first peoples to inhabit the region, Amerindians, succumbed very early to European conquest, there are no indigenous religions in the Caribbean, in the sense that the term is used to describe religions of native peoples in Latin and North America. Rather, all Caribbean religions have undergone transformation over time and derive from predecessor religions that were variegated in their belief and practice. Yet because of the legacy of cultural creolization, the Caribbean represents a major crucible of creole, or syncretic, religions.

As in other parts of the world, religion has offered the peoples of the Caribbean a way to interpret and engage past and present social conditions and forms of inequality. Among the most well known examples is the role of vodou priests and priestesses in slave revolts, such as Boukman's 1791 insurgency, which is thought to have initiated the Haitian Revolution. Similarly, in 1884, in response to British colonial curtailments, the insistence of Trinidadian Muslims and Hindus on carrying on Hosay (the Caribbean version of Muharram, the Shi'a Muslim ritual mourning the martyrdom of the Prophet Mohammed's grandson, Imam Hussain) resulted in Trinidad's "Hosay Riots."

At the same time, Caribbean religions offer alleviation of natural and supernatural distress, notably problems of health, success, and fidelity. For example, brujería in Puerto Rico—a blend of popular Catholicism, Afro-Latin religions, French spiritism, and folk Protestantism—engages in healing, advocacy, and solving both metaphysical and practical problems among populations who have few alternatives or who avail themselves of a number of religious options (Romberg 2003). Although they possess their own distinctive histories, characteristics, and modes of practice, vernacular religions such as Haitian vodou, Cuban Santería, and Trinidadian orisha also serve such needs. And institutionalized forms of religious practice such as Christianity, Islam, Judaism, and Hinduism have found fertile ground in the region. Associated with European colonizers, the Catholic and Protestant churches have worked to conserve their formal traditions and doctrines even under the forces of transformation and syncretism. Hindu and Muslim communities in the region have sponsored missionaries and educators from India since the mid-19th century and from Pakistan in the 20th.

Caribbean religions are among the most complex examples of the emergence and transformation of cultural lifeworlds in the Americas. Given their numerous sources and formations, and their tendency to eschew orthodox axioms in favor of heterodox practices guided by a few broad principles, religions emerging from the Caribbean are characterized by amalgamation and recombination. Added to syncretic or creole religions deriving from the Caribbean context are religions whose doctrines and belief systems, themselves varied and changing over time, derive from "Old World" origins. Thus, today even a cursory list of religions in the region would be long—Catholicism, Protestantism, evangelical and Pentecostal movements, Judaism, Hinduism, vodou, Santería, Islam, espiritismo, Rastafari, and orisha—made even longer by a number of demographically smaller but socially significant traditions such as Kali worship in Guyana, brujería and Mita worship in Puerto Rico, Quimbois in Martinique, and Winti in Suriname.

Equally important are historical and contemporary magical practices (often subsumed under the term "obeah") that involve supernatural powers, deriving largely from West African divination and healing practices and, to a lesser extent, Hindu and Christian cosmologies. The meaning of obeah has changed over the centuries. Among 17th- to 19th-century Africans and Afro-Caribbeans it was associated with salutary objectives, such as alleviating illness, protecting against harm, and avenging wrongs. Euro-colonial and local bourgeois ideologies emphasized the dangerous aspects of obeah, often equating it with Judeo-Christian interpretations of evil forces. Often, positive and negative assessments existed simultaneously, making local opinion about obeah ambiguous. Today, as in earlier eras, its practice represents tensions between the ways in which practitioners interpret obeah's methods and objectives, and the ways in which those methods and objectives are perceived by outsiders.

Caribbean religions are expressions of traditions of creativity, resistance, and flexibility that continuously build on as well as disassemble older and current forms of knowledge, heritage, and custom. The challenge in understanding them is to grasp that difference and similarity exist at the same time. Hinduism, as practiced by the progeny of indentured laborers, reflects both the remembered traditions that early immigrants brought with them from India and a contemporary global Hinduism that travels across the Hindu diaspora. While Caribbean Hindus may interpret their forms of worship as replicating those in India, they also recognize that certain transformations and syncretisms have occurred for almost 170 years in the Caribbean.

In contrast, Rastafari's origins are in Jamaica, where religious movements based in Afro-Caribbean folk Christianity, the pan-Africanism of Marcus Garvey, grassroots reinterpretations of the Old Testament, and the veneration of Haile Selassie of Ethiopia coalesced in the 1930s, giving rise to the religious, philosophical, and political worldview of today's Rastafari movement. In it, Africa plays a great symbolic role as a place of desired return and the antithesis of "Babylon"—all places and forms of consciousness in which predatory relationships and "mental slavery" abound. Yet although thus memorialized, Africa is not literally remembered by many Rastafari, the vast majority of whom have never had direct experience with societies and cultures in Africa or Ethiopia (two terms often used synonymously). Nonetheless, Africa/Ethiopia represents for them an indispensable emblem of unity, self-determination, authenticity, and morality.

Islam, meanwhile, first came to the Caribbean as the religion of some African slaves. With the advent of indentured laborers from India, Islam gained an increased presence in the region. Notable today are the numerous *masjids* (mosques) that dot the landscape of many countries, from Trinidad to Guyana, Puerto Rico, and Suriname. Some masjids are humble, built to serve small communities and local villages; others are grand, built as centers of learning as well as centers of worship for larger populations in the towns and cities. In these places of worship that serve *jamaats* (congregations) large and small, imams (religious leaders) work to preserve the *Sunnah* (Muslim way of life). At the same time, Islam in the Caribbean encapsulates the simultaneous inclusiveness and exclusions of a religion claimed by different ethnic groups, practiced according to divergent interpretations of doc-

Figure 27.2 A tadja at Hosay in St. James, Trinidad. Photograph by Dr. Ted Hill (1950s).

trine, and, in certain contexts, participated in by non-Muslims. This is perhaps best seen in the ritual of Hosay, the Caribbean version of Shi'a Islam's commemoration, Muharram.

Historically spread throughout the Anglophone Caribbean, today Hosay is practiced on a major scale only in Trinidad, where it is simultaneously an important religious event, a freighted political statement, an embattled heritage claim, and a multicultural symbol. Mourners of Hussain march with enormous, elaborate representations of the *tadjas* (*tazzias*, or representations of the martyrs' tombs; see fig. 27.2). This procession has been treated by some local participants less like a sacred commemoration than like a parade, where music and general revelry may occur on the sidelines. Despite its Muslim origins, Hosay in Trinidad also has always involved Hindus and Afro-Trinidadians. Hindus have long been key participants in the building of the tadjas, and Afro-Trinidadians traditionally have played a significant role as drummers as well as bearers (along with Hindu and Muslim Indo-Trinidadians) of the tadjas in procession. Moreover, Hindus sometimes make their own vows and offerings during Hosay. This ritual was the only significant element in the Indian cultural repertoire that provided a social bridge to the rest of 19th-century Trinidadian society (Singh 1988, 4). Given its multiple interpretations and diverse participants, Hosay lends a distinctive religious and cultural tenor to Trinidad's national culture. The combination of participants and their varied forms of involvement has given rise to debates among Muslims and non-Muslims about the authenticity of Hosay and its appropriateness in Islam. Other observers argue that this ceremony's heterogeneity and cooperation counters the divide-and-rule antagonism among subordinate groups (notably Afro- and Indo-Caribbeans) encouraged by British colonizers, offering a natural space for a creole unity.

Religion is just one of innumerable examples of the ways in which Africa, Europe, and Asia have together produced the 20th-century Caribbean. In the organization of labor, language, group identities, and kinship as well as religion, these Old World continents inspired the creation of many multidimensional New World cultures and societies. The productive relationship between "old" (existing) and "new" (emerging) that gave rise to the Caribbean of today must be understood as a consequence of the protracted and often painful tension between domination (initiated by the articulation of colonialism and capitalism, which significantly defined the region) and resistance (local forms of accommodation and challenge) to that domination. The 20th-century Caribbean represents one of the most diverse places on earth; this diversity is richly symbolic of the workings of the human imagination in both felicitous and forbidding circumstances.

WORKS CITED

Andrews, George Reid. 2004. *Afro-Latin America, 1800–2000*. New York: Oxford University Press.

Bernabe, Jean, Patrick Chamoiseau, and Raphael Confiant. 1989. *Eloge de la creolite*. Paris: Gallimard.

Brathwaite, Edward Kamau. 1971. *The Development of Creole Society in Jamaica, 1770–1820*. Oxford: Clarendon Press.

Conway, Dennis. 2003. "The Caribbean Diaspora." In *Understanding the Contemporary Caribbean*, edited by Richard S. Hillman and Thomas J. D'Agostino, 333–53. Boulder, CO: Lynne Rienner.

De la Fuente, Alejandro. 2001. *A Nation for All: Race, Inequality, and Politics in Twentieth-Century Cuba*. Chapel Hill: University of North Carolina Press.

Glissant, Edouard. 1995. "Creolization in the Making of the Americas." In *Race, Discourse, and the Origin of the Americas*, edited by V. L. Hyatt and R. Nettleford, 268–75. Washington, DC: Smithsonian Institution Press.

Helly, Dorothy, ed. 1993. *The Cuba Commission Report: A Hidden History of the Chinese in Cuba*. Baltimore: Johns Hopkins University Press.

Khan, Aisha. 1993. "What is 'a Spanish'? Ambiguity and Mixed Ethnicity in Trinidad." In *Trinidad Ethnicity*, edited by Kevin Yelvington, 180–207. Knoxville: University of Tennessee Press.

Knight, Franklin. 1995. *Race, Ethnicity, and Class: Forging the Plural Society in Latin America and the Caribbean*. Waco, TX: Markham Press Fund.

Look Lai, Walton. 1993. *Indentured Labor, Caribbean Sugar*. Baltimore: Johns Hopkins University Press.

Nicholls, David. 1980. *Arabs of the Greater Antilles*. New York: Research Institute for the Study of Man.

Ortiz, Fernando. 1995. *Cuban Counterpoint: Tobacco and Sugar*. Durham, NC: Duke University Press.

Romberg, Raquel. 2003. *Witchcraft and Welfare: Spiritual Capital and the Business of Magic in Modern Puerto Rico*. Austin: University of Texas Press.

Schuler, Monica. 1980. *"Alas, Alas, Kongo": A Social History of Indentured African Immigration into Jamaica, 1841–1865*. Baltimore: Johns Hopkins University Press.

Singh, Kelvin. 1988. *Bloodstained Tombs: The Muharram Massacre 1884*. London: Macmillan Caribbean.

Trouillot, Michel-Rolph. 1992. "The Caribbean Region: An Open Frontier in Anthropological Theory." *Annual Review of Anthropology* 21:19–42.

Wilson, Peter. 1973. *Crab Antics: A Caribbean Case Study of the Conflict between Reputation and Respectability*. New Haven: Yale University Press.

PART 6

The New Empire

28

Building US Hegemony in the Caribbean

BRENDA GAYLE PLUMMER

US interest in the Caribbean dates to the era of the American Revolution. Despite various imperial restrictions designed to ensure that most colonial revenues returned to Britain, North American prosperity depended heavily on trade with the islands. This commerce continued after American independence, since monocrop agriculture kept the islands' plantation economies dependent on imports. British and French activity west of the Appalachians and the Spanish presence in Florida limited opportunities for territorial expansion of the fledgling United States and increased its interest in the Caribbean and other regions controlled by European powers. US policy makers speculated about seizing Cuba or the wealthy French colony of Saint-Domingue (after 1804, Haiti). When the slaves in the latter colony rebelled, the Americans supplied the rebels with arms in the unrealized hope that their revolt would drive France from the area. With Saint-Domingue lost, Americans sought the vast Louisiana territory.

President James Monroe's December 2, 1823, message to Congress outlining the Monroe Doctrine is a foundational statement of US policy toward the Americas. Monroe issued his statement well after European powers ceased to threaten US survival, however, and thus it represented a consequence rather than a cause of US intentions. When revolutions erupted in Latin America after 1810, the United States pursued neutrality, hoping to eventually gain territory at Spain's expense. Britain also remained neutral because it had important commerce in the Americas to protect, and it persuaded France to refrain from supporting Spain. While the British navy easily could have demolished US pretensions in the Americas in the 1820s, the crown allowed its former possession to pull its chestnuts out of the fire. These combined actions contributed to the loss of most of Spain's empire. The Monroe Doctrine thus seconded, rather than determined, a policy of noninterference by extrahemispheric powers. In later years, however, the United States became strong enough to invoke the doctrine regardless of other nations' aims, and to enforce it.

The United States reached its current continental boundaries by 1898 and began to rival Britain and Germany in industrial output. It competed in the Caribbean to supplant former British, French, and Spanish agricultural and commercial interests. Finance and technology proved important partners as US-financed railroads moved sugar and fruit to ports, especially in Cuba. Certain US opinion makers, most notably Admiral Alfred Thayer Mahan, campaigned for the development of a larger fleet to ensure the security of national interests abroad, allow the United States to dominate the Caribbean and Central American regions, and make its navy competitive with British and German counterparts in the Pacific. Mahan's widely consulted book *The Influence of Sea Power upon History, 1600–1783* (1892) described the eminence that had accrued to nations with strong navies. Such navalists as Mahan and Assistant Secretary of the Navy Theodore Roosevelt also advocated building a canal through the Central American isthmus to radically reduce shipping time and stimulate Asian trade. As European nations increasingly turned their attention to colonial possessions in Africa and Asia, they allowed the United States to patrol the Caribbean and secure their interests for them. Washington officials coupled this informal control over the region with a commitment to a free-trade policy referred to as the Open Door.

The Impact of the Spanish-American War

The destruction of the USS *Maine* in the Havana harbor on February 15, 1898, was the ostensible cause of the Spanish-American War. Decades later, the explosion that wrecked the ship was determined to have resulted from faulty storage of combustibles, but at the time, Americans were convinced that Spain had blown it up in retaliation for US sympathies with rebelling Cuban nationalists. Navalist advice seemed to have paid off when, after declaring war on Spain, the US Navy effectively blockaded

Havana. In the Pacific, Commodore George Dewey neutralized the Spanish army in the Philippines and seized the island of Guam and the island kingdom of Hawaii, which US sugar interests already dominated. The Caribbean theater of the Spanish-American War resolved itself in only three months with the defeat of the Spanish army. Spain signed a treaty on December 10, 1898, placing Cuba and Puerto Rico under US military control. The rapid victory strengthened the view held by many Americans that war could accelerate political transformation and instill the American way of life even in nations with radically different cultures.

Figure 28.1 Cartoon image of Cuba as the lovely mestiza in distress, awaiting rescue by the United States. Drawing by Louis Dalrymple (1898). Source: Art Resource, NY.

Prevalent thinking about race and gender also quickened the pace of US hegemony in the Caribbean. The belief in the inherent savagery and inferiority of non-European peoples justified the wars and punitive expeditions carried out against them. In the United States lynch law, the Plains Wars against Native Americans, and discrimination against Asian immigrants illustrated the nature of a society obsessed with efforts to preserve racial hierarchy through such practices as eugenics and segregation. Social Darwinism, the application of evolutionary ideas to society, gave a scientific veneer to racial bias and helped legitimize it.

The visual culture of the popular press stimulated the American public's support for Cuban independence. Cartoonists frequently depicted Cuba as an innocent and beautiful female victim of Spanish rapacity in need of rescue by American men (figure 28.1). The image was intended not only to arouse sympathy but also to point out

Figure 28.2 Despite Theodore Roosevelt's racial attitudes, his Rough Riders were aided by African American troops in their battle against the Spanish in Cuba. Print (ca. 1898). Source: Art Resource, NY.

the disparate power relations between the hapless and dependent sufferer and her valiant would-be saviors. The trope of the damsel in distress had a venerable lineage in US thought: the female captivity narrative dated back to 17th-century Indian wars. The foil of the distraught Cuban maiden in the popular graphic press was the stalwart American who exemplified the cult of virility as espoused by Roosevelt. Worried about the racial impact of immigration on the national character and the decline of the old Anglo-Saxon stock, Roosevelt encouraged whites to have more children and white men to increase their vitality through physical culture and cultivation of manly military virtues. Roosevelt followed up on his convictions, suspending his cabinet service to lead a regiment, known as the Rough Riders, in the Spanish-American War. White supremacy, then, helped rationalize US ascendancy over the Caribbean, a region whose peoples often appeared in illustrations as wayward children or savages and who, as Roosevelt notoriously said, deserved spanking when they misbehaved. Armed with supremacist beliefs, and shored up by the evidence of European victories over nonwhite peoples in Africa and Asia, Americans premised their authority on ideological as well as political foundations.

At the turn of the 20th century, racism was not limited to the great powers. The legacy of slavery also influenced opinion and social practice in Latin America and the Caribbean. Societies in the Americas retained substantial ambivalence about their mixed-race heritage as well as considerable adulation of the customs, mores, and traits of the empires that had colonized them. Panama, for example, denied citizenship to persons of African descent, wishing to maintain an identity as a white nation. As Dominican society did not readily acknowledge its own African heritage, preferring to attribute dark skin to Amerindian ancestry, Haitian immigrants and their offspring encountered racial discrimination. In Haiti, the prosperous classes modeled themselves on the French bourgeoisie. Countries that rejected black immigrants extended a welcome to Europeans in the hopes of modernizing and "improving" the national phenotype. While Caribbean racism did not share the singular violence and rigidity of the North American variant, its collusion with it abetted the growing US mastery of the region.

Another practice that facilitated and increased the power and influence of Europeans and North Americans derived from the circumstances of coups d'état and revolutions. Severe social inequality in many Caribbean countries all but guaranteed that episodes of civil violence would entail attacks on private property. The business community, both foreign and native-born, attempted to shield itself through appeals to metropolitan powers for protection. A French trader in trouble, for example, might seek the assistance of the French consul, who in turn might request a visit from a French gunboat. In Haiti and the Dominican Republic, some indigenous merchants sought foreign citizenship to receive the advantages enjoyed by expatriates. The long-term result was the devaluation of local nationalities and the privileging of foreign identities that conveyed security, prosperity, and status.

The same reasoning that justified US control could also support arguments against it. Not all Americans wanted the United States to keep the territories it had annexed during the war with Spain, or seek other colonies populated by people of color. Some, like author Mark Twain, objected to imperialism on ethical and moral grounds, as it deprived subject nations of the liberties that Americans assumed for themselves. Some objected to the vociferous patriotism, called jingoism, that marked expansionist rhetoric. A strand of pacifism underlay the anti-imperialism of some critics. Others did not believe that people of radically different race and culture could or should assimilate into American life.

Bowing to these reservations in the run-up to war with Spain, Congress in April 1898 adopted the Teller Resolution, a statement disavowing any intent to make Cuba a colony of the United States. While Cuba remained technically sovereign, the United States expanded its empire between 1898 and 1934 while simultaneously maintaining the fiction that it was not a colonial power. Speaking of US rule as guardianship over subjects too politically immature for self-government held out the promise that such stewardship would have a foreseeable end. This did not differ substantially from the self-serving oratory of other colonial powers, which US advocates of intervention overlaid with a view of the United States as an exception to the behaviors that guided other nations. They evoked divine providence to explain in mystic terms why the United States was destined for the benevolent domination of inferior peoples.

The United States maintained a protectorate over Cuba from 1898 to 1901, during which time it suppressed nationalist revolts and forced the legislature to adopt laws known in the United States as the Platt Amendment to the Cuban constitution. Once finalized by treaty in 1903, the laws stipulated that Cuba could not enter into foreign relations or initiate financial agreements with other powers without express US consent. Cuba gave the United States a right to intervene in its internal affairs and to establish a naval base at Guantanamo Bay. The Platt Amendment governed Cuban-American relations until 1934 and provided the pretext for several armed interventions conducted by US forces.

Military occupation did not solve Cuba's political problems or make it more amenable to US ideas about governance. Puerto Rico, however, provided an early model of the desired relationship. Spain ceded the island as part of the terms of the Treaty of Paris in 1898. US military rule ended in 1900, and the Foraker Act of April 2 of that year set in motion the evolution of Puerto Rico's current status. The law created a bicameral Puerto Rican legislature whose upper house would consist of US appointees, most of them Americans. While islanders could vote for members of the lower chamber, the US president would name their governor. Soon thereafter, US sugar interests and local capitalists boosted by free trade began creating large-scale plantations. In spite of spirited efforts by some local leaders to promote independence, US authorities did not face nationalist resistance in Puerto Rico of the same magnitude as in Cuba, and they more easily imposed a colonial structure on Puerto Rican society. Pro-independence activities nevertheless continued both within and outside the constitutional structure the Americans had devised. In 1917, when the United States entered World War I, Congress passed the Jones Act, which bestowed US citizenship on Puerto Ricans, preempting European subversion and undercutting local sentiment for independence. Still, nationalism flourished in Puerto Rico during the 1920s and 1930s under the leadership of Dr. Pedro Albizu Campos. The Nationalist Party's challenge to US hegemony was ruthlessly put down and Albizu Campos was jailed in federal prison for the presumptive crime of sedition.

Political unrest in the Philippines proved more difficult to contain. After Admiral Dewey's fleet quickly dispatched the Spanish navy, the US military confronted a full-fledged nationalist uprising. The Philippines provided the methods and metaphors for American counterinsurgency campaigns for years to come. Warfare took on racist overtones, as the dehumanization of Filipino rebels as "gooks" rationalized the taking of hundreds of thousands of lives. US forces finally crushed native resistance in 1902 and set up government administration on the Puerto Rican model.

The United States also monitored the actions of powers that had not accepted the principle of US hegemony in the Americas. Washington officials suspected that Germany had not abandoned designs on acquiring territory in the region. A diplomatic solution to the problem of German ambition presented itself when Venezuela defaulted on loans to European creditors, who persuaded the governments of Britain, France, and Italy to blockade major ports and shell Venezuelan defenses in December 1902. Venezuela's president, Cipriano Castro, evoked the Monroe Doctrine in appealing for US assistance. The Roosevelt administration did not sympathize with Castro, but saw in the crisis a chance to foil German as well as other European schemes. Secretary of State John Hay took the high road in persuading all powers to accept arbitration of the Venezuelan dispute in the international court at The Hague. In this instance, the United States avoided an active intervention and gained respect for statesmanlike behavior.

US Policy in the Caribbean, 1903–12

The United States proved in the war with Spain that it could defend a Central American isthmian canal. Roosevelt became vice president in 1901 and succeeded to the presidency upon the assassination of William McKinley. As president, he seized the opportunity to act on his longstanding desire to initiate a canal project. He understood that some residents of Panama, then part of Colombia, harbored separatist aspirations. Among them were individuals who had invested in the speculative New Panama Canal Company. The Roosevelt administration encouraged the Panamanians to secede. Private parties in the United States, including noted attorney William Nelson Cromwell, helped the insurrectionists obtain aid. US Navy gunboats kept Colombian troops out of Panama while it declared independence on November 4, 1903. Widespread bribery of Colombian forces had ensured the absence of serious fighting, and Washington extended formal recognition of the new republic the following week. The subsequent Hay-Bunau-Varilla Treaty, signed on November 18, granted to the United States in perpetuity a 10-mile strip of land on which it would establish the Canal Zone. In exchange, the United States guaranteed Panama's independence.

Roosevelt justified his actions in Panama in the name of progress and modernization. Canal construction began in May 1904 with labor heavily recruited from the British West Indies. Black workers found themselves worked endlessly, paid little, exploited, and ignored by their consular representatives. By the time the Panama Canal opened in 1914, US authorities had created in the Canal Zone a replica of racially segregated American life. Canal authorities housed, schooled, and paid employees according to race, with the greatest benefits accruing to white Americans.

Cuba began its precarious independence with the presidency of Tomás Estrada Palma, whose pro-American inclinations outweighed the nationalist credentials he had amassed as a revolutionist. His efforts to retain power when his term ended were met with opposition and political violence. In an action legitimated by the Cuban-American treaty, the United States moved troops to the island on September 29, 1906, to impose calm. For nearly three years an American proconsul, Charles Magoon, ruled a provisional government before restoring control to Cubans. The US Marines returned in 1912 to suppress black Cuban dissidents who were indignant at their growing exclusion from national political life.

Just as civil disorder provided a justification for US military forays in the Caribbean, a debt crisis in the Dominican Republic in 1904 revived US fears that European nations would intervene. Rather than witness Europeans running customs houses and collecting revenues in the region, the Roosevelt administration preferred that the United States serve as the collection agency. In line with the Monroe Doctrine's principle of noninterference, Washington sought and the Dominican government agreed to discharge the Dominican public debt by means of a customs regime. As Roosevelt framed it, the United States had succeeded to "the exercise of an international police power." Political cartoonists seized on the constable image, augmented by another Roosevelt adage: "Walk softly and carry a big stick." The president failed to achieve congressional approval of the arrangement, whose underlying principles—US preemptive action to avoid European interference in case of default or civil unrest—became known as the Roosevelt Corollary to the Monroe Doctrine. The customs regime continued for two years under the cover of executive fiat and proved effective at relieving bondholders and protecting foreign property. As a result, in 1907 Congress acquiesced to a treaty that perpetuated it.

Caribbean countries suffered from widespread political unrest and indebtedness during this period. Washington saw the failure to create governments that effectively addressed the region's poverty, social stratification, and economic underdevelopment as a hemispheric security threat. Success in the Spanish-American War had strengthened the notion that prompt military action could resolve specific crises. Sending in the US Navy to repel particular challenges to the Monroe Doctrine, however, provided only a short-term solution. Roosevelt's successor, William Howard Taft, took a longer view of the issue, identifying lack of money as the cause of Caribbean weakness. Good administration and defense capabilities would end civil wars and European intrigues. The resulting peace would put these nations on the road to stable development. Taft encouraged North American banks to extend credit to perennially cash-short republics. This so-called dollar diplomacy did not require much federal initiative. Instead, it enlarged the playing field for the US

Figure 28.3 Cartoon image of Roosevelt's famous adage, "Walk softly and carry a big stick." Drawing (ca. 1904). Source: Library of Congress.

banking industry to expand overseas, helped steer countries in the region toward US rather than European sources of capital, and ensured that indebtedness to American interests would check fiscal irresponsibility. Banks considered many Caribbean governments to be risky clients and exacted high rates of interest from them, thus furthering their dependency. In cases where the United States declined to create receiverships or customs regimes, the possibility that it might do so in the event of future default kept debtor governments in line.

Wilsonian Gunboat Diplomacy and Military Occupations

Private banks increased their powerful role in Caribbean economies after Woodrow Wilson became president in 1913. Wilson had campaigned as a reformer on domestic issues, but in foreign policy he expanded federal assistance to financial institutions operating overseas, especially the First National City Bank of New York. Wilson deplored revolutionary regime change, and he endorsed his predecessor's belief that only stable constitutional governments, capable of satisfying their creditors, merited support. Deep social fissures and economic and political structures inherited from colonial times and reaffirmed in the present, however, prevented Caribbean states from achieving the conditions that Wilson thought ideal.

Wilson delineated his policy for Latin America and the Caribbean in a major address delivered on October 27, 1913. With seeming sympathy, he praised the Mexican Revolution of 1910 and compared the experience of the Latin American republics to that of the United States in its infancy. All had known colonial oppression and had revolted against it. The Americas had inherited a common resentment of encroachment by European powers, which, he asserted, continued their practices of exploitation through draconian loans and political subversion. American nations could resist them through alliances with the United States, which was powerful enough to repel both financial opportunists and military aggression. Wilson's speech did not refer to the many incidents in which the United States itself had meddled in the internal affairs of other republics or condoned harsh lending practices by US banks. During the Taft years alone, the United States had helped overthrow Nicaragua's president, established a customs receivership in Honduras, supported an extortionate banking contract in Haiti, sent troops to respond to fears of a black Cuban insurrection, and obstructed business between Mexico and Japan. In spite of Wilson's criticisms of dollar diplomacy, his administration continued it. Changing world conditions, however, demanded some modifications.

Europe plunged into war in August 1914. The United States maintained neutrality until April 1917, but public sympathies lay strongly with Britain and France in their struggle against Germany and other members of the Central Powers alliance. Conflict in the Atlantic seaways and disruption of transatlantic trade meant that fighting could spill over into the Caribbean, threatening US control and providing opportunities for Europeans to establish beachheads. The American purchase of the Danish Virgin Islands in 1917 preempted their possible seizure by Germany.

Washington leaders became increasingly concerned about preventing regional insurgencies and depriving extrahemispheric powers of a foothold in troubled countries. Rather than allow the British or Germans to land marines to protect their nationals, the United States assumed this responsibility. In Haiti, where a cycle of coups and countercoups had undermined civil society and deprived the government of revenues needed for development, the US State Department tried to coax Port-au-Prince into yielding control of customs revenues to American administrators. In July 1914, US Marines armed with sticks physically removed funds from the Haitian central bank and conveyed them to the United States on a warship. Such draconian efforts failed to stem Haiti's political crisis, which climaxed with the assassination of its president in January 1915. This time the Marines returned and remained in Haiti for 20 years.

World war provided the rationale for the military occupation of Haiti and its neighbor, the Dominican Republic, in 1916. In Haiti, the Marines immediately set out to defeat the peasant armies called *cacos* and to co-opt their leaders. US leaders held that deprivation caused Caribbean unrest, and that unemployment and landlessness motivated peasant enlistment in private armies. Military officers accord-

Figure 28.4 The US consul
at Cap Haïtien, an African
American, surrounded by white
officers of the US Navy. Photograph (1915). Source: Naval
Historical Center.

ingly pledged jobs to guerrillas who agreed to disarm. They
promised that labor on the US-owned and financed National
Railroad and employment with the proposed rural constabulary would provide prosperity. Several important insurgent
leaders accepted a truce on September 29, 1915. Yet the US
Marine Corps could not control every remote corner of the
rugged country where guerrillas raided foreign-controlled estates and challenged US patrols. Responding to the likelihood
of renewed *caco* activity, the Marines launched punitive expeditions against bandits
in the countryside, claiming thousands of Haitian lives. In the cities and towns, they
enforced curfews, censored the press, and introduced American-style racial segregation in public places.

The Marine Corps accepted no soldiers of color during this era. The Wilson administration sent political appointees with mediocre qualifications to staff Haitian
ministries and newly conceived bureaucracies at Haitian expense. Key officers and
"experts" hailed from the US South or held racist opinions—a major source of friction with Haitians. They were chosen on the assumption that they knew how to
handle "Negroes." The Haitian legislature, at gunpoint, elected a president who followed US orders. In February 1916, the US Senate consented to a treaty that permitted American control over Haitian finances and authorized training of a native
guard, the Gendarmerie d'Haïti. Brute force kept Haiti relatively quiescent for the
first three years of the occupation, but peasant resistance revived in 1919 when US
authorities forced rural Haitians to build roads, paying and housing them poorly,

often removing them far from their homes and making it impossible for them to tend their farms. Violence perpetrated by the Marines and forced labor so resembled slavery that both city and countryside supported the *caco* war of 1919–20.

The insurrection took place primarily in north and central Haiti, and while the most famous leader, Charlemagne Péralte, was from the privileged class, most of the fighters came from rural communities. Urban opposition took on a different character. Affluent individuals who formerly had disparaged their own Caribbean roots now experienced foreign invasion, in author Léon Laleau's words, as a "shock." Haiti was the first Latin American republic to declare independence and throw off the yoke of slavery as well as that of colonialism. Its history of internal strife had created the bond that united Haitians in defense of national sovereignty. While some members of the bourgeoisie furtively financed the rural war, others chose constitutional means of protest. They reached out for support to anti-imperialists and civil liberties groups in the United States, forming the Union Patriotique, an organization modeled on the National Association for the Advancement of Colored People (NAACP). The embrace of national unity and the rejection of racism and imperialism contributed to a new literature in which writers probed the history and culture of their own countries. Works included Jean Price-Mars's *La vocation de l'élite* (The Vocation of the Elite, 1919) and Laleau's *Le choc* (1932). These texts appeared just as the worldwide "Negro renaissance" of the 1920s began taking shape and fed the stream of what would later be termed *négritude* literature, produced in the Americas by such Francophone Caribbean authors as the Haitians Jacques Roumain, Normil Sylvain, and Carl Brouard; the Martinican Aimé Césaire; and the Guadeloupian Léon Damas.

Continuing fiscal disputes and Washington's fears that the Dominican Republic would fall prey to European wartime machinations led to the occupation of the Dominican Republic by US troops in 1916–24. During this period, the US government made infrastructural improvements that facilitated the expansion of modern cane plantations, but the majority of Dominicans remained poor, including those who had lost their land to sugar and subsequently joined the guerrilla movement. Corporations brought in Haitian immigrants to work the land. Their slavery-scale wages and harsh treatment underwrote the exports that enriched US companies. The Marines treated Dominicans with the same bigotry, brutality, and highhandedness they were practicing in Haiti. The Dominican response also resembled that of Haiti: urban professionals established a protest organization, the Unión Nacional Dominicana, while eastern peasants engaged in armed struggle. Insurgents challenged US hegemony in a war that engulfed the eastern part of the country in 1917. Haitian and Dominican insurgents fought together against the Americans on the frontier between the two countries. The Americans found themselves in a classic guerrilla war in which there were few victories and the enemy successfully recruited rural communities to its cause. A 1922 ceasefire disarmed the Dominican rebels in exchange for pardons.

The Haitian and Dominican experiences were not unique. The US Marines returned to Cuba in 1917 and occupied it until 1922. American investors' considerable interest in the sugar fields joined Washington's attention to hemispheric security in wartime. US officials also faced increasing radicalism in the region, precipitated by World War I and the Bolshevik Revolution. Huge fortunes were made in sugar from this period through the 1920s. The "Dance of the Millions," as the boom and subsequent bust were called, attracted thousands of immigrant workers, but as in the colonial era, the wealth thus generated benefited few Cubans.

In Honduras, the US Marine Corps guarded banana plantations belonging to US firms. The United States also sent Marines to Nicaragua in 1912 to support a conservative regime. They remained there until 1925 and returned in 1927. Nicaraguans did not view these interventions passively. Augusto César Sandino was one of the most determined opponents of US control, and his resistance inspired subsequent generations of Nicaraguans for whom the term Sandinista connoted nationalist authenticity and power. The figure of the rebel appears frequently during this period in the greater Caribbean and Central American region, and it includes the Mexican soldier Pancho Villa, who skirmished on the border with US military authorities during World War I. Nations under US rule understood that their struggles encompassed the region. The experience of one individual exemplified an emerging international critique of imperialism. Gregorio Urbano Gilbert, although among those who received amnesty in the Dominican Republic in 1922, continued to reject the status quo of American domination and went into exile in Cuba. Urbano Gilbert expressed solidarity with Puerto Rican advocates of independence and in 1928 traveled to Nicaragua to fight with Sandino.

A New Model of Control

The ideological rationale of white supremacy played a major role in US interventions in the Caribbean. Another powerful set of beliefs also underwrote Washington's policies. Many American leaders subscribed to an almost religious faith in modernization and in the power of technology to generate social and political change. This thinking stemmed from the contemporaneous domestic reform impulse in the United States. The first two decades of the 20th century formed part of what US historians call the Progressive Era. Activists repelled by rampant corruption in government, urban decay, low standards of education, and unregulated business sought to institute managerial standards and professionalism in politics and corporate behavior. President Wilson achieved electoral success by endorsing this agenda. The transfer of "progressive" ideas to the Caribbean entailed eradi-

Figure 28.5 US officer inspecting Haitian constabulary. Photograph (ca. 1920). Source: Marine Corps History Division.

cating what US administrators perceived as the inefficiency, fraud, and backwardness that had retarded the area's development. They pinpointed one source of trouble in the public and private armies that in many countries had been a stepping-stone to power and a cause of instability. US planners believed that these armies should be disbanded and replaced by wholly professional police and national defense forces which, as the US military putatively did, would remain uninvolved in politics and subservient to civil authority. Military officers from the United States accordingly began to train such units. The Gendarmerie d'Haïti, later called the Garde d'Haïti, and the Guardia Nacional of the Dominican Republic and of Nicaragua, were products of the conviction that the United States could export political culture to nations with different values and traditions.

After the Allied victory in World War I, the United States emerged as the world's premier military power. Nationalists in the Caribbean and Central America nevertheless continued to resist the "protectorates" exercised over their countries. The *cacos* and *gavilleros*, and clamor from US anti-imperialists, forced Warren G. Harding's administration to modify the political structure of these regimes. Congressional hearings on Haiti and the Dominican Republic in 1921 and 1922 led to modest reforms. By the end of the 1920s, pressures intensified to replace Americans in the civil service and military of the occupied countries with indigenous people. The onset of global economic depression in the late 1920s made the occupations increasingly expensive, even when impoverished host countries shouldered much of the administrative cost.

Definitive changes occurred after the Cuban Revolution of 1933. In 1924, Gerardo Machado had won the presidency as an anti-American advocate of reform, but had enacted few positive changes; he held onto repressive power until ousted in 1933. Rejecting Machado's US-endorsed successor, Cubans rallied around the candidacy of Ramon Grau San Martín in September 1933. The power behind the new president's throne was an army sergeant, Fulgencio Batista. Washington proved hostile to the nationalist Grau San Martín and, with the connivance of Batista, forced his resignation in 1934. The United States had performed an about-face. In spite of its heralded opposition to military involvement in politics, it had conspired with a common soldier to effect regime change.

As the Depression worsened, President Franklin D. Roosevelt elaborated a policy initially sketched by his predecessor, Herbert Hoover. The Good Neighbor Policy, officially unveiled in Roosevelt's March 4, 1933, inaugural address, foreswore punitive expeditions, interventions, and occupations in the Americas. Congress repealed the Platt Amendment in 1934, and the Marines left Haiti the same year. The United States nevertheless retained its claim to regional hegemony, including continuing control over some nations' customs revenues. Yet indigenous people would increasingly do the work of securing American interests themselves, as US expatriates yielded civil service and military posts to locals. Caribbean defense forces, trained by US officers, were the chosen instruments. In Cuba, Haiti, the Dominican Republic, and Nicaragua, strongmen emerged from the ranks of the military to assume leadership or wield power behind the scenes. In Cuba it was Batista; in the Dominican Republic, Rafael Trujillo; and in Nicaragua, Anastasio Somoza. These men soon established ruthless dictatorships. In Haiti, the powerful Major Armand Durcé began reconverting the Garde d'Haïti into the conventional army the Americans had earlier dismantled. Political repression dissolved Progressive Era hopes that armed forces would abstain from politics, as Caribbean aspirations for democracy and prosperity were postponed.

Conclusion

American opinion leaders and policy makers between 1898 and 1934 often spoke as if the United States had received special dispensation to impose its decisions on Caribbean nations. Some pointed to divine providence, and others to special characteristics that they felt made the United States an exception to the patterns of political behavior that governed other great powers. In the final analysis, however, US dominance derived from a combination of fortuitous circumstances, none of them mystical or resistant to factual explanation. In the 19th century, the United States had synchronized its policies with Britain, whose naval power—rather than American force—had restrained the New World ambitions of continental European powers. Widespread ideological acceptance of both white supremacy and modernization not only by the technologically advanced nations, but also by many citizens of the developing states of the Caribbean, also benefited the Americans. An association of whiteness with prestige had roots in prior colonial history, and the identification of whiteness with progress in the 20th century further accentuated it. After 1898, an industrializing United States held its own militarily in the region, largely with the approval of other powers that could now tend their colonies elsewhere and rest assured that the United States would maintain order and mind their interests in the Americas. By the mid-1930s, economic conditions favored the replacement of the US protectorates with indigenous authoritarian regimes that served as subcontractors for these same tasks.

29

The American Sugar Kingdom, 1898–1934

CÉSAR J. AYALA

Two institutions have characterized, like no others, the history of the Caribbean since the European discovery and conquest: the plantation and slavery. While slavery in the archipelago ended at different points in the 19th century, the plantation endured and even thrived after abolition. Perhaps the most dramatic example of this trend comes from Cuban sugar production. In the early 1890s, less than a decade after the last slaves achieved freedom in Cuba, the island produced the formidable and unprecedented amount of one million tons of sugar per year.

By the time the United States occupied Cuba and Puerto Rico in 1898, the Cuban sugar industry had been almost totally destroyed by insurgents seeking independence from Spain, but it quickly recovered as Cuban sugar received favorable tariff preference in the US market. In 1905, the United States also placed the Dominican Republic—the third country of the Spanish Caribbean—within its sphere of influence through a "customs receivership," and from 1916 to 1924 its troops occupied the country. The specific political mechanisms through which US colonial power was established in the region varied from island to island. Cuba became a semi-independent republic under the restrictions imposed by the Platt Amendment, while Puerto Rico became a colonial possession of the United States—an "unincorporated territory," in the colonial language of the time, which remains to this day—and its residents were declared US citizens in 1917. The Dominican Republic, which regained its "sovereignty" in 1924, remained firmly within the US colonial orbit. But while the political arrangements of US power differed in each country, the economic impact of its intervention in the region resulted uniformly in the expansion of sugar plantations and sugar monoculture.

It was ironic that the displacement of a second-tier European colonial power, Spain, by a modernizing and economically dynamic power from the Americas resulted in the strengthening of the institution most responsible for Caribbean underdevelopment. To some observers, the expansion of plantation agriculture represented a continuation of colonial structures the inhabitants of the Caribbean had fought so long to eliminate. Other observers pointed out that the new plantations differed from all previous systems in the archipelago. For example, whereas in the British Caribbean indentured servitude from India and China had replaced slavery as the principal form of coerced labor and ended only at the end of World War I in 1918, in the Spanish Caribbean the new plantations primarily used wage labor. In this sense, the type of "extra-economic" coercion that had been characteristic of all previous plantation systems seemed to be absent from what historian Eric Williams later dubbed the American Sugar Kingdom (Williams 1984, 428–42).

Nevertheless, many other evils of plantation agriculture survived. The extreme land concentration, the huge income inequalities, the impoverishment of the rural workers, the dependence of the islands on one export crop at the expense of diversified agriculture, the thwarting of urban development by plantations—all continued under the plantation system that developed as the Spanish Caribbean nations became increasingly integrated into the economic structures of the United States as colonial producers of raw material. The system also exhibited such traits as metropolitan control of the colonial economy as an exclusive region of trade, such that the colony's exchange with other metropolitan economies was limited or nonexistent; concentration of production on "terminal" activities that generated little added value; metropolitan control of the financial system and of all shipping; and imperial tariff preference, which characterized all plantation economies (Best 1968). Still, the plantation system of the American Sugar Kingdom was different from previous such systems in that workers were free, in the sense that all wage workers are free to enter into contracts and free from ownership of independent means of production. Formal freedom mattered immensely to the men and women—former slaves, indentured servants, and peasants—who actually planted, cut, and hauled the cane in the fields.

At the macro level of the world economy, the emergence of a new kind of plantation agriculture in the 20th century also signified a reversal of the domination of beet sugar in the world market. From 1870 to 1900, beet sugar production advanced in Europe and North America, and by 1900, 65% of the sugar sold came from beets. But a new wave of technological innovation and imperial expansion—by Japan in Taiwan, the Netherlands in Java, and the United States in Hawaii and the Philippines as well as the Spanish Caribbean—reinvigorated tropical plantation agriculture after 1900. By 1930 tropical cane had reemerged as the principal source of sugar (62%) in the world market (Ayala 1999, 28–29).

The new imperialism was characterized by important changes in the metropolitan economies that determined patterns of investment in the colonial world and shaped the new configuration of metropole-satellite relations. The advances in energy, materials, chemicals, and medicine associated with the Second Industrial Revolution (1870–1914) transformed the technological basis of industrial production and with it the forms of organization of capital, the size of the enterprises, and the structures of markets. As investments in sophisticated machinery became more expensive and the fixed-capital outlays required for up-to-date industrial enterprises became more formidable, the owner-operated factories of the 19th century gave way to the corporations of the 20th. Management became a progressively specialized function, often with a degree of autonomy from ownership. In many industries only a few large-scale enterprises remained, eliminating the competitive markets of the previous epoch and replacing them with oligopolistic markets in which a few firms dominated in each industry (Eichner 1969). In the United States, sugar refining was not only one of the industries thus transformed by technology but also an organizational pioneer in the emergence of the modern corporation.

Horizontal Consolidation and Vertical Integration

Through a long period of competitive expropriation, the number of sugar refineries in the United States had decreased until, by the 1880s, fewer than 20 enterprises produced the bulk of the industry's output. Thus began a process of consolidation in which the remaining refiners merged their interests and colluded to fix prices. This process required challenges to existing legal structures and particularly to the emerging tenets of antitrust doctrine, as embodied in the Sherman Antitrust Act of 1890. When the original legal form of the "trusts" became illegal, the emerging corporations reorganized themselves as holding companies incorporated in New Jersey to avoid antitrust restrictions.

As in many other industries, the consolidation of American sugar took place under the leadership of one captain of industry—in this case, Henry O. Havemeyer of New York. In 1887, Havemeyer merged 17 sugar refineries into a single enterprise, the American Sugar Refining Company, which controlled 84% of the refining capacity east of the Rocky Mountains and quickly raised prices. From 1888 to 1891, Havemeyer's "Sugar Trust" engaged in a price war with a West Coast competitor, Claus Spreckels, who owned not only refineries in California but also plantations in Hawaii and transportation and shipping facilities to bring the raw sugar from Hawaii into California (Adler 1966). Spreckels's vertically integrated complex of plantations, railroads, shipping lines, and refineries allowed him to withstand the predatory price war and even to establish refineries on the East Coast. Havemeyer heeded the advantages of vertical integration, and soon after his Sugar Trust finally merged with Spreckels's business in 1891, he began to invest in Cuban sugar plantations. After the merger, the American Sugar Refining Company controlled 98% of the US refining capacity. This almost-perfect monopoly soon evolved into an oligopoly in which a few competitors shared markets and administered prices.

Thus, by the time the Spanish-American War of 1898 brought Cuba, the Philippines, and Puerto Rico into the orbit of the United States—and increasingly within reach of its investors—the US sugar refining industry had undergone processes of both horizontal consolidation (mergers between refiners) and vertical integration (refineries acquiring interests in sugar plantations). The industry had also begun experimenting with the innovative corporate form of the "holding company," through which one enterprise could own the stock of another—in this case, refiners owning stock in companies that owned Caribbean sugar mills. Having learned the organizational lessons of the preceding decade, the refiners proceeded to build an impressive empire of vertically integrated sugar plantations in the Caribbean.

US economic policies toward the Spanish Caribbean also aided the growth of the American Sugar Kingdom. The United States granted free trade to Puerto Rican sugar in 1900, and soon thereafter lowered the tariff on Cuban sugar to 80% of the rate applied to products from other countries. These tariff advantages induced metropolitan investment in both Puerto Rico and Cuba. US companies also set up shop in the Dominican Republic during this period. Native capitalists, especially in Puerto Rico and Cuba, benefited as well from US tariff policies and investments.

Before the Spanish-American War, Puerto Rico's main export had been coffee. The sugar tariff and the lack of tariff protection for coffee quickly upset the established ranking of the principal export crops. Sugar exports soared, followed by tobacco (which also enjoyed tariff protection), but coffee production declined after 1898. Although coffee's decline was not permanent, the industry never reclaimed its primacy from sugar. This reversal signified a dramatic restructuring of productive structures and encouraged internal migration from the coffee- to the sugar- and tobacco-producing zones.

In Cuba, railroad construction advanced, linking larger portions of the previously isolated central and eastern provinces of Camagüey and Oriente to the more populous western provinces and the port of Havana (Zanetti 1998). Some US-owned sugar mills were initially established in the east with steamboat connections to US markets but no overland connections to the country's central railroad grid. The expansion of the railroad network soon linked these coastal mills to Cuba's central railroad and to private railroad grids that carried cane inside immense sugar plantation complexes housing thousands of workers. In the Dominican Republic, US investments in Barahona, San Pedro de Macorís, and La Romana generated an expansion similar to those in Cuba and Puerto Rico, although the Dominican Republic's overall sugar production remained below that of its two neighbors.

On paper, scores of seemingly independent US-owned sugar companies operated in the three islands, each one incorporated under its own name. Some of these corporations owned more than one sugar mill. The composition of their boards of directors, however, revealed important links to and control by US refiners. Typically, a company's board would include important figures from the refining industry and from the large US banks associated with the refineries. Thus, for example, in 1921 James Howell Post, president and director of the National Sugar Refining Company, was also a director of National City Bank and of the American Colonial Bank of Porto Rico; a director of three of the four largest US-owned sugar corporations doing business in Puerto Rico; vice-president and director of the Cuban American Sugar Company, a holding company that in turn controlled mills in Cuba and refineries in Cuba and Louisiana; and director of the West India Sugar Finance corporation, which owned 10 mills in the Dominican Republic, representing more than half of the sugar output of that country. Clearly, Post sat on the boards of these Caribbean companies representing something more than his own personal investments. He actually served as an institutional linkage between the US sugar refineries, the Caribbean plantations that produced raw sugar, and the most important US bank in the Spanish Caribbean, National City Bank. Because the plantations produced the principal input of the sugar refining business, this system of holding companies linking Caribbean plantations to US refineries was a form of international vertical integration in the industry.

The percentage of the output of the American Sugar Kingdom that was owned or controlled by the US refining industry increased during World War I, when the destruction of European beet crops led to high sugar prices. In January 1916, for example, Manuel Rionda, an established New York sugar broker, traveled to Cuba with financial resources provided by a consortium of banks, and in one month purchased 17 large sugar mills whose combined output surpassed that of all the mills in the Dominican Republic, at a cost of over $48 million. The Cuba Cane Sugar Corporation instantly became the largest raw sugar producer in the world and made formidable profits as the price of raw sugar soared from an average of 3 cents a pound before 1914 to almost 20 cents a pound in 1920. Many local sugar companies also profited during this period, but by the end of the war, US companies owned more than half of the sugar-producing capacity of Cuba, about 80% of that of the Dominican Republic, and about 55% of that of Puerto Rico.

When the European beet crops recovered, the price of sugar in the world market collapsed. Beginning in December 1920, many Cuban sugar mill owners who had acquired huge debts to expand capacity in the context of soaring prices began to go bankrupt, and many of their mills were taken over by US sugar companies and banks. Through this dynamic, the network of refiners and bankers who controlled most of the assets of the Spanish Caribbean's plantation economy could deepen its control of the sugar industry in crisis as well as in boom times.

Colonos

Like so many plantation economies, the American Sugar Kingdom was a place where wealth was highly concentrated into a few hands and social inequality was profound. However, between the immensely powerful corporations that owned the sugar mills and the poorly paid cane workers stood a complex layer of intermediate farmers who delivered cane to the sugar mills under diverse contractual conditions. These farmers, known as *colonos*, were a sort of "middle class" of the plantation world, though they were not a homogeneous group. The word *colono* referred to small-scale farmers who planted cane only with the help of their immediate families. But it also referred to cane farmers who owned thousands of acres of land, hired hundreds of workers, and sold their cane to the mills. Thus the *colonato* (system of satellite cane farming) consisted of a few large landowners and many small farmers who had a common interest against the sugar mills, which tried to pay as little as possible for their cane.

The class of colonos emerged after emancipation. It was most developed in Cuba before the Spanish-American War, and much less so in the Dominican Republic and Puerto Rico. Before emancipation in 1886, many *ingenio* (sugar mill) owners in Cuba had operated both cane farms and sugar mills, which were designed to grind all the cane harvested by slaves on their farms. But improved technologies allowed newer mills to process much more cane than the older facilities, leading to a post-abolition differentiation of ingenio owners. The more prosperous owners developed high-capacity mills called *centrales*, but since neighboring farms were occupied by other owners, they could not consolidate enough land to produce all the cane that their new mills could grind. Their less successful neighbors, meanwhile, closed their obsolete grinding mills but retained their land, specializing now in the production of cane for delivery to the modernized centrales. These cane producers, who were the majority of the ingenio owners, became colonos. The separation of milling from cane growing was defended by contemporaries as an advance corre-

sponding to the principle of the division of labor, but it reflected post-abolition capital shortages and the difficulties of overhauling land allotments that corresponded to the grinding capacity of an earlier era. This internal transformation of the Cuban planter class took place before 1898.

Figure 29.1 Sugar mill at Aguacate, Cuba. Photograph (ca. 1904). Source: Library of Congress.

After 1898, US corporations erected gigantic sugar mills on virgin lands in eastern Cuba, in the provinces of Camagüey and Oriente. This land was not fragmented by an existing plantation system and often had to be cleared for first-time planting. Some of the new sugar companies owned tens of thousands of acres. Initially they sought to function as unitary enterprises, although on a much larger scale than the ingenios of the epoch of slavery. They tried planting all the land under the management of the sugar mill, in a system known as *tierras de administración*. Very soon, however, mill managers realized that placing thousands of cane cutters under one management structure was a call for easy unionization and labor unrest. They then turned to a new type of colono known as the *colono financiado* or *colono controlado* (financed or controlled colono).

The colonos of the gigantic mills of eastern Cuba were renters of land, not owners. They could not make mills compete for their cane, as had happened among colonos in Cuba's western provinces. Instead, their leases stipulated how much cane they had to deliver and at what price. The US owners of the mills also effectively subcontracted their labor problems to this new group of colonos financiados, who were in charge of recruiting and paying workers, often in charge of providing housing for them, and generally in debt to the mills that advanced the money for the operation of the farms.

Despite the diversity in their ranks, colonos managed to organize for certain reforms. After the Cuban Revolution of 1933, for example, they fought for state regulation of the percentages of sugar in the cane that could kept by the colono and by the mill, and for the employment of state-hired—as opposed to mill-hired—chemists, thus guaranteeing an impartial measuring of the cane's sugar content. Regardless of whether the colonos were independent or financed by the mills, the very existence of the colono class buffered the relationship between Caribbean labor and metropolitan capital, often allowing foreign mill owners to avoid struggles with local workers. On issues of working conditions and wages, laborers typically directed their demands at their immediate employer, who was more often than not a local Cuban, Puerto Rican, or Dominican colono.

Labor and Migration

The expansion of sugar production in the Spanish Caribbean after 1898 was formidable. The combined sugar production of the islands increased from 433,000 tons in 1900 to 1,127,000 tons in 1902. Output then doubled between 1902 and 1910, and again between 1910 and 1919, reaching 5,033,000 tons. Thus, in a short span of two decades, sugar production increased by a remarkable 1,062%. This dizzying rate of expansion was accompanied by a feverish colonization of virgin lands, especially in central and eastern Cuba and in the Dominican Republic (Barahona and La Romana). Such colonization often meant that great numbers of cane cutters were required in areas that had previously been only sparsely populated. Thus, some regions of the American Sugar Kingdom resorted to the importation of workers from other regions of the Caribbean.

Migratory flows of workers changed the ethnic and linguistic composition of the populations of these zones. From the smaller British islands of the Lesser Antilles, tens of thousands of workers migrated to the Dominican Republic and Cuba in search of employment. Most migrated seasonally, but over time many stayed and settled in their working places. These workers were known at the time as *cocolos*, a pejorative term that has been recovered by some island populations and turned into a popular source of pride among their descendants. The cultural legacy of these populations in the islands is rich. For example, Dominican baseball, which today produces more excellent players for the US major leagues per capita than any region of the United States itself, originated as a cricket league that eventually evolved into a baseball league among second-generation Dominicans of West Indian extraction. The West Indians, explains sports historian Rob Ruck (1991), had their "holy trinity": (1) mutual aid societies, (2) Garveyism, and (3) cricket.

The migratory flows were large and complex. Jamaicans and Haitians migrated to Cuba, as did workers from Spain and the Canary Islands (Ayala 1999, 148–82). British West Indians and Haitians migrated to the Dominican Republic. Here the Haitian workers were recruited and worked under conditions that can certainly be characterized as unfree (Plant 1987; Lemoine 1987). They were also subjected to inordinate levels of violence: in 1937, for example, at least 12,000 Haitian workers were killed in a genocidal massacre in the Dominican Republic (Roorda 1996).

The only region of the American Sugar Kingdom that did not experience massive immigration was Puerto Rico. There, much higher population densities than those in Cuba or the Dominican Republic and the existence of an already largely dispossessed peasantry allowed the sugar mills to find enough workers no matter how much production expanded. In fact, even as the industry was booming, Puerto Rican workers left for the Dominican Republic, Cuba, and Hawaii in search of employment. Some cocolos from the Lesser Antilles migrated to Puerto Rico, notably to the island of Vieques in the 1870s, but the numbers never matched the flows into Cuba and the Dominican Republic.

These labor flows indicate the relative scarcity of workers in different regions of the Hispanic Caribbean. In Cuba, an entrenched agricultural proletariat in the provinces of Pinar del Río, Havana, Matanzas, and Santa Clara provided much of the manpower for the sugar mills. However, in Camagüey and Oriente, which experienced explosive growth during World War I, the establishment of plantations in virgin zones forced mills to rely on immigrant harvesters. By the mid-1920s these eastern provinces were producing more sugar than the rest of Cuba. Labor scarcity due to the mills' explosive growth and competition for workers—to the point of poaching each other's skilled labor—provided workers with a measure of bargaining power. Tens of thousands of workers came to Cuba yearly for the harvest, and many stayed and settled. The absence of a dispossessed peasantry and the presence of a highly mobile immigrant labor force granted workers more power of resistance than is generally assumed (Carr 1998).

In the Dominican Republic, similarly, the lack of a dispossessed peasantry compelled planters to seek workers in the British Caribbean and in Haiti. Although labor scarcity may have given workers a measure of bargaining power with the mills and colonos, their working conditions have not been studied. In Puerto Rico, the existence of a large mass of dispossessed rural proletarians guaranteed that the mills had an adequate supply of labor without having to resort to the importation of workers. Labor organizing by the Federación Libre de Trabajadores (FLT, or Free Federation of Workers), which was affiliated with the American Federation of

Labor, provided some protection, but for the most part Puerto Rican agricultural workers remained an unorganized group. The Great Depression of the 1930s generated militant responses and organizing among the workers in Cuba and Puerto Rico—particularly during the harvest of 1933–34, during which Cuban sugar workers participated in the revolutionary overthrow of the Machado regime (Carr 1996), while their Puerto Rican counterparts participated in a wildcat general strike in alliance with the Nationalist Party of Pedro Albizu Campos against the leadership of the FLT (Taller de Formación Política 1984).

As a system of plantations, the American Sugar Kingdom was a heterogeneous social formation that combined highly centralized investment by metropolitan capital with diverse local conditions. By the early 20th century, it was operating on an unprecedented scale. The Guánica mill of the South Porto Rico Sugar Company in Puerto Rico, for example, produced 93,031 tons of sugar in the harvest of 1926–27 and more than 100,000 tons yearly in the 1930s. It ground sugarcane from all of southwestern Puerto Rico as well as sugarcane shipped by barge from the Dominican Republic over the Mona Passage. It produced more sugar in one year than all the combined sugar mills of Puerto Rico in any year of the 19th century. That is, the annual capacity of this sugar mill was more than that of all the ingenios of the slavery epoch, or even of the the larger mills that existed between emancipation (1873) and the Spanish-American War (1898).

From the epoch of slavery to the end of World War I, the gravitational center of the Cuban sugar industry had gradually shifted eastward, from Matanzas to Camagüey and Oriente, where US sugar companies built mills on the magnitude of Guánica. The Chaparra and Delicias mills of the Cuban American Sugar Company probably represented the largest sugar complex in the archipelago. Cunagua and Jaronú, of the American Sugar Refining Company, produced more than 95,000 tons of sugar each. The mills of the Punta Alegre Sugar Company and the United Fruit Company in Cuba were also on this scale. In the Dominican Republic, La Romana Sugar Mill, which is still in operation, surpassed all others in output and was one of the giants of the Spanish Caribbean.

Economic Collapse and Revolution

The onset of the Great Depression strained the structures of the American Sugar Kingdom, which had been laid out in the period between 1898 and 1929. Beginning in the 1920s, price competition became more acute internationally, and producers of raw sugar faced difficulties, especially in Cuba. Both Puerto Rico and Cuba enjoyed imperial preference in tariffs, but to different degrees. That difference seemed to matter little until 1921. As a US territory, Puerto Rico enjoyed unlimited free entry for its products into the US market, while the nominally independent republic of Cuba enjoyed a 20% tariff reduction. In the 1920s, US beet producers requested and received increased tariff protection from Congress; meanwhile, tariffs on raw sugar were raised several times, slowly displacing Cuban sugar from the US market. The big winners were the Philippines and Puerto Rico, which, together with the beet producers, now enjoyed increased protection from Cuban competition. And each time the Philippines and Puerto Rico increased their share of the US market and continental beet producers felt displaced, tariffs were raised again in a self-propelling cycle.

By the 1930s the situation of Cuban sugar was dire. Its share of the US market had decreased, and in an attempt to increase prices through voluntary reductions of output, the country's total sugar production had declined. In 1933 the Cuban polity exploded in a revolution against dictator Gerardo Machado. The revolution spread to the sugar mills and combined militant action by hundreds of thousands of sugar workers with broader calls for reform, for the derogation of the Platt Amendment and the return of sovereignty to Cuba, and for regulation of the sugar industry. Similarly, in January 1934 a general strike in Puerto Rico mobilized the sugar proletariat of that island in a wildcat, unapproved action against the conservative union leaders, who sat in the local legislature and in the governor's cabinet. The period of expansion of the American Sugar Kingdom thus ended with the social upheavals caused by the Great Depression.

Responses to the crisis varied from island to island. Despite the fact that the American Sugar Kingdom included one US territory and two presumptively sovereign nations, the economic solutions offered by the metropolitan state treated them all as part of a larger US economic sphere. The Jones-Costigan Act of 1934 allocated sugar quotas to the different sugar-producing regions that supplied the United States (continental beet producers; Louisiana cane growers; the US territories of Hawaii, the Philippines, and Puerto Rico; and "sovereign" Cuba). Under the terms of the act, each region was guaranteed the purchase of a set amount of sugar at a fixed price. Quantities of sugar above these limitations were not guaranteed that price, and sold for less. This solution was part of the increased state regulation initiated by the Roosevelt administration to initiate a recovery from the ravages produced by unrestricted, largely unregulated functioning of the so-called "free" market.

This free market, in its plantation form, had never brought real prosperity to the inhabitants of the islands, particularly the small farmers and the sugar workers. Now, with the Depression, conditions became abysmal. To solve the problems of overproduction, for example, cane crops were restricted and even destroyed. During the crisis, critics of the free market system that had produced these plantations began to voice their concerns, not only in the colonial islands but within the metropole itself. "As our economic system works . . . it seems the greater the surplus of wheat in Nebraska farms, the longer the breadlines in New York," noted US Secretary of Agriculture Henry Wallace. "To have to destroy a crop is a shocking commentary on our civilization" (Wallace 1934, 172, 138–39). For once, the colonial subjects of the islands of the American Sugar Kingdom could add their voices to those of their counterparts inside the metropole, and reply: "Indeed."

WORKS CITED

Adler, Jacob. 1966. *Claus Spreckels: The Sugar King in Hawaii.* Honolulu: University of Hawaii Press.

Ayala, César J. 1999. *American Sugar Kingdom: The Plantation Economy of the Spanish Caribbean, 1898–1934.* Chapel Hill: University of North Carolina Press.

Best, Lloyd. 1968. "The Mechanism of Plantation Type Societies: Outlines of a Model of Pure Plantation Economy." *Social and Economic Studies* 17, no. 3: 283–326.

Carr, Barry. 1996. "Mill Occupations and Soviets: The Mobilization of Sugar Workers in Cuba, 1917–1933." *Journal of Latin American Studies* 28:129–58.

———. 1998. "'Omnipotent and Omnipresent'? Labor Shortages, Worker Mobility, and Employer Control in the Cuban Sugar Industry, 1910–1934." In *Identity and Struggle at the Margins of the Nation State: The Laboring Peoples of Central America and the Hispanic Caribbean*, edited by Aviva Chomsky and Aldo Lauria Santiago. Durham, NC: Duke University Press.

Eichner, Alfred S. 1969. *The Emergence of Oligopoly: Sugar Refining as a Case Study* Baltimore: Johns Hopkins University Press.

Lemoine, Maurice. 1987. *Azúcar amargo: Hay esclavos en el Caribe.* Santo Domingo: CEPAE.

Plant, Roger. 1987. *Sugar and Modern Slavery: A Tale of Two Countries.* London: Zed Books.

Roorda, Eric Paul. 1996. "Genocide Next Door: The Good Neighbor Policy, the Trujillo Regime, and the Haitian Massacre of 1937." *Diplomatic History* 2, no. 3.

Ruck, Rob. 1991. *The Tropic of Baseball: Baseball in the Dominican Republic.* Westport, CT: Meckler.

Taller de Formación Política. 1984. *¡Huelga en la caña!* Río Piedras, PR: Editorial Huracán.

Wallace, Henry. 1934. *New Frontiers.* New York: Reynal and Hitchcock.

Williams, Eric. 1984 [1970]. *From Columbus to Castro: The History of the Caribbean, 1492–1969.* New York: Vintage Books.

Zanetti, Oscar, and Alejandro García. 1998. *Sugar and Railroads: A Cuban History, 1837–1959.* Chapel Hill: University of North Carolina Press.

30

Culture, Labor, and Race in the Shadow of US Capital

WINSTON JAMES

In 1885 a remarkable book, *De l'égalité des races humaines,* was quietly published in Paris. Apart from its intrinsic qualities, the book was remarkable because its author, Anténor Firmin (1850–1911), was a black Haitian, and its appearance marked the emergence onto the public stage of newly self-confident African Caribbean intellectuals. Three years later, five African Jamaicans collaborated on another important book aimed at combating racist stereotypes of black Jamaicans. *Jamaica's Jubilee* was indicative of a trend that continued over the two generations following Firmin's book. From at least the 18th century, Caribbeans of mixed descent—"coloreds" and "mulattoes"—had had greater access to education, and thus to the wherewithal for intellectual combat, than their black compatriots. Those of supposedly "un-mixed African blood"—"Negroes"—emerged as intellectuals later, generally a generation or two after emancipation. Significantly, the rise of the black Caribbean intellectual was overdetermined by racist and imperialist provocation between 1880 and 1930, when the peoples of the Caribbean, especially those of African descent, suffered the dual burden of amplified racist calumny and new imperial aggression.

Racism, paradoxically, became more intense in the aftermath of slavery, as former slaves pressed for greater autonomy from their erstwhile masters, who struggled for control over an unruly labor force newly untethered from the formal bonds of slavery. In this battle over the concrete meaning of freedom, racist ideologues endeavored to tip the scales in favor of the ruling class and against the former slaves. Meanwhile, the extraordinary growth of capitalism in Europe and North America propelled imperial expansion into the non-European world in search of raw materials, agricultural commodities, and new markets for manufactured goods. Racism and new overseas adventures went hand in hand in a diabolical dialectic—the racism provided ideological cover for a resurgent imperialism, which in turn spawned even more outlandish racist ideas aimed at legitimating the existence of that imperialism, not to mention its "excesses." Even after the emergence of the United States as the dominant power in the Caribbean, the imperial drama remained the same in all essentials as it had been under European hegemony. But one of the most distinguishing features of the period was the remarkable extent to which those on the receiving end of this onslaught responded through cultural, intellectual, and broadly ideological counterattacks and political organization.

Carlyle, Froude, and the Burden of Black Response

In 1849 the British intellectual Thomas Carlyle had published "Occasional Discourse on the Negro Question," a notoriously racist diatribe against the newly emancipated Africans of the British Caribbean. Carlyle viewed emancipation as a failure attributable to the inherent racial characteristics of Africans and, to a lesser extent, the misguided interference of British abolitionists. Black Caribbeans provided no immediate response to Carlyle's views—unsurprisingly, since, apart from a besieged Haiti, they had only in 1838 begun staggering out of slavery. Another racist outrage was perpetrated in the 1860s by novelist Anthony Trollope. In *The West Indies and the Spanish Main*, Trollope turned Carlyle's précis on the "nigger question" into a book, using his predecessor's offensive language. Their compatriot Charles Kingsley's *At Last: A Christmas in the West Indies* (1871) also caused offense, but despite Kingsley's condescension and evident racism, his book was more complex and contradictory than Carlyle's and Trollope's. Kingsley saw sugar as a "sweet malefactor" and adjudged the large sugar plantations as the "bane of the West Indies." Moreover, he explicitly described himself as "an advocate of 'petite culture'" (smallholdings) and the development of a black peasantry (Kingsley [1871] 1889, 319). But the Caribbean intelligentsia was quickly coming of age, and unlike Carlyle, Trollope, and

Kingsley it received a vigorous response from black and colored intellectuals armed with newspaper and magazine outlets of their own.

An even more vociferous response greeted publication of James Anthony Froude's 1888 travelogue, *The English in the West Indies, or the Bow of Ulysses*. Froude, Carlyle's protégé and biographer, especially singled out the black peasantry, the black middle class, and Haitians for attack. Black Caribbeans widely condemned Froude's book, especially in Trinidad, which had the most prosperous black middle class and enjoyed the most vibrant black press in the late-19th-century Caribbean. The most famous and sustained critique of Froude was written by a Trinidadian of self-described "unmixed African blood," John Jacob Thomas (ca. 1840–89), who considered it his "patriotic duty" as a "representative of Her Majesty's Ethiopic West Indian subjects" to undertake "our self-vindication" against "our assailant" (Thomas [1889] 1969, 56–58). His book *Froudacity: West Indian Fables by James Anthony Froude* was a systematic and efficient dismantling of the house that Froude had built. With wit and sarcasm, Thomas challenged not only Froude's "facts" but also his outlandish interpretations and baneful political extrapolations.

But Thomas was by no means Froude's only Caribbean critic. A host of others wrote critical reviews in the local press. Of special note is "Mr. Froude's Negrophobia; or Don Quixote as a Cook's Tourist," a 40-page critique by N. Darnell Davis (1846–1915), a colored Grenadian working in the civil service of British Guiana. Apparently unknown to Thomas and his literary circle in Trinidad, it was published in a Georgetown (British Guiana) journal, *Timehri*, in 1888 and also separately as a pamphlet. With a polemical style similar to Thomas's, Davis had in fact used the terms "Froudacity" and "Froudacious" before Thomas did.

But neither Thomas nor Davis performed an effective exorcism on Froude's specter of black Haiti. From its birth in 1804, Haiti had been a negative symbol to slaveholders and racists. As Theophilus Scholes, the distinguished African Jamaican scholar, noted in 1899, the nation was put to a variety of uses by the enemies of black people and black advancement. Instead of challenging the falsehoods spread by those enemies, both Thomas and Davis were more anxious to separate themselves and the British Caribbean from association with Haiti. We English West Indians, they argued, are not like the Haitians, despite the "sameness of our ancestry and the colour of our skin." And what was the distinction? Well, they are savages and we are not. Thus Thomas, who was far more progressive on Haiti than Davis, took great exception to the Haitian comparison—"perversity gone wild in the manufacture of false analogies"—but for the wrong reasons: "He [Froude] calls upon us to believe that, in spite of being free, educated, progressive, and at peace with all men, we West Indian Blacks, were we ever to become constitutionally dominant in our native islands, would emulate in savagery our Haytian fellow-Blacks." Despite praising the Haitians who "so gloriously conquered their merited freedom," Thomas went on: "We saw them free, but perfectly illiterate barbarians, impotent to use the intellectual resources of which their valour had made them possessors, in the shape of books on the spirit and technical details of a highly developed national existence" (Thomas [1899] 1969, 53–55).

In the end, then, the Haitians were largely left undefended by their "British" Caribbean brothers, and would have to defend themselves. A long and distinguished line of Haitian intellectuals countered the notion of black inferiority, of whom the most distinguished was Firmin, author of *De l'égalité des races humaines*. In a work drawing upon the most up-to-date findings from different disciplines, Firmin systematically countered the racist theories of Arthur de Gobineau (1816–1882), who is frequently referred to as the "father" of modern racism (Biddiss 1970). Contrary to Gobineau's assertion in *Essai sur l'inégalité des races humaines*, Firmin argued that humans everywhere "are endowed with the same qualities and defects, without distinction based on color or anatomical shape. The races are equal; they are all capable of rising to most noble virtues, of reaching the highest intellectual development; they are equally capable of falling into a state of total degeneration" ([1885] 2002, 450). But Firmin intended a general critique of racist reasoning and only incidentally a defense of Haiti itself.

The latter task was undertaken by J. N. Léger, a Haitian diplomat based in Washington, D.C. Explicitly aiming to correct erroneous ideas about Haiti, Léger devoted two-thirds of *Haiti: Her History and Her Detractors* to its history, emphasizing the peculiar hardships and unique accomplishments of the second independent state in the Americas and the first black republic forged by the heroic efforts of former slaves. According to Léger, at the root of the "unceasing and persistent calumnies" against Haiti was the fact that, in overthrowing slavery, the slaves of Saint-Domingue had committed "an unpardonable crime" in the eyes of the slaveholding world. This crime was rendered all the more monstrous as any black person "upon setting foot on the Haitian soil would be considered as a freedman." Citing the political history of western European nations, Léger argued forcefully that the so-called political instability of Haiti was no different than what other nations had experienced at a similar stage of development. He challenged the charges of Haitian cannibalism and illustrated the way in which malicious rumor and hearsay take on a life of their own. While acknowledging the positive role that vodou played in the slave insurrection of 1791, Léger went out of his way to assert that it was dying out. Haiti, he argued, was not relapsing into barbarism but advancing in "civilization" (Léger 1907, 300–71).

Like Firmin and the Haitian intellectuals before him, Léger challenged the notion of black inferiority and made the case for the ancient African roots of "civilization" while largely separating himself from contemporary Africa and supposed African cultural forms in the New World. As one scholar has observed, these intellectuals "rarely challenged the superiority of European culture and they minimised the role of African elements in the heritage of the Haitian people" (Nicholls 1996, 128–29). But the prolonged American occupation of Haiti (1915–34) would serve as a catalyst to elevate the status of popular cultural forms and their connection with Africa.

Empire, Labor, Black Contact Zones, and Resistance

The year 1898 is rightly regarded as a watershed year in the history of the Americas. In many ways the end of the Spanish-American War and the annexation of Puerto Rico and de facto colonization of Cuba by the United States simply marked the culmination of long-standing trends. However, this assumption of control of the state apparatus in the former Spanish colonies cleared the way for more rapid and systematic penetration of American capital into the region. A new economic era emerged in the Spanish-speaking Caribbean, marked by large-scale sugar production using modern techniques. In contrast, the non-Hispanic Caribbean—especially the older British colonies—continued in a long economic decline. Thus the period was marked by conspicuously uneven development. In some areas sugar plantations were in secular decline, while in others there was almost exponential growth; in some areas there was an emergent—at times even prosperous—peasantry, while in others there were virtually no peasants at all; in some areas land was cheap, in others very expensive; and in some areas wages were several times higher than in others.

Little wonder, then, that during the late 19th and early 20th centuries the region was also characterized by enormous waves of labor migration from the peasantless regions where wages were low to the ones where wages were higher and land was relatively cheap. Islands such as Barbados and Antigua were among those that experienced high emigration, while Trinidad, British Guiana, and the expanding capitalist economies of the Spanish-speaking Caribbean—especially Cuba—became the primary destinations. The expanding banana enclaves of Central America, opened and developed by US capital during this period, would also become an important magnet for migrants. And from the 1880s until its completion in 1914, the Panama Canal construction project attracted hundreds of thousands of Caribbean workers, including a substantial number from the French islands of Guadeloupe and Martinique.

Although black migrants earned substantially higher wages on the sugar plantations of Cuba, on the banana plantations of Costa Rica, or in the Panama Canal zone than in labor-exporting societies such as Jamaica and Barbados, racism was even more overt in these settings, and life even cheaper. Conditions conspired to generate a racial consciousness where one had hardly existed before. These men—and they were overwhelmingly male—had hardly, if ever, heard the word "nigger" in their home societies. Here, the expression was commonplace, along with a humiliating segregation also unheard of in their home countries. Many of the migrants, especially the Jamaicans, had never met people from islands such as Barbados and Guadeloupe. Thrown together by the necessity of the labor process and the common affliction of racism, these workers developed not only a Caribbean consciousness but also a black and in many instances pan-Africanist one. After all, they were being discriminated against not because they were Barbadian or Martinican, but because they were black. The starkness and centripetal power of racism transformed them profoundly.

In response, they developed structures and institutions of mutual support and solidarity. On the large centrales in San Pedro de Macorís, Dominican Republic, workers from the eastern Caribbean established friendships that "extended beyond their home islands as black men from all over the Lesser Antilles became acquainted with one another" (Richardson 1983, 129). In the barracks, those who were most literate wrote letters home for others. They played music to provide diversion after a day's labor. They shared island stories and learned of the similarities and differences that existed among the islanders. And the same dynamic of community formation developed in Panama, Costa Rica, Cuba, and similar locations.

These locations served as "black contact zones"—sites at which peoples of African descent from different geographic spaces met, interacted, and commingled with one another, often for the first time. Metropolitan cities such as London, Paris, and New York also operated as black contact zones. Within these areas, smaller and more intimate units—such as barracks, hostels, workingmen's halls or clubs, lodges, mutual aid societies, and churches—facilitated denser networks of interaction between their members. Black contact zones were often sites of shared suffering and black solidarity, congenial spaces for the development of black internationalism and pan-Africanism. Not surprisingly, organizations such as the Universal Negro Improvement Association (UNIA) found ready adherents and recruits in such environments.

Founded in Kingston, Jamaica, in 1914, the UNIA moved its headquarters to Harlem, New York, in 1916. Its leader, Marcus Garvey, a man of the Caribbean diaspora himself, had lived and traveled in Europe and had worked on banana plantations in Costa Rica. He had developed a racial consciousness during his travels, and felt the need to form an organization that addressed the general suffering, complaints, and aspirations of black people around the world. Not for nothing did he name his organization the *Universal* Negro Improvement Association, for its appeal extended beyond his fellow Jamaicans and African Caribbeans to all Africans—those at home and those abroad, as he put it. The organization grew meteorically, to as many as two million members and supporters and almost 1,100 chapters on every continent, most of them in the United States. A disproportionate number of UNIA

Figure 30.1 Marcus Garvey. Lithograph (ca. 1920).

chapters within the circum-Caribbean were located in black contact zones: Cuba and Panama had by far the most (101 out of 221), while Costa Rica, Honduras, Guatemala, Nicaragua, the Dominican Republic, and Puerto Rico collectively had 55 in 1926. Thus, US imperialism in the region—whether in the form of the ICC in Panama, or of the United Fruit Company in Costa Rica, or of its many incarnations in Cuba, the Dominican Republic, and Puerto Rico—created a black working-class counterpoint in the form of the UNIA, which in Panama, Cuba, and the Dominican Republic was often inseparable from black labor unions.

Occupied Haiti and Expressions of Black Affirmation

Haiti again came to the fore of black Caribbean consciousness with the US invasion in 1915. Despite the US government's declaration that the intervention was taking place for humanitarian reasons—to prevent anarchy and bloodshed—its real motivations were geopolitical and economic, driven by the logic of the Monroe Doctrine, which had informed US relations with the rest of the Americas since the 1820s. The Panama Canal (then under construction) and its economic and strategic importance gave this policy even greater urgency. In Haiti the Americans not only suppressed the recalcitrant black peasantry but also alienated the black and colored middle class, much of which had at least tacitly supported the takeover. The national humiliation and racist degradation contributed to a radical reassessment of Haitian national identity and culture, ending with the most unequivocal affirmation of its African connections.

Jim Crow landed with the Marines in Haiti. The chief civilian administrators were all from the Deep South, chosen for their political loyalty rather than their competence. The Americans disparaged all Haitians, whether *mulâtre* or *noir*, as "niggers" and "gooks." They barred all nonwhites, including the mulatto Haitian president, from the American Club. The few Americans who had the courage to marry Haitian women were ostracized by their fellow countrymen. The colored Haitian elite were shocked by the racism of the occupiers. Indeed, the Americans had a special animus toward this class, whose members did not offer the level of deference expected by white Marines.

The Marines' conduct in the countryside was brutal. The hated *corvée* forced-labor system elicited resistance by the peasantry, which organized in rural guerrilla groups known as *cacos* and fought back with primitive arms and meager resources. The leader of the resistance, Charlemagne Péralte, a former officer in the disbanded army and a landowner, was captured and murdered by the Marines, his corpse placed on display to intimidate others. During the first five years of the occupation, US authorities estimated that 2,250 Haitians were killed, in contrast to "14 to 16" Marines. But Haitian sources put the number killed at no fewer than 6,000 peasants, with another 5,500 dying in "forced labor camps" (Schmidt 1971, 103; Trouillot 1990, 107).

In 1932, two years before the occupation ended, a young black Haitian writer, Lorimer Denis, noted that there was a "profitable" aspect to the situation: in the face of the invaders, Haitians had been forced to unify their interests and their efforts (Nicholls 1996, 165). The occupation indeed triggered an unprecedented level of self-examination among the Haitian intelligentsia, black and colored alike. It propelled what became known as the ethnological movement, which generated a burst of literary expression despite American censorship. This movement, begun by Justin Dorsainvil before the American occupation, aimed at identifying and analyzing the distinctive features of Haitian life. It focused on the culture of the majority of Haitians, particularly the peasantry.

The most distinguished of the ethnologists was Jean Price-Mars (1876–1969), scion of a long line of distinguished black Haitians. After attending college and medical school in Port-au-Prince and earning a doctorate in Paris, Price-Mars embarked upon a career as school master, doctor, university lecturer and rector, deputy, senator, diplomat, presidential candidate, cabinet minister, and prolific author. He became the doyen of Haitian intellectuals.

Price-Mars is remembered primarily for his remarkable volume, *Ainsi parla l'oncle*, which was first published in 1928 but had largely been presented years before as lectures. Addressing the Haitian people, especially the elite, Price-Mars sought to help rescue the nation from its "collective bovaryism," its tendency to see itself as something other than what it really was. This condition, he argued, had existed from the birth of Haiti in 1804, which had involved the "absurd and grandiose task" of becoming "'colored' Frenchmen." Through "a disconcerting paradox," the Haitians who had "if not the finest, at least the most binding, the most moving history of the world," felt an "embarrassment barely concealed, indeed shame, in hearing of their distant past." The architects of black slavery had spread the idea abroad that "Negroes were the scum of society, without history, without morality, without religion, who had to be infused by any manner whatsoever with new moral values, to be humanized anew." After their heroic and astonishing triumph, the "simplest choice" for the Haitian revolutionaries, "badly in need of national cohesion, was to copy the only model that they comprehended." They thus "donned the old frock of western civilization shortly after 1804." In this undertaking, "we forgot we were simply Haitians . . . men born of determined historic conditions, having collected in their minds, just as all other human groups, a psychological complex that gives to the Haitian society its specific physiognomy."

Price-Mars aimed to replace this view by presenting Haiti with a mirror held up to itself. He sought to "collect the facts of our social life, to assess the gestures, the attitudes of our people, however humble they may be, to compare them to those of other peoples, to examine their origins, and to situate them in the general life of man on the planet" (Price-Mars [1928] 1983, 7–10). He mobilized all the pertinent human sciences—anthropology, linguistics, musicology, sociology, history, and literary criticism—to bring to light what he called, somewhat erroneously, the "indigenous" (black) culture of Haiti. He analyzed Haitian folklore and examined Kreyol as a fully formed language. Similarly, he attended to the music of rural Haiti and to the practice of vodou, the widely disparaged religion that infused so much of Haitian culture. Unlike many of his predecessors, Price-Mars acknowledged the heterogeneity of African cultural forms and affirmed without apology the extraordinary debt that Haitian culture owed to African ancestral roots. He also considered Haitian linkages to contemporary Africa.

Perhaps because of the prevailing censorship, Price-Mars made only passing reference to the occupiers of his country. But in a 1922 speech used as the coda for the volume, he remarks, "I cannot keep from shuddering with horror at the thought of the carnage and destruction which have been pursued so implacably in this country and on the old continent by those who boast of themselves as being a superior humanity and who now dare to reproach the black race for its savagery and the instability of its institutions." *Ainsi parla l'oncle* had a profound impact on Price-Mars's Haitian compatriots—especially the educated youth, who pressed on with the effort of cultural self-knowledge and reclamation. Among them, one of the most prolific was Jacques Roumain, who had been educated in Europe and returned to Haiti in 1927, at age 20. Roumain was variously described as having come from "the smartest Houbigant scented aristocracy," and as being a *"grand bourgeois"* (Fowler 1980, 42). But he soon awoke and determined to join the struggle against the "detested Yankees." He appealed above all to the youth to unite and resist, and called upon Haitians to bridge their class differences in the name of national unity. Not surprisingly, he was persecuted by the American authorities and spent time in jail between 1928 and 1932. Realizing the limitations of Haitian nationalism and its manipulation by opportunistic politicians, he eventually became a Marxist. *"Je suis communiste,"* he baldly declared in 1932. "The son of owners of extensive landholdings, I have renounced my bourgeois origins" (Fowler 1980, 140).

The protagonist of Roumain's most celebrated novel, *Gouverneurs de la rosée*, is Manuel, a poor peasant who has left Haiti to work on Cuba's sugar plantations before returning home. Implementing the lessons of political organization acquired during his Cuban years, Manuel helps the peasants of his village realize the power of their collective action during a desperate drought. Roumain's is undoubtedly a political novel, but also an exquisitely realized work of art. Soon translated into more than a dozen languages, the English edition was rendered by Roumain's African American friends, Langston Hughes and Mercer Cook, as *Masters of the Dew*, appearing in 1947.

Carl Brouard, another scion of the colored elite and close friend of Roumain, was described as "perhaps the most interesting and gifted poet" of the period. Brouard assailed his bourgeois forebears and aligned his sympathy with the struggling black Haitians, even embracing vodou. He also helped facilitate the emergence of an important group of black Haitian intellectuals—Louis Diaquoi, Lorimer Denis, and François Duvalier, known collectively as les Trois D (later the Griots)—who began meeting in the late 1920s to discuss the implications of the ethnological movement for their generation and their class. Price-Mars inspired and encouraged the group. "It is in his work," declared Diaquoi, "that we find our Gospel" (Nicholls 1996, 169). Yet over time the group departed from Price-Mars's position, believing instead that the biology of a racial group determined its psychology, and in turn its "collective personality." Duvalier went so far as to agree with de Gobineau that races were biologically different. This essentialist strand of cultural black nationalism, generally referred to as *noiriste*, predated the 1930s version of *négritude*.

The Roots of Transformation

Haiti may have been the forerunner in reconsidering the place of Africa and African-derived cultural forms within the life of the Caribbean and the Caribbean diaspora, but it was not unique. Afro-Cubanism or *afronegrismo*, which developed in the late 1920s and 1930s, articulated the same valorization of African cultural forms and expressions. Fernando Ortiz, the great ethnologist, linguist, and musicologist, was the Price-Mars of Cuba, providing historical and cultural evidence of the profound impact of Afro-Cubans, and by extension Africans, on all aspects of Cuban society. He also provided a theoretical framework for this cultural history and sociology, and encouraged younger writers, artists, and musicians—such as poet Nicolas Guillén—to draw upon Cuban material and cultural forms. Meanwhile, in Puerto Rico, the white poet Luis Palés Matos also drew upon and celebrated that island's African cultural forms.

In the United States, Jamaican emigrant Claude McKay emerged as one of the most important writers of the Harlem Renaissance. Even before leaving Jamaica in 1912, McKay had used the local vernacular form as a medium for his poetry and celebrated Jamaican black working-class and peasant culture. His poetry and novels produced in exile continued the valorization of blackness and the promotion of black pride and pan-Africanist sensibilities and solidarity. His 1929 novel *Banjo*, set among the multinational black working class of Marseilles, had a profound influence upon the *négritude* movement, which developed in Paris in the 1930s among such Caribbean and West African intellectuals as Aimé Césaire (from Martinique), Léon-Gontran Damas (from French Guiana), and Léopold Senghor (from Senegal).

Several factors accounted for this sudden valorization of the African connection. The newly positive ethnological appraisal of African culture and history within European intellectual circles had a profound impact. Through careful and detailed research on the continent itself, scholars such as Leo Frobenius, Maurice Delafosse, Mary Kingsley, and Caribbean-born Edward Wilmot Blyden presented an Africa that, contrary to prevailing stereotypes, had produced cultures and civilizations worthy of respect and even wonder and emulation. Meanwhile, greater exposure to African art, especially sculpture and carving, profoundly affected modernist art beginning in the 1890s. The work of Picasso and Modigliani, for instance, bore the acknowledged imprint of West African influences, which added prestige to African art and thus helped legitimize the endeavors of Caribbean artists such as the Cuban Wilfredo Lam, who became a close friend of Picasso. Beyond the visual arts, Césaire's poetry also carried the imprint of Africa.

But probably the most important external influence on this new appreciation of African cultural forms and black political assertiveness was World War I. The resulting carnage severely diminished the prestige of Europe and so-called Western civilization. McKay's assessment that the war epitomized the "blind brute forces of tigerish tribalism which remain at the core of civilized society" was typical of his generation of radical Caribbean intellectuals. The war even provided him with a key piece of evidence against racist ideologues such as H. G. Wells: "It is entirely too funny to think—seven years after the appallingly beastly modern white savagery of 1914–18—of Mr. Wells naïvely wondering whether the Negro is capable of becoming a civilized citizen of a world republic" (McKay 1937, 55, 123). Writing in 1922, German historian Oswald Spengler observed: "It was not Germany that lost the World War; the West lost it when it lost the respect of the colored races" (Spengler 1963, 210). Spengler's *Decline of the West*, with its diagnosis of European declension and supersession, brought cheer to these Caribbean intellectuals and exercised remarkable influence upon artistic movements in the region.

But the Great War, as contemporaries called it, also had a more directly political impact upon the region, especially the British Caribbean. More than 15,000 Caribbean men were mobilized by Britain to serve in Egypt, Iraq, Palestine, and, to a lesser extent, Europe. Exposed to an astonishing level of racism by their British officers, they resisted and even mutinied, and returned to the Caribbean changed men, disillusioned and radicalized. Disenchanted with empire and armed with a new pan-Caribbean and pan-Africanist consciousness, many played leading roles in a series of strikes and protests in Trinidad, Belize, Jamaica, and elsewhere in 1919–20. A large number joined the labor movement and the black nationalist UNIA, becoming leading activists not just in the Caribbean but also in the wider diaspora, especially in the United States.

The Bolshevik Revolution in Russia, one of the fruits of the global disequilibrium occasioned by World War I, also provided political and symbolic inspiration to Caribbean intellectuals such as McKay, who called it "our golden hope" (1920). Césaire, who joined the French Communist Party, insisted that the *négritude* movement was a movement of the left despite its appeal to race pride; Guillén was a man of the left in Cuba and later welcomed the *fidelista* revolution of 1959; and Roumain, who founded the Communist Party of Haiti, recognized that Haiti's maladies extended beyond racial bovaryism and required not just the appreciation and reclamation of cultural resources, but also the radical redistribution of economic ones.

Finally, these new cultural, ideological, and political transformations were facilitated and enhanced by the development of solidarity and comradeship transcending national and colonial boundaries. Roumain, for instance, established close friendships with Hughes in the United States and Guillén in Cuba. And the Garveyites established an extraordinarily dense network of transnational solidarity among their hundreds of chapters around the world.

Conclusion

The half century from 1880 to 1930 was one of remarkable intellectual, cultural, and political ferment within the Caribbean. It marked the birth and emergence of a combative black intelligentsia willing and able to counteract the racist belittling of peoples of African descent. In response to the hegemonic rise of United States imperialism within the region and the cataclysm of World War I, the period also witnessed the development of pan-Caribbean, pan-African, and in some cases anti-capitalist and even socialist consciousness.

The struggle for political independence and wider anti-imperialist efforts in the Caribbean during the interwar period and after World War II grew out of these earlier developments. The Garveyites of the 1920s, many of whom had spent time in Central America and the United States, became prime movers behind the development of Rastafarianism in Jamaica in the 1930s; in later decades this movement would in turn become an international phenomenon. Meanwhile, black veterans from World War I and many of those who had spent time abroad in Cuba, Central America, and the United States formed the leadership of the labor movement in the Anglophone Caribbean, which in turn spearheaded the struggle for self-government and independence. Organizations within the diaspora, such as the Harlem-based Jamaica Progressive League, played a disproportionate role in these political struggles within the Caribbean from the 1930s right up to political independence more than a generation later.

Of course, not all the legacies of the period were positive ones. The later tragedy of Duvalierism in Haiti can be at least partially accounted for, as Michel-Rolph Trouillot and others have argued, by the essentialist *noiriste* ideology that emerged in the 1920s and helped underpin François Duvalier's opportunistic and authoritarian goals. Few, however, would contest the conclusion that the political and cultural bequests of the period were resoundingly positive for the people of the Caribbean.

WORKS CITED

Biddiss, Michael D. 1970. *Father of Racist Ideology: The Social and Political Thought of Count Gobineau.* London: Weidenfeld and Nicolson.

Davis, N. Darnell. 1888. "Mr. Froude's Negrophobia, or Don Quixote as a Cook's Tourist." *Timehri: Journal of the Royal Agricultural & Commercial Society of British Guiana,* vol. 2 (new series): 85–129.

Firmin, Anténor. [1885] 2002. *The Equality of the Human Races.* Translated by Asselin Charles. Urbana: University of Illinois Press.

Fowler, Carolyn. 1980. *A Knot in the Thread: The Life and Work of Jacques Roumain*. Washington, DC: Howard University Press.

Froude, James Anthony. 1888. *The English in the West Indies, or the Bow of Ulysses*. London: Longemans, Green, and Co.

Kingsley, Charles. [1871] 1889. *At Last: A Christmas in the West Indies*. London: Macmillan.

Léger, J. N. 1907. *Haiti: Her History and Her Detractors*. New York: Neale.

McKay, Claude. 1920. "To 'Holy' Russia." *Workers' Dreadnought*, February 28.

———. 1937. *A Long Way from Home*. New York: Lee Furman.

Nicholls, David. 1996. *From Dessalines to Duvalier: Race, Colour and National Independence in Haiti*. New Brunswick: Rutgers University Press.

Price-Mars, Jean. [1928] 1983. *So Spoke the Uncle*. Translated by Magdaline W. Shannon. Washington, DC: Three Continents Press.

Richardson, Bonham. 1983. *Caribbean Migrants: Environment and Human Survival on St. Kitts and Nevis*. Knoxville: University of Tennessee Press.

Schmidt, Hans. 1971. *The United States Occupation of Haiti, 1915–1934*. New Brunswick: Rutgers University Press.

Scholes, Theophilus E. S. 1899. *The British Empire and Alliances; or, Britain's Duty to Her Colonies and Subject Races*. London: Elliot Stock.

Spengler, Oswald. 1963. *The Hour of Decision, Part One: Germany and World-Historical Evolution, Vol. 1*. Translated by Charles Francis Atkinson. New York: Alfred A. Knopf.

Thomas, J. J. [1889] 1969. *Froudacity: West Indian Fables by James Anthony Froude Explained*. London: New Beacon Books.

Trouillot, Michel-Rolph. 1990. *Haiti: State against Nation—The Origins and Legacy of Duvalierism*. New York: Monthly Review Press.

31

Labor Protests, Rebellions, and the Rise of Nationalism during Depression and War

The Great Depression, which began in the United States in 1929, had a huge economic, social, and political impact throughout the Caribbean. In the 1930s the resiliency of capitalist economies was challenged, and countries responded in various ways to the resulting threat of social instability. This crisis in capitalism had a profound impact throughout the region because Caribbean economies, whether colonial or not, were closely tied to metropolitan economies in the United Kingdom and France as well as in the United States. Most Caribbean territories are small and highly vulnerable to external influences, and the plantation system created largely monocrop economies that depended on exporting a single product and importing everything else. Even Cuba, which is by far the largest island and was nominally independent after 1902, was an economic dependency of the United States. In these circumstances, a wide spectrum of Caribbean society questioned the legitimacy of the political system that supported the bankrupt economies. Most places witnessed a rise in labor militancy and nationalism, but the long-term outcome, which was also affected by World War II, varied greatly from one place to another.

The economic dislocations of the Depression threatened a complete breakdown in the predominantly monocultural economies of the Caribbean, leading to social instability and political crisis. Throughout the region unemployment increased, wages and incomes declined, and the standard of living for the great majority of the population—especially agricultural workers—worsened. Even in better times most agricultural workers, who were employed only seasonally, lived in chronic insecurity and dire poverty. During the Depression the prices of many necessities increased while wages and chances of employment decreased. Moreover, while emigration had offered opportunities for thousands of Caribbean people to work in Panama, Costa Rica, Cuba, the Dominican Republic, and the United States in the four decades before the Depression, many returned home when their work was no longer needed, often returning to economies that were worse than when they had left.

Numerous protests, strikes, riots, and rebellions occurred throughout the region in the 1930s. Many of these produced new leaders, labor organizations, and political parties. Most were nationalistic in orientation, so emerging nationalist movements often had a strong base in, and overlapping leadership with, labor movements. Over time, working people gained more liberal civil rights and labor regulations as well as improved wages and working conditions, but they generally lost the political initiative they had achieved in the 1930s. Responses to the crisis included reforms—economic and legal first, political and constitutional later—that required legislation and state intervention, so workers became increasingly dependent on the technocrats, lawyers, politicians, and administrators who organized and implemented the reforms. By the late 1940s and 1950s, these middle-class people controlled the changes that had been initiated by the working class.

Everywhere, the state responded to social protests and political instability with a mixture of repression and concessions. Working-class leaders were co-opted or suppressed, and reforms stopped—or at least postponed—potential revolutions, while economies remained dependent and metropolitan capital remained dominant. The economic and social structures remained essentially the same, recognizably similar to those during the period of slavery, but most territories experienced constitutional changes. The nature of these changes varied widely, however, because of local factors and differences in the history of relations with the metropoles. The changes made in political systems and constitutional status in the 1940s and 1950s had long-term effects in most territories, from the integrated status of the French West Indies, through the more autonomous status of Puerto Rico to the independence of most British colonies. The Dutch colonies moved in different directions, independent Haiti and the Dominican Republic moved hardly at all, and the Cuban

Revolution of 1933 was interrupted, to resume in the 1950s. Understanding what happened in the 1930s and 1940s is essential for understanding the subsequent history of the Caribbean.

West Indian Colonies before 1929

The economies of British, French, and Dutch colonies in the Caribbean were structurally similar to those of the American Sugar Kingdom in the early 20th century. Along with competition from European beet sugar, the growth of sugar production in the Hispanic Caribbean (aided by US investments and markets) and in Brazil led to an economic crisis in the colonies that remained dependent on sugar. In the late 19th and early 20th centuries, this crisis led to social unrest, demands for new social policies and political reforms, accelerated urbanization and emigration, and increasing race and class consciousness.

At least 20 serious strikes and disturbances occurred between 1884 and 1912, many in Jamaica and British Guiana, and others in British Honduras, Dominica, Grenada, Guadeloupe, Martinique, Montserrat, St. Kitts, St. Lucia, St. Vincent, and Trinidad. Many attempts were made to create labor organizations, but trade unions were illegal or severely restricted and the colonial administrators and plantation managers viewed labor conflict as a matter for the police. Any protest, demonstration, or strike by working people was promptly defined by British authorities as a riot, so the colonial state strengthened its police forces to coerce workers and suppress disorders. When governments used force in this way, however, they provoked people to question the legitimacy of the colonial system that defended injustices. Racial and class consciousness increased in most of the British West Indies after World War I as a result of persistent economic hardship and government oppression, the return of demobilized soldiers of the British West Indies regiment who were bitter about the racial discrimination they had encountered, and the growing and widespread influence of Garveyism.

Marcus Garvey, a Jamaican who participated in a short-lived printers' union between 1907 and 1909, traveled in Central America and to the United Kingdom between 1910 and 1914. Having developed a strong sense of racial consciousness, he returned to Jamaica in 1914 and founded the Universal Negro Improvement Association (UNIA) and African Communities League. He emigrated to the United States in 1916 and developed the UNIA into a major international organization appealing to racial pride and self-reliance. Many people in the Caribbean and Central America gained their first experience of organizing and public speaking in its branches. In 1925 Garvey was imprisoned in the United States. Deported to Jamaica in 1927, he formed the People's Political Party in 1928, founded a newspaper—the *Blackman*—in 1929, and created the Jamaican Labourers and Workers Association in 1930. He was elected to the Kingston and St. Andrew Corporation, as the city council was called, in 1929 and 1931 but was defeated when he tried to win a seat on the colony's Legislative Council in 1930. His efforts were frustrated by legal constraints on trade unionism, a very limited franchise that excluded most of his followers, and the colonial government's opposition, so he relocated to London in 1935. In the Caribbean he was eclipsed as a labor leader long before his death in 1940, but his ideas and organization had an important and lasting impact not only in the English-speaking territories but also among West Indian migrants in places like Cuba, Panama, and Costa Rica. Many labor and political leaders of the 1930s and 1940s were, or had been, Garveyites in Barbados, British Honduras, Trinidad, and Jamaica, and some returning migrants from Cuba and Costa Rica had been influenced by Garveyism and had gained experience in the UNIA.

Even as class and racial consciousness increased, working people lacked organizations to effectively channel their needs and demands into political action. In the British and French West Indies, a variety of friendly societies and mutual associations served some social and economic needs of working people, and some more politically oriented organizations were created before the 1930s. Outside Cuba and Puerto Rico, however, trade unions were generally the result, rather than a source, of the labor protests and rebellions of the 1930s. Two exceptions occurred, paradoxically, in two colonies with the most racially divided working classes, namely British Guiana and Trinidad and Tobago. The Trinidad Workingmen's Association (TWA) was one of the earliest and longest-lasting organizations of working people in the British Caribbean. Founded in 1897, its core consisted of skilled workers, but it sought also to include and represent unskilled workers, such as those employed on the railways and waterfront. Engaging in trade union activities and reformist politics, the TWA pioneered the way for the stronger labor and political organizations created in the 1930s and 1940s. The British Guiana Labour Union (BGLU) was founded in 1919 by Hubert Critchlow, who, as a young dock worker, was involved in a strike in 1906 and led a massive demonstration in 1918. The BGLU barely survived a crisis in the early 1920s but was still functioning in the 1940s. Both the TWA and the BGLU suffered from the fact that, in drawing their members and support largely from people of African descent, they neglected to organize workers of Indian (South Asian) origin. Both organizations had become less effective by the late 1920s, but together they began to create a regional labor movement by convening the first British Guiana and West Indies Labour Conference in Georgetown, British Guiana, in 1926. In 1945 Critchlow was elected the first vice president of the regional Caribbean Labour Congress.

The aspiration for trade unions and political parties representing working people was emerging in these colonies, and the experiences gained from the early protests, strikes, and various organizations would be important in the 1930s, but it was the economic distress and consequent social instability after 1929 that gave rise in the West Indies to modern trade unions and political parties, many of which still exist.

The Impact of the Great Depression

The Wall Street crash of 1929 triggered the Great Depression, which created a crisis in the capitalist world and hit the vulnerable Caribbean region at the heart of the sugar industry. In the 1920s, US investments had helped Cuba become the world's biggest sugar producer, but the price of sugar began to fall in the mid-1920s, from 4.2 cents per pound in 1924 to 2.6 cents in 1926. Cuba responded by trying to curtail production, but instead of raising the value of sugar, this move stimulated sugar production elsewhere and the price continued to drop. Once the Depression arrived, the United States did not extend loans or increase investments to offset the declining price of sugar. In 1928 sugar was 2.18 cents per pound, and by 1932 it reached a record low of 0.57 cents. For Caribbean territories that were inordinately dependent on sugar, this trend spelled disaster.

In Cuba, sugar production fell from 4.67 million tons in 1930 to under 2 million in 1933, and it remained below 3 million tons per year for the rest of the decade. National income fell from 571 million pesos in 1929 to 294 million in 1933. As commerce declined, other businesses and factories closed, public employees were laid off, and many civil servants who were fortunate enough to have work received half pay. Unemployment soared, and wages fell by as much as 75%. Some 250,000 heads of families, who were responsible for about one-quarter of Cuba's four million people, were totally unemployed. In 1933, 30% of the population earned marginal wages of $300–600 per year, and 60% earned even less. A 1932 survey reported that wages were "the lowest since the days of slavery."

In Puerto Rico, where the GNP fell from $176 million in 1929 to $134 million in 1933, the economic pangs were not felt equally by all. Agriculture's share of national income fell from $87 million (49.4%) in 1929 to $59 million (30.1%) in 1933. While wages and salaries declined from $131 million to $95 million, annual dividend payments on stocks and bonds remained unchanged at $3 million, and net interest and rent actually increased from $6 to $7 million. Puerto Rican workers, like their Cuban counterparts, were among the first to launch labor protests in the 1930s.

In the British colonies about half the population was engaged in agriculture. Many workers depended on seasonal labor on sugar plantations, often for less than half the year. The endemic unemployment and underemployment that was always characteristic of these economies, and which resulted in widespread and persistent poverty, became dramatically worse in the 1930s. Sugar workers and their families suffered, as did workers dependent on forest products in British Honduras and bananas in Jamaica. For the many people whose work was seasonal or intermittent, daily wage or piecework rates do not accurately reflect actual income. A daily wage that appears satisfactory was really not, if the possibility of earning it was restricted to two or three days a week. Seasonal and casual employment and low wage rates created insecurity and poverty for many urban workers, such as dockworkers, as well as rural laborers.

Working conditions were poor, in terms of both the physical environment and the lack of respect and frequent abuses that characterized the traditionally author-itarian supervision of labor. Living conditions—housing, nutrition, and health—were generally appalling, especially for poor children. When members of a royal commission made a report to the British government on the terrible conditions they observed throughout the West Indian colonies in 1938 and 1939, the war cabi-net suppressed its publication for fear it could provide useful information for enemy propaganda. Some particularly dangerous sections of the report, such as those on housing and the position of women, were cut from the published version. The gov-ernment passed the Colonial Development and Welfare Act in 1940, and 60% of the fund available to the whole British Empire was allocated to the Caribbean colonies between 1940 and 1944, which was a relatively high amount per capita. However, wartime conditions limited the scope and effectiveness of the assistance offered, and the implementation of the act emphasized the welfare aspects more than long-term development, to demonstrate the empire's benevolence. Most of the funds went to projects such as water supply, housing, medical services, public health, and education, reflecting the government's political motives and concern about the po-tential for more disturbances.

In the Caribbean, per capita income declined dramatically in the early 1930s and only began to approach the 1930 level toward the end of the decade, but that was merely a measurement in nominal value. The war increased the Caribbean's prob-lems, not least because of threats to shipping. Colonial trade, already depressed in the 1930s, declined further as a result of the war, reaching its lowest point in the Caribbean between 1940 and 1942. In the import-dependent Caribbean, the prices of most imports, including such essentials as flour, increased, as did the cost of liv-ing in general, and the war made imports unreliable as well as more expensive. The great majority of the population experienced a decline in the standard of living.

In the early 20th century, many thousands of Caribbean workers sought em-ployment through migration, both within and outside the region. In general they moved according to the demands of US capital, as the application and withdrawal of that capital largely dictated labor needs. Thus, thousands of West Indians, espe-cially Jamaicans and Barbadians, worked on the construction of the Panama Canal, and when that wound down, many moved to work on expanding US banana plan-tations in Costa Rica and Honduras. Other West Indians, including Haitians, mi-grated to work on expanding sugar plantations in Cuba and the Dominican Repub-

lic. Between 1910 and 1929 there was a net migration of 217,000 Haitians and Jamaicans to Cuba. Many Caribbean people migrated to the United States until 1924, when a new immigrant quota law abruptly curtailed this opportunity. The Depression then had a massive effect on the migration of labor within the Caribbean as local people complained that migrants took jobs away from them. Haitian and Jamaican

Figure 31.1 Living conditions in the El Fanguito slum of San Juan, Puerto Rico, in the wake of depression and war. Photograph by Jack Delano (1941). Source: Library of Congress.

workers in Cuba were persecuted, and thousands were deported. In the Dominican Republic at least 12,000 and perhaps as many as 20,000 of the Haitians who lived and worked on sugar plantations were massacred in 1937. The closing of opportunities to migrants, and the return home of many West Indians who had migrated in more prosperous years, swelled the ranks of the unemployed in the 1930s. Some of these returning migrants, who may have acquired experience of trade unionism, politics, or Garvey's UNIA while abroad, now became active in the labor protests and rebellions that broke out in, among other places, British Honduras, St. Kitts, Jamaica, and Trinidad. The impact of the Depression was not only direct, therefore, in terms of the deteriorating conditions, but also indirect because it caused many people, some of whom had been influenced by radical new ideas and organizations, to return home.

Labor Protests and Rebellions

Labor protests and strikes occurred throughout the Caribbean in the 1930s. In Cuba they were so extensive that, combined with an army mutiny, they brought down the government. In Trinidad and Jamaica, island-wide protests that involved resistance to the government constituted labor rebellions. Other protests and strikes occurred in Puerto Rico, Suriname, British Honduras, St. Kitts, St. Vincent, St. Lucia, Barbados, Antigua, and British Guiana. Wherever these protests occurred, they initiated a new period of modern politics in which working people became more organized and succeeded in placing their demands on the national agenda. In most places this led to lasting social and political reforms.

The chief exceptions to this pattern were Haiti and the Dominican Republic, probably because the former was largely a peasant society and in the latter about two thirds of the sugar workers were Haitians. In both countries authoritarian governments remained firmly in control. In Haiti there were some early efforts to organize shoe workers and construction workers, and an attempt to form a drivers' union in 1937 was broken up by the government. A trade union movement did not develop in Haiti until after 1946. In the Dominican Republic no working class movement or major industrial action occurred in the 1930s. The dictatorial government of Rafael Trujillo, which lasted from 1930 to 1961, granted the Dominican Labor Federation official status and made the governor of each region a president ex-officio of the provincial labor organization. Trujillo's government passed some labor laws concerning wages, working hours, vacations, and social security, but it did not permit labor to have an independent voice. In 1937 the 21,370 foreigners among 31,956 sugar workers were especially vulnerable to persecution, but Dominicans may have been a higher proportion of the labor force in the eastern region, where sugar workers organized a series of strikes in 1942, 1945, and 1946, demanding an increase in wages, regulation of working hours, and a reduced work load. Some increase in wages was conceded, but the government suppressed further union activity, killing, jailing, and driving into exile the leaders. Mauricio Báez, who led the 1946 strike, was killed on Trujillo's orders four years later while in exile in Cuba. Due to extreme government control and repression, very few unions formed until after Trujillo's death in 1961.

The Cuban economy was already faltering by 1929 when President Gerardo Machado was inaugurated for a second term. The economic conditions "set the stage for political confrontation and social conflict on a scale unprecedented in the republic" (Pérez 1995, 254). Cigar workers and electrical workers established trade unions in 1927 and 1928, respectively, and sugar workers established a national union in 1932. The Cuban Communist Party, created in 1925, was active in organized labor. A series of hunger marches, demonstrations, and strikes occurred, including a general strike that paralyzed the island in 1930. Workers and soldiers fought, scores of demonstrators were killed and injured, and strike organizers were arrested. Political rallies and student demonstrations broadened the opposition to the government, which declared a state of siege in November 1930. Repression, far from quelling opposition, provoked it further. Labor militancy and strikes increased until open warfare broke out in 1931, when hundreds of political leaders, including the moderate opposition, were imprisoned. The labor movement became a revolution.

In July 1933 the US ambassador, Sumner Welles, tried to mediate the political crisis to circumvent a revolution, but it was too late. A general strike led to clashes with police, and scores of demonstrators were killed or injured. On August 12 the army, fearing a US intervention similar to those of 1906 and 1912, moved against Machado, who promptly went into exile. Carlos Manuel de Céspedes, Machado's successor, lacked popularity and support. Strikes spread across the island, and workers seized sugar mills. On September 4 some mutinous soldiers led by Sergeant Fulgencio Batista, supported by anti-government groups, overthrew Céspedes in the "Sergeants' Revolt." When a revolutionary government was formed on September 5, US fears were realized.

Members of the new government, led by Ramón Grau San Martín, had long been active in the reformist movement, and for the next hundred days they turned their earlier demands into decrees. Women received the vote, and laws established a minimum wage for cane-cutters, an eight-hour work day, workers' compensation, and compulsory labor arbitration. A Nationalization of Labor decree required that at least half of all employees in industry, commerce, and agriculture should be Cuban citizens, and labor contracts with Haiti and Jamaica were canceled. Although these measures were reformist rather than revolutionary, the United States refused to recognize Grau's government. The army was reorganized, with newly promoted Colonel Batista at its head. With encouragement from Welles, Batista threw the army's support behind Carlos Mendieta, a liberal politician who had broken from Machado in 1927, and he was installed as president in January 1934. The United States recognized his government in five days.

A general strike in 1935 forced Mendieta's resignation, and Batista nominated each of the three presidents who rapidly succeeded him. Batista, with US sup-

Figure 31.2 Sergeant Fulgencio Batista greets Ramón Grau San Martín. Photograph (1933).

port, was the dominant political figure in Cuba for six years before he was elected president in 1940. He made peace with the Communist Party, which acquired legality and permission to organize labor in return for supporting Batista. The Workers' Confederation of Cuba, which claimed a membership of 350,000, was a powerful political force and, as economic conditions improved, Batista's social reforms restored political tranquility. The army became increasingly influential through its extensive involvement in education and the implementation of social reforms throughout the country. Cuba was a highly authoritarian democracy in which Batista assumed "the mantle of defender of national sovereignty and protector of national honor" (Pérez 1995, 279), but opposition grew in the late 1940s.

While Cuba had become independent in 1902, Puerto Rico remained a US colony. In 1917 Puerto Ricans became US citizens, but with limited rights in the federal system. The Nationalist Party (PN), founded in 1922, expressed the *independentista* aspirations of many Puerto Ricans, but the dominant group in the island between 1932 and 1940 was La Coalición, an electoral pact between the Republican and Socialist parties in which the former was the primary voice. This coalition brought together the wealthy agricultural and commercial middle classes (including sugar estate and other large landowners, import-export merchants, bankers, clothing contractors and exporters, and US corporations) with the lawyers and bureaucrats who controlled the Socialist Party and the AFL-affiliated Free Federation of Workers (FLT). The coalition sought to achieve statehood and to maintain "industrial peace," which put it increasingly at odds with new labor leaders and the more militant working class of the Depression years.

A series of protest marches in 1931 was followed by protests and strikes by tobacco workers, women in needlework factories, coffee and sugar workers, road and construction workers, and car and truck drivers. Between July and December 1933, 85 strikes occurred in various sectors, directed not only against employers but also as protests against the government's failure to respond adequately to the crisis. In late 1933 and early 1934 the entire sugar industry, including field, mill, and port workers, went on strike against both their employers and the FLT. Sugar workers in the east organized their own union and invited Pedro Albizu Campos, president of the PN, to lead the strike. This placed the Nationalists, who demanded immediate and unconditional independence, at the center of political events and so led to "one of the most repressive periods of US rule" (Dietz 1986, 148).

On October 24, 1935, police fired on a car containing Nationalists, killing four occupants and one bystander. The PN vowed revenge and on February 23, 1936, the island's chief of police was assassinated. Two Nationalists accused of his murder were taken to the San Juan jail and killed. Federal charges of "sedition and conspiring to overthrow the federal government" were brought against Albizu Campos and seven others. After the first trial resulted in a hung jury, the jury in the second trial—which had been packed with North Americans—found the defendants guilty. They were sent to the federal jail in Atlanta. On Palm Sunday, 1937, police fired on a Nationalist parade in Ponce, killing 20 people in what became known as the Ponce Massacre. The PN, now decimated by official violence and repression, was supplanted by those who sought for Puerto Rico greater autonomy within a colonial relationship with the United States. The labor struggles, which continued through the 1930s and included an island-wide waterfront strike in 1938, had played a part in questioning the legitimacy of colonial rule, but they did not produce the basis for a successful nationalist movement.

Perhaps because Britain was a remote and declining imperial power in contrast to the nearby and increasingly powerful United States, the labor movement that emerged in the British colonies became the basis for successful independence movements. Beginning in Trinidad, British Honduras, and British Guiana in 1933 and 1934, a series of protests and demonstrations, strikes and rebellions gave rise to new labor organizations, including trade unions and political parties. In many cases the unions provided rank-and-file support for the parties, often with overlapping leadership, but even when this was not the case, the new nationalist parties sought to appeal to labor. Thus, the politics of labor was at the center of the rise of nationalism in the British colonies in the 1930s and 1940s.

In Trinidad and Tobago, the Trade Union Ordinance of 1932 permitted the registration of trade unions, but did not permit peaceful picketing or protect unions from legal actions arising rom strikes—protections that already existed in the United Kingdom. The TWA, which had pioneered labor organization, was not registered as a trade union but was renamed the Trinidad Labour Party (TLP) in 1934. As labor struggles expanded in the 1930s new leaders emerged, and militants saw the TLP as an obstacle to the further development of the labor movement. A series of demonstrations began in 1933 and strikes broke out on sugar estates in 1934, but the predominantly Indian sugar workers did not succeed in uniting with the urban unemployed and hunger marchers, who were largely of African descent. Beginning in 1935, oil fields became the center of the labor rebellion. A Grenadian-born former oil field worker, Tubal Uriah "Buzz" Butler, became the leader of the movement. When police tried to arrest Butler at a public meeting in June 1937, they triggered widespread rioting. Troops augmented the police forces, but strikes spread throughout the island and became a prolonged general strike. With Butler in hiding, the Oilfield Workers' Trade Union (OWTU) was created in July 1937, and a lawyer of Indian origin, Adrian Cola Rienzi, was elected its president. This union has remained one of the most powerful in the country.

Five other unions were registered before the end of the year, representing building workers, seamen and waterfront workers, sugar estate and factory workers, public works and public service workers, and others. Butler was the most charismatic labor leader, but Rienzi, who led three of these unions, was the most competent builder of lasting organizations. By the end of 1938, following more strikes, 10 trade unions were registered in Trinidad and Tobago. While employers still opposed unionization, the colonial government and the Colonial Office supported what they defined as "responsible leadership" in order to prevent further disorder. This became crucial when Britain sought to secure vital supplies of aviation fuel from Trinidad with the coming of World War II. In just five years the labor movement had become organized, led by Trinidadians of Indian and African descent, and it was poised to influence the movement to independence.

The Jamaican labor rebellion, which began in 1935, peaked in 1938 with island-wide strikes, riots, and demonstrations among sugar and banana workers as well as dock and transport workers. Aware of what had happened in other islands, labor leaders in Jamaica sought to organize people throughout the country. One of these leaders, Alexander Bustamante, was already establishing a reputation in 1937, and when sugar workers went on strike in January 1938, he became involved. A riot and strike on a sugar estate in April led to protests, riots, and an uprising in Kingston between May 2 and May 28 and many demonstrations, riots, and rolling strikes throughout the island between May 23 and June 11. British troops and the Royal Navy were called in to help restore order. Official reports claimed that crowds were fired on 13 times and at least 12 people were killed.

In contrast to the many trade unions of Trinidad, one large union, the Busta-mante Industrial Trade Union (BITU), dominated the scene in Jamaica and ac-quired about 8,000 members, mostly sugar and dock workers, even before it was officially registered in January 1939. With Bustamante its "president for life," this powerful body became a lasting political force as the basis of the Jamaica Labour Party (JLP), which was launched in 1943. Meanwhile, Norman Washington Manley and others had created a reform-oriented party, the People's National Party, in Sep-tember 1938. When this party created its own trade union base, these two men and their organizations constituted the central rivalry that divided Jamaicans even as they moved toward independence.

Rising Nationalism and Constitutional Changes

Nationalism existed in the Caribbean before the 20th century, but the impact of the Depression and the effects of World War II enhanced national aspirations in most of the region during the 1940s. However, the varieties of constitutional status and the historical differences in the relations each territory had with its respective metro-pole were reflected in the different aspirations around the region.

Both Haiti and the Dominican Republic had become independent in the 19th century and were occupied by the United States early in the 20th—the former from 1915 to 1934, the latter from 1916 to 1924. These extended occupations, following the invasions of Cuba and Puerto Rico in 1898 and followed by the purchase of the Danish Virgin Islands in 1917, were part of the US strategy for control of the Carib-bean and Central America. A rebellion broke out in Haiti in 1918, but it was ruth-lessly suppressed by 1920, and most subsequent national resistance in that country came in the form of legal and ideological responses by intellectuals, divided sharply between Marxists and "race-conscious" *noiristes*. Many elite Haitians, however, opposed the nationalist movements and welcomed the Americans. The government of President Sténio Vincent (1930–41) cultivated the small but increasingly influential black middle class, but the mulatto elite remained powerful. In the absence of unity, an attempt at revolution in 1946 led to the exile of President Elie Lescot (1941–46) and the election of President Dumarsais Estimé (1946–50), but not to any major changes.

Before withdrawing from the Dominican Republic, the United States created a National Guard there whose leader, Trujillo, began his tyrannical rule after ousting the incumbent president in 1930. With a handful of US companies, Trujillo virtually owned the country and succeeded in suppressing opposition from all quarters until his assassination in 1961. The Cuban case was similar in some ways, but it had a different outcome. After the revolution of 1933, the army and its leader, Batista, dominated Cuba with US support, but powerful opposition grew in the late 1940s. In 1947 Eduardo Chibás broke with Grau's party to form the Cuban People's Party, or Ortodoxos, but he committed suicide in 1951. The year after Batista seized power in a military coup in 1952, a young Ortodoxo, Fidel Castro, attacked the Moncada Barracks in Santiago. Castro's revolution, which succeeded in 1959, unified nationalist aspirations with socialist ideology and thus extended the goals of the frustrated 1933 revolution.

Puerto Rico, as a small US colony, faced a vastly different situation. With the decline of the Socialist Party and the repression of the Nationalist Party in the 1930s, a new party, the Popular Democratic Party, or Populares, led by Luis Muñoz Marín, won the 1940 election and led the economic, social, and political transformation of the country in a way that was acceptable to the United States. Puerto Rico's economic base was rapidly transformed from agriculture to industry, and government became the largest employer, while the cities grew and thousands of people migrated to the mainland. In 1950, uprisings occurred in several Puerto Rican towns and nationalists attacked Blair House in Washington, where President Truman was temporarily staying. In 1954 a group of nationalists shot at congressmen from a balcony in the House of Representatives chamber at the US Capitol. Although aspirations to political nationalism were crushed, cultural nationalism became acceptable, even including the official use of Puerto Rico's flag, which had been a nationalist symbol. Constitutional changes allowed Muñoz Marín to become the first elected governor in 1948, and by 1952, over nationalist objections, Puerto Rico gained more autonomy in its new status as a *estado libre asociado*, or "commonwealth." Muñoz Marín and his Populares continued to steer Puerto Rico on this path until his death in 1980.

The French, Dutch, and British colonies, less dominated by relations with the United States, moved in different directions. The Depression had affected the French

colonies, and social unrest and strikes occurred in Martinique and Guadeloupe, but these events did not lead to an independence movement. On the contrary, French West Indians, who had had the right to vote since 1870 and trade union rights since 1919, sought through closer integration with the colonial power to be accorded the same rights and social benefits as citizens in France. Trade unions that emerged in Martinique and Guadeloupe, tied institutionally with French unions, agitated for the advantages enjoyed by the French working class. The shock of losing civil rights under the Vichy regime in 1940

Figure 31.3 Alexander Bustamante (far left), Norman Manley (far right), and British officials celebrate the conclusion of the Jamaica Independence Conference, 1962. Source: John Franks/Hulton Archive/Getty Images.

strengthened their demand for total and unqualified French citizenship after the war. A tradition of faith in and adherence to the idea of a universalist and egalitarian France—born in the 1789 revolution, and strengthened by emancipation in 1848 and voting rights in 1870—led the French West Indies to integration into the French Republic with departmental status in 1946. The Dutch colonies, meanwhile, moved more slowly and less decisively toward constitutional change. There were protests in Suriname in 1933, but they died out after the leader, Anton De Kom, was arrested and expelled to the Netherlands (he died in a Nazi concentration camp in 1945). In 1954 the colonies became part of the Kingdom of the Netherlands, integrated but with a degree of autonomy. Suriname became independent in 1975, after 40% of its population had emigrated, but the rest of the Netherlands Antilles remained part of the Kingdom.

British Caribbean colonies, unlike French ones, moved through stages of increasing self-government in the 1940s and 1950s. Most of the political parties that had emerged in the 1930s and 1940s, many based on the labor movement, sought independence as the best route to social and economic development. The war delayed the nationalist movement—partly due to residual loyalty to the "mother country," but also because many militant leaders, including Butler and Bustamante, were imprisoned. Jamaica and Trinidad and Tobago were the first to be granted universal adult suffrage, in 1944 and 1946 respectively, leading to a degree of self-government. Great Britain was in rapid decline after the war, the British Empire was disintegrating, and by 1954 all the British Caribbean colonies had adult suffrage. In Jamaica, Bustamante's JLP won the elections of 1944 and 1949 before Manley's PNP won in 1953. Those two parties have alternated in power ever since. In Trinidad and Tobago none of the political parties formed in the 1940s has survived, but soon after Eric Williams created the People's National Movement in 1956, it became the center of national politics. In 1962 these two countries became the first British Caribbean colonies to become independent, and all the others, except the smallest, followed.

WORKS CITED

Dietz, James L. 1986. *Economic History of Puerto Rico: Institutional Change and Capitalist Development*. Princeton, NJ: Princeton University Press.

Pérez, Louis A. 1995. *Cuba: Between Reform and Revolution*. 2nd ed. New York: Oxford University Press.

32

Toward Decolonization

ANNE S. MACPHERSON

Impulses, Processes, and Consequences since the 1930s

When labor rebellions swept much of the Caribbean in the 1930s, there were only three independent nation-states in the region—Haiti, the Dominican Republic, and Cuba—and their sovereignty was clearly compromised by the United States in economic, political, and military terms. Those Caribbean peoples still formally colonized in the 1930s—in the French, American, Dutch, and British-held territories—showed a marked impulse toward political decolonization in subsequent decades. But that impulse was not ubiquitous, it never took revolutionary form, and only sometimes did it equate decolonization with nation-state sovereignty. Since 1962, 13 former colonies have gained "flag" independence, others have negotiated various new statuses that have been pitched as decolonization by their proponents, and a few clearly remain colonized (table 32.1).

The bitter commonalities of neocolonialism—economic dependency, inequality and poverty, emigration to former or current metropoles, and the effective exclusion of non-elites from meaningful political participation—continue to plague the region. The

Table 32.1 Status of former Caribbean colonies as of 2011

Territory	Intermediate Step(s)	Current Status
DECOLONIZED AND SOVEREIGN		
A. Former British colonies that participated in the West Indies Federation		
Jamaica		independent (1962)
Trinidad and Tobago		independent (1962)
Barbados		independent (1966)
Grenada	associated statehood (1967–1974)	independent (1974)
Dominica	associated statehood (1967–1978)	independent (1978)
St. Lucia	associated statehood (1967–1979)	independent (1979)
Antigua & Barbuda	associated statehood (1967–1981)	independent (1981)
St. Kitts-Nevis	associated statehood (1967–1983)	independent (1983)
St. Vincent	associated statehood (1969–1979)	independent (1979)
B. Former British Colonies that did not participate in the West Indies Federation		
Guyana		independent (1966)
Bahamas		independent (1973)
Belize		independent (1981)
C. Former Dutch colony		
Suriname	overseas Territory (1945–54); partner in Kingdom of the Netherlands (1954–75)	independent (1975)
"DECOLONIZED" BUT NON-SOVEREIGN		
A. Former French colonies		
Guadeloupe		overseas department (1946); overseas region (1983)
Guyane		overseas region (1983)
Martinique		overseas region (1983)
B. Former Dutch colonies		
Aruba	Dutch overseas territory (1945–54); part of Netherlands Antilles (1954–86)	partner in Kingdom of the Netherlands (1954)
Netherlands Antilles	Dutch overseas territory (1945–54)	partner in Kingdom of the Netherlands (1954)
C. Former US unincorporated territory		
Puerto Rico		commonwealth (*estado libre asociado*; 1952)

Territory	Intermediate Step(s)	Current Status

COLONIZED

A. British colonies that participated in the West Indies Federation

Anguilla	associated statehood as part of St. Kitts-Nevis (1967–78)	British overseas territory (2002)
Montserrat		British overseas territory (2002)
Turks & Caicos		British Overseas Territory (2002)

B. British colonies that did not participate in the West Indies Federation

Bermuda		British overseas territory (2002)
Cayman Islands		British overseas territory (2002)
British Virgin Islands		British overseas territory (2002)

C. US unincorporated territory

US Virgin Islands

diversity of "decolonization" points to the region's internal differentiation. Five general outcomes can be discerned among those parts of the Caribbean that were still formally colonized in 1940: absorption into the metropole for France's colonies, "limbo" status for Puerto Rico, partnership with Holland for Dutch colonies, independence for many British colonies and eventually Suriname, and ongoing colonial rule in other British colonies and the US Virgin Islands.

Complex political conflicts, negotiations, and unique conjunctures produced these outcomes. Imperial intentions and capabilities, local elites' preferences and unanimity, and the degree of popular classes' mobilization and alliance with local and imperial elites all mattered. France, the United States, and the Netherlands had quite clear policies, but the Netherlands, like the more muddled Britain, had less success in implementing them. American pressure for decolonization, articulated in the Atlantic Charter of 1941 and stemming from a desire for open markets, also played a significant role. Local political elites varied greatly, from the near-unanimous advocacy of departmentalization in the French Caribbean in 1946 to the profound ongoing disagreements among elites favoring statehood, commonwealth, and independence in Puerto Rico. Popular mobilization sometimes strengthened imperial intentions but also sometimes successfully ran counter to them, as was the case with pro-independence struggles in Britain's colonies in the 1950s and anti-independence pressures in parts of the Dutch Caribbean from the 1970s to the 1990s. Caribbean women were often active, particularly where popular mobilization was strong (Macpherson 2007). Their political positions varied considerably, but they seem to have shared a limited ability to fundamentally contest male political authority in decolonization processes. Post-1970 Caribbean feminist movements have developed critiques of the gendered limits of decolonization.

Impulses and Processes

The French Caribbean

In March 1946 a constituent assembly in France voted unanimously for the three French Caribbean colonies to be absorbed into France; the new status was formalized in October 1946 when they were named overseas departments (*départments d'outre mer*, or DOMs). In 1947 the United Nations removed Guadeloupe, Guyane, and Martinique from its list of non-self-governing territories. The impulses behind this earliest, swiftest version of post-1940 Caribbean decolonization lay in long-term patterns of political development in the French Caribbean and in the particular conjuncture of political forces in France just after World War II. While there was minimal and diffuse opposition to departmentalization in 1946, a broader critique of political assimilation only emerged in the late 1950s. There were some small radical, even violent nationalist groups in the 1960s and 1970s, but as most critics demanded greater autonomy rather than independence, they were satisfied by the decentralization reforms of 1982, when each DOM gained the additional status of a *region d'outre mer*, or ROM.

Proposals for departmentalization were brought to the Constituent Assembly in March 1946 by elected deputies from the three Caribbean colonies and Réunion in the Indian Ocean—in particular, Aimé Césaire and Léopold Bissol from Martinique and Gaston Monnerville from Guyane. The dominance of the pro-departmentalization view stemmed from France's granting of full citizenship rights, manhood suffrage, and elected representation in the French parliament to the colonies beginning in the late 19th century. These rights helped to create and consolidate a black and mulatto political elite that embraced all things French: identity, marriage and family norms, education, and political belonging. This was not simply cultural alienation, but also faith in the universal promise of the French revolutionary tradition and a strategic cultivation of metropolitan power to check the economic dominance of local white landowners.

Césaire (1913–2008) was a product of this particular history. Born into the black lower middle class in Martinique, he received a colonial education in Fort-de-France and then went to university in Paris. Radicalized there, he became famous as the cofounder of the literary-political *négritude* movement, characterized by its insistence on racial difference and pride. But this never translated into a nationalist politics, and Césaire's enormous popularity with Martinicans embodied a linkage of black pride with assimilation into France via communist politics. Throughout his long political career as mayor of Fort-de-France, deputy in the French parliament, and head of Martinique's Regional Council, he never made the ultimate break with France, culturally or politically.

The urban and rural poor of the French Caribbean played no significant independent role in the departmentalization process. Manhood suffrage created a stake in the relationship with France, and the chief enemy was identified as local landowners and employers. There was no basis for a strong popular critique of French colonialism or for a radical nationalist alternative to integration. Certainly the dominant popular and elite response in all three colonies to the fall of France in 1940 was to rally to the support of the occupied motherland—and to demand the restoration of prewar political rights.

With the achievement of DOM status came expectations of complete equality with residents of metropolitan France. Women's suffrage, achieved in France in 1944, came into force in the DOMs in 1946. But several negative trends quickly emerged: the decline of local agricultural and artisan production, rising unemployment, growing dependence on public assistance and state employment, and an inferior level of public assistance. Living standards were rising, but on the basis of aid from France, not real local development.

By the mid-1950s the "assimilationist consensus" was over. Local civil servants had struck for equality with their metropolitan counterparts. Nationalist groupings formed among French Caribbean students in France and returned home with them. Notable among these was the Guyanese People's Union. Césaire resigned from the French Communist Party and denounced the DOM for fostering economic stagnation and undermining freedom in the French Caribbean. But his new Progressive Party of Martinique was pro-autonomy, not nationalist. Constitutional reform in 1960, which allowed for a greater measure of local decision-making, did not satisfy the pro-autonomy camp and small, mostly leftist nationalist groups engaged in elections, protests, and violence throughout the 1960s and 1970s. They had some success in fostering new kinds of Guadeloupian, Martinican, and Guyanese cultural nationalist identities, but few advocated a complete break with France.

The achievement of ROM status in 1982 resulted in the absorption of many separatist activists into the new bureaucracy and electoral machinery, leaving the remaining nationalists even more marginalized. While the fundamental problems of departmentalization—overwhelming dependence on French imports (including food), unemployment and underemployment, migration as a safety valve, and a standard of living based on budgetary transfers from France—have deepened, hope in the capacity of decentralization to spark local economic development endures. Since the mid-1950s, most pressures for change in the "decolonization" of 1946 have taken the form of demands for greater autonomy, not sovereign independence.

Puerto Rico

Puerto Rico occupies a unique position among the Caribbean territories under discussion in this chapter, because no real constitutional change occurred there. Rather, the political process that resulted in the status of commonwealth (estado libre asociado, or ELA) has been constructed as a myth of constitutional decolonization, one that has been endlessly contested by scholars, politicians, activists, and even US courts, yet not quite discredited. The ELA was inaugurated on July 25, 1952, and in November 1953 the United Nations General Assembly narrowly voted to remove Puerto Rico from its list of non-self-governing territories. The process leading to this apparent decolonization began concretely in 1946, when President Harry S. Truman appointed the first Puerto Rican governor. In 1947 the US Congress passed legislation paving the way for the founder and leader of the Popular Democratic Party, Luis Muñoz Marín, to become Puerto Rico's first elected governor in 1948. Next, Congress passed the Puerto Rico Federal Relations Act, which authorized a constituent assembly in Puerto Rico to write a new constitution for the island. When voters approved this constitution—after alteration by Congress—in 1952, the ELA formally came into being.

The impulses behind the process leading to ELA status were complex. All major parties desired the appearance of change, the United States rejected both independence and statehood, and Muñoz Marín was prepared to repackage colonial rule and sell it as decolonization. A writer, journalist, former island senator, and New Deal enthusiast, Muñoz Marín had long worried that independence in defiance of the United States would ruin most Puerto Ricans economically. In the mid-1940s he became convinced that the United States would never offer an economically viable path to independence. In 1946 he sanctioned a dominion-like status proposal and declared that PPD votes in 1948 would endorse that option. Simultaneously, Muñoz Marín abandoned pro-labor economic nationalist policies and criticisms of US capital's exploitation of Puerto Rican workers, consumers, and resources, and began to focus more exclusively on population control and emigration as solutions to poverty. The launching of Operation Bootstrap in 1947 as "a market-propelled modernization" and industrialization (Ayala and Bernabe 2007, 150–51) and the red-baiting and surveillance of nationalists from the late 1940s were part and parcel of the historic choice made by Muñoz Marín and the PPD.

US authorities benefited enormously from PPD cooperation, but maintained control of the repackaging process throughout. Bolstering their global image and leverage—as both the Cold War and pressures for decolonization intensified— depended on assuring the appearance of real change. Their rejection of statehood or independence with economic guarantees effectively killed those options. They limited the elected governor's powers, maintained legislative veto power, and safeguarded all existing federal powers on the island, including the power to alter the commonwealth constitution. Skeptics from 1952 on have noted that establishment of the ELA was merely a reorganization of Puerto Rico's internal government, not a fundamental constitutional change.

Nationalist opposition to the illusion of constitutional change was not sufficiently rapid, consistent, or popular to slow or modify the process. Once ELA status was achieved and the economic growth and mass emigration of the 1950s had occurred, nationalist movements, parties, and armed groups faced even greater difficulties in making their case to the Puerto Rican people. Some ex-Populares, disillusioned with Muñoz Marín and then expelled from the PPD, founded the Partido Independentista Puertorriqueño (PIP) in 1946–47 under the charismatic leadership of Gilberto Concepción de Gracia, a lawyer and longtime Nationalist Party member. The PIP's ability to alter the course of events was sharply reduced by the delay in breaking with the PPD—a delay that allowed Muñoz Marín to consolidate his alliances with the United States and a critical mass of the island electorate, and which slowed the organization of pro-independence forces island-wide. The PIP also lacked influential allies in the US Congress or the Truman administration. That there was a latent electoral nationalism in Puerto Rico is suggested, however, by the PIP's achievement of 19.1% of the vote in the November 1952 elections (Anderson 1965, 109).

Between 1947 and 1950, Nationalist Party activists planned an armed insurrection to embarrass the PPD and the United States and to raise doubts at the UN about the legitimacy of the ELA process. The insurrection occurred in late October and early November 1950, and it resulted in 25 deaths. At least 1,000 others—Nationalist Party members, other *independentistas*, and Communists—were arrested. Further armed violence in 1954 and in the 1970s through the mid-1980s—particularly by the Ejército Popular Boricua, also known as Los Macheteros—proved the durability of this kind of nationalist struggle. The bloody FBI killing of Macheteros leader Filiberto Ojeda Ríos in 2005 unleashed a wave of patriotic anger in the island.

Since 1959, however, there has been no mass popular support for either armed nationalist struggle or the legal unarmed nationalist movements and political parties. The latter, including some leftist groups, have been limited in their effectiveness by factionalism, inconsistent labor politics, skyrocketing dependence on federal social assistance, government repression, and the threat of a resurgent statehood movement, which has won island elections intermittently since 1968 and has at times forced parts of the independence movement into the arms of the PPD. Whether on plebiscites on the status question or in regular elections, the PIP garners only between 2.1% and 5.2% of the vote.

In 1953 only 43.4% of the UN's 60 members voted to remove Puerto Rico from the UN's list of non-self-governing territories, while 26.6% voted against and 30% abstained. More recent international doubts about the validity of the process leading to the "decolonized" status of the ELA, and the responses of American legislators and administrations to those doubts, may open a creative path toward true self-government for Puerto Rico. If so, it will leave Puerto Ricans facing the same challenging questions about economic development and cultural identity that real constitutional change in the French, Dutch, and British Caribbean left unanswered.

The Dutch Caribbean

In late 1954 the Charter of the Kingdom of the Netherlands came into force, creating a tripartite kingdom formed of three theoretically equal partners: Holland, the Netherlands Antilles (NA), and Suriname. Accordingly, in 1955 the UN deemed the Dutch Caribbean to be decolonized.

The most potent impulses bringing about this unique form of "decolonization" were mainly external to the Dutch Caribbean. They originated with an intense Dutch concern to prevent Indonesian independence by offering Indonesians autonomy within a federated kingdom. In 1940 Queen Wilhelmina and the Dutch cabinet fled to London as Germany occupied Holland, and in 1942 Japan occupied Indonesia. That year the cabinet—facing the strain of two fascist occupations, Indonesian nationalism, and US pressure for decolonization via the Atlantic Charter—persuaded Wilhelmina to promise the colonies a postwar conference on autonomy and partnership in a restored kingdom. Indonesian nationalism continued unabated and, despite war with the Dutch, Indonesia became sovereign in 1949. Commitments of autonomy and partnership, however, applied to and were welcomed by the people of Suriname and the NA.

From 1945 to 1954 a slow, sporadic, acrimonious process ensued, dominated until 1949 by Holland's efforts to hold onto Indonesia and afterward by the shock of Indonesia's independence (Oostindie and Klinkers 2003, 74–84). The Dutch renamed the colonies as overseas territories in 1945, committed to respecting their right to self-determination in early 1946, mandated universal suffrage in 1948, and granted them full internal autonomy in 1949. The last of these moves, intended to create the appearance of progress, was not actually implemented until 1951. Although real constitutional change did occur, in practice kingdom policy has been made in Holland.

Suriname's eventual independence was certainly foreshadowed by its assertive stance in negotiations resulting in the Kingdom Charter, but it was ultimately made possible by an unusual conjuncture in the early 1970s. In the late 1950s and the 1960s, Afro-Surinamese political nationalism had been muted by an electoral alliance with the Hindu Party, which preferred continued Dutch influence through the kingdom to protect Surinamese of Asian descent from black dominance. Cultural nationalism made some progress in these years, with the 1959 adoption of national symbols and an anthem as well as the rising status and formal recognition of Sranantongo as a lingua franca. A few small, openly pro-independence parties formed as well, and the presence of one of these, the Party of the Nationalist Republic (PNR), in the coalition government elected in 1973, contributed greatly to Suriname becoming independent in 1975.

That coalition, led by Henk Arron, was formed entirely of Creole-based parties; for the first time, no Asian-based parties, with their strategic opposition to independence, played any role in government. The PNR held a handful of seats critical to the coalition and was able to push it in a strongly nationalist direction. It is unlikely that this would have had much impact, however, if in 1972 Dutch voters had not made Labor Party leader Joop den Uyl prime minister. Concerned with disturbances in Suriname and Curaçao in 1969, wanting to join the global trend toward full decolonization, and worried by immigration from the NA and Suriname to Holland, the Dutch legislature had voted in 1971 to grant sovereignty to Suriname and the NA. Both Arron and den Uyl nurtured the decolonization process eagerly. The process was relatively quick but not harmonious; only after grueling negotiations in 1974–75, heightened ethnic hostilities, a huge wave of Hindustani emigration to Holland, and a tripling of Dutch aid proposals did independence occur in November 1975. The reluctance of both the Dutch and Surinamese authorities to slow down the process in order to take seriously the opposition's concerns caused deep anger among Surinamese of Asian descent. A proposal by Hindustani politician Jagernath Lachmon of the Progressive Reform Party for a 10-year transition to develop a more integrated Surinamese national identity was dismissed out of hand. Lachmon's party remained in opposition until the military coup of 1980, an event that would underscore just how involved the Dutch government remained in Suriname's internal affairs.

In the NA, the 1970s and 1980s were dominated by Aruba's desire to secede from the six-island federation while remaining part of the kingdom. Holland, wanting the NA to move toward independence as a unified whole, resisted strenuously, but strike action, attention from the UN, and pressure from local leaders like Benito Croes and Henny Eman eventually forced the Dutch to concede. Aruba's separate status began in 1986 and was made permanent in 1996, Aruban pressure having forced Holland to abandon the goal of independence. The kingdom is again formed of three partners, but in 2010 the NA were dissolved, with two islands gaining separate status within the kingdom and three being absorbed into Holland as special municipalities. Political nationalism in the region remains extremely marginal.

The British Caribbean

Full political decolonization in the post-1940 Caribbean was concentrated in the British zone, with 12 new nations emerging. This pattern resulted from long-term conditions that fueled strong labor movements and anti-British identities, and also from Britain's own poorly funded and contradictory efforts to prevent or indefinitely delay independence. The wave of national independence began in 1962 in Jamaica and Trinidad and Tobago, continued in 1966 in Barbados and Guyana and in 1973 in the Bahamas, and ended in the early 1980s in Belize and the eastern Caribbean. Each declaration and recognition of national sovereignty resulted in the UN removing Britain's former colonies from its list of non-self-governing territories.

Several long-term patterns nurtured the possibility of effective nationalism in these colonies. First, Britain's failures and refusals to promote economic diversification, labor and voting rights, or social security gave few any meaningful stake in the colonial relationship. Second, radicalizing processes were at work from the early 20th century: the modest expansion of secondary education, the development of mutual-aid organizations, countless women's and men's work migration experiences, Garveyite mobilization and ideology, service during World War I, the effects of meeting fellow "colonials" while working or studying in Britain, and the impact of the Bolshevik revolution. As a direct consequence of these patterns labor identity, organization, and action erupted across the region between 1934 and 1939. Not all labor leaders and unions were explicitly nationalist at first, and in a few colonies nationalist political parties developed without much prior mobilization of labor groups, but overall labor organization laid the basis for a mass nationalism in which the popular classes had real, if temporary, clout. British Caribbean reformers also had strong allies in the metropole. These included social democrats in and around Parliament as well as West Indian migrants in and around the League of Coloured Peoples. Finally, Britain responded to unrest with a combination of repression and underfunded moralistic reform that pushed grievances in a more strongly nationalist direction.

Beginning in the mid-1940s and continuing into the 1950s, Britain sought to indefinitely delay independence by simultaneously granting colony-by-colony constitutional advance, and planning for a region-wide federation. The former was intended to prepare colonies for the latter, but instead it undermined federation by strengthening nationalist identities and political parties during the decade of planning (1947–58). The West India Federation of 1958–62 failed in part because it lacked the popular support that labor-nationalist movements enjoyed, not only because of intercolonial rivalries but also because Britain never promised that federation would lead to independence within a clear and reasonable time frame.

Colony-by-colony constitutional decolonization, pushed by mass nationalist movements, proceeded in a relatively set pattern. Except in Barbados, which had preserved its colonial legislature, the process began with establishing and then expanding the proportion of elected members on the legislative and executive councils. Universal suffrage followed, between 1944 and 1954, with most women and men gaining voting rights simultaneously. Next came ministerial government, with a cabinet of elected legislators headed by a premier. Finally, internal self-government was achieved, between 1959 and 1967, with the British governor retaining responsibility only for defense and external relations. In several colonies political parties developed before the achievement of universal suffrage, in others not until after that milestone, but at some point in most colonies, popular mobilization began to pressure the British for faster and more meaningful change. In some colonies one political party was dominant initially, in others two-party systems emerged quickly, while Trinidad and Tobago stood out for its multiplicity of parties, especially until the mid-1950s. Of the three colonies with two or more major ethnic groups, only British Hounduras managed to avoid ethnic partisan division during constitutional decolonization; both British Guiana and Trinidad and Tobago developed ethnically defined party systems by about 1960.

In that same year, the secretary of state for the colonies announced that Jamaica was ready for independence; it pulled out of the Federation in 1961 and became independent in 1962. Thus, in the early 1960s, British policy switched toward accepting and even promoting independence, but with little economic aid and no right to immigrate to Britain. Its volte-face resulted in part from its success in shaping what kinds of nation-states would emerge. Along with some more repressive tactics, persuasion played a significant role. The very process of gradual, peaceful, negotiated decolonization trained the emerging political elites and national electorates in moderate Westminster-style politics and capitalist economic policies. A cohort of strong populist male leaders, often from the black and mixed-race middle class, was central to the largely orderly decolonization process. Many of the leaders were never radical, while others shed at least some of their radicalism to become acceptable negotiating partners to the British. Those produced in part by large popular nationalist movements—George Price in Belize, Albert Gomes in Trinidad and Tobago, Norman Manley in Jamaica—had particularly to harness and control popular militancy in order to have both leverage and credibility with British officials. Cheddi

Jagan of Guyana stands out for his more authentic and enduring labor-left radical-ism, but Britain exacted a high price for his obstinacy.

Several of these populist leaders joined Britain in repressing or marginalizing the labor-left version of British Caribbean nationalism that was alive in the region, especially in the Caribbean Labour Congress, which was destroyed by 1952. Grant-ley Adams of Barbados colluded with the British governor in denying the socialist nationalist Wynter Crawford his rightful place on the Executive Council in the mid-1940s, and then took credit for the achievement of universal suffrage, for which Crawford had fought hard. In 1952 Norman Manley and his People's National Party in Jamaica expelled the party's left wing, which was led by Richard Hart, Arthur Henry, and Ken and Frank Hill. In 1953 British Guiana's first universal suffrage legislative elections saw a victory for the socialist, nationalist, multiracial People's Progressive Party under Jagan, a US-trained dentist and son of a sugar plantation foreman, and Forbes Burnham, a lawyer trained in England. A few months later Britain sent in troops, suspended the constitution, and imposed an appointed Legis-lative Council. Jagan, who unlike Burnham refused to give up mass politics, was jailed in 1954. His political career revived, but multiracial nationalism rooted in a strong labor movement ended, as the British fostered both a bitter Indian/black divide and Burnham's moderate black leadership, which turned murderously dicta-torial after independence.

Political federation failed and a compromised form of national independence prevailed, belatedly supported by British leaders who were confident that popular mass nationalism had been tamed. Anticipating neocolonialism even before the region's independence process was complete, critical voices like those of C. L. R. James, the Marxist, pan-Africanist novelist, historian, and sports writer, and Walter Rodney, an Afro-Guyanese historian and activist who promoted multiracial worker-based democratic politics, spoke strongly beginning in the 1960s against the limita-tions of the process. Rodney's assassination in 1980 during the Burnham dictator-ship epitomized both those limits and the authoritarianism they had bred.

Consequences

The four paths to "decolonization" outlined above have led to some significant dis-tinctions among the Caribbean territories under discussion, yet those differences are balanced by a common set of dilemmas.

By some measures, national independence is associated with poverty. While sta-tistical methodologies vary, a 2006 ranking of Caribbean nations and territories from highest to lowest gross domestic product per capita is typical in finding non-sovereign territories monopolizing the top 8 spots and independent nation-states, including Suriname and seven former British colonies, occupying the bottom

11 spots. Even in the middle group, non-sovereign territories tended to be ranked higher. Yet even the relatively well off non-sovereign areas of the Caribbean are plagued by high unemployment and underemployment, especially among young people. This commonality speaks to the inability of Caribbean economies to absorb workers, a phenomenon that has intensified since the 1940s and is linked to the withering of agriculture across much of the region. Moreover, all the Caribbean territories discussed here are at risk from global trade liberalization, which threatens their preferential treatment in certain export markets. Both wage rates and economies of scale make them uncompetitive among underdeveloped countries.

Poverty and unemployment fuel emigration, and the Caribbean has the highest percentage of emigrants of any world region (Erisman 2003, 173). A clear pattern of difference among the four metropoles under discussion is that only Britain closed the door on Caribbean immigrants. Puerto Ricans and US Virgin Islanders have the right of free migration to the United States, as do DOM residents to France and NA and Aruba residents to Holland. Even Surinamese migration to Holland continued after independence. But Britain, which recruited West Indian labor in the 1950s, ended that legal flow with the Commonwealth Immigration Act of 1962. Even so, this difference pales in significance next to the commonality of ongoing emigration. After 1962, British Caribbeans began moving to Canada and the United States, both of which eased their restrictions on Caribbean immigration in the 1960s and 1970s. In 1990 the ratio of Caribbean people living abroad relative to the size of population in the home country was 75:100 for Puerto Rico, 54:100 for Suriname, almost 49:100 for Martinique (including those of island ancestry), 42:100 for Jamaica, and 30:100 for the NA (Baronov and Yelvington 2003, 233). A wave of emigration from the NA to Holland in the 1990s led to a 10% decrease in Curaçao's population. For some of the smaller British Caribbean nations, the emigrant community's size actually exceeds that of the nation. Of the three open-immigration metropoles, only Holland has recently witnessed public calls for limitations on immigration, and these are not primarily aimed at Caribbean migrants (Oostindie and Klinkers 2003, 190–91).

Heavy emigration, despite its often temporary or circular nature, complicates the articulation and consolidation of nationalist identities, whether or not flag independence has been won. Yet a colonial ambience survives only in the NA and the DOMs, and there most strongly in Martinique. The DOMs are relatively isolated from their Caribbean neighbors and are oriented overwhelmingly toward France in terms of material consumer culture and identity. Still, traditional family support networks survive despite European-style public assistance provisions. Puerto Rico and the British Caribbean, despite bombardment by North American mass consumer culture, do not feel like extensions of the United States, not least because Caribbean cultures shaped in part by Spain and Britain are notably different from those influenced by the United States. In Puerto Rico the persistence of the Spanish language adds to the island's distinctiveness, and ironically it has contributed to the growth of both cultural nationalism and pro-statehood opinion since the 1960s. British culture in its colonies was long held at bay by deeply rooted Afro-Caribbean popular cultures, which, along with the more recent middle-class and intellectual embrace of black national identity, have had a similar effect on American culture. In the most strikingly multiracial parts of the British Caribbean, indigenous, mestizo, and Asian communities have created other kinds of cultural difference.

Three of the independent countries discussed here stand out for their experiences of dictatorship. In Guyana, Britain's favored moderate, Forbes Burnham, turned authoritarian immediately after the country achieved independence in 1966. Consolidating control via fraudulent elections, police and military power, and a self-serving nationalization of the economy in the name of socialism, Burnham furthered racial division, deepened poverty, and provoked massive emigration. He died in office in 1985. Grenada devolved into dictatorship in the 1960s and 1970s under Eric Gairy, whose brutal regime ended in the 1979 coup by middle-class Marxists led by Maurice Bishop and Bernard Coard. Their revolutionary government imploded just prior to the US invasion of 1983, and although it had strong popular support, it did not create a new constitution or hold elections. Finally, Suriname endured military rule and civil war from 1980 to 1988 under Desi Bouterse, who later backed a coup that briefly returned him to power in 1990, and who in July 2010 was elected president despite facing trial for the 1982 murders of 15 political opponents.

Yet authoritarianism extends well beyond these three extreme cases. Control by the French and Dutch of their former colonies has persisted not so much despite decolonization as because of the manner in which it unfolded. France's harsh treatment of pro-independence activists is particularly notable. In Puerto Rico, PPD rule from 1940 to 1968 allowed for a creeping authoritarianism most evident in the harassment and surveillance of peaceful *independentistas*. Since then, the alternations in power between the PPD and the pro-statehood party have hardly eliminated corruption. And the dozen nations of the former British Caribbean have not developed as strong civil democracies. Popular disaffection has increased, with voter turnout and party identification declining, both damaged by the inability of post-independence patron-client networks to absorb economic crisis. Whether this will translate into a resurgence of popular organization and a broadening of electoral politics as set up by controlled British decolonization is still unclear.

None of these patterns of decolonization has definitively solved the problems that the peoples of the Caribbean face as inheritors of a brutal 500-year history. Skepticism of the nation-state in the region takes two broad forms: that of Surinamese and British Caribbean critics, who lived through the bitter disappointments of flag independence, and that of most people living in the non-sovereign territories, who fear that their economic well-being would be jeopardized by separation from the metropoles. Those in the former group are profoundly oriented toward struggling for a more meaningful, democratic, and prosperous national sovereignty; in the British Caribbean, they can turn to a history of robust popular struggle as an inspiration and resource in that ongoing endeavor.

WORKS CITED

Anderson, Robert. 1965. *Party Politics in Puerto Rico.* Stanford, CA: Stanford University Press.

Ayala, César, and Rafael Bernabe. 2007. *Puerto Rico in the American Century.* Chapel Hill: University of North Carolina Press.

Baronov, David, and Kevin Yelvington. 2003. "Ethnicity, Race, Class, and Nationality." In *Understanding the Contemporary Caribbean*, edited by Richard Hillman and Thomas D'Agostino. Boulder, CO: Lynne Rienner.

Erisman, H. Michael. 2003. "International Relations." In *Understanding the Contemporary Caribbean*, edited by Richard Hillman and Thomas D'Agostino. Boulder, CO: Lynne Rienner.

Macpherson, Anne S. 2007. *From Colony to Nation: Women's Activism and the Gendering of Politics in Belize, 1912–1982.* Lincoln: University of Nebraska Press.

Oostindie, Gert, and Inge Klinkers. 2003. *Decolonizing the Caribbean: Dutch Politics in a Comparative Perspective.* Amsterdam: Amsterdam University Press.

33

The Caribbean and the Cold War

DAVID SHEININ

Between Reform and Revolution

Given the persistence of grinding poverty and the dramatic failure of regional development projects in the Caribbean, the Cold War era proved to be a period of shared harshness of life for most people in the region, punctuated by promises of reform tied to great power international political projects that, for the most part, generated few results. Often, scholars have presented such failed promise as a backdrop to Cold War conflict while subsuming national and regional historical processes to a larger history laced with super-power competition. This chapter posits an alternative approach; without setting aside Cold War historical processes as they touched the Caribbean, the analysis will focus in the first instance on local, regional, and national histories in explaining the Caribbean during the Cold War.

The Cold War Caribbean as a proving ground for superpowers is particularly evident in many studies of revolutionary change in Cuba and, to a lesser extent, Grenada. But it also applies more generally to how Caribbean history is understood. Historians have often gauged the historical significance of local events in reference to Cold War touchstones. They have cast military dictatorships (such as in Haiti and the Dominican Republic) as a consequence of Washington's aversion to a putative international communist menace, as though military and other domestic political cultures were tertiary to the denial of democracy. Longstanding political contests (such as that between Michael Manley and Edward Seaga in Jamaica) and how they shaped democratic processes have been described unsatisfactorily as a reflection of varying influence of one or another of the superpowers in the region; and development strategies, whether in Grenada after 1978 or in Puerto Rico throughout the Cold War, have been cast inadequately as a measure of great power ideological and strategic initiatives.

The Great Yardstick

Cuba is the yardstick by which Caribbean Cold War history has been measured, and the Cuban Revolution is the central Caribbean narrative against which others are brought into relief. Once an advocate for social reform linked to a limited redistributive politics, Cuba's Fulgencio Batista had by the 1950s become a brutal dictator. Mired in monocultural sugar exports and overwhelmed by US capital whose interests extended from agriculture, banking, and public utilities to prostitution, organized crime, and casinos, Batista's Cuba became increasingly repressive in defense of the divide between extreme wealth and devastating poverty. In 1953, after leading a famously aborted attack on the dictatorship, the young lawyer Fidel Castro went to jail for two years and then into exile, from where he tried again, in 1956, to bring down the Batista regime. This time most of Castro's band was killed by Cuban soldiers. But a small number made it to the Sierra Maestra Mountains, where they began the revolutionary process that overthrew the dictatorship in 1959.

Change came quickly. The new revolutionary government outlawed race-based discrimination, increased wages, set and achieved modest health care and educational improvement targets that outpaced those of neighboring island nations, and nationalized key enterprises. The 1959 Agrarian Reform (nationalizing and redistributing land as cooperatives and state-owned enterprises) and an early 1960 agreement with the Soviet Union for the sale of sugar convinced American leaders that in Castro's Cuba they were facing the Soviet enemy. When the revolutionary government took over the facilities of Texaco and Standard Oil, the United States ended its decades-old sugar quota. The Cubans nationalized more American companies; American exports to Cuba all but ended. And in 1961, the United States broke diplomatic relations with Cuba, forcing it reluctantly into much stronger ties with the Soviet Union.

In April 1961 the United States launched the Bay of Pigs invasion, which hinged on the fantasy that with a little prodding the Cuban people would rise up against their supposed government oppressor. The Central Intelligence Agency (CIA) had organized some 1,200 Cuban exiles, most from South Florida, to overthrow Castro. To the surprise of American officials, when the surreptitious force landed on April 17 there was no popular uprising. The attackers were routed.

By 1963 some 200,000 Cubans, for the most part white and privileged, had left the island for the United States. Citing the Bay of Pigs and other perceived US threats, the revolutionary government became more authoritarian in tone and practice, purging former allies, gutting university faculties, and locking away political opponents. In 1962 American spy plane photos showed that the Soviet Union intended to arm Cuba with nuclear missiles capable of striking US targets, prompting perhaps the most dramatic international confrontation of the era. While in the Cuban case, as in so many others, American officials incorrectly assumed that social revolution or reform was socialist in character, the Cuban missile crisis transformed the Caribbean into a Cold War stage for Soviet-American hostility with global as well as local implications.

Castro never forgave the Soviets for withdrawing their offer of a missile defense system. Still, the crisis ushered in three decades of a conflictive Cuban-Soviet alliance. In 1975, when Cuba became involved in Angola's liberation war—a war that echoed the Vietnam War in the United States for the trauma of loss it engendered in Cuba—American officials assumed falsely that the Cubans were fighting a proxy war for the Soviets. In fact, Cuba had always prosecuted its own agenda in Africa. Its multiple objectives included the development of ties to other peoples through, for example, effective and inexpensive health care offered by Cuban physicians. By mid-1977 the Soviet Union had begun to press Cuba to withdraw from Angola, recognizing that the United States would never be convinced that Cuba was acting alone and that a continued Cuban military presence in Africa would jeopardize the latest round of US-Soviet arms reduction talks. But Castro stayed his course in Africa, much to the consternation of Moscow.

In literacy, health care, education, and other areas in which the state intervened to improve the lives of Cubans, the revolution was a success, especially when compared to other Caribbean societies in which these social indices often remained abysmal. From the early 1960s through the late 1980s, thousands of Haitians, in much more dire straits than their Cuban neighbors, crossed the narrow strait separating the two nations in search of a better life in eastern Cuba. But attracting poverty-stricken Haitians can only be read as a subjective success for the revolution. Still, Cuba's Cold War development models, artificially backed by Soviet sugar purchases and oil supplies, never produced the desired results.

Shortly after coming to power in Cuba, the revolutionary government broke with the past by ending reliance on the plantation economy for exports. Following a decision to pursue industrial diversification, the government nationalized foreign holdings in energy and related sectors. By the mid-1960s the diversification plan had failed dramatically, due in part to the US economic blockade. With the failed promise of industrialization models, the revolution returned to Cuba's traditional export crop, sugar. Gone were the large private plantations that had monopolized good land and sharply limited domestic food production before 1959. But despite the end of earlier forms of exploitative plantation agriculture, by the mid-1960s economic growth depended entirely on steadily increasing sugar production. Without attention to international prices or demand, Cuba became quickly and entirely dependent on consumption by the Soviet Union and its allies.

Sugar production—the quintessential Caribbean economic project, accounting for rampant and persistent poverty—now gave the island a steady source of income and, to some extent, protected it from the vagaries of the market. But in two respects Cuba paid a high price for its ongoing reliance on sugar. First, like other Caribbean economies dependent on declining commodity prices, it suffered drops in export earnings over time, most notably in the mid-1980s. When the impact turned severe at the end of the Cold War, Cuba had to fend for itself on international markets for the first time in three decades. The result was widespread impoverishment and social disarray. The second price it paid was that of having to heed Soviet strategic concerns that as a leading nation in the non-aligned movement it would otherwise not have followed.

As in the period before World War II, the United States continued to play a crucial cultural role in Cuba during the Cold War. The 1950s marked an apogee in strong Cuban attraction to American popular culture, even as Cuban animosity toward the Batista regime—identified with longstanding American exploitation on the island—mounted. These tensions culminated in Fidel Castro's 1959 question, "How could we import rice and buy Cadillacs?" (Pérez 1999, 480), and abated somewhat with the coming of the revolution.

An Opposing Narrative

If in the US narrative of the Cold War, Cuba represented a Soviet surrogate, Puerto Rico represented the opposite—an opportunity for Washington to develop a Caribbean nation within its own nation. Puerto Rico became a hub of modernization policy, even as Puerto Ricans sought greater authority in an evolving context of US colonialism. Luis Muñoz Marín won the island's first gubernatorial elections in 1948 hard on the heels of "Operation Bootstrap," a Washington-backed project designed to lift Puerto Rico out of poverty through rapid industrial growth. This project presaged similar modernization plans for other Latin American nations, and reflected continuing US stereotyping of Puerto Ricans and other Latin Americans as "backward." Supporting modernization, Muñoz Marín governed through 1964, during which time Puerto Rico experienced uneven development through an industrialization model that drew on tax breaks, low wages, and the fantasy of an end to colonialism through commonwealth status, obtained in 1952. In the race for Caribbean modernization, Puerto Rico became Cuba's antagonist.

But the attention many critics lavished on Puerto Rico's economic failures reflected an undue emphasis on the Caribbean as an "American backyard" during the Cold War, and the historical record belies false binary models of success or failure for societies under American or Soviet sway. Responses to colonialism and foreign influences varied across time and space. There were remarkable, if limited successes to US-initiated or backed programs in the region that defied the norm and reflected forceful political agency on the part of participants; for example, the 1940s land distribution program in Puerto Rico afforded recipients and their families a range of opportunities. The latter half of the 20th century was also characterized by new grassroots movements and the strengthening of Puerto Rican cultural nationalism. While the revolutionary group Los Macheteros, for example, could never be cast as a popular movement, its shift from armed resistance to vociferous peaceful protest marked the long-term dissatisfaction of many Puerto Ricans over colonial abuses, including the US use of the inhabited island of Vieques for naval exercises and bombings.

The image of islands as bombing grounds contradicts a different Cold War–era Caribbean fantasy: the islands as paradise. No economic project has had as profound an impact on the region as tourism, both inside and outside the contexts of Cold War competition. As Cuba became a key tourist destination for Canadians and Europeans in the 1980s and 1990s, for example, firms capitalizing that sector became a central target of US ire. This intricate link between tourism and Cold War conflicts was also in evidence in Puerto Rico. An important tourist destination for Americans since the 1920s, this island took on new significance in the aftermath of the Cuban Revolution. During the 1960s, when tourism in revolutionary Cuba collapsed, more visitors went to Puerto Rico than to anywhere else in the region. But, as in other Caribbean nations, the rise of tourism in Puerto Rico also reflected generations of failed attempts ot develop industrialization. Through the 1960s and 1970s, the nature of work changed in Puerto Rico as the nation shifted away from industry. As offshore production continued to rise exponentially around the globe, Puerto Rico became less and less competitive, in part because it was constrained by American minimum-wage requirements. Tourism emerged to fill an economic gap that brought the illusion of economic success, creating some employment for local residents, but little opportunity for most to change their lives substantially.

A Second Cuba

Inspired in part by the Cuban model, a second Cold War–era revolution in the Caribbean came in a strikingly different context. With a population of only 89,000 at the time of its revolution in 1979, Grenada had never figured prominently in the imperial designs of any nation. There were no widespread demands for land reform. Even so, the New Jewel Movement led by Maurice Bishop enjoyed widespread support when it overthrew the increasingly corrupt and authoritarian government of Eric Gairy. Like its Cuban counterpart, the new People's Revolutionary Government began introducing notable change to Grenada by ending traditional dependence on agricultural exports and ongoing imperial relationships (the island had gained independence from the United Kingdom five years earlier). Also like Cuba in the early stages of revolution, Grenada's leaders looked to economic diversification focused on tourism, some industry, and food production as a panacea.

Perhaps Grenada's most pronounced contrast with Cuba came in its more hesitant project for revolutionary change. Even though Washington regarded Grenada as a Cuba-like threat, Prime Minister Bishop's revolution was not explicitly socialist in direction; its objectives were more modest than the massive state intervention implemented by the Cuban government after 1962. A small handful of banks were nationalized. State ownership of land increased but remained limited to a minority of good, arable land. About half of all public utilities were already in government hands by the time Bishop had come to power. The government planned for economic reform in stages that would lead not to state economic dominance, but rather to state direction of the economy with modest intervention; there would be a slow shift from agricultural exports to a new tourism industry capitalized by the state and foreign investors, as well as some mechanization of agriculture. For example, taking over one important foreign-owned hotel was a first step toward the imagined government-directed tourist economy. A Marketing and National Importing Board was established to further help make private investment feasible and profitable. But while such private investment in the economy increased in 1981 and 1982, grumblings about a greater state role in the economy were beginning.

As in Cuba, social reforms, including dramatic increases in health-related spending, bore quick results. But many projects stalled. A program to bring unused land into production did not increase output substantially. Some economic successes were offset by the region-wide problem of stagnant or declining commodity prices. Hopes for a revitalized tourist trade remained unfulfilled as reports of "communism" in the American media prompted a decline in travelers from the United States. In an act perfectly in keeping with the revolution's mandate for a public-private mix, the government made two related decisions. To attract more tourists and more foreign investment in the tourist sector, it began building a new airport with a longer runway to compete with other island nations for the charter airline industry. The government also sought Cuban investment beyond sources in the private sector. This latter decision, combined with the growing strength of hardliners within the New Jewel Movement, stoked the reactionary resurgence of the Cold War in the minds of early Reagan administration officials, opening the door for the US invasion in 1983 and the destruction of Grenada's revolution. What Cuban leaders had feared in their country—insufficient time for revolutionary reform to take hold in the face of US pressure—had played out in Grenada.

Dictatorship

During the Cold War, while American leaders and their friends throughout the hemisphere were griping about communism, military dictatorship swept the Caribbean and parts of Latin America. Right-wing authoritarian rule was intimately tied to the Cold War itself, and to how that conflict shaped the region. In Cuba, for example, Batista's regime was characterized by gross abuses of force, persistent poverty, and political corruption so great that it alienated large sectors of the US Congress, in turn enabling revolution. Both François "Papa Doc" Duvalier in Haiti and Rafael Trujillo in the Dominican Republic had emerged from National Guard units established decades earlier by the United States to ensure regional political and economic stability. In a hemisphere beset by Cold War–era military dictatorship—with its hallmarks of state terror, ferocious anti-Communism, and Washington's support in the era of national security doctrine—what distinguished these two nations were the local racial and social hierarchies on which the dictators thrived.

Having seized presidential power in 1930, Trujillo quickly undertook repressive authoritarian measures to ensure his rule. He set the country on a kleptocratic economic course directed from the presidential palace, stressed friendly relations with the United States, and set in place what quickly became a grotesque caricature of an intensely personalist regime featuring mammoth statues of the dictator and other gargantuan tributes to his own leadership. Trujillo's power derived not only from a keen understanding of Dominican racial hierarchies, but also from his willingness to combine terror, an awareness of popular discourses on race, and the fostering of existing divisions that linked race to class. While lining his own pockets and those of his friends, Trujillo left in place the sugar industry, which had long been dominated by the United States. In Brazil, Argentina, and other Latin American nations, military leaders faced insurmountable pressures for a transition to democracy as World War II drew to a close, yet Trujillo was able to sidestep such pressures because of his rigorous suppression of political dissent over the previous decade, the weakness of social movements, and the willingness of the US government to overlook repression in the Dominican Republic in the context of an emerging Cold War conflict.

Ironically, in light of how such measures were perceived by Washington in nations where leftist reformers held sway, Trujillo practiced a limited form of import substitution industrialization during the 1950s that did in fact lead to some modest growth in various industrial sectors. More surprising still, the traditionally US-dominated sugar industry came to be controlled by Trujillo and his cronies. What kept Americans supportive of Trujillo for so long was his Cold War anticommunism. But even that became less important to Washington after 1959, when weighed against the threat of "another Cuba" in the Dominican Republic, and what many Americans began to see as the signs of impending communist doom in that country—a poverty-stricken peasantry, growing political dissent, and the dictator's unabated corruption.

As pressures on the regime mounted, emboldened former allies assassinated Trujillo in 1961. But little reform on par with the wave of social change that swept Cuba in the 1960s occurred during the subsequent presidency of Joaquín Balaguer, save the excision of Trujillo and his cronies from control of the national economy. In 1965, fearing that political uncertainty and Balaguer's incompetence might lead to revolution, the United States invaded the Dominican Republic. For many, this Cold War return to the era of gunboat diplomacy as an American solution to "unrest" in the Caribbean was a shocking surprise. US President Lyndon Johnson's approach to the region left little to interpretation; asked about the possibility of an Organization of American States peacemaking mission in lieu of the US Marine invasion, Johnson famously retorted that "the OAS couldn't pour piss out of a boot if the instructions were written on the heel" (Brands 1987–88).

An even more stark case of dictatorship and social inequality in the shadow of anticommunism and Cold War conflict came in Haiti, where American authorities propped up brutal authoritarianism for fear of social revolution in the region. More so than in either Cuba or the Dominican Republic, race was crucial to the emergence of dictatorship in Haiti. A physician who had gained prominence as health minister for his campaign against malaria, François Duvalier identified early in his political career with the nationalist *noiriste* movement that accurately linked class inequalities with racial divisions in society. When he sought and won the presidency in 1957, Duvalier stressed the mulatto origins of his opponent and the concentration of wealth in the hands of light-skinned Haitians.

Like Trujillo, Duvalier crafted a personality cult in asserting dictatorial authority over Haiti. But his self-deification was less hierarchical, at least in the beginning, and more tied to popular identities and politics. In addition to promoting vodou and other popular cultural manifestations of the black majority, Duvalier promoted a vision of his own rule as related to the cult of Baron Samedi, Lord of the Dead. His creation of the Tontons Macoutes, a paramilitary squadron exclusively loyal to himself, had the quadruple function of weakening Haiti's armed forces as a potential threat to his extended rule, orchestrating a reign of terror that would keep him in power, perpetuating popular animosity toward an ambiguously defined mulatto elite, and cementing the link between his politics and a vodou-inspired popular imaginary.

Far more than Batista or Trujillo, Duvalier crushed any semblance of a syndical or political opposition. Although the Caribbean was experiencing a modest economic boom as measured by gross domestic production, the Haitian economy shrunk abysmally. In addition to staggering poverty, results of that decline included Haiti's international isolation and growing emigration, especially to the United States. When "Papa Doc" died in 1971, his son Jean-Claude ("Baby Doc") Duvalier took power. The illusion of a more benevolent rule encouraged the development of extremely low-paying offshore industries that led to a dramatic economic shift, but no abatement in the ongoing decline in living standards.

As he oversaw the ongoing decimation of the agricultural sector in the late 1970s and early 1980s, Baby Doc critically altered the race-based politics his father had painstakingly nurtured. When he married Michelle Bennett Pasquet, who had family connections to the mulatto elite that Papa Doc had always reviled, Jean-Claude jeopardized his ties to the black middle and working classes and to an older group of backers inside and outside government that had stood with his father. Moreover, the perception of Michelle as a spendthrift only confirmed the public's view of Jean-Claude's corruption, excess, and concentration of power.

The Other Caribbean

In the mid-1970s, already wealthy but not yet an international celebrity, Bob Marley moved from the poor Kingston sector of Trenchtown to a wealthy neighborhood where Prime Minister Michael Manley lived. This move broke a range of class, racial, and religious barriers in Jamaica, as did the narratives that emerged from Marley's music. Marley's transgressive success far beyond Jamaica underscored a Cold War parallel between the English- and Spanish-speaking Caribbean on race, class, and persistent poverty. Throughout the Caribbean, and despite US-led Cold War modernization projects, most people of color continued to live in poverty. In part, the popularity of Marley's music drew on narratives tied to the singer's personal ascent, which broke down assumptions implicit in Caribbean societies that made race and class a determinant of social and economic hierarchies. On other levels, however, the English-speaking Caribbean—dominated in land mass and population by Jamaica and by Trinidad and Tobago—had a radically different trajectory from those of Haiti, the Dominican Republic, Puerto Rico, and Cuba. Farther from the core Cold War preoccupations of the United States, the English-speaking Caribbean nonetheless evolved in a context shaped by the economic and political developments of that larger conflict.

Both Jamaica and Trinidad won full independence in 1962 and subsequently established British-style parliamentary systems, avoiding military dictatorships. Still, a Jamaican governmental and electoral system that juxtaposed the conservative Jamaican Labour Party (JLP) and the left-of-center People's National Party (PNP) made few dents into two large sets of problems that also afflicted other island nations. First, poverty was grinding and unrelenting. Second, class was tied to race. When Kingston experienced violent rioting in 1966 and again in 1968, parliamentary leaders began to reflect on their distance from popular politics and on the dual problems of racial oppression and poverty.

Under Michael Manley's leadership, the PNP gradually shifted further left, identifying itself with democratic socialism. It won the 1976 general elections on a platform of sweeping social reform, inspired in part by earlier change in Guyana and Cuba. However, Manley's increasing rapprochement with Cuba alienated important sectors of the local elite and, in turn, led the JLP to emphasize an anticommunist stance that played well in the United States, whose leaders were bent on marginalizing—and possibly destabilizing—the Manley government. Yet given a lack of funds to implement social programs, little did change in Jamaica—and when, on the eve of the 1980 election, the leaders of the two major parties signed an antiviolence pact, the document merely marked the end of a period of ideological conflict and a return to governance from the center-right by the JLP under Edward Seaga. Mounting electoral apathy was matched by increasing violence in sprawling Kingston slums and elsewhere in the country.

If Jamaica's formal parliamentary politics remained woefully inadequate to redress social pressures, its music expressed race- and class-based conflict not only on the island but around the globe. Lee "Scratch" Perry was among many who had preceded Marley, expressing Jamaica's African-Christian cultural roots in dub music that, according to artist Philip Maysles, became "a language that manages to retain, consolidate, and communicate cultural memory in an environment determined to silence all traces of Africa" (Maysles 2002, 92). Dub music made Jamaica's African heritage political in a process that evoked the musician's journey itself. Perry's move from the countryside to the city in 1960, like Marley's later move within Kingston, formed part of a massive urban migration in the Caribbean during the Cold War—one that politicized poor urban slums, reemphasized the links between race and poverty, and revolutionized musical expression of these connections in dub, ska, and reggae.

Race was at the core of how Trinidadian politics were institutionalized after independence. As in Jamaica, a two-party Trinidadian British-style parliamentary democracy made few dents in the nation's persistent poverty. Unlike in Jamaica, however, Trinidad's Cold War–era politics was firmly divided along racial lines. The People's National Movement, led by Eric Williams, drew on the backing of a black majority and, to some extent, mixed-race Trinidadians, while the more conservative Democratic Labour Party, and later the United Labour Front, held the support of generally more prosperous Indians, descendants of indentured workers who had been brought to the island after emancipation. In 1970, responding in part to economic uncertainty and government sloth, a loose agglomeration of university students, militant union leaders, and disaffected members of the Trinidad Defense Force—the Black Power movement—rose against Williams. The government quickly suppressed the resulting strikes, marches, and limited military actions. And while Williams responded in the aftermath by stating his sympathy for Black Power and removing government ministers from office, he also implemented new legislation restricting the right to march and other civil rights.

Failed Promise

The end of the Cold War came with failed promise for the Caribbean. Like other nations in the region, Jamaica had, after the end of Manley's government, tied its star to late Cold War American visions for prosperity through the free market. Edward Seaga had come to the Jamaican presidency in October 1980, only days before the election of Ronald Reagan. Having chased Manley's democratic socialists from office, Seaga assumed power intending to shift the country firmly to the right. He became the first head of state to visit the newly installed Reagan in 1981, and his pro-free-market positions brought Jamaica firmly into line with US economic and strategic policies.

At his meeting with Reagan, Seaga suggested a Marshall Plan–like infusion of capital for the region. Reagan agreed, and the Caribbean Basin Initiative (CBI) was launched a year later. The program included a forceful reassertion of US military objectives, such as massive military aid for the government of El Salvador, but US government funding generally was minimal. The core of the program was similar to what had been promoted in Puerto Rico for years—large tax breaks for American investors in the region, and duty-free offerings to Caribbean entrepreneurs looking for North American markets.

US investment in Seaga's Jamaica was staggering, particularly in light of the relative paucity of such government and business interest in other Caribbean nations. Before the US Congress passed the CBI, Washington had given $100 million to Seaga's government, and in short order Jamaica ranked fifth per capita among recipients of American aid. In stark contrast to the difficulties Manley's government had faced in winning the backing of the International Monetary Fund and private lenders during the 1970s, the Seaga administration was showered with credit. At the same time, Seaga expelled Cuban health professionals who had been working at the invitation of the Manley government, slashed public spending, ended price and rent controls, and terminated a host of import substitution policies initiated by Manley. The model for success was to be the rapidly expanding economies of Southeast Asia, which were geared for export and peopled with low-wage workforces.

From Washington's standpoint, Seaga was a success. But by all other measures, the Jamaican shift to the right was a dramatic failure. Wages and the standard of living fell. Prices rose sharply as the gross domestic product declined year by year through the mid-1980s, spearheaded by a predictable drop in industrial production. Foreign debt rose steadily, as did unemployment, and the much-anticipated flow of foreign investment never materialized.

If one event marked the culmination of Cold War–era policy failures in the Caribbean, it was the tacit post–Cold War alliance between Dominican President Balaguer and his longtime opponent, Juan Bosch of the Dominican Liberation Party. When the two leaders came together in June 1996 to forge an alliance, the National Patriotic Front, against a common adversary, José Francisco Peña Gómez of the Dominican Revolutionary Party, it signaled the remarkable end to what appeared to have been 30 years of rivalry.

In 1966, Balaguer had won the presidency over the more left-leaning Bosch in tainted elections one year after the US invasion. Balaguer consolidated his power by sending paramilitary units to slaughter thousands of Bosch supporters in poor Santo Domingo neighborhoods. Bosch boycotted subsequent elections in 1970 and 1974, claiming that they were unwinnable under Balaguer's authoritarian rule. Then in the 1980s he shifted hard to the political right, coming out in favor of a Seaga-like program of privatizations and foreign capital inflows. Balaguer successfully defeated him in the 1990 presidential election by reminding Dominicans of the instability of the 1960s, which ostensibly had been the work of Bosch.

In seeking explanations for the Balaguer-Bosch entente, scholars have found them in the leaders' social and racial background. Despite their emergence in the early 1960s as "polar opposites" in a political system inherited from Trujillo, their background and ethnicities—middle-class and white—were politically and socially similar in a nation that was severely divided on class and racial lines. Both Balaguer and Bosch were noted authors and intellectuals in the Dominican context, and they practiced a variety of personalist politics, viewing their parties as vehicles for their own quests for power. More important, to avoid that most feared of Cold War–era threats—widespread armed conflict—the two leaders worked within unstated political bounds that were defined by an ongoing series of pacts which led, in the first instance, to Bosch's voluntary exile in 1966.

In the end, Balaguer and Bosch combined to present a Dominican political system that was less authoritarian than the Trujillo dictatorship—less violent, less dogmatic, more democratic, and more determined to correct the country's ills, beginning with the persistent poverty. Ultimately, however, the political system they defined remained a staunch Cold War ally of the United States, furthered American economic and strategic objectives in the region and beyond, and failed to produce any substantial results in changing the lives of most Dominicans.

This Cold War end point was not unlike developments in most Caribbean nations, and it reflected more general trends in the hemisphere in the 1990s. The fall of the Soviet Union helped create the conditions for the emergence of the Washington Consensus, by which American, Caribbean, and Latin American business and government leaders reached informal understandings of the sort US officials had sought for years. The consensus stressed the value of political stability in the region as a precondition for withdrawal of government regulation of national economies and the opening of national borders to much freer capital and commercial flows. As in the cases of the Dominican Republic and Jamaica, the political center shifted right throughout the Americas. While some nations experienced limited sector-specific economic growth (often dependent on a continuation of low-wage labor conditions and other "advantages" to foreign investors, including lax environmental rules), more commonly nations like Grenada and Haiti saw none of the growth that advocates of the consensus had promised and no end to the long-standing linkages between race, class, and increasing urban impoverishment that the Cold War and its aftermath of neoliberal reforms had helped to cement.

WORKS CITED

Brands, H. W., Jr. 1987–88. "Decisions on American Armed Intervention: Lebanon, Dominican Republic, and Grenada." *Political Science Quarterly* 102, no. 4: 607–24.

Maysles, Philip. 2002. "Dubbing the Nation." *Small Axe* 6, no. 1: 91–111.

Pérez, Louis A. Jr. 1999. *On Becoming Cuban: Identity, Nationality, and Culture.* New York: Ecco Press.

PART 7

The Caribbean in the Age of Globalization

34

The Long Cuban Revolution   Michael Zeuske

The largest island in the Caribbean has been a site of political and economic struggles for centuries. Long before its historic 20th-century revolution, Cuba and its port city, Havana, served as an important link between the Americas, the Caribbean, and the Atlantic, as well as between the region and its dominating world powers. In fact, nearly all great empires with an interest in the region sought control over the island.

At the same time, internal pressures constantly roiled a Cuba turned wealthy and powerful, one of the most advanced, modern, and lucrative agricultural producers in the world, with a rich culture and complex African heritage. In many non-sugar-producing regions of the island, the *guajiros* (often free colored people or poor whites in alliance with local elites) formed small agricultural settlements, little influenced by the great plantations. Other such zones marginal to the plantation complex were characterized by *cimarronaje* (slave flight) and resistance against the expansion of the big sugar culture with its symptomatic institutions, like the *ingenio* (the agro-industrial complex of sugar fields and factories) and the slave barracoons of the port cities. Already in the 19th century, Cuban proponents of independence and nationalist elites, particularly in the eastern parts of the island, had formed alliances with free farmers, ex-slaves, workers, and the urban poor and middle classes against the conservative Hispano-Cuban planter class, the colonial bureaucracy, and the Catholic Church. Their most effective tool in the conflict over independence, nation, and sovereignty was the *ejército libertador cubano*, one of the largest transracial armies the Western Hemisphere had ever seen, whose traditions have lasted until the present day.

After Spain lost control over Cuba in 1898, the United States occupied the island twice (1899–1902 and 1906–9) and intervened on various occasions. Even after independence, the Cuban people had to deal with limitations on their sovereignty imposed by the US government through the Platt Amendment to the Cuban constitution of 1901. The first two Cuban presidents were imposed by the occupiers (in 1902 and 1909), and the constitutional system, only in theory fully implemented, masked harsh social and racial hierarchies.

The years between 1902 and 1925 witnessed official and unofficial conflicts among the Cuban elites, split as they were between *militares* and *doctores* (soldiers and intellectuals), liberals and conservatives, centralists and regionalists. In addition, and despite much racially inclusive rhetoric, there were hidden conflicts between "white" and "colored" elites. The first presidents were all white independence fighters. Racial conflicts were brought into the open only in one case, the Guerrita de los Negros of 1912, when the Partido Independiente de Color, an all-black political party, was suppressed with deadly force. Many protests and struggles for provincial or central power were carried out in the tradition and rhetoric of the independence wars—that is, through armed protest under the leadership of military elites (in the countryside) or civilian ones (in the cities). When the uprisings were suppressed, resistance took shape in the form of banditry and lawlessness, particularly in the *sierras* of Oriente.

In the 1920s, under Geraldo Machado's dictatorial rule, new forms of political participation and organization arose from the struggle against the alliance between a conservative military and the United States. These new forms, such as parties and cultural organizations, together with collective mass actions, a rebellion in the army, and the older forms of rural protest, played decisive roles in the socialist-inspired revolution of 1933, which was aborted under US pressure after only a few months. It is in this context—especially the attempt of rebel leader Antonio Guiteras Holmes to defend the doomed mass revolution through direct military action in rural terrains—that one can see the roots of the *fidelista* movement of the 1950s. Other former revolutionaries of military origin soon began using terrorist methods and effectively became bands of gangsters, especially in Havana. The years between

1933 and 1940 were a period of political, social, and institutional instability; within this period, Cuba had five presidents. The situation only stabilized under Fulgencio Batista, the first colored leader in highest office, initially as dictator and later (1940–44) as elected president.

One of the lasting results of the aborted revolution was the formation of a new party, the Partido Auténtico de la Revolución Cubana (the Auténticos), under Ramón Grau San Martín, the former president of the revolutionary government of 1933. During World War II, Batista formed new alliances, including with the communists of the Partido Unión Revolucionaria Comunista (PURC). The moderately radical nationalist Auténticos then won the elections of 1944 and 1948 against Batista and formed a new government that could be characterized as social democrat. Yet their leaders soon took to corrupt political maneuvers and—despite their radical and nationalistic rhetoric—assumed a pro-United States position early in the Cold War.

Struggling to maintain control of Cuba, the Auténtico government endured a series from challenges: from high-ranking military groups with contacts to Batista; from communists leading the unions; and from a new section of the Auténtico Party, called the *Ortodoxos*, under the leadership of Eduardo Chibás (1907–1951), who aimed to restore Cuban nationalism by returning to the teachings of José Martí (1853–1895), the 19th-century intellectual and champion of Cuban independence. Chibás had been one of the student leaders of 1933 and was a brilliant anticommunist speaker. But the most important goal of his "orthodox" *martianismo* was the critique of corruption under the Auténticos. The young Fidel Castro and his fellow comrades began their political career as Ortodoxos, admirers of Chibás, and members of the "generation of 1953," a designation honoring the centennial of Martí's birth.

In 1952 Batista once more took power in a coup. During the second *Batistiato*, the United States used a militarily subordinated Cuba to secure its own power over Caribbean states like Venezuela, by then one of the world's most important oil producers. But even though Batista proved less astute and skillful than during his first period in power, the older political leaders and organizations in the opposition made little headway against the *dictadura*. This was the historical moment for direct action by young politicians.

Toward the Revolution

On July 26, 1953, a group of students and workers led by Castro launched an attack on the army's Moncada Barracks in Santiago de Cuba. Although it failed, the attack demonstrated the willingness of Batista's adversaries to die for their ideal of a new nationalism embracing all social classes and groups, including the *campesinos* (both plantation workers and small farmers) and urban workers. After his imprisonment and eventual release, Castro could not stay in Cuba. Batista and the Batistianos had long used terror to repress urban resistance, political parties, parts of the unions, and civil enemies, including the Auténticos. So Castro, his brother Raúl, and their core group of supporters emigrated to Mexico, after founding the Movimiento 26 de Julio. There they began military and political training and met Ernesto "Ché" Guevara, who had participated in failed revolutions in Bolivia and Guatemala. After an adventurous return to Cuba in the yacht *Granma* in 1956, Castro's group took refuge in one of the most important regions of resistance against elite and state power, the Sierra Maestra mountains in eastern Cuba, where they transformed themselves into a guerrilla movement.

At this time, the Sierra Maestra, a small but relatively high mountain range, was still covered with primary subtropical forest, its very narrow valleys difficult to enter even with mules. The only major points of access were controlled by the cities of Manzanillo, Bayamo, and Santiago de Cuba. It was not easy for the mostly urban fidelistas to survive in this hostile environment, nor was it easy for them to form alliances with the people of the Sierra—a population of small farmers, refugees, smugglers, and bandits. The guerrilla fighters presented themselves in the tradition of the *mambises* (rebel fighters) from the anticolonial struggles of the 19th century and the rural conflicts against the oligarchic republic, combining this "invented tradition" with a strong hostility against US-owned plantation companies like the United Fruit Company. Beginning in 1957, the Castro guerrillas succeeded in organizing local camps as institutions of a new, revolutionary power, defending the guajiros of the Sierra against state terror and taking military initiatives against the army. Thus, the struggle in the Sierra became a symbol of armed resistance against the local agents of dictatorship.

Nevertheless, until April of 1958, the leadership of the struggle against Batista remained concentrated in urban environments, controlled by leftist student organizations, parts of the Ortodoxos, the communists, and parts of the unions. Only after a failed general strike and a number of failed written *pactos* (agreements among opposition groups and organizations) did the Sierra and Castro attain undisputed leadership over nearly all opponents of Batista. The faction of the communist party (Partido Socialista Popular, or PSP) under Carlos Rafael Rodríguez, who sympathized with the guerrillas, made contact with the Marxist wing of the fidelistas (foremost among them Guevara, but also Raúl Castro and Ramiro Valdés).

At this time Guevara viewed Castro as "the authentic leader of the leftist bourgeoisie." Cuba had strong national middle classes and powerful organizations of workers. Simultaneously faced with an economic crisis in the sugar sector, a crisis of Cuban identity, a crisis of relations with the United States (evident in conflicts between the CIA, the Pentagon, and the State Department over policy toward

Figure 34.1 Fidel Castro and his guerrilla fighters in the Sierra Maestra, 1958. Source: Andrew Saint-George/Magnum Photos.

Figure 34.2 Castro in Washington, DC, 1959. Photograph by Warren K. Leffler. Source: Library of Congress.

Cuba), and an institutional crisis, nearly all Cubans in 1958 shared the feeling that a renewed Cuban nationalism would improve their future (Pérez 1999).

That year, after an attack by Batista's army on the Sierra failed to crush Castro and his comrades, the guerrilla units took the strategic initiative and sent military columns under the commandants Guevara, Camilo Cienfuegos, Raúl Castro, and Juan Almeida to other Cuban regions, thus "invading" the whole island. In many territories, the forces of the *llanos* (anti-Batista forces from the lowlands) took power before—or, in some instances, in coalition with—the Castro guerrillas. In one of the other Cuban mountain ranges, the Escambray, Eloy Gutiérrez Menoyo created a "Second National Front." After a major defeat in the Battle of Santa Clara in December 1958, Batista fled to the Dominican Republic, handing over the army to General Eulogio Cantillo, who proposed to Castro the formation of a military junta. Castro refused. Declaring "*¡Revolución sí, golpe militar, no!*" (Revolution yes, military coup, no!), he called for a general strike, forcing the generals to retreat. The fidelistas then marched into Santiago de Cuba, and Guevara and Cienfuegos moved on Camp Columbia, the central military institution, and the Cabaña fortress in Havana.

On January 2, 1959, Castro gave a historic speech in Santiago de Cuba, remembering the 1898 occupation of the city by American troops and crying out: "This time it is a real revolution!" He declared Santiago the provisional capital of the island and proclaimed the liberal Manuel Urrutia president of the republic. The same day, Cienfuegos overtook Camp Columbia, capturing the most influential generals of the Batista army. In the following days, Castro moved in a triumphal procession across the 1,000 kilometers from Santiago to Havana. The political and military phase of the struggle thus came to an end, but it proved to be just the first chapter of the long Cuban Revolution.

The First Steps, 1959–73

The period immediately following Castro's military triumph was one of revolutionary improvisation. This was the era of major social reforms and of the destruction of capitalist forms of property and production, with assumption of control over them by the state. Linked to these changes were the expansion of political power over the whole of the island, the defense of the revolution against external threats, and a military projection of the Cuban model of guerrilla revolution to Latin America and parts of Africa. The revolutionaries regarded the internal processes in Cuba only as a first step toward a "world revolution."

The fidelistas attained national power while rapidly transcending the bourgeois nationalism (and middle-class constituencies) that had helped them win the military revolution. After extended conflicts within the Movimiento 26 de Julio, and with other nationalist forces in the government, Castro and his allies formed a revolutionary government controlled by left-wing guerrillas of the Sierra and, to a lesser degree, Communist and non-Communist activists from the Directorio Estudiantil Revolucionario.

The new government immediately implemented agrarian reform, which was overseen by the Instituto Nacional de Reforma Agraria (INRA). Private land was limited first to 400 hectares and later to 67, resulting in the nationalization of vast landholdings. Because the Cuban revolutionaries portrayed themselves as champions of the poorest Cuban farmers and sugar workers, the agrarian reform and the redistribution of land formed the core of this phase of the revolution, and the INRA became a type of parallel government in the first two years after the military victory.

In the long run, however, the problem with this reform was that "modern" agrarian ideology favored large-scale, mechanized, and industrialized production, aided by large quantities of chemical fertilizers, which could not be achieved on the newly limited plots. Gradually rural landholders, urban elites, and parts of the middle classes (as well as competing military leaders, like Gutiérrez Menoyo) began to rebel against such policies of the fidelistas, using the guerillas' own methods. Other dissenters emigrated to the United States and other countries of the hemisphere.

At this point, the late Eisenhower and early Kennedy administrations began to support the diverse forms of resistance that had developed against the fidelistas, first by economic and political means, then with Secret Service and military methods, using Cuban counterrevolutionary immigrants as mercenaries. Still, the US government, many political analysts, and Cuban exiles initially underestimated, neglected, or overlooked the solid alliance that had emerged between the fidelistas and the great mass of the Cuban population, primarily the urban and rural working classes but also large parts of the lower middle class. This alliance found symbolic expression in the strong position of Castro as the *comandante en jefe* (commander in chief) with *mando único* (single-handed command), and was based on revolutionary militias including all classes, genders, and institutions, which drew mass participation in the tradition of Western revolutions since 1776.

In April 1961, the Cuban revolutionary militia thus successfully repelled the invasion of Playa Girón (Bahía de Cochinos, or "Bay of Pigs") near Cienfuegos, which counterrevolutionaries had launched in the hope of activating other internal enemies of the fidelistas. The invasion was a total failure for the Cuban counterrevolution, the CIA, and the hawks in the US administration, and a great victory for Castro, his supporters, the Cuban militias, and the new Cuban army.

Such incidents also drove Cuba further into the arms of the Cold War rival of the United States. At the onset of the invasion Castro had reaffirmed the "the socialist and Marxist-Leninist character" of the Cuban revolution. Because of the hostile economic measures of the Eisenhower administration, which included a halt to sugar imports and conflicts over oil, the Cuban government had already nationalized 37 banks and 382 international and national companies. At the same time, Cuba and the Soviet Union agreed to expand commercial relations. At the core of their agreements stood a fixed sugar quota and the delivery of oil from the Soviets. Close relations to the *rusos* or *soviéticos* expanded quickly into political and even military alliances.

In 1962 Soviet premier Nikita Khrushchev installed nuclear missiles and tactical weapons in Cuba. The Kennedy administration, which had stationed the same type of weapons in Turkey, near the Soviet border, responded with a military sea blockade of Cuba. In late October 1962, the world stood on the brink of a nuclear war. The US administration eventually gave the unwritten assurance that it would not attack or invade Cuba. The Soviets, in turn, withdrew their missiles—without the consent of the Cuban government.

In the following years, Cuba independently propagated and exported the "Cuban model" of revolution to the Caribbean, Africa, and Latin America, beginning with Venezuela. Even though the "export" effort did not immediately succeed, it had great ideological significance for those who resisted US power in the region. For its part, US diplomacy succeeded in expelling Cuba from the Organization of American States and similar groups.

Meanwhile, the revolutionaries proposed the formation of the *hombre nuevo*, or "new man," in Cuba under the doctrine of revolutionary nationalism and idealism. Between 1964 and 1973, the Cuban state subsidized the costs of transportation, telephone service, and other infrastructure as well as schools, social security, health care, and everyday needs such as bread, milk, meat, rice, potatoes, soap, cigarettes, clothes, and shoes. In return for this "historical loan," Cuba's men and women were expected to work voluntarily and transform themselves into "new" socialist citizens through labor, study, and service in the Fuerzas Armadas Revolucionarias (FAR) or other institutions to defend the revolution. The state also proposed nationwide reforms to the Cuban educational and medical systems and new infrastructure connecting the countryside and the cities. Urban reform enabled many Cubans to buy their homes, while rents on flats and apartments were fixed at a low rate. As minister of industry, Guevara strove to create a proper industrial base and to diminish the economy's dependence on sugar.

At first, the reform process was creative and open, because Cuba had not just a single revolutionary party for the whole country but rather many different national organizations (for youth, students, women, farmers, artists) and neighborhood committees for the defense of the revolution (Comités de Defensa de la Revolución). Connecting the traditionally strong regionalisms of the six provinces were the National Militia (until 1962) and later the FAR. A socialist culture that promoted national education also linked the people of Cuba.

But industrialization and the short-term formation of "new men" failed, as did such efforts as the creation of a new breed of cattle, which was supposed to improve milk and meat production. The result was a famine, alleviated only by rice purchases from China. In 1962, partly in response to the US trade embargo, Cuba began a giant distribution program, giving fixed rations of daily necessities to all households. At a time when the state needed the income from sugar exports for its ambitious social programs, the sugar harvest stood without enough workers because nobody would "voluntarily" do the extremely hard work in the cane fields. The state had to resort to drafting army personnel, prisoners, students, and members of the state bureaucracy for the harvesting, and it also relied on international volunteers who came to Cuba to help.

Between 1960 and 1968, Havana became the capital of world revolution, attracting numerous members of the international left. The question of whether the Cuban revolution was specific to the island or part of a coming world revolution against imperialism was symbolized by the figure of Guevara and a relatively small but influential group of his followers. On the one hand, Guevara was Cuba's minister of industry and director of the national bank, a core institution of the national state; on the other, he traveled the world in search for new foci of global revolution and trained guerrillas in Cuba for this purpose.

But the international politics of revolution—as expressed in Castro's Declaration of Havana (1962) and the theoretical works of Guevara, which were in line with Maoist doctrine between 1965 and 1968—proved too expensive for Cuba. After the failure of the direct export of the Cuban model of revolution to Argentina, Algeria, Somalia, Congo, Venezuela, and finally Bolivia, where Guevara died in 1967, the Cuban government decided to resolve its inner crisis by means of a "revolutionary offensive": first, the nationalization of all services, restaurants, shops, and petty commercial installations, and second, a revival of sugar agriculture planned to culminate in 1970 with a model harvest, called the *gran zafra,* with a production goal of 10 million tons of sugar. The harvest failed, however, and in a public speech Castro offered to resign. But the great performance of preparing the gran zafra had demonstrated the achievements of revolutionary nationalism and organization. In the midst of the turbulent international context of 1968–74, with its worldwide political crisis and democratic student movements, Cuba entered a new era. It began with a search for new orientations, strong repression against critics of the "mistakes" of the period of revolutionary voluntarism, and new forms of institutionalization, centralization, and bureaucratization. The state of revolutionary emergency came to its end.

Socialism in the New World, 1975–89

The second period after the military revolution was one of socialist institutionalization and international projection, linked to the building of the first New World welfare state with the highest degree of social security in the Americas. The fidelistas now saw their revolution as an original and creative part of the "real socialism" that existed in the Soviet Union and Europe. They also conceived of Cuba as the "first socialist territory in the Americas," with an important function as a model for Africa and Asia. This period witnessed Cuba's engagement with the non-aligned movement and its intense military intervention in Angola (1975–89), among other adventures in Africa.

Yet from 1968–70 (the 100th anniversary of the first anticolonial revolution) onward, the revolutionaries embarked on a "concentration on Cuba and its revolutionary traditions" that entailed increasing institutionalization, a new constitution and legal reform, the final formation of a national communist party (Partido Comunista de Cuba), and the consolidation of a socialist economy (in reality a form of centralist state economy). The revolution of 1959 acquired a very long history. The result was a fidelista-guided process of constitution-building from the ground up (*poder popular,* "people's power," as enshrined in the socialist constitution of 1976), a political integration into the socialist network dominated by the Soviet Union, and an economic integration into the communist organization COMECON. The only remnants of formal private property were small plots called *fincas,* used in a type of socialist subsistence agriculture, which represented about 20% of Cuba's arable land. The Communist Party began to formally rule Cuban society, with Castro as head of the army, the state, the council of ministers, and the party. But he and the leading group of former guerrillas also began to develop an informal double system of power: Castro was the visible head, the spokesman, and the international strategist while his brother Raúl would become more and more the chief of personnel, the head of the armed forces and the secret services. As such, he played an extremely important role in managing the revolution.

Meanwhile, Cuba's ongoing policy of supporting revolutionary movements elsewhere—not only by military power or mere "export," but also through education of cadres within Cuba (particularly on the Isla de Pinos, also known as the Isla de la Juventud) and a combination of military, medical, educational, and organizational assistance—was successful. Sending Cubans on internationalist missions abroad was also an important element in the solution of the island's inner problems between 1970 and 1975. Castro took the initiative to support Marxist revolutionaries in Angola, declaring Cuba an "Afro-Latin country." He launched "Operation Carlota," a military, political, and cultural initiative in support of the MPLA (People's Movement of Liberation of Angola); from then until 1990, 400,000 Cubans operated in Angola.

Caribbean countries such as Jamaica under Michael Manley (1972–80) and Grenada under Maurice Bishop (1979–83) also figured prominently in Cuba's strategy of aiding other Third World nations. In the latter case, the experiment ended on a sour note with the assassination of Bishop and a subsequent US invasion. Cuba's greatest success along these lines was the Sandinista victory in Nicaragua (1979–90). Although the Sandinistas were ousted from power in 1990, events such as these quite plausibly laid the basis for the leftist turn, after the so-called lost decades of the 1970s and 1980s, of many Latin American countries including Brazil, Argentina, Venezuela, and Ecuador at the end of the 20th century and beginning of the 21st. When in 1979 the non-aligned states of the world held their summit meeting in Havana, Castro was elected president of the organization, confirming his role as a leader of the Third World.

As Cuba became firmly integrated into the communist world, it became increasingly isolated in the West but also alienated from the European left and from sympathetic Western governments. A short renewal of relations between Cuba and the United States under President Jimmy Carter (1977–81) ended with the election of Ronald Reagan as Carter's successor. Castro also feared that a reformist policy toward the United States would undermine Cuban unity, as indeed occurred in 1981 when 125,000 Cubans fled the island in a massive wave of illegal emigration to the United States, termed the "Mariel exodus."

The growth of Cuban institutions signaled a period of increasing bureaucratization and centralization of schools and universities, as well as the repression of cultural and artistic liberties during what became known as the *quinquenio gris* (the "grey half-decade") between 1971 and 1975. During the 1970s the government restructured provincial administration and privileged rural development, while inadequate housing remained a pressing social problem. But the greater centralization of society, together with the credit, goods, and oil provided by the Soviet Union, East Germany, and other socialist countries, enabled the government to maintain and extend the socialist welfare state. In Cuba nobody went hungry, and medical care and education were free. In fact, Cuba became a social, educational, and medical success story, with demographic indicators comparable to those in Western European welfare states. It is therefore not surprising that against the backdrop of the 1990s crisis, many Cubans later remembered the period between 1970 and 1990 as the "golden years" of a modest but stable "tropical socialism."

That situation, however, was not as stable as it seemed. In 1981 sugar prices fell to levels similar to those in 1920. Cuba had giant debts and was technically bankrupt. The centralist economy was inefficient and it failed to produce enough to maintain the country's expensive social and foreign policies. The government allowed semi-private farmers' markets (*agromercados*) to soften the food problems. Cuba's survival rested on the solidarity of other socialist countries. But the Eastern bloc had its own problems, which the Soviet Union aimed to resolve with the reforms of glasnost and perestroika under leader Mikhail Gorbachev. The reaction in Cuba was the onset of conflict within the revolutionary leadership, followed by a new period of economic voluntarism (the expectation that citizens work for little or no pay to help advance socialism) and the increasing glorification of Guevara. In 1986, Castro himself decided to put an end to the remnants of a market economy in Cuba, such as farmers' markets, in what he called a "rectification of errors."

As this phase of the revolution drew to a close in 1989, Cuban troops began to retreat from Angola after military victory. However, that same year, General Arnaldo Ochoa, chief of the troops and a veteran guerrilla, was convicted of involvement in international drug trafficking and executed—an event that many analysts have interpreted as the elimination by members of Castro's inner circle of a competing leader sympathetic to Soviet perestroika and Gorbachev.

A Permanent Revolution, 1990–Present

The most recent period in Cuban history, dating from 1990, has been marked by crisis, the institutionalization of a wartime economy, retreat, reforms, and recentralization. With the breakdown of the Soviet Union (1989–91), Cuba lost its ties to a third consecutive empire. It also became the only surviving "real socialist" nation in the West (at least until 2006, when Hugo Chávez declared his brand of Bolivarian socialism in Venezuela). The Cuban revolutionaries, under the direct leadership of Castro until his resignation in February 2008, strengthened a new discourse of "permanent revolution." The term, once conceptualized by Guevara (and, even earlier, by Leon Trotsky), now included a dose of real nationalism as envisioned by Martí and was linked to new forms of economic performance as well as a new relationship with the Latin American left—Venezuela primarily, but also Bolivia and Ecuador.

The years between 1986 and 1989 had already been a time of severe problems for Cuba, but the breakdown of socialist states in the Soviet Union and Eastern Europe ushered in a period of deep crisis. While maintaining the discourse of permanent revolution, Castro declared a "special period" of wartime austerity measures in a time of peace. Informally, the centralized state had to accept local and provincial assistance in organizing economic performance and food production. The national transportation infrastructure and even the urban transport systems collapsed, while food distribution shrunk to dangerously low levels.

The black market, which at other times had been of minor significance, expanded greatly and imbued the US dollar with a new and important role, even though the possession of dollars was proscribed in Cuba. By 1993 the illegal-exchange rate had risen to 130 Cuban pesos per US dollar, which led the Cuban counterrevolution and parts of the Cuban exile community to expect the imminent breakdown of Castroism. In 1996, the US Congress passed the Cuban Liberty and Democratic Solidarity Act (known as the Helms-Burton Act after its sponsors, Senators Jesse Helms and Dan Burton), which strengthened the US trade embargo in hopes of hastening a collapse.

The Cuban state reacted by legalizing the possession of US dollars for individuals in 1993, fixing the official exchange rate at around 20 to 30 pesos per dollar, and establishing official exchange bureaus (*casas de cambio*). In the following years it also embarked on a program of economic reforms, facilitating limited international investment in certain sectors (maintaining 51% ownership by the Cuban state) as well as joint ventures, most extensively in the tourist sector but also in mining and in the marketing of Cuban cigars, pharmaceuticals, and rum. Domestically, the state reinstated farmers' markets, allowed the opening of small private restaurants (*paladares*), and permitted minor economic activities on a "self-employment" basis (*por cuenta propia*). Cubans who had jobs in the hotel and tourist sector, or who received remittances from relatives in the United States or other parts of the exile community, achieved special status, giving rise to new social hierarchies despite persistent rhetoric emphasizing revolutionary equality.

The state filled this growing gap between reality and rhetoric with a retreat to the core program of Cuban nationalism, *martianismo*, and permanent *revolución*. At the 1991 Party Congress it rehabilitated religious practices, including both institutionalized denominations and Afro-Cuban religions such as Santería, Palo Monte, Abakuá, and vodou. At the same time, the state sought to develop a new system of taxation, implement programs to save electricity and water, and modernize the sugar industry. All of these attempts failed to one degree or another.

Within Cuba a variety of minor opposition groups arose, largely centered on reformist programs for the future of the island. Many Cubans, especially younger people, sought to emigrate by whatever means possible—marrying foreigners or tourists, staying in other countries after an *internacionalista* mission, or fleeing to Florida aboard rickety boats and even more precarious rafts. But even during the most difficult times, when many Cubans suffered acute hunger or deficiency diseases, the Cuban state never stopped the *internacionalista* program of university education in Cuba for Latin American, Caribbean, or African students, particularly in medicine. In 1998 Castro, who had never totally broken with the social program of the Catholic Church, invited Pope John Paul II to Cuba. Clearly, the Cuban revolution retreated but did not collapse.

One important ally with revolutionary sympathies during the later years of this period was Venezuela, where Chávez had proclaimed himself a leader of the "Bolivarian revolution." After a failed counterrevolutionary coup against Chávez in 2002 and the victory of the Chavistas in a national referendum in 2004, the relationship between Venezuela and Cuba became even closer. Chávez ramped up aid to Cuba and sent cheap oil and other goods in exchange for Cuban doctors in social missions, sports, and education.

Internal reforms in 1993, 1997, and 2003 aimed at reasserting national control over financial and economic activities, particularly private farmers' markets. These reforms ended more or less with the state's decision to grant entrepreneurial privileges to the army. Since then, the Revolutionary Armed Forces (FAR) have controlled important parts of the economy. Its members receive higher salaries, paid partly in convertible currency, which allows their families to purchase goods from dollar shops (*tiendas de la recaudación de divisas*, or TRDs). The police force has been modernized and reinforced. A group of younger politicians surrounding the civilian academic Carlos Lage formed a kind of socialist technocracy and intelligentsia, which played an important role in the making of the "reforms in socialism" during the "special period" and facilitated the creation of centers of new technologies (mainly biotechnology, but also computer programming and medical research).

Between 2002 and 2005, the neoconservative administration of George W. Bush curtailed remittances from the United States to Cuba and controlled the contacts of US citizens with Cuba. In 2004, Castro ended the era of the dollar as a legal currency in Cuba, replacing it with the convertible Cuban peso (CUC), and he levied a fee of between 8% and 20% on every foreign currency transaction, thus ending the reforms for which "dollarization" had become a symbol.

Castro's supporters in the higher army echelons reasserted power over the whole island by repressing the moderate internal opposition and continuing to cut down the possibilities for free enterprise based on the US dollar, even as industrial sugar production practically collapsed. At the same time, the state opened important spaces—literally and metaphorically—for debate (especially for the National Union of Writers and Artists, UNEAC) and made it possible for those elites regarded as "revolutionaries" to make money in new civil (medical, technical, and cultural) internationalist missions to foreign countries, particularly Venezuela. The recentralization of national power also benefited the broader population. Between 2005 and 2009 the transport infrastructure, schools, hospitals, and universities were renovated, and many Cuban households received new power-saving domestic equipment (refrigerators, stoves, lamps) at very low cost.

But nearly a half-century after their military victory, Castro and members of his circle faced the realities of their age. In 2007 Castro missed the official celebration of his 80th birthday because of an acute intestinal illness, appearing only in short television images from the hospital. This event perhaps serves as a metaphor for his place in history and the popular imagination. In Cuban public discourse he remains an undisputed iconic presence; in private conversations, however, his name may be met with silence or even jokes. Outside Cuba, he is a mythical figure—one of evil for parts of the Cuban exile community and their political allies; one of revolution, devotion to his country, and improvement of social conditions for the poor to many people in the Caribbean and the Third World in general.

Castro's younger brother Raúl, who had controlled all armed forces since 1989, took provisional power over the island in the middle of 2006 and was confirmed as president in February 2008. He started a new round of "reforms in socialism," aimed at stabilizing the economic core of Cuban society. Productivity in Cuba is still extremely low, with as much as 50% of the land uncultivated. The lack of food production in times of rising prices is opening more and more gaps between imports and local production. Ironically, many of those imported foodstuffs originate in the

United States. Cuba also suffered reverberations from the global financial crisis of 2008.

In January 2009, the 50th anniversary celebrations of the Triumph of the Revolution in Santiago de Cuba featured all the elements of the present-day revolution: pride in a great tradition, sovereignty, thrift (no army parade), virtual quotations from the absent Castro, loud speeches on "revolution," and quiet discourses on new reforms, such as the possibility of buying homes, one of the greatest problems facing young Cubans. But as was made clear by the anniversary celebrations and subsequent events of 2009—the increasing presence of the army in the government, and the removal from government of the group of reformers associated with Carlos Lage and Pérez Roque—the government of Raúl Castro retains control over the nation and territory of Cuba.

WORKS CITED

Pérez Jr., Louis A. 1999. *On Becoming Cuban: Identity, Nationality, and Culture.* Chapel Hill: University of North Carolina Press.

Zeuske, Michael. 2004. *Insel der Extreme: Kuba im 20. Jahrhundert* (Island of Extremes: Cuba in the 20th Century). Zurich: Rotpunktverlag.

35

Independence and Its Aftermath

ANTHONY P. MAINGOT

Suriname, Trinidad, and Jamaica

The struggle for political power in parliamentary systems characterized by pluralistic and well-developed parties very often has meant the subordination of programs to the exigencies of electioneering. Such was the case in several West Indian societies as they passed from colonial to independent status: Jamaica and Trinidad in 1962, and Suriname in 1975. By then all had institutionalized the trappings of the parliamentary models of their colonizers; most had internalized a number of the values and norms that make these models function. Indeed, in the Anglophone Caribbean, the Westminster parliamentary model suited the urban, "middle-class" background (an important part of which was British-influenced education) of many of the new elites. And in terms of Westminster-based criteria, these countries have been successful.

Yet this model, though admirably suited to managing political and ideological pluralism and conflict, was less appropriate for mediating conflict originating in both class and race. And race—or, at a minimum, color—was by far the dominant factor in West Indian political strife. In both Suriname and Trinidad, parties and traditional patronage-distributing mechanisms (though officially "non-racial" in nature) became the articulators and aggregators of ethnic interest. In Jamaica political patronage generated a kind of violent zero-sum game. And since both parties in Jamaica were fundamentally polyclass in composition, it was difficult to establish a clear-cut racial cleavage in political terms—which did not stop perceptions of racial differences from being a major part of the ongoing tensions.

By the first decade after independence, the elites of these societies had overcome the foremost challenge to the system by which they had opted to rule—the ideological challenge from the radical left. A review of socialist initiatives of the 1970s indicates that the new West Indian left came up against a wall of ethnic and racial allegiances that they could not overcome. Indeed most, if not all, the violence centered on ethnic, not ideological, rivalries and competitions for power.

Suriname

The 64,000-square-mile colony of Suriname (originally Dutch Guiana) was first settled by the Dutch in 1602. With brief interruptions by the British, the Dutch ruled it as a classical capitalist slave plantation system, abolishing slavery only in 1863. But slave flight into the densely forested backlands, which make up 90% of the colony's territory, had been endemic from the start. There the fugitives formed a series of maroon settlements that resisted every effort at conquest, forcing the Dutch to eventually conclude peace treaties with the three largest groups (Saramaka, Ndyuka, Paramaka) in the 1750s and 1760s. After abolition, labor scarcity led to the contracting of labor from China, India, and, between 1890 and 1939, very large numbers from Java in Dutch-governed Indonesia, giving Suriname a multiethnic population.

In 1954 the Netherlands reformed its colonial system, granting internal autonomy to Suriname and the Netherlands Antilles. Accompanying that political move was an infusion of Dutch development monies, especially in education, which helped generate a high standard of living and, in turn, a politically active middle class that competed for power by organizing ethnically based parties. The first of the three "traditional" parties was the Suriname National Party (NPS in its Dutch acronym), followed by the "Creole" sector of the population (colored people and blacks who were largely Christians). NPS members, the first to join the civil service and mobilize politically, claimed to be the "true national" party and favored eventual independence. Second, the Progressive Reform Party (VHP) was led and sustained by the British Indian or Hindustani population, which feared and resisted independence under Creole leadership. Third came the Kaumtani Persantuan Indonesia (KTPI), led and championed by the Javanese community, also largely opposed to independence.

There were also small groups (usually led by students returned from the Netherlands) of Maoist, Albanian, Soviet, and later, pro-Cuban orientation, which never received even half of the 1% support specified by the constitution but later had an important intellectual influence under military rule. The Netherlands, apprehensive of the enormous migration of Surinamese to the metropole, eagerly encouraged independence, which was granted in 1975, with the Creole elite of the NPS in a leadership position. By then politics was so firmly based on ethnic parties that Suriname could be considered a system of "ethnic fixations" (Dew 1978, 201).

Independence came at a time when the intellectuals of Suriname and the Caribbean were engaged in intense debates on ethnic pluralism and governance. The central question was whether, absent the "umbrella" of colonial domination, these multiethnic states could evolve peacefully. Two clear positions existed. Some argued that democratic frameworks and structures did not lend themselves to the resolution of intense, conflicting ethnic interests. They maintained that ambitious politicians not included in multiethnic coalitions, and therefore motivated to pursue communal rather than national interests, would seek to "outbid" any ambiguous (that is, more ideological) multiethnic coalition (Kabushka and Shepsle 1972). Taking an opposite position were those who argued that ethnic accommodation was indeed possible—and existent, as in the Netherlands—in what Dutch scholar Arend Lijphart (1977) called "a Consociational Democracy." The foremost scholar of this group, Edward Dew, argued that "Surinam is second to none in the Caribbean for bearing the strains of development without severe turbulence" (1978, 202). He maintained that one of the conditions for stability was the existence of elites and communities desirous of establishing or maintaining democratic rule.

Unfortunately for Suriname, the politics of ethnic patronage and special dealing began to spin out of control. As anthropologist Gary Brana-Shute (1990) put it, the new elites displayed an inability to govern but an immense appetite for graft. The development fund from the Netherlands, an alleged $1.5 billion "golden handshake," had kept the urban portion of society afloat. The legitimacy of the government was eroding quickly, however, and on February 25, 1980, Sergeant Desi Bouterse and 16 noncommissioned officers (all recruited and trained in the Netherlands Army) carried out a coup d'état. Initially well received by the populace, the National Military Council that Bouterse headed soon began to lose support. Two events in particular undermined the military's legitimacy: first, the speedy and ostentatious arrival of outside "advisers" (mainly Cuban, Libyan, and Dutch radicals); and, second and most tragically, the imprisonment, torture, and execution of 15 prominent Surinamese intellectuals, artists, and entrepreneurs in December 1982.

These "December murders" represented a fundamental break with Suriname's civil tradition, and were widely associated with revolutionary trends in the rest of the Caribbean that enjoyed no support either in Suriname or in the Surinamese diaspora in the Netherlands. Yet initial rumors that the murders had been committed by Cuban military advisors in the country were soon proven incorrect, and blame was squarely placed on Bouterse. The most complete journalistic investigation of the murders exonerated the Cubans and pointed to Bouterse and the army as the culprits (Boerboom and Oranje 1992). Similarly, two reports of the Inter-American Commission on Human Rights (1983, 1985) accused "high government officials" of the crime.

The government of the Netherlands immediately condemned the atrocity and cut off further development assistance (Hoefte and Oostindie 1991). The most immediate and ultimately fatal result of these events, however, was the rebellion of virtually all the *bosnegers* (maroons) in a special unit protecting Bouterse and his lieutenants. Led by Ronny Brunswijk, a member of the large Ndyuka maroon community, followers of the revolt came from the other large maroon groups, Saramaka and Paramaka. They formed what became known as the "Jungle Commando" with full maroon support, and with financing mainly from Surinamese exiles in the Netherlands. Controlling as much as three-quarters of the forested backlands (Thoden van Velzen 1990) and the loyalty of the local population, and vowing to overthrow the regime in the capital, Brunswijk and his men engaged in the first and only civil war in the 20th-century Caribbean.

The war lasted two and-a-half years and was finally ended by the Kourou Accords, arranged by France and the United Nations High Commission for Refugees. In November 1987 the government agreed to hold elections. With 88% of the electorate participating, the coalition of the traditional parties—those that had existed before the coup—received 83% of the vote. Bouterse's new National Democratic Party (NDP) secured only a handful of votes in the three interior districts that had been depopulated by the war. But Bouterse had negotiated a special status for himself and the military: article 177 of the New Constitution (1987) stated that the military was "the vanguard of the people," which "labours for the national development and for the liberation of the nation," and so merited special recognition (Dew 1989, 144). Bouterse and his followers also kept control of the rice marketing board and much of the gold trade—which kept them content until 1990, when a new element made inroads into Surinamese society: the Colombian-controlled drug trade.

Not wanting to lose the monopoly over this source of monumental riches, the military carried out another coup d'état in December 1990. After securing immunity from extradition to the Netherlands, they allowed new elections in 1991. By then, financially able to purchase votes, the military party secured 12 seats in the 51-seat National Assembly. The post-civil war pattern of the Surinamese political and economic system had consolidated. Creoles, maroons, East Indians, even back-land Amerindians were now "in business," with serious money acquired through money laundering, pyramid-like banking schemes, and facilitating narcotics transport. "In a mutually reinforcing, interlocking relationship, East Indian capital supports Creole state control, and vice-versa," argues Brana-Shute (2000, 108).

By 2008, Bouterse was rubbing shoulders in Parliament with his erstwhile enemy Brunswijk, who heads his own political party and, like Bouterse, is wanted by the Dutch and Interpol for drug trafficking. Sadly for Suriname, both Bouterse and Brunswijk enjoy immunity from extradition and appear to have little interest in confronting each other. On July 19, 2010, Bouterse was elected president of Suriname with key support from Brunswijk. Corruption is clearly functional in this plural society. As Brana-Shute observed with the irony born of experience: "Who says the races cannot get along in a plural society?"

Trinidad and Tobago

The last of the major British conquests in the Caribbean (1797), the twin-island Republic of Trinidad and Tobago consists of 2,000 square miles with a population of 1,213,000. Because it was conquered by the Spanish and settled by French planters before the British conquest, and had a short history of African slavery and a longer history of East Indian indentureship, it now has a much diversified population. As in Suriname, the resulting ethnic and cultural pluralism is more than just of folkloric interest: it influences every aspect of life on the island, from electoral politics to short- and long-range macroeconomic policies.

The more educated and urban black and colored middle class organized first into a mass-based party, the People's National Movement (PNM). They came to power in 1956 when autonomy was granted, took the country into independence in 1962, and, except for two brief interludes in the 1990s, have continued to dominate the political front. As in Suriname, this racially divided system has never allowed space for purely ideological parties.

In the 1956 general elections for the Legislative Council, for example, the Marxist West Indian Independence Party (WIIP) contested only one of a possible 24 seats, receiving 3.8% of the vote in that working-class district. In 1961 the WIIP ran no candidate. In the 1966 parliamentary elections, the radical groups ran under the banner of the Workers and Farmers Party (WFP) and competed in 35 of the 36 constituencies with a mix of black, Indian, colored, and white Trinidadians, all with strong personal ties with different parts of the island. Additionally, many of the candidates were intellectual luminaries of the left and had long histories of direct or indirect ties with the labor movement. This radical alliance, however, did not elect a single member; its total vote was 3.46%. Already Trinidad politics had become a racial matter in which ideology played a minimal role. After two successive PNM governments, the number of declared Marxist-Leninists had been reduced to insignificance; in 1965 they were calculated to number 15 (Report of the Commission of Enquiry 1965, 19).

Understanding the racial basis of politics, and in keeping with a "critical support" program followed by other Marxist movements in the Caribbean at the time, the left changed tack. In the 1975 elections they appealed to the Indian vote through a "popular front" of labor unions called the United Labour Force (ULF). Led by the charismatic Indian lawyer Basdeo Panday, they won 10 of the 36 seats—all in predominantly Indian areas. But the socialist revolutionaries had not given up hope of leading the party, and in early 1977 a group of Marxist-Leninists united in a semi-secret organization called the National Movement for the True Independence of Trinago (NAMOTI) carried out an anti-Panday coup within the ULF. It soon became evident, however, that the radical left was not united and lacked mass support. Panday, who in early 1978 recaptured command of the party, reassessed the political-ideological terrain and opted for command rather than revolutionary politics. "These armchair ideologists," he told the *Trinidad Express*, "have no conception of how our people feel and think. They mislead themselves into believing that the working class care what is happening in China, Cuba, and the Soviet Union or that our people are ready to accept, lock, stock and barrel, these foreign systems."

As in Suriname, there was little interest in Trinidad in socialist revolution, despite the radical ideas already spreading from Cuba to much of the Western Hemisphere. But as the PNM government of Eric Williams soon discovered, other forms of political mobilization were possible.

In 1970 Williams wrote that the path taken by his government since independence was sui generis—the "Trinidad Model." It differed, he said, from the two other prominent models in the Caribbean in that it had not sacrificed national identity for economic growth (like Puerto Rico) and was not totalitarian (like Cuba). Instead, Trinidad's domestic program was a state-directed mixed economy in which the growth of state-created employment opportunities had been balanced with the greatest amount of freedom for the native and foreign private sector. Though foreign investment was encouraged, the emphasis was on "localization"—eventual government ownership of majority shares in all sectors.

This program continued unchallenged into the late 1960s, but its fundamental flaws were all too evident; unemployment seemed to grow with the economy, especially among young urban blacks. By 1970, between 20 and 25% of the workforce was unemployed, and for the first time in its history the island showed an out-migration trend. Discontent was generalized, including serious charges that while the population suffered, members of the regime were enriching themselves through corrupt schemes. There was discontent in the predominantly Indian sugar-growing areas, tension between professionals and politically appointed officers in the army, seething anger among young and unemployed urban blacks, and a rebellious mood among University of the West Indies students.

Two external incidents had slow but eventually explosive reverberations in Trinidad. In 1968, rioting broke out in Jamaica when authorities banned the Guyanese professor and Black Power advocate, Walter Rodney, from entering the country. A year later Trinidad students, claiming discrimination, rioted at Sir George Williams University in Canada and were expelled. Students in Trinidad responded to both these events with protests of their own. With the regime seemingly suffering a paralysis of will, these protests grew into mass mobilizations calling for Williams's resignation, and for restructuring of the island's economic and ownership system. The movement, by now called the "Black Power Revolt," came to a head when the military rebelled and attempted to reach the students who had assembled in the capital's central square. What was the nature of this social movement? It included, to be sure, "a cadre of revolutionaries" inspired by Marxist-Leninist doctrines of socialist revolution and Cuban notions of guerrilla warfare (Brown 1995). But the Black Power Revolt was led by young blacks much more interested in the *négritude* of Aimé Césaire and Frantz Fanon than in Marx and Lenin, and inspired by the writings of Rodney, the most influential Black Power thinker in the Caribbean. "Black Power," he declared in 1969, "is a doctrine about black people, for black people, preached by black people."

The student and military revolts petered out once they were rejected by the colored middle class and the rural Indian community. In their aftermath the movement leadership turned itself into a political party with a Black Power platform, but it had no appeal in a society already divided between a black party and an Indian one. By 1974 Trinidad was back to politics as usual: Williams was stronger than ever and he had the funds to accelerate his "localization" development plans, starting with the oil industry (Maingot 1998).

The partial nationalization of the petroleum industry was made possible by the dramatic increase in oil revenues resulting from the OPEC-induced price of oil in 1973. Petroleum revenues in 1973 were TT$130 million. By 1977 they had reached TT$1,540 million, a sensational development best understood when taking into account that 23% of the government's revenues of TT$474 million in 1973 had come from oil, whereas only two years later the government collected TT$1,687 million—70% of the total—from oil.

Proving that rising economic growth rates do not necessarily quell popular discontent were two critical events at the end of the 1980s. First, the PNM lost power to a coalition of the black and colored middle class and the Indians, the National Alliance for Reconstruction (NAR). Soon, however, the Indian sector of the leadership began accusing the black prime minister of favoring black projects. Despite these accusations, social discontent was strongest among the black urban working class and the legions of unemployed. Joining the call for a change in the system was a group of former Black Power members from the 1970 crisis, now converted to Islam. Through Islam, they argued, the black man could break his dependence on the white "racists" (Ryan 1991; Maingot 2007). The speeches of their leader, Lennox Phillips, who took the name Yasin Abu Bakr, differed little from those of the Black Power leaders, yet the Black Muslim ("Jamaat-al-Muslimeen") leaders of 1990 did not enjoy popular support. Having planned and trained in Libya, and armed themselves with guns bought in Florida, their idea was not a popular antigovernmental front but a well-executed coup.

On August 27, 1990, 125 of these men bombed the police headquarters, captured Parliament (along with the prime minister and virtually the whole cabinet), and took control of the television station, killing 33 people without losing a single man. After a siege of three days, the movement failed for three fundamental reasons: First, it received no support from either the intellectual community or the general public. Second, it was roundly condemned by the existing, traditional Islamic community. Third—and fatal to any coup attempt—the Muslimeen decided to accept government amnesty instead of facing a full assault by the police and army, which had remained loyal to the government.

Not unlike Bouterse in Suriname, Abu Bakr is, as of this writing, on trial—not for the 1990 coup attempt, but for subsequent efforts to purchase weapons in Miami and for threatening the lives of prominent Muslims on the island. No one seems to know the origins of his fortune, calculated in 2007 at TT$40 million. Meanwhile, Trinidad's politics are more racially divided than ever, while the spreading drug trade and drug culture have engendered a level of corruption and violence never seen in the island's history.

Jamaica

The Jamaican case exemplifies a process of conventional political conflict escalating into systemic violence. Such conflict dates from the beginning of party politics in the late 1930s and the closely linked widespread labor unrest of those years. A crucial result was the rise to political prominence of charismatic trade unionist Alexander Bustamante (né William Alexander Clarke) and his half-cousin, the lawyer and intellectual Norman Manley, whose Fabian socialism would provide the counterpoint to Bustamante's populism. Their political rivalry shaped Jamaican politics up to the early 1970s.

While both Bustamante and Manley originally organized on the labor front, only Manley moved politically, and his People's National Party (PNP) was the first serious Jamaican effort at a mass-based political party. In 1940, the PNP declared itself a socialist party. To Manley at that time, socialism meant "a demand for the complete change of the basic organization of the social and economic conditions under which we live" (Nettleford 1971b, 61), including the notion that "all means of production should in one form or the other come to be publicly owned and publicly controlled." Though clearly labor unrest played a major role in awakening native leadership, foreign ideological influence was vital in providing that leadership with a perspective: the Fabian socialism then current in Britain.

By the mid-1950s Manley wrote that he was a democratic socialist in the tradition of British socialism (Nettleford 1971a). This approach held a wide appeal for the middle class, especially the intellectuals. They joined the PNP, as Jamaican journalist Wilmot Perkins noted in the *Sunday Gleaner*, because it "appropriated not only the country's leading intellectuals and artists . . . but the very idea of intellectualism in politics." Indeed, Bustamante's Jamaican Labour Party (JLP), founded in 1943, could never rival the PNP in terms of the glamour of its following. The JLP, Perkins continued, was "repellent to the status-conscious 'brown skinned' intelligentsia."

Manley demonstrated his adherence to democratic parliamentary principles and his aversion to "alien" ideologies in 1952, when he expelled some of his most important left allies from the PNP on the grounds that they had formed a Marxist caucus within the party. Yet he and his party remained vulnerable to opposition on two grounds—the "foreign" origins of the party's philosophy, and race. To the opposition the PNP was a party of socialist, middle-class "brown men." As one observer noted, Bustamante was "elected to fight the PNP on the issue on which they were most vulnerable and one which they themselves had interjected, namely, ideology. . . . Socialism was equated with Communism, and Communism meant tyranny and slavery" (Eaton 1975, 106–7).

The issue of a "brown" middle class, so frequently mentioned in JLP platforms, was always a convenient fiction to insert race—or rather, skin color—into the competition. Yet the breakdown (in percentages, not total numbers) of the island's racial composition shows that both parties had to secure votes from all groups, blacks and colored. The reality was that when Jamaica decided to leave the West Indies Federation (1957–61) and declare independence in 1962, it had a solid multiracial two-party system. What differentiated it from Suriname and Trinidad, then, was that the competition for spoils and patronage was geared toward the same large racial group. Even today, both parties show a polyclass composition for the simple reason that there has been very little popular polarization along ideological lines.

Though race cannot be dismissed as a source of ongoing social conflict, there is evidence that it is secondary to material and economic issues across all occupational groups (Stone 1973, 14–15). This conclusion holds despite the evident correlation between class and skin color, and the substantial concentration of corporate ownership in the hands of highly visible and long-entrenched Jewish, Lebanese, and Chinese minorities. Thus, in a 1974 poll only 9% of a representative class and community sample admitted hostility or anger toward whites (Stone 1974, 79), and in a 1978 poll by the *Weekly Gleaner* of the 84% percent of urban Jamaicans who perceived conditions to be "getting worse," 70% blamed "the government" first, whereas only 17% put the blame on "capitalists and political enemies of the government." In a poll earlier that year, "governmental mismanagement" and "radical talk" consistently outpolled the "private sector" as the main culprits in the opinion of those who saw the situation as deteriorating. One has to question, therefore, the widely held assumption that all social conflict takes place along clear class lines.

The nature of political conflict in Jamaica, especially in the 1970s, is perhaps better explained by reference to the competition between the "middle sector" served by both parties, for it is to this sector that an active and expanding government appeals most. PNP leader Michael Manley never ignored this problem of political pressures for an expanding state machinery in both capitalist and socialist economies. "The astonishing growth in bureaucracies the world over during the last two centuries," he said, "does not only represent itself by asexual fission: it demonstrates the unending demand made on the political arm that it experiment with forms of intervention" (Manley 1976, 191). Correct, no doubt. Since independence, but especially since 1972, there has been a steady increase in full-time civil servants. Whereas in 1970 public administration accounted for 8.4% of the gross domestic product (J\$82 million), in 1975 the figure was 14.3% (J\$358 million). The number of civil servants increased from 8,750 in 1962–63 to 15,570 in 1975 (Bell and Gibson 1978, 10). But the ever-increasing levels of violence explain why the most dramatic increases in budget were for the police and military services—from J\$7,220,000 in 1971–72 to J\$86,462,875 in 1978–79. This had nothing to do with "revolutionary" movements, and much to do with competition for drug monies.

Concerned with issues of "revolution" and "dependency," even moderate and well-informed scholars of Jamaica refused to confront the issue of the international criminal threat. As late as April 1988, for example, political scientist Carl Stone expressed distress that, in a year when Jamaicans were electing a new government, "we are spending as much time agonizing over petty US gossip about supposed mafia-type links between local politics and drug dons," calling for a discussion of "the real issues" instead. Exactly one year later, after Jamaican voters had elected a new government without any serious debate or discussion of the Jamaican drug problem, Stone demonstrated a dramatically changed perception of the threat. The drug dealers, he wrote, were "crippling Jamaica . . . the very future and livelihood of this country and its people are at risk." He urged that steps be taken "in a hurry" to stop the trade, including making "any constitutional changes necessary" (Stone 1990, 35–40).

Especially serious threats came from Jamaica's highly organized criminal gangs, known as "posses" or "crews," which were occasionally romanticized in song, film, fiction, or history. Only the writings of courageous journalists have revealed the dimensions of a problem that had become a major source of friction between Jamaica, the United States, Canada, and the United Kingdom. In late 1994, *Jamaican Gleaner* columnist Dawn Ritch started to reveal the links between the drug trade, crime, and the political protection both parties provided to the gangs. Despite considerable pressure to keep quiet, Ritch published facts taken from police records showing a total of 54 criminal gangs and "garrison" constituencies that were allied with major leaders of both parties. Jamaicans call these local communities "garrison constituencies" because the gangs exercise such control that the police have to be "garrisoned" in fortified stations. Not unlike under civil war conditions, the state exercises little if any control over these areas, yet there were no clear ethnic divisions and no one was interested in overthrowing the state.

Understandably, Jamaicans want to protect their reputation and that of the all-important tourist industry. Yet, the reality of Jamaican criminality could no longer be swept under the carpet as the island's first full-fledged professional criminologist, Anthony Harriott, pointed out in 1996:

> The development of a critical mass of professional criminals (sufficient to alter the social organization of crime) is a post 1977 development. Safe havens where externally directed criminality is accepted have been in existence for some 30 years. These are the garrison communities of the Kingston Metropolitan Area and Spanish Town which are characterized by political homogenous populations, tight integration between local party structures and criminal gang organizations which exercise a highly centralized control over social and political activity in these communities and a fair measure of political protection from police actions. A new generation has grown up under these conditions, in a milieu in which the internalized moral inhibitors against criminality are considerably neutralized (Harriott 1996, 71).

Only four decades after independence did Jamaicans finally begin mobilizing for what they now started calling the "war on drugs." By then, however, the problem had become systemic because the levels of patronage and spoils demanded by the political clients had outgrown the capacity of the parties to satisfy them. Drug "dons," controlling "garrison" communities, began to fill the need.

Conclusion

The three case studies presented here demonstrate that five decades after independence, these societies face some intractable problems, leading to a region-wide redefinition of what "social problems" are (Maingot 2000). In the early 21st century, social problems are post–Cold War issues related to globalization and "viability" in all its dimensions: crime (domestic and international), drugs, corruption, and violence are what agitate the Caribbean the most.

There is a growing awareness that crime negatively affects a range of developmental necessities; it scares away investments and undermines the work ethic. There is also concern that organized crime, with its deep pockets from the drug trade and easy access to guns, is forcing the business community to resort to "criminal adaptations and corrupt innovations" that could have longer-term consequences for the governability of these societies (Francis, Gibbson, Harriott, and Kirton 2009, 32–33).

If the first true step toward dealing with a social problem is honesty and realism in confronting its dimensions, these societies have taken that first step. There are, of course, many more steps to take, given the seriousness of the problem. Nevertheless, there is one solid reason to be optimistic about an eventual favorable outcome: the fact that these societies have chosen the democratic system of governance. Democracy is arguably slower and even messier than authoritarian systems in dealing with such grave social ills, but history has shown it to be ultimately more effective.

WORKS CITED

Bell, Wendell, and J. William Gibson, Jr. 1978. "Independent Jamaica Faces the Outside World." *International Studies Quarterly* 22.

Boerboom, Harmen, and Joost Oranje. 1992. *De 8-December-Moorden*. 's-Gravenhage: Uitgeverij BZZTOH.

Brana-Shute, Gary. 1990. "Old Shoes and Elephants: Electoral Resistance in Suriname." In *Resistance and Rebellion in Suriname: Old and New*, edited by Gary Brana-Shute. Williamsburg, VA: Studies in Third World Societies, no. 43.

———. 2000. "Narco-Criminality in the Caribbean." In *The Political Economy of Drugs in the Caribbean*, edited by Ivelaw L. Griffith. Houndsmills, UK: Macmillan Press.

Brown, Deryck. 1995. "The Coup that Failed: The Jamesian Connection." In *The Black Power Revolution, 1970*, edited by Selwyn Ryan and Taimoon Stewart. St. Augustine, Trinidad: Institute of Social and Economic Research.

Dew, Edward. 1978. *The Difficult Flowering of Surinam*. The Hague: Martinus Nÿhoff.

———. 1989. "Suriname." In *1989 Yearbook on International Communist Affairs*, edited by Richard F. Staar. Stanford, CA: Hoover Institution.

Eaton, George E. 1975. *Alexander Bustamante and the Modern Jamaica*. Kingston: Kingston Publishers.

Francis, Alfred, Godfrey Gibbison, Anthony Harriott, and Claremont Kirton. 2009. *Crime and Development: The Jamaican Experience*. Mona, Jamaica: Sir Arthur Lewis Institute of Social and Economic Studies.

Harriott, Anthony. 1996. "The Changing Social Organization of Crime and Criminals in Jamaica." *Caribbean Quarterly* 42, nos. 2, 3.

Hoefte, Rosemarijn, and Gert Oostindie. 1991. "The Netherlands and the Dutch Caribbean: Dilemmas of Decolonization." In *Europe and the Caribbean*, edited by Paul Sutton. London: Macmillan Education.

Inter-American Commission on Human Rights. "Second Report on the Situation of Human Rights in Suriname," October 2, 1985, and "Report on the Situation of Human Rights in Suriname," October 5, 1983.

Kabushka, Alvin, and Kenneth A. Shepsle. 1972. *Politics in Plural Societies: A Theory of Democratic Instability*. Columbus, OH: Charles E. Merrill.

Lijphart, Arend. 1977. *Democracy in Plural Societies: A Comparative Exploration*. New Haven: Yale University Press.

Maingot, Anthony P. 1998. *Global Economics and Local Politics in Trinidad's Divestment Program*. Miami: The North-South Agenda, No. 34.

———. 2000. "Changing Definitions of 'Social Problems' in the Caribbean." In *Security in the Caribbean Basin*, edited by Joseph S. Tulchin and Ralph Espach. Boulder, CO: Lynne Rienner.

———. 2007. "Transnacionalización de identificaciones raciales y religiosas en el Caribe." *Nueva Sociedad*, no. 177.

Manley, Michael. 1976. *The Search for Solutions*. Edited by John Hearne. Toronto: Maple House Publishing Company.

Nettleford, Rex. 1971a. *Manley and the Politics of Jamaica*. Mona, Jamaica: Institute of Social and Economic Research, University of the West Indies.

Nettleford, Rex, ed. 1971b. *Manley and the New Jamaica, Selected Speeches and Writings, 1938–1968*. London: Longman Caribbean.

Report of the Commission of Enquiry into Subversive Activities in Trinidad and Tobago. 1965. Port of Spain: House Paper no. 2.

Rodney, Walter. 1969. *The Groundings with My Brothers*. London: Bogle L'Ouverture.

Ryan, Selwyn. 1991. *The Muslimeen Grab for Power*. Port of Spain: Inprint.

Stone, Carl. 1973 . *Class, Race, and Political Behaviour in Urban Jamaica*. Mona, Jamaica: Institute of Social and Economic Research, University of the West Indies.

———. 1974. *Electoral Behavior and Public Opinion in Jamaica*. Mona, Jamaica: Institute of Social and Economic Research, University of the West Indies.

———. 1990. *National Survey on the Use of Drugs in Jamaica*. Kingston, Jamaica.

Thoden van Velzen, H. U. E. 1990. "The Maroon Insurgency: Anthropological Reflections on the Civil War in Suriname." In *Resistance and Rebellion in Suriname: Old and New*, edited by Gary Brana-Shute. Williamsburg, VA: Studies in Third World Societies, no. 43.

36

The Colonial Persuasion

HUMBERTO GARCÍA MUÑIZ

Puerto Rico and the Dutch and French Antilles

After more than 400 years of imperial control under Spain and the United States, Puerto Rico is arguably the oldest colony in the world, while the Dutch and French Antilles have been under the same metropolitan powers since the 1630s. Colonialism does not mean a common history, however: unlike Puerto Rico and the French Antilles, for example, the Dutch Antilles did not experience the sugar plantation complex. Originally part of extensive territorial empires in the Western Hemisphere, the Dutch and French Antilles were reduced over time by warfare, revolution, and decolonization. Only for a few decades did these islands possess economic, strategic/military, or symbolic value to their metropolitan powers. Now they are in the midst of redefining their place within the constitutional systems of the United States, France, and the Netherlands.

This chapter discusses these three cases of Caribbean societies characterized by asymmetrical dependency relationships with their metropolitan powers. Aware of the difficulties experienced by neighboring independent states, their populations are reluctant to sever ties with their metropoles. Neither independent nor wholly colonial, these territories strive for an alternative, non-sovereign political path with economic and social development that preserves their own cultural identities. In their relationships with their respective metropoles, they share certain commonalities: metropolitan citizenship; freedom of movement; common defense, market, and currency (with one exception); and metropolitan transfer payments and expenditures. These ties strengthen metropolitan-territorial links while weakening connections with other Caribbean territories.

Colonial Puerto Rico under the United States, 1898–1945

Although the United States offered to buy Puerto Rico from Spain in 1868, its real interest surfaced with the isthmian canal project later in the century. While trade between the island and the United States had been strong, no sizable American investments had found their way into its depressed agricultural export economy. But Puerto Rico's strategic location protected key access routes to the planned Panama Canal, and US forces invaded the island on July 25, 1898. By the Treaty of Paris—signed on December 11, 1898, and ratified on April 11, 1899—Spain ceded and the United States annexed Puerto Rico.

The political elites' favorable reception of US forces soured almost immediately with the establishment of a military government (1898–1900) and the enactment of the colonial Foraker Act in April 1900. Compared to the short-lived Autonomic Charter granted by Spain on November 25, 1897, the Foraker Act was found wanting; it established a civil government and the principles of the US–Puerto Rico relationship. Several of its provisions, which are still in operation today, were a federal court with proceedings in English, a customs union and the application of US coastwise shipping laws, the exemption of Puerto Rico from the application of US internal revenue laws, and a nonvoting "resident commissioner" in the US Congress. One important proviso also remains in full force today as part of the Federal Relations Act: the extension of all federal laws to Puerto Rico unless found to be locally inapplicable. No federal law has yet been deemed inapplicable.

Colonialism proved controversial in the republican United States. As a consequence of the Insular Cases brought before the US Supreme Court between 1901 and 1905, Puerto Rico was branded an "unincorporated territory"—that is, a possession that was not part of the United States, yet belonged to it and fell under the plenary powers of the US Congress and the executive.

Political forces in Puerto Rico responded much as they had under Spain. Some sought a wider form of self-government within the colonial status of the Foraker Act, while others favored assimilation through admission of Puerto Rico as a US

Figure 36.1 Pedro Albizu Campos. Photograph (1936).

state, or through independence under a US protectorate. Like Spain before it, the new colonial power repressed the pro-independence forces. One of the reasons for the imposition of US citizenship in the Jones Act of 1917 was to defuse a growing call for independence. In the 1920s, this pro-independence sector grew and became more militant under the Nationalist Party, headed by a Harvard-trained mulatto lawyer, Pedro Albizu Campos. During the economic crisis of the 1930s, political violence increased. It culminated in the assassination in 1936 of Francis Riggs, the American chief of police; the imprisonment of Albizu Campos as "intellectual author" of the crime; and the firing on peaceful Nationalist marchers by the insular police on March 21, 1937. This incident, known as the Ponce Massacre, left 17 Nationalists and two policemen dead.

During the 1930s two new US governmental actors entered onto the insular stage: the FBI and federal relief programs. Close surveillance by the FBI paired with repressive measures by the police against the Nationalists and pro-independence supporters became commonplace. The New Deal programs distributed food surpluses and other direct aid, and launched emergency programs to reduce unemployment. World War II alleviated the economic crisis, and the island's role in US regional and military strategy increased.

Diversity of the Dutch Antilles

The term "Netherlands Antilles" (hereafter NA) conceals significant differences between two sets of islands that had little contact until the 20th century. Inhabitants of the Windwards—St. Maarten (shared with France), St. Eustatius, and Saba—speak English, while those in the Leewards—Curaçao, Aruba, and Bonaire—communicate mainly in Papiamentu, a vernacular made up principally of Spanish, Portuguese, Dutch, English, and French. Catholicism predominates in the Leewards, Protestant denominations in the Windwards. Up to the early 20th century, the colonies remained under the direct control of the Kingdom of the Netherlands, ruled by an appointed governor with strong executive powers. But political stagnation did not prevent economic and social change. By the 1920s Shell and Esso had established oil refineries in Curaçao and Aruba, respectively, taking advantage of their stability and security under the Netherlands, in contrast to nearby Venezuela. As World War II neared, the strategic value of the Dutch Leewards increased.

In 1936 new statutory regulations gave the Dutch Antilles a largely elected local council, with only 5% of the population enfranchised. The regulations catered to Aruba's interest in autonomy by stating that local governments could be established free from direct control of the central administration in Curaçao, the largest and most populous island. Political parties began to be organized. But in spite of early calls by Curaçaoan lawyer Dr. Moises da Costa Gomez for extending the franchise, autonomy and representative parliamentary democracy were nowhere in sight on the eve of World War II.

Assimilation in the French Antilles

France's policy oscillated for most of the 19th century between making the French Antilles—Martinique, Guadeloupe, St. Bartholomew, and half of St. Martin—an integral (i.e., assimilated) part of France, or administering them separately as colonial possessions. Emancipation, declared for good in 1848, transformed slaves into citizens. By 1870 each island had elected one deputy to the National Assembly. Unlikely to be elected, white planters refrained for the first time from participating. Between 1890 and 1923, black and mulatto Martinican and Guadeloupean deputies and senators introduced various bills in Parliament asking for the transformation of both islands into full-fledged but separate departments of France. French Antilleans backed their demand of "total Frenchness" by willingly enlisting in the French army in 1914 and 1939.

Consequently, it came as no surprise that on March 19, 1946, two Martinican deputies and members of the French Communist Party—the young, renowned poet and writer Aimé Césaire, founder of the *négritude* literary movement, and the labor leader Leopold Bissol—introduced the Law of Assimilation in the National Assembly, by which both islands became, as of January 1, 1948, two *départements d'outre-mer* (DOM), the equivalent of US states. Césaire—who also served as mayor of Fort-de-France, a position he held until his retirement in 2001—fully supported *départementalisation*. Assimilation, or decolonization through statehood within France, meant application to the DOM of social measures approved in the 1930s and in 1945, which the *bekés* or white planters opposed, and the removal of the islands from the list of non-self-governing territories stipulated under article 73(e) of the United Nations Charter.

In the short run, the Constitution of the French Union, approved on October 26, 1946, failed to transform the empire into a commonwealth by creating various kinds of territories linked to the French Republic. In the end, only the French Antilles, Guyane, and St. Pierre and Miquelon in the Western Hemisphere remained part of France; several other territories attained independence, some by way of bloody wars (for example, Vietnam and Algeria). The constitution confirmed that the legal structure in the DOM was "the same as that of all metropolitan departments, other than for exceptions determined by law." The law meant that every DOM had the same institutions as those in the metropole: a prefect (instead of a governor); a regional council elected by adult suffrage; representation in the Senate, Chamber of Deputies, and Economic and Social Council; the same legal codes and system of justice. But the conditional clause meant that exceptions to legislation could be made. All laws passed after 1946 would be automatically applicable to the DOM, unless otherwise specified, but earlier laws had to have been especially promulgated by the prefect to be applicable. Thus, legal disparities between the metropole and the DOM never disappeared. In Guadeloupe, serious social and political consequences erupted in at least two instances: first in 1967 due to the wider powers given to the prefect, and again in 2009 because of the high cost of gasoline and an unemployment rate of 22.7%.

The Netherlands Antilles under the Kingdom's Charter

As with the French and US empires, World War II gave impetus to changes in the relationship between the Netherlands and its colonies. The German occupation forced the London-exiled Dutch government to govern the overseas territories without the Dutch parliament's assistance. In December 1942, Queen Wilhelmina said the future relationship of the kingdom would be directed "towards a commonwealth in which the Netherlands, Indonesia, Surinam, and Curaçao" would participate with "internal autonomy" and "full partnership." No mention was made of self-determination as in the pronouncement aimed to keep Japanese-occupied Indonesia within the kingdom.

The call from political parties for autonomy in the Dutch Antilles and Surinam increased as soon as the war ended, as the Netherlands tried and failed to impede Indonesia's independence. By 1947 the first change took place with the appointment by the governor of Curaçao of da Costa Gomez as representative in the Dutch Ministry of Overseas Affairs. Also introduced were universal suffrage and a controversial executive council to function as a ministerial cabinet. From 1948 to 1954, two round table conferences were held to discuss the new constitutional order of the kingdom, with delegations from the NA and Surinam representing their own interests. A draft charter was approved in the Dutch House of Commons and the Antillean and Surinamese parliaments, and promulgated in December 1954.

The 61-article charter made the Netherlands, the NA, and Surinam equal and autonomous parts of the Kingdom of the Netherlands, a federal state bound to mutual assistance and to management of common affairs on an equal footing. The Netherlands handled exclusively the designated domains of citizenship, defense, and foreign relations. Among the kingdom's affairs were the "observance of human rights and freedoms," "the rule of law," and "integrity of administration," issues now falling under the contemporary term "good governance." A central parliament and island councils, elected by universal suffrage and based on proportional representation, were set up in the NA. A minister plenipotentiary represented the NA in The Hague with the right to meet with the Council of Ministers when matters of their concern were under consideration. The charter also gave the NA specific prerogatives in international affairs. Thus, international agreements negotiated by the Netherlands would be nonbinding to territories that considered them detrimental; the metropole would be required to cooperate in international agreements that applied exclusively to the islands; and the NA would gain membership in international organizations. Two key provisions of the document placed military service under the jurisdiction of each territory and gave people of the Dutch territories freedom to move to and from the Netherlands, a right the Netherlanders themselves did not have.

In December 1955 the United Nations accepted the claim that the Netherlands Antilles and Suriname had attained a full measure of self-government by free association and removed them from the list of non-self-governing territories. For almost half a century, the charter operated as an agreeable compromise to all parties, leaving a range of areas (education, public health, social welfare, and economic development) in the hands of the autonomous parties, open to cooperation and assistance by the other partners, if so desired.

Puerto Rico as *Estado Libre Asociado*

Meanwhile, the US approach to Puerto Rico dramatically changed during World War II. With the building of army, naval, and air installations, the island became for the next half-century the center of US military operations in the Caribbean. Yet the new pro-independence Popular Democratic Party (PDP), led by Luis Muñoz Marín, a charismatic leader who had lived in the United States in his early years and maintained close relations with Democratic leaders, dominated the political panorama.

At first, colonial governor Rexford G. Tugwell and Muñoz Marín, as president of the Senate, implemented a progressive, government-supported development program. By 1948 a new program, known as Operation Bootstrap, began promoting industrialization with private (mostly US) capital. A symbol of economic and social success, it would soon be hailed as an example for other developing countries. For the next two decades, Muñoz Marín worked with the US Congress and president on the passage of the elective governor law (1948), the adoption by Puerto Rico of its own constitution (1950–52), the creation of commonwealth status (1952), the removal of Puerto Rico from the UN list of non-self-governing territories (1953), and the celebration of the first (1967) of three plebiscites on status preference.

During the war years, the political ferment of the island did not abate, particularly the demand by the independence forces for a plebiscite. Mindful of US opposition—particularly by the military establishment—to any real self-determination, Muñoz Marín pushed for a freezing of the status debate to focus on the dire economic and social situation of the island. With this platform, the PPD handily won the elections of 1944 and 1948, when Muñoz Marín became the first Puerto Rican elected governor. That year the legislature approved the Gag Law, a local version of the US Smith legislation of 1940, which punished with fines or incarceration any advocacy of "overthrowing, paralyzing, or destroying the insular government, or any political subdivision of this, by means of force of violence." The law, enforced rigidly against the Nationalist Party, stifled public expression for independence until its repeal in 1958.

Public Law 600, the bill to permit Puerto Ricans to write their own constitution, was approved on July 3, 1950. It consisted of two parts. The first spelled out the procedure for drafting a constitution: the islanders would elect delegates to a constitutional convention that would approve or reject the finished document and then submit it to the US president and Congress for approval. The second part, known as the Federal Relations Act, compiled all the fiscal, economic, and political principles unilaterally enacted by the US Congress regarding the US–Puerto Rico relationship,

Figure 36.2 Luis Muñoz Marín, seated in center, campaigning among the peasants. Photograph (ca. 1947). Source: Fundacion Luis Muñoz Marín.

most of them contained in the Foraker Law of 1900 and retained in the Jones Law of 1917. They included citizenship, immigration, currency, coastwise shipping, commercial treaties, tariff policy, defense and military issues, and foreign relations. In case of a conflict, federal acts would prevail over Puerto Rico's constitution. No wonder the Dutch UN representative protested in 1953 that the Netherlands Antilles had far greater autonomy than Puerto Rico. That year, only US pressure and outright deception obtained the approval of a UN resolution that withdrew Puerto Rico from the list of non-self-governing territories.

Meanwhile, the independence forces actively opposed the process, to no avail. The Nationalist Party used violent methods, including shootings in Congress, attempts on President Truman and Muñoz Marín, and an uprising in the town of Jayuya; the Puerto Rican Independence Party (PIP), a PPD splinter party founded in 1946, voted or used boycotts against them. While Public Law 600 and the constitution were approved by large majorities—76.5% and 80%, respectively—Albizu Campos and his followers ended up in jail either for violations to the Gag Law or for their participation in the shooting attempts, and the PIP became the main legislative opposition.

On July 25, 1952, the 54th anniversary of the US invasion, Puerto Rico proclaimed itself an *estado libre asociado*, or commonwealth, as the term was officially translated. Throughout the process, Muñoz Marín and congressional leaders differed in their interpretations of this event. For Muñoz Marín, the nature of the relationship with the United States changed because of the consent voted by the Puerto Rican people, even though he admitted to Congress that the official relationship remained unchanged. Congress, however, believed that Puerto Rico remained under the "territorial clause" of the Constitution, and it continued to exert plenary powers over the island. In the ensuing years, all PDP attempts to modify or enhance commonwealth status bumped against either a reluctant Congress or an uncooperative president; it could never synchronize both powers to attain its objectives. Meanwhile, large-scale migration to the mainland and the extension of new federal programs such as the minimum wage, food stamps, Medicare, and mortgage and rent programs further linked the island to the United States. The more the commonwealth remained the same, the more it became integrated into the United States.

Simultaneously, the PIP and other pro-independence groups promoted their case on the international scene (mainly in the UN). The PIP's electoral support dwindled, falling slowly and consistently from 19% in 1956 to 2% in the 2008 elections, losing for the third time their electoral franchise, with no leader of any stature in sight. The PPD's electoral support declined from majorities of over 60% in the Muñoz Marín era to around 45%. The statehood party has been the only movement steadily gaining support in the electoral field; its candidate won the governorship in 2008 with 53% of the vote.

Although diasporas to the metropoles also characterize the Dutch and French Antilles, only in Puerto Rico's case did stateside communities, led by Puerto Rican congressional representatives, demand participation in the island's decolonization process. And the numbers are significant: of 8 million Puerto Ricans in 2007, about 4.1 million resided in the mainland (2.7 million born there) and 3.9 million on the island. No study has been conducted of the emigrés' status preference. Meanwhile, immigration from the neighboring, independent Dominican Republic has further fueled the travails of independence.

These trends notwithstanding, plebiscites in 1993 and 1998 indicated a stalemate between the pro-commonwealth (49%) and pro-statehood (46%) forces. Pro-statehood forces will probably continue holding plebiscites until they gain a majority for a statehood petition, while simultaneously blocking, as in the past, any attempt by the PDP to enhance commonwealth status.

Moreover, Puerto Rico's symbolic and strategic value to the United States diminished with the 2008 economic crisis and the loss of federal tax incentives and exemptions. The closures of US military installations and of the naval range on the island of Vieques further distanced Puerto Rico more from its metropole. The prevalence of the Spanish language—the basis of a strong cultural nationalism—and the low percentage of bilinguals make statehood a difficult choice for the US

Congress to support, apart from other considerations, such as the number of seats it would wield in the House of Representatives, which would diminish other states' congressional delegations.

Another growing factor is the control by Puerto Rican statehood supporters of the local field offices of the Justice Department, the federal courts, and, more recently, the FBI, which has always intervened strongly against independence, either with repressive measures or with counterintelligence actions against organizations and individuals. On September 23, 2005, the anniversary of the 1868 independence revolt, FBI operatives carried out the murder of Filiberto Ojeda Ríos, a leader of the clandestine pro-independence group Los Macheteros. In the early 21st century, US attorneys in Puerto Rico have won numerous cases of corruption against pro-statehood politicians, but in March 2009 they failed to convict a former PPD governor in what was seen as a case of political persecution. As with the NA, "good governance" is an issue in the US–Puerto Rico relationship, especially given the large amounts of metropolitan transfers and the high incidence of drug-related crimes.

The Quest for Autonomy in the French Antilles

In the French Antilles, the first serious expressions of discontent with departmentalization came from Césaire, who broke with the French Communist Party in 1956 and formed the Parti Progressiviste Martiniquais (PPM) in 1958. Césaire now advocated autonomy, meaning a large measure of self-government within the context of an ambiguous relationship with France. The first student movements sponsoring independence began at this time in France and later in each of the French Antilles. All were left-leaning and lacked popular backing. In 1967 a workers' strike supported by the Groupe d'Organisation Nationale de la Guadeloupe (GONG) turned violent, and white French security forces killed more than 100 people. No official inquiry was ever called. During the 1970s and early 1980s bombing campaigns by the Alliance Revolutionnaire Caraïbe (ARC) were carried out in Guadeloupe and Martinique as well as in France, but violent political actions eventually fizzled and the ARC dissolved.

In the meantime, tourism and public administration became important in the economy, with the majority of the labor force employed in the service and public sectors. The traditional economy (sugar, bananas, and pineapples) declined, and most food began to be imported and sold at much higher prices than in France. Because of public and social transfers from France, both Guadeloupe and Martinique experienced significant economic growth, faster than most independent insular economies in the region and at times even faster than France. Yet unemployment stood at 25% in each island near the end of the 1970s, with most people depending on social allowances.

In 1982 the government of François Mitterand introduced a decentralization law creating an elected regional council alongside the existing elected general council for each Caribbean department, effectively transferring decision-making power from the prefects to these bodies. As a result, unlike metropolitan France, where several departments combined into a region, each of the French Antilles became a region unto itself, with the new regional council becoming the most important local assembly. Decentralization also allowed the creation of agencies for local development, the opening up of local media outlets, and inclusion of the creole language in the educational curriculum. Césaire claimed that the new policies fulfilled his struggle for autonomy, started to work within the system, and called for a moratorium of status politics. In practical terms, for a time, any impulse toward independence or a significant change in status was quelled by Mitterand's decentralizing reforms.

Alfred Marie-Jeanne, founder and president of the Mouvement Indépendantiste Martiniquais (MIM), was reelected as head of the regional executive in 2004 and as a deputy to the French National Assembly in 2007. Yet independence sentiment in the French Antilles is marginal, and in 2003 Martinique (with 51% of the vote) and Guadeloupe (73%) each rejected in a referendum the option of becoming a "territorial collectivity" (*collectivité territoriale*), choosing instead to remain under article 73 with greater powers transferred to the islands. To the surprise of most political leaders—especially Lucette Michaux-Chevy, the charismatic president of Guadeloupe's regional council—the electorate voted for the status quo. On the other hand, the residents of St. Martin and Saint-Bartholomew (with a mainly white population of descendants of the original French settlers and a high-priced tourism economy) voted overwhelmingly to become "overseas collectivities" (*collectivités d'outre-mer*, COM), severing in this way their administrative links with Guadeloupe. On February 7, 2007, Parliament passed a bill granting COM status to both islands. Guadeloupe and Martinique kept their separate place as DOM within the French political system, side by side with St. Martin and St. Bartholomew as COM.

As part of France, the DOM are legally part of the European Union (EU). This new constitutional arrangement served as the mechanism through which a significant amount of the EU's structural funds have been allocated to the islands as less developed regions of the EU. But these large transfers of monies from France, and now increasingly from the EU, have fostered welfare-based dependency rather than development. And such interest in the French Antilles goes further than their symbolic value as the vestiges of global empire and a projection of French and EU power and culture in the Caribbean. The islands also represent an extensive, exclusive maritime economic zone and play a role in intercontinental air travel and telecommunications.

In January 2009, a violent general strike began in Guadeloupe and lasted 44 days.

People protested prices that were higher, and wages that were lower, than in the metropole, and unemployment rates of more than 20%. The strike pitted white French riot police against a coalition of 48 organizations—trade unions, environmental groups, and so forth—named Lyannaj Kont Pwofitasyon (LKP), loosely translated as the Alliance against Profiteering. The LKP signed an agreement with the French government on 165 demands, including a US$250 increase in the monthly minimum wage.

As the labor turmoil spread to Martinique and other DOM, French President Nicholas Sarkozy launched an unprecedented consultation on the overseas territories, calling on the people of the DOM themselves and the diaspora in France to participate through the Internet. In Martinique a referendum was held in January 2010 "not about independence [but] about setting the right level of autonomy." With a 55% turnout, 79.3% voted against the proposal for more autonomy, as the "no" campaign managed to conflate a vote for more autonomy with a vote for independence. Apart from the traditional "divide and rule" policy, Sarkozy's referendum offer to Martinique, which left out Guadeloupe (the LKP boycotted the consultation), indicates that each island generally moves to its own rhythm, with little or no coordination between political groups. No movement exists toward the integration of the islands and their 350,000 or so people into one political entity, although recently the diasporic associations have begun to represent the French Caribbean in general, not just individual islands. Amid labor turbulence, calls for further individual insular equality within the French economic system and for more local power based on each island's identity are the order of the day in the French Caribbean.

Fragmentation and Autonomy in the Dutch Antilles

In the 1960s, labor troubles in Curaçao ushered a new era in the relationship between the Netherlands and its Caribbean territories. On May 30, 1969, a strike for higher wages against the Shell refinery turned into massive disturbances and looting in Willemstad by black workers and the unemployed, which led to the immediate deployment of the Dutch military, the eventual downfall of the Democratic Party administration, and the resignation of its long-time white leader, Dr. Ephraim Jonckheer. Since then, politics in Curaçao has been dominated by black leaders from two parties, the Worker's Liberation Front (Frente Obrero de Liberación, or FOL), formed by labor leaders, and the New Antillean Movement (Movimiento de Antiyas Nobo, or MAN), formed by socialist-oriented intellectuals.

The May 1969 riots had significant consequences on relations between the Netherlands and the Dutch Caribbean and among the islands themselves. First, Dutch policy, contrary to that of France and the United States, centered on the promotion of decolonization via independence. Suriname, in a convoluted process,

followed through in 1975. To separate itself from the rest of the Netherlands Antilles, particularly the larger and more populous Curaçao, Aruba's highly popular
"Betico" Croes, of the Movimiento Electoral di Pueblo (MEP), reluctantly agreed
to take that road by 1996. It was only a bluff, however, because as soon as Aruba
attained *status aparte* in 1986—meaning that it became an autonomous country in
the kingdom on similar and equal terms as the NA—it made it clear that it had no
interest in going through with the change. A 1993 protocol between the Netherlands and Aruba suspended the granting of full independence, which was originally
scheduled for 1996. Aruba accepted several conditions guaranteeing "good governance" and abstained from restricting the admissions of Dutch citizens. Earlier, in
1990, a money-laundering situation linked with drug trafficking and offshore banking had led to the intervention of the Netherlands government in Aruba. Meanwhile, the economy prospered, based on a strong tourism sector, oil transshipment,
offshore banking, and remittances. In 2000 the Netherlands and the United States
exchanged diplomatic notes for a 10-year agreement giving access to the airports of
Aruba and Curaçao for counternarcotics operations.

Dutch intervention in issues of "good governance" led to the action of the
Curaçao-based Antillean government in 1992 to end the corrupt 40-year authoritarian rule of Claude Wathey on the Dutch side of St. Maarten. Metropolitan intervention in the form of monitoring and monies to Curaçao stopped the downturn of the
tourist and offshore banking sectors and the financially troubled and environmental
hazardous refinery leased to Petróleos de Venezuela (PDVSA). The Netherlands'
policy, termed "recolonization" by various critics, resulted in promoting "good governance" by curtailing the financial autonomy of the Dutch Caribbean islands and
establishing new individual constitutional relationships with The Hague, furthering
interisland fragmentation and separatism.

The 50-odd-year experiment of the "Netherlands Antilles" failed. The islands
wanted a different relationship with the Netherlands and among themselves.
Between 2000 and 2005, referendums held in St. Maarten (70%) and Curaçao
(68%) resulted in votes for *status aparte*; in Saba (59%) and Bonaire (86%), for
closer ties with the Netherlands; and in St. Eustatius (76%), for remaining within
the Netherlands Antilles. A May 2009 referendum in Curaçao turned the situation
more fluid, as only 52% percent voted for that island to become, like Aruba, an autonomous country within the Kingdom of the Netherlands and to have the Netherlands absorb a large portion of Curaçao's US$2.7 billion debt in return for financial
and judicial controls.

Thus, The Hague granted *status aparte* to Curaçao and St. Maarten with financial supervision and improvements in law enforcement, while Bonaire, St. Eustatius, and Saba (together known as BES) were slated to become part of the Netherlands, with their island councils as local council, their governors as mayors, their

residents entitled to vote in Dutch and European elections, and the US dollar as their national currency, effective in January 2011. BES retained a "special municipality" status because, as Dutch Prime Minister Jan Peter Balkenende put it, "We are different; at home, we speak different languages. Whereas one person grew up among palm trees, the other among tulip fields." The Netherlands agreed to preserve the islands' culture, with Dutch, English, and Papiamentu being the accepted languages. By October 10, 2010, a new Kingdom of the Netherlands would be in place, including a more fragmented Dutch Caribbean with no common language or culture either within itself or with its main federation partner, the Netherlands. For the moment, the diaspora in the Netherlands—consisting of some 130,000 people (25% of them second-generation), mainly from Curaçao—remained marginal to the status discussions.

Conclusion

In the early 21st century, Puerto Rico and the French and Dutch Antilles, although constitutionally diverse, are redefining their relationship with their metropoles, either for greater integration or for autonomy under "good governance" and sound economic administration with metropolitan supervision. Metropolitan citizenship, when allowing for cultural nationalism, is valued more than sovereignty. Voters do not favor the independence option, particularly in the French Antilles and Puerto Rico. The metropoles' repression of independence movements in Puerto Rico and the French Antilles and the difficult economic situation of sovereign Caribbean nations make independence an unattractive, distant goal—especially in the case of the Dutch and French Antilles, where insularism makes integration a difficult prospect.

France and the Netherlands have been more active than the United States in ascertaining by direct negotiations and popular consultations their dependencies' wishes and presenting their own alternatives for discussion. The results might not be crystal clear or definitive for any option, but for the moment autonomy and integration under a watchful and intervening metropole have the upper hand. In both the French and Dutch cases, intraisland fragmentation prevails, as the smallest islands leave their larger islands' associations to integrate into the metropoles.

Puerto Rico is afflicted by a lack of consensus among insular political parties on substantive questions (which commonwealth: an enhanced version, or the present one?) and procedural issues (referendums or constitutional assemblies?). In the United States, an open, real discussion about whether to incorporate a Spanish-speaking, ethnically and culturally distinct nation as a state has not taken place, even though its increasingly English-speaking diaspora is more and more a part of the US mainstream.

For these non-sovereign Caribbean islands, economic growth has meant strengthening of the service (mainly tourist) and public sectors, to the detriment of manufacturing, traditional export crops, and food production for local consumption. All these islands rely for their main nourishment on imports from the metropoles, acutely so wherever urban sprawl and environmental degradation have claimed the limited lands that are suited for agriculture. The status options open to these societies are few. For the moment, autonomy seems to be the preferable political condition, for it allows the expression of cultural nationalism as a way to defuse an asymmetrical situation. Certainly, future change will also depend on political will and public opinion in the metropolitan states. The role played by the diasporas from these islands may increasingly be a key factor in any decision, final or otherwise.

37

An Island in the Mirror

PEDRO L. SAN MIGUEL

The Dominican Republic and Haiti

The watershed in Hispaniola's modern history was the US occupation of Haiti from 1915 to 1934 and of the Dominican Republic from 1916 to 1924. Both nations endured similar hardships during this dual occupation. The invaders imposed puppet presidents in Haiti and a military government in the Dominican Republic, and they enforced policies that increased dependence on the United States. In both Haiti and the Dominican Republic, the Americans also sought to strengthen the state by upgrading transportation and restructuring the military and the government. As part of their "conquest of the tropics," Americans tried to improve education, health, and agriculture, although these programs had limited effects on the population at large.

Other measures had more direct repercussions, particularly for peasants. By the early 20th century, both Haiti and the Dominican Republic had sizable peasantries that cultivated foodstuffs and export crops (coffee in Haiti, cacao and tobacco in the Dominican Republic), and both governments relied on export duties on these

553

crops as their main income source. Merchants, meanwhile, purchased peasant harvests for export at miserly prices. By maintaining this predatory system, each state besieged its peasantry, acting thus "against the nation" (Trouillot 1990)—or at least against the bulk of the population.

US intervention reinforced the predatory role of the state and helped subdue the peasantry, whose restlessness stirred political instability. Haitian and Dominican elites depicted the rural world as barbarous and in need of domestication to achieve modernization. Particularly in the Dominican Republic, this notion was intertwined with racial ideas: peasants of African ancestry were believed to occupy the lowest rung in the social scale. Such local conceptions were reinforced by US racism, mixed with a large dose of imperial "paternalism" (Renda 2001). The invaders took measures to subdue the overwhelmingly black and mulatto peasantries of Hispaniola, disarming them and forcing them to labor in public works. Though partly based on previous local practice, the *corvée* system of compelled labor—implemented during the occupation—became one of the foremost sources of the peasants' distress.

Attempts to alter land tenure had analogous effects. In the Dominican Republic, US companies established sugar plantations on lands often acquired fraudulently or by outright force. In Haiti, similar schemes had uneven results. In both countries, the extreme fragmentation of holdings, the transportation problems, the inadequate labor supplies, and the qualms of US investors mired the growth of large holdings.

Rural dwellers did not remain impassive; armed resistance erupted in both countries. In Haiti, *cacos* (peasants long opposed to central power) launched a guerrilla war, especially fierce in 1918–21, which waned after the murders of leaders Charlemagne Péralte and Benoit Batraville. In the Dominican Republic, armed peasants called *gavilleros* initiated a similar movement in the eastern part of the country. US forces, assisted by local troops, launched a brutal campaign against rebels in both countries. Villages were destroyed, properties confiscated, and innocent civilians harassed, clustered, and tortured. Suspects were often executed on the spot.

Shrouded in a civilizing discourse, the campaign against the peasantry took on religious overtones—especially in Haiti, where elites viewed religious practices associated with vodou as barbarous. But the US "civilizing" crusade had unforeseen outcomes. Although some local intellectuals shared many of the occupiers' biases, they also resented the vicious campaigns against *cacos* and *gavilleros*, denounced land grabs as an "imperial" ploy, and rejected American disapproval of the countries' ethnic and cultural makeup. Haitian writers, scholars, and artists thus disputed the ideological tenets of the occupation and condemned the peasants' expropriation. They harshly criticized the educational policies of the occupiers and decried "the racial prejudices of the Americans" (Nicholls 1996, 150).

In his masterwork *Ainsi parla l'oncle* (1928), which advocated vodou as a full-fledged religion, Haitian writer Jean Price-Mars triggered a nationalist movement representing the peasantry as "that which is authentically and specifically Haitian" (Nicholls 1996, 159). *Négritude*, a movement claiming that all people of black/African ancestry shared spiritual and cultural qualities, was part of this cultural revival. No corresponding cultural renaissance took place in the Dominican Republic, however. Social and intellectual elites in both countries continued to deplore the "backwardness" of the rural masses.

The US intervention left indelible marks on the island. It indeed contributed to social peace in both Haiti and the Dominican Republic, although at a high cost: the states reinforced their dominance upon the peasantry, military caudillos were subdued, and professional armies replaced traditional militias. Although changes in social structure were relatively small, the strengthened states and economic growth prompted the emergence of new middle classes. Since urban centers were few and quite small, members of the middle classes acquired an unusual degree of relevance as political cadres, state bureaucrats, military officers, intellectuals, artists, and professionals. Because of their lower-class origins, these groups acted as liaisons with the urban populace and the peasantry. In the aftermath of the US intervention, the aspirations and actions of the middle classes became crucial in both Haitian and Dominican societies.

The Dominican Republic

A Dictator Dubbed *"el Jefe"*

Between 1924 and 1929, following the US withdrawal, the Dominican Republic experienced a period of relative calm. Party politics was restored, and the country enjoyed economic stability. But old habits die hard, and by the late 1920s traditional politics resurfaced when Rafael L. Trujillo, Sr., emerged as the opposition to President Horacio Vásquez. A person of modest origins, Trujillo had served in the constabulary during the US occupation, and he eventually became chief of the national army and a leading political figure. Betraying Vásquez as well as his own political allies, and terrorizing his opponents, Trujillo seized power in 1930 after rigged elections, and ruled until his assassination in 1961. Throughout his three decades in power, Trujillo created a totalitarian state capable of controlling Dominicans regardless of social class. Elites, middle classes, workers, and peasants all felt the ominous presence of *el Jefe* (the Boss).

When Trujillo took power, the Dominican Republic was in the throes of the Great Depression and the added devastation caused by a hurricane. Trujillo quickly imposed rigorous measures to improve the countryside. The state coerced peasants to cultivate the land and build irrigation channels, roads, and pathways. Quickly, production of foodstuffs increased, economic collapse was prevented, and starvation and social unrest were avoided. During the 1930s, the *trujillista* state further enhanced agriculture and implemented an agrarian reform of sorts. By blending compulsion with paternalism, Trujillo enlarged his base of support. Town dwellers enjoyed a steady supply of rural goods, merchants profited from cheap and abundant crops, and landlords benefited from an inexpensive and submissive work force. Thousands of peasants, meanwhile, gained access to the land.

Trujillo also gained the support of the middle classes—particularly bureaucrats, the military, and intellectuals. At times, intellectuals were enticed into serving the government through rewards, social recognition, and political clout. They supplied the ideological underpinnings of the *trujillato* by interpreting Dominican history as a series of "tragedies" and portraying Trujillo as a savior. One of his major feats, clarifying and marking the border with Haiti, was accomplished in 1935–36, when he and Haitian President Sténio Vincent signed a frontier treaty. Nonetheless, in 1937 thousands of Haitians who had settled in the Dominican Republic were slaughtered. This hideous enterprise was perpetrated by the military and civilian militias following Trujillo's orders, and was justified by claiming that Haitians were marauders who pillaged Dominican properties. The massacre was in line with the anti-Haitianism that became central to the Trujillo regime (Mateo 2004). Manuel A. Peña Batlle and Joaquín Balaguer played major roles in articulating the nationalist discourse that condemned the Haitian "pacific invasion" of the Dominican Republic and justified the ethnic cleansing. Nonetheless, the massacre was handled nonchalantly by Vincent. After cursory inquiries, the Haitian government accepted US$750,000 as indemnity (US$525,000 was ultimately paid).

Manufacturing expanded in the Dominican Republic after 1940, although the country retained its agrarian character. By 1960, more than 60% of the population lived in rural areas, and three-fourths of the people were illiterate. Tokens of modernity sprouted in the cities, but extreme poverty and social inequality were rampant. Meanwhile, Trujillo co-opted or repressed all potential sources of resistance. The Catholic Church, one of the few formally independent institutions left, was complacent. Totalitarianism and lack of liberties became an issue among the younger generations. Opponents of Trujillo's dictatorship were few but active. Some fled the country; conspiring from abroad, they organized several attempts to overthrow Trujillo—to no avail.

By the late 1950s, signs of distress were surfacing repeatedly. In June 1959 invading rebels attempted, unsuccessfully, to lead an uprising. The insurgents were decimated; survivors were tortured and in most cases killed. Nonetheless, malcontents and dissenters multiplied because of the regime's brutality. Underground organizations, like the June 14 Movement, plotted against Trujillo. In the Caribbean,

Figure 37.1 Rafael L. Trujillo, Sr. (left) with Haitian Minister Elie Lescot, 1939. Source: Thomas D. McAvoy/Time & Life Pictures/ Getty Images.

political circumstances also turned inauspicious for him, as democratic forces in the region targeted him for removal. The despot made costly mistakes, like trying to assassinate Venezuelan President Rómulo Betancourt in 1960; the attack won him an embargo by the Organization of American States that worsened the Dominican economy, which was already shaken by the government's wasteful spending. The OAS's resolution concealed an even more disturbing fact: Trujillo's alliance with the United States—based largely on anticommunism—had been shattered.

Internally, Trujillo's repressive apparatus had also become implacable. The November 1960 assassination of Minerva, Patria, and María Mirabal—sisters linked to the underground opposition—generated widespread indignation. Even the Catholic Church distanced itself from *el Jefe*. Plots against the tyrant increased, even among his cronies. One such group of conspirators, with US backing by the CIA, finally executed Trujillo on May 30, 1961. His reign had certainly ended, but the pernicious legacies of his rule proved harder to eradicate.

Quandaries of Contemporary Dominican Society

The period after Trujillo's death was one of the most dramatic in the history of the Dominican Republic. At first, Dominicans were astounded and apprehensive. For decades they had lived under the fist of a menacing ruler whose tyranny forced them to withhold their political views. But soon citizens began to defy the remnants of *trujillismo*. Massive demonstrations and strikes forced the family and inner circle of the tyrant—including Balaguer, Trujillo's last puppet president—into exile. A state council ruled until Juan Bosch was elected president in December 1962. His election attests to the prodigious political transformations taking place.

A gifted writer, Bosch had exiled himself in 1938 and, like other political émigrés, he returned to the country after Trujillo's fall. As candidate of the Partido Revolucionario Dominicano (PRD, or Revolutionary Dominican Party), which had been founded by exiles in 1939, Bosch was elected by a staggering 60% of voters. As president he strengthened democracy, fought corruption, and encouraged social reforms. The military, the state bureaucracy (where trujillistas still thrived), and the upper classes loathed the president's populism; the all-pervading Catholic Church accused him of atheism and communism. Bosch soon became another casualty of the Cold War. In the wake of the Cuban Revolution, he was reluctant to become a US puppet, and on September 25, 1963, he was overthrown and deported. A right-wing triumvirate exercised power until April 24, 1965, when sectors of the armed forces rebelled, seeking to restore Bosch's constitutional government. Hundreds of civilians willingly partook in the conflict.

So did the "Caribbean's watchdog," the United States, which immediately sent 23,000 troops to Santo Domingo and forced the constitutionalists to accept a provisional government. Elections were scheduled for June 1966, and Bosch once again ran for the presidency. But this was not 1962: it was Balaguer, the "US candidate," who prevailed in an irregular contest. Thus began Balaguer's Twelve Years, which constituted a mockery of democracy. Balaguer became the head of a conservative regime in which, especially from 1966 to 1974, paramilitary gangs and the armed forces harassed, arrested, kidnapped, tortured, and murdered thousands of opponents. Balaguer prompted modernization through foreign investment and state outlays. His economic policies privileged public works, light industry, tourism, and banking, essentially ignoring the countryside. Ironically, though, his enforcement of the "agrarian laws" during the early 1970s briefly allowed him to retain the peasantry's support.

Combining fraud, repression, and pervasive corruption, and benefiting from the opposition's inner quarrels, Balaguer stayed in power until 1978, when he was forced to step down thanks in part to the diplomatic intervention of US President Jimmy Carter. From 1979 to 1986 the PRD's candidates, Antonio Guzmán and Salvador Jorge Blanco, occupied the presidency. During their administrations, public liberties improved but economic policies were unsuccessful and corruption continued unbridled. The PRD's government reached its nadir in April 1984 when it raised the prices of commodities. Popular uproar met with fierce state repression, and hundreds of protesters were killed or wounded, leading to Balaguer's political rebirth.

Throughout Balaguer's new administrations (1987–96), corruption and economic chaos reached unforeseen heights. Devaluation and inflation became unmanageable, and the country's infrastructure verged on collapse. Meanwhile, the government embarked on several pharaonic projects such as the Columbus Lighthouse, a massive building on the outskirts of Santo Domingo, planned by Trujillo, that ironically celebrates the Dominicans' "Spanishness." Nonetheless, Balaguer stayed in power thanks to sweeping corruption, repression, and the opposition's flaws. By the late 1980s, the Partido de la Liberación Dominicana (PLD, or Dominican Liberation Party), founded by Bosch, began appealing to the lower and middle classes. In the 1994 election, initial ballot counts favored Bosch, but Balaguer was eventually proclaimed the winner. A deadlock ensued, and finally a compromise was reached: Balaguer stayed in office until 1996.

The 1996 election was a threshold in recent Dominican history: for the first time since 1966, Balaguer was absent from the ballot, though his influence remained. The main candidates for the presidency were the PRD's José Francisco Peña Gómez and the PLD's Leonel Fernández. With Balaguer's blessing, Fernández won the presidency by exploiting racism and anti-Haitianism against Peña Gómez, who was of Haitian parentage but adopted and raised by a Dominican couple. Because of constitutional restrictions, Fernández could not be reelected in 2000, but after a disastrous term by Hipólito Mejía of the PRD, he returned to power in 2004, and thanks to constitutional reform, he was reelected in 2008 for another four-year term.

Dominican politics got a much-needed facelift during the 1990s, though some of its age marks are still quite visible. State corruption, for instance, remains unabated. But the end of the Cold War favored the rise of political parties, like the PRD and the PLD, that previously had been curbed by the United States. The relationship between the Dominican Republic and the United States changed also as consequence of economic and social transformations. Manufacturing, tourism, and the service sector have become the main drivers of the economy, but drug trafficking and money laundering have also contributed to economic expansion; so have remittances from abroad, especially from the United States. Emigration increased during the 1960s for political reasons, and since the 1980s for economic ones, and as of 2008 nearly half of Dominican households reportedly had a member abroad. Remittances, whether legitimately or illicitly earned, comprise vital income for countless families. Internal migration, similarly, has altered the country's makeup: most Dominicans now live in urban areas. Santo Domingo, the capital, concentrates 30% of the national population of more than nine million; in 1960 it had fewer than 400,000 residents. Lifestyles have changed accordingly. Like most of their Caribbean neighbors, Dominicans now live under the omnipresent influence of the United States.

One significant feature of migration patterns is the constant inflow of Haitians. How many are settled in Dominican territory, legally or otherwise, is a matter of controversy; figures range from 500,000 to more than a million. Moreover, while previous generations of Haitian immigrants were mostly sugar workers clustered in a few regions of the country, members of the current wave are conspicuous in urban settings as day laborers, peddlers, and vagrants, thus augmenting the perception that Haitians are "invading" the Dominican Republic. Haitian immigrants and their Dominican-born progeny comprise a sizeable ethnic group that is the target of chauvinism, legal and cultural discrimination, and all kinds of abuse. Dominicans claim that their country is incapable of shouldering Haiti's tribulations as well as their own. This somber reality creates an excruciating dilemma for both countries.

Haiti

A Tyrant Nicknamed "Papa Doc"

After the departure of US forces in 1934, Haiti enjoyed a period of relative tranquility. Surely there were events that perturbed the country, like the massacre of Haitians along the Dominican border in 1937 and the "anti-superstition campaign" against vodou launched by Elie Lescot's government and the Catholic Church in 1941–42, which stirred considerable violence. Allegedly this movement was a crusade for civilization against African-inspired barbarism. However, it barely concealed an attempt by the mulatto elite, francophile in its cultural outlook, to reaffirm its social and political clout, which was challenged by (mostly) black and radical intellectuals who spoke on behalf of peasants and workers.

Following the US occupation, the position of the black middle classes was downgraded in the state and in society. But during the 1940s, in reaction to Lescot's pro-mulatto measures, "anti-*mulâtre* resentment" reached new heights among black intellectuals, politicians, civil servants, and military personnel as well as among students and urban masses. Articulated in the "language of color," the opposition to Lescot generated "an ideological tidal wave" that put Dumarsais Estimé in power (Trouillot 1990, 133–34). During Estimé's presidency, schooling expanded and civil liberties improved, though repression and state-sponsored violence did not disappear altogether. Even labor unions and radical organizations benefited from an enhanced public environment. All these developments seemed to augur a rupture with traditional politics—until the army, Haiti's real authority, ousted Estimé in 1950.

Paul Magloire, one of Haiti's strongmen and a firm ally of the United States, suc-ceeded Estimé. Under his leadership Haiti's economy improved, thanks to high cof-fee prices and expanding tourism. With foreign financial and technical backing, the government enhanced the country's infrastructure. But other features of Haitian life remained untouched: corruption ran high in Magloire's administration, and by allying himself with the mulatto elite and the Catholic Church, he alienated the black middle classes.

From the beginning Magloire faced the antagonism of populist leader Daniel Fignolé and *noiriste* crusader François Duvalier. When Magloire exiled himself in 1956, both activists became presidential candidates. Following several months of in-stability, violence, and political trickery, Duvalier was proclaimed president in 1957. A black physician of middle-class origins, "Papa Doc" was known for his *noiriste* ad-vocacy and his ethnological work. Exploiting a two-tier discourse based on race and class, Duvalier attracted Haiti's poor classes, who were traditionally discriminated against because of their black ancestry and poverty. His propaganda also appealed to the black middle classes. Finally, having gained the support of the armed forces, Duvalier then proceeded to create a paramilitary corps, the terrifying Tonton Ma-coutes, that reported directly to him.

The Tonton Macoutes were useful to Papa Doc in several ways. First, they were a means of counterbalancing the army, which Duvalier also undermined by pitting high officers against one another and dismissing or banishing potential challeng-ers. Second, the Macoutes acted as a terrorist organization that intimidated oppo-nents regardless of social position, political stance, age, or gender. Whole families were slaughtered and their belongings ravaged by the Macoutes. The Volontaires de la Sécurité Nationale (VSN), as the Macoutes became officially known in 1962, served to keep in place all sectors of Haitian society, and to disseminate the creed of Duvalierism. The distinctive outfit of the Macoutes (sunglasses and blue-and-white uniforms), as well as their prepotency and cockiness, bestowed on them an aura of dominance and impunity. These traits attracted not a few Haitians, men and women, to the ranks of active Duvalierists.

Ideological concerns also played a part in shaping the Macoutes. Duvalierism shrouded itself in a nationalist and *noiriste* discourse that traced its origins to the founding of the republic, especially to the figure of Jean-Jacques Dessalines. There-fore, the Macoutes could conceive of themselves as warriors for a transcendental national and ethnic cause. Yet being a Macoute also brought tangible benefits, like influence in state agencies, unusual sway in everyday dealings, and opportunities for material gain. To the black middle-class Haitians who comprised the bulk of the organization, being a Macoute meant partaking in the "Duvalierist revolution" while reasserting their own political and social standing.

Besides the army, other organizations were constrained by Duvalier. The Catholic

Figure 37.2 François "Papa Doc" Duvalier (seated at right) with a group of Tonton Macoutes in their distinctive outfits. Photograph (ca. 1964).

Church suffered the onslaught of the dictator, who claimed that it represented an antinational institution. Several priests were deported; others were stalked and harassed. The position of the church improved after 1966, thanks in part to the Haitianization of its hierarchy—meaning that it had become subservient to the tyrant. Meanwhile, civic organizations were banished or subjugated, and the state's legislative and judicial branches were subdued as Duvalier aimed to hamper any potential source of resistance. Even vodou was put at his service: Duvalier cloaked himself in a mysterious veil, suggesting that he had extraordinary powers derived from vodou, though he persecuted those *bocors* and *hougans* (vodou priests) who opposed him. In 1964 he felt strong enough to proclaim himself president for life.

One of Duvalier's most striking attributes was his capacity to outmaneuver international adversaries and gain US support in the Cold War era. Shortly after he became president, Fidel Castro took power in Cuba, and in 1961 Trujillo was assassinated. These events reverberated in Haiti: from 1958 to the early 1960s Duvalier confronted and crushed several plots against his regime. During Bosch's rule in the Dominican Republic, when Haitian exiles launched several invasions from Dominican territory, tensions between the countries rose, not to diminish until after Bosch's downfall. The US invasion of the Dominican Republic in 1965, prompted by anticommunist sentiment, further benefited Duvalier. Exploiting an ambiguous discourse that oscillated between pro-Americanism and nationalism, Duvalier established a symbiotic relationship with the United States. In exchange for safeguarding Haiti from communism, he received US acquiescence as well as weapons, military assistance, and substantial amounts of money.

Indeed, Haiti's national income relied heavily on international—mostly US—subsidies. Since Haiti's infrastructural and institutional deficiencies hampered investments, Duvalier depended on foreign monies to run the country. Loans, grants, humanitarian help, and every conceivable form of donation or funding became central to state finances. Few of these funds benefited citizens; most were pocketed by state functionaries and by the dictator's cronies and relatives. Unsurprisingly, Haiti's economy was in disarray during the 1960s and 1970s. Agriculture was in a particularly dire condition, hampered by soil exhaustion and erosion (among Haiti's most pressing problems), technological backwardness, and lack of financial support and transportation. A swelling population added to the countryside's predicaments.

Haiti in the Wake of Papa Doc's Rule

As part of the second phase of the "Duvalierist revolution," by the late 1960s the Haitian government had begun promoting tourism and manufacturing, which attracted foreign capital, mainly from the United States. However, Papa Doc did not live to witness the consequences of these measures: he died in April 1971 and was swiftly replaced by his 19-year-old son and heir, Jean-Claude. Under "Baby Doc," the new economic measures produced some changes. Attracted by a cheap and subservient workforce and by other economic incentives, foreign light industry increased in Haiti in the 1970s. Thousands migrated from the provinces to Port-au-Prince, the capital, in search of jobs. Workers' living quarters, already pitiful, now became dreadful. The peasantry and the countryside continued to be neglected. Meanwhile, opulent mansions sprouted in Port-au-Prince's affluent neighborhoods.

Baby Doc himself embodied the lavish lifestyle of the economic elites. Lacking his father's political aptitude and shrewdness, the junior Duvalier was mainly a bon vivant. Yet Jean-Claude's rule constituted a renewed compromise between Duvalierism and the Haitian bourgeoisie. In exchange for its new sources of income—based on manufacturing, tourism, and government corruption—the bourgeoisie buried its resentment against Duvalierism, an antipathy based more on racial and power issues than on economic ones. US endorsement of Baby Doc helped to lessen the elite's animosity against him. The new bond between Duvalierism and the *haute bourgeoisie* was symbolized by Jean-Claude's marriage to Michèle Bennett, a light-skinned *mulâtresse*. Their sumptuous wedding, profusely covered by the international press, was portrayed as a symbol of the "new Haiti."

But the ceremonies only increased popular resentment against Baby Doc, and the black middle classes and hard-core Duvalierists felt rejected by him. After US President Jimmy Carter enforced a human-rights policy against Haiti, repression did diminish, and Jean-Claude made adjustments that, though minute, conveyed the impression that he was steering Haiti's transformation. Underneath, what was actually changing was society itself.

Emigration swelled in the 1980s as a result of the profound social crisis. In spite of the increasing pressure against Haitians in the Dominican Republic, thousands continued crossing the border. Boat people sought refuge in the United States or other Caribbean countries; the better-off emigrants headed by other means to France, Canada, and Mexico. Suffering from lack of opportunities, hundreds of professionals abandoned Haiti. Massive emigration had contradictory implications: it deprived the country of thousands of skilled and purposeful citizens, yet it allowed emigrants to denounce Haiti's plight and fight against its wrongdoers.

Other aspects of Haitian reality also had unforeseen implications. The Haitianization of the Catholic priesthood, one of Papa Doc's victories in his quarrel with the Vatican, ultimately boomeranged against Jean-Claude. The church sponsored cooperatives that endowed peasants and workers with organizational expertise. Moreover, several priests became social activists who voiced popular demands, while Radio Soleil, a Catholic radio station, broadcast programs that upset the government. Criticism of the government became more acute by the early 1980s, when rising prices and food shortages worsened the already dismal living conditions of the Haitian masses. Food riots finally erupted in 1984. The government resorted to its accustomed harshness, but this time the members of the repressive machinery acted reluctantly, and Jean-Claude paid the price for having belittled traditional Duvalierists. Protests continued throughout 1985, especially in the provinces. For the first time in decades the Haitian masses rallied on their own behalf. On February 7, 1986, abandoned even by the United States, Baby Doc fled the country.

Once again the military stepped in and used repression and carnage to keep citizens at bay. Civilians answered violently, targeting Macoutes and Duvalierists; a new constitution was enacted and elections were set for November 1987. But on election day armed gangs, reluctant to see Haiti transformed, attacked voters. Most citizens stayed home next time, in January 1988, when Leslie Manigat became president as result of army-run elections, only to be deposed a few months later. After two years of unsteady military rule, Jean-Bertrand Aristide (known as Titid), a former Catholic priest, was elected president in 1990 by two-thirds of the vote.

Initially, Aristide followed a compromising path as chief of state, notwithstanding his previous radical discourse and some outbursts after becoming president. Yet his rule was hard to swallow for those who feared that his presidency presaged the loss of their traditional privileges and power. Their fears seemed ratified by Aristide's political movement, Lavalas (meaning flood or torrent), which pressured, harassed, and punished his opponents, including the legislature. Even honest citizens and convinced democrats were shocked by this performance, reminiscent of Duvalierism's genesis. In September 1991 the military, the Catholic hierarchy, social elites, corrupt functionaries, and deep-seated Duvalierists coalesced, with documented CIA support, in overthrowing Aristide.

After three years in exile, Aristide returned to the presidency backed by international support, including US troops, but stayed in the position just a few months. He was succeeded by René Preval, an agronomist who tried to implement reforms, including land distribution, but was burdened with political discord in his government. After attempting to dominate Preval from behind the scenes, Aristide officially returned to the presidency in 2001.

Despite his popularity, Aristide's second term in office was marred by widespread violence, ineffectiveness, and corruption. He was even accused of dishonesty and despotic proclivities. Aristide's misdeeds, real or not, were stage-managed by his adversaries—who also sponsored a rebel force composed of disreputable elements—to convey the image of an unstable and unreliable ruler. Food and fuel shortages added to the president's troubles. With ample sectors of the population discontented, protests erupted, and on February 28, 2004, under international pressure, Aristide abandoned the country. He later claimed that he had been abducted by US forces and unwillingly transported to Africa. In any event, the United States maintained an ambivalent position toward Aristide: though formally recognizing his government, it covertly acted to impair him.

During the next two years, Haiti was headed by an interim government sustained by UN military forces. Armed squads of different political tendencies, most of them essentially gangsters, acted uncontrollably. Lavalas activists were hunted down by police, paramilitaries, and even UN "peacekeeping" squads. Finally, elections were held in 2006 and Preval returned to office.

Yet electing a democratic government was but a minor step toward solving the country's daunting problems. By early 2010, Haiti had a devastated ecology as result of centuries of intensive soil utilization. While agriculture was thus endangered, manufacturing was embryonic. Consequently, most of Haiti's nine million inhabitants faced daunting material constraints. Social conditions were appalling. Cité Soleil, one of Port-au-Prince's slums, was home to more than a quarter million people. Education and health concerns were overwhelming. Haiti had the highest rate of HIV/AIDS in the Americas, an argument often used to impede Haitian immigration to the United States. Obviously, political instability hampered Haiti's capacity to adequately face these maladies—and it also fostered new problems, like drug trafficking, which had increased over the preceding decades. A significant portion of the narcotics entering the United States was passing through Haiti. And then conditions took a major turn for the worse.

A Shaken Country

On January 12, 2010, a magnitude 7.0 earthquake struck Haiti, devastating Port-au-Prince and its surroundings. The Presidential Palace, the Cathedral, and the National Assembly collapsed; schools, hospitals, banks, industries, and business structures crumbled; thousands of dwellings were destroyed or damaged; the country's infrastructure broke down. Material losses ranged between $8 and $14 billion. The number of victims was staggering: nearly 220,000 dead, over 300,000 wounded, more than a million (half of the capital's inhabitants) homeless. Overall, one-third of the country's population was affected by the quake.

The earthquake shattered Haiti's already fragile political institutions. Before the tragedy, authority had rested mainly on UN and US troops, while the government lacked resources to assist citizens. Though international relief began to arrive soon after the quake, little of it reached the needy; meanwhile, corpses piled on the streets, augmenting the danger of disease. Fleeing from hellish conditions, about 500,000 Haitians ran away from Port-au-Prince. The images spread by news media produced awe; governments and citizens around the world responded with massive donations. By April 2010 governments and international organizations had pledged more than $10 billion for reconstruction.

The tragedy put to the test Haiti's relationship with the Dominican Republic, which responded promptly to its neighbor's plight. The Dominican government took measures to help the injured, and Dominican citizens donated money and supplies. Analysts argued that the catastrophe might encourage a more congenial relationship between the two countries and that Haiti's rebuilding could further their economic bonds. Yet many Dominicans feared a massive exodus of Haitians to the Dominican Republic, adding to the friction between the two countries.

But reconstructing Haiti would be a complex task entailing much more than feeding and housing a destitute population, upgrading infrastructure, increasing production, and generating jobs. It also implies revamping Haiti's institutional makeup, as well as combating long-standing political and social problems. Such ingrained practices as corruption, bossism, racial and social discrimination, and authoritarianism threaten to channel resources into the wrong hands, deepening Haitians' poverty and frustration. Rampant corruption has also historically jeopardized the understanding

between the countries that share the island of Hispaniola. The involvement of the international community in Haiti's reconstruction offers some hope of overcoming these challenges. Haitians would not be left out, of course, but given the scale of their needs and the scarcity of resources, they would have to rely on international assistance. Long ago, after Haiti achieved independence, the great powers castigated it for having carried out a revolution that smashed slavery and colonialism. A suffering but heroic people who had tested enlightened notions of liberty was outcast by Western nations. Ironically, those same nations were left with little choice but to collaborate in the remaking of Haiti after the earthquake of 2010.

Figure 37.3 Devastation in Port-au-Prince in the wake of the January 2010 earthquake. Source: Marco Dormino/United Nations Development Programme.

To make things worse, in 2010 a cholera epidemic broke out, killing thousands. Augmenting Haiti's woes, after 25 years in exile "Baby Doc" Duvalier unexpectedly returned to the country in January 2011, claiming that he just wanted to "help" in the remaking of Haiti. His assertions did not minimize the anxieties of those citizens who feared that he might try to return to power, further muddying Haitian politics. Some Haitians maintain that "Baby Doc" ought to be prosecuted for human rights violations as well as for corruption and embezzlement. However, it is dubious whether Haitian institutions are capable of prosecuting the ex-dictator. The political scenario might be further aggravated if Jean-Bertrand Aristide also returns from exile; actually, he has already expressed such intention.

One Island, Two Histories

The island of Hispaniola is uncommon among Antillean territories, in that it comprises two nation-states. The thorniness of the relationship between Haiti and the Dominican Republic only serves to emphasize the distinctiveness of each country. In Haiti, the story of the slave uprising (1791) and the birth of the republic (1804) act as founding narratives; their outcomes—including the very existence of the Haitian nation—are conceived as a vindication of the "black race." Consequently, Haiti is deemed a besieged citadel surrounded by hostile forces—the West, imperialism, white power—that have impeded its development (Nicholls 1996; Bellegarde-Smith 1990).

Dominican national histories also partake in this siege syndrome, but with some twists. The narratives portray the early colonial period as a golden age in which Dominican society acquired its essential cultural and ethnic makeup, allegedly of Spanish stock. The main threat to this legacy is posed by Haiti, which is deemed "an extension of Africa," and thus the antithesis of the "Spanish" Dominican Republic. From the colonial period onward, Dominicans endured Haitian land seizures, raids, conquest, illegal immigration, and cultural and ethnic encroachment. In Dominican sagas, the nation is represented as a community assailed by its aggressive neighbor, an unrelenting foe.

Both of these historical outlooks have had profound implications for cultural, racial, and ethnic questions, for national politics, and for state policies. They have sustained a "doctrine of retaliation," according to which the two countries are "national essences" confronting each other (San Miguel 2005, 96). Thus, while Haiti and the Dominican Republic share a geographical space, they have usually conceived of themselves as adversaries rather than as partners. This stance has led to denial that their histories have common threads, and to affirmation of features that differentiate one nation from the other. Yet it is possible to identify analogous historical patterns between the two countries. As if gazing at a mirror, Dominicans and Haitians may glimpse facets of their respective histories reflected in each other's past. Furthermore, it has been argued that Haiti's dilemmas cannot be tackled unless the international community—especially the United States and France—takes clear and honest measures to face them. Since Haiti and the Dominican Republic share the island of Hispaniola, any answer to the former's predicaments will inevitably impinge on the neighboring country. For this reason alone, Haitians and Dominicans should ask themselves whether the face they reluctantly glimpse in the mirror is really that of a foe.

WORKS CITED

Bellegarde-Smith, Patrick. 1990. *Haiti: The Breached Citadel*. Boulder: Westview Press.

Mateo, Andrés L. 2004. *Mito y cultura en la Era de Trujillo*, 2nd ed. Santo Domingo: Editora Manatí.

Nicholls, David. 1996. *From Dessalines to Duvalier: Race, Colour and National Independence in Haiti*. New Brunswick, NJ: Rutgers University Press.

Renda, Mary A. 2001. *Taking Haiti: Military Occupation and the Culture of U.S. Imperialism*. Chapel Hill: University of North Carolina Press.

San Miguel, Pedro L. 2005. *The Imagined Island: History, Identity, and Utopia in Hispaniola*. Translated by Jane Ramírez. Chapel Hill: University of North Carolina Press.

Trouillot, Michel-Rolph. 1990. *Haiti, State against Nation: Origins and Legacy of Duvalierism*. New York: Monthly Review Press.

38

Tourism, Drugs, Offshore Finance, and the Perils of Neoliberal Development

ROBERT GODDARD

In its early colonial days, the Caribbean was a notoriously un-healthy place to reside. Endemic outbreaks of mosquito-borne diseases like yellow fever and malaria decimated locals and visitors alike. The armies of Napoleon lost 1,000 men a day to disease during a hopeless campaign to restore French control of what is now Haiti. And while some territories like Barbados had the beginnings of a tourism industry as early as the late 19th century (or even before, if George Washington's only foreign excursion, to Barbados in 1751, can be thought of as a tourist trip), this form of tourism was typically medical in nature, appealing to people convalescing from tuberculosis, for example. For that reason, the main tourist installations were on the windy Atlantic coasts, where the bracing sea breezes were considered healthful. It took large-scale mosquito eradication programs, beginning with one in Cuba during the US occupation from 1899 to 1902, together with improvements in public sanitation to set the scene for the growth of the Caribbean as a mass tourism destination. These improvements in health conditions were indispensable to a change in the perception of the Caribbean as a tropical paradise rather than a graveyard.

Not long after this, World War I interrupted travel between the US and Europe, redirecting elite vacationing toward what came to be known as the "American Mediterranean." In 1919 the Cuban government established the National Tourist Commission to promote travel to the island. Railway and steamship companies saw the potential, and worked together to develop routes from major metropolitan centers to Havana. One typical service picked up travelers at New York's Pennsylvania Station and took them by railway car to Key West before arriving by steamship in Havana 56 hours later. Other travelers coming from the West and Midwest went by train to New Orleans before transferring to ship.

Air travel between Key West and Havana began in 1921, and within decades a number of airlines—among them Braniff, Cubana, and Pan American Airways— were operating regularly scheduled flights between Havana and New York, Miami, and Chicago, among other cities. US visitor arrivals in Cuba grew from 33,000 in 1914 to 90,000 in 1928 and 178,000 in 1937. Tourist traffic temporarily halted during World War II, but by 1950 it had recovered to prewar levels, and in 1957 tourist arrivals from the United States hit a record of 356,000.

Some of the spectacular growth in Cuban tourism was due to the beautiful natural surroundings, pleasant weather, and proximity to the US market. But another critical element was the adoption of the 18th Amendment to the US Constitution in 1920, which banned the sale, manufacture, and distribution of alcohol. Prohibition had the effect of driving many distillers, hoteliers, restaurateurs, nightclub owners, saloon keepers, and others involved in the liquor business to Cuba, where they stimulated the growth of an industry that allowed US tourists to indulge in pleasures banned at home.

These pleasures came to include not only alcohol but also gambling, illegal drugs, and prostitution—activities that grew enormously in scale during the 1950s as North American gangsters relocated to Cuba in response to heightened scrutiny by US law enforcement agencies. But, as Cuban songwriter Carlos Puebla put it, "*se acabó la diversion* [the party was over]" once the Castro revolution displaced the accommodating Batista regime. The assimilation of the Cuban economy into the Soviet orbit made the Cuban tourist industry virtually disappear for the first few decades of the revolution. Much of the Cuban market was diverted to nearby destinations like Puerto Rico, the US Virgin Islands, and Jamaica.

The disappearance of Soviet support in 1989, however, forced the Cuban government to reevaluate the industry, and tourist arrivals have been growing rapidly since then, reaching 2.5 million in 2005 and contributing 50% of the island's total foreign exchange earnings. Much of the growth has come in the form of joint venture partnerships with foreign companies, like Spain's Sol Melía. Yet state control is still critical to the Cuban government, and Gaviota, one of the major hotel companies, is directly controlled and operated by the Cuban armed forces. Recent decisions have further centralized direction of the industry in the hands of the military. Future growth of Cuban tourism has become a great imponderable. Some estimates suggest that 60% of the 1.6 million US tourists who visit the Caribbean region each year could be diverted to Cuba in the wake of trade liberalization between the two countries. On the other hand, Cuba has one of the lowest rates of repeat tourism of any destination in the world, and demand has appeared to soften in the early 21st century, as Cuba's reputation for poor food and service counteract the positives of historical interest and scenic beauty.

Nearby territories like Jamaica, the Bahamas, and Bermuda followed a trajectory somewhat similar to that of Cuba. There was minimal tourism investment until the early 20th century, when improvements in transportation and communications—in particular, the wide adoption of steamships and the telegraph—reduced the length and uncertainty of oceanic travel.

In the case of Jamaica, the early development of tourism was linked to the growth in the banana trade. The forerunner to the United Fruit Company was established in the scenic Portland district of Jamaica's north coast in the 1880s. This company grew bananas on its own land in Jamaica and shipped the fruit on its 30-ship fleet to distributors in Boston, Philadelphia, Baltimore, and New York. These same ships could be used to take paying passengers to and from Jamaica at limited marginal costs, amounting to $60 in 1892, which led to investments in hotel construction as well, notably a 150-room facility in Port Antonio.

By the early 20th century, therefore, certain lineaments were already established for the development of the Caribbean tourism industry. First, regional governments were positively disposed toward tourism as an engine of economic growth. Second, the capital for tourism development was assumed to come from outside the Caribbean territories themselves. And third, as the Jamaican government demonstrated as early as 1890, foreign investors could count on a variety of fiscal incentives to encourage them to set up operations in the Caribbean. By the 1920s, the tourist trade in Jamaica was the fourth largest foreign exchange earner, after bananas, sugar, and coffee.

The real boom came with the deployment of long-haul jet passenger craft in the 1960s and a decisive shift in consumer preferences toward holidays centered on beaches and sun rather than mountain retreats. Other countries followed the lead of Cuba, Jamaica, and the Bahamas, with Barbados and Antigua among the newer destinations for which tourism became a leading industry in the 1960s and 1970s.

Tourism is now the major engine of economic growth for Caribbean countries. Direct and indirect employment affiliated with the sector has been estimated at just over 15% of the total, and it generates about the same proportion of the region's gross national product. Stay-over arrivals range from over three million in the Dominican Republic to under 10,000 for Montserrat. The United States is the main market for the Bahamas, Jamaica, the US Virgin Islands, and Puerto Rico, while Europe dominates the trade to Cuba, Barbados, and the Dominican Republic.

The growth of tourism has allowed some Caribbean countries to successfully diversify their economies away from agricultural exports while investing in infrastructure and improving health services and educational resources. Overall in the region, life expectancy is a reasonable 70 years, and literacy rates are between 80% and 90% for all countries except Haiti. Tourism-dependent economies like Antigua and Barbuda, the Bahamas, and Barbados enjoy per capita incomes of US$10,000 or more, poverty rates of 10% or under, and high rankings for government effectiveness. Yet unemployment rates remain high throughout most of the Caribbean, and growth rates, while positive overall, have not kept pace with those in other developing areas in Asia and elsewhere, and are only slightly ahead of those in Latin America.

Even with its positive attributes, there are some concerns about the future of Caribbean tourism. The Caribbean tourism industry, while growing, has been losing market share as a destination. And what growth there has been has been largely concentrated in the Hispanic territories of Cuba, Puerto Rico, and especially the Dominican Republic. One constraint to future growth is the region's dependence on foreign-based airlines to provide most of the carrying capacity to service the industry. One airline, American, accounts for more than a third of flights into the Caribbean and has announced plans to reduce the size of its central hub in Puerto Rico, although other airlines have since entered the Caribbean market, including US Airways, Continental, and Delta. The Dominican Republic, which receives more than three million tourists a year, does not have its own carrier, leaving it vulnerable to changes in lift capacity imposed from outside. Caribbean-owned airlines, including Air Jamaica, LIAT, Cubana, and Caribbean Airlines, exist only because they are heavily subsidized, with Air Jamaica's losses in 2007 amounting to US$171 million.

Cruise ship arrivals are an important and growing sector of the tourism industry, with arrivals in 2007 at 19.5 million, only slightly behind the 22.55 million arrivals that year by air. But cruise passengers are less valuable than other visitors to the host country, as most of their spending is kept by the cruise company. The crews are all non-nationals, and virtually all cruise ship supplies except fuel are sourced from outside the region. Cruise passengers are also exempt from many of the taxes and fees imposed on tourists arriving at airports, reducing their value as a revenue source for government. Consequently, receipts from cruise ship activity amount to only 10% of the total generated by tourism in the Caribbean. Market concentration is also a worry, as the cruise ship market in the region is now dominated by two companies, Carnival and Royal Caribbean, which have 75% market share and have so far refused to contribute to regional marketing programs or to the environmental levies to which hotels are liable.

Tourism growth has brought with it other issues that transcend the purely economic. Jamaicans complained of a color bar aboard the banana boats carrying travelers to North America as early as the 1920s. And both local Jamaicans and British colonial officials complained that the presence of US tourists tended to corrupt the moral tenor of the country, turning the island into "a perverted hell," rife with crime, consumerism, and sexual promiscuity. These complaints were even more pronounced, of course, in the case of 1950s Cuba, where mobsters from the United States found a congenial home for their investments in casino gambling.

The long-term consequences of tourism development on Caribbean society and the Caribbean environment have been debated ever since. For example, analysis of tourism's supposed links with crime depends a great deal on how crime itself is understood. Arguably, many tourists travel for the purpose of conducting illegal or improper activity, such as drug use and prostitution, and tourist arrivals can increase local demand for criminal activity. Even tourists who have no criminal intent may unintentionally provoke criminal behavior by leaving expensive property like cameras in plain view. On the other hand, the economic growth that follows tourism development can be seen as part of modernization, which in a more general way has been associated with higher crime rates as the traditional bonds that hold society together are loosened. In any event, some of the most spectacular crimes committed in recent Caribbean history have taken place in a tourist setting. In 1972 six masked gunmen burst into a clubhouse at the Fountain Mountain Valley Course in St. Croix, in the US Virgin Islands, and robbed the 16 people inside before opening fire and killing eight. The fact that all the gunmen were black and all but one of the victims were white added a racial dimension to the event, sending shock waves throughout the Caribbean tourism industry. But spectacular incidents like this are unusual, and in general crimes committed against tourists are quite low, with figures of 0.01% for Jamaica and 0.07% for Barbados in 1999 being fairly representative.

New Economic Challenges and Opportunities

If some Caribbean crime can be arguably linked to the growth of the tourism sector, not all of it can. Much of the violence that has traumatized Jamaica in recent decades, for example, stems from the rivalry between the two main political parties, which have each sponsored armed gangs that effectively control "garrison constituencies" in the capital, Kingston. Even more important to the growth of the crime rate in the Caribbean is the area's geographical position as a transit point for narco-trafficking between South American producers and North American consumers. Income from such trafficking generates an estimated US$3.3 billion a year, or just over 3% of the region's GNP. Most of the trade is in cocaine, whose share of the market has been steadily increasing at the expense of marijuana, and 90% of which is reexported to the United States. The Caribbean is also a producer of illegal drugs, mostly marijuana, although not nearly on the same scale as previously. Jamaica, for example, was ranked as the world's leading ganja producer during the 1970s, but the region's contribution to global marijuana production has fallen to just over 4% from 18% a generation ago.

The drug trade has doubtless played a part in the rising incidence of violent crime, as a long-established pattern of crime in the Caribbean has shifted away from an almost exclusive incidence of property crime to crimes against persons. The homicide rate in the Caribbean is now 30 per 100,000 of population annually, giving it one of the highest murder rates of any region in the world. Other new forms of criminal activity, such as extortion and kidnapping, have also now become a worrisome feature of Caribbean life, especially in Haiti and Trinidad and Tobago. Trinidad's kidnapping rate has grown from 10 per year in 2001 to 150 per year in 2004, which in a population of 1.3 million means that Trinidad, at the time, had the highest abduction rate in the world after Colombia. The wave of kidnappings has played into existing ethnic tensions, as most of the victims are from the country's East Indian population.

The vast sums involved in drug trafficking have also tempted public officials to accept bribes, and in many parts of the Caribbean, proven and unproven allegations of drug-linked corruption are a staple of political discussion. Among the best known cases of public corruption has been the naming of former Bahamian Prime Minister Lynden Pindling in an antidrug probe by US authorities and the 1989 trial and subsequent execution of high-ranking Cuban officials, including General Arnaldo Ochoa, for their alleged role in drug smuggling. And while many have speculated that Ochoa's trial was motivated in part by the Castro brothers' concerns about Ochoa's political ambitions, a number of Ochoa's codefendants offered testimony suggesting high-level involvement with drug trafficking among Cuban officials.

The drug trade has also stimulated the growth of white-collar crime, as traffickers endeavor to "launder" receipts from the distribution of narcotics through financial intermediaries, especially Caribbean offshore banks. The Caribbean has become a center for offshore financial services for a number of reasons. For one, many Caribbean territories are in the same time zone as the Eastern seaboard of the United States. The Anglophone countries typically have legal systems based on common law, which is also the foundation of US commercial law. In addition, some Caribbean countries have earned a reputation for political stability, an indispensable asset for attracting international business. Yet another reason is that the development of communications technology has deterritorialized commerce.

In general, offshore financial centers (OFCs) provide financial services to nonresidents, which can include the establishment of offshore banks, corporations, and insurance companies as well as tax planning and asset management. Looked at in this way, almost any financial center, including London and New York, could be described as offshore, since much of the financial business that takes place in those cities occurs on behalf of nonresidents. Yet the OFC classification is normally reserved for those jurisdictions where the majority of financial services are rendered between nonresidents and are far larger than needed for the local economy, and where the majority of financial institutions are owned by nonresidents.

In 1936 the Bahamas became the first offshore financial center in the Western Hemisphere, as British and Canadian interests sought to manage the investments of wealthy clients. These offshore banking operations eventually became part of Britain's National Westminster Bank, and offshore operations spread to other British territories including Anguilla, the British Virgin Islands, and the Cayman Islands. In the 1960s the Bahamas OFC grew enormously as a result of tax measures taken by the US Treasury during the Johnson administration to restrict dollar exports. One of these, Regulation Q, penalized non-US residents who tried to buy US domestic dollar bonds, thus inhibiting US banks from borrowing on the domestic US money market. Another regulation made it unattractive for US residents to invest in non-US securities, thus inhibiting the growth of non-US portfolios on the part of US banks and driving US banking business out of the country. The larger banks tended to focus their energies on the emerging Eurodollar market, but the smaller ones found it more effective to operate out of an offshore jurisdiction in the Caribbean. The Bahamas thus eventually became host to more than 600 offshore banks and trusts, loosely regulated under a 1909 act that lacked the legal power to adequately supervise the activities of this newly important sector.

As the Bahamas moved toward independence in 1973, many investors, unnerved by this political change, moved their holdings elsewhere. The main beneficiary was the Cayman Islands, a non-self-governing overseas territory ruled by a governor appointed from London. The Caymans became one of the world's largest banking centers, home to 10,000 hedge funds and controlling assets of more than US$1.3 trillion as of June 2008. Other Caribbean jurisdictions followed this lead, with Barbados passing enabling legislation in 1980, and offshore companies appearing in Antigua and Barbuda two years later and in Nevis shortly thereafter. Dominica began turning itself into an OFC in 1996, Grenada in 1997, and St. Lucia and St. Kitts at the start of the millennium.

The economic impact of OFCs is certainly perceived to be positive, given the impetus added to the sector by the regional governments, but the effect on employment is not especially high, given that many of the financial entities exist only on paper and have no physical presence in the host country. OFC employment in Dominica thus was estimated at 100, or 0.5% of the workforce in 2000. Corresponding figures for Antigua and Barbuda, which has specialized in online gambling, are 2,500, or 8% of the workforce. But the importance of the OFCs as financial contributors to Caribbean economies is greater. The British Virgin Islands, the world market leader in incorporation of International Business Corporations (IBCs), relied on OFC fees for 55% of government revenues and 13% of GNP. Elsewhere the effect on government revenues is smaller, ranging from 7% in Antigua and Barbuda to no more than 1% in the Bahamas and Barbados. These estimates do not take into account indirect benefits to the local economies, such as demand for professional services, rental space, tourism products, and utility services, which would certainly present an even more positive impression. On the other hand, there are costs to managing OFCs that should also be considered and for which accurate data does not exist at the moment. These costs stem from the increasingly onerous regulatory requirements needed to supervise OFCs.

OFCs have also attracted concern in recent decades as governments in North America and Europe have begun to consider the possible threat posed by OFCs to their own tax bases and to the integrity of the international financial system. For example, many Caribbean OFCs have no laws against tax evasion for the simple reason that there is no income tax. In August 2005 the US Internal Revenue Service won a major court case against the accounting firm KPMG for peddling phony tax shelters in the Cayman Islands and elsewhere that generated US$11 billion in phony tax losses. KPMG admitted to criminal tax fraud and paid a US$456 million fine.

More disturbing is the opportunity presented by OFCs for money laundering—that is, moving money from illegal activity into the banking system so that any trace of the original transaction and the parties to it is removed. In 2000, a number of Caribbean territories were criticized by an international agency, the Financial Action Task Force (FATF), for failing to properly supervise their OFCs. The FATF found that the Bahamas, the Caymans, Dominica, St. Kitts and Nevis, and St. Vincent and the Grenadines failed in some way to monitor suspicious transactions. As a result, Caribbean OFCs had to modify existing legislation and increase staffing of the supervisory agencies responsible for overseeing the sector. Subsequent reviews by the FATF have found that Caribbean OFCs have made the necessary changes to be removed from the list of "noncooperative" territories.

The Caribbean has also explored non-tourism service export possibilities, among them "informatics," in which Caribbean workers perform various back-office functions for North American companies. Beginning in the 1980s, informatics was pursued by a number of Caribbean countries hoping to match highly educated workforces and advanced telecommunications infrastructure to compete in a high-tech field. American Airlines established Caribbean Data Services in Barbados, which had 1,500 employees by 1990, and Call Centers Antigua Limited counted 200 workers around the same time, bringing total employment in informatics to 6,500 by

1994. But multinationals eventually took their operations to other lower-cost locations, especially in Asia.

A similar experience has tended to characterize export manufacturing, with foreign companies establishing themselves in low-tax enclaves in the Caribbean but eventually migrating in search of lower-cost labor markets. A striking example of this phenomenon occurred in apparel manufacturing, which expanded enormously as a result of the so-called 807 provision of the US Customs Code which benefited Caribbean exporters. The program was exploited most successfully by Jamaica and the Dominican Republic, each country doubling its apparel exports between 1989 and 1994, to a total of US$2 billion. But this impressive growth stalled in the late 1990s after the North American Free Trade Act (NAFTA) treaty took effect, giving Mexico a competitive advantage over the Caribbean as a location for enclave manufacturing. The effect on the Caribbean was immediate, with 23 factories closing in Jamaica during 1995–96 and 15,000 workers losing their jobs. Puerto Rico had a similar experience with enclave manufacturing under the terms of Section 936 of the US Tax Code. Section 936 encouraged mainland companies, principally in the pharmaceutical and electronics sectors, to invest in the island, but when the 936 provisions were finally withdrawn in 2005, manufacturing investment shrank. The Caribbean Basin Initiative, introduced by the Reagan administration after the Grenada invasion, never provided much stimulus to regional economies as it excluded certain goods—such as sugar, textiles, and leather goods—in which the Caribbean enjoyed a comparative advantage over US manufacturers.

The Fate of Export Agriculture

Despite the growth of service industries and manufacturing, however, traditional agriculture has remained important in the Caribbean—especially the production of sugar and bananas. These commodities were important enough in the past to warrant the cost of long-distance trade, the subsidized transport of labor, and the garrisoning of troops and naval protection on the part of the metropolitan centers of power, and they laid the basis for continuing trade links between Europe, the United States, and the Caribbean.

The iconic Caribbean plantation crop, sugar, has always depended on market access for success. Caribbean sugar producers have flourished when granted preferential access to export markets, and struggled when those preferences are curtailed. Thus the British West Indies suffered after the UK adopted free trade in 1846, allowing sugar producers with lower costs to outcompete British possessions for market share in Britain itself. Likewise, Cuba prospered with privileged access to the sugar markets of the United States, and more recently to those of the former Soviet Union.

The English islands had their preferential access to the British market formalized in the aftermath of World War II under the terms of the Commonwealth Sugar Agreement of 1951. British authorities wanted to end sugar rationing at home while keeping sugar purchases within the Sterling area to minimize foreign exchange losses. This arrangement was carried over as the Sugar Protocol to the Lomé Convention when Britain joined the European Union in 1974. The Sugar Protocol established a series of export quotas and guaranteed prices for Caribbean sugar producers.

Protected from the extreme market fluctuations characteristic of commodity exports, the sugar producers of the Commonwealth Caribbean successfully refinanced their industries and expanded operations, from 400,000 tons in the early 1930s to 1.3 million tons in the mid-1960s. The extra revenues also permitted the Caribbean sugar industry to invest in new technologies, reducing the number of factories by half to 50 and increasing per-factory output by a factor of six.

But costs also increased during this time, partly as a consequence of a tide of nationalization that swept the Caribbean sugar industry in the 1960s and 1970s. From Cuba to Guyana, Jamaica, and Trinidad and Tobago, sugar industries came under state control and management controls were loosened. Costs rose and production fell, while the Caribbean's share of world sugar production declined from almost 40% in the 1950s to 20% in the 1970s.

Together with declining industry performance, Commonwealth Caribbean sugar exporters began to lose preferential market access. The United States began reducing access to its domestic markets in the 1990s, and quotas for the region fell from 2,624,150 tons in 1982 to under 1,300,000 tons in 2001. Even more serious for the Commonwealth Caribbean has been the changes to the EU sugar regime. Following complaints to the World Trade Organization (WTO) from sugar exporters like Brazil and Australia, the EU has agreed to steep cuts of 36% in the guaranteed price it will pay regional growers. Largely as a consequence of this decision, the government of Trinidad and Tobago has opted to close the country's sugar industry. The sugar industry of St. Kitts and Nevis has also been closed, and the future of the Barbados sugar industry is uncertain. Guyana is one exception to the dramatic contraction of the regional sugar industries, as costs in that country are relatively low since successive currency devaluations have reduced local labor costs to internationally competitive levels.

Banana exports from the region—principally Jamaica, Dominica, St. Lucia, Grenada, and St. Vincent and the Grenadines—are also in jeopardy for similar reasons. Preferential market access to the EU was challenged at the WTO by US banana companies on behalf of Central American growers, and as a result the EU has been forced to reduce tariffs on Central American fruit.

The Cuban sugar producers, once the largest in the world, faced the same problems as the Anglophone Caribbean with regard to beet competition in the late 19th century, and their salvation also resided in market access outside the region, this time with the United States. The 1902 reciprocity treaty gave Cuban producers a three-cent-per-pound advantage on raw sugar exports over other foreign suppliers, and for the rest of the decade almost all of Cuba's sugar exports went to its neighbor to the north. Prices and US investment grew during this time, especially as supplies tightened among European beet producers during World War I. But declining prices in the interwar period, especially during the Great Depression, forced Cuba, acting in concert with other major sugar exporters, to restrict exports in order to reduce overstocks and improve prices. These measures had limited effect, as other producers took advantage of the situation to increase production behind protectionist walls. Cuban access to the US market itself was restricted during this period, to the benefit of producers on the US mainland and dependent territories like Hawaii, the Philippines, and Puerto Rico. Cuba's share of the US market dropped from 58% in 1924 to 25% in 1933.

The stresses caused by this economic dislocation were made more acute by the extreme differentials—in terms of landholding, capital resource, and production capacity—that existed at the time in Cuba between the smaller cane growers, or *colonos*, and the larger sugar factory companies, or *centrales*. This economic gulf between *colonos* and often US-owned *centrales* become a major political issue, as economic nationalists concluded that the factory companies did not have the interests of the Cuban nation at heart. In response to intense political pressure, in 1937 the Cuban government passed a piece of far-reaching legislation called the Law for Sugar Coordination, which decisively intervened in the sugar economy on behalf of the *colono* community. Production quotas were established that favored *colonos*, who also won the absolute right to occupy their land as long as the land was kept in sugar cultivation, superseding the property rights of the *centrales* who owned the land and often used their position as landlords to threaten *colonos* with eviction.

Like World War I, World War II stimulated demand in the United States as supplies from European beet growers were interrupted, and Cuba had no trouble disposing of its crop, as well as carryovers from earlier crops. However, the US-imposed price controls kept prices artificially low, while prices elsewhere in the Cuban economy rose quickly, owing to wartime inflation. As a result, margins on the crop were quite low, even though Cuba's share of the US market recovered to more than 44%. Also, Cuba's close cooperation with the United States during the war was remembered when the 1947 US Sugar Act was drafted, giving Cuba access to the US market vastly superior to that enjoyed by any foreign supplier. Output grew to six million tons in 1952, and the period between the late 1940s and early 1950s was one of prosperity. Although overproduction and changes to the US sugar quota system weakened Cuba's position later in the decade, total receipts from sugar exports were averaging half a billion dollars a year, up from 100 million in the early 1940s.

The coming of the 1959 Cuban Revolution changed the ownership structure of the sugar industry but not the central importance of sugar to the Cuban economy. An Agrarian Reform Law resulted in the expropriation of land from large- and medium-scale owners, and effective control passed to state-controlled collectives. The Cuban government briefly attempted to diversify the island's economy away from sugar and toward industry in the early 1960s, but these efforts stalled and sugar exports became ever more important to the country. Sugar production reached 8.5 million tons in 1970, a remarkable output, although lower than the much-publicized target of 10 million tons. As in the prerevolutionary period, the Cuban sugar industry depended on guaranteed market access to a major sugar importer, this time the Soviet Union rather than the United States. Under the terms of a 1960 trade pact, the USSR committed itself to purchasing a minimum of 1 million tons of sugar a year from Cuba, with 80% of the price being in the form of merchandise goods manufactured in the USSR. This barter arrangement continued until the fall of the Soviet Union, providing 400,000 jobs and earning US$5 billion worth of oil and other essentials. The loss of the Soviet market forced the Cuban government to dispose of its sugar crop on the world market at much lower prices, and revenues fell 90% to just over US$400 million. At these prices, the Cuban authorities had no choice but to radically shrink the industry, closing almost half of the island's 156 factories after the 2002 crop. More recently, production has hovered around 1.4 million tons per year, enough to satisfy the 700,000-ton local market and a 400,000-ton export quota to China. Employment also had to be trimmed, with at least 100,000 out of about 500,000 workers losing their jobs. Half of these former sugar workers were kept on the payroll, while more than 30,000 were enrolled in schools to continue their education.

The decline of export agriculture in most of the Caribbean mirrors larger political and economic processes. The early 21st century finds the Caribbean confronting a world in which national self-determination—a political rallying cry for decades, pursued through control of sugar agriculture—seems outmoded. The forces of economic globalization have undermined the autonomy of small states in the Caribbean, and indeed those countries that most aggressively asserted their geopolitical independence have lost the most ground. Cuba under Fidel Castro, Jamaica under Michael Manley, and Guyana under Forbes Burnham were among the slowest nations to adapt to the new economic realities, and living standards in these countries have declined since the late 1980s, as have the prestige and credibility of the governing regimes themselves. Paradoxically, the territories that have been most accommodating to external political and economic forces have experienced the most robust growth and gains in the delivery of goods and services by the state.

39

Caribbean Migrations and Diasporas

CHRISTINE M. DU BOIS

Shaping Caribbean history since the pre-Columbian era, migration has intensely and repeatedly added complexity to the region's societies. Flows of people into, within, out from, and returning to the area—both forced and voluntary—are major, foundational aspects of the islands' social lives and cultures. Although tragedies have impelled these migrations and resulted from them, Caribbean peoples have demonstrated extraordinary resilience and adaptability as they have moved about. The past century of their migrations illustrates well this adaptability, and the considerable effects of their movements on sending and receiving societies alike.

The Early 20th Century

Prior to World War II, Caribbean migrations primarily responded to the need for labor in shifting locales. From 1904 to 1914, American construction of the Panama Canal drew some 60,000 Barbadians and 85,000 Jamaicans to the Canal Zone, along with thousands of laborers from other islands. Many of these workers eventually returned home. Others went on to other American-financed projects in the Caribbean Basin: railroad construction in Costa Rica, banana plantations in Honduras, and sugar plantations in Cuba and the Dominican Republic. Still other migrants perished; in Panama probably more than 15,000 British West Indians died before 1920 (Richardson 1989, 210).

The migrants sent steady remittances home, thereby continuing the postemancipation tradition among Afro-Caribbean men of going to where the money flowed at any given time and then sending some back to their families, only on a grander scale. The participation of some 20,000 British West Indians in World War I, primarily in the Palestine campaign, was also a source of earnings. The remittances cushioned economic downturns on the home islands, and enabled some wives and mothers to purchase the means of small-scale economic production—for example, fishing boats or land. The early 20th-century migrations thus aided working-class households on the sending islands, reinforcing both their economic transnationalism and the female-dominated decision-making of their day-to-day living. For a time the migrations, along with US capital, also hugely stimulated the local economies of the Latin American countries that received them. They led to lasting communities of West Indian origin in Panama and in the Costa Rican province of Limón.

British West Indians also migrated to the mainland United States in search of employment. The first cohort began arriving around 1900, peaking with the admittance of some 12,000 individuals in 1924. More than half these immigrants settled in New York City and many others went to Boston. Although the original population came mostly from the working class, in time more educated West Indians chose to migrate, and by the 1930s they represented "a disproportionately high percentage of those in the professional, economic, and political leadership of New York's black community" (Kasinitz 1992, 24–25).

At that time, when American racialized barriers were so firm in law and social attitudes, these ambitious immigrants found scant political or economic value in publicly emphasizing their cultures of origin, as they would tend to do in later decades. In the early 20th century, the "fact" of "blackness" was so overwhelmingly important in American social relations that clinging to a Caribbean-based ethnic identity at the expense of cooperative relationships with African Americans was not generally fruitful. Although jealousies and conflicts between immigrant and native-born blacks did exist during this period, for the most part in the public arena this first West Indian cohort emphasized black solidarity.

To that end, they produced several early black leaders. The Jamaican Marcus Garvey created the Universal Negro Improvement Association (UNIA), with a pioneering pan-African philosophy, four million followers, and a newspaper with international circulation. Until the US government convicted Garvey of mail fraud in what was widely seen as a politically motivated trial, sent him to jail, and then deported him, the UNIA played a seminal role in the development of black consciousness in the United States. Other prominent West Indian immigrants included writers, leaders of black nationalist movements, labor organizers, and radical activists.

Meanwhile Haitians were also on the move, to the United States, France, Cuba, and especially the neighboring Dominican Republic. Attracted by employment opportunities in the burgeoning Dominican sugar industry, Haitians emigrated there by the tens of thousands, as they had in earlier periods and would continue to do throughout the 20th century. Despite their willingness to take arduous cane-cutting jobs that Dominicans eschew, Haitians and their descendants in the Dominican Republic have faced generations of resentment and discrimination. In 1937, tensions boiled over in the massacre of Haitian immigrants under the leadership of Dominican dictator Rafael Trujillo. The exact number of the dead is unknown, but evidence is clear that many thousands perished. Nevertheless, Haiti's relative poverty continues to encourage both legal and illegal migration across the Dominican border. Estimates place the population of Haitian descent in the Dominican Republic today at some 800,000, with the possibility of a significant rise in the wake of the catastrophic Haitian earthquake of 2010.

Sugarcane production also propelled Puerto Rican migration in the early 20th century. The island's plantations were devastated by hurricanes in 1899, leaving skilled sugar workers without employment and the world market with an unexpectedly short supply of the much-desired sweetener. American economic, political, and military might provided a solution startlingly similar to the transport of Asians to Caribbean isles in prior decades and the transport of Africans to the New World before then: the sending of Puerto Rican laborers to the developing sugar plantations of Hawaii. Within a few years about 5,000 Puerto Ricans settled in Hawaii, forming the base of what today is a community of more than 30,000.

Sugar proved an unreliable source of employment for Caribbean peoples, however. During World War I the sugar market was stable, and in Cuba there was even a labor shortage in the sugar industry, leading to renewed permission for Chinese to immigrate there. But following the end of US and British wartime price controls, speculation and competition within the capitalist system caused such instability in prices that many sugar mills were financially ruined. Cane workers were thrown out of work.

Some sugar laborers found new opportunities in the construction of oil refineries on the Dutch islands of Curaçao and Aruba. Apart from these isles, however, economic opportunities in the Caribbean became scarce, particularly during the Great Depression. Without the outlet of labor migration and the cushioning by remittances from abroad, massive underemployment and deprivation led to rioting, violence, and—in some cases—modest economic and political reforms.

The region had to wait until 1940 for the creation of new jobs for tens of thousands, as the United States undertook military construction on several British islands. As in so many migratory movements of the past, Caribbean men drew on their maritime skills to arrive in small sailing ships at the US bases, ready for work. These jobs proved short-lived, however. The era of mass, long-term migrations was yet to come.

Migrations after World War II

During the latter 20th century and into the 21st, migration from the Caribbean has continued to be economically motivated. But wrenching wars and substantial legal changes have also had major impacts on the flow of people during this period.

Events in the United States and Britain produced large shifts in the movements of English speakers from the Caribbean. Having been devastated during World War II, Britain by the 1950s sought enormous manpower to rebuild the country. Almost simultaneously, an isolationist and xenophobic mood in the United States produced the McCarran-Walter Act of 1952, drastically reducing the number of West Indians allowed to immigrate. West Indians responded to these conditions by emigrating in droves across the Atlantic—until the Commonwealth Immigrants Act shut the door to Britain in 1962. More than half of these hundreds of thousands of migrants came from Jamaica, but all the British islands participated in the outflow of between 5% and 30% of their populations (Richardson 1989, 216; Gmelch 1992, 43).

In the Caribbean, the staunching of the West Indian labor flow to Britain might eventually have reproduced the underemployment and economic frustration of the 1930s, except that in 1968 a sea change in US immigration law went into effect, redirecting the flow to North America. The economic strength of the United States, cheaper air travel, and legal changes combined to produce a wave of immigration from the West Indies (and many other developing countries) far larger than any of the law's framers expected. By the 1980s, approximately 50,000 legal immigrants were entering the United States from the Anglophone Caribbean every year, and perhaps an equal number were migrating without legal permission. West Indians have continued to settle in great numbers in New York, but have also formed vibrant communities in many other US cities.

In contrast with the varying flow of Anglophone West Indians, Hispanophone migration has been more unifocal. The Cubans present an unusually dramatic case. The triumph of Fidel Castro in 1959, his subsequent alliance with the Soviet Union, and the nationalization of US businesses on the island spurred Cubans of the middle and upper classes to leave their homeland, with the US government's encouragement. In the revolution's early years, some 60,000 Cubans emigrated to the United

States annually. These migrants were eventually accorded a facilitated legal pathway to permanent US residence.

In fits and starts, the Cuban emigration has continued for decades. Cubans unhappy with the revolution have sought a better life in Miami and its environs, and prior to the fall of the Soviet Union, the US government wished to maintain Cold War consistency by treating anyone fleeing a Communist country as a deserving political refugee. Politics internal to Cuba and the United States have also powerfully affected the immigrant flow, as the Cuban government has found relief in exporting its political opponents, while American presidential candidates—mindful of the need to win Florida's electoral votes—have courted the Cuban-American vote with promises of continued openness to Cuban migrants.

The most startling moment in this already singular migration history came in 1980. For many months the Cuban government had expressed frustration over the fact that whenever disaffected Cubans hijacked a vessel in Cuban waters and forced it to US territory, the United States received the hijackers as heroic refugees rather than criminals who had just put others' lives in danger. The Cuban government's irritation with this policy, its need to deal with its restless population during an economic downturn, and a tit-for-tat desire to harass the American government— which had recently applauded the 10,000 Cubans who had sought asylum in the Peruvian embassy—all convinced Castro to permit a sealift of any Cubans wishing to leave.

On April 18 the Communist government phoned Cuban exile leaders in Miami to inform them that they could freely pick up Cuban emigrés at the port of Mariel. By April 19 the first two boats had arrived. Before the sealift ended in October, some 125,000 Cubans had left the island (Smith 1987, 197–237). They were generally of lower socioeconomic standing than the first waves of exiles, and 2 to 3% of them were criminals and mentally ill individuals whom the Cuban government forced the arriving boats to accept. Yet over time the "marielito" Cubans have integrated reasonably well into American society. They have fit into working-class occupations in the robust, internationally important Miami economy that the first wave of Cubans built up. But their competition for jobs with African Americans and with Haitian, Jamaican, Dominican, and other Latin American immigrants has at times produced serious ethnic tensions in the city.

By contrast with the Cuban case, Puerto Rican emigration to the United States has been calm. Puerto Ricans have been freely coming to the American mainland since 1900, when their island became an unincorporated US territory. This migration increased gradually in the first three decades of the 20th century, but dropped off during the Great Depression. Beginning in 1945, however, this flow was greatly augmented as job opportunities and the inauguration of low-cost flights from San

Juan to the mainland encouraged Puerto Ricans to try life in the north, particularly in New York City. The peak decade was 1950–60, when an estimated 470,000 Puerto Ricans—21% of the island's population—emigrated north (Acosta-Belén and Santiago 2006, 81).

The Puerto Rican migrations have had a strikingly cyclical character, with many individuals shuttling frequently back and forth between island and mainland life. On the mainland they have often taken unskilled and semiskilled jobs in light industry, the garment trade, and hotel and restaurant service. They have struggled with the language barrier, the lack of high-quality schools both in Puerto Rico and on the mainland, and racial prejudice in New York and elsewhere in the United States. Yet migration from Puerto Rico continues to be commonplace, in part because of some inspiring success stories from the mainland—for example, elevation to the US Supreme Court of Judge Sonia Sotomayor, the daughter of two Puerto Ricans without high school educations who emigrated during World War II. The continuing migration from Puerto Rico constantly refreshes the cultural identity of the more than four million mainland Americans of Puerto Rican origin or descent.

In the latter 20th century, migration from the Dominican Republic has also been pronounced. Prior to the assassination of the dictator Trujillo in 1961, few Dominicans were permitted to leave their country. With the collapse of the Trujillo regime, however, new legal permission to emigrate combined with economic and political instability as instigators of mass Dominican migration. The majority of these migrants have settled in New York City, but others have chosen Puerto Rico, Miami, Providence, and Boston. Meanwhile, Dominicans have a large community in Spain and a growing presence in Venezuela, St. Martin, Antigua, Curaçao, St. Thomas, Italy, Switzerland, and other European countries (Sagás and Molina 2004, 2).

In the United States, Dominicans have taken up residence both legally and illegally and have tended to occupy low-status jobs. In comparison with other American Hispanophones, they have the lowest median family incomes; by contrast, Cubans have among the highest. Unfortunately, nearly 30% of Dominicans in the United States live in poverty, a function of their poor education in the Dominican Republic, their struggle with English (they are among the least confident of US Hispanophones in their own English skills), and their frequent employment in declining industries hard hit during economic downturns (Ramírez 2004, 10–16; Sagás and Molina 2004, 17–18). They occupy a socioeconomic position similar to that of Puerto Ricans on the mainland, with one crucial difference: all Puerto Ricans are legally on the mainland, whereas many Dominicans are not and therefore cannot avail themselves of the benefits that legal status confers.

Processes similar to those taking place among Puerto Ricans have occurred for migrants from Guadeloupe and Martinique to metropolitan France, since like Puerto Ricans they are citizens of the mainland country yet are culturally distinct.

This migration has been substantial since 1946, when the isles legally exchanged their colonial status for full incorporation into France. By 1999 more than 200,000 individuals living in mainland France had been born on the small overseas *départements* of Guadeloupe or Martinique (Byron and Condon 2008, 35).

In other ways, however, the experience of these migrants has differed significantly from that of the Puerto Ricans. For one thing, the French government has generally taken a much more organized approach to the migration than its American counterpart. After World War II the French government directly encouraged "les Antillais" to migrate, as a way to relieve population pressures on the islands and to provide unskilled and semiskilled laborers for the state bureaucracy in the metropole. The government initially sent these workers to training camps in various French towns, although eventually most Antilleans ended up settling in the Paris region.

Another significant difference between the experiences of Antillean migrants in France and those of Caribbean migrants to Britain and the United States lies in the way the migrants have been received: "The ideology of assimilation into the French nation that pervaded French policy-making facilitated the incorporation of these colonial societies who had been acculturated as French people over a period of more than 300 years. The approach was paternalistic and exploitative of their labour power, but at no time were the Caribbean migrants perceived by the state as 'other than French,' and their right to share in the resources of the French nation were not disputed" (Byron and Condon 2008, 48–49). Moreover, the French experience has been unusual in that the French generally do not consider "race" an acceptable or even meaningful measure of differences among peoples. Thus dark-skinned Caribbean migrants to mainland France are more often upset by insults to their cultural self-definition and practices than by a sense that their skin color is an inescapable marker of inferiority in the eyes of the metropolitan French (Beriss 2004).

Migrants from the Dutch-speaking region of the southern Caribbean—the "ABC islands" of Aruba, Bonaire, and Curaçao—have also encountered a relatively generous reception in the European metropole. Although economically successful oil refining, mining, and tourism have made these isles a migration destination for job seekers from elsewhere in the Caribbean and Latin America, ABC islanders do emigrate to the Netherlands to take advantage of education and employment opportunities. In the Netherlands today the population of ABC islanders, including the second generation, numbers some 100,000. Although they do at times encounter discrimination, these Antilleans tend to be more economically successful in the metropole than the Turkish, Moroccan, and Surinamese migrants with whom Dutch employers compare them (Reubsaet 1988). They sometimes return to live in the ABC islands, which also receive European Dutch pensioners eager to settle in a sunny clime.

Reminiscent of the exodus from Cuba, the migration from Suriname presents a special case. Like the adjacent South American countries of Guyana and French Guiana, Suriname shares many historical and cultural ties with the island societies of the Caribbean. But whereas Guyana and French Guiana have generally experienced steady, modest emigration (primarily to Britain, the United States, and Canada in the former case, and to France in the latter), Suriname has witnessed sudden spikes in emigration to the Netherlands in 1974–75 and 1979–80 due to interethnic tensions, political turmoil, economic failures, and changes in Dutch law.

Around the time of Suriname's political independence from the Netherlands in 1975, many descendants of East Indians and Javanese, who had been brought to Suriname well into the early years of the 20th century to work on plantations, fled South America. They feared ill treatment under the politically ascendant Afro-creole population. Many Afro-creole Surinamese also migrated at that time, since after independence it would become harder to migrate legally and benefit from perceived greater economic opportunities in the metropole. Today more than 300,000 Dutch residents claim Surinamese descent.

Unfortunately, the Surinamese have often had lower educational attainment at the time of immigration than the ABC islanders, and they have often migrated without clear job prospects in Europe (Cross and Entzinger 1988). They have tended not to fare as well in the metropole as the ABC Afro-creoles. Economic struggles have been particularly acute for refugees migrating illegally to the Netherlands in the wake of Suriname's brutal civil war of the late 1980s. Yet their distress has not been as severe as that of some 10,000 war refugees who settled in makeshift housing in French Guiana. Eventually many of these migrants returned, often under duress, to a precarious political and economic future in Suriname.

Also fleeing great political and economic hardships have been the Haitian "boat people," who arrived in US waters during the 1970s and 1980s in a constant trickle that increased alarmingly after Haitians were declared unwelcome in the much closer Bahamas. Over the last four decades, the American government has rescued migrants in danger from overcrowded boats, but only occasionally, under pressure, has it welcomed them into the United States. Frequently, the migrants have been sent home—by plane, when necessary—as unqualified for legal refugee status. During the Reagan administration the US Coast Guard, with the consent of the Haitian government, even patrolled Haiti's waters to stop migrants from leaving. The contrast with the treatment of Cuba's "boat people," particularly during the Mariel crisis, has galled many international observers.

Most social scientists disagree with policymakers' assessments of the Haitian boat people. The academics ask: If political tyranny and instability in your homeland has produced such economic malfunction that you can no longer feed your children, and you are desperate enough to navigate a small fishing boat across 650

Figure 39.1 Haitian "boat people" attempting to migrate to the United States are intercepted by the US Coast Guard and ultimately sent back to Haiti, 2005. Source: US Coast Guard/John Edwards.

miles of open sea—a trip that you, as a person from a seafaring tradition, realize is quite dangerous—is it fair to classify you merely as an economic migrant, rather than as someone escaping political repression? Even the US government, by its actions, has tacitly acknowledged that attempting to separate the tangled political and economic factors that "push" people out of Haiti is frequently not a useful exercise. Thus the United States has taken political action to stem a supposedly purely economic flow. After Haitian president Jean-Bertrand Aristide was ousted in 1991 and three years of political terror and economic chaos followed, the United States invaded Haiti to restore Aristide to power. His return, it was felt, would help stem the new tide of boat people arriving in US waters. But to ensure that the tide would indeed be staunched, the US Coast Guard also resumed patrolling Haitian waters (Conway 2005). By invitation, the US military also intervened after the 2010 earthquake; this was not only humanitarian aid but also, once again, an effort to prevent a flotilla of distraught, unauthorized migrants.

The question of why any Caribbean peoples have migrated in the past century is, in fact, enormously complex. Policymakers prefer straightforward explanations that make their jobs of categorizing people simpler, although most do understand that realities are always messier "on the ground" or in the sea. The complexity stems in part from the multi-stranded motivations of people, and from the ways in which categories in sending and receiving countries do not always match. For example, if a young West Indian woman comes to the United States on a tourist visa and then remains as an illegal worker to provide economically for the legally resident—but cancer-stricken—stepgrandmother who raised her, is the young woman an illegal economic migrant, or is she legitimately reuniting with a family member who does not fit the narrow definitions of family in US immigration law?

Cultural variability in categorizations is paralleled by variability in academics' emphases. Some scholars focus on the "push" factors within countries that motivate people to leave, the "pull" factors that attract them to particular locales at particular times, or both. But in recent years other scholars, particularly anthropologists, have emphasized not only push and pull factors, but also Caribbean "cultures of migration." These are sets of shared expectations in which Caribbean peoples consider migration a commonplace part of a successful life. Along with these expectations comes a whole series of educational preparations, social supports, learned responsibilities and obligations, information networks, economic systems, and family arrangements surrounding the propensity to voyage.

Prospective migrants—particularly those less educated—also often have extremely positive, unrealistic expectations about life abroad. Such perceptions arise from a combination of foreign television shows depicting idyllic lifestyles, the flashy generosity of previous emigrants who come "home" for vacation (and who often fear that if they do not display ostentatious generosity they will be belittled as migration failures), and wishful thinking.

Although scholars can characterize broad patterns of movement, the number of factors affecting individual migrants makes it difficult to predict who will or will not migrate and who will or will not return to live back home in the Caribbean after many years abroad. As one group of observers has noted, a migrant tends to lack "single or simple reasons" for return migration: "His experiences are influenced by nostalgic memories of the island home, by a range of critical assessments of his present situation, by comparisons between places, between societal milieus, between social networks, work experiences, among many other complexities. [Or] her personal goals for emigration may have been met, not yet met, were unrealistic in the first place, or may have had to be drastically altered. [Or] his plans to return may have had to be changed because of changes in circumstances. Conditionality reigns!" (Conway, Potter, and Phillips 2005, 5). It is these same interwoven processes of push, pull, culture, and unpredictable personal and societal contingencies that have led to the formation of Caribbean communities far beyond the Caribbean Sea.

In the 20th and 21st centuries, Canada has joined the countries of the European colonizers, the United States, and areas within the Caribbean and circum-

Caribbean mainland penetrated by US business or military interests as an important destination for Caribbean migrants. Prior to 1967, few individuals from the Caribbean could settle in Canada due to racist immigration restrictions, but once the laws were changed, a substantial number arrived. Canada has become the second most important destination for the islands' migrants after the United States. More than 300,000 Caribbean-born individuals now live there, with heavy concentrations of English speakers in the Toronto area and of Haitians in Quebec.

Canadian law favors the settlement of skilled and professional workers, refugees, and family members of legal residents. Hence, the Caribbean migrant population there has a relatively high educational profile. Although even in avowedly multicultural Canada these immigrants do encounter discrimination, on the whole they appreciate the opportunities for educational and job advancement they encounter there. Unfortunately, their exodus to Canada, as to other countries, has had a mixed impact on the islands from which they came. Remittances sent "home" are the economic lifeblood of many island families, but the "brain drain" has often left these societies bereft of much-needed trained personnel.

In all the receiving societies, the migrants are acutely aware that their job prospects and well-being depend on their access to civil rights. As in the early 20th century, Anglophone West Indians have played prominent roles in the US struggle for equal treatment. In the 1960s, the Trinidadian American Stokely Carmichael was a leader in the Student Nonviolent Coordinating Committee, which organized sit-ins and marches to protest Jim Crow laws in the South. He later became affiliated with the radical Black Panther Party. Similarly, the second-generation Grenadian American Malcolm X became an extremely influential black separatist Muslim leader, followed later by Louis Farrakhan, who was raised in Boston's West Indian community by a mother from St. Kitts and Nevis. Although these leaders' Caribbean backgrounds likely contributed to their boldness (families from black-majority societies often display a very visible racial self-confidence), all three emphasized pan-black solidarity, downplaying their Caribbean origins.

In recent decades, however, as more opportunities have opened up to people of color in the United States, some West Indians have taken a different tack. They recognize that economic success can depend on ethnic reputations. Discrimination is sometimes tied to negative ethnic imagery, which the migrants try to combat in various ways, while good prospects in the metropole can be tied to positive ethnic reputations, which the migrants work hard to enhance. Some West Indians have found it useful to subtly distance themselves from African Americans when interacting with "whites"—for example, by clinging to their accents or mentioning their island origins at the beginning of a first conversation. Their hope is that whites will prefer them over African Americans, and this is indeed sometimes the case. The migrants are quick to point out the success of individuals of West Indian origin, such as General and former Secretary of State Colin Powell and Nobel laureate in literature Derek Walcott.

But their ethnic reputations have at times proved to be a liability. During the 1980s, for example, a string of stories about violent Jamaican cocaine dealers in US cities cast a pall over the ethnic reputation of Jamaicans—and, because many Americans do not differentiate between Jamaicans and other West Indians, over the reputation of all Anglophone Caribbean migrants. Ironically, the Jamaican drug dealers actively cultivated a reputation for violence as a way of intimidating rival dealers, even as the vast majority of West Indian immigrants—including the substantial numbers who do not have legal permission to work in the United States but do so anyway, often at more than one low-paying job—have no interest in criminal activity and intensely desire that Americans notice their many positive contributions to US society (Du Bois 2004).

In Britain there have been black communities in Liverpool, London, and Bristol—including individuals from the Caribbean—since the 18th century, yet the vast majority of blacks who live in Britain today owe their British citizenship to the post–World War II Caribbean migration to the metropole. When comparisons are made between black Caribbean British and other minorities, therefore, the tendency is to measure the integration of the former into British society against that of Muslim immigrants rather than against that of the few non-Caribbean blacks. A parallel process occurs in France, which also has a large Muslim immigrant population. In both cases, such comparisons can work to the Caribbean population's advantage.

Nevertheless, among the working class and the poor, black incorporation into British society has been difficult. In 1919 anti-black riots broke out in several port cities when black West Indian seamen and white British soldiers returning from World War I competed for jobs and women. Then, in 1958, white youths repeatedly attacked West Indians in the Notting Hill area of London. The now-famous Notting Hill Carnival was founded the following year in response, to build Afro-Caribbean pride and showcase immigrants' talents to the larger society. The festival now draws hundreds of thousands of visitors annually.

In 1981, inner-city blacks rioted in London and Liverpool. Hundreds of injuries, vehicle burnings, arrests, and damages to buildings occurred at the hands of blacks frustrated with unemployment, poverty, and especially harsh policing. The riots eventually prompted changes in police training, although the research into disturbances occurring in later years suggests that police reforms have been insufficiently implemented. Such conflicts can contribute to islanders' more negative view of Britain than of the United States or Canada (Thomas-Hope 1992, 6, 145–46), although of course racial disturbances that include West Indians are not unknown in those other two countries. In 1991 West Indians, with considerable African

American participation, memorably clashed with Hasidic Jews and police in the Crown Heights section of New York City. Yet such incidents should not obscure the fact that Caribbean migrants regularly succeed and daily make valuable contributions to their adopted societies. Arguably it is the ardent transnationalism of these varied migrants that enables them to enrich the economic, artistic, linguistic, culinary, musical, and educational milieus to which they move. They embrace dual—or multiple—identities and at times dual citizenship, which may even permit them to vote in more than one country. On their trips back and forth between their home and adopted societies they disseminate goods, ideas, and community news and are constantly willing to adapt while also embracing their Caribbean heritage. They embody a cosmopolitanism with the potential to enhance every neighborhood to which they move. Unfortunately, their complex adaptations are not always appreciated by those around them. There are difficulties in the metropole, and sometimes also among people back "home" who reject return migrants out of jealousy, or out of a perception that the returnees are no longer culturally suited to island life. Yet Caribbean migration continues, and individual migrants persevere. Their remarkable resilience merits respect.

WORKS CITED

Acosta-Belén, Edna, and Carlos E. Santiago. 2006. *Puerto Ricans in the United States: A Contemporary Portrait.* Boulder, CO: Lynne Rienner.

Beriss, David. 2004. *Black Skins, French Voices: Caribbean Ethnicity and Activism in Urban France.* Boulder, CO: Westview.

Byron, Margaret, and Stéphanie Condon. 2008. *Migration in Comparative Perspective: Caribbean Communities in Britain and France.* New York: Routledge.

Conway, Dennis, Robert B. Potter, and Joan Phillips. 2005. "The Experience of Return: Caribbean Return Migrants." In *The Experience of Return Migration: Caribbean Perspectives,* edited by Robert B. Potter, Dennis Conway, and Joan Phillips, 1–26. Burlington, VT: Ashgate.

Conway, Frederick J. 2005. "Haiti and Refugees." In *Immigration and Asylum: From 1900 to the Present,* edited by Matthew J. Gibney and Randall Hansen, 281–84. Santa Barbara: ABC-CLIO.

Cross, Malcolm, and Han Entzinger. 1988. "Caribbean Minorities in Britain and the Netherlands: Comparative Questions." In *Lost Illusions: Caribbean Minorities in Britain and the Netherlands,* edited by Malcolm Cross and Han Entzinger, 1–33. London: Routledge.

Du Bois, Christine M. 2004. *Images of West Indian Immigrants in Mass Media: The Struggle for a Positive Ethnic Reputation.* New York: LFB Scholarly.

Gmelch, George. 1992. *Double Passage: The Lives of Caribbean Migrants Abroad and Back Home.* Ann Arbor: University of Michigan Press.

Kasinitz, Philip. 1992. *Caribbean New York: Black Immigrants and the Politics of Race.* Ithaca, NY: Cornell University Press.

Ramírez, Roberto R. 2004. *We the People: Hispanics in the United States*. Washington, DC: US Census Bureau.

Reubsaet, Theo. 1988. "On the Way Up? Surinamese and Antilleans in the Dutch Labor Market." In *Lost Illusions: Caribbean Minorities in Britain and the Netherlands*, edited by Malcolm Cross and Han Entzinger, 106–25. London: Routledge.

Richardson, Bonham. 1989. "Caribbean Migrations, 1838–1985." In *The Modern Caribbean*, edited by Franklin Knight and Colin Palmer, 203–28. Chapel Hill: University of North Carolina Press.

Sagás, Ernesto, and Sintia E. Molina. 2004. Introduction to *Dominican Migration: Transnational Perspectives*, edited by Ernesto Sagás and Sintia E. Molina, 1–28. Miami: University Press of Florida.

Smith, Wayne S. 1987. *The Closest of Enemies: A Personal and Diplomatic Account of U.S.–Cuban Relations since 1957*. New York: W.W. Norton & Co.

Thomas-Hope, Elizabeth. 1992. *Explanation in Caribbean Migration*. London: MacMillan.

ACKNOWLEDGMENTS

Every author contracts debts of gratitude too diffuse and numerous to properly acknowledge. All the more is this so in a publication of this nature. Obviously, we owe thanks first and foremost to the authors of the contributions to this volume. They all took time out of their busy schedules to help us realize our vision of compiling a state-of-the-art compendium of Caribbean history that would be accessible to a non-specialist audience. The expertise and insights they generously shared is what will hopefully render this volume not only useful but intellectually stimulating.

Thanks of a different but equally important nature go to the members of the University of Chicago Press's editorial staff who shepherded this project from its inception. We cannot imagine more inspiring editors than those who have worked with us over the past several years. Paul Schellinger was enthusiastic about the project from the beginning, helping us imagine the book that was needed and conveying the general stipulations of our work. Realizing that some of the tasks involved in anthologizing scores of authors could be difficult, he imparted a creative mix of kindness and firmness that helped ease our way to completion. Kira Bennett fulfilled the role of editorial assistant marvelously well, supporting the editorial team in all aspects of the project, and Jenny Gavacs finished the job. Anthony W. Burton carried out the thankless task of locating and evaluating the illustrations and, after a hiatus, returned to lend a hand when we most needed him. Our thanks likewise go to our patient manuscript editor, Renaldo Migaldi, whose critical eye and stylistic brilliance we learned to appreciate and depend on. The true hero of this complex project, however, was Mary E. Laur. The most accomplished editors keep projects on schedule, remind authors and volume editors of their responsibilities, teach them best practices to follow, and improve the intellectual and literary content of the work. Mary did all of this with superb efficiency, diligence, and sense of humor. We are indebted to these professionals for their invaluable assistance, and most of all to Mary, known to one of us as the green-and-gold fan who keeps her sporting preferences under wraps while laboring in rival territory. Finally we want to express our gratitude to the staff at the University of Wisconsin Cartography Lab, who generously offered their time and expertise to design, according to our specifications, the general maps included in the front matter.

Francisco wishes to thank the University of Wisconsin System for a sabbatical that allowed him to complete his work on the manuscript. As always, he thanks Olga, who graciously avoided his (short-lived) instances of frustration and was always waiting on the other side with a smile on her face and a short memory. Stephan's thanks go to Doris for her love and unflagging support.

Finally, we would like to recall the judgment of an early reviewer of this project who assured the University of Chicago Press that Scarano and Palmié were "gentlemen" who would work together in a pleasant, effective, and intellectually productive manner. We think we proved him right.

Stephan Palmié, Murnau am Staffelsee
Francisco A. Scarano, Fajardo, Puerto Rico
August 2010

GLOSSARY

afronegrismo
Also known as Afro-Cubanism; a literary and artistic movement that developed in Cuba and Puerto Rico in the late 1920s and 1930s and aimed at valorizing African-derived cultural forms and expressions.

Age of Revolution
A period lasting from the late 18th to the early 19th century during which independence wars and political revolutions were prevalent in American colonies and European states.

amelioration
Attempt on the part of the British imperial state, beginning in 1823, to rid the colonies of what were perceived as the worst excesses of the slave system and to improve the slaves' living and working conditions.

annexationism
Nineteenth-century political ideology in the United States and among some sectors of Spanish Caribbean societies advocating US annexation of these islands.

apprenticeship
A system instituted after the 1833 passing of the Act for the Abolition of Slavery in Britain, which bound former slaves to their former masters for a projected four or six years.

asiento
Exclusive import license granted to a series of foreign contractors to introduce specified numbers of slaves into Spain's New World possessions.

Baptist War
An 1831–32 slave revolt in Jamaica, also known as the "Christmas Rebellion."

boucan
A campfire with a wooden grill that was a traditional cooking mechanism for Jamaican Amerindians and, later, buccaneers and maroons.

Bourbon Reforms
Administrative and policy reforms introduced in Spain and Spanish America by the Bourbon monarchs, from Philip V (monarch, 1700–1724) to Charles III (1759–88). They led to greater governmental efficiency and, in the Spanish Caribbean, to vigorous growth in population and economy.

bozales
Spanish term for slaves born in Africa; called "saltwater slaves" in the Anglophone Caribbean.

buccaneers
Sea rovers and outlaws who, in the 17th-century circum-Caribbean region, mixed the raiding of coastal settlements with more settled activities, like tobacco growing. They were based on the island of Tortuga, off the northwest coast of Hispaniola, from which they gradually began the colonization of the portion of the island that later became French Saint-Domingue and then Haiti.

cacos
Haitian peasant armies that resisted US Marines during and after the 1915 invasion.

Caribs
Disparaging name given to the native inhabitants of the Lesser Antilles by the early Spanish chroniclers. In these accounts, which initiated a discourse of denunciation against the natives, the Caribs were deemed warlike and even cannibalistic, claims that have never been proven.

cacicazgo
Taino chiefdom.

caciques/cacicas
Taino chiefs (male/female).

Casa de Contratación
Spain's central commercial clearing house, regulating trade and navigation with Spanish America.

centrales
High-capacity sugar mills employing myriad technological advancements. Inaugurated in the Caribbean in the second half of the 19th century, each of them replaced several preexisting mills. They transformed productive and social relations between workers and capital.

coartación
Spanish American institution that allowed enslaved men and women to purchase their freedom in installments.

cognatic kinship
Afro-creole form of reckoning descent that, by allowing kinship networks and inheritance rights to run through both the father's and the mother's side, helped to maximize scarce land rights and kinship ties among the enslaved.

colonos
Satellite cane farmers who grew sugarcane for sale to a nearby mill (*central*), often under onerous contractual conditions. The colono system reached its peak in the first half of the 20th century.

commercial capitalism
An economic system practiced by the major European trading nations between the 16th and 18th centuries. It was premised on the idea that colonial wealth, based on systems of labor exploitation like slavery and on high-value goods like sugar or precious metals, would enrich the core nations, particularly if hoarded within exclusive trading circuits.

commercial exclusivism
During the early modern era (16th to 18th centuries), the prohibition against trading with foreign nationals, barring a special permit.

Consejo de Indias
Crown council that advised the monarch in all matters related to trade, justice, and administration in Spain's overseas dominions.

conuco agriculture
Traditional cultivation practice in which small plots are fertilized with organic crop and household residues, often in mounds, to grow manioc and other subsistence crops.

creole languages
Languages that blend lexical, grammatical, and morphosyntactic elements of parent languages into a new, stable language that is spoken natively.

creoles
Children of first-generation Old World migrants to the New World (both African slaves and European colonists) born in the Americas.

creolization
Processes of indigenization of foreign populations, languages, and cultures, usually entailing considerable historical transformation.

departmentalization (*départamentalisation*)
The incorporation of the former French Antillean colonies into the French state as *départements d'outre-mer* (overseas departments), beginning in 1946.

dollar diplomacy
The policy of the US government, under William Howard Taft (1909–13) and later presidents, to use its diplomatic and, if need be, its military might to create conditions that allowed US financial and commercial interests to penetrate weaker countries, particularly in the Caribbean and Latin America.

Dutch West India Company
A joint-stock firm of Dutch merchants charted in 1621 to carry out warlike commercial relations in the Americas. It attacked and pillaged several Spanish and Portuguese possessions including, most prominently, the sugar-producing areas of Pernambuco in northeast Brazil, which the Dutch held from 1624 until 1654.

East India Company
An English joint-stock company founded in 1600 to compete with the Dutch in the spice trade from the East Indies. It remained in existence until 1857.

encomenderos
Under the encomienda system, Spaniards entrusted by the crown with groups of Indians to exploit.

encomienda
In the early years of Spanish conquests, the institution by which Spaniards obtained tribute and labor from Indians in exchange for food, clothing, and religious instruction. An encomienda consisted of a group of Indians and their native leader (a cacique or some other authority figure), entrusted to one of the leading members of the conquering group. See also *repartimiento*.

engagé
An indentured worker in the French Caribbean.

estado libre asociado
Translated into English as "commonwealth," this Puerto Rican political entity was created by a constitutional convention in 1952, vetted by a majority of the island's electorate, and later ratified by the US Congress. Its scope and powers have remained under contention to this day.

exclusif
The law in French-governed territories, inspired in mercantilism and championed by Minister of Finance Jean-Baptiste Colbert (1619–83), which dictated that the majority of their trade must be with France.

family land
Traditional form of land tenure among many Caribbean peasantries involving the equal inheritance of land and its usufruct rights among all members of the cognatic descent group.

feitorías
Portuguese trading posts in Africa and Asia.

fidelista
A supporter of Fidel Castro.

filibustering

Participating in a private military action in a foreign country, with the intent of changing that country's political system.

Foraker Act

Act passed by the US Congress in 1900 that established a civil government in Puerto Rico and the neocolonial principles of the US–Puerto Rico relationship.

free people of color

Caribbean people of African descent who were either born outside the institution of slavery or were emancipated from it. In the French colonies, such people were called *gens de couleur*.

free trade

A less restrictive trading environment that developed as industrial capitalism challenged the colonial system in the 19th century.

free village system

A system of land tenure established in post-emancipation Jamaica in response to state/planter legislation obstructing rights to plantation house yards and provision grounds. Free villages were often established through the purchase of ruined estates by missionaries, who subdivided the land and sold it to ex-slaves in their congregations.

French and Indian War

The conflict between Great Britain and France, and between their colonial and Indian allies, fought in North America between 1754 and 1763. In 1756 it sparked a larger conflict, known in Europe and the Caribbean as the Seven Years' War, which historians consider to have been the first-ever world war.

garrison constituencies

Jamaican urban areas controlled by criminal gangs, so named because the gangs exercise such control that the police have to be "garrisoned" in fortified stations.

Garveyism

The near-global black nationalist movement established by Marcus Mosiah Garvey (1887–1940), formally known as the United Negro Improvement Association (UNIA). Its broad antiracist and anticolonialist agenda emphasized global political solidarity among all black people, economic independence, a vigorous appeal to identification with Africa, and a positive black self-image.

gens de couleur

See *free people of color*.

grand marronage

Pattern of slave flight aimed at permanent separation from the plantation and the subjugation it dictated (as opposed to "petit marronage," which designated temporary flight).

Guanches

The original inhabitants of the Canary Islands, who were violently subjugated and practically exterminated in the Spanish conquest of the Canaries in the 15th century.

gunboat diplomacy
The display, threat, or use of naval force for political or diplomatic purposes. In the Caribbean it was most prevalent in the late 19th and early 20th centuries as a tool of US foreign policy.

indentured servant
A European migrant laborer who was contractually bound to the highest bidder for a period of three to seven years in exchange for passage to the New World. While under contract, such a laborer could be sold or passed down like any movable good.

ingenio
Spanish term applied between the 16th and the 19th centuries to the agroindustrial complex comprising both sugarcane fields and the processing plant.

Jones Act
Act passed by the US Congress in 1917 that bestowed US citizenship on Puerto Ricans, preempting European subversion and undercutting local sentiment for independence.

ladinos
In late medieval and early modern times, Africans born in Iberia who had been baptized, had adopted Christian customs and the Castilian language, and had taken Spanish names.

Laws of Burgos
Spanish laws, implemented in 1512 and amended the following year, intended to curb rampant abuse of native populations by identifying the natives as "vassals of the crown."

Leeward Islands
The northern islands of the Lesser Antilles.

liberated Africans
Enslaved Africans on ships heading for the Americas that were intercepted by the British Navy and freed as part of the 19th-century British campaign against the foreign slave trade.

maroons
Deriving from the Spanish *cimarrones,* which originally designated communities of runaway natives, this term soon came to mean African slaves who fled their masters.

Maroon Wars
Periods of military conflict in Jamaica, identified more specifically as the First (1729–39) and Second (1795–96) Maroon Wars, that saw two groups of escaped slaves, known as the Leeward and Windward maroons, engage in hostilities with the British colonial state and later enter into peace treaties with it.

marronage
The general practice of running away from enslavement.

mercantilism
Early modern economic doctrine centering on the concentration of bullion in metropolitan treasuries. Legislation inspired by mercantilist doctrines drastically restricted colonies from trade with foreign nationals.

mestizaje

Process of biological and cultural hybridization.

mestizos

Persons of mixed Native American and European descent. The term is also sometimes used for people of undefined mixed descent.

metropole

Core territory of an imperial state.

mixed labor regime

A system of labor, employed in the 19th century, that centered on slavery but was supplemented by free or bound workers imported from Europe.

Monroe Doctrine

A principle of US foreign policy articulated by President James Monroe in 1823 stating that any further European colonization or appropriation of territory in the Western Hemisphere would be regarded as an act of aggression on the United States and would prompt US retaliation.

Moret Law

The 1870 Spanish law that freed children born into slavery in Cuba and Puerto Rico, along with persons 60 years or older.

mulatto

A person of mixed African and European descent.

myalism

Ritual practices usually associated with religious movements aiming to counteract malignant sorcery in post-emancipation Jamaica.

naborías

Members of the lowest stratum of Taino society who were assigned the most difficult and dangerous chores in agriculture and war.

Navigation Acts

Mercantilist legislation passed by Britain in 1650, 1651, and 1660 that severely curtailed colonists' rights to trade with foreign nationals.

négritude

A literary-political movement of the early 20th century characterized by its insistence on racial difference and pride. Its key figures were Aimé Césaire of Martinique, Léopold Senghor of Senegal, and Léon Damas of French Guiana.

new empire

The US attempt after 1898 to turn overseas territories into formal or informal dependencies.

Nine Years' War

A conflict (1688–97) between France and a coalition of European powers, among them England, Holland, and Spain. In 1697, the Treaty of Ryswick put an end to the conflict, transferring sovereignty over the western third of Hispaniola (later the colony of Saint-Domingue, and now Haiti) to France.

nitaínos
Members of a privileged or "noble" stratum of Taino society, who were accorded special economic and ceremonial functions alongside the caciques, or chieftains.

noirisme
Haitian literary and political movement in the early 20th century that extolled the virtue of blackness and was critical of the light-skinned elite. Its key figures were Louis Diaquoi, François Duvalier, and Lorimer Denis.

obeah
A vague term designating a wide array of ritual practices, thought to be of amoral if not immoral nature, in the British Caribbean.

Pact of Zanjón
The agreement that ended Cuba's Ten Years' War for independence (1868–78).

papal bull of 1493
Papal decree, titled *Inter caetera*, which granted the Spanish crown dominion over the newly encountered lands 100 leagues west of the Azores and Cape Verde islands, under the condition that their inhabitants be converted to Catholicism.

Partido Independiente de Color
Political party, founded by black veterans of the second Cuban war of independence in Havana in 1908, that fought for equal rights and greater representation of Afro-Cubans in the Cuban government. It was legally prohibited in 1908 and brutally repressed in 1912.

petit marronage
Pattern of short-term slave flight (rather than permanent escape) from the plantation, which sometimes ended with capture and punishment or a negotiated return.

pirates
Sailors engaged in naval aggression (including contraband trade) unsanctioned by international maritime laws.

plantation
Agroindustrial type of enterprise specializing in monocultural production of tropical staples for export onto the world market that played a prominent role in the colonization of the Caribbean region.

Platt Amendment
US-sponsored amendment imposed in 1901 on Cuba's first republican constitution and ratified the following year. Among other things, it reserved the right of the United States to intervene in Cuban affairs if political order or American property were threatened.

privateers
Pirates in the service of whatever state would temporarily license their activities, principally active in the 17th and 18th centuries.

proto-peasants

Slaves, particularly in the British and French Caribbean, who developed a peasant-like existence and carved out areas of relative freedom within the institution of slavery through the practice of provision-ground agriculture.

proto-slavery

The situation of indentured servants caught in the sugar regime, who in Old World contexts would have been considered slaves.

provision grounds

Parcels of land often set aside by plantation owners where estate slaves could grow their own food for consumption or sale.

reconquest

The eight-centuries-long (711–1492) process of intermittent warfare during which Christian forces gradually displaced and drove out Muslim rule on the Iberian peninsula.

reducciones

Resettlement in planned villages of Native American groups and individuals who had survived the Spanish conquest and the destruction of their previous social and political structures.

repartimiento

In the early years of Spanish conquests, the crown's allotment of a group of Indians to a Spaniard to exploit for labor and tribute in exchange for food, clothing, and religious instruction. See also *encomienda*.

Roosevelt Corollary

An addition to the Monroe Doctrine, articulated in 1904 by President Theodore Roosevelt, establishing the US right to intervene anywhere in the Western Hemisphere to stabilize political and financial crises that could lead to intervention by foreign nations.

seasoning

The period during which newly arrived enslaved Africans were supposed to adjust to slavery and the plantation regime.

Seven Years' War

A 1756–63 conflict between world powers that extended from India to Europe and the Americas. Considered by some historians to be the first world war, it was fought across the globe by all the major European powers. The Treaty of Paris of 1763, which ended the conflict, dealt a major blow to France and its allies, including Spain, while Great Britain and its allies (Prussia in particular) came out victorious.

South Atlantic System

"A complex economic organism centered on the production in the Americas of tropical commodities for consumption in Europe and grown by the labor of Africans." Term coined in 1955 by the historian Philip Curtin.

Spanish-American War

A war fought between the United States and Spain in 1898, in which the former was an easy victor. In the aftermath, the United States gained possession of Puerto Rico, the Philippines, and other territories in the Pacific and enhanced its influence on an eventual Cuban republic. Also known as the *Spanish-Filipino-Cuban-American War*.

Sugar Revolution
The demographic, economic, social, and political transformations brought about by the advent of large-scale sugar production on the basis of unfree labor in the middle decades of the 17th century.

Tacky's Revolt
A series of slave rebellions in Jamaica in 1760, begun by Tacky, a Coromantee slave, and inspired by obeah religious beliefs.

Tainos
Native inhabitants of the Greater Antilles.

Ten Years' War
Cuba's first war for independence, fought between 1868 and 1878.

transculturation
The multiplicity of histories, cultures, languages, religions, and worldviews constitutive of Caribbean social life. The term, coined by Fernando Ortiz, expresses the various phases of the transition from one culture to another.

trapiche
An animal-powered sugar mill.

Treaty of Paris of 1763
The treaty that ended the Seven Years' War.

Treaty of Paris of 1898
The treaty between the United States and Spain that ended the Spanish-American War (or, more precisely, the Spanish-Filipino-Cuban-American War).

Treaty of Ryswick
The 1697 treaty that ended the Nine Years' War.

Treaty of Tordesillas
A 1494 treaty excluding Spain from direct trade with Africa.

Treaty of Utrecht
The 1713 treaty that ended the War of Spanish Succession.

triangular trade
A pattern of trade whereby Europeans exported commercial goods to Africa for the purchase of slaves, who were then exchanged against plantation products in the Americas, which were subsequently shipped to European markets.

UNIA
The Universal Negro Improvement Association, founded in Kingston, Jamaica, in 1914 and led by Marcus Garvey. See also *Garveyism*.

unilinear kinship

Pattern of reckoning descent only along the maternal or paternal line.

vodou

Religious practices that evolved in Haiti from the fusion of various African and some Catholic elements.

War of Austrian Succession

A war fought among major European powers between 1740 and 1748 over succession to the Habsburg throne, exacerbated by economic struggles over Caribbean colonial possessions.

War of Jenkins' Ear

A war fought between Great Britain and Spain between 1739 and 1748 over commercial holdings, so named because it broke out after British captain Robert Jenkins accused Spanish forces of having severed his ear when they boarded his vessel.

War of Spanish Succession

A war fought between 1701 and 1713 (1702–13 in the Caribbean) among major European powers over control of the Spanish throne.

Williams thesis

Historian (and later Trinidadian leader) Eric Williams's economic interpretation of the importance of the slave trade and Caribbean plantation economies in the rise of European capitalism, outlined in his 1944 book *Capitalism and Slavery*.

Windward Islands

The southern islands of the Lesser Antilles.

BIBLIOGRAPHY

General Caribbean

Blackburn, Robin. 1997. *The Making of New World Slavery: From the Baroque to the Modern.* London: Verso.

Crosby, Alfred W. 1972. *The Columbian Exchange: Biological and Cultural Consequences of 1492.* Westport, CT: Greenwood Publishing Co.

Curtin, Philip. 1990. *The Rise and Fall of the Plantation Complex.* New York: Cambridge University Press.

Deerr, Noël. 1949–50. *The History of Sugar.* 2 vols. London: Chapman and Hall.

Eltis, David. 2000. *The Rise of African Slavery in the Americas.* New York: Cambridge University Press.

Eltis, David, David Richardson, Stephen D. Behrendt, and Herbert S. Klein. 1999. *The Trans-Atlantic Slave Trade: A Database on CD-ROM.* Cambridge: Cambridge University Press.

Hanke, Lewis. 1949. *The Spanish Struggle for Justice in the Conquest of America.* Philadelphia: University of Pennsylvania Press.

Henry, Paget, and Paul Buhle, eds. 1992. *C. L. R. James's Caribbean.* Durham, NC: Duke University Press.

James, C. L. R. 1963. *The Black Jacobins: Toussaint L'Ouverture and the San Domingo Revolution.* 2nd ed. New York: Vintage Books.

Jong, Lammert de, and Dirk Kruijt, eds. 2005. *Extended Statehood in the Caribbean: Paradoxes of Quasi-Colonialism, Local Autonomy and Extended Statehood in the USA, French, Dutch and British Caribbean.* Amsterdam: Rozenberg Publishers.

Knight, Franklin W. 1990. *The Caribbean: The Genesis of a Fragmented Nationalism*. 2nd ed. New York: Oxford University Press.

Knight, Franklin, and Colin A. Palmer, eds. 1989. *The Modern Caribbean*. Chapel Hill: University of North Carolina Press.

Lewis, Gordon K. 1983. *Main Currents in Caribbean Thought: The Historical Evolution of Caribbean Society in Its Ideological Aspects, 1492–1900*. Baltimore: Johns Hopkins University Press.

Mintz, Sidney W. 1966. "The Caribbean as a Socio-Cultural Area." *Journal of World History* 9, no. 4.

———. 1974. *Caribbean Transformations*. New York: Columbia University Press.

———. 1985. *Sweetness and Power: The Place of Sugar in Modern History*. New York: Penguin Books.

Mintz, Sidney W., and Richard Price. 1992. *The Birth of African-American Culture*. Boston: Beacon Press.

Mintz, Sidney W., and Sally Price, eds. 1985. *Caribbean Contours*. Baltimore: Johns Hopkins University Press.

Moya Pons, Frank. 2007. *History of the Caribbean: Plantations, Trade, and War in the Atlantic World*. Princeton, NJ: Markus Wiener Publishers.

Ortiz, Fernando. 1947. *Cuban Counterpoint: Tobacco and Sugar*. New York: Alfred A. Knopf.

Parry, J. H. (1971) 2000. *Trade and Dominion: The European Overseas Empires in the Eighteenth Century*. London: Phoenix Press.

Parry, John H., and Robert J. Keith, eds. 1984. *New Iberian Worlds: A Documentary History of the Discovery and Settlement of Latin America to the Early Seventeenth Century*. New York: Times Books.

Price-Mars, Jean. (1928) 1983. *So Spoke the Uncle*. Translated by Magdaline W. Shannon. Washington, DC: Three Continents Press.

Stepan, Nancy Leys. 1991. *The Hour of Eugenics: Race, Gender and Nation in Latin America*. Ithaca, NY: Cornell University Press.

Trouillot, Michel-Rolph. 1992. "The Caribbean Region: An Open Frontier in Anthropological Theory." *Annual Review of Anthropology* 21:19–42.

———. 1995. *Silencing the Past: Power and the Production of History*. Boston: Beacon Press.

UNESCO. 1997–2010. *General History of the Caribbean*. 6 vols. New York: Palgrave Macmillan.

Verlinden, Charles. 1970. *The Beginnings of Modern Colonization*. Ithaca, NY: Cornell University Press.

Watts, David. 1987. *The West Indies: Patterns of Development, Culture, and Environmental Change since 1492*. Cambridge: Cambridge University Press.

Williams, Eric. 1944. *Capitalism and Slavery*. Chapel Hill: University of North Carolina Press.

———. (1970) 1984. *From Columbus to Castro: The History of the Caribbean, 1492–1969*. New York: Vintage Books.

Wilson, Peter. 1973. *Crab Antics: A Caribbean Case Study of the Conflict between Reputation and Respectability*. New Haven: Yale University Press.

Wolf, Eric R. 1982. *Europe and the People without History*. Berkeley: University of California Press.

Part 1: The Caribbean Stage

Barker, David, and Duncan F. M. McGregor, eds. 1995. *Environment and Development in the Caribbean: Geographical Perspectives*. Kingston: University of the West Indies Press.

Brierley, John S., and Haime Rubenstein, eds. 1988. *Small Farming and Peasant Resources in the Caribbean*. Manitoba Geographical Studies, no. 10. Winnipeg: University of Manitoba.

Curet, L. Antonio. 2005. *Caribbean Paleodemography: Population, Culture History, and Sociopolitical Processes in Ancient Puerto Rico*. Tuscaloosa: University of Alabama Press.

Dacal Moure, Ramón, and Manuel Rivero de la Calle. 1996. *Art and Archaeology of Pre-Columbian Cuba*. Pittsburgh: University of Pittsburgh Press.

Donovan, S. K., and T. A. Jackson, eds. 1994. *Caribbean Geology: An Introduction*. Kingston: UWIPA.

Fewkes, Jesse W. (1907) 2009. *The Aborigines of Puerto Rico and the Neighboring Islands*. Tuscaloosa: University of Alabama Press.

Galloway, J. N. 1989. *The Sugar Cane Industry: An Historical Geography from Its Origins to 1914*. Cambridge: Cambridge University Press.

Higman, Barry W. 2008. *Jamaican Food: History, Biology, Culture*. Kingston: University of the West Indies Press.

Hofman, Corinne L., Menno L. P. Hoogland, and Annelou L. van Gijn, eds. 2008. *Crossing the Borders: New Methods and Techniques in the Study of Archaeological Materials from the Caribbean*. Tuscaloosa: University of Alabama Press.

Keegan, William F. 1992. *The People Who Discovered Columbus*. Gainesville: University of Florida Press.

McGregor, Duncan F. M., David Dodman, and David Barker, eds. 2009. *Global Change and Caribbean Vulnerability: Environment, Economy and Society at Risk*. Kingston: University of the West Indies Press.

Newsom, Lee A., and Elizabeth S. Wing. 2004. *On Land and Sea: Native American Uses of Biological Resources in the West Indies*. Tuscaloosa: University of Alabama Press.

Oliver, José R. 2009. *Caciques and Cemí Idols: The Web Spun by Taino Rulers between Hispianola and Puerto Rico*. Tuscaloosa: University of Alabama Press.

Phillips, William D., Jr. 1985. *Slavery from Roman Times to the Early Transatlantic Trade*. Minneapolis: University of Minnesota Press.

Potter, Robert B., David Barker, Dennis Conway, and Thomas Klak. 2004. *The Contemporary Caribbean*. New York: Pearson/Prentice Hall.

Richardson, Bonham C. 1992. *The Caribbean in the Wider World, 1492–1992: A Regional Geography*. Cambridge: Cambridge University Press.

Rouse, Irving B. 1986. *Migrations in Prehistory: Inferring Population Movement from Cultural Remains*. New Haven: Yale University Press.

Rouse, Irving B. 1992. *The Tainos: Rise and Decline of the People Who Greeted Columbus*. New Haven: Yale University Press.

Schwartz, Stuart B., ed. 2004. *Tropical Babylons: Sugar and the Making of the Atlantic World, 1450–1680*. Chapel Hill: University of North Carolina Press.

Watson, Andrew M. 1983. *Agricultural Innovation in the Early Islamic World: The Diffusion of Crops and Farming Techniques*. Cambridge: Cambridge University Press.

Wilson, Samuel M. 2007. *The Archaeology of the Caribbean*. Cambridge: Cambridge University Press.

Part 2: The Making of a Colonial Sphere

Acosta, José de. 2002. *Natural and Moral History of the Indies*. Edited by Jane E. Mangan; translated by Frances Lopez-Morillas. Durham, NC: Duke University Press.

Andrews, Kenneth R. 1978. *The Spanish Caribbean: Trade and Plunder, 1530–1630*. New Haven: Yale University Press.

Atkinson, Lesley-Gail. 2006. *The Earliest Inhabitants: The Dynamics of the Jamaican Taino*. Kingston: University of the West Indies Press.

Boucher, Philip P. 1992. *Cannibal Encounters: Europeans and Island Caribs, 1492–1763*. Baltimore: Johns Hopkins University Press.

Campbell, Mavis C. 1988. *The Maroons of Jamaica, 1655–1796: A History of Resistance, Collaboration, and Betrayal.* Granby, MA: Bergin & Garvey.

Carney, Judith A. 2001. "African Rice in the Columbian Exchange." *Journal of African History* 42, no. 3: 337–96.

Cook, Noble David. 2002. "Sickness, Starvation, and Death in Early Hispaniola." *Journal of Interdisciplinary History* 32, no. 3: 349–86.

Crosby, Alfred W. 1986. *Ecological Imperialism: The Biological Expansion of Europe, 900–1900.* Cambridge: Cambridge University Press.

Curtin, Philip D. 1969. *The Atlantic Slave Trade: A Census.* Madison: University of Wisconsin Press.

Davis, Ralph. 1973. *The Rise of the Atlantic Economies.* Ithaca, NY: Cornell University Press.

Diouf, Sylviane A., ed. 2003. *Fighting the Slave Trade: West African Strategies.* Athens, OH: Ohio University Press.

Elliot, John H. 1970. *The Old World and the New, 1492–1650.* Cambridge: Cambridge University Press.

Fernández de Oviedo y Valdés, Gonzalo. 1959. *Natural History of the West Indies.* Translated by Sterling Aubrey Stoudemire. Chapel Hill: University of North Carolina Press.

Forte, Maximillan, ed. 2006. *Indigenous Resurgence in the Contemporary Caribbean: Amerindian Survival and Revival.* New York: Peter Lang.

Funes Monzote, Reinaldo. 2008. *From Rainforest to Cane Field in Cuba: An Environmental History Since 1492.* Chapel Hill: University of North Carolina Press.

Guitar, Lynne A. 1999. "Willing It So: Intimate Glimpses of 'Encomienda' Life in Early Sixteenth-Century Hispaniola." *Colonial Latin American Historical Review* 7, no. 3: 244–63.

Hanke, Lewis. 1935. *The First Social Experiments in America: A Study in the Development of Spanish Indian Policy in the Sixteenth Century.* Cambridge, MA: Harvard University Press.

Haring, Clarence Henry. 1910. *The Buccaneers in the West Indies in the XVII Century.* London: Methuen.

Heuman, Gad J., ed. 1986. *Out of the House of Bondage: Runaways, Resistance, and Marronage in Africa and the New World.* London: Cass.

Hulme, Peter. 1986. *Colonial Encounters: Europe and the Native Caribbean.* London: Methuen.

Keegan, William F. 2007. *Taino Indian Myth and Practice.* Gainesville: University Press of Florida.

Lane, Kris E. 1998. *Pillaging the Empire: Piracy in the Americas, 1500–1750.* Armonk: M. E. Sharpe.

La Rosa Corzo, Gabino. 2003. *Runaway Slave Settlements in Cuba: Resistance and Repression.* Translated by Mary Todd. Chapel Hill: University of North Carolina Press.

Las Casas, Bartolomé de. 1971. *History of the Indies.* Translated by Andrée Collard. New York: Harper & Row.

Linebaugh, Peter, and Marcus Rediker. 2000. *The Many-Headed Hydra: Sailors, Slaves, Commoners, and the Hidden History of the Revolutionary Atlantic.* Boston: Beacon Press.

McNeill, John. 2008. *Epidemics and Geopolitics in the American Tropics, 1640–1920.* New York: Cambridge University Press.

Pané, Fray Ramón. 2000. *An Account of the Antiquities of the Indians.* Edited by José Juan Arrom; translated by Susan Griswold. Durham, NC: Duke University Press.

Pennell, C. R., ed. 2001. *Bandits at Sea: A Pirates Reader.* New York: New York University Press.

Perez-Mallaína, Pablo E. 1998. *Spain's Men of the Sea: Daily Life on the Indies Fleets in the Sixteenth Century.* Baltimore: Johns Hopkins University Press.

Pike, Ruth. 2007. "Black Rebels: The Cimarrons of Sixteenth-Century Panama." *The Americas* 64, no. 2 (October): 243–66.

Price, Richard, ed. 1996. *Maroon Societies: Rebel Slave Communities in the Americas.* 3rd ed. Baltimore: Johns Hopkins University Press.

Rediker, Marcus. 2004. *Villains of All Nations: Atlantic Pirates in the Golden Age.* Boston: Beacon Press.

Reid, Basil A. 2009. *Myths and Realities of Caribbean History.* Tuscaloosa: University of Alabama Press.

Sauer, Carl O. 1966. *The Early Spanish Main.* Berkeley: University of California Press.

Seed, Patricia. 1995. *Ceremonies of Possession in Europe's Conquest of the New World, 1492–1640.* New York: Cambridge University Press.

Siegel, Peter E., ed. 2005. *Ancient Borinquen: Archaeology and Ethnohistory of Native Puerto Rico.* Tuscaloosa: University of Alabama Press.

Stevens-Arroyo, Antonio M. 2006. *Cave of the Jagua: The Mythological World of the Tainos.* 2nd ed. Scranton, PA: University of Scranton Press.

Sued-Badillo, Jalil. 1995. "The Theme of the Indigenous in the National Projects of the Hispanic Caribbean." In *Making Alternative Histories: The Practice of Archaeology and History in a Non-Western Setting,* edited by Peter Schmidt and Tom Patterson. Santa Fe: School of American Research Press.

Sued-Badillo, Jalil. 2001. *El Dorado borincano: La economía de la Conquista, 1510–1550.* San Juan: Ediciones Puerto.

Thornton, John. 1998. *Africa and Africans in the Making of the Atlantic World, 1400–1800.* 2nd ed. New York: Cambridge University Press.

Van Lier, Rudolf Asveer Jacob. 1971. *Frontier Society: A Social Analysis of the History of Surinam.* The Hague: Martinus Nijhoof.

Whitehead, Neil L., ed. 1995. *Wolves from the Sea: Readings in the Anthropology of the Native Caribbean.* Leiden: KITLV Press.

Wilson, Samuel M. 1990. *Hispaniola: Caribbean Chiefdoms in the Age of Columbus.* Tuscaloosa: University of Oklahoma Press.

Part 3: Colonial Designs in Flux

Beckles, Hilary McD. 1989. *White Servitude and Black Slavery in Barbados, 1627–1715.* Knoxville: University of Tennessee Press.

———. 1998. "'The Hub of Empire': The Caribbean and Britain in the Seventeenth Century." In Nicholas Canny, ed., *The Oxford History of the British Empire.* New York: Oxford University Press.

Boucher, Philip P. 2008. *France and the American Tropics to 1700: Tropics of Discontent?* Baltimore: Johns Hopkins University Press.

Carrington, Selwyn H. H. 2002. *The Sugar Industry and the Abolition of the Slave Trade, 1750–1810.* Gainesville: University of Florida Press.

De la Fuente, Alejandro, with César García del Pino and Bernardo Iglesias Delgado. 2009. *Havana and the Atlantic in the Sixteenth Century.* Chapel Hill: University of North Carolina Press.

Dunn, Richard S. 1972. *Sugar and Slaves: The Rise of the Planter Class in the English West Indies, 1624–1713.* Chapel Hill: University of North Carolina Press.

Egerton, Douglas R., Alison Games, Kris Lane, and Donald R. Wright. 2007. *The Atlantic World: A History, 1400–1888.* Wheeling, IL: Harlan Davidson, Inc.

Games, Alison. 1999. *Migration and the Origins of the English Atlantic World.* Cambridge, MA: Harvard University Press.

Garrigus, John. 2006. *Before Haiti: Race and Citizenship in French Saint-Domingue.* New York: Palgrave Macmillan.

Goslinga, Cornelis Ch. 1971. *The Dutch in the Caribbean and on the Wild Coast, 1580–1680.* Gainesville: University of Florida Press.

———. 1985. *The Dutch in the Caribbean and the Guianas, 1680–1791.* Assen/Maastricht: Van Gorcum.

Higman, Barry W. 2000. "The Sugar Revolution." *Economic History Review,* 2nd series, 53: 213–38.

Klein, Herbert S. 1986. *African Slavery in Latin America and the Caribbean.* Oxford: Oxford University Press.

Klooster, Wim. 1997. *The Dutch in the Americas, 1600–1800.* Providence, RI: John Carter Brown Library.

Norton, Marcy. 2008. *Sacred Gifts, Profane Pleasures: A History of Tobacco and Chocolate in the Atlantic World.* Ithaca, NY: Cornell University Press.

Paquette, Robert L., and Stanley L. Engerman, eds. 1996. *The Lesser Antilles in the Age of European Expansion.* Gainesville: University Press of Florida.

Phillips, Carla Rahn. 1986. *Six Galleons for the King of Spain: Imperial Defense in the Early Seventeenth Century.* Baltimore: Johns Hopkins University Press.

Postma, Johannes Menne. 1990. *The Dutch in the Atlantic Slave Trade, 1600–1815.* Cambridge: Cambridge University Press.

Pritchard, James. 2004. *In Search of Empire: The French in the Americas, 1670–1730.* New York: Cambridge University Press.

Sheridan, Richard. 1974. *Sugar and Slavery: An Economic History of the British West Indies, 1623–1775.* Kingston: University of the West Indies Press.

Stein, Robert Louis. 1979. *The French Slave Trade in the Eighteenth Century: An Old Regime Business.* Madison: University of Wisconsin Press.

Tomich, Dale. 1990. *Slavery in the Circuit of Sugar: Martinique in the World Economy, 1830–1848.* Baltimore: Johns Hopkins University Press.

Part 4: Capitalism, Slavery, and Revolution

Besson, Jean. 1992. "Freedom and Community: The British West Indies." In *The Meaning of Freedom: Economics, Politics, and Culture after Slavery,* edited by Frank McGlynn and Seymour Drescher, 183–219. Pittsburgh: University of Pittsburgh Press.

———. 2002. *Martha Brae's Two Histories: European Expansion and Caribbean Culture-Building in Jamaica.* Chapel Hill: University of North Carolina Press.

Blackburn, Robin. 1988. *The Overthrow of Colonial Slavery, 1776–1848.* London: Verso.

Burnard, Trevor. 2004. *Mastery, Tyranny, and Desire: Thomas Thistlewood and His Slaves in the Anglo-Jamaican World.* Chapel Hill: University of North Carolina Press.

Bush, Barbara. 1989. *Slave Women in Caribbean Society, 1650–1832.* Bloomington: Indiana University Press.

Childs, Matt. 2006. *The 1812 Aponte Rebellion in Cuba and the Struggle against Atlantic Slavery.* Chapel Hill: University of North Carolina Press.

Craton, Michael J. 1982. *Testing the Chains: Resistance to Slavery in the British West Indies.* Ithaca, NY: Cornell University Press.

Curtin, Philip. 1970. *Two Jamaicas: The Role of Ideas in a Tropical Colony 1830–1865.* New York: Atheneum.

Davis, David Brion. 1975. *The Problem of Slavery in the Age of Revolution, 1770–1823.* Ithaca, NY: Cornell University Press.

Drescher, Seymour M. 1977. *Econocide: British Slavery in the Era of Abolition.* Pittsburgh: University of Pittsburgh Press.

Dubois, Laurent. 2004. *A Colony of Citizens: Revolution and Slave Emancipation in the French Caribbean, 1787–1804.* Chapel Hill: University of North Carolina Press.

———. 2004. *Avengers of the New World: The Story of the Haitian Revolution*. Cambridge, MA: Harvard University Press.

Elliot, John H. 2006. *Empires of the Atlantic World: Britain and Spain in America, 1492–1830*. New Haven: Yale University Press.

Fick, Carolyn. 1990. *The Making of Haïti: The Saint-Domingue Revolution from Below*. Knoxville: University of Tennessee Press.

Gaspar, David Barry. 1985. *Bondmen and Rebels: A Study of Master-Slave Relations in Antigua, with Implications for Colonial British America*. Baltimore: Johns Hopkins University Press.

Geggus, David. 2002. *Haitian Revolutionary Studies*. Bloomington: Indiana University Press.

Goveia, Elsa V. 1965. *Slave Society in the British Leeward Islands at the End of the Eighteenth Century*. New Haven: Yale University Press.

Hall, Catherine. 2002. *Civilising Subjects: Metropole and Colony in the English Imagination, 1830–1867*. Cambridge: Polity Press.

Hall, Neville A. T. 1992. *Slave Society in the Danish West Indies: St. Thomas, St. John and St. Croix*. Edited by Barry W. Higman. Kingston: University of the West Indies Press.

Hamilton, Douglas J. 2005. *Scotland, the Caribbean, and the Atlantic World, 1750–1820*. Manchester, UK: Manchester University Press.

Higman, Barry W. 1976. *Slave Population and Economy in Jamaica, 1807–1834*. Cambridge: Cambridge University Press.

———. 1984. *Slave Populations of the British Caribbean, 1807–1834*. Baltimore: The Johns Hopkins University Press.

Holt, Thomas C. 1992. *The Problem of Freedom: Race, Labor, and Politics in Jamaica and Britain, 1832–1938*. Baltimore: Johns Hopkins University Press.

Jennings, Lawrence C. 2000. *French Antislavery: The Movement for the Abolition of Slavery in France, 1802–1848*. Cambridge: Cambridge University Press.

Knight, Franklin W. 1969. *Slave Society in Cuba during the Nineteenth Century*. Madison: University of Wisconsin Press.

Kuethe, Allan J. 1986. *Cuba, 1753–1815: Crown, Military, and Society*. Knoxville: University of Tennessee Press.

Lambert, David. 2005. *White Creole Culture, Politics and Identity during the Age of Abolition*. Cambridge: Cambridge University Press.

McNeill, John Robert. 1985. *Atlantic Empires of France and Spain: Louisbourg and Havana, 1700–1763*. Chapel Hill: University of North Carolina Press.

Moitt, Bernard. 2001. *Women and Slavery in the French Antilles, 1635–1848*. Bloomington: Indiana University Press.

Olwig, Karen Fog. 1985. *Cultural Adaptation and Resistance on St John: Three Centuries of Afro-Caribbean Life*. Gainesville: University of Florida Press.

Oostindie, Gert, ed. 1995. *Fifty Years Later: Antislavery, Capitalism, and Modernity in the Dutch Orbit*. Leiden: KITLV Press.

O'Shaughnessy, Andrew J. 2000. *An Empire Divided: The American Revolution and the British Caribbean*. Philadelphia: University of Pennsylvania Press.

Palmié, Stephan, ed. 1995. *Slave Cultures and the Cultures of Slavery*. Knoxville: University of Tennessee Press.

Paquette, Robert L. 1988. *Sugar Is Made with Blood: The Conspiracy of La Escalera and the Conflict between Empires over Slavery in Cuba*. Middletown, CT: Wesleyan University Press.

Pares, Richard. (1936) 1963. *War and Trade in the West Indies, 1739–63*. London: Frank Cass.

Paton, Diana. 2004. *No Bond but the Law: Punishment, Race, and Gender in Jamaican State Formation, 1780–1870*. Durham, NC: Duke University Press.

Petley, Christer. 2009. *Slaveholders in Jamaica: Colonial Society and Culture during the Era of Aboli-tion*. London: Pickering & Chatto.

Price, Richard. 1990. *Alabi's World*. Baltimore: Johns Hopkins University Press.

Schloss, Rebecca Hartkopf. 2009. *Sweet Liberty: The Final Days of Slavery in Martinique*. Phila-delphia: University of Pennsylvania Press.

Schuler, Monica. 1980. *"Alas, Alas, Kongo": A Social History of Indentured African Immigration into Jamaica, 1841–1865*. Baltimore: Johns Hopkins University Press.

Solow, Barbara L., and Stanley L. Engerman, eds. 1987. *British Capitalism and Caribbean Slavery: The Legacy of Eric Williams*. Cambridge: Cambridge University Press.

Stinchcombe, Arthur L. 1995. *Sugar Island Slavery in the Age of Enlightenment: The Political Economy of the Caribbean World*. Princeton, NJ: Princeton University Press.

Turner, Mary. 1982. *Slaves and Missionaries: The Disintegration of Jamaican Slave Society, 1787–1834*. Urbana: University of Illinois Press.

Viotti da Costa, Emilia. 1994. *Crowns of Glory, Tears of Blood: The Demerara Slave Rebellion of 1823*. New York: Oxford University Press.

Part 5: A Reordered World

Andrews, George Reid. 2004. *Afro-Latin America, 1800–2000*. New York: Oxford University Press.

Baralt, Guillermo A. 2007. *Slave Revolts in Puerto Rico*. Princeton, NJ: Markus Wiener Publishers.

Bergad, Laird. 1990. *Cuban Rural Society in the Nineteenth Century: The Social and Economic His-tory of Monoculture in Matanzas*. Princeton, NJ: Princeton University Press.

Berlin, Ira, and Philip Morgan, eds. 1991. *The Slaves' Economy: Independent Production by Slaves in the Americas*. London: Frank Cass.

Brathwaite, Edward Kamau. 1971. *The Development of Creole Society in Jamaica, 1770–1820*. Oxford: Clarendon Press.

Brereton, Bridget, and Kelvin Yelvington, eds. 1999. *The Colonial Caribbean in Transition: Essays on Postemancipation Social and Cultural History*. Gainesville: University Press of Florida.

Bronfman, Alejandra. 2004. *Measures of Equality: Social Science, Citizenship, and Race in Cuba*. Chapel Hill: University of North Carolina Press.

Browne, Katherine. 2007. *Creole Economics: Caribbean Cunning under the French Flag*. Austin: University of Texas Press.

Candelario, Ginetta E. B. 2007. *Black behind the Ears: Dominican Racial Identity from Museums to Beauty Shops*. Durham, NC: Duke University Press

Casanovas, Joan. 1998. *Bread or Bullets: Urban Labor and Spanish Colonialism in Cuba, 1850–1898*. Pittsburgh: University of Pittsburgh Press.

Cooper, Frederick, Thomas C. Holt, and Rebecca J. Scott. 2000. *Beyond Slavery: Explorations of Race, Labor, and Citizenship in Post-Emancipation Societies*. Chapel Hill: University of North Carolina Press.

The Cuba Commission Report: A Hidden History of the Chinese in Cuba. 1993. Baltimore: Johns Hopkins University Press.

De La Fuente, Alejandro. 2000. *A Nation for All: Race Inequality and Politics in Twentieth-Century Cuba*. Chapel Hill: University of North Carolina Press.

Dorsey, Joseph. 2003. *Slave Traffic in the Age of Abolition: Puerto Rico, West Africa, and the Non-Hispanic Caribbean, 1815–1859*. Gainesville: University Press of Florida.

Ferrer, Ada. 1999. *Insurgent Cuba: Race, Nation, and Revolution, 1868–1898*. Chapel Hill: Univer-sity of North Carolina Press.

Fradera, Josep Maria. 2005. *Colonias para después de un imperio*. Barcelona: Edicions Bellaterra.

Freeman, Carla. 2000. *High Tech and High Heels in the Global Economy: Women, Work, and Pink-Collar Identities in the Caribbean*. Durham, NC: Duke University Press.

Glissant, Edouard. 1989. *Caribbean Discourse*. Charlottesville: University Press of Virginia.

Helg, Aline. 1995. *Our Rightful Share: The Afro-Cuban Struggle for Equality, 1886–1912*. Chapel Hill: University of North Carolina Press.

Heuman, Gad. 1994. *The Killing Time: The Morant Bay Rebellion in Jamaica*. London: Macmillan.

Hill, Robert A., and Marcus Garvey. 1983–. *The Marcus Garvey and Universal Negro Improvement Association Papers*. 10 vols. (ongoing) Berkeley: University of California Press.

James, Winston. 1999. *Holding Aloft the Banner of Ethiopia: Caribbean Radicalism in Early Twentieth-Century America*. London: Verso.

Kirk, John M. 1983. *José Martí: Mentor of the Cuban Nation*. Tampa: University Press of Florida.

LaFeber, Walter. 1963. *The New Empire: An Interpretation of American Expansion, 1860–1898*. Ithaca, NY: Cornell University Press.

Look Lai, Walton. 1993. *Indentured Labor, Caribbean Sugar: Chinese and Indian Migrants to the British West Indies, 1838–1918*. Baltimore: Johns Hopkins University Press.

Martínez-Fernández, Luis. 1994. *Torn between Empires: Economy, Society and Patterns of Political Thought in the Hispanic Caribbean, 1840–1878*. Athens, GA: University of Georgia Press.

Matibag, Eugenio. 2003. *Haitian-Dominican Counterpoint: Nation, State, and Race in Hispaniola*. London: Palgrave Macmillan.

Mohammed, Patricia. 2002. *Gendered Realities: Essays in Caribbean Feminist Thought*. Kingston: University of the West Indies Press.

Moore, Robin Dale. 1997. *Nationalizing Blackness*. Pittsburgh: University of Pittsburgh Press.

Moya Pons, Frank. 1998. *The Dominican Republic: A National History*. Princeton, NJ: Markus Wiener Publishers.

Nicholls, David. 1980. *Arabs of the Greater Antilles*. New York: Research Institute for the Study of Man.

Palmié, Stephan. 2002. *Wizards and Scientists: Explorations in Afro-Cuban Modernity and Tradition*. Durham, NC: Duke University Press.

Pérez, Louis A. Jr. 1982. *Cuba between Empires, 1878–1902*. Pittsburgh: University of Pittsburgh Press.

———. 1986. *Cuba under the Platt Amendment, 1902–1934*. Pittsburgh: University of Pittsburgh Press.

———. 1999. *On Becoming Cuban: Identity, Nationality, and Culture*. Chapel Hill: University of North Carolina Press.

Price, Richard. 2006. *The Convict and the Colonel: A Story of Colonialism and Resistance in the Caribbean*. Durham, NC: Duke University Press.

Putnam, Lara. 2002. *The Company They Kept: Migrants and the Politics of Gender in Caribbean Costa Rica, 1870–1960*. Chapel Hill, NC: University of North Carolina Press.

Rodney, Walter. 1981. *A History of the Guyanese Working People, 1881–1905*. Baltimore: Johns Hopkins University Press.

Scarano, Francisco A. 1984. *Sugar and Slavery in Puerto Rico: The Plantation Economy of Ponce, 1800–1850*. Madison: University of Wisconsin Press.

———. 1996. "The *Jíbaro* Masquerade and the Subaltern Politics of Creole Identity Formation in Puerto Rico, 1745–1823." *American Historical Review* 96:1398–431.

Schmidt-Nowara, Christopher. 1999. *Empire and Antislavery: Spain, Cuba, and Puerto Rico, 1833–1874*. Pittsburgh: University of Pittsburgh Press.

Scott, Rebecca J. 1985. *Slave Emancipation in Cuba: The Transition to Free Labor, 1860–1899*. Princeton, NJ: Princeton University Press.

———. 2005. *Degrees of Freedom: Louisiana and Cuba after Slavery.* Cambridge, MA: Harvard University Press.

Singh, Kelvin. 1988. *Bloodstained Tombs: The Muharram Massacre, 1884.* London: Macmillan Caribbean.

Smith, Angel, and Emma Dávila-Cox, eds. 1999. *The Crisis of 1898: Colonial Redistribution and Nationalist Mobilization.* New York: St. Martin's.

Stolcke, Verena. 1974. *Marriage, Class, and Colour in Nineteenth-Century Cuba: A Study of Racial Attitudes and Sexual Values in a Slave Society.* New York: Cambridge University Press.

Thompson, Krista A. 2006. *An Eye for the Tropics: Tourism, Photography, and Framing the Caribbean Picturesque.* Durham, NC: Duke University Press.

Tone, John Lawrence. 2006. *War and Genocide in Cuba, 1895–1898.* Chapel Hill: University of North Carolina Press.

Veeser, Cyrus. 2002. *A World Safe for Capitalism: Dollar Diplomacy and America's Rise to Global Power.* New York: Columbia University Press.

Part 6: The New Empire

Allahar, Anton, ed. 2001. *Caribbean Charisma: Reflections on Leadership, Legitimacy, and Populist Politics.* Boulder, CO: Lynne Rienner.

Anderson, Robert. 1965. *Party Politics in Puerto Rico.* Stanford, CA: Stanford University Press.

Ayala, César J. 1999. *American Sugar Kingdom: The Plantation Economy of the Spanish Caribbean, 1898–1934.* Chapel Hill: University of North Carolina Press.

Ayala, Cesar, and Rafael Bernabe. 2007. *Puerto Rico in the American Century: A History since 1898.* Chapel Hill: University of North Carolina Press.

Baptiste, F. A. 1988. *War, Cooperation, and Conflict: The European Possessions in the Caribbean, 1939–1945.* Westport, CT: Greenwood Press.

Bolland, O. Nigel. 2001. *The Politics of Labour in the British Caribbean: The Social Origins of Authoritarianism and Democracy in the Labour Movement.* Kingston: Ian Randle.

Calder, Bruce J. 1984. *The Impact of Intervention: The Dominican Republic during the U.S. Occupation of 1916.* Austin: University of Texas Press.

Chomsky, Aviva. 1995. *West Indian Workers and the United Fruit Company of Costa Rica, 1870–1940.* Baton Rouge: Louisiana State University Press.

Conniff, Michael L. 1985. *Black Labor on a White Canal: Panama, 1904–1981.* Pittsburgh: University of Pittsburgh Press.

Cross, Malcolm, and Gad Heuman, eds. 1988. *Labour in the Caribbean: From Emancipation to Independence.* London: Macmillan.

Dash, J. Michael. 1981. *Literature and Ideology in Haiti, 1915–1961.* Totowa, NJ: Barnes & Noble.

De la Fuente, Alejandro. 2008. "The New Afro-Cuban Cultural Movement and the Debate on Race in Contemporary Cuba." *Journal of Latin American Studies* 40:697–720.

Derby, Lauren. 2009. *The Dictator's Seduction: Politics and the Popular Imagination in the Era of Trujillo.* Durham, NC: Duke University Press.

Dietz, James L. 1986. *Economic History of Puerto Rico: Institutional Change and Capitalist Development.* Princeton, NJ: Princeton University Press.

Eaton, George E. 1975. *Alexander Bustamante and Modern Jamaica.* Kingston: Kingston Publishers.

Edmondson, Belinda, ed. 1999. *Caribbean Romances: The Politics of Regional Representation.* Charlottesville, VA: University Press of Virginia.

García Muñiz, Humberto, and Jorge Rodríguez Beruff. 1994. "U.S. Military Policy Toward the Caribbean in the 1990s." *Annals of the American Academy of Political and Social Science* 533:112–24.

Hart, Richard. 1999. *Towards Decolonization: Political, Labour, and Economic Development in Jamaica, 1938–1945.* Mona, Jamiaca: Canoe Press.

———. 2004. *Time for a Change: Constitutional, Political, and Labour Developments in Jamaica and Other Colonies in the Caribbean Region, 1944–1955.* Kingston: Arawak Publications.

Hintzen, Percy. 1989. *The Costs of Regime Survival: Racial Mobilization, Elite Domination, and Control of the State in Guyana and Trinidad.* Cambridge: Cambridge University Press.

Ibarra, Jorge. 1998. *Prologue to Revolution: Cuba, 1898–1958.* Boulder, CO: Lynne Rienner.

Jennings, Eric T. 2001. *Vichy in the Tropics: Pétain's National Revolution in Madagascar, Guadeloupe, and Indochina, 1940–1944.* Stanford, CA: Stanford University Press.

Khan, Aisha. 2004. *Callaloo Nation: Metaphors of Race and Religious Identity among South Asians in Trinidad.* Durham, NC: Duke University Press.

Macpherson, Anne S. 2007. *From Colony to Nation: Women Activists and the Gendering of Politics in Belize, 1912–1982.* Lincoln: University of Nebraska Press.

Mars, Perry. 1998. *Ideology and Change: The Transformation of the Caribbean Left.* Detroit: Wayne State University Press.

Meléndez, Edwin, and Edgardo Meléndez, eds. 1993. *Colonial Dilemma: Critical Perspectives on Contemporary Puerto Rico.* Boston: South End.

Nicholls, David. 1996. *From Dessalines to Duvalier: Race, Colour, and National Independence in Haiti.* New Brunswick, NJ: Rutgers University Press.

Oostindie, Gert, and Inge Klinkers. 2003. *Decolonizing the Caribbean: Dutch Politics in a Comparative Perspective.* Amsterdam: Amsterdam University Press.

Pérez, Louis A. Jr. 2003. *Cuba and the United States: Ties of Singular Intimacy,* 3rd ed. Athens: University of Georgia Press.

Plant, Roger. 1987. *Sugar and Modern Slavery: A Tale of Two Countries.* London: Zed Books.

Plummer, Brenda Gayle. 1988. *Haiti and the Great Powers, 1902–1915.* Baton Rouge: Louisiana State University Press.

Post, Ken. 1978. *Arise Ye Starvelings: The Jamaican Labour Rebellion of 1938 and Its Aftermath.* The Hague: Martinus Nijhoff.

Post, Ken. 1981. *Strike the Iron: A Colony at War: Jamaica, 1939–1945.* Atlantic Islands, NJ: Humanities Press.

Price, Richard. 2008. *Travels with Tooy: History, Memory, and the African American Imagination.* Chicago: University of Chicago Press.

Quintero Rivera, Angel. 1976. *Workers' Struggle in Puerto Rico: A Documentary History.* New York: Monthly Review Press.

Reddock, Rhoda E. 1994. *Women, Labour, and Politics in Trinidad and Tobago: A History.* London: Zed Books.

Renda, Mary. 2001. *Taking Haiti: Military Occupation and the Culture of U.S. Imperialism.* Chapel Hill: University of North Carolina Press.

Richardson, Bonham. 1983. *Caribbean Migrants: Environment and Human Survival on St. Kitts and Nevis.* Knoxville: University of Tennessee Press.

Romberg, Raquel. 2003. *Witchcraft and Welfare: Spiritual Capital and the Business of Magic in Modern Puerto Rico.* Austin: University of Texas Press.

Roorda, Eric Paul. 1998. *The Dictator Next Door.* Durham, NC: Duke University Press.

Routon, Kenneth. 2010. *Hidden Powers of State in the Cuban Imagination.* Gainesville: University Press of Florida.

Schmidt, Hans. 1971. *The United States Occupation of Haiti, 1915–1934.* New Brunswick, NJ: Rutgers University Press.

Singh, Kelvin. 1994. *Race and Class Struggles in a Colonial State: Trinidad, 1917–1945.* Calgary: University of Calgary Press.

Thoden van Velzen, and Wilhelmina van Wetering. 2004. *In the Shadow of the Oracle: Religion as Politics in a Surinamese Maroon Society.* Long Grove, IL: Waveland Press.

Thomas, Deborah. 2004. *Modern Blackness: Nationalism, Globalization, and the Politics of Culture in Jamaica.* Durham, NC: Duke University Press.

Trouillot, Michel-Rolph. 1990. *Haiti: State against Nation—The Origins and Legacy of Duvalierism.* New York: Monthly Review Press.

Turits, Richard L. 2003. *Foundations of Despotism: Peasants, the Trujillo Regime, and Modernity in Dominican History.* Stanford, CA: Stanford University Press.

Whitney, Robert. 2001. *State and Revolution in Cuba: Mass Mobilization and Political Change, 1920–1940.* Chapel Hill: University of North Carolina Press.

Williams, Brackette. 1991. Stains on My Name, War in My Veins: Guyana and the Politics of Cultural Struggle. Durham: Duke University Press.

Wirtz, Kristina. 2007. *Ritual, Discourse, and Community in Cuban Santería: Speaking a Sacred World.* Gainesville: University Press of Florida.

Zanetti, Oscar, and Alejandro García. 1998. *Sugar and Railroads: A Cuban History, 1837–1959.* Chapel Hill: University of North Carolina Press.

Part 7: The Caribbean in the Age of Globalization

Acosta-Belén, Edna, and Carlos E. Santiago. 2006. *Puerto Ricans in the United States : A Contemporary Portrait.* Boulder, CO: Lynne Rienner.

Beriss, David. 2004. *Black Skins, French Voices: Caribbean Ethnicity and Activism in Urban France.* Boulder, CO: Westview.

Brana-Shute, Gary, ed. 1990. *Resistance and Rebellion in Suriname: Old and New.* Williamsburg, VA: Studies in Third World Societies, No. 43.

Burton, Richard, and Fred Reno, eds. 1995. *French and West Indian: Martinique, Guadeloupe, and French Guiana Today.* London: Macmillan Caribbean.

Byron, Margaret, and Stéphanie Condon. 2008. *Migration in Comparative Perspective: Caribbean Communities in Britain and France.* New York: Routledge.

Clegg, Peter, and Emilio Pantojas-García, eds. 2009. *Governance in the Non- Independent Caribbean: Challenges and Opposition.* Kingston: Ian Randle Publishers.

Collier, Michael W. 2005. *Political Corruption in the Caribbean Basin.* New York: Routledge.

Cross, Malcolm, and Han Entzinger, eds. 1988. *Lost Illusions: Caribbean Minorities in Britain and the Netherlands.* London: Routledge.

Dew, Edward. 1978. *The Difficult Flowering of Surinam.* The Hague: Martinus Nÿhoff.

Du Bois, Christine M. 2004. *Images of West Indian Immigrants in Mass Media: The Struggle for a Positive Ethnic Reputation.* New York: LFB Scholarly.

Dupuy, Alex. 1989. *Haiti in the World Economy: Class, Race, and Underdevelopment since 1700.* Boulder, CO: Westview Press.

———. 2007. *The Prophet and Power: Jean-Bertrand Aristide, the International Community, and Haiti.* Lanham, MD: Rowman & Littlefield Publishers.

Farmer, Paul. 2003. *The Uses of Haiti.* 2nd ed. Monroe, ME: Common Courage Press.

Gleijeses, Piero. 1978. *The Dominican Crisis: The 1965 Constitutionalist Revolt and American Intervention.* Baltimore: Johns Hopkins University Press.

Gmelch, George. 1992. *Double Passage: The Lives of Caribbean Migrants Abroad and Back Home.* Ann Arbor: University of Michigan Press.

Griffith, Ivelaw L., ed. 2000. *The Political Economy of Drugs in the Caribbean*. Houndsmills, UK: Macmillan Press.

———. 2004. *Caribbean Security in the Age of Terror*. Kingston: Ian Randle.

Hall, Kenneth, and Denis Benn, eds. 2000. *Contending with Destiny: The Caribbean in the 21st Century*. Kingston: Ian Randle Publishers.

Hartlyn, Jonathan. 1998. *The Struggle for Democratic Politics in the Dominican Republic*. Chapel Hill: University of North Carolina Press.

Hillebrink, Steven. 2008. *The Right to Self-Determination and Post-Colonial Governance: The Case of Netherlands Antilles and Aruba*. The Hague: T.M.C. Press.

Hillman, Richard S., and Thomas J. D'Agostino, eds. 2009. *Understanding the Contemporary Caribbean*. 2nd ed. Boulder, CO: Lynne Rienner.

Holt, Thomas C. 2000. *The Problem of Race in the 21st Century*. Cambridge, MA: Harvard University Press.

Johnson, Paul C. 2007. *Diaspora Conversions: Black Carib Religion and the Recovery of Africa*. Berkeley: University of California Press.

Kasinitz, Philip. 1992. *Caribbean New York: Black Immigrants and the Politics of Race*. Ithaca, NY: Cornell University Press.

Klak, Thomas, ed. 1998. *Globalization and Neoliberalism: The Caribbean Context*. Lanham, MD: Rowman & Littlefield.

Maingot, Anthony P. 1994. *The United States and the Caribbean: Challenges of an Asymmetrical Relationship*. Boulder, CO: Westview Press.

Martínez, Samuel. 1995. *Peripheral Migrants: Haitians and Dominican Republic Sugar Plantations*. Knoxville: University of Tennessee Press.

McAlister, Elizabeth. 2002. *Rara! Vodou, Power, and Performance in Haiti and Its Diaspora*. Berkeley: University of California Press.

Oostindie, Gert. 2005. *Paradise Overseas: The Dutch Caribbean and its Transatlantic Legacies*. London: Macmillan Caribbean.

Pattullo, Polly. 2005. *Last Resorts: The Cost of Tourism in the Caribbean*. London: Cassell.

Payne, Anthony J. 1994. *Politics in Jamaica*. Kingston: Ian Randle Publishers.

Richman, Karen. 2005. *Migration and Vodou*. Gainesville: University Press of Florida.

Rivera Ramos, Efrén. 2001. *The Legal Construction of Identity: The Judicial and Social Legacy of American Colonialism in Puerto Rico*. Washington, DC: American Psychological Association.

Rodney, Walter. 1969. *The Grounding with My Brothers*. London: Bogle L'Ouverture.

Ryan, Selwyn. 1991. *The Muslimeen Grab for Power: Race, Religion, and Revolution in Trinidad and Tobago*. Port of Spain: Inprint.

Sagás, Ernesto. 2000. *Race and Politics in the Dominican Republic*. Gainesville: University Press of Florida.

Sagás, Ernesto, and Sintia E. Molina, eds. 2004. *Dominican Migration: Transnational Perspectives*. Gainesville: University Press of Florida.

San Miguel, Pedro L. 2005. *The Imagined Island: History, Identity, and Utopia in Hispaniola*. Translated by Jane Ramírez. Chapel Hill: University of North Carolina Press.

Sheinin, David. 1999. "The New Dollar Diplomacy in Latin America." *American Studies International* 37, no. 3: 81–99.

Smith, Wayne S. 1987. *The Closest of Enemies: A Personal and Diplomatic Account of U.S.-Cuban Relations since 1957*. New York: W.W. Norton & Co.

Stone, Carl, and Aggrey Brown, eds. 1977. *Essays on Power and Change in Jamaica*. Kingston: Jamaica Publishing House.

Sweig, Julia E. 2002. *Inside the Cuban Revolution: Fidel Castro and the Urban Underground*. Cambridge, MA: Harvard University Press.

Thomas-Hope, Elizabeth. 1992. *Explanation in Caribbean Migration: Perception and the Image: Jamaica, Barbados, St. Vincent*. London: MacMillan.

Trías Monge, José. 1997. *Puerto Rico: The Trials of the Oldest Colony in the World*. New Haven: Yale University Press.

Zeuske, Michael. 2004. *Insel der Extreme. Kuba im 20. Jahrhundert*. [*Island of Extremes. Cuba in the 20th Century*]. 2nd ed. Zuerich: Rotpunktverlag.

CONTRIBUTORS

CÉSAR J. AYALA is professor of sociology at the University of California, Los Angeles. He is the author of *American Sugar Kingdom: The Plantation Economy of the Spanish Caribbean, 1898–1934*, and coauthor of *Puerto Rico in the American Century: A History Since 1898.*

DAVID BARKER is a professor in the Department of Geography and Geology at the University of the West Indies at Mona, Jamaica. He is the coauthor or coeditor of several books, including *The Contemporary Caribbean* and *Global Change and Caribbean Vulnerability: Environment, Economy, and Society at Risk.*

HILARY MCD. BECKLES is a historian and principal of the campus at the University of the West Indies at Cave Hill, Barbados. His many works on Caribbean history include *White Servitude and Black Slavery in Barbados, 1627–1715*, and *Natural Rebels: A Social History of Enslaved Black Women in Barbados.*

JEAN BESSON is professor of anthropology at Goldsmiths College, University of London. She is the author of *Martha Brae's Two Histories: European Expansion and Caribbean Culture-Building in Jamaica* and co-editor of, among other books, *Caribbean Land and Development Revisited.*

O. NIGEL BOLLAND is Charles A. Dana Professor of Sociology and Caribbean Studies Emeritus at Colgate University. His published works include *The Politics of Labour in the British Caribbean: The Social Origins of Authoritarianism* and Democracy in the Labour Movement and *The Birth of Caribbean Civilisation: A Century of Ideas about Culture and Identity, Nation and Society.*

PHILIP BOUCHER is Distinguished Professor of History Emeritus at the University of Alabama-Huntsville. He is the author of *Cannibal Encounters: Europeans and Island Caribs, 1492–1763,* and *France and the American Tropics to 1700: Tropics of Discontent?*

SELWYN H. H. CARRINGTON is professor of history at Howard University. He is the author of *The Sugar Industry and the Abolition of the Slave Trade, 1775–1810,* and the co-author of *Capitalism and Slavery Fifty Years Later: Eric Eustace Williams—A Reassessment of the Man and His Work,* as well as a contributor to the African Burial Ground Project.

ELIZABETH COOPER is curator in the Americas Department within Scholarship and Collections at the British Library and lecturer in history at Birkbeck, University of London. She is the author of a chapter in *Obeah and Other Powers: The Politics of Caribbean Healing and Religion.*

L. ANTONIO CURET is curator of circum-Caribbean archeology at the Field Museum of Natural History in Chicago, as well as adjunct professor in the Department of Anthropology and Program in Geology at the University of Illinois. His published works include *Caribbean Paleodemography: Population, Culture History, and Sociopolitical Processes in Ancient Puerto Rico.*

ISAAC CURTIS is a doctoral candidate in history at the University of Pittsburgh, working on the subject of piracy in the early colonial Caribbean.

CHRISTINE M. DU BOIS is the author of *Images of West Indian Immigrants in the Mass Media: The Struggle for a Positive Ethnic Reputation,* and co-editor of *The World of Soy.*

LAURENT DUBOIS is professor of Romance studies and history at Duke University. His published works include *A Colony of Citizens: Revolution and Slave Emancipation in the French Caribbean, 1787–1804,* and *Avengers of the New World: The Story of the Haitian Revolution.*

JOSEP M. FRADERA is University Professor at Universitat Pompeu Fabra in Barcelona. He is the author of *Colonias para después de un imperio* (Colonies for the aftermath of empire) and *Gobernar colonias* (To govern colonies).

REINALDO FUNES MONZOTE works for the Antonio Nuñez Jiménez Foundation in Cuba, and teaches history at the University of Havana. He is the author of *From Rainforest to Cane Field in Cuba: An Environmental History since 1492* and editor of *Naturaleza en declive: Miradas a la historia ambiental de América Latina y el Caribe* (Nature in decline: Studies on the environmental history of Latin America and the Caribbean).

ALISON GAMES is Dorothy M. Brown Distinguished Professor of History at Georgetown University. Her book publications include *The Web of Empire: English Cosmopolitans in an Age of Expansion, 1560–1660,* and *Migration and the Origins of the English Atlantic World.*

HUMBERTO GARCÍA MUÑIZ is director and senior researcher of the Institute of Caribbean Studies, University of Puerto Rico. He is coauthor of *La ayuda military como negocio: Estados Unidos y el Caribe* (Military aid as business: The United States and the Caribbean).

ROBERT GODDARD is lecturer in Latin American and Caribbean studies at Emory University.

LYNNE A. GUITAR teaches in CIEE's liberal arts program at Pontificia Universidad Católica Madre y Maestre, Santiago, Dominican Republic. She has contributed chapters to *Slaves, Subjects, and Subversives: Blacks in Colonial Latin America* and *Indigenous Resurgence in the Contemporary Caribbean: Amerindian Survival and Revival.*

DOUGLAS HAMILTON is RCUK fellow and lecturer in the Wilberforce Institute for the Study of Slavery and Emancipation and the Department of History at the University of Hull. He is the author of *Scotland, the Caribbean, and the Atlantic World, 1750–1820* and co-editor of *Representing Slavery.*

GAD HEUMAN is emeritus professor of history at the University of Warwick and editor of the journal *Slavery & Abolition: A Journal of Slave and Post-Slave Studies.* He is the author of *The Killing Time: The Morant Bay Rebellion in Jamaica,* and co-editor of *Contesting Freedom: Control and Resistance in the Post-Emancipation Caribbean.*

WINSTON JAMES is professor of history at the University of California, Irvine. He is the author of *The Struggles of John Brown Russwurm: The Life and Writings of a Pan-Africanist Pioneer, 1799–1851,* and *Holding Aloft the Banner of Ethiopia: Caribbean Radicalism in Early Twentieth-Century America.*

AISHA KHAN is an associate professor of anthropology at New York University. She is the author of *Callaloo Nation: Metaphors of Race and Religious Identity among South Asians in Trinidad* and co-editor of *Empirical Futures: Anthropologists and Historians Engage the Work of Sidney W. Mintz.*

ANNE S. MACPHERSON is associate professor of history at the College at Brockport—State University of New York. She is the author of *From Colony to Nation: Women Activists and the Gendering of Politics in Belize, 1912–82.*

ANTHONY P. MAINGOT is professor emeritus of sociology at Florida International University. His many publications include *The United States and the Caribbean: Challenges of an Asymmetrical Relationship* and *Small Country Development and International Labor Flows: Experiences in the Caribbean.*

LUIS MARTÍNEZ-FERNÁNDEZ is professor of history at the University of Central Florida. He is the senior editor of the *Encyclopedia of Cuba: People, History, Culture* and the author of *Protestantism and Political Conflict in the Nineteenth-Century Hispanic Caribbean* and *Torn between Empires: Economy, Society, and Patterns of Political Thought in the Hispanic Caribbean, 1840–1878.*

DUNCAN MCGREGOR is senior lecturer in geography at Royal Holloway, University of London. He has co-edited such works as *Resources, Planning, and Environmental Management in a Changing Caribbean* and *Global Change and Caribbean Vulnerability: Environment, Economy, and Society at Risk.*

PHILIP MORGAN is the Harry C. Black Professor of History at The Johns Hopkins University. He is the author of *Slave Counterpoint: Black Culture in the Eighteenth-Century Chesapeake and Lowcountry* and coeditor of *Cultivation and Culture: Labor and the Shaping of Slave Life in the Americas.*

RONALD C. NOEL is a graduate student in the Department of History at Howard University. His previous work at the University of the West Indies at St. Augustine focused on Henry Sylvester Williams.

STEPHAN PALMIÉ is professor of anthropology and social sciences at the University of Chicago. Among many other publications, he is the author of *Wizards and Scientists: Explorations in Afro-Cuban Modernity and Tradition* and the editor of *Slave Cultures and the Cultures of Slavery*.

DIANA PATON is reader in Caribbean history at Newcastle University. She is the author of *No Bond but the Law: Punishment, Race, and Gender in Jamaican State Formation, 1780–1870*, and editor of *A Narrative of Events since the First of August, 1834, by James Williams, an Apprenticed Labourer in Jamaica*.

WILLIAM D. PHILLIPS, JR. is a professor of history at the University of Minnesota. He is the author of, among other books, *Slavery from Roman Times to the Early Transatlantic Trade* and the coauthor of *The Worlds of Christopher Columbus*.

BRENDA GAYLE PLUMMER is professor of history at the University of Wisconsin–Madison. Her published works include *Rising Wind: Black Americans and U.S. Foreign Affairs, 1935–1960*, and *Haiti and the Great Powers, 1902–1915*.

PEDRO L. SAN MIGUEL teaches in the Department of History at the University of Puerto Rico, Río Piedras. He is the author of, among other books, *The Imagined Island: History, Identity, and Utopia in Hispaniola* and *Crónicas de un embrujo: Ensayos sobre historia y cultura del Caribe hispano* (Chronicles of a spell: Essays on the Hispanic Caribbean's history and culture).

FRANCISCO A. SCARANO is professor of history at the University of Wisconsin–Madison. He has coedited several volumes on Caribbean history and culture, including *Colonial Crucible: Empire in the Making of the Modern American State*, and is the author of *Sugar and Slavery in Puerto Rico: The Plantation Economy of Ponce, 1800–1850*.

CHRISTOPHER SCHMIDT-NOWARA is professor of history at Fordham University. His most recent book is *Slavery, Freedom, and Abolition in Latin America and the Atlantic World*.

DAVID SHEININ is professor of history at Trent University and a member of the Academia Nacional de la Historia de la República Argentina. He is the author of *Argentina and the United States: An Alliance Contained* and the editor of *Beyond the Ideal: Pan Americanism in Inter-American Affairs*.

JALIL SUED BADILLO is professor of social sciences at the University of Puerto Rico, Río Piedras. He has published, among others, the books *El Dorado borincano: La economía de la Conquista, 1510–1550* (The Puerto Rican El Dorado: The economy of the conquest, 1510–1550) and *Los caribes: ¿Realidad o fábula?* (The Caribs: Reality or myth?).

DALE TOMICH is professor of history and sociology at the State University of New York at Binghamton. His publications include *Slavery in the Circuit of Sugar: Martinique in the World Economy, 1830–1848* and *Through the Prism of Slavery: Labor, Capital, and World Economy*.

ROBERT WHITNEY is a professor of history at the University of New Brunswick–Saint John. He is the author of *State and Revolution in Cuba: Mass Mobilization and Political Change, 1920–1940*.

MICHAEL ZEUSKE is professor of history at the University of Cologne and the author of several books, most recently *Insel der Extreme. Kuba im 20. Jahrhundert* (Island of extremes: Cuba in the 20th century).

INDEX

Abakuá, in Cuba, 520
Abbad y Lasierra, Iñigo, 336
abolition of slavery, 3, 15, 17, 289–300; in
America, 275, 298; and anticolonial struggles,
363; apprenticeship replacing slavery, 296,
300, 315, 347, 349–50, 389, 390; in Aruba,
300; in Bonaire, 300; in Brazil, 275, 312;
by Britain, 291–92, 296, 311–12, 315, 387;
and Christian missionaries, 292, 322–24,
324–28; compensation of slaveholders, 296;
in Cuba, 17, 275, 312, 342–43, 344–45, 366,
367; in Curaçao, 300; decline thesis, 306;
by Denmark, 299–300; economic motive
for, 306, 307, 308; fear of re-enslavement,
352–53; by France, 289, 290–91, 296–97,
298–99, 312, 314; free birth law, 299–300; in
French Antilles, 540; in French Guiana, 291,
299; gradual reforms leading to, 289–90; in
Guadeloupe, 298, 299; in Haiti, 15, 275, 282–
83, 284, 285–86, 400; and Haitian Revolution, 295; humanitarian theory of, 305, 306,
311; and imperialism, 4, 15; and industrial
capitalism, 241–42, 290; in Jamaica, 275; in
Martinique, 298, 299, 355; and myalism, 320;
by Netherlands, 299, 300; by Portugal, 312;

in Puerto Rico, 342, 343–44, 367; and racism,
390, 446; in Saint-Domingue, 290; by Spain,
312, 337–39, 389–90; in St. Croix, 299, 300;
in St. John, 299; in St. Martin, 299, 300; in
St. Thomas, 299; in Suriname, 300, 524; in
United States, 344
Abu Bakr, Yasin, 530
Aburrazach, Thahin, 75
Accarra, 227–28
Account of the Antiquities of the Indians, An
(Pané), 98
Account of the Destruction of the Indies (Las
Casas), 98
achira, 64
ackee, 40
Adams, Grantley, 486
Adams, John Quincy, 373
Adja-Fon slaves, 249–50
Africa: pirates and, 160; in South Atlantic Sys-
tem, 232
African Americans, and Caribbean immigrants,
593–95
African blood, unmixed, 445–46
African colonies, 7–9. *See also* slavery
African Communities League, 461

colonialism in, 138, 146, 171, 191, 194, 207, 220, 263; head tax on laborers, 350–51; labor movement in, 473; migration from, 588–89; Mouvement Indépendantiste Martiniquais, 547; nationalism in, 487; as neutral port, 268; Panama Canal workers, 449; Parti Progressiviste Martiniquais, 546; plantation agriculture in, 225, 227; political assimilation in, 540–41; population statistics, 35; Progressive Party, 479; Quimbois in, 409; sharecropping in, 355–56; slave rebellions in, 229, 297–98; slavery in, 172, 200, 207, 222, 251; slaves as spoils of war, 262; social protests and strikes in, 461; status of, 476, 478; sugar plantations on, 158, 217, 218, 224, 291, 314; tourism in, 48; unemployment in, 546, 548; urbanization of, 36; volcanic eruptions, 28

Mártir de Anglería, Pedro, 123, 127
Martyr, Peter, 88, 97–98
Marx, Karl, 2, 9, 239–40
Masters of the Dew (Hughes and Cook), 454
matelotage, 196–97
mateship, 196–97
Matos, Luis Palés, 455
matrimonios desiguales, 184
Mauritius, 314; indentured Asian laborers in, 315; indentured laborers from, 390; Indian laborers in, 357; sugar plantations in, 291
Maximilian of Mexico, 376–77
Mayobanex, 110
Maysles, Philip, 500
McCarran-Walter Act of 1952, 586
McGregor, Duncan, 39–40
McKay, Claude, 455, 456
McKinley, William, 380, 423
McKinley tariff of 1890, 377
medicine: African, 318; obeah used in healing, 409–10; plants used in, 66, 102, 193–94; sugar used in, 71
Meillacan people, 61
Mejía, Hipólito, 559
melons, 91
Mendieta, Carlos, 467
meningitis, spread by colonizers, 90
mercantilism, 232, 238, 239, 241, 262, 309; and American Revolution, 309–10; and Haitian Revolution, 310–11
mestizos, 115, 120; demographic predominance, 7–8
metallurgy, and South Atlantic System, 231, 232
Methodist missions, 292, 317, 321–22, 325
metropoles, 2
Mexican-American War, 374
Mexico: enclave manufacturing in, 579; enco-

mienda system in, 106; European forces invading, 376; fidelistas' emigration to, 510; Gadsden strip, 375; gold mining in, 106, 167; Haitian immigration to, 564; independence wars in, 341; Japan's relations with, 426; mineral resources of, 137; mining in, 106; slaves from, 105; state system in, 102; sugar production in, 107; US expansionist plans, 375
Miami, immigrants living in, 587, 588
Michaux-Chevy, Lucette, 547
Middle East, sugar production in, 72, 73
Middle Passage, journey of captives through, 236
Mier, Fray Servando Teresa de, 338
migration, 37, 591–92; and natural disasters, 37; and poverty, 37; and unemployment, 487. *See also specific countries*
military reform, in Spanish American societies, 336
military units, freed slaves serving in, 342
Mina, 248
mineral resources, 37–38; agriculture and mining, 165–66; in Cuba, 38, 46; in Dominican Republic, 38, 46; extractive industries, 46; in Guyana, 38, 46; in Haiti, 30, 46; in Hispaniola, 88; in Jamaica, 38, 46; in Mexico, 106, 137; in Peru, 106, 137; in Puerto Rico, 30; in Suriname, 46; Tainos' management of, 102; in Trinidad and Tobago, 38, 46. *See also specific minerals*
mining. *See* mineral resources
Minorca, British loss of, 264
Mintz, Sidney W., 13, 135, 251, 348, 386; on modernism, 16
Miquelon, 541
Mirabal, Minerva, Patria, and María, 557
Mirabeau, Honoré de, 275, 278
Mita worship, in Puerto Rico, 409
Mitterand, François, 547
modernism, 9, 11–12; demodernization, 16; sugar plantations in establishing, 13
modernity, 12; and creolization, 19; global regimes of, 15; postmodernity, 19; precocious modernity, 13
Modigliani, Amedeo, 455
molasses and rum, 198, 219; Cuban exports, 520; and mercantile system, 309–10; and South Atlantic System, 237
Môle St. Nicholas, 380
Monardes, Nicolás, 193–94
Moncada, Guillermo, 370
monetary system, bimetallic system, 103–4
money laundering, 559, 576
Monnerville, Gaston, 478
Monroe, James, 417–18

Made in the USA
Middletown, DE
23 August 2023

37250619R00402